Love Sonnets of Ghālib

Mirza Ghalib is to the Urdu language what William Shakespeare is to the English language. And the most widely read Urdu book in the world is a collection of the love sonnets of Ghalib. These sonnets resonate with the voices of maestros through the corridors of history. Ghalib is not just an Asian phenomenon and his sonnets are loved and studied worldwide. Ranking with the likes of Omar Khayyam and Rumi, his sonnets promise to win the hearts of millions, and because of their reflections associated with love and loving, they are, and always will be, universal. Now, for the first time, the complete collection of the love sonnets of Ghalib has been translated into English by Dr Sarfaraz K. Niazi. Artistic renditions by one of Asia's most famous artists, Sadequain, beautifully depict the themes and aura of some of these timeless verses.

Love Sonnets of Ġhālib

Translations by
Dr Sarfaraz K. Niazi

Introduction by
Dr Farman Fatehpuri

Aristic Renditions by
Sadequain

RUPA

Published by
Rupa Publications India Pvt. Ltd 2002
7/16, Ansari Road, Daryaganj
New Delhi 110002

Sales centres:
Allahabad Bengaluru Chennai
Hyderabad Jaipur Kathmandu
Kolkata Mumbai

In collaboration with the Ghalib Academy of America, P.O. Box 176,
Deerield, Illinois, 60015-0176, USA

ISBN: 978-81-291-4852-0

Third impression 2022

10 9 8 7 6 5 4 3

Typeset by Mindways Design, New Delhi.

Printed in India

To the memory of my father
Padmabhushan Allama Niaz Fatehpuri

Contents

Preface

The most widely read book in the Indian Subcontinent next to the Gita and Qur'an, representing one-fifth of the world population, is Divan-e-Ghalib, the collection of *Urdū* love sonnets by the 19th century poet, *Ġhālib*. The sonnets of *Ġhālib* resonate in the voices of maestros from street-side cafes to elegant courtly palaces throughout Asia, making *Ġhālib* a poet of the people. *Ġhālib* is not merely an Asian phenomenon; scores of scholars from Moscow University to the University of Chicago have based their doctoral theses on the style and thoughts of *Ġhālib*; they have critiqued his style and compared him to the best poets of the world: Rumi, Sa'adi, Hafiz, Shakespeare, Shelley, Pope. Those who have grown up in the Indian Subcontinent or who have ever lived there cannot avoid exposure to *Ġhālib*'s verses in their daily lives. Required reading in schools and colleges, *Ġhālib* is labored upon by millions trying to decipher the mystery and magic of his two-line couplets that range from spontaneous expression to extremely complex and convoluted poetic thoughts that but a few can visualize, let alone understand. Regardless of the simplicity or difficulty encountered in his verses, nothing is ever straightforward; there are nuances, there are similes, there are traps hidden in every couplet that *Ġhālib* wrote. This is part of what makes him so challenging to read and so thrilling to understand.

Love Sonnets of Ġhālib is the first complete English translation, explication, lexicon, and transliteration of *Ġhālib*'s *Urdū* love sonnets. The difficulties in translating across cultures and languages were overcome by including a detailed explication, keeping the translation on a literal level because of the pragmatic difficulties of a rhyming translation, though several have been attempted. A detailed glossary of terms and lexicon is included in the book to clarify oft-repeated themes that might be new to some readers. Notably, the glossary contains many compound words created by *Ġhālib* that require special clarification. This book can serve as a reference for readers of *Ġhālib*'s *Urdū ġhazals* in any language. Those able to read the *Urdū* script are abetted in understanding word meanings and their subtle nuances as used by *Ġhālib*. The transliteration aids with pronunciation and the use of *izāfat* or connections between letters. The transliteration is also of benefit to those who are not fluent in *Urdū* script, and this falls in line with transliteration in other scripts such as Hindi, Bangla, etc.

A book of this scope could not have been written without the help, motivation, and assistance of many people. Foremost here was the encouragement given to me by *Dr. Farmān Fatehpūrī*, the most widely recognized *Urdū* scholar of our time. When I showed him my limited work years ago, he patiently read every word and while encouraging me to improve on it, he challenged me by asking why no one had yet published a complete translation and explication as I was contem-plating? The answer was that it would present an undertaking of mammoth proportions. I accepted this challenge, and whenever I came up against an obstacle, I returned to *Dr. Farmān Fatehpūrī*, who assured me I could do this if I studied the dictionaries well and not relied upon the interpretations of others, who may have assumed many meanings. As it turned out, as I looked up just about every difficult word in the dictionaries published in *Ġhālib*'s time, I was able to identify many differences in the *Urdū* authoritative texts that did not conform to present-day dictionaries. I read through most available *Urdū* explanations of *Ġhālib*'s *Urdū* poetry authored by renowned scholars, I poured over most of the works published on *Ġhālib* in English, including sporadic translations, rhyming and literal, as well as other books written by the Western and Eastern authors on the subject of South Asian poetry. I consulted with the faculty teaching *Urdū* and Persian in American universities and had the rare opportunity of having my long-time friend and associate, *Vidā Salehī*, a published Persian poetess herself, review and critique my choice of words in the translation and explication sections. She also secured for me old Persian literature by traveling to Iran to help understand some of the most complex compound constructions in *Ġhālib's* work. She also took on the most difficult and patient task of teaching me Persian and demonstrated to me the difference between "*raft*" and "*būd*," as *Ġhālib* would have liked to see it done. I am also thankful, in a very special way, to my long-time confidant and friend *Sīmā Khān*, who, in her own way, helped me understand the meaning of many verses.

Many obligations are due to *Dr. Farmān Fatehpūrī*, my life-time mentor, for writing the Introduction and for his affectionate style that inspired me with the energy I needed badly to complete this work.

This was a labour of love for me. It took several years to complete, having undergone scores of revisions. The fine editing and critique by *Subūhī Sultān* was pivotal in identifying the errors in transliteration, grammatical issues in the explication and translation. The detailed editing by Karl Monger was exemplary. My incessant critic *GulAfshāñ* did more than just pursue me in completing this work—she made sure that I did it. My friend Steven E. Shear's appreciation of this work was important to me. Many others have assisted me with their labour and suggestions including *Arshad Ḳhattak*, who worked on the digital files, *Sīmā Jamshed*, who typed the most difficult section on transliteration. My brother *Riāz*, who diligently poured over the glossary and lexicon section. Above all, I am thankful to my family, who endured through the trials and tribulations of writing this book that resulted in the inevitable transformation of *Sarfirāz K. Niazī* from an ordinary mortal into a *Ġhālib* addict. Alain De Botton's, "How Proust Can Change Your Life" can be easily replicated for "How *Ġhālib* Can Change Your Life." How the thoughts of *Ġhālib* affect the lives of his readers is remarkable as I experienced it the hand. I am deeply indebted to Dr. Frances Pritchet at Columbia University for offering many suggestions to me along with her continuous admonishings that a perfect translation of *Ġhālib*'s verses into English cannot exist. I agreed with her and it was this clear appreciation that made me combine a literal translation with explication to achieve my design.

I am thankful to *Sultān Ahmed*, nephew of Sadequain and heir to the works of Sadequain, for giving me permission to reproduce the works of Sadequain in this book that are surely rare and totally delightful. I am thankful to the editors at Rupa & Co., for their incessant efforts in making this work as error-free as possible and for the appreciation of Rupa and Co., for bringing this work to the readers.

Whereas many people and institutions have helped me correct the mistakes in the book, it is inevitable that a work of this nature cannot be error-free; any remaining errors are altogether mine, however. I hope that the readers of this book will be kind enough to point these errors to me and offer their suggestions on improving this work for future editions. I can be reached at niazi@niazi.com, or through Rupa & Co. or Ghalib Academy of America. The translation put forth in this book qualifies for a literal translation wherein I have tried to capture the subtleties of the construction of thought. The choice of words may often seem abrupt but it remains an accurate reflection, as best I could come up with, of how the verse had been written—subtle, and often abrupt. I have translated the couplets into two lines, which may or may not be joined. In the case of continuous thought with no need for a pause, the two lines form a single sentence but with the capitalization of the first letter of the second line. In some instances, a pause was necessary and it was provided by a comma, hyphen, or a semicolon. In Persian and *Urdū*, there is no capitalization of words; as a result, all transliteration is in lower case except for proper names, merely for ease in reading rather than for correctness of transliteration. The Glossary and Lexicon section contains a dictionary and a description of various topics. In arranging it, I have followed the serial order of the *Urdū* alphabet. The delicate and deliberate choice of addressing the beloved as female was made despite many objections that can be rightfully raised since in *Urdū* poetry, the beloved is traditionally addressed as either male or as a neutral gender, the latter more in line with the lack of gender differentiation found in Persian. The fact that in some instances, the beloved *is* a male is elaborated in the explication section.

Sarfaraz K. Niazi
Deerfield, Illinois, USA
July 2001

Introduction
Ġhālib, the genesis of *Urdū* Poetry and *Dr. S. K. Niāzī*

Great poets are distinguished by their thought and diction—ready hallmarks are but two of the many qualities shared by great poets. If we examine the classical *Urdū* poetry from the times of *Walī* to *Iqbāl* (from the first poetry to the mid-20th century) and introspectively analyze the fundamental aspects of those poets who came to fame before, during, and after *Ġhālib*, we find a mosaic of thoughts clearly displayed. Thus, appreciating the characteristics of *Urdū* poetry (as displayed by these great poets) allows us to form a collective opinion about each one of them. For example, we can say about *Walī Deccanī* that he is entirely a poet of corporeal love. *Khwajā Mīr Dard*, among the finest of poets and contemporary of such giants as *Mīr* and *Saudā*, espouses a style of diction quite peculiar and different from that of *Mīr* and *Saudā*. In him, we find the dark shadow of Sufism; he is not a corporeal lover, but a lover of the Almighty. From *Mīr*, perhaps the greatest poet of *Urdū ġhazal*, we hear a prolonged lamentation on the decay of cultural life and simultaneously sense the profound imprints of philosophic thoughts; no lover of an imaginary beloved, he loves a real human being. Although *Hasrat Mohanī* also declares his love for the Almighty, he is in reality a lover of beauty, not the beloved. *Fanī Badayunī*, a poet of the ecstasy and joy, draws from sorrow. *Yaganā* has a loud and bold script, and *Asghar Gondvī* aches for the love of his beloved. The most prominent *Urdū* poet of the last century is *Mohammad Iqbāl*, who preaches a life of discipline and self-respect; in this regard he is a philosopher-poet of the highest order.

Ġhālib's poetry encapsulates the full range of styles and artistic concerns of these prominent *Urdū* poets. To this repertoire, he adds peculiarities found nowhere else. In the realm of life, *Ġhālib* is a poet who questioned its logic and expends much creative energy addressing the dilemmas of human existence. Philosophy is a peculiar characteristic of *Ġhālib*'s poetry, but his mind is not restricted merely to his surroundings, contemporary thoughts, or oft-repeated themes. He exceeds these things and, contrary to *Iqbāl*, *Ġhālib* emerges as a poet-philosopher. After *Dr. Abdur Rahmān Bijnori* declared that in India there were only two divinely inspired books—the collection of *Ġhālib*'s poetry and the Holy Ved (the bible of Hindus)—*Ġhālib* became a topic of discussion everywhere, and a mass movement to dissipate his thoughts emerged, disseminating *Ġhālib* to Britain, Russia, France, and other European countries. Impressionable minds worldwide absorbed *Ġhālib* quickly despite the ire that he faced, mostly from his contemporaries back in his homeland. Hundreds of books published on *Ġhālib* attest to his popularity, the likes of which has not been seen for any poet or writer of the *Urdū* language. The question arises: why did his contemporaries ridicule him and withhold the recognition he deserved? This can be answered by examining the times, the people, and the society in which *Ġhālib* lived.

Ġhālib's perceptions and sensitivity, political vision, style of diction, and analytical thinking were exceedingly progressive. Thus, it comes, as no surprise that a poet so advanced in his thinking would be widely misunderstood, particularly by his contemporaries, who lived in a time when anarchy was rampant. *Ġhālib*'s originality in itself was enough to cast him beyond the grasp of most, making it easy for many to overlook his worth, his potential, and his value to literature. *Ġhālib* was indeed unique, his vision, futuristic. Whereas most poets of his time took pride in the royal past of India and lamented the fact that it had begun to vanish, *Ġhālib* looked to the future and was farsighted enough to acknowledge that the Western technological revolution was here to stay—through the lens of his singular poetry, he had viewed the writing on the wall: he was able to predict the future. There was no need, in his view, to stick to the orthodoxy of the East, a common theme among many of his contemporaries. *Ġhālib*'s ode to the new culture was not limited to his poetry and spilled into his prose writings as well. His futuristic vision was so strong that he even denounced the most liberal and dynamic leader of that time, *Sir Syed Ahmad Ḳhān*, calling him ritualistic and orthodox. We can compare *Ġhālib*'s poetic philosophy to *Iqbāl* and others and readily see the superiority of freshness and straightforwardness in *Ġhālib*'s thinking. He was an optimist and looked forward to a bright future. Many of his verses, condemned by his contemporaries, reveal a path to future, including splitting the atom, landing on the moon, and the rise of the West. One criticism that has been leveled at *Ġhālib* has been his complexity of expression and the mental gymnastics employed in his verses. The fact is that to this day, those attempting to decipher these verses have scarcely been able to scratch the surface. He was a complicated man, one who was not concerned about how others saw him. All he could manage was to contain the entire ocean between the two halves of a seashell. Two centuries after being commited to paper, his thoughts retain their original freshness; readers still find new meanings, just as compelling, with every reading of *Ġhālib.* Every new invention has the look of something *Ġhālib* had predicted; every rise and fall of political fortune smacks of something *Ġhālib* wrote about long ago; mankind's unending strife and self-directed atrocities make us tremble: for their poetic horror and because they underscore the accuracy of *Ġhālib*'s portents.

Ġhazal is a genre of *Urdū* in which love prevails. The verses (more like hemistitches) of *ġhazals* contain within them an entire ocean of thought, representing the traditions and trends of cultural impressions; culture and social style are entailed in these verses, and because cultures and languages cannot exist without the other, it is easy to understand the difficulties inherent in translating *ġhazals* into other languages. One can readily arrive at a literal correspondence for every word, but a translation of a *ġhazal* that truly captures the emotional essence or message of the genre is a hearty task. How does one translate into another language soulful, whimsical, cultural, and situational word arrangements that are entirely indigenous and colloquial? Translating *ġhazals* can be an arduous and often impossible task unless the translator has a firm grasp of the subtleties involved in the construction and design of this genre.

It seems *Ġhālib* was introduced to Europe by the writings of the famous French scholar Garcin de Tassy, author of "History of Hindi and Hindustani Literature", the first edition of which appeared in French in 1839. The introduction of *Ġhālib* into the English language is somewhat more of a mystery that I will avoid dwelling on; but what has been so far published about *Ġhālib* (most of which I have seen), comprises only sporadic commentary and selected translations from his *Urdū* and Persian works; in some instances these translations include limited critical explication. The story of the translation of *Ġhālib*'s *Urdū* Ghazals begins in 1969, the first centenary of his birth, when we find sporadic translations of selections of his *ġhazals*, although no one at the time dared to write a complete translation and explication of his Divan of *Urdū ġhazals*. The work of Dr. Yusuf Husain Khan is noteworthy but it lacks the essential explication.

The first complete translation and explication, written by *Dr. Sarfiraz Niāzī*, you now hold in your hands. It is not only comprehensive, but also describes in detail the characteristics of *Ġhālib*'s poetry—the body and meaning of *Ġhālib*'s monumental efforts together in a single volume for the first time in over 200 years. To date, this is by far the most successful translation of *Ġhālib*'s *Urdū ġhazals*. The translator and explicator relied heavily on his familiarity with Eastern and Western literature, culture, and etiquette. Following his undergraduate education in India and Pakistan, *Dr. Niāzī* received his postgraduate degree in healthcare sciences in the U.S. A recognized scholar in his field, he has triumphed in completing a work that, while perhaps removed from his academic profession, is nonetheless closer to his heart. Through his mastery of both *Urdū* and English, his love for his parent culture and land, and above all his reverence for poetry (in particular *Ġhālib*), *Dr. Niāzī* was able to realize this work. Also abetting *Dr. Niāzī* in this work was his membership in one of the most prominent literary families of the Indian subcontinent. His father, *Niaz Fatehpurī* (d. 1966), was a recognized scholar, critic, and writer, and known for his mastery of English, Arabic, Persian, and Turkish, broadly recognized as the ultimate authority of the *Urdū* language during the 20th century, when his knowledge, vision, and style dominated debate on the subject. He wrote an explicatory book oṅ *Ġhālib*'s *Urdū ġhazals*, but this was an abbreviated effort, limited to a handful of verses, particularly those he considered most difficult to understand. Dr. *Niāzī*'s grandfather, *Amīr Mohammad Ḳhān*, was another ardent fan of *Ġhālib*, and he corresponded with *Ġhālib* frequently. This was from the home where *Sarfarāz* was raised, steeped in an atmosphere of appreciating literature, poetry, and, particularly, the phenomenon of *Ġhālib*. The impression left on him by his home environment is amply evident in the achievement of this text. At the outset of his book, *Niāzī* examines *Ġhālib*'s life and works, communicating to the reader some sense of the environs and cultural situation *Ġhālib* lived in and of the events most formative to his life and thinking. Another noteworthy aspect of this work is the style of presentation; first *Niāzī* presents the verses in Roman, using special diacritical fonts in order to pronounce the verse properly, and then offers a two-line translation of the verse, which is then followed by a comprehensive yet compact explication, emphasizing various subtleties of meaning. This method sheds an illuminating light on *Ġhālib*'s linguistic labyrinth and dispels the haze of uncertainty, priming the mind of the reader to absorb meaning. This book uniquely enables poetry lovers to form their own interpretations without having to decipher the nuances in expression that have for too long kept secular minds at a remote distance from *Ġhālib*. Through *Niāzī*'s presentation, we are free to imbibe the beauty of *Ġhālib*'s verses and arrive at our own meaning by avoiding the obstacles of obsolete words, obscure idioms, and classical references. Among the many significant books written about *Ġhālib* in English, *A Critical Introduction*, by Captain *Fayyāz Mahmūd*, is noteworthy. At over 500 pages, the book was published in 1969 at the centenary of *Ġhālib*'s birth and includes explications of many verses and simultaneous translations of a few *ġhazals*. Following are some examples of *Mahmūd*'s translations, along with the corresponding translations by *Niāzī*.

shikan-e zulf-e 'añbariñ kioñ hai
nigah-e chashm-e surmah sā kyā hai (163:6; #991)

Why are the curls of her tresses smelling of amber?
What is the purpose of those antimony-blackened eyes?—*Niāzī*

Why does the beloved's perfumed hair curl into such ringlets?
What is the nature of the bewitching power of the dark flashing eye of the beloved?—*Mahmūd*

sabza(h)-o-gul kahāñ se āe haiñ
abr kyā chīz hai, havā kyā hai (163:7; #992)

From where have the flowers and greenery come?
What are the clouds made up of? What is the substance of air?—*Niāzī*

Where have the greenery and flowers of the world come from?
What is colour and what role does the air play? (in our distraction)—*Mahmūd*

ham ko un se vafā kī hai 'umid
jo nahiñ jānte vafā kyā hai (163:8; #993)

I am hopeful for faithfulness from her,
Who does not even know what faithfulness is.—*Niāzī*

(Why do) we except [sic] fidelity from persons who do not even
know the meaning of the word?—*Mahmūd*

hāñ bhalā kar terā bhlā hogā
aur darvesh kī ṣadā kyā hai (163:9; #994)

Yes! Do good deeds to get good deeds in return;
Or what else is the call of a dervish?—*Niāzī*

(I can only say) Yes, do good, so that good be done to you.
What else can a dervish (one who has renounced the world)
want?—*Mahmūd*

jān tum par nis̄ār kartā hūñ
maiñ nahīñ jāntā du'ā kyā hai (163:10; #995)

I offer my life to you;
I know not what is the prayer of blessing.—*Niāzī*

I am prepared to lay down my life for you;
I do not know what prayers are!—*Mahmūd*

maiñ ne mānā kih kuchh nahiñ Ġhālib
muft hāth āe to burā kyā hai (163:11; #996)

I acknowledge that it is not much of anything, *Ġhālib*;
But it is not bad if you get it for free.—*Niāzī*

I admit that *Ġhālib* is a mere nothing, but if he costs you
nothing, what harm can there be in accepting him?—*Mahmūd*

Clearly, the fluidity of literal translation is captured well by *Niāzī*. Another book worth mentioning is *Hundred Gems from Ġhālib*, a look at about 100 of *Ġhālib*'s verses by *Matlūbul Hasan Sayyed*, who has translated hundreds of verses that have appeared in many publications. It is of little benefit to compare the rhyming translations with the work of *Niāzī*, who translates them literally. The work of *Sayyed* appears more an attempt to impress the reader with his own command of the English language rather than to present the material in a straightforward manner. This leads the reader quickly to confusion for two reasons: (a) the rhyming translation loses the subtlety of the original verses and (b) invariably, the translator ends up adding his or her own version of an explanation. This tendency makes it harder for the reader to discern and appreciate the original content. *Niāzī* presents in a straightforward manner a literal translation and then follows it up with a simple clarification rather than imposing his own interpretation. This allows the reader to bypass the pitfalls of diction and focus on the thoughts that lay beneath the words. Also, *Sayyed*'s work is restricted to some of the most popular verses whereas *Niāzī* tackles the entire collection, during which process he travailed some of the most difficult jungles of thoughts. Those who have executed selected translations were blessed with the luxury of circumventing many of the intellectual predicaments that *Niāzī* undoubtedly faced. The short verses of *Ġhālib* are widely recognized as being more difficult than the long ones; some *ġhazals* are also brief, comprising just one or two verses, wherein we find some of the most difficult passages, such as the following, which has been handled exquisitely by *Niāzī*:

Asad ham vuh junūñ jaulāñ gadā'-e be sar-o-pā haiñ
kih hai sar panj'a(h)-e mizhgān-e āhū pusht ḳhār apnā (24:1; #156)

Asad, we are those wanderers in madness, roguish paupers,
To whom the eyelids of the deer serve as the handy back-scratching claw.

Scholars of *Urdū* have invariably encountered difficulty in deciphering into their native tongue such verses, which in fact abound in *Ġhālib*'s *ġhazals*. Imagine the difficulty that faced *Niāzī* in translating and interpreting them into another language. This further indicates not only his keen understanding of *Urdū* and Persian, but also a remarkable command over the English language. His ability to grasp the poetic and philosophic aspects of *Ġhālib*'s *ġhazals* reveals his key position as a *Ġhālib* scholar as well as the degree to which he embraces literary thoughts—two qualities that compelled him to work for so many years to produce the exemplary work of beauty and incision you now hold—a book that entails the first 21st century work on *Ġhālib* worth emulating. *Niāzī* herein introduces *Ġhālib* to the English speaking audience in an unprecedented and accessible manner. There can exist no greater tribute to a great poet. *Niāzī*'s work reminds me of one of *Ġhālib*'s own verses:

kaun hotā hai ḥarīf-e mai mard afgan-e ʿishq
hai mukarrar lab-e sāqī meñ ṣalā mere baʿd (58:7: 353)

"Who dares to taste the heady wine of love that knocks men out?"
Repeated is the call on the lips of the cupbearer after my death.

Let us see who would come to challenge the work of *Niāzī*.

Dr. Farman Fatehpuri
January 2001
Karachi, Pakistan.

List of Ghazals

First verse

naqsh fa ryādī hai kis kī shoḳh'ī taḥrīr kā
kāġhażī hai pairahan her paikar-e taṣvīr kā (1:1; #1)

jirāḥat toḥfa(h), almās ārmuġhāñ, dāġh-e jigar hadīya(h)
mubārakbād Asad, ġhamḳh(v)ār-e jān-e dardmand āyā (2:1; #6)

juz Qais aur koī' na(h) āyā ba(h) rūekār
ṣaḥrā magar ba(h) tangī' chashm-e ḥusūd thā (3:1; #7)

kahte ho na(h) deñ ge ham, dil agar paṛā pāyā
dil kahāñ kih gum kīje, ham ne mudda'ā pāyā (4:1; #13)

dil merā soz-e nihāñ se be muḥābā jal gayā
ātish-e ḳhāmosh ke mānind goyā jal gayā (5:1; #20)

shauq, har rang raqīb-e sar-o-sāmāñ niklā
Qais taṣvīr ke parde meñ bhī 'uryāñ niklā (6:1; #26)

dhamkī meñ mar gayā jo, na(h) bāb-e nabard thā
'ishq-e nabard pesha(h) ṭalabgār-e mard thā (7:1; #32)

shumār-e sabḥ marġhūb-e but-e mushkil pasand āyā
tamāshā-e ba(h) yak kaf burdan-e ṣad dil, pasand āyā (8:1; #39)

dahr meñ naqsh-e vafā vajh-e tasallī na(h) hu'ā
hai yih vuh lafẓ kih sharminda'a(h) ma'nī na(h) hu'ā (9:1; #42)

sitāish gar hai zāhid is qadar jis bāġh-e riẓvāñ kā
vuh ik guldasta(h) hai ham be-ḳhudoñ kih ṭāq-e nisyāñ kā (10:1; #49)

na(h) hogā yak bayābāñ māndgī se żauq kam merā
ḥabāb-e mauj'a(h)-e raftār hai naqsh-e qadam merā (11:1; #61)

sarāpā rahn-e ʽishq-o-nāguzīr-e ulfat-e hastī
ʽibādat barq kī kartā hūñ aur afsos ḥāṣil kā (12:1; #63)

maḥram nahīñ hai tū hī navā hā-e rāz kā
yāñ varna(h) jo ḥijāb hai, parda(h) hai sāz kā (13:1; #65)

bazm-e shāhanshāh meñ ashʽār kā daftar khulā
rakhyo yārabb yih dar-e ganjina(h)' gohar khulā (14:1; #72)

shab kih barq-e soz-e dil se zahrah' abr āb thā
shoʽla(h) javāla(h) har ik ḥalq'a(h)-e girdāb thā (15:1; #82)

nāla(h)' dil meñ shab andāz-e aṡar nāyāb thā
thā sipand-e bazm-e viṣl-e ġhair, go betāb thā (16:1; #90)

ek ek qaṭre kā mujhe denā paṛā ḥisāb
ḳhūn-e jigar vadīaʽt-e mizhgān-e yār thā (17:1; #97)

baskih dushvār hai har kām kā āsāñ honā
ādmī ko bhī mayassar nahiñ insāñ honā (18:1; #102)

shab ḳhumār-e shauq-e sāqī rastḳhez andāza(h) thā
tā muḥīṭ-e bāda(h) ṣurat ḳhāna(h)' ḳhamyāza(h) thā (19:1; #111)

dost ġham ḳh(v)ārī meñ merī saʽī farmāeñ ge kyā
zaḳhm ke bharne talak nāḳhun na(h) baṛ(h) jāeñ ge kyā (20:1; #116)

yih na(h) thī hamārī qismat kih viṣāl-e yār hotā
agar aur jīte rahte yahī intiẓār hotā (21:1; #123)

havās ko hai nishāṭ-e kār kyā kyā
na(h) ho marnā to jīne kā mazā kyā (22:1; #134)

dar ḳhor-e qahr-o-ġhaẓab jab koʽī ham sā na(h) huʽā
phir ġhalat kyā hai kih ham sā koʽī paidā na(h) huʽā (23:1; #147)

Asad ham vuh junūñ jaulāñ gadā' be sar-o-pā haiñ
kih hai sar panj'a(h)' mizhgān-e āhū pusht ḳhār apnā (24:1; #156) pa'e

nażr-e karam toḥfa(h) hāi sharm-e nārasā'ī kā
ba(h) ḳhūñ ġhalṭīd'a(h)-e ṣad rang da'vā pārsā'ī kā (25:1; #157)

gar na(h) andoh-e shab-e furqat bayāñ ho jāe gā
be takalluf dāġh-e mah mohr-e dahāñ ho jāe gā (26:1; #165)

dard minnat kash-e davā na(h) hu'ā
maiñ na(h) achhā hū'ā, burā na(h) hu'ā (27:1; #174)

gila(h) hai shauq ko dil meñ bhī tangī' jā kā
gohar meñ meḥv hu'ā iẓṭirāb daryā kā (28:1; #184)

qaṭra(h)-e mai baskih ḥairat se nafas parvar hu'ā
ḳhaṭ-e jām-e mai sarāsar, risht'a(h)' gohar hu'ā (29:1; #192)

jab ba(h) taqrīb-e safar yār ne maḥmil bāndhā
tapish-e shauq ne har żarre pa(h) ik dil bāndhā (30:1; #194)

maiñ aur bazm-e mai se yūñ tashna(h) kām āu'ñ
gar maiñ ne kī thī tauba(h), sāqī ko kyā hu'ā thā (31:1; #198)

ghar hamārā jo na(h) rote bhī to vīrāñ hotā
baḥar gar baḥar na(h) hotā to bayābāñ hotā (32:1; #201)

na(h) thā kuchh to ḳhudā thā, kuchh na(h) hotā to ḳhudā hotā
ḍuboyā mujh ko hone ne, na(h) hotā maiñ to kyā hotā (33:1; #204)

yak żarra(h)-e zamīñ nahiñ bekār bāġh kā
yāñ jāda(h) bhī fatīla(h) hai lale ke dāġh kā (34:1; #207)

vuh merī chīn-e jabīñ se ġham-e pinhāñ samjhā
rāz-e maktūb ba be rabṭī-e u'nvāñ samjhā (35:1; #214)

phir mujhe dīda(h)' tar yād āyā
dil, jigar tashnah' faryād, āyā (36:1; #222)

hu'ī tāḳhīr to kuchh bā'is-e tāḳhir bhī thā
āp āte the, magar ko'ī 'ināñgir bhī thā (37:1; #232)

lab-e ḳhushk dar tashnagī murdagāñ kā
ziyārat kada(h) huñ dil āzurdgāñ kā (38:1; #243)

tū dost kisī kā bhī sitamgar! na(h) hu'ā thā
auroñ pa(h) hai vuh ẓulm kih mujh par na(h) hu'ā thā (39:1; #245)

shab kih vuh majlis furoz-e ḳhilvat-e nāmūs thā
risht'a(h)' har shama' ḳhār-e kisvat-e fānūs thā (40:1; #252)

ā'īna(h) dekh apnā sā mun(h) le ke rah ga'e
ṣāḥib ko dil na(h) dene pa(h) kitnā ġhurūr thā (41:1; #256)

'arẓ-e niyāz-e 'ishq ke qābil nahiñ rahā
jis dil pa(h) nāz thā mujhe, vuh dil nahiñ rahā (42:1; #258)

rashk kahtā hai kih us kā ġhair se iḳhlāṣ ḥaif
'aql kahtī hai kih vuh be mahar kis kā āshnā (43:1; #266)

żikr us parīvash kā, aur phir bayāñ apnā
ban gayā raqīb āḳhir, thā jo rāzdāñ apnā (44:1; #272)

surma(h)' muft-e naẓar hūñ, merī qīmat yih hai
kih rahe chashm-e ḳharīdār pa(h) iḥsāñ merā (45:1; #280)

ġhāfil ba(h) vahm-e nāz ḳhud ārā hai varna(h) yāñ
be shān'a(h)' ṣabā nahiñ ṭurra(h) gīyāh kā (46:1; #282)

jaur se bāz āeñ, par bāz āeñ kyā
kahte haiñ ham tujh ko muñh dikhlāeñ kyā (47:1; #287)

laṭāfat be kaṡāfat jalva(h) paidā kar nahīñ saktī
chaman zangār hai ā'īna(h) bād-e bahārī kā (48:1; #294)

'ishrat-e qaṭra(h) hai daryā meñ fanā ho jānā,
dard kā ḥad se guzarnā hai davā ho jānā. (49:1; #296)

phir hu'ā vaqt kih ho bālkushā mauj-e sharāb
de baṭ-e mai ko dil-o-dast-e shinā mauj-e sharāb (50:1; #306)

afsos kih dandāñ kā kīyā rizq falak ne
jin logoñ kī thī dar ķhor-e ʿaqd-e gohar angusht (51:1:318)

rahā gar ko'ī tā qiyāmat salāmat
phir ik roz marnā hai ḥaẓrat salāmat (52:1; #321)

mund gai'ñ kholte hī kholte āñkheñ Ġhālib
yār lāe merī bālīñ pa(h) use, par kis vaqt (53:1; #325)

āmad-e ķhat se hu'ā hai sard jo bāzār-e dost
dūd-e shamaʿ-e kushta(h) thā shāyād ķhaṭ-e ruķhsār-e dost (54:1; #326)

gulshan meñ band-o-bast ba(h) rang-e dīgar hai āj
qumrī kā ṭauq ḥalqa(h)' berūn-e dar hai āj (55:1; #337)

lo ham marīẓ-e ʿishq ke bīmār dār haiñ
achhā agar na(h) ho to masīḥā kā kyā ʿilāj (56:1; #340)

nafis na(h) anjuman-e ārzū se bāhar khainch
agar sharāb nahiñ, intiẓār-e sāġhar khainch (57:1; #341)

ḥusn ġhamze kī kashākash se chhuṭā mere baʿd
bāre, ārām se haiñ ahl-e jafā mere baʿd (58:1; #347)

balā se, haiñ jo ba(h) pesh-e naẓar dar-o-dīvār
nigāh-e shauq ko haiñ bāl-o-par dar-o-divār(59:1; #356)

ghar jab banā liyā tere dar par kahe baġhair
jāne gā ab bhī tū na(h) merā ghar, kahe baġhair (60:1; #366)

kioñ jal gayā na(h) tāb-e ruķh-e yār dekh kar
jaltā huñ apnī ṭāqat-e dīdār dekh kar (61:1; #375)

laraztā hai merā dil zaḥmat-e mahr-e daraķhshāñ par
maiñ hūñ vuh qaṭra' shabnam kih ho ķhār-e bayābāñ par (62:1; #387)

hai baski(h) har ik un ke ishāre meñ nishāñ āur
karte haiñ muḥabbat to guzartā hai gumāñ aur (63:1; #395)

ṣafāe ḥairat-e ā'īna(h) hai sāmān-e zang āḳhir
taġhaiyur āb-e bar jā mānda(h) kā pātā hai rang āḳhir (64:1; #406)

junūñ kī dastgirī kis se ho, gar ho na(h) 'uryānī
garebāñ chāk kā ḥaq ho gayā hai merī gardan par (65:1; #408)

sitam kash maṣlaḥat se hūñ kih ḳhūbāñ tujh pa(h) 'āshiq haiñ
takalluf barṭaraf mil jāe gā tujh sā raqīb āḳhir (66:1; #414)

lāzim thā kih dekho merā rastā ko'ī din aur
tanhā gae kioñ, ab raho tanhā ko'ī din aur (67:1; #415)

fāriġh mujhe na(h) jān kih mānind-e ṣubḥ-o-mahr
hai dāġh-e 'ishq zīnat-e jeb-e kafan hanoz (68:1; #425)

ḥarīf-e maṭlab-e mushkil nahiñ fusūn-e niyāz
du'ā qubūl ho yārabb, kih u'mr-e Ḳhiẓr darāz (69:1; #428)

vus'at-e sa'ī-e karam, dekh kih sar tā sar-e ḳhāk
guzre hai ābla(h) pā abr-e gohar bār hanūz (70:1; #433)

kioñ kar us but se rakhūñ jān 'azīz
kyā nahiñ hai mujhe imān 'azīz (71:1; #435)

na(h) gul-e nāġhma(h) huñ, na(h) parda(h)' sāz
maiñ hūñ apnī shikast kī āvāz (72:1; #438)

muzhda(h), ai żauq-e asīrī kih naẓar ātā hai
dām ḳhālī qafas-e murġh-e giraf tār ke pās (73:1; #448)

na(h) leve gar ḳhas-e johar ṭarāvat sabza(h)' ḳhaṭ se
lagā de ḳhana(h)' ā'ina(h) meñ rū'e nigār ātish (74:1; #455)

jād'a(h) rah ḳhor ko vaqt-e shām hai tār-e shua'
charḳh vā kartā hai māh-e nau se āġhosh-e vidā' (75:1; #457)

ruḳh-e nigār se hai soz-e jāvedānī' shama'
hu'ī hai ātish-e gul, āb-e zindigānī' shama' (76:1; #458)

mahrbāñ ho ke bulā lo mujhe, chāho jis vaqt
maiñ gayā vaqt nahiñ hūñ kih phir ā bhī na(h) sakūñ (90:1; #534)

ham se khul jā'o ba(h) vaqt-e mai parastī ek din
varna(h) ham chheṛeñ ge rakh kar ʽużr-e mastī ek din (91:1; #537)

ham par jafā se tark-e vafā kā gumāñ nahiñ
ik chheṛ hai vagarna(h) murād imteḥāñ nahiñ (92:1; #542)

mānaʽ-e dasht navardī ko'ī tadbīr nahiñ
ek chakkar hai mere pāuñ meñ, zanjīr nahiñ (93:1; #554)

mat mardomak-e dīda(h) meñ samjho yih nigāheñ
haiñ jamaʽ suvaidāe dil-e chashm meñ āheñ (94:1; #561)

bar shikāl-e girya(h)' ʽāshiq hai, dekhā chāhiye
khil ga'ī mānind-e gul sau jā se dīvār-e chaman (95:1; #562)

ʽishq tāšīr se naumīd nahiñ
jāñ sipārī shajar-e baid nahiñ (96:1; #564)

jahāñ terā naqsh-e qadam dekhte haiñ
ḳhiyābān, khiyābāñ iram dekhte haiñ (97:1; #570)

miltī hai ḳhūe yār se nār' iltihāb meñ
kāfir hūñ, gar na(h) miltī ho rāḥat ʽażāb meñ (98:1; #576)

kal ke liye kar āj na(h) ḳhissat sharāb meñ
yih sūī' ẓann hai sāqī' kaušar ke bāb meñ (99:1; #589)

ḥairāñ huñ, dil ko ro'uñ kih pīṭuñ jigar ko maiñ
maqdūr ho to sāth rakhuñ nauḥa gar ko maiñ (100:1; #600)

żikr merā ba(h) badī bhī use manẓūr nahīñ
ġhair kī bāt bigaṛ jāe to kuchh dūr nahīñ (101:1; #610)

nāla(h), juz ḥusn-e ṭalab ai siṭam ījād, nahīñ
hai taqāẓāe jafā, shikva(h)' bedād nahīñ (102:1; #619)

donoñ jahān de ke vuh samjhe yih ḳhush rahā
yāñ āpaṛī yih sharm kih takrār kyā kareñ (103:1; #629)

hoga'ī hai ġhair kī shīrīñ bayānī kārgar
'ishq kā us ko gumāñ ham be zabānoñ par nahīñ (104:1; #632)

qiyāmat hai kih sun lailā kā dasht-e Qais meñ ānā
ta'jub se vuh bolā: yūñ bhī hotā hai zamāne meñ (105:1; #633)

dil lagā kar lag gayā un ko bhī tanhā baiṭhnā
bāre apnī bekasī kī ham ne pā'ī dād yāñ (106:1; #635)

yih ham jo hijr meñ dīvār-o-dar ko dekhte haiñ
kabhī ṣabā ko kabhī nāma(h) bar ko dekhte haiñ (107:1; #637)

nahiñ kih mujh ko qiyāmat kā i'tiqād nahiñ
shab-e firāq se roz-e jazā ziyād nahīñ (108:1; #641)

tere tausan ko ṣabā bāndhte haiñ
ham bhī mazmūñ kī havā bāndhte haiñ (109:1; #648)

zamāna(h) saḳht kam āzār hai, ba(h) jāne Asad
vagarna(h) ham to tuvaqqu' ziyāda(h) rakhte haiñ (110:1; #656)

dā'im paṛā hu'ā tere dar par nahiñ hūñ main
ḳhāk aisī zindagī pa(h) ke patthar nahiñ hūñ main (111:1; #657)

sab kahāñ, kuchh lāla(h)-o-gul meñ numāyāñ ho gaī'ñ
ḳhak meñ, kyā ṣūrateñ hoñgī kih pinhāñ ho gaī'ñ (112:1; # 665)

dīvāngī se dosh pa(h) zunnār bhī nahīñ
ya'nī, hamāre jeb meñ ik tār bhī nahīñ (113:1; #681)

nahiñ hai zaḳhm ko'ī baḳhye ke dar ḳhūr mere tan meñ
hu'ā hai tār-e āshk-e yās rishta(h) chashm-e sozan meñ (114:1; #691)

maze jahān ke, apnī nazar meñ ḳhāk nahīñ
sivāe ḳhūn-e jigar, so jigar meñ ḳhāk nahīñ (115:1; #700)

dil hī to hai, na(h) sang-o-ḳhisht, dard se bhar na(h) āe kioñ
roeñ ge ham hazār bār, ko'ī hameñ satāe kioñ (116:1; #707)

ġhunchah' nā shagufta(h) ko dūr se mat dikhā, kih yuñ
bose ko puchhtā huñ maiñ muñh se mujhe batā kih yūñ (117:1; #716)

ḥasad se dil āgar āfsurda(h) hai, garm-e tamāshā ho
kih chashm-e tang shāyad kas̊rat-e naz̤z̤āra(h) se vā ho (118:1; #726)

ka'be meñ jā rahā, to na(h) do ta'na(h), kyā kaheñ
bhūlā hūñ ḥaqq-e ṣoḥbat-e āhl-e kunisht ko (119:1; #729)

vārasta(h) us se haiñ kih muḥabbat hī kioñ na(h) ho
kīje hamāre sāth a'dāvat hī kioñ na(h) ho (120:1; #733)

qafis meñ huñ, gar achhā bhī na(h) jāneñ mere shevan ko
merā honā burā kyā hai navāsanjān-e gulshan ko (121:1; #743)

dhotā huñ jab meñ pīne ko us sīm tan ke pāuñ
rakhtā hai z̤id se, khaiñch ke bahar lagan ke pāuñ (122:1; #755)

vañ us ko haul-e dil hai, to yāñ maiñ huñ sharmsār
ya'nī, yih merī āh kī tās̊ir se na(h) ho (123:1; #763)

vāñ pahuñch kar jo ġhash ātā pa'e ham hai ham ko
ṣad rah āhang-e zamiñ bos-e qadam hai ham ko (124:1; #765)

tum jano, tum ko ġhair se jo rasm-o-rāh ho
mujh ko bhī puchhte raho to kyā gunāh ho (125:1; #776)

ga'ī vuh bāt kih ho guftagū to kioñkar ho
kahe se kuchh na(h) hu'ā, phir kaho to kioñkar ho (126:1; #783)

kisī ko de ke dil ko'ī navāsanj-e fuġhāñ kioñ ho
na(h) ho jab dil hī sīne meñ to phir muñ(h) meñ zabāñ kioñ ho (127:1; #793)

rahīe ab aisī jagah chal kar jahāñ ko'ī na(h) ho
ham suḳhan ko'ī na(h) ho āur ham zabāñ ko'ī na(h) ho (128:1; #804)

az mahr tā ba(h) żarra(h) dil-o-dil hai ā'ina(h)
ṭūṭī ko shish jahat se muqābil hai ā'īna(h) (129:1; #807)

hai sabza(h) zār har dar-o-divār-e ġhamkada(h)
jis kī bahār yih ho phir us kī ḳhizāñ na(h) pūchh (130:1; #808)

ṣad jalva(h) rū-ba(h)-rū hai, jo mizhgāñ uṭhāiye
ṭāqat kahāñ kih dīd kā eḥsāñ uṭhāiye (131:1; #810)

masjid ke zer-e sāya(h) ḳhirābāt chāhiye
bhauñ pās āñkh, qibla(h)' ḥājāt chāhiye (132:1; #814)

bisāṭ-e 'ijz meñ thā ek dil, yak qaṭra(h) ḳhūñ vuh bhī
so rahtā hai ba(h) andāz-e chakīdan sar nigūñ vuh bhī (133:1; #823)

hai bazm-e butāñ meñ suḳhan āzurda(h) laboñ se
tang āe haiñ ham, aise ḳhushāmad ṭaloboñ se (134:1; #830)

tā, ham ko shikāyat kī bhī bāqī na(h) rahe jā
sun lete haiñ, go żikr hamārā nahiñ karte (135:1; #834)

ghar meñ thā kyā, kih terā ġham use ġhārat kartā
vuh jo rakhte the ham ik ḥasrat-e ta'mīr, so hai (136:1; #836)

ġham-e dunyā se gar pāī' bhī furṣat sar uṭhāne kī
falak kā dekhnā taqrīb tere yād āne kī (137:1; #837)

ḥāṣil se hāth dho baiṭh, ai ārzū ḳhirāmī
dil josh-e girya(h) meñ hai ḍubī hū'ī asāmī (138:1; #844)

kyā tang ham sitam zadgāñ kā jahān hai
jis meñ kih ek baiẓah' mūr āsmān hai (139:1; #846)

dard se mere hai tujh ko beqarārī, hāi hāi
kyā hū'ī ẓālim terī ġhaflat shi'ārī, hāi hāi (140:1; #854)

sar gashtagī meñ 'ālam-e hastī se yās hai
taskīñ ko de navīd kih marne kī ās hai (141:1; #866)

gar ḳhāmoshī se fāida(h) iḳhfāe ḥāl hai
ḳhush hūñ kih merī bāt samajhnī moḥāl hai (142:1; #872)

tum apne shikve kī bāteñ na(h) khod khod ke pūchho
ḥaẓar karo mere dil se kih is meñ āg dabī hai (143:1; #879)

ek jā ḥarf-e vafā likkhā thā, so bhī miṭ gayā
ẓāhiran kāġhaż tere ḳhaṭ kā, ġhalaṭ bardār hai (144:1; #881)

pīnas meñ guzarte haiñ jo kūche se voh mere
kandhā bhī kahāroñ ko badalne nahiñ dete (145:1; #887)

merī hastī faẓā'e ḥairat ābād-e tamannā hai
jise kahte haiñ nāla(h) vuh isī 'ālam kā 'anqā hai (146:1; #888)

raḥam kar ẓālim kih kyā būd-e charāġh-e kushta(h) hai
nabẓ-e bīmār-e vafā dūd-e chirāġh-e kushta(h) hai (147:1; #892)

chashm-e khūbāñ ḳhāmshī meñ bhī navā pardāz hai
surma(h) tū kahv-e kih, dūd-e shola(h)' āvāz hai (148:1; #894)

'ishq mujh ko nahiñ, vaḥshat hī sahī
merī vaḥshat, terī shohrat hī sahī (149:1; #897)

hai ārmīdgī meñ nikuhish bajā mujhe
ṣubḥ-e vaṭan hai ḳhanda(h)' dandāñ numāñ mujhe (150:1; #907)

zindagī apnī jab is shakl se guzrī Ġhālib
ham bhī kyā yād kareñ ge kih ḳhudā rakhte the (151:1; #912)

us bazm meñ mujhe nahiñ bantī ḥayā kīye
baiṭhā rahā, agarchi(h) ishāre hūv'ā kīye (152:1; #913)

raftār-e 'umr qaṭa'-e rah-e iẓṭirāb hai
is sāl ke ḥisāb ko barq āftāb hai (153:1; #922)

dekhnā qismat kih āp apne pe rashk ājāe hai
maiñ use dekhūñ, bhlā kab mujh se dekhā jāe hai (154:1; #929)

be iʻtidālyoñ se subuk sab meñ ham hu'e
jitne ziyādah hogae utne hi kam hu'e (168:1; #1028)

jo na(h) naqd-e dāġh-e dil kī kare sho'lah pāsbānī
to fusurdagī nehāñ hai ba(h) kamīn-e be zabānī (169:1; #1038)

zulmat kade meñ mere shab-e ġham kā josh hai
ik shamaʻ hai dalīl-e ṣaḥar so ḳhamosh hai (170:1; #1041)

āḳih merī jān ko qarār nahiñ hai
ṭāqat-e bedād-e intiẓār nahiñ hai (171:1; #1054)

ḥujūme gham se yān tak sarnigūni mujh ko ḥāsil hai
kih tāre dāman-o-tāre nazar meñ farq mushkil hai (172:1; #1061)

pā ba(h) dāman ho rahā hūñ baska(h) maiñ ṣaḥrā navard
ḳhār-e pā haiñ johar-e āʻina(h)' zānū mujhe (173:1; #1064)

jis bazm meñ tū nāz se guftār meñ āve
jāñ kā lubd-e ṣurat-e dīvār meñ āve (174:1; #1067)

ḥusn-e mai garchih bah hangām-e kamāl achhā hai
us se merā mah-e ḳhurshīd jamāl achhā hai (175:1; #1078)

na(h) hu'ī gar mere marne se tasallī, na(h) sahī
imteḥāñ aur bhī bāqī ho to yih bhī na(h) sahī (176:1; #1088)

ʻajab nishāṭ se jallād ke chale haiñ ham āge
kih apne sāe se, sar pāuñ se hai do qadam āge (177:1; #1095)

shikve ke nām se be mahar ḳhafā hotā hai
yih bhī mat kah, kih jo kahīye to gilā hotā hai (178:1; #1102)

har ek bāt pa(h) kahte ho tum kih tū kyā hai
tumhiñ kaho kih yih andāz-e guftagū kyā hai (179:1; #1115)

maiñ unheñ cheṛūñ, aur kuchh na(h) kaheñ
chal nikalte jo mai pīye hote (180:1; #1125)

ġhair leñ maḥfil meñ bose jām ke
ham rahaiñ yūñ tashna(h) lab paiġhām ke (181:1; #1129)

phir is andāz se bahār ā'ī
kih hu'e mahr-o-ma(h) tamāshā'ī (182:1; #1136)

taġhāful dost hūñ, merā damāġh-e 'ijz 'ālī hai
agar pahlū tahī kije to jā merī bhī ḳhālī hai (183:1; #1143)

kab vuh suntā hai kahānī merī
aur phair vuh bhī zabānī merī (184:1; #1145)

naqsh-e nāz-e but-e ṭannāz ba(h) āġhosh-e raqīb,
pāe ṭā'ūs pae ḳhām'a(h) mānī māñge. (185:1; #1154)

gulshan ko terī ṣoḥbat az baskih ḳhush āī hai
har ġhunche kā gul honā āġhosh kushā'ī hai (186:1; #1157)

jis zaḳhm kī hosaktī ho tadbīr rafū kī
likh dijiyo yārabb use qismat meñ 'adū kī (187:1; #1160)

sīmāb pushtgarmī' ā'ina(h) de hai, ham
hairāñ kiye hu'e haiñ dil-e beqarār ke (188:1; #1165)

hai vaṣal hij r 'ālam-e tamkīn-o-ẓabṭ meñ
ma'shūq-e shoḳh-o-'āshiq-e dīvāna(h) chāhiye (189:1; #1167)

chāhiye achhoñ ko, jitnā chāhiye
yih agar chāheñ to phir kyā chāhīye (190:1; #1169)

har qadam dūrī' manzil hai numāyāñ mujh se
merī raftār se, bhāge hai bayābāñ mujh se (191:1; #1179)

nukta(h) chīñ hai, ġham-e dil us ko sunā'e na(h) bane
kyā bane bāt, jahāñ bāt banā-e na(h) bane (192:1; #1189)

chāk kī ḳh(v)āhish agar vaḥshat ba(h) 'uryānī kare
ṣubḥ ke mānind zaḳhm-e dil girebānī kare (193:1; #1198)

vuh āke ḳh(v)āb meñ taskīn-e iẓṭirāb to de
vale mujhe tapish-e dil majāl-e ḳh(v)āb to de (194:1; #1203)

tapish se merī vaqf-e kash-ma-kash har tār-e bistar hai
merā sar ranj-e bālīñ hai merā tan bār-e bistar hai (195:1; #1208)

ḳhaṭar hai rishtah-e ulfat rag-e gardan na(h) ho jāve
ġhurūr-e dostī āfat hai, tū dushman na(h) ho jāve (196:1; #1214)

faryād kī ko'ī lae nahiñ hai
nālah pāband-e lae nahiñ hai (197:1; #1216)

na(h) pūchh nusḳha(h)' marham jirāḥat-e dil kā
kih us meñ rezah' almās juzv-e a'zam hai (198:1; #1223)

ham rashk ko apne bhī gavārā nahiñ karte
marte haiñ, vale un kī tamannā nahiñ karte (199:1; #1225)

kare hai bāda(h) tere lab se kasb-e rang-e furoġh
ḳhaṭ-e piyāla(h) sarāsar nigāh-e gulchīñ hai (200:1; #1228)

kioñ na(h) ho chashm-e butāñ maḥv-e taġhāful, kioñ na(h) ho
ya'nī is bīmār ko naẓẓāre se parhez hai (201:1; #1232)

diyā hai dil agar us ko, bashar hai kyā kahīye
hu'ā raqīb to ho, nāma(h) bar hai, kyā kahīye (202:1; #1235)

dekh kar darparda(h) garm-e dāman afshānī mujhe
kar gaī' vābasta(h)' tan merī 'uryānī mujhe (203:1; #1244)

yād hai shādī meñ bhī hangāma(h)-e "yārabb!" mujhe
subḥa' zāhid huvā hai ḳhanda(h) zere lab mujhe (204:1; #1253)

ḥuẓūr-e shāh meñ ahl-e suḳhan kī āzmāi'sh hai
chaman meñ ḳhūshnavāyān-e chaman kī āzmāish hai (205:1; #1258)

kabhī nekī bhī us ke jī meñ gar ājāe hai mujh se
jafāeñ kar ke āpnī yād sharmā jāe hai mujh se (206:1; #1268)

vuh āke ḳh(v)āb meñ taskīn-e iẓṯirāb to de
vale mujhe tapish-e dil majāl-e ḳh(v)āb to de (194:1; #1203)

tapish se merī vaqf-e kash-ma-kash har tār-e bistar hai
merā sar ranj-e bālīñ hai merā tan bār-e bistar hai (195:1; #1208)

ḳhaṯar hai rishtah-e ulfat rag-e gardan na(h) ho jāve
ġhurūr-e dostī āfat hai, tū dushman na(h) ho jāve (196:1; #1214)

faryād kī ko'ī lae nahiñ hai
nālah pāband-e lae nahiñ hai (197:1; #1216)

na(h) pūchh nusḳha(h)' marham jirāḥat-e dil kā
kih us meñ rezah' almās juzv-e a'zam hai (198:1; #1223)

ham rashk ko apne bhī gavārā nahiñ karte
marte haiñ, vale un kī tamannā nahiñ karte (199:1; #1225)

kare hai bāda(h) tere lab se kasb-e rang-e furoġh
ḳhaṯ-e piyāla(h) sarāsar nigāh-e gulchīñ hai (200:1; #1228)

kioñ na(h) ho chashm-e butāñ maḥv-e taġhāful, kioñ na(h) ho
ya'nī is bīmār ko naẕẕāre se parhez hai (201:1; #1232)

diyā hai dil agar us ko, bashar hai kyā kahīye
hu'ā raqīb to ho, nāma(h) bar hai, kyā kahīye (202:1; #1235)

dekh kar darparda(h) garm-e dāman afshānī mujhe
kar gaī' vābasta(h)' tan merī 'uryānī mujhe (203:1; #1244)

yād hai shādī meñ bhī hangāma(h)-e "yārabb!" mujhe
subḥa' zāhid huvā hai ḳhanda(h) zere lab mujhe (204:1; #1253)

ḥuẓūr-e shāh meñ ahl-e suḳhan kī āzmāi'sh hai
chaman meñ ḳhūshnavāyān-e chaman kī āzmāish hai (205:1; #1258)

kabhī nekī bhī us ke jī meñ gar ājāe hai mujh se
jafāeñ kar ke āpnī yād sharmā jāe hai mujh se (206:1; #1268)

hazāroñ kh(v)āhisheñ aisī kih har ḳh(v)āhish pe dam nikle
bahut nikle mere armān lekin phir bhī kam nikle (220:1; #1357)

koh kih hūñ bār-e ḳhāṭir, gar ṣadā ho jāīye
be takalluf ai sharār-e jasta(h)! kyā ho jāīye (221:1; #1366)

mastī, ba(h) żauq-e ġhaflat-e sāqī, halāk hai
mauj-e sharāb, yak mizhah' ḳh(v)ābnāk hai (222:1; #1368)

lab-e 'isā kī junbish kartī hai gahvāra(h) junbānī
qiyāmat kushta(h)' la'l-e butāñ kā ḳh(v)āb-e sangiñ hai (223:1; #1371)

āmaa-e sailāb-e ṭūfān-e ṣadā-e āb hai
naqsh-e pā jo kān meñ rakhtā hai unglī jāda(h) se (224:1; #1372)

huñ maiñ bhī tamāshāī' nairang-e tamannā
maṭlab nahiñ kuchh is se kih maṭlab hī bar āve (225:1; #1374)

siyāhī jaise gir jāve dam-e tḥrīr kāġhaż par
merī qismat meñ yūñ taṣvīr hai shab hāi hijrāñ kī (226:1; #1375)

hujūm-e nālah, ḥairat 'ājiz-e 'arẓ-e yak afġhāñ hai
ḳhamoshī reshah' ṣad nīstāñ se ḳhas badandāñ hai (227:1; #1376)

ḳhamoshīyoñ meñ tamāshā adā nikaltī hai
nigāh dil se terī surmah sā nikaltī hai (228:1; #1381)

jis jā nasīm shāna(h) kash-e zulf-e yār hai
nāfa(h) damāġh-e āhūe dasht-e tattār hai (229:1; #1384)

ā'īna(h) kioñ na(h) dūñ kih tamāshā kaheñ jise
aisā kahāñ se lāuñ kih tujh sā kaheñ jise (230:1; #1394)

shabnam ba(h) gul-e lālah na(h) ḳhālī ze adā hai
dāġh-e dil-e be dard, naẓargāh-e ḥayā hai (231:1; #1401)

manẓūr thī yih shakl tajallī ko nūr kī,
qismat khulī tere qad-o-ruḳh se ẓuhūr kī. (232:1; #1412)

ġham khāne meñ būdā dil-e nākām bahut hai
yih ranj kih kam hai ma'i gulfām bahut hai (233:1; #1421)

muddat hu'ī hai yār ko mahmāñ kīye hu'e
josh-e qadaḥ se bazm charāġhāñ kīye hu'e (234:1; #1430)

navīd-e amn hai bedād-e dost jāñ ke liye
rahī na(h) ṭarz-e sitam ko'ī āsmāñ ke liye (235:1; #1447)

1

نقش فریادی ہے کس کی شوخیِ تحریر کا!
کاغذی ہے پیرہن ہر پیکرِ تصویر کا

naqsh faryādī hai kis kī shoḳhī' taḥrīr kā
kāġhażī hai pairahan her paikar-e taṣvīr kā (1:1; #1)

Against whose playful writing are the words complainants?
Made of paper is the attire of the countenance of every image.

naqsh: mark, word; *faryādī*: pleader, crier; *shoḳh*: playful, mischievous; *kāġhaż:* paper; *taḥrīr*: writing; *pairāhan:* attire, clothes; *paikar*: face, countenance, figure, mould, model, form, portrait, likeliness, an idol-temple; *taṣvīr*: forming, fashioning, painting, limning, picture, image, effigy, likeness, sketch, drawing.

This opening verse of *Ġhālib's Urdū ġhazal divān* is critical of God in a rather unusual manner—with an element of surprise! In it, *Ġhālib* alludes to God's neglect and obliviousness towards us. "Whose mischief was it to create this Universe?" the first line asks in a rather perplexed manner. This would have been a straightforward ode to the Lord if in the first verse the poet had not raised the question, "who has done it?" but instead stated, "He did it." This would have been in line with the tradition of making the first verse an ode to the Lord. This is followed by a description of the sheer helplessness of humankind—all that is visible (or corporeal) in the Universe is clad in "paper dress," as if pleading or bowing before the Lord in awe. This construction of "pleading in paper attire" is drawn from an old Persian tradition in which the men would enter the courts of their kings wearing clothing made of paper in order to display their humility. In this sense, *Ġhālib* implies that we stand before God in a similarly humbled (not humble) way. Another literary support to the construction of paper attire comes from the word "candidate," derived from Latin and means someone who is presenting his or her credentials wearing "white" attire.

In *Ġhālib*'s own words, this verse illustrates that the existence of man itself is the reason for his sorrow and despair. In the first line, *Ġhālib* talks about the Universe as if it were a thoughtless creation, a careless stroke of a pen, an undesirable graffiti, wherein each "word" of that "graffiti" ponders the purpose for its creation. If the end were sorrow and grievance, then what was the need to create us? In the second line, *Ġhālib* talks about everything in the Universe being "wrapped in paper". This draws a beautiful correlation between God's writing and God's creation of humanity—the humility of paper dress and the humility of the written word (i.e., our being) on the paper (i.e., this world) are in a sense synonymous. (Note: paper is also impermanent; writing on paper as opposed to carving on stone is displayed here as a source of its impermanence.) In the first line, there is a plea to know the cause for this injustice while the second line expresses the extreme insignificance of human existence. (In the Bible there is a famous quote that reads, "God's ways are not our ways", meaning, we cannot understand the sense of this senselessness, this suffering.) It is clear that this verse is more ironic than claiming man's position in the Universe; even while *Ġhālib* questions, "who has done it," he leaves room for us to ponder that perhaps it was God?

کاوکاوِ سخت جانیہاے تنہائی، نہ پوچھ
صبح کرنا شام کا، لانا ہے جوئے شیر کا

kāvkāv-e saḳht jānī hāi tanhā'ī, na(h) pūchh
ṣubḥ karnā shām kā, lānā hai jū'-e shīr kā (1:2; #2)

Inquire not of my forebearance to the incessant hammering in the loneliness.
Turning night into day is like unearthing a channel of milk.

kāvkāv: continuous beating of hard stone with a sharp object; [some interpreters have wrongly read it as *kā'o ka'o* or *kāv-e kāv-e* meaning sheer labor]; *saḳht jānī hāi:* ability to bear extreme agony—expressed as surviving the state of extreme commotion and agitation; *jū-e shīr*: channel of milk. (Referring to the legendary lover *Farhād*'s digging the channel of milk out of the mountain for *King Khusrāo*, as a condition of having his wife, *Shīrīn*. See *Shīrīn-Farhād*; Glossary).

The deeply inflicted pain of being away from the beloved, spending lonely nights without her, is no less formidable than digging a channel of milk, as the legendary hero, *Farhād* did. The poet asserts that in the path of love, one has to be just as dedicated, tough, and forbearing. While *Farhād* did this only once, the poet suffers daily, belittling the efforts of the legendary lover and magnifying the pain of the nights of separation. Here, *Ġhālib* compares the intensity of his passion and desire with the legendary lover, *Farhād*. In this way, he implies that the severity of his pain is at par with the intensity of the lover's. While the pain of *Farhād*'s work was physical, the poet's agony is mental or spiritual in nature. In both instances, however, extreme resilience is needed to survive. Note how the poet makes a play on words using continuous tapping as if with a sharp object. It is almost like the mountain digger was digging, hardening the heart like a callous by the tapping.

جذبۂ بے اختیارِ شوق دیکھا چاہیے
سینۂ شمشیر سے باہر ہے دم شمشیر کا

jazb'a(h)-e be iḳhtiār-e shauq dekhā chāhīye
sīn'a(h)-e shamshīr se bāhar hai dam shamshīr kā (1:3; #3)

Worth seeing is the spirit of my uncontrollable desire,
Causing the edge of the sword to unfurl from its sheath.

dam: breath; *dam-e shamshīr*: edge of sword.

My desire to sacrifice myself is so intense that the sword edge has come out of its casing. The sword finds me so ripe for sacrifice that it cannot control itself to grant me my wish. The expulsion of breath further symbolizes an expression of extreme desire to act.

آگہی دامِ شنیدن جس قدر چاہے بچھائے
مدعا عنقا ہے اپنے عالمِ تقریر کا

āgāhī dām-e shanīdan jis qadar chāhe bichhāe
mudda'ā u'nqā hai apne 'ālam-e taqrīr kā (1:4; #4)

No matter how awareness spreads its nets of hearing,
The meaning is the nonexistent bird in the style of my expression.

āgāhī: awareness; *dām*: net; *shanīdan*: to hear, listen, or attend to; *mudda'ā*: whatever is meant; *u'nqā:* legendary bird that does not exist (*alá* Unicorn).

No matter how hard one tries to understand *Ġhālib*'s verses, they shall remain unfathomable; trying to understand them is like catching a bird that does not exist. The net of reasoning and intelligence cannot catch my thoughts. *Ġhālib* was oft blamed for adducing complex thoughts. He openly admits that it is difficult, even for a genius, to understand the true meaning of his verses.

بسکہ ہوں غالب اسیری میں بھی آتش زیر پا
موئے آتش دیدہ ہے حلقہ مری زنجیر کا

baske hūñ Ġhālib asīrī meñ bhī ātish zer pā
mūe ātish dīda(h) hai ḥalqa(h) merī zanjīr kā (1:5; #5)

Even in bondage, there is fire under my feet, *Ġhālib*,
The chains that bind me are merely curls of singed hair.

baske: whereas; *ātish zer pā*: impatient, cinders (fire) under feet; *mūe ātish*: heat-damaged hair (not burned), hair, singed, fragile; *ḥalqa(h)*: ring.

O' *Ġhālib*, even in bondage I am so impassioned that the links of the chain tying me down are like curls of singed, fragile hair. The complexity of the verse depends on "fire" and "singed hair." Having reached my ultimate desire of surrendering to you, I am impatient for the pain of suffering. The heat of my desire and passion has weakened the rings of the chain, allowing me imminent freedom to begin suffering this pain again. The images of fire beneath the feet (an illustration of impatience and passion) and the curls of damaged hair (not burned) so close to "fire" are remarkable. Impatience, bondage, chain-links, fire, singed hair —all parts of a very complex visualization. The personality of the lover who does not long for bondage, who is a free soul, is eloquently expressed here.

2

جراحت تحفہ ، الماس ارمغاں ، داغِ جگر ہدیہ
مبارک باد اسدؔ ، غمخوارِ جانِ دردمند آیا

jirāḥat toḥfa(h), almās ārmuġhāñ, dāġh-e jigar hadīya(h)
mubārakbād Asad, ġhamḳh(v)ār-e jān-e dardmand āyā (2:1; #6)

The gift of wound, the souvenir of a diamond,
the offering of a scarred heart.
Congratulations, Asad! Your sympathetic, compassionate
beloved has arrived.

jirāḥat: wound; *ġhamḳh(v)ār*: consoler; *toḥfa(h)*: gift; *almās*: diamond; *armuġhāñ*: souvenir; *dāġh*: scar (in heart); *jān-e dardmand*: sympathetic beloved; *hadīya(h)*: offering.

Calling the cruel beloved sympathetic is not merely sarcasm here, but actually an appreciation of the gifts that will deepen his pain. This is exactly what the lover wants; having them bestowed by the beloved makes them even more valuable. The diamond is here for you to swallow, for it will lacerate your body from inside. The sharp knife is here for you to carve fresh wounds. The dark scar is here to signify a heart on fire, hot with passion. The beloved has brought all that is needed to test the resolve of a true lover. This is the moment to congratulate the lover. Having fallen in love, these elements of pain are very comforting. The arrival of the beloved is not corporeal; it only signifies the introduction of the gift of love.

3

جز قیس اور کوئی نہ آیا بہ روے کار
صحرا مگر بہ تنگیٔ چشم حسود تھا

juz Qais aur ko'ī na(h) āyā ba(h) rūekār
ṣaḥrā magar ba(h) tangī' chashm-e ḥusūd thā (3:1; #7)

Except for Qais, no one ever came face to face.
The wilderness was perhaps like a narrow jealous eye.

juz: except; *Qais*: *Majnūn* (literally meaning lunatic; the legendary lover from Arabia); *ba(h) rūekār*: to come face to face; *tangī*: tightness, narrowness; *ḥusūd*: jealousy; *tang'ī chashm*: narrowness of vision (heart), anemic eye.

No one ever came forward as a lover except *Qais* (the legendary lover from Arabia) from the wilderness. Why were not there more lovers? Despite its vast expanse, there wasn't room in the wilderness to allow them to wander, thus they could not perfect their act. Why was there not room enough in the wilderness? The wilderness was very tight and closed, like a jealous eye. Why was wilderness like a jealous eye? It wanted to guard its sanctity by allowing only the best, most lunatic ones, to come into the desert. This is a circular argument that simply means except for *Qais* and me, there are no other qualified lunatics. The words critical to this verse are "tightness of the wilderness" and "tightness of an eye". A jealous eye is also called a narrow eye, similar to a narrow heart.

آشفتگی نے نقشِ سُوَیدا کیا دُرُست
ظاہر ہُوا کہ داغ کا سرمایہ دُود تھا

āshuftagī ne naqsh-e suvaidā kīyā durust
ẓāhir hū'ā kih dāġh kā sarmāya(h) dūd thā (ß:2; #8)

Lunacy healed the black spot in my heart;
Its essence, like swirls of smoke, was thus revealed.

āshuftagī: lunacy; *naqsh:* mark, spot, scar; *suvaidā*: black spot in heart; *durust:* making it proper, correcting, fixing [used here to denote removing]; *ẓāhir*: manifest; *dāġh*: spot, scar; *sarmāya(h)*: asset, substance; *dūd*: cloud, smoke.

The lunacy of my love erased the dark spot in my heart, revealing that this dark spot was blown away as easily as smoke. The dark spot refers to the branding of the heart from the callousness of the beloved. The heart burns a black spot from pleading with, yearning for the beloved. Especially remarkable is the connection made between lunacy and the dark spot as smokestack. It points to the impermanence of such spots in the heart. The hurt from lost love is as impermanent as it is remarkable, provided there is lunacy to go with it. "Lunacy" here refers to divine desire.

تھا خواب میں خیال کو تجھ سے مُعاملہ
جب آنکھ کھُل گئی، نہ زیاں تھا نہ سُود تھا

thā ḳh(v)āb meñ ḳhayāl ko tujh se muʿāmla(h)
jab āñkh khul ga'ī, na(h) ziyāñ thā na(h) sūd thā (ß:3; #9)

Within the dream, we were exchanging thoughts.
When the eyes opened, there was neither any gain nor any loss.

ḳh(v)āb: dream, *muʿāmla(h)*: interaction; *ziyāñ*: loss; *sūd*: profit.

My effort to understand nature from life's events proved to be just a dream; my ignorance remained. There was neither gain nor loss in my ignorance. I couldn't be enlightened and I couldn't be made more ignorant. This is clearly a divine verse, though some have read it as a dialogue with the beloved. Understanding that which cannot be understood is the theme of this verse. Because we do not know what needs to be known, we cannot say that we are wiser today than we were yesterday. When you do not know where you are going, taking steps in any direction does not help you gauge the distance between you and your destination. The construction, "opening of the eye," also means, "coming to know the reality". Einstein once remarked that if we knew what is there to know, there would be miniscule difference between those who claim to know it all and those who plead ignorance.

لیتا ہوں مکتبِ غمِ دل میں سبق ہنوز
لیکن یہی کہ رفت گیا اور بود تھا

letā hūñ maktab-e ġham-e dil meñ sabaq hanoz
lekin yahī kih raft gayā āur būd thā (3:4; #10)

Still taking lessons in the school of broken hearts,
That what is gone, is lost now, and what I had is mine no more.

maktab: school; *hanoz*: still; *raft*: gone; *būd*: was; *gayā*: gone; *thā*: was.

Still an amateur in the school of love, I have only successfully learned the first two lessons in the meaning of "gone," and "was". I do not know when I had my heart and when it was gone. The learning in the field of love goes on. Even though I have come a long way, I still consider myself just a beginner, for there is much to learn.

ڈھانپا کفن نے داغِ عیوبِ برہنگی
میں ورنہ ہر لباس میں ننگِ وجود تھا

ḍhāñpā kafin ne dāġh-e ʿayūb-e barahnagī
maiñ varna(h) har libās meñ nang-e vajūd thā (β:5; #11)

The shroud concealed the brandings of embarrassing nakedness.
In any other attire, I were a disgrace to my existence.

kafin: shroud; *ʿayūb*: defects; *nang-e vajūd*: disgrace to own existence.

While living, I was a disgrace due to my nakedness. This means that my exposed sins made me a target of profanity from many. My death was the only way to stop this embarrassment; therefore, my shroud ended it all. Notice that the use of nakedness in the first line is necessary to support the shroud as a cloak. Here "nakedness" means sins and the cloak of death brought it all to an end. In any other situation, I would have been an embarrassment.

تیشے بغیر مر نہ سکا کوہکن، اسدؔ
سرگشتۂ خمارِ رسوم و قیود تھا

tīshe baġhair mar na(h) sakā kohkan, Asad
sargashta(h)' ḳhumār-e rusūm-o-quyūd thā (β:6; #12)

Without the axe, *Farhād* could not take his own life, Asad,
For he was lost in the intoxication of traditions and restrictions.

tīsha(h): axe; *kohkan*: mountain digger; *Farhād*: the legendary lover who was out to dig a channel of milk; *sargashta(h):* lost; *ḳhumār:* hangover, intoxication; *rusūm-o quyūd:* traditions and restrictions.

To kill himself, *Farhād* needed the assistance of an axe. When told by an old woman (who was actually a man dressed as an old woman) that his beloved had passed away, he axed himself and ended his life. To wait for such a scenario to develop would make him extremely desperate. Then, using a typical method of suicide is not in the tradition of true lovers. *Farhād* was more of a traditionalist. He was a common man, no one to boast about. True lovers give their life without any obvious reasons and without the use of any implement. They can think themselves into dying. This is one of several verses where *Ġhālib* has belittled *Farhād*. The meanings of this verse go beyond *Farhād* and his beloved. *Ġhālib* points to how we remain tied to the traditions of the world at the cost of bringing out the best in us. People like to trek traditional paths, for they dread inviting criticism. That humans are not sure of themselves is the theme of this verse.

4

کہتے ہو نہ دیں گے ہم، دل اگر پڑا پایا
دل کہاں کہ گم کیجے، ہم نے مدعا پایا

kahte ho na(h) deñ ge ham, dil agar paṛā pāyā
dil kahāñ kih gum kīje, ham ne muddaʿā pāyā (4:1; #13)

You vow not to return it if you found my heart lying around,
But where is this heart to lose? We already found our destiny?

muddaʿā pāyā: understood well, reached the goal.

You say coquettishly that if you found my heart, you would take it and never return it to me. How could you do that? You've already got my heart, as was my goal. The many ways in which a beloved teases are amply presented here. The statement about not returning his heart is an admission of keeping the lover's love. The lover thinks he understands the meaning of these words. *Ġhālib* takes into account the childish singsong "finders keepers, losers weepers", and makes original a rather simple scenario.

عشق سے طبیعت نے زیست کا مزا پایا
درد کی دوا پائی، دردِ بے دوا پایا

ʿishq se tabīʿat ne zīst kā maza(h) pāyā
dard kī davā pā'ī, dard-e be davā pāyā (4:2; #14)

Through love, I savoured the taste of life.
Curing one pain, it yielded another incurable one.

dard: pain (of life).

Before I knew real love, my life was full of pain. Now, after having fallen in love with you, that pain has been cured and I am relieved. However, this pain has been replaced with the pain of love for which there is no cure. At least now I do not have to strive to relieve myself of the first pain, a turmoil that had wrought much suffering upon me. The pain of love replaces the pain of life. In the first instance, I was searching for a cure, which made me suffer more. I know now that there *is* no cure for the pain of love, and so I can sit back and enjoy it.

دوستدارِ دشمن ہے، اعتمادِ دل معلوم!
آہ بے اثر دیکھی، نالہ نارسا پایا

dost ḍār-e dushman hai, `itimād-e dil ma`lūm
āh be ās̤ar dekhī, nāla(h) nārasā pāyā (4:3; #15)

Befriended by my enemy, the faithfulness of heart was revealed,
Seeing that my sighs were ineffective, my plaints unheard.

*dost dār:*one caring for the beloved; *`itimād-e dil*: trust in heart; *nālah*: plaint; *nārasā*: unheard.

My beloved is my enemy and joining her is, surprisingly, my own heart. This explains why my sighs have no impact and my complaints go unheard. What can I expect when my own heart is beyond me? The sighs coming from my heart are ineffective because she is the one who holds my heart. People develop associations with the things they hold. The poet is hopeful that someday the defecting heart will become the heart of the beloved and she will turn kind.

سادگی و پرکاری، بیخودی و ہشیاری
حسن کو تغافل میں جرأت آزما پایا

sādgī-o-purkārī, beḳhudī-o-hushyārī
ḥusn ko taġhāful meñ jurr'at āzmā pāyā (4:4; #16)

Deceptively innocent, alert in rapture
I found the beauty daring me in her unmindfulness.

sādgī-o-purkārī: simplicity and deception; *beḳhudī-o-hushyārī*: obliviousness and cunningness; *taġhāful*: unmindfullness, being unaware, indifferent; *jurr'at āzmā*: daring.

Do not be fooled by the simplicity of beauty or her flirtatious demeanor. She is testing him, appearing out of self-control to see how her lover will approach her and how far he would go to win her over. Watch out! She is setting her snare.

غنچہ پھر لگا کھلنے، آج ہم نے اپنا دل
خوں کیا ہوا دیکھا، گم کیا ہوا پایا

ġhuncha(h) phir lagā khilne, āj ham ne apnā dil
ḳhūñ kīyā hu'ā dekhā, gum kīyā hu'ā pāyā (4:5; #17)

The bud began to blossom again and thus today I saw my heart.
What was lost before, I now find wounded and bleeding.

Buds blossoming into bright red flowers remind me of my bleeding heart. Looking at it I feel as though I have retrieved my lost heart. Comparing the wounded heart to red flowers is an oft-repeated simile. The emphasis on this as a repeated experience refers to the repeated ordeal of the lover.

حالِ دل نہیں معلوم، لیکن اس قدر یعنی
ہم نے بارہا ڈھونڈا، تم نے بارہا پایا

ḥāl-e dil nahiñ ma'lūm, lekin is qadar ya'nī
ham ne bārhā ḍhūndā, tum ne bārhā pāyā (4:6; #18)

Surely, the whereabouts of my heart are not known, but even,
As I searched for it over and over, you found it, again and again.

I do not know the whereabouts of my heart. Despite searching for it, I cannot find it anywhere. However, you have been able to find my heart time and time again. You have stolen my heart, so it is easy for you to find. The lover seems to be saying, let things stay as they are between us.

شورِ پندِ ناصح نے زخم پر نمک چھڑکا
آپ سے کوئی پوچھے: تم نے کیا مزا پایا!

shor-e pand-e nāṣiḥ ne zaḳhm par namak chiṛkā
āp se ko'ī pūchhe: tum ne kyā mazā pāyā (4:7; #19)

The preacher's boisterous reprimands threw salt on my wounds.
Would someone please ask him, "What savor you got out of it?"

pand: advice, moral admonition; *nāṣiḥ*: preacher.

The preacher's loud response to me is to give up loving. This is like rubbing salt into my wounds. It is a bitter pill to swallow. Let me ask him, what pleasure did he draw from this act? Giving up loving is a more painful proposition than to continue loving in desperation. How would the preacher know this? The theme of this verse questions the motives of the preacher while complaining aloud. There is also an indication that the preacher was attempting to admonish other prospective lovers with his loud tone.

5

دل مرا سوزِ نہاں سے بے محابا جل گیا
آتشِ خاموش کے مانند گویا جل گیا

dil merā soz-e nihāñ se be muḥābā'jal gayā
ātish-e ḳhāmosh ke mānind goyā jal gayā (5:1; #20)

The hidden heat of love burned my heart unkindly;
Like a smoldering fire, it withered away to ashes.

soz-e nihāñ: hidden heat (of love); *be muḥābā'*: unkindness; *ātish-e ḳhāmosh*: smoldering fire.

The hidden fire of love burned my heart, cruelly, like that of a smoldering fire. Lovers are not supposed to display their hurt feelings and should instead suffer in silence. That is what my heart did. No one saw the leaping flames; the quiet fire did the work.

دل میں ذوقِ وصل و یادِ یار تک باقی نہیں
آگ اِس گھر میں لگی ایسی کہ جو تھا جل گیا

dil meñ żauq-e viṣl-o-yād-e yār tak bāqī nahiñ
āg is ghar meñ lagī aisī kih jo thā jal gayā (5:2; #21)

Neither longings for bliss of union nor the memory of my beloved remain.
A fire raged such that whatever there was in this house burnt down.

The fire of longing in my home (heart) was so intense that it burned my heart entirely. With it went the most valuable asset in my home, my desire to be united with her. There was nothing left, not even the desire for my beloved.

میں عدم سے بھی پرے ہوں، ورنہ غافل! بارہا
میری آہِ آتشیں سے بالِ عنقا جل گیا

maiñ ʿadam se bhī pare hūñ, varna(h) ġhāfil! bārhā
merī āh-e ātishiñ se bāl-e ʿunqā jal gayā (5:3; #22)

I am beyond non-existence, else O! Unmindful one;
My fiery sighs would frequently burn the feathers of Unqa.

ʿadam: nonexistence; *āh-e ātishiñ* fiery breath, fiery self.

My fiery soul was enough to burn the feathers of *Unqa* (the legendary nonexistent, imaginary bird) when I was in the state of nonexistence. Now that I have traveled beyond nonexistence, I would rather not talk about what I have left behind. (I do get unmindful, but think of it often). This verse alludes to *Sufism's* concept of nonexistence and its highest stage of "give up, give up" or going beyond nonexistence. Comparison with the nonexistent bird and nonexistence of being is a play upon words here. This verse also declares the supremacy of man. When my fiery breath burns what does not exist yet spares my existence, I must be a superior soul.

عرض کیجے جوہرِ اندیشہ کی گرمی کہاں؟
کچھ خیال آیا تھا وحشت کا کہ صحرا جل گیا

ʿarẓ kīje jauhar-e andesha(h) kī garmī kahāñ
kuchh ḳhayāl āyā thā vaḥshat kā kih saḥrā jal gayā (5:4; #23)

How can I express humbly the intensity of my thoughts,
When the mere thought of my despair consumed the desert?

jauhar: power; *andesha(h)*: thought; *vaḥshat*: despair.

How can I describe to you the intensity of my thoughts? As I began to think of the wilderness, the wilderness began to burn. This is an exaggeration of the thought here. "Despair" is related to wandering, which conveys heat brought about by walking. However, *Ġhālib* says that just *thinking* about wandering will bring down the wilderness. This is incredible.

دل نہیں، تجھ کو دکھاتا ورنہ داغوں کی بہار
اس چراغاں کا کروں کیا، کار فرما جل گیا

dil nahiñ tujh ko dikhātā varna(h) dāġhoñ kī bahār
is chirāġhāñ kā karuñ kyā, kār farmā jal gayā (5:5; #24)

With no heart left to show you the landscape of wounds,
What shall I do with this display of lamps when its guardian got burnt?

chirāġhāñ: display of many lamps (not a plural of lamp); *kār farmā*: ruler, guardian.

My heart is gone. If I had it I would have shown it to you so that you could see how the blooming wound appears like lamps burning all around. What am I to do with this magnanimous branding when its caretaker, my heart, is gone? Who will care for it now? A rather convoluted connection is present here. The heart nurtured the wounds, so with it gone, I am left with only the memory of being branded. This is vivid in my imagination; however, I cannot show it to anyone.

میں ہوں اور افسردگی کی آرزو، غالبؔ! کہ دل
دیکھ کر طرزِ تپاکِ اہلِ دنیا جل گیا

maiñ hūñ āur afsurdagī kī ārzū Ġhālib! kih dil
dekh kar ṯarz-e tapāk-e āhl-e dunīyā jal gayā (5:6; #25)

Now it is me and my longing for suffering, *Ġhālib*,
As my heart, seeing the greeting style of people, got burnt.

afsurdagī: sadness; *ṭarz-e tapāk*: welcoming style (dishonesty of people).

The deception and dishonesty of this world saddens my heart. All desires and wishes are gone. I can only look forward to more sadness, for in the end that is what the world always hands you. *Ġhālib* speaks with deep sarcasm about how people welcome him with kindness, while in the back of their minds they mean ill. It is like the story of Brutus and Caesar. Having the heart burnt also means losing all love for people.

6

شوق، ہر رنگ رقیبِ سروساماں نکلا
قیس تصویر کے پردے میں بھی عریاں نکلا

shauq, har rang raqīb-e sar-o-sāmāñ niklā
Qais taṣvīr ke parde meñ bhī ʿuryāñ niklā (6:1; #26)

Passion, in every form proved to be enemy to life and belongings.
***Qais*, even in the illusion of pictures, was portrayed naked and forlorn.**

Qais: see *Majnūn*; *ʿuryāñ*: naked.

Falling in love, in any form, presented a sure recipe for disaster, to lose all that one possessed. Even in the portrait of *Qais* (the legendary lover from Arabia), he is always shown naked or in tattered clothing, indicating the material promised by the desire for love.

زخم نے داد نہ دی تنگیِ دل کی یارب
تیر بھی سینۂ بسمل سے پَرافشاں نکلا

zaḳhm ne dād na(h) dī tangī' dil kī yārabb
tīr bhī sīna(h)' bismil se par afshāñ niklā (6:2; #27)

The wound did not appreciate the tightness of the heart, O! Lord. Even the arrow came out of the wounded chest with broken feathers.

zaḳhm: wound; *dād*: praise, appreciation; *tangī*: narrowness; *yā*: O!; *rabb*: Lord (in *Urdū* and Persian, it means someone who is the highest of all beings); *tīr:* arrow; *bismil*: wounded; *par*: feather; *afshāñ*: wounded.

The wound did not honor the "tightness" of the heart, as reflected in how the heart did not allow the arrow to pass through without losing its feathers (feathers being scattered). The entire verse hinges on the concept of tightness, meaning the sorrow of heart. My heart was so full of sorrow, which results from the injustices of the world, that even the beloved's arrow could not relieve it. In other words, the lover's arrow had become so trivial compared to the realities of life that its passing did not create a large enough wound to vent my romantic sighs.

بُوئے گُل، نالۂ دِل، دُودِ چراغِ محفل
جو تری بزم سے نکلا سو پریشاں نکلا

būe gul, nāla(h)' dil, dūd-e chirāġh-e maḥfil,
jo terī bazm se niklā so pareshañ niklā. (6:3; #28)

The scent of a flower, the sighs of the heart and the smoke from the lamps of your assembly;
Whosoever wandered out of your gathering, departed perturbed.

būe gul: scent of flower; *nāla(h)' dil*: sighs of heart; *dūd:* smoke; *maḥfil*: gathering; *pareshañ*: worried, disturbed, perturbed.

Smells, the echoes of plaint, and a streak of fresh lamp smoke have something in common: they all dissipate into thin air. Coming out of your assembly in one piece is impossible.

دلِ حسرت زدہ تھا مائدۂ لذّتِ درد
کام یاروں کا بہ قدرِ لب و دنداں نکلا

dil-e ḥasrat zada(h) thā mā'ida(h)' lażżat-e dard,
kām yāroñ kā ba(h) qadr-e lab-o-dandāñ niklā. (6:4; #29)

A heart filled with despair offered a feast of delights of pain;
However, the friends satisfied their satiety by just tasting it.

ma'ida(h): feast; *lażżat*: delicacy; *ba(h) qadr-e lab-o-dandāñ*: to the extent that only lips and teeth can enjoy the delicacy, tasting only.

My desperate heart was like a feast of painful delicacies, which many had the chance to enjoy, but people only tasted it (only teeth and lips experienced it) and did not swallow. The feast represents poetry, meaning that understanding my poetry required studious commitment (swallowing). People did not understand me and thus could not enjoy it.

اے نو آموزِ فنا ہمتِ دُشوار پسند!
سخت مُشکل ہے کہ یہ کام بھی آساں نکلا

ae nau āmūz-e fanā himmat-e dushvār pasand
saḳht mushkil hai kih yih kām bhī āsāñ niklā (6:5; #30)

O! You novice to extinction, your courage to invite difficulties
Proved this to be an easy task; that's the greatest difficulty.

nau: new; *āmūz*: experience; *fanā*: extinction; *himmat*: courage; *dushvār pasand*: liking difficulty, hardship lover.

My courage to bear great suffering is telling me that, "O!, you novice who has just been through the stage of extinction, that was an easy task." Now what things can we find that would be more difficult than extinction in order to satisfy your fondness for difficulty. In *Sufism,* reaching the stage of extinction is a lofty achievement, but the ultimate is extinction-extinction (often called "beyond extinction"). The stage of *fanā* was considered a difficult milestone and was attempted to satisfy our desire for difficulties; here, the poet has achieved it with little difficulty. The play on words here: the difficulty is that it proved to be easy.

دِل میں پھر گریے نے اِک شور اُٹھایا غالِب
آہ جو قطرہ نہ نِکلا تھا سو طُوفاں نِکلا

dil meñ phir girye ne ik shor uṭhāyā Ġhālib
āh jo qaṯra(h) na(h) niklā thā so ṯūfāñ niklā (6:6; #31)

Crying has again created a tumult in your heart, *Ġhālib*;
As the teardrop, unshed before, escaped like a raging storm.

girya(h): crying.

Once again, I began to cry and the drop of an original tear issued forth like a storm. The "unshed tear" was the nucleus that stirred up an ocean of tears. It would be like a single cancerous cell left after surgery that had the potential to turn into a life-threatening tumor. Misery loves company; a lone tear managed to muster many more.

7

دھمکی میں مر گیا جو، نہ بابِ نبرد تھا
عشقِ نبرد پیشہ طلبگارِ مرد تھا

dhamkī meñ mar gayā jo, na(h) bāb-e nabard thā
ʿishq-e nabard pesha(h) ṯalabgār-e mard thā (7:1; #32)

The one killed by threats alone was not qualified for the battle;
Love for fighting hardships demanded a real man.

dahmkī: challenge, threat; *bāb-e nabard*: someone qualified to contest; ***nabard pesha(h)***: fond of fighting and contests; *ṯalabgār*: demanding; *mard*: man.

In the arena of love, only those who can bear extreme hardship should enter and not those who give up early. Loving is not for everyone; it requires great courage. It is implied that it takes a mature, tough, strong man to truly love a woman. Those who are scared into complaining during the initial stages of love lack the necessary strength and should not consider themselves lovers.

تھا زندگی میں مرگ کا کھٹکا لگا ہوا
اڑنے سے پیشتر بھی مرا رنگ زرد تھا

thā zindagī meñ marg kā khaṭkā lagā hū'ā
uṛne se peshtar bhī merā rang zard thā (7:2; #33)

While living, there remained the fear of death;
Even before the flight of my soul, my complexion had turned pale.

marg: death; *khaṭkā*: paranoia of unknown happening; *peshtar*: before; *rang*: color; *zard*: pale.

My paranoia of death kept me pale throughout life. Whereas most would become pale *in* death, I was made pale *before* the fact. There are many pitfalls to understanding this verse. It is a mistake to let whatever is inevitable (the death) to provoke fear or paranoia. The complexion was pale before the flight of the soul because of the multitude of deaths (humiliations) that the poet endured throughout life, almost daily.

تالیفِ نسخہ ہائے وفا کر رہا تھا میں
مجموعۂ خیال ابھی فرد فرد تھا

tālīf-e nusḳha(h) hāi vafā kar rahā thā meñ
majmūʿa(h)' ḳhayāl abhī fard fard thā (7:3; #34)

I was compiling the volumes on the theme of devotion,
Even when my thoughts were scattered, and my musings fragmented.

tālīf: compiling; *nusḳha(h)*: manuscript, volume; *vafā*: faithfulness; *majmūʿa(h)*: collection; *ḳhayāl*: thought; *fard fard*: scattered, incoherent.

Even when my thoughts about love and devotion were scattered and beyond my conscious reach, my devotion was exemplary. Now that I have passed through the initial stages of love and devotion, there is no limit to my faithfulness. I was gifted with the ability to be an exemplary lover. Writing about or compiling information on any subject is possible only if you know the subject well. The juxtaposition of scattered thoughts and scattered pages collected into a bound manuscript is clever and insightful.

دل تا جگر کہ ساحلِ دریاے خوں ہے اب
اس رہگزر میں جلوۂ گل آگے گرد تھا

dil tā jigar kih sāḥil-e daryāe ḳhūñ hai ab
is rahguzar meñ jalva(h)' gul āge gard thā (7:4; #35)

The shores of the sea of blood now stretch from my heart to my liver.
Before this, the track was so colorful it put flowers to shame.

rahguzar: track, path; *gard thā*: was like dust, inferior.

Devastated by my feelings for the beloved, a river of blood runs from my heart to my liver—meaning I am now totally consumed by love. Before this event, I was a happy man (no blood flowing); a colorful man. But now I am filled with sadness. Before, my personality was without equal—Now, I am shattered. I am as sad now as I once was joyful.

جاتی ہے کوئی کشمکش اندوہِ عشق کی
دل بھی اگر گیا تو وہی دل کا درد تھا

jātī hai ko'ī kash-ma-kash andoh-e 'ishq kī
dil bhī āgar gayā to vohī dil kā dard thā (7:5; #36)

Does the strife of love's anguish ever end?
Even when the heart is gone, the pain of heart still remains.

kash-ma-kash: tussle, strife; *andoh*: pain, grief.

As long as my heart was with me, it was the source of all pain and sorrow; now that it is gone, I am sorrowful for having lost it. The meaning here is that the struggle against sorrow is never won—if it is not one thing, it's another. The lover wants his heart to be stolen by his beloved; and when it *is* the lover is still not happy, because now, he is left with nothing to lament over. The interplay of the ideas of the "heart going" and wanting the "grief to be gone" is intriguing.

احباب چارہ سازیِ وحشت نہ کر سکے
زنداں میں بھی خیال بیاباں نورد تھا

aḥbāb chāra(h) sāzī' vaḥshat na(h) kar sake
zindāñ meñ bhī ḳhayāl bayābāñ navard thā (7:6; #37)

Friends could not find a solution to my madness;
Even in the prison, my mind kept wandering in the wilderness.

chāra(h) sāzī: resolution of problem; *bayābāñ navard*: wanderer of wilderness.

The only way friends could help me get rid of this lunacy was to lock me up so I would not flee into the wilderness. But while I was locked up, my thoughts themselves took to the wilderness. You cannot imprison the thoughts of a man, though you chain his body.

یہ لاشِ بے کفن اسدِ خستہ جاں کی ہے
حق مغفرت کرے عجب آزاد مرد تھا

yih lāsh-e be kafan Asad-e ḳhasta(h) jāñ kī hai
ḥaq maġhfirat kare ʽajab āzād mard thā (7:7; #38)

This shroudless corpse is that of tired soul, Asad.
May God forgive him, a strangely carefree man that he was.

kafan: shroud; *ḳhasta(h) jāñ*: tired, wounded, afflicted; *ḥaq*: God; *maġhfirat*: forgiveness; *ʽajab*: strange, unsual; *āzād*: free; *mard*: man.

This shroudless body is that of Asad, a broken and tired man. May God bless his soul, for surely he was a carefree man. Lacking a shroud connotes having no friends; the poet is drawing attention to inequities that have inflicted enough suffering on the deceased already. "Strangely carefree" means that, in his own peculiar way, he cared little about the world, which had much to do with his misery. He, however, never gave in to these inequities. He faced them bravely, and was hurt in the end; nevertheless, he stood tall when alive.

8

شمارِ سُبحہ مرغوبِ بُتِ مُشکل پسند آیا
تماشائے بہ یک کف بُردنِ صد دِل، پسند آیا

shumār-e subḥ marġhūb-e but-e mushkil pasand āyā
tamāshā' ba(h) yak kaf burdan-e ṣad dil, pasand āyā (8:1; #39)

I liked my difficult beloved's fondness for rotating the rosary;
I liked watching her hold a hundred hearts in her palm.

shumār: count; *subḥ*: rosary; *marġhūb*: liked; *but-e mushkil*: difficult idol, beloved; *kaf burdan*: in the palm; *ṣad dil*: hundred hearts.

I like very much that my hardship-giving beloved's passion to rotate her rosary beads is not devotional. It is her way of clutching a hundred hearts in her hand. This appeals to me because it shows that she likes to keep her lovers; she relishes them. Note: there are one hundred beads in the rosary and thus the connection to a hundred hearts is obvious.

بہ فیضِ بیدلی نو‌میدیٔ جاوِید آساں ہے
کشائش کو ہمارا عُقدۂ مُشکل، پسند آیا

ba(h) faiẓ-e bedilī naumīdī' jāvaid āsāñ hai
kushā'ish ko hamārā 'uqda(h)' mushkil pasand āyā (8:2; #40)

Thanks to pessimism, the hopelessness of life is easier to bear.
My efforts to open knots liked this difficult argument of mine.

ba(h) faiẓ: by the grace of; *bedilī*: pessimism; *naumidī-e javed*:

hopelessness of life; *kushā'ish*: opening, aperture, cheerfulness, gaiety; *'uqd'a(h)-e mushkil*: difficult knot, difficult argument, difficulties.

Continuous disappointments and hopelessness is difficult to bear in life. However, because of my content nature and my heart's reluctance to seek solace, this pain is easier to bear. If something is not supposed to happen, then I have no reason to sulk when it does not happen. This stance helps to dissolve the difficult knots of life (sorrows of life). Even if the mystery of my misfortunes remains unsolved, I will be perfectly at peace.

ہوائے سیرِ گل آئینہ بے مہریِ قاتل
کہ اندازِ بہ خوں غلتیدنِ بسمل پسند آیا

havā'ī sair-e gul ā'īna(h)' be mahrī' qātil
kih andāz-e ba(h) ḳhūñ ġhaltīdan-e bismil pasand āyā (8:3; #41)

Stroll in the garden reveals the callousness of a murderer,
As she relishes the sight of blood-laced wounded hearts.

havā: desire; *ba(h) ḳhūñ ġhaltīdan*: laced with blood; *bismil*: wounded.

Her penchant for roaming around in the garden just to appreciate the flowers reveals her cunning nature in that the red flowers remind her of hearts laced with blood—the hearts of her lovers. She savors the sight; she is blood hungry, a barracuda!

9

دہر میں نقشِ وفا وجہِ تسلی نہ ہوا
ہے یہ وہ لفظ کہ شرمندۂ معنی نہ ہوا

dahr meñ naqsh-e vafā vajh-e tasallī na(h) hu'ā
hai yih vuh lafẓ kih sharminda(h)' maʿnī na(h) hu'ā (9:1; #42)

The word fidelity did not bring solace in the world;
For it is a word that has escaped fulfilling its meaning.

dahr: world represented as a terrible place (see Glossary);
sharmind'a(h) maʿnī: fulfilling its meaning.

Faithfulness as practiced today was not to my liking; the way it is expressed does not honor its meaning. It is a debauchery to use the word "faithfulness" in this world. In complaining about a terrible world, the poet is asserting that "faithfulness" is merely a label and not a reality.

سبزۂ خط سے ترا کاکلِ سرکش نہ دبا
یہ زمرد بھی حریفِ دمِ افعی نہ ہوا

sabza(h)' ḳhaṭ se terā kākul-e sarkash na(h) dabā
yih zumurrud bhī ḥarīf-e dam-e afʿī na(h) hu'ā (9:2; #43)

The green line of your face could not quell your rebellious tresses.
Even this emerald could not confront the breath of a black cobra.

sabz'a(h): greenery; *zumurrud*: emerald (legend says it blinds snakes);
ḥarīf: opponent; *afʿī*: black snake (compared here to tresses).

The greenish tinge of your facial hair is like the emerald that cannot face the black snake of your tresses; even though your beauty has started to dwindle, you retain the killer's instinct. The legend goes: the appearance of an emerald, which is green, can blind a black cobra, which is black; here the greening of the face is likened to the emerald, and the tresses to the black cobra. The appearance of the emerald has not harmed the cobra, your long black and lovely tresses. This is a difficult verse to interpret. If we take literally the masculine beloved (as is the case in all of classic *Urdū ġhazal*), then the greening of the face is quite acceptable; if you consider this to be a female beloved, then only *Ġhālib* has dared to offer such subtle "insults."

مَیں نے چاہا تھا کہ اندوہِ وفا سے چھُوٹوں
وہ ستمگر مرے مرنے پہ بھی راضی نہ ہُوا

maiñ ne chāhā thā kih andoh-e vafā se chhūṭūñ
vuh sitamgar mere marne pa(h) bhī rāẓī na(h) hu'ā (9:3; #44)

I had wanted to be freed from the pain of fidelity,
But, that cruel temptress did not agree to even award me death.

andoh: sorrow; *sitamgar*: punisher

I wanted to rid myself of the pain of loving her, for it had become too much to bear. However, my "torturer" would not agree to let me die. A delicate aspect here is that the lover considers death only a reprieve; being separated from his beloved means even greater suffering. Death or nothing! Why does the beloved not award death? First, to avoid the disgrace that would accompany the knowledge of the connection, and second, she wants to keep the lover alive—on whom else to practice her tyranny?

دِل گزرگاہِ خیالِ مے و ساغر ہی سہی
گر نفس جادۂ سرمنزلِ تقوی نہ ہُوا

dil guzargāh-e ḳhayāl-e ma'i-o-sāġhar hī sahī
gar nafis jāda(h)' sar manzil-e taqvā na(h) hu'ā (9:4; #45)

Better that the heart remains on the path of wine and goblet,
If I could not get onto the path to the destiny of abstinence.

guzar gāh: passage; *nafas*: soul; *jāda(h)*: path; *taqvā*: abstinence

Because I lack the fortune to be on the path of abstinence and piety, I might as well settle for the wine and goblet, since only one of these paths can exist for me. They are mutually exclusive. So, as I take to the bottle, it is because abstinence is not in my fate; and if it is not in my fate, then it is not my fault that I choose wine and goblet. The play of words here is between abstinence and not abstaining; if you drink, you are not abstaining, and vice versa. The argument left open here is: does he drink because he could not be pious, or can he not be pious because he drinks.

ہوُں ترے وعدہ نہ کرنے میں بھی راضی کہ کبھی
گوش منّت کشِ گلبانگِ تسلّی نہ ہُوا

hu'ñ tere va'da(h) na(h) karne meñ bhī rāẓī kih kabhī
gosh minnat kash-e gul bāng-e tasallī na(h) hu'ā (9:5; #46)

Agreeable I am that you did not make a promise, for
This way, my ears were not obliged by such a call of assurance.

minnat kash: obliged; *bāng-e tasallī*: call of assurance.

It is perfectly fine with me that you promised never to come; at least this way, I did not await your arrival. If you had instead made false promises using consoling words to give me false hope, then I would have had to wait, even if in the back of my mind I knew you were not coming. If you had promised to come, my ears would have been under the obligation, hearing the good news. Your lack of a promise kept my ears from incurring this obligation to you.

کس سے محرومیٔ قسمت کی شکایت کیجے
ہم نے چاہا تھا کہ مر جائیں، سو وہ بھی نہ ہوا

kis se maḥrūmī' qismat kī shikāyat kīje
ham ne chāhā thā kih mar jā'eñ so vuh bhī na(h) hu'ā (9:6; #47)

To whom shall I complain of my ill fate?
I had wanted to die but even that did not happen.

maḥrūm'ī qismat: deprivation of fate (ill fate).

I am so deprived of good fate that I did not even get the wish nobody wants—which is to die. This is the ultimate misfortune. To whom and where would I even go to lament it? When I cannot be granted the least desirable of all human wishes, why should I bother entertaining desirable wishes, such as a union with the beloved?

مر گیا صدمۂ یک جنبشِ لب سے غالب
ناتوانی سے حریفِ دمِ عیسیٰ نہ ہوا

mar gayā ṣadma(h)' yak junbish-e lab se Ġhālib
nā tavānī se ḥarīf-e dam-e ʿisā na(h) hu'ā (9:7; #48)

The shock of a single movement of lips killed *Ġhālib*;
The weakness prevented facing the breath of Jesus.

nā tavānī: weakness; *ḥarīf*: opponent; *ʿīsā:* Christ.

My beloved with Jesus' instinct (to give life to the dead) came to me, but I was so frail that just the movement of her lips was sufficient to kill me. Meaning that my condition was so hopeless that nothing could change it; even a panacea offered little hope.

10

ستائش گر ہے زاہد اس قدر جس باغِ رضواں کا
وہ اک گلدستہ ہے ہم بیخودوں کے طاقِ نسیاں کا

sitāish gar hai zāhid is qadar jis Bāġh-e Riẓvāñ kā
vuh ik guldasta(h) hai ham be-ḳhudoñ kih ṯāq-e nisyāñ kā (10:1; #49)

The garden of paradise, so highly praised by the preacher
Is merely a bouquet left in the forgotten cupola, to us lost in ecstasy.

sitāish: praise; *zāhid*: preacher; *is qadr*: so much; *bāġh*: garden; *guldasta(h)*: a bouquet; *be ḳhud*: in ecstasy; *ṯāq*: cupola; *nisyāñ*: amnesia, forgetfulness.

Whereas the preacher is building mountains of praise for paradise, it is like the bouquet that we have left in the cupola and forgotten about—it is a long forgotten memory. The coupling of the bouquet and paradise is compared with the luxuries of paradise; bouquets are also left to dry out in cupolas in homes. In this case, the cupola is forgotten. Such is the obliviousness to the thought of the preacher's paradise. The verse points to *Ġhālib*'s indifference to the idea of paradise, because his own ambitions and thoughts are too lofty to get excited about the concept.

بیاں کیا کیجیے بیدادِ کاوش ہائے مژگاں کا
کہ ہر اک قطرۂ خوں دانہ ہے تسبیحِ مرجاں کا

bayāñ kyā kijiye bedād-e kāvish hāi mizhgāñ kā
kih har ik qaṯra(h)' ḳhūñ dāna(h) hai tasbīḥ-e marjāñ kā (10:2; #50)

What can I say of the cruel efforts of her eyelashes that
Each drop of my blood is like a bead in her coral rosary?

mizhgāñ: eye lashes; *marjāñ*: red stone coral; *tasbiḥ*: rosary.

What can I say about the relentless efforts of her eyelashes to unleash cruelty on me? She has caused each drop of my blood to turn into a rosary bead. A rosary of red stones, which she rotates in her hand, represents the blood drawn from my body by her piercing eyelashes. The blood drops were pierced by her eyelashes to allow the thread to pass—this is indeed the ultimate in cruelty.

نہ آئی سطوتِ قاتل بھی مانع میرے نالوں کو   لیا دانتوں میں جو تنکا، ہوا ریشہ نیستاں کا

na(h) āʼī siṭvat-e qātil bhī maʼnī mere nāloñ ko
liyā dāñtoñ meñ jo tinkā, huʼā reshā nīstāñ kā (10:3; #51)

Even the reverence to the murderer could not arrest my lamentations. As I held the straw in my teeth, it turned into the fiber of a flute.

siṭvat: reverence; *maʼnī*: holding; *tinkā*: straw (holding straw between teeth is an old tradition to show submissiveness; see also the Persian idiom: *rīsha(h) dar dandān giraftan*); *resha(h)*: fiber; *nistāñ*: flute, a jungle of reed

I presented myself before the murderer, holding straw in my teeth as a sign of submissiveness. The straw then turned into a flute that began playing my heart's lament, despite my reverence to her. Here we have the very difficult comparison of the fiber of a flute and straw held in teeth. Fiber also means what something is made up of, meaning that the straw provided the substance for the making of a flute. The straw was there as a sign of submissiveness, but instead, it rebelled and turned into a flute. Nothing could hold back my lamentations.

دکھاؤں گا تماشا، دی اگر فرصت زمانے نے   مرا ہر داغِ دل اک تخم ہے سروِ چراغاں کا

dikhāūñ gā tamāshā, dī agar furṣat zamāne ne
merā har dāġh-e dil ik tuḳhm hai sarv-e chirāġhāñ kā (10:4; #52)

If given the time, I would unveil before the world,
That each scar on my heart is the seed to a cluster of lamps.

sarv-e chirāġhāñ: a grand or multiple lamps arrangement or display; the word *chirāġh* (lamp) also refers to punishmen in ancient times when the guilty had a hole drilled in their head to carry a lit candle in it. Both meanings are intended here.

I shall display the condition of my heart, should circumstances permit, showing that every scar in it is a seed of a chandelier of lighting. A dark spot in the heart serves as a seed to other spots, just like one lamp lighting leads to another and so on, giving greater pleasure, by illuminating the heart. Darkness from the branding of the heart (from too many scars) gives rise to an abundance of lit lamps illuminating my heart. The illumination refers to the joy that comes from the pain of love. The presence of scars illuminates my heart (it gladdens me).

کیا آئینہ خانے کا وہ نقشہ تیرے جلوے نے   کرے جو پرتوِ خورشید، عالم شبنمستاں کا

kīyā ā'īna(h) ḳhāne kā vuh naqsha(h) tere jalve ne
kare jo partau-e ḳhurshīd, 'ālam shabnamistāñ kā (10:5; #53)

Your display boldly transfigured the house of mirrors,
Like sunrays transforming the dew-covered earth.

partau: shine; *shabnamistāñ*: dew covered land.

The rays of the morning sun brighten the dew and evaporate it as well; the same happens when the beloved arrives in the assembly hall. The ubiquitous mirrors are brightened by the reflection of the beautiful beloved; her reflection also causes them to melt. This couplet brims with conceptual connections—mirror, dew, luster, and melting. The melting of the mirrors presents another connection to the warmth of her beauty. This is indeed an extremely bright and fluid verse.

مری تعمیر میں مضمر ہے اک صورت خرابی کی
ہیولیٰ برق خرمن کا ہے خونِ گرم دہقاں کا

meri ta'mīr meñ muẓmir hai ik ṣūrat ḳharābī kī
hayūlā barq-e ḳhirman kā hai ḳhūn-e garm dehqāñ kā (10:6; #54)

Hidden in my constitution is the cause of my own destruction. The flash of lightning striking the granary is the toil of the peasantry.

muẓmir: hidden; *hayūlā*: real matter (here meaning flash); *barq-e ḳhirman*: lightning striking crop; *ḳhūn-e garm*: toil; *dehqāñ:* farmer.

Who will hear about my devastation when the fault lies in my own constitution, just like the toil of a peasant results in the growth of grain, which in turn invites the lightning to strike the crops? The fact that I exist is reason enough for the devastation to strike. A cause, effect, and irony is presented here. The peasant plants the seeds, which become newly grown grain, which later and ironically gets struck by lightening. The fault lies in me, not my stars. Note that hard threshing of crop often results in sparks that burn the crop.

اُگا ہے گھر میں ہر سُو سبزہ، ویرانی تماشا کر
مدار اب کھودنے پر گھاس کے ہے میرے درباں کا

ugā hai ghar meñ har sū sabza(h), virānī tamāshā kar
madār ab khodne par ghās ke hai mere darbāñ kā (10:7; #55)

Lush weeds growing all around the home. Desolation! See yourself! Digging out grass is all the guard is left to do now.

vīranī: desolation; *tamāshā*: to see, an spectacle; *madār*: depended on; *darbāñ*: guard.

Addressing desolation, the poet challenges: "see what have you done to my abode?" wild grass grows everywhere in my home, an utterly desolate place because of neglect, since I have gone off to wander in the wilderness. The guard to my house is not expecting anyone to enter, so he is busy digging out the grass to justify his job. The guard was assigned to protect the house, but now, since everything in the house has gone to ruin, there is nothing left to guard, and no visitors are expected, either. All the guard can do now is cut the grass. *Ġhālib*'s humor in the second line is extremely exquisite.

خموشی میں نہاں خوں گشتہ لاکھوں آرزوئیں ہیں   چراغِ مردہ ہوں میں بے زباں، گورِ غریباں کا

ḳhamoshī meñ nihāñ ḳhūñ gashta(h) lākhoñ ārzūeñ haiñ
chirāġh-e murda(h) hūñ maiñ be zabāñ, gor-e ġharībāñ kā (10:8; #56)

Hidden in the silence are millions of desires that have been bled out;
I am just a silent, snuffed-out lamp at the grave of a stranger.

ḳhūñ gashtah: been bled–no hope of its coming to fruition; *charāġh-e murdah*: burnt out lamp; *gor-e ġharibāñ*: stranger's grave.

In my silence are buried hundreds of thousands of desires and aspirations that were killed and will never reach fruition; I am like a burnt out lamp at the grave of a stranger. Because a stranger's grave is rarely visited, no one would ever attend or pay attention to me. The silence of the poet in the first line, and that of a lonely lamp in the second, creates a devastating aura. The graveyard is quiet and there are burnt out lamps all over, bereft of life, like the place's inhabitants.

ہنوز اک پرتوِ نقشِ خیالِ یار باقی ہے   دلِ افسردہ گویا حجرہ ہے یوسف کے زنداں کا

hanoz ik partau-e naqsh-e ḳhayāl-e yār bāqī hai
dil-e afsurda(h) goyā ḥujra(h) hai yusuf ke zindāñ kā (10:9; #57)

Still her dazzling reflection remains vivid in my imagination.
The saddened heart is, like the enclave of Joseph's prison.

partau: reflection, brightness; *ḥujra(h)*: cell, enclave; *zindāñ*: prison.

The reflections of my beloved live on in my thoughts even though my aspirations have been extinguished. My heart is like a prison cell. The darkened cell has been illuminated by the vivid and bright reflections of her memory like the cell in which Joseph was confined. Joseph's legendary beauty had brightened the cell. The thought of the beloved is illuminating like Joseph.

بغل میں غیر کی آج آپ سوتے ہیں کہیں ورنہ   سبب کیا خواب میں آ کر تبسم ہائے پنہاں کا

baġhal meñ ġhair kī āj āp sote haiñ kahiñ varna(h)
sabab kyā, ḳh(v)āb meñ ākar, tabassum hāe pinhāñ kā (10:10; #58)

You must have been sleeping in the arms of my rival, otherwise,
Why do you visit me in my dreams with that sheepish smile?

tabassum hāe pinhāñ: hidden smile (smiling sheepishly).

You must have been sleeping with my rival; why else would I see you in my dreams smiling sheepishly? Suspecting the beloved of sexual indiscretions, the clue comes from her sheepish, guilt-laden smile—the word on which the whole verse is constructed. Note that the word "sheepish" has some element of guilt as well. The poet is assuming, rather audaciously, that since there is guilt in her appearance, she still has some feelings left for him, even though she has been sleeping with the stranger.

نہیں معلوم کس کس کا لہو پانی ہوا ہوگا   قیامت ہے سرشک آلودہ ہونا تیری مژگاں کا

nahiñ maʿlūm kis kis kā lahū pānī huʾā hogā
qiyāmat hai sar-e shak ālūda(h) honā terī mizhgāñ kā (10:11; #59)

I do not know how many would have had their blood turned to water;
Doomsday it is to see your eyelashes laced with tears.

lahū pānī honā: to suffer in pain and sorrow; *ālūda(h):*laced; *mizhgāñ*: eyelashes.

God knows how many would have suffered the direst pain to see you with tears on your eyelashes—it must have been like doomsday for your lovers. It is noteworthy that the eyelashes continue to do their task of piercing the hearts of lovers to extract the blood. Blood turning into water suggests spilling it out like water, meaning extreme suffering. The concept of Doomsday in *Urdū* poetry is related to that of chaos, turmoil, and extreme suffering combined. The tears in the eyes of the beloved may signifying her falling in love with someone else, yet the suffering of her lovers survives.

نظر میں ہے ہماری جادۂ راہِ فنا، غالب
کہ یہ شیرازہ ہے عالم کے اجزائے پریشاں کا

nazar meñ hai hamārī jāda(h)' rāh-e fanā, Ġhālib
kih yih shirāza(h) hai `ālam ke ajzā'e pareshāñ kā (10:12; #60)

In my vision stretches the path leading to extinction, *Ġhālib*, For this is the binding thread of all the perturbed elements of the Universe.

ajzāe pareshāñ: elements of perturbation; *jāda(h)*: path; *shirāzah*: thread used to bind parts of book together.

From my perspective there is but one ultimate goal, the path to extinction, for this path presents the only thread capable of binding all the elements that keep life perturbed. All things around us tied together with a common end—their demise—and that proves to be the only connection among them. *Life* is just another name for *discontent* to *Ġhālib,* and we are wary until we reach the state of extinction where all turmoil wanes. Notice the analogy between the path—the straight-line of it—and the thread that binds books. Often wrongly interpreted as death being the end of all perturbation, this verse refers to the path to extinction. This path as described in *Sufism*, requires relinquishing all desires and, thus, all suffering, bringing harmony to life. Remarkable is this verse's blending of *Sufism, Buddhism, Hinduism,* and an account of human frailty.

11

نہ ہوگا یک بیاباں ماندگی سے ذَوق کم میرا
حَبابِ مَوجۂ رَفتار ہے نقشِ قدم میرا

na(h) hogā yak bayābāñ māndgī se żauq kam merā
ḥabāb-e mauja(h)' raftār hai naqsh-e qadam merā (11:1; #61)

Extreme weariness shall not lessen my passion to wander;
The bubbles on the fast moving waves are my footprint.

yak bayābāñ māndgī: tiredness equivalent to desert, extreme tiredness; *żauq:* passion (to wander in wilderness); *kam*: less; *mauj:* wave, tide; *maujah'-e raftār:* fast wave; *naqsh-e qadam*: foot prints.

Regardless of how tired I am, my passion to wander in the wilderness shall not lessen. The impressions made by my feet are like the bubbles on a fast moving wave of water, appearing and disappearing; they continue. How can I possibly get tired? Comparing footprints to bubbles needs more reflection, though. Both are temporary in nature. Further, a bubble is also a blister on the feet. This is an interesting combination of thoughts used by *Ġhālib* to express his resolve to wander the wilderness.

محبّت تھی چمن سے لیکن اب یہ بے دِماغی ہے
کہ موجِ بُوے گُل سے ناک میں آتا ہے دَم میرا

muḥabbat thī chaman se lekin ab yih be damāġhī hai
kih mauj-e būe gul se nāk meñ ātā hai dam merā (11:2; #62)

In love with the garden though I once was, now I am spiritless
So much that even the wave of fragrance coming from flowers disgusts me.

be damāġhī: spiritless; *nāk meñ dam*: to feel sick of.

Once I was in love with the garden, but I have since grown tired of it. Even the smell of flowers now makes me sick. I once used to enjoy ordinary things that others enjoyed, but the frustrations of life have taken away my ability to appreciate the beautiful things in life. "Feeling sick" expressed as "breath coming to nose," creates a play on words that makes the verse very aromatic.

12

سراپا رہنِ عشق و ناگزیرِ اُلفتِ ہستی
عبادت برق کی کرتا ہوں اور افسوس حاصل کا

sarāpā rahn-e ʿishq-o-nāguzīr-e ulfat-e hastī
ʿibādat barq kī kartā hūñ aur afsos ḥāṣil kā (12:1; #63)

Head to toe I am pledged to love and inevitably in love with myself
Is like praying for lightning and then repenting the outcome.

rahn: mortagage, pledge; *npā* ba(h) *āguzīr*: inevitable; *ulfat*: love *afsos:* repent.

I pledge to love her, but at the same time, I wish to preserve and enjoy my life. It is like praying for lightning and then worrying about the wrath of it. Falling in love requires total devotion; one must be prepared to give up everything else. The comparison to lightning makes sense, for it destroys everything in a flash, just like the first fire of love.

بقدرِ ظرف ہے ساقی! خمارِ تشنہ کامی بھی
جو تو دریائے مے ہے تو میں خمیازہ ہوں ساحل کا

baqadr-e ẓarf hai sāqī! ḳhumār-e tashna(h) kāmī bhī
jo tū daryā-e mai hai to main ḳhamyāza(h) hūñ sāḥil kā (12:2; #64)

O' Cupbearer! Equal to the ability to imbibe is the intoxication of thirst;
If you are the river of wine, then we are the expanse of its shore.

ẕarf: courage; *tashna(h) kāmī*: thirst for wine; *ḳhamyāza(h)*: expanse.

Only those who desire have the capacity to hold that, which they desire, O! Cupbearer, If you have the wine, we have the thirst to drink it all. Like banks, we can contain the entire river of wine.

13

محرم نہیں ہے تُو ہی نوا ہاے راز کا
یاں ورنہ جو حجاب ہے، پردہ ہے ساز کا

maḥram nahīñ hai tū hī navā hā-e rāz kā
yāñ varna(h) jo ḥijāb hai, parda(h) hai sāz kā (13:1; #65)

Knowing you are not of the mysteries of hidden voices;
Here, otherwise, the veil that hides is a musical chord.

maḥram: knowing; *navā hā-e rāz*: calls from unknown; *ḥijāb*: veil, curtain; *parda(h)*: veil, curtain, music note, music chord; *sāz*: musical instrument.

The veil that hides the realities of the other world from us would turn into music, revealing through its sounds the truth about the world beyond, if only we were conditioned to understand these notes. If we knew what to hear we would know the truth, and every veil would prove to be evidence in itself. We need vision to see the evidence of the Almighty. It is all around. Everything in the Universe emanates a melody; if we could hear it, we would know the universe. Can we know what a bat "sees" with its sonar signals?

رنگِ شکستہ صبحِ بہارِ نظارہ ہے
یہ وقت ہے شگفتنِ گل ہاے ناز کا

rang-e shikasta(h) subḥ-e bahār-e naẓāra(h) hai
yih vaqt hai shagiftan-e gul hāi nāz kā (13:2; #66)

The pale complexion is evoking the blooming display of dawn;
The time is now for the flowers of coquetry to bloom.

rang: color; *shikasta(h):* pale, weak; *subḥ*: dawn; *bahār*: prime, bloom, glory delight; *naẕārah*:sight, view, vista; *shaguftan:* blooming; *nāz:* coquetry.

O! Beloved, look at your face after making love to my rival. Look how it has brightened with flushing, obviously due to embarrassment. An interesting analogy is drawn between the paleness of dawn and the blooming of flowers. The paleness of her face is likened to the arrival of dawn. This coincides with the hour the beloved walks home, causing her cheeks to bloom. This is the time when the flowers of her coquetry might bloom, now when she is full of ecstasy and joy. The beloved might appear coquettish simply to hide her embarrassment. The phrasing lends a tone of melancholy if we extend the paleness of the beloved's face to a reason. Most interpreters have left it without expounding on the reason.

تو اور سوئے غیر نظرہائے تیز تیز
میں اور دکھ تری مژہ ہائے دراز کا

tū aur sūe ġhair naẕar hāi tez tez
main aur dukh terī mizha(h) hāi darāz kā (13:3:#67)

You and your looking towards stranger angrily;
I, and my pain from your long eyelashes.

sū: towards; *naẕar tez tez*: bold glance, angry look; *mizha(h) hāi darāz*: long lashes.

The beloved is upset with the rival and looks at him angrily, which makes the poet jealous. The long eyelashes directed towards the rival are piercing the heart of the lover with jealousy.

صرفہ ہے ضبطِ آہ میں میرا، وگرنہ میں
طعمہ ہوں ایک ہی نفسِ جاں گداز کا

ṣarfa(h) hai ẓabṯ-e āh meñ merā, vagarna(h) maiñ
ta'ma(h) hūñ ek hī nafis-e jāñ gudāz kā (13:4; #68)

Better it is for me to hold on to my sighs; otherwise,
I am just a bite of a heart-rending breath.

ṣarfa(h): profitable; *ta'ma(h)*: greed, avarice, a bite.

It is best that I hold onto my sighs, or else I may end up as a single bite of my own breath. It is so hot with sorrow that it can immolate me immediately. A sigh is enough to melt me and thus I must hold on. Immolation by a sigh signifies the intense heat of expression.

ہیں بسکہ جوشِ بادہ سے شیشے اچھل رہے
ہر گوشۂ بساط ہے سر شیشہ باز کا

haiñ baske josh-e bāda(h) se shishe uchhal rahe
har gosha(h)' bisāṯ hai sar shīsha(h) bāz kā (13:5; #69)

Whereas, intoxicated by the chaotic wine, the goblets are skipping;
Every corner of the tavern is like the head of a goblet juggler.

bisāṯ: place, floor; *shīsha(h) bāz:* juggler who dances with wine glass on his head.

Intoxication by wine is causing the goblets to appear to bounce. In fact, the whole tavern appears to be the head of the juggler on which the glasses are bouncing. This is an unusual analogy used to describe the chaotic intoxication of drunkards.

کاوش کا، دل کرے ہے تقاضا کہ ہے ہنوز
ناخن پہ قرض اس گرہِ نیم باز کا

kāvish kā, dil kare hai taqāẓā kih hai hanoz
nāḳhūn pa(h) qarẓ us girah-e nīm bāz kā (13:6; #70)

The heart is insisting to make a greater effort, for there is still
A debt owed by the fingernails to the half-opened knot.

kāvish: effort; *girah-e nīm bāz*: half opened knot.

My heart insists that I continue to undo the knot of grief in it. My nails owe this favor to the half-opened knot as they have not finished releasing it. The nails bring me comfort by digging into wounds. They make the wound deeper by relieving me of the knot of sorrow in my heart. Note the use of nails to open ordinary string knots. Nails can also be used to dig into the knot of sorrow in the heart.

تاراجِ کاوشِ غمِ ہجراں ہوا، اسدؔ
سینہ، کہ تھا دفینہ گہر ہاے راز کا

tārāj-e kāvish-e ġham-e hijrāñ hu'ā, Asad
sīna(h), kih thā dafīna(h) gohar hāi rāz kā (13:7; #71)

Devastated by the impact of the sorrow of separation, Asad,
A chest that was once a buried treasure of pearls of secrets.

tārāj: devastation, destruction; *dafīna(h)*: buried place, treasure; *gohar*: pearl.

O! Asad, my chest was once full of pearls of secrets, but the sorrow of separation has destroyed this treasure. The secret pearls buried in my heart were the offerings of my love; how I had planned to love and cherish you. Because of our separation, all of these thoughts have been devastated and destroyed. I no longer remember how I had planned to serve you, love you, and cherish you.

14

بزمِ شاہنشاہ میں اشعار کا دفتر کھلا   رکھیو یارب یہ درِ گنجینۂ گوہر کھلا

bazm-e shāhanshāh meñ ash'ār kā daftar khulā
rakhyo yārabb yih dar-e ganjina(h)' gohar khulā (14:1; #72)

In the assembly of the Emperor, the contest of verses opened.
O! Lord, keep this door to treasure of pearls open.

ganjīna(h): treasure.

The contest of verses opens in the court of the Emperor. O! Lord, keep the door of treasure open. Verses are referred to as pearls. May the King continue to have a taste for poetry!

شب ہوئی، پھر انجمِ رخشندہ کا منظر کھلا   اِس تکلف سے کہ گویا بتکدے کا در کھلا

shab hu'ī, phir anjum-e rakhshinda(h) kā manzar khulā
is takalluf se kih goyā butkade kā dar khulā (14:2; #73)

The fall of night again brought a display of brightly shining stars,
With a ceremonial formality of the opening of doors to a house of idols.

anjum: star; *rakhshinda(h)*: bright, shining; *takalluf*: formality, observance of etiquette, ceremoniously.

As night fell, the sky lit up with bright, shining stars. This appeared formally, as if the doors to the house of idols had opened up. The idols in the house are, of course, the beloved, and the coming of night makes the poet think of her bright shiny face. Temples where idols are housed often keep their doors locked, only opening them to supplicators on special occasions. It is only when the doors are open that we can see the face of our beloved.

گرچہ ہوں دیوانہ، پر کیوں دوست کا کھاؤں فریب   آستیں میں دشنہ پنہاں، ہاتھ میں نشتر کھلا

garcheh hūñ dīvāna(h), par kioñ dost kā khāuñ fareb
āstiñ meñ dashnah pinhāñ, hāth meñ nishtar khulā (14:3; #74)

Though a lunatic I may be, why should I be deceived by friends?
Bearing healing lancets in hand, they hide daggers up their sleeves.

āstiñ: sleeve; *dashna(h)*: dagger; *nishtar*: knife (healing lancets used to let out blood).

I may be a lunatic, but my friends, who bear lancets in their hands to drain me of my insanity, will not deceive me? They also hold daggers (with which to kill me) up their sleeves. This refers to an old tradition of bloodletting that was believed to remove bad elements from the body. *Ġhālib* warns here that we should not be fooled by the apparent good intentions of people. They may be out to get you. Trust no one, he is saying, especially friends.

گو نہ سمجھوں اُس کی باتیں، گو نہ پاؤں اُس کا بھید   پر یہ کیا کم ہے کہ مجھ سے وہ پری پیکر کھلا

go na(h) samjhūñ us kī bāteñ, go na(h) pāūñ us kā bhed
par yih kyā kam hai kih mujh se vuh parī paikar khulā (14:4:75)

Though I understand not her words, though I catch not her clues,
Is not it enough that the fairy persona opened up to me?

parī paikar: fairy persona; *khulā:* became informal.

Though I do not understand her words, or the reason behind her attention towards me, I am satisfied that she has become informal with me. It is enough that the fairy persona dropped her veil of formality. I have hope that we will open up to each other after a few more meetings.

ہے خیالِ حُسن میں حُسنِ عمل کا سا خیال　　خُلد کا اک در ہے میری گور کے اندر کھُلا

hai ḳhayāl-e ḥusn meñ ḥusn-e ʿamal kā sā ḳhayāl
ḳhuld kā ik dar hai merī gor ke andar khulā (14:5; #76)

The thought of beauty surely merits virtue of a pious action,
As a door to paradise has opened inside my grave.

ḳhuld: heaven; *gor*: grave; *ḥusn-e ʿamal*: good deed.

The reward of direct access from the grave to heaven comes from good deeds in life. Keeping this in mind, *Ġhālib* says that he entered the grave thinking only of her as opposed to the usual good deeds, but still, the door to heaven opened in his grave. Thinking about her is a good deed in itself. More realistically, thinking of her is heaven enough, grave or no grave.

مُنہ نہ کھُلنے پر ہے وُہ عالم کہ دیکھا ہی نہیں　　زُلف سے بڑھ کر نقاب اُس شوخ کے مُنہ پر کھُلا

muñh nā khulne par hai vuh ʿālam kih dekhā hī nahiñ
zulf se baṛh kar naqāb us shoḳh ke muñh par khulā (14:6; #77)

Without seeing her face, it is a sight never seen before.
More than her tresses, the veil suited the face of that sweet beloved.

vuh ʿālam: what a spectacle; *muñh par khulnā*: for something to suit on face.

In her covered face, I see a spectacle never before seen. First, her face used to be partially covered with tresses in a dazzling display of beauty.

Now she has begun wearing a veil, which enhances her charm, for it, suits her face even more. When her face was shown just partially, I wanted to see the rest of it. Now, fully veiled, I desire to see even more of her. Her veil has done more than what her tresses used to do.

در پہ رہنے کو کہا اور کہہ کے کیسا پھر گیا   جتنے عرصے میں مرا لپٹا ہوا بستر کھلا

dar pa(h) rahne ko kahā āur kah kih kaisā phir gayā
jitne ʿarṣe meñ merā lipṭā hu'ā bistar khulā (14:7; #78)

Having told me to stay at her threshold, see how she has reneged,
Just in time, as I laid out my rolled bed.

phir gayā: reneged.

She told me I could remain at her threshold, but by the time I unrolled my bed, she reneged and I was told to pack and go. She was both flirtatious and callous. She lets me come close, and then she pushes me away causing much frustration. This is one of the livelier, almost wanton, verses of *Ġhālib.*

کیوں اندھیری ہے شبِ غم ہے بلاؤں کا نزول   آج اُدھر ہی کو رہے گا دیدۂ اختر کھلا

kioñ andherī hai shab-e ġham, hai balāoñ kā nuzūl
āj udhar hī ko rahe gā dīda(h)' aḳhtar khulā (14:8:79)

Why is the night of sorrow so bleak? Calamities are descending upon me;
Today the eyes of the stars shall remain fixed upwards.

andherī: dark; *balā:* calamity; *nuzūl:* coming down; *aḳhtar*: star.

Why is the night of sorrow so dark? It is because calamities are descending from heaven, so the stars have their face towards the sky leaving a dark shadow on the earth. It may also be interpreted as stars shutting their eyes with fear. As calamities begin falling, they cannot bear to watch. This verse falls classically in line with some of the most imaginative writings of *Ġhālib*.

کیا رہوں غربت میں خوش، جب ہو حوادث کا یہ حال نامہ لاتا ہے وطن سے نامہ بر اکثر کھلا

kyā rahūñ ġhurbat meñ ḳhūsh, jab ho ḥavādiṡ kā yih ḥāl
nāma(h) lātā hai vaṭan se nāma(h) bar akṡar khulā (14:9:80)

How can I be happy in this foreign land, while misfortunes happen so frequently,
That often the mailman brings open letters from home?

ġhurbat: living in alien land; *ḥavādiṡ*: accidents; ***nāma(h)***: letter.

The reference is to an old tradition of sending unsealed letters that announce bad news. How can I be happy in a foreign land where I am poor and when most letters I receive from home arrive already open?

اُس کی اُمت میں ہوں مَیں، میرے رہیں کیوں کام بند
واسطے جس شہ کے غالب گنبدِ بے دَر کھلا

us kī ummat meñ hūñ maiñ, mere raheñ kioñ kām band
vāsṯe jis shah ke Ġhālib gunmbad-e be dar khulā (14:10; #81)

I am a follower of him, why would not things work out for me?
O, *Ġhālib*! The King for whom the doors opened to the door-less dome.

ummat: people, followers of a Prophet; *gunmbad-e be dar*: dome without door, heaven

I am a follower of the Prophet Mohammed. How could my works be hindered? For him, entering the dome without a door is not an obstacle. The door-less dome refers to heaven that was opened to him on the night of "journey." Through his bestowing of blessings, things will work out for me, too.

15

شب کہ برقِ سوزِ دل سے زہرۂ ابر آب تھا
شعلۂ جوّالہ ہر اک حلقۂ گرداب تھا

shab kih barq-e soz-e dil se zahrah' abr āb thā
sho'la(h) javāla(h) har ik ḥalqa(h)' girdāb thā (15:1; #82)

Last night, the lightning heat of my heart's anguish melted the clouds;
Each vortex of the whirlpool was a leaping flame.

zahr'a(h)-e abr āb: melting out of clouds; *sho'la(h) javāla(h)*: leaping flame; *girdāb*: whirlpool.

Last night my heart was so tender with pain that it made lightning. This heat caused the clouds to melt and swirl like a whirlpool with leaping flames in its vortex. The remarkable imagination illustrated here is matched only by the verse's extreme exaggeration. The heat of anguish filled my spleen like a whirlpool spewing out flames.

واں کرم کو عذرِ بارش تھا عناں گیرِ خرام
گریے سے یاں پنبۂ بالش کفِ سیلاب تھا

vāñ karam ko 'uzr-e bārish thā 'inān gīr-e ḳhirām
girye se yāñ pumba(h)' bālish kaf-e sailāb thā (15:2; #83)

There, to the beloved, rain was the excuse keeping her from coming over;
Here, from the tears, the cotton of my pillow became the foam of a flood.

karam: kindness (beloved!); *'ināñ gīr*: one stopping; *ḳhirām*: stroll; *pumbah'-e bālish*: cotton of pillow; *kaf*: foam.

Her excuse for not coming to see me was that it was raining. Out of sheer disappointment, my tears created such a storm that the cotton of my pillow appeared like the foam on flooding waters. A flood flows like tears; wet cotton and foam are similar, also. Simply, because she could not come because of rain, I cried on my pillow and created my own storm.

واں خود آرائی کو تھا موتی پرونے کا خیال
یاں ہجومِ اشک میں تارِ نگہ نایاب تھا

vañ ḳhud ārā'ī ko thā motī pirone kā ḳhayāl
yāñ hujūm-e ashk meñ tār-e nigāh nāyāb thā (15:3; #84)

There, self-adorning was busy with stringing pearls;
Here, with the onslaught of tears, the line of sight was rare.

hujūm-e āshk: crowding of tears; *tār-e nigāh*: thread of sight.

There, in self-adornment, she was stringing pearls in her hair. Here, I was waiting for her and crying. This caused the crowding of tears to block the line of my vision, as if it were a thread. Note the references to thread and hair, pearls in hair, and tears in thread. Tears stringed onto eyelashes block the sight also. Tears are compared to pearls, and stringing pearls to the presence of tears on eyelashes. *Ġhālib* frequently speaks of sight as if it were a string coming out of eyes.

جلوۂ گُل نے کیا تھا واں چراغاں آبجُو
یاں رواں مژگانِ چشمِ تر سے خُونِ ناب تھا

jalva(h)-e gul ne kīyā thā vāñ charāġhāñ ābjū
yāñ ravāñ mizhgān-e chashm-e tar se ḳhūn-e nāb thā (15:4; #85)

There, it was a display of flowers illuminating the waterway,
Here, a channel of fresh blood was flowing from my eyelashes of bedewed eyes.

jalva(h)-e gul: display of flowers; *chashm-e tar:* bedewed eyes; *ḳhūn-e nāb*: pure and clean blood.

The flowers along the banks of the lake were offering bright reflections upon the water and appeared to be burning lamps. All the while, I cried in desperation letting my tears flow. The reflection of red flowers in the water makes it appear as if blood were flowing. Tears, which are fluid, were flooding with great pain, also like blood. "Tears of blood" is an expression used to illustrate extreme pain. Simply put, there were celebrations in her assembly while I was suffering intensely.

یاں سرِ پُر شور بیخوابی سے تھا دِیوار جُو
واں وُہ فرقِ ناز محوِ بالشِ کمخواب تھا

yāñ sar-e pur shor be ḳh(v)ābī se thā dīvār jū
vāñ vuh firq-e nāz maḥv-e bālish-e kamḳh(v)āb thā (15:5; #86)

Here, with a splitting headache due to sleeplessness, I was looking for a wall;
There, that prideful beauty was asleep on a silken pillow.

dīvār-e ju: looking for a wall.

Unable to sleep a wink, my frustration made me want to bang my head against the wall. There, in the comfort of her abode, she had her head on a silken pillow sleeping quietly. Love makes it difficult to sleep, whereas the beloved, having given this tumult to her lover, can sleep in comfort.

یاں نفَس کرتا تھا روشن، شمعِ بزمِ بیخودی
جلوۂ گُل واں بساطِ صُحبتِ احباب تھا

yāñ nafas kartā thā roshan, sham'-e bazm-e beḳhudī
jalva(h)' gul vāñ bisāṭ-e soḥbat-e iḥbāb thā (15:6; #87)

Here, my breath was lighting up lamps in the assembly of rapture,
There, the floor was lined with flowers in the company of friends.

nafas: breath; *roshan*: to light up; *bazm-e beḳhudī*: assembly of rapture; *bisāṭ*: floor.

Here, with each breath, I light candles in the state of my rapture. There, in the company of her friends, she enjoys the splendor of flowers. Here, I am barely keeping the candle lit because I am suffocating. There, though, in the company of strangers, it is delightful as if flowers are blooming all over. Lit candles and blooming flowers are being compared. Another way of looking at this verse is to see that the heat of emotions is so strong that it only takes breathing to light the candle of rapture which is my only company. In her assembly, there are flowers lining the floor and she enjoys the company of her friends.

فرش سے تا عرش واں طُوفاں تھا مَوجِ رنگ کا
یاں زمیں سے آسماں تک سوختن کا باب تھا

farsh se tā 'arsh vāñ ṭufāñ thā mauj-e rang kā
yāñ zamiñ se āsmāñ tak soḳhtan kā bāb thā (15:7; #88)

There, from floor to heaven was a storm of colored waves;
Here, from land to sky, it was a chapter of burning.

sokhtan: jealousy, burning; *bāb:* door, chapter.

There, from the earth to heaven, were arrangements of all luxuries and enjoyment. Here, though, there was only jealousy. In the expanse of her assembly, there was nothing but ultimate joy. This caused me to feel extreme jealousy and I wanted to burn all I had.

ناگہاں اِس رنگ سے خُوننابہ ٹپکانے لگا
دل کہ ذوقِ کاوشِ ناخُن سے لذّت یاب تھا

nāgahāñ is rang se ḳhūnnāba(h) ṭapakne lagā
dil kih żauq-e kāvish-e nāḳhun se lażżat yāb thā (15:8; #89)

Unexpectedly then, the fresh blood began dripping with such intensity,
That the heart began savoring for the sweet pain of the nail's efforts.

nāgahāñ: unexpected; *ḳhūnnāba(h)*: pure blood (meaning tears of blood); *żauq-e kāvish nāḳhūn*: taste for the efforts of nails, sweet pain of the nail's laceration.

My heart was lavished with joy because my nails made the wounds deeper and offered greater pain. Such all-consuming pain that gives joy was too much, and so a storm of tears (of blood) began to flow. The storm of tears can also be taken as fresh verses coming from an extremely saddened heart.

16

نالۂ دل میں شب اندازِ اثر نایاب تھا
تھا سپندِ بزمِ وصلِ غیر، گو بے تاب تھا

nāla(h)-e dil meñ shab andāz-e aṡar nāyāb thā
thā sipand-e bazm-e viṣl-e ġhair, go betāb thā (16:1; #90)

Last night, the sighs of my heart were hardly effective;
Though it cracked, the rue seed proved a good omen for my rival's union with beloved.

āṡar: effect; *nāyāb*: nonexistent, rare; *sipand:* black rue seed thrown in fire; if cracks down, it protects from evil.

Last night my sighs proved totally ineffective. In fact, they served as an omen, which blessed the union of my beloved with my rival. If my sighs were at all sincere, they would have prevented, not graced, the union. My sighs were also restless like the black rue seed as it cracked in fire. Black rue seed that crackles in fire is known to serve as protection from evil. I was burning in my own fire and my laments, as tumultuous as they may be, encouraged the beloved to teach me a lesson. Just to make me feel greater pain, she went ahead with a union with my rival. My sighs, therefore, proved blissful for the rival. Notice the restlessness of the sigh and the crackling of rue seeds in fire. My restless sigh proved a good omen for my rival. My efforts backfired.

مقدمِ سیلاب سے دل کیا نشاط آہنگ ہے
خانۂ عاشق، مگر سازِ صدائے آب تھا

maqdam-e sailāb se dil kyā nishāṯ āhang hai
ḳhāna(h)ʼ ʻāshiq, magar sāz-e ṣadāʼ āb thā (16:2; #91)

How the arrival of a flood has enraptured my heart.
The lover's home was but a resonating water reed.

maqdam-e sailāb: arrival of flood; *nishāṯ āhang:* glad; *ḳhāna(h):* home; *sāz-e ṣadā-e āb:* water reeds.

I was so glad to see the flood destroying my home that my heart began to sing. The sound of water gushing through my ruined home was like the sound of a water reed to me. Singing heart and resonating water reed are notable, as is the arrival of a flood, which connotes the arrival of something calamitous. Here, the broken frame of the house acts as a reed.

نازشِ ایامِ خاکستر نشینی کیا کہوں
پہلوئے اندیشہ وقفِ بسترِ سنجاب تھا

nāzish-e ayām-e ḳhākastar nashīnī, kyā kahūñ
pahlūʼe andesha(h) vaqf-e bistar-e sanjāb thā (16:3; #92)

What to say of the pride and comfort of the days of humbleness
When worried thoughts used to rest on a bed of mink?

nāzish: pride; *ḳhākastar nashinī*: humbleness; *andesha(h)*: worry; *vaqf*: dedicated; *bistar*: bed; *sanjāb*: mink.

The days of humble living were my pride. Contentment prevailed and my thoughts rested on a bed of mink. I enjoyed myself ecstatically with no worry at all. This means that when we live a life of simple virtue, life is a soft dream, both physically and mentally.

کچھ نہ کی اپنے جنونِ نارسا نے، ورنہ یاں
ذرہ ذرہ روکشِ خورشیدِ عالم تاب تھا

kuchh na(h) kī apne junūn-e nārasā ne, varna(h) yāñ
żarra(h) żarra(h) rūkash-e ḳhurshīd-e ʿālam tāb thā (16:4; #93)

My incomplete, ineffective devotion did little, or else here,
Every particle was the coating for the world-illuminating sun.

kuchh na(h) kī: did little; *junūn-e nārasāñ*: incomplete and ineffective devotion; *rūkash*: covering surface layer, coating.

The power of love is such that it can polish ordinary dust to a shine; I could not do anything to make my love shine. I could not shine the particles of existence because of my imperfect love and devotion. The sun is the beloved and particles of the universe shine as an expression of devotion. My untrue love did not sharpen my skills of devotion adequately. I did not shine before my beloved.

آج کیوں پروا نہیں اپنے اسیروں کی تجھے؟
کل تلک تیرا بھی دِل مہر و وفا کا باب تھا

āj kioñ parva(h) nahiñ apne asīroñ kī tujhe
kal talak terā bhī dil mahr-o-vafā kā bāb thā (16:5; #94)

Why today, do you care little for those in your bondage,
When till yesterday, your heart too was the door to affection and fidelity?

asīr: in bondage; *bāb*: door, chapter.

Why aren't you concerned any longer with those who are in your bondage? It was only yesterday that your heart was full of sincerity, and being callous to your lovers was not your style. Why, now?

یاد کر وہ دن کہ ہر اِک حلقہ تیرے دام کا
اِنتظارِ صید میں اِک دیدۂ بے خواب تھا

yād kar vuh din kih har ik ḥalqa(h) tere dām kā
intiẓār-e ṣaid meñ ik dīdah' beḳh(v)āb thā (16:6; #95)

Think of those days when every ring of your snare
Was waiting for its prey like a wide-open sleepless eye.

ḥalqa(h): ring; *dām*: net; *ṣaid*: catch, prey.

Do you remember when your net used to be empty? You had left it open while hunting for game as if it were a wide-open, insomniac eye. This period is gone now that you have caught so many in your net; you need not think of any new catches. Observe the reference to the opening of the net and the unblinking insomniac eye. This represents a rather desperate situation on the part of the beloved. You have enough lovers in your net, the lover is informing her. Another meaning is that the lover is reminding the beloved of the days when she would be up all night thinking about how to catch lovers.

مَیں نے روکا رات غالبؔ کو، وگرنہ دیکھتے
اُس کے سیلِ گریہ میں گردُوں کفِ سیلاب تھا

maiñ ne rokā rāt Ġhālib ko, vagarna(h) dekhte
us ke sail-e girya(h) meñ gardūñ kaf-e sailāb thā (16:7; #96)

Last night I restrained *Ġhālib*, otherwise you would have seen
The flow of his tears turn the sky into the foam of flood.

girya(h): crying; *kaf*: foam.

Had I not stopped *Ġhālib* from crying last night, the tears would have turned into such a great flood that the sky would appear as the foam of rushing waters. Note how the clouds are the foam of an infinitely deep ocean, which is the sky. Foam appears in water only when the flow is fast; that is how *Ġhālib* compares his shedding of tears to foam in the sky.

17

ایک ایک قطرے کا مجھے دینا پڑا حساب
خونِ جگر ودیعتِ مژگانِ یار تھا

ek ek qaṭre kā mujhe denā paṛā ḥisāb
k͟hūn-e jigar vadīʿat-e mizhgān-e yār thā (17:1; #97)

I was forced to account for each and every drop, as
The blood of my liver was held in trust for her eyelashes.

vadiʿat: something in trust.

The blood of my liver was merely a deposit in trust on behalf of her eyelashes. It belonged to her exclusively. However, having spent my tears of blood elsewhere, I had to be accountable and start working all over just to return her property. The connection between eyelashes and blood refers to the poet having assured her that only her eyelashes would be allowed to pierce his liver. However, having shed blood-tears elsewhere (falling in love elsewhere), the lover still had to be true to his promise. Some have interpreted it as tears of blood flowing uncontrollably, leaving no blood in the liver, but that creates the problem of how to connect this loss to her eyelashes. Essentially, the lover has misappropriated the trust and is now afraid of how he will come up with what is lost. Some have interpreted it simply as the tears were hers to have and in this way I have had to account for it all.

اب میں ہوں اور ماتمِ یک شہرِ آرزو
توڑا جو تو نے آئنہ، تمثال دار تھا

ab maiñ hūñ aur mātam-e yak shahar-e ārzū
toṛā jo tū ne ā'īna(h), timṡāl dār thā (17:2; #98)

Now, it is I and my laments for countless lost aspirations,
As you shattered the mirror that reflected myriad images.

mātam: lamenting; *shahr-e ārzū*: city of aspiration (many aspirations); *ārzū*: desire; *ā'īna(h)*: mirror; *timṡāl dār*: reflection producing.

My heart, like a mirror, reflected your image and thus contained my desire for you. Having shattered my heart, you have converted it into thousands of mirrors, each one with your image in it. What was a single lost desire has turned into thousands of desires that would be lost. I lament that you converted it into a larger loss for me to bear. I am now left holding a whole "city of desires."

گلیوں میں میری نعش کو کھینچے پھرو، کہ میں
جاں دادۂ ہوائے سرِ رہگزار تھا

galīyoñ meñ merī na'sh ko khenche phiro, kih maiñ
jāñ dādah' havā-e sar-e rahguzar thā (17:3; #99)

Take my corpse and drag it through the alleys, for I
Was desirous of dying along the path frequented by her.

galīyoñ: alleys; *na'sh*: corpse; *jāñ dāda(h)*: who is willing to give his life; *havā*: desire.

Drag my corpse along her route to remind her of who I was and how much I loved her, and to let her know that I achieved my goal.

Dragging my corpse disgraces me and induces her to feel ashamed for not paying attention to me. Different alleys indicate places where she visited the lover's rivals. The beloved may come across the lover's corpse somewhere. In addition, the desire to be dragged through many alleys indicates the places where she used to visit the rivals, where she might come across my corpse.

موجِ سرابِ دشتِ وفا کا نہ پُوچھ حال
ہر ذرّہ، مثلِ جوہرِ تیغ، آب دار تھا

mauj-e sarāb-e dasht-e vafā kā na(h) pūchh ḥāl
har żarra(h), miṡl-e johar-e teġh, ābdār thā (17:4; #100)

Ask not about the waves of mirage in the desert of loyalty.
Each particle was shining like the edge of a sharp sword.

sarāb: mirage; *johar-e teġh*: edge of sword; *ābdār*: shiny, sparkling.

The shining grains of sand produce an illusion of waves of water, a mirage that comforts thirsty wanderers. For wanderers in the wilderness of love, there is a mirage of comfort in the company of the beloved. Each particle that creates the mirage is actually the edge of a sword, so to go through the wilderness of love is to walk over these swords. Along the path to loyalty, any comfort is a mirage leading to more heartbreak. In the vast mirage of beloved's loyalty, each particle of sand is like a sharp sword that lover grabs believing it is water (love).

کم جانتے تھے ہم بھی غمِ عشق کو، پر اب
دیکھا تو کم ہوئے پہ غمِ روزگار تھا

kam jānte the ham bhī ġhame ʿishq ko, par ab
dekhā to kam hu'e pa ġham-e rozgār thā (17:5; #101)

Little did we appreciate the sorrows of love, but I now
See that when it was lessened, the sorrows of livelihood took its place.

The lessening of sorrow of love is quickly made up with other sorrows, particularly the sorrow of everyday living. The pain of love has lessened, but the gap is quickly filled by other sorrows of life. When in love, devotion makes all other sorrows appear insignificant. I did not know the grief of love before, when I had to contend with just one sorrow. Now I have to worry about so many. Now I have other sorrows that do not carry with them the pleasure of love.

18

بسکہ دشوار ہے ہر کام کا آساں ہونا   آدمی کو بھی میسّر نہیں انساں ہونا

baskih dushvār hai har kām kā āsāñ honā
ādmī ko bhī mayassar nahiñ insāñ honā (18:1; #102)

Whereas it is difficult for everything to work out easily,
A man cannot even afford to be a human.

baskih: whereas, though; *dushvār*: difficult; *mayassar:* affordable.

It is difficult for anything to work out easily. If man cannot afford to act like a human being, how can one expect all else to work out naturally? It is actually a very arduous task to act human, though it is the closest thing to his being. What to ask of other things? A great deal of sarcasm is infused here. Man, behaving as a human being, is more an irony than reality. As we learn from the history of mankind, man is more like an animal. The verse points to the pitfalls in thinking that there are things that we know to be true. For example, it is not fair for the lover to suffer so much. However, fairness does not prevail in this world. Difficulties arise when we assume things. Someone said, "the more I learn about human nature, the more I like nature."

گریہ چاہے ہے خرابی مرے کاشانے کی   در و دیوار سے ٹپکے ہے بیاباں ہونا

girya(h) chāhe hai ḳharābī mere kāshāne kī
dar-o-dīvār se ṭapke hai bayābāñ honā (18:2; #103)

The crying is threatening to destroy my home;
The walls and doors are dripping with the signs of a wilderness in the making.

girya(h): crying; *kāshāna*: home.

My tears have endangered my home. The doors and walls are dripping with evidence that they will be wiped out by waves of tears, leaving my home to ruin. The flood of tears has destroyed the doors and walls. Complete destruction is my fate.

واے دیوانگیِ شوق کہ ہر دم مجھ کو   آپ جانا اُدھر اور آپ ہی حیراں ہونا

vāe divāngī' shauq kih har dam mujh ko
āp jānā udhar aur āp hī ḥairāñ honā (18:3; #104)

Alas! The intensity of desire that again and again I would
Drive myself there and then get lost in amazement.

vāe: Alas!; *divāngī' shauq*: intensity of desire.

Alas! The intensity of my desire continuously drags me to her. Then, upon reaching her, I am stunned when I realize her lack of attention. I am surprised because her aloofness proves that my desires may not have been sincere or intense enough. I am surprised at myself for being so inarticulate and ineffective.

جلوہ از بسکہ تقاضاے نگہ کرتا ہے   جوہرِ آئینہ بھی چاہے ہے مژگاں ہونا

jalva(h), az baskih taqāẓā-e nigāh kartā hai
johar-e ā'īna(h) bhī chāhe haī mizhgāñ honā (18:4; #105)

The display of beauty, of its own accord, demands to be seen.
The lines in the mirror also wish to become eyelashes.

az baskih: because; *taqāẓā*: insisting; *johar-e ā'īna(h)*: lines formed at the time of coating in the steel mirror.

Your display of beauty demands that everyone look at you so much that the lines in the mirror coating have turned into eyelashes hoping to catch a glimpse of you. The beloved is looking into the mirror and the mirror wants to look back at her desperately. To do that, the coating of the mirror has creased into the shape of eyelashes. A small difficulty arises here since eyelashes do not see. This is the function of eyes. If the coating of the mirror had turned into a pupil it would be clearer, but then it would not be *Ġhālib.* The poet just wanted to play with straight lines in the mirror that appear in the shape of eyelashes. Note: Metallic mirrors in the times of the poet used to develop imperfections in the shape of lines.

عشرتِ قتل گہِ اہلِ تمنا مت پوچھ　　عیدِ نظارہ ہے شمشیر کا عریاں ہونا

ʿishrat-e qatl gah-e ahl-e tamannā mat pūchh
ʿīd-e naẓẓāra(h) hai shamshīr kā ʿuryāñ honā (18:5; #106)

Ask not of the joy on the killing fields, to those with desire;
A sheer delight it is to see the sword unsheathed.

ahl-e tamannā: having desire (to get sacrificed for their beloved); *ʿīd-e naẓẓāra(h)*: sight of sheer happiness.

The joy of willing lovers upon reaching the fields of murder is indescribable. When the naked sword rises to strike them, they are elated, for they have reached their destiny of being killed by their beloved. Those who stand firm in the path of their belief have much to be proud of for they leave behind a legacy for others to follow. The construction of Eid crescent to describe happiness is similar to the shape of a sword as well.

لے گئے خاک میں ہم داغِ تمنائے نشاط　　تُو ہو اور آپ بہ صد رنگ گلستاں ہونا

le ga'e ḳhāk meñ ham dāġh-e tamannā-e nishāṯ
tū ho āur āp baṣad rang gulistāñ honā (18:6; #107)

We took to the grave the scars of the longing for happiness,
Wishing you to rejoice in hundreds of ways.

baṣad: hundreds; *gulistāñ honā*: to rejoice.

O! Beloved, we have taken to our graves our unfulfilled desire for the ecstasy of any joy. We wish you well in your merriment and joy. May you bloom in hundreds of ways!

عشرتِ پارۂ دل، زخمِ تمنا کھانا   لذتِ ریشِ جگر، غرقِ نمکداں ہونا

'ishrat-e pāra(h)' dil, zaḳhm-e tamannā khānā
lażżat-e resh-e jigar, ġharq-e namakdāñ honā (18:7; #108)

The joy of pieces of heart is to get wounded from lost hopes.
The joy of the liver's wounds is to be drowned in a saltshaker.

pār'a(h): shatter; *resh:* wound.

The heart's joy comes when it is shattered after being wounded by unfulfilled desires. Rubbing salt into wounds enhances the pain therefore, the joy, so much so that we may as well bring the wounds right into the salt shaker, instead of bringing salt to the wounds.

کی مرے قتل کے بعد اس نے جفا سے توبہ   ہائے اس زود پشیماں کا پشیماں ہونا

kī mere qatl ke ba'd us ne jafā se tauba(h)
hāi us zūd pashemāñ kā pashemāñ honā (18:8; #109)

After killing me, she vowed never again to be cruel.
Alas! The repentance of an early repentant!

zūd pashemāñ: who repents readily

After killing me, my beloved vowed never to kill again with her cruelty. Alas! She did not repent early enough to save me. Early repentant is central to the theme and is sarcastic. This is one of the most widely quoted verses of *Ġhālib*.

حیف اُس چار گرہ کپڑے کی قسمت غالبؔ!
جس کی قسمت میں ہو عاشق کا گریباں ہونا

ḥaif us chār gira(h) kapṛe kī qismat Ġhālib
jis kī qismat meñ ho ʿāshiq kā garebāñ honā (18:9:110)

Pity the fate of the foot-long parcel of cloth, *Ġhālib*;
In the fate of which it is to end up becoming the lover's collar.

haif: pity; *girah*: equivalent to 3 inches; *garebāñ:* collar.

Pity! That foot of cloth, O' *Ġhālib*, which by its ill fate ends up as the collar of the lover, for it will be repeatedly torn in agony. The lovers are continuously tearing and sewing their collar so the cloth bears the pain of lovers' agony.

19

شبِ خمارِ شوقِ ساقی رستخیز اندازہ تھا
تا محیطِ بادہ صورت خانۂ خمیازہ تھا

shab ḳhumār-e shauq-e sāqī rastḳhez andāza(h) thā
tā muḥīṭ-e bāda(h) ṣurat ḳhāna(h)' ḳhamyāza(h) thā (19:1; #111)

Last night, the hangover waiting for the cupbearer was like the end of the world;
Even the wine was splashing at the meniscus as if it were yawning.

ḳhumār: intoxication; *shauq:* desire; *sāqī:* cupbearer, beloved; *rastḳhez andāza(h):* like the Day of Resurrection; *tā muḥīṭ-e bāda(h):* even the wine, the meniscus mark; *ṣurat-e ḳhāna(h)-e ḳhamyāza(h):* as if yawning or stretching arms.

Last night, as I longingly waited for my beloved to arrive, an air of intoxication and boredom hung about the tavern. Even the wine splashed about in the decanter as if it were yawning and stretching. The air resembled the chaos of Doomsday. The poet has made some very difficult comparisons, from using Resurrection of the dead with stretching arms to the splashing of wine in the glass, which could also be said to raise its arms. In *Urdū* poetry, the air on the day of Resurrection is chaotic and unbearable. In brief, the poet wants to convey the feeling of a hangover with a cupful of exaggeration.

یک قدم وحشت سے درسِ دفترِ امکاں کھلا
جادہ، اجزائے دو عالم دشت کا شیرازہ تھا

yak qadam vaḥshat se dars-e daftar-e imkāñ khulā
jāda(h), ajzā'e do ʿālam dasht kā shīrāza(h) thā (19:2; #112)

Only one foot into frenzy revealed a world of possibilities,
The path to the elements of the two worlds was the thread tying the wilderness together.

vaḥshat: solitude, frenzy; *dars*: lesson; *daftar-e imkāñ*: world of possibilities; *jāda(h)*: path; *shīrāza(h)*: thread that binds a book.

As I stepped into the wilderness of solitude and frenzy, I came to know the reality of the world beyond. It was revealed to me that the path to understanding the elements of here and hereafter is actually a string (path) of frenzy, not reason, or intelligence. Notice the similarity in the physical display of thread and path and what happens when the thread is pulled: it comes off. The binding thread holds a book together. If it is pulled out, all the pages come off. The path to frenzy is just that thread which keeps all elements together. Noticeable is the declaration that this revelation came just when he began his journey on this long path. He understood it well and quickly and quite early in his career as a lover.

مانعِ وحشت خرامیہائے لیلیٰ کون ہے؟
خانۂ مجنونِ صحرا گرد بے دروازہ تھا

mānīʿ-e vaḥshat ḳhirāmī hāi lailā kaun hai
ḳhāna(h)' majnūn-e ṣaḥrā gard be darvāza(h) thā (19:3; #113)

Who is keeping *Lailā* from her frenzied walks?
The home of *Majnūn*, the desert wanderer, had no doors.

mānī́: preventing; *ḳhirām*: walk; *ṣaḥrā gard*: wanderer of wilderness, the character of *Majnūn*; *ṣaḥrā:* desert.

Majnūn's place was in the wilderness where there were no doors and no obstacles. Why didn't *Lailā* reach him then? Who prevented her arrival? Keep in mind that *Lailā* loved *Majnūn* as well and wanted to meet him. The only way for *Lailā* to reach *Majnūn* would be for her to adopt the state of frenzy also, or else she would not know where to find him. What stopped her? The sanctity of her love was not as supreme as that of *Majnūn*, the poet concludes. On a more physical level, if there were no doors to the home of *Majnūn*, what could have prevented *Lailā* from entering it?

پُوچھ مت رُسوائیِ اندازِ استغنائے حُسن
دست مرہُونِ حنا، رُخسار رہنِ غازہ تھا

puchh mat rusvāī' andāz-e istaġhnā-e ḥusn
dast marhūn-e ḥinā, ruḳhsār rahn-e ġhāza(h) thā (19:4; #114)

Ask not what embarrassment is wrought to beauty by the simple style;
When hands owed to *henna*, and face was pawned to face powder.

rusvā'ī: disgrace; *istaġhnā*: obliviousness; *marhūn*: indebted to; *rahn*: pawn.

Simplicity, as a style, is subject to challenge and disgrace for she is indebted to *henna* for the red color of her hands and to face powder for the beauty of her cheeks. Real beauty does not need any implements to enhance it. If the beloved must use *henna* and face powder to enhance her beauty, then acting simple is hypocritical.

نالۂ دل نے دِیے اَوراقِ لختِ دل بہ باد
یادگارِ نالہ اک دیوانِ بے شیرازہ تھا

nāla(h)' dil ne đīye aurāq-e lakht-e dil ba(h) bād
yādgār-e nālah ik divān-e be shīrāza(h) thā (19:5; #115)

The sighs of heart gave the pages of the pieces of my heart to the breeze.
The memory of my sighs was a volume of unbound collection of verses.

lakht-e dil: pieces of heart; *ba(h) bād*: given to breeze; *đīvān*: collection of verses.

The sighs of my heart shattered it into many pieces that flew away on the breeze, like the pages of a book from which the binding had been removed. The shattered pieces of my heart were my verses. The memory of my sighs was the collection of my verses, which are now scattered, its pages disjointed. With these gone, no memory of the sighs remains. This verse refers to the loss of *Ġhālib*'s work during the mutiny of 1857.

20

دوست غمخواری میں میری سعی فرمائیں گے کیا
زخم کے بھرنے تلک ناخن نہ بڑھ جائیں گے کیا

dost ġham ḳh(v)ārī meñ merī saʿī farmāeñ ge kyā
zaḳhm ke bharne talak nāḳhun na(h) baṛ(h) jāeñ ge kyā (20:1; #116)

What could the friends do to help console me in my suffering?
Would the nails not grow back till the wounds heal?

ġham ḳh(v)ārī: consoler; *saʿī*: help.

What can friends do to comfort me in my suffering and pain? The most they can do is to trim my nails so I will not scratch my wounds. But do they not know that by the time my wounds heal, my nails will have grown back and I will return to scratching my wounds? All measures to ward off the misery of loving are but temporary; it is a permanent wound. Somehow, I will keep getting newer problems as the old ones resolve.

بے نیازی حد سے گزری بندہ پرور کب تلک
ہم کہیں گے حالِ دل اور آپ فرمائیں گے کیا

be niyāzī ḥad se guzrī banda(h) parvar kab talak
ham kaheñ ge ḥāl-e dil aur āp farmāeñ ge kyā (20:2; #117)

Obliviousness, gone beyond limits, for how long, you affable beloved?
I would tell my heart's tale and you would respond, "What?"

banda(h) parvar: concerned about others, affable beloved (sarcastically).

O! Beloved, your obliviousness to me has gone beyond all limits. Tell me, how long will it last? When I tell you the condition of my heart, the only response I get from you is, "What?" This sarcastic response destroys all seriousness. The poet is trying to make her listen to him seriously. This is typical of *Ġhālib*'s wanton style.

حضرتِ ناصح گر آئیں، دیدہ و دل فرشِ راہ
کوئی مجھ کو یہ تو سمجھا دو کہ سمجھائیں گے کیا؟

ḥaẓrat-e nāsiḥ gar āeñ, dīda(h)-o-dil farsh-e rāh
ko'ī mujh ko yih to samjhā do kih samjhāeñ ge kyā (20:3; #118)

Should the honorable preacher arrive, I shall welcome him with my eyes and heart to the floor.
Would someone explain, what could he possibly do to make me understand?

dīda(h)-o-dil farsh-e rāh: (eyes and heart spread in the path) highest regards.

If the revered preacher wants to visit me, I will welcome him with highest regard, but will someone please tell me exactly what he can make me understand? Absolutely nothing can change me, but if he wants to waste his time, he is welcome to try. He can say all he wants to, but I am beyond the stage where advice would do any good.

آج واں تیغ و کفن باندھے ہوئے جاتا ہوں میں
عذر میرے قتل کرنے میں وہ اب لائیں گے کیا

āj vāñ teġh-o-kafan bāndhe hu'e jātā huñ maiñ
'użr mere qatl karne meñ vuh ab lāeñ ge kyā (20:4; #119)

Armed with sword and shroud, I go there today.
What excuse will she bring for not killing me this time?

kafan: shroud.

Getting killed by the beloved is the ultimate desire of the lover. The beloved continues to give excuses like "I cannot kill you for I do not have a sword," or "there is not any arrangement to bury you," etc. The lover is determined, carrying both sword and shroud with him to her assembly. I am anxious to see what excuse she would adduce now. A very delicate relationship is expressed here. The beloved does not want to kill her lover, only wound him. The lover, however, wants to get it over with as he has had enough.

گر کیا ناصح نے ہم کو قید، اچھا یُوں سہی
یہ جنُونِ عشق کے انداز چھُٹ جائیں گے کیا

gar kīyā nāseḥ ne ham ko qaid, achhā yuñ sahī
yih junūn-e ʿishq ke andāz chhuṭ jāen ge kyā (20:5; #120)

If the preacher gets me imprisoned; so be it.
Would we quit our style of the frenzy of love?

If the preacher has me imprisoned, so be it. That cannot arrest the craziness of my frenzy. Wandering around may be one way to express my frenzy, which he can check by locking me up, but there are so many other ways to express my frenzy in the prison. The preacher has gone overboard, beyond his authority, but the poet does not mind it for he knows himself to be incorrigible. As soon as he were released from prison, he would return to his old ways. Even in the prison, the lover can do many things to harm himself.

خانہ زادِ زُلف ہیں، زنجیر سے بھاگیں گے کیوں
ہیں گرفتارِ وفا، زنداں سے گھبرائیں گے کیا

ḳhāna(h) zād-e zulf haiñ, zanjīr se bhageñ ge kioñ
haiñ giraftār-e vafā, zindāñ se ghabrāeñ ge kyā (20:6; #121)

Slave to your tresses we are; how can we run from those chains?
Arrested in devotion, how can we be worried about prison?

ḳhāna(h) zād-e zulf: being enslaved by the tresses.

Enslaved by her tresses, I have developed a special affection for them. I shall not run away from the chain of your tresses. Arrested by my fidelity to her, I am least bothered by the prison offered by these tresses. I am perfectly happy with that.

ہے اب اِس معمُورے میں قحطِ غمِ اُلفت اسدؔ
ہم نے یہ مانا کہ دِلّی میں رہیں، کھائیں گے کیا؟

hai ab is ma'mure meñ qaḥṯ-e ġham-e ulfat Asad
ham ne yih mānā kih dillī meñ raheñ, khāeñ ge kyā (20:7; #122)

This settlement is now in the grip of a famine of sorrow of love, Asad;
Given that I desire to live in *Delhī*, but what will I eat?

ma'mure: settlement; *qaḥt*: famine.

There is a famine in the settlement of the sorrow of love. I want to live in *Delhī*, but if I did, what would there be to eat? The sorrow of love is my only staple. With that gone, I will starve. When the people around me have lost all sense of loving, this is no longer a place to live. This verse refers to the callousness of his peers towards him. The staple poet is longing for is the appreciation of his work.

21

یہ نہ تھی ہماری قسمت کہ وصالِ یار ہوتا　　اگر اور جیتے رہتے یہی انتظار ہوتا

yih na(h) thī hamārī qismat kih viṣāl-e yār hotā
agar aur jīte rahte yahī intiẓār hotā (21:1; #123)

It wasn't in my fate to have union with the beloved;
Had I lived, the waiting would still have been the same.

viṣāl: union.

Union with her was not my fate. It is better that I died, for if I had kept on living it would have been a life of continuous waiting. The pain of waiting would have been worse than the one time agony of death. It worked out better for me that I died.

ترے وعدے پر جیے ہم تو یہ جان جھوٹ جانا　　کہ خوشی سے مر نہ جاتے اگر اعتبار ہوتا

tere vaʻde par jīye ham, to yih jān, jhūṭ jānā
kih ḳhūshī se mar na(h) jāte agar iʻtibār hotā (21:2; #124)

Had I lived on your pledge, I would surely have lost life
Out of sheer joy and ecstasy, if I had believed in it.

If I had believed in your promise, the joy would have killed me. The fact that I am living is proof that I did not believe you. The word "life," has a dual meaning. In calling the beloved "my life," *Ġhālib* is saying, "if I die I will lose both my life and my beloved."

تری نازکی سے جانا کہ بندھا تھا عہد بودا کبھی تُو نہ توڑ سکتا، اگر اُستوار ہوتا

terī nāzukī se jānā kih bāndhā thā ʿahd būdā
kabhī tū na(h) toṛ saktā, agar ustuvār hotā (21:3; #125)

Your delicate nature revealed why the pledge you gave was so fragile;
You would not have been able to break it, had it been firm.

ʿahd: promise; *būdā*: weak; *ustuvār:* permanent.

Everything is delicate about you, which explains why your promise was weak, for if it had been firm you would not have been able to break it. This is an extremely "delicate" way to relieve the beloved of her embarrassment at breaking her pledges. "It was not your fault. Your delicate nature made it inevitable. Since you cannot be anything but delicate, your pledges are fragile. It is not your fault. It is all right."

کوئی میرے دل سے پُوچھے ترے تیرِ نیم کش کو یہ خلش کہاں سے ہوتی جو جگر کے پار ہوتا

ko'ī mere dil se pūchhe tere tīr-e nīm kash ko
yih ḳhalish kahāñ se hotī jo jigar ke pār hotā (21:4; #126)

Would someone ask my heart about your half-drawn arrow;
From where would this sweet pain have come, had it gone through the liver?

tīr-e nīm kash: half drawn arrow; *ḳhalish*: pinch, hurt.

O! Beloved, ask my heart the doings of your half-drawn arrow. A hurtful pinch continues to emanate from my liver, for it did not go all the way through. If the arrow had gone through, such a beautiful pain would not have been created. A half-drawn arrow is her half-hearted amorous glance; the hurt comes from anticipation of her full glance.

یہ کہاں کی دوستی ہے کہ بنے ہیں دوست ناصح　　کوئی چارہ ساز ہوتا، کوئی غمگسار ہوتا

yih kahāñ kī dostī hai kih bane haiñ dost nāṣiḥ
ko'ī chāra(h) sāz hotā ko'ī ġhamgusār hotā (21:5; #127)

What sort of friendship is this that the friends have turned preachers?
There should have been someone to resolve my predicament and to console my heart.

What kind of friendship turns friends into preachers? What I needed was someone to mend my broken heart by resolving my problems. I needed people who could console me, give me hope that someday she will be kind to me. Preaching neither helps me resolve my problems nor gives support to my heart. The first line has often been interpreted as preacher becoming a friend. The second line will then not interpret correctly because of *Ġhālib*'s perpetual tiffs with the preacher.

رگِ سنگ سے ٹپکتا وہ لہو کہ پھر نہ تھمتا　　جسے غم سمجھ رہے ہو یہ اگر شرار ہوتا

rag-e sang se ṭapaktā vuh lahū kih phir na(h) thamtā
jise ġham samajh rahe ho yih agar sharār hotā (21:6; #128)

It would have dripped from the veins of stone, the blood that would not stop.
Had it been a spark, what you think is the sorrow.

rag: vein; *sang:* stone; *sharār*: spark.

Blood would drip from the veins of stone and would not stop if my sorrow becomes a spark and enters the body of stone. Imagine if it can make a stone bleed. How do you suppose the sorrow rends my heart and hurts me? *Ġhālib* has been very precise in the way he chooses to express the intensity of his sorrow. Stones, like marble, often have lines running through them that resemble veins. The poet says that if the stone is sparked by the intensity that rivals my sorrow, that stone will begin to bleed inside. Not only that, but blood will begin to ooze out. Such will be the intensity of this pain. We all know how hard it is to squeeze water, let alone blood, out of a stone. Only the intensity of the poet's pain can make it happen.

غم اگرچہ جاں گُسل ہے، پہ بچیں کہاں کہ دل ہے
غمِ عشق گر نہ ہوتا، غمِ روزگار ہوتا

ġham agarcheh jāñ gusil hai, pa(h) bacheñ kahāñ kih dil hai
ġham-e ʿishq gar na(h) hotā, ġham-e rozgār hotā (21:7; #129)

Though sorrow is life-taking, we cannot escape it, for there is a heart;
Had there not been the sorrow of love, the worries of living would still be there.

jāñ gusil: killing; *ġham-e rozgār:* worries of livelihood.

Sorrow kills, but you cannot avoid it when dealing with affairs of the heart. If it were not the sorrow of love, your heart would have wanted other worldly things. It is better to have the sorrow of love than the sorrow of disappointment from the material world. If it is not one, then it is another; somehow, woes continue.

کہوں کس سے مَیں کہ کیا ہے، شبِ غم بُری بلا ہے
مجھے کیا بُرا تھا مرنا، اگر ایک بار ہوتا

kahūñ kis se maiñ kih kyā hai shab-e ġham burī balā hai
mujhe kyā burā thā marnā, agar ek bār hotā (21:8; #130)

To whom shall I tell what it is, that the night of separation is a bad calamity?
What was wrong if I were to die, but only once?

balā: affliction, misfortune, distress.

To whom and what shall I say about the distresses of the night of separation? Would not it have been better to die once and get it over with than to die repeatedly, all night, with each breath, waiting for her to arrive? The night of separation continues to kill.

ہوئے مر کے ہم جو رسوا، ہوئے کیوں نہ غرقِ دریا　　نہ کبھی جنازہ اُٹھتا، نہ کہیں مزار ہوتا

hu'e mar ke ham jo rusvā, hu'e kioñ na(h) ġharq-e daryā
na(h) kabhī janāza(h) uṭhtā, na(h) kahiñ mazār hotā (21:9; #131)

Having died, I invited disgrace; why didn't I just drown in the river?
For then, no coffin had to be raised, nor any grave built.

janāza(h): coffin, a type of open coffin wherein the corpse is clad in white shroud and carried by pallbearers.

When I died, nobody came to console or offer a eulogy; this was, of course, a matter of great disgrace to my dead body. Had I drowned it would have spared my corpse the embarrassment since there would not have been a need to arrange a funeral or dig a grave for me. Note that pallbearers to the graveyard carry a coffin. This would have been embarrassing since few would volunteer to "give shoulder" to the coffin of the lover.

اُسے کون دیکھ سکتا کہ یگانہ ہے وُہ یکتا　　جو دُوئی کی بُو بھی ہوتی تو کہیں دوچار ہوتا

use kaun dekh saktā kih yagāna(h) hai vuh yaktā
jo dū'ī kī bū bhī hotī to kahīñ dochār hotā (21:10; #132)

Who could see Him? For He is unique, for He is alone,
Had there been a faint whiff of duality, we surely would have run into Him somewhere!

yagāna(h): alone; *yaktā*: unique; *dū'ī*: duality; *dochār*: a sudden and unexpected meeting, encounter, or interview.

God is unique and alone; there is no existence like His. Had there been even a faint reality to duality, I certainly would have seen Him somewhere. Since the singularity of God is absolute, seeing Him amounts to duality. Since He is part of everything, including myself, my seeing Him would mean that He is not alone. As a result, no one can see Him. If God is in everything and everything is God, then to demand to see Him in order to believe negates the very concept of singularity. A remarkable clarity of thought is presented in this verse. An inevitable challenge is thrown to Moses. The word used to indicate running into God has many colloquial meanings including the mathematical meaning of two pairs of eyes meeting to make them four. If God were not part of us, we would then have many images, two, and four being no exception.

یہ مسائل تصوّف، یہ ترا بیان غالب
تجھے ہم ولی سمجھتے جو نہ بادہ خوار ہوتا

yih masā'il-e taṣavvuf yih terā bayān Ġhālib
tujhe ham valī samajhte jo na(h) bāda(h) ḳh(v)ār hotā (21:11; #133)

These maxims of mysticism and your sublime oration, *Ġhālib*;
We would have taken you for a saint had you not been a wine-drinker.

masā'il: maxim, aphorism, problems; *taṣavvuf*: mysticism; *valī*: saint; *bāda(h) ḳh(v)ār*: wine-drinker.

These maxims of mysticism and your exposition of them are so divine that had you not been a winedrinker, we would have thought of you as a saint. Being a winedrinker, however, strips you of your credibility.

This is the most common explanation. The meaning of this verse is opposite from what is commonly assumed. A saint can only explain things that are simple; it takes a drunkard, not a saint, to reach the state of resolving maxims of mysticism. Since you explained many mysteries to us, we thought of you as merely a saint, but when we found out that you are a drunkard, we knew you were talking about something of a greater value.

22

ہوس کو ہے نشاطِ کار کیا کیا　　نہ ہو مرنا تو جینے کا مزا کیا

havās ko hai nishāṯ-e kār kyā kyā
na(h) ho marnā to jīne kā mazā kyā (22:1; #134)

Avarice is busy with what a multitude of lively affairs?
If there were not death, then life would not be worth the joy.

havas: avarice; *nishāṯ-e kār*: desire to accomplish.

Avarice prompts a desire to work, to achieve worldly things. The driving force for avarice to exist is the imminence of death. If we knew there would always be a tomorrow, we would not do things today. If there were no death, there would be no rush to accomplish anything; it could always wait. Life is so much more interesting knowing that we shall all die. By using the word "avarice," poet states that we are greedy to accumulate worthless things because we are racing against time. That "life would not be worth living if it were not for death" is craftily worded.

تجاہل پیشگی سے مدعا کیا　　کہاں تک اے سراپا ناز کیا کیا

tajāhul peshgī se mudda'ā kyā
kahāñ tak ai sarāpā nāz kyā kyā (22:2; #135)

What is the intent in appearing ignorant knowingly?
For how long O!, You all-coquettish-thing would say, "What, what?"

tajāhul peshgī: knowingly appear ignorant; *sarāpā nāz*: cornpletely coquettish.

Like a stranger, you ask me, "what, what?" whenever I speak to you, as if you do not know anything. What do you mean by this? I know it is nothing but an act of purposely appearing ignorant. The beloved knows well what the lover wants but to ward him off she keeps saying "what" as if she did not hear or understood him. This is irritating to the lover.

نوازِشہائے بیجا دیکھتا ہوں   شِکایتہائے رنگیں کا گِلا کیا

navāzish hāi bejā dekhtā hūñ
shikāyat hāi rangīñ kā gilā kyā (22:3; #136)

I see favors bestowed undeservedly.
Why should then you complain of lover's plaints?

navāzish: favors; *bejā*: undeserved; *shikāyat hāi rangīñ*: lover's plaint; *gilā*: complain.

Whenever I complain to you, my love, you get upset with me. As a result, I keep quiet. I see how you extend favors to my rival undeservedly. I am still quiet. There is a desperate effort by the lover to draw attention of the beloved to say that these favors should be directed towards him instead. However, the lover is not threatening to break it off. He just wants to use the situation of being the underdog to gain attention.

نگاہِ بے مُحابا چاہتا ہُوں   تغافُلہائے تمکیں آزما کیا

nigāh-e be muḥābā chāhtā hūñ
taġhāful hāi tamkīñ āzmā kyā (22:4; #137)

An uninhibited glance is what I long for.
Why then this indifference to test my patience?

be muḥābā: uninhibited; *taġhāful hāi tamkīñ āzmā:* indifference to test patience.

Your indifference towards me is extremely trying. You test my patience by showing indifference, trying to hurt me. If you really want to hurt me, you need only look at me unabashedly just once. An intimate glance can hurt me more than your indifference. The lover is trying to trick the beloved into becoming informal with him.

فروغِ شعلۂ خس یک نفس ہے ہوس کو پاسِ ناموسِ وفا کیا

faroġh-e shola(h)' ḳhas yak nafas hai
havas ko pās-e nāmūs-e vafā kyā (22:5; #138)

In a single breath, the straw goes up in flames;
What respect would desire have for the sanctity of fidelity?

faroġh: flaring; *faroġh-e sho'la(h)-e ḳhas*: brightness of straw flame; *ḳhas*: straw; *havās*: desire lust; *pās*: consideration; *nāmūs*: sanctity; *vafā*: faithfulness.

Intense desire (lust) of the rivals is like straw catching fire and flaring into the air momentarily (in a single breath.) How can you expect such people to show any faithfulness to you? They are like flaring straw, gone quickly. You should not trust them. Instead, you should pay more attention to your real lover, me.

نفس موجِ محیطِ بیخودی ہے تغافلہائے ساقی کا گلا کیا

nafas mauj-e muḥīṯ-e beḳhudī hai
taġhāful hāi sāqī kā gilā kyā (22:6; #139)

Each breath is ecstatic on the whirl of rapture.
Why then should I complain of cupbearer's indifference?

nafis: breath; *muḥīṯ*: encompassing.

My every breath is a tide in the ocean of ecstasy. Why should I complain about Cupbearer's indifference toward me that she does not give me wine? It makes no difference in my ecstasy. The intoxication of love is so deep that even if Cupbearer gives me no wine, I stay intoxicated in my thoughts. My every breath is full of intoxication; I can go into ecstasy by myself without needing any wine to take me there.

دماغِ عطرِ پیراہن نہیں ہے   غمِ آوارگیہائے صبا کیا

damāġh-e ʿiṯr-e pairāhan nahīñ hai
ġham-e āvārgī hāi ṣabā kyā (22:7; #140)

If I cannot bear the scent of her attire,
Then why should I sulk at the vagabond breeze?

ʿiṯr-e pairāhan: perfume of clothing; *damāġh na(h) honā*: inability to bear; *ṣabā*: breeze.

Why should I complain to the breeze for carrying the scent of my beloved's attire everywhere except towards me? Had it wafted towards me, I would not be able to bear it anyway, for mixed with the perfume would be the smell of my enemy (rival) also. An alternate meaning is that this perfume reminds me of her and that I cannot bear. Knowing *Ġhālib,* he is probably complaining about the beloved's union with the rival. Some have interpreted it as a competition between vagabond lovers searching for the scent of the beloved's perfume on a vagabond breeze.

دلِ ہر قطرہ ہے سازِ "انا البحر"   ہم اُس کے ہیں، ہمارا پوچھنا کیا

dil har qaṯra(h) hai sāz-e "an-al-baḥar"
ham us ke haiñ, hamārā puchhnā kyā (22:8; #141)

The heart of every drop sings, "I am the ocean."
What to ask of me? I belong to Him.

an-al-baḥar: "I am the ocean." (Arabic)

Whereas it is not improper for a drop of water to declare, "I am the ocean," likewise, it would not be wrong for me to declare that I am part of the Almighty. A beautiful description of the concept of God: One in all and all in one.

مُحابا کیا ہے، مَیں ضامن، اِدھر دیکھ   شہیدانِ نگہ کا خُوں بہا کیا

muḥābā kyā hai, maiñ ẓāmin, idhar dekh
shahīdān-e nigah kā ḳhūñbahā kyā (22:9; #142)

What do you fear? I am the guarantor; look towards me.
What is the blood money for the martyrs of your glance?

muḥābā: fear; *ẓāmin*: guarantor; *shahid*: martyr; *ḳhūñbahā*: blood money.

Fear not, my love and look towards me. I guarantee that nothing will happen to you for no blood money is offered for bringing your lover to martyrdom by sight alone. To be required to pay blood money requires proof of the murder weapon. Your eyes cannot be defined as a weapon, and so there would be no evidence after my death. Who would know of it? The poet is daring the beloved to kill him.

سُن اے غارتگرِ جنسِ وفا، سُن   شکستِ قیمتِ دِل کی صدا کیا

sun ai ġhāratgar-e jins-e vafā, sun
shikast-e qīmat-e dil kī ṣadā kyā (22:10; #143)

Listen you, O! Plunderer of the commodity of fidelity, listen:
What is the plaint of a heart devalued?

ġhāratgar: plunderer; *jinas:* commodity; *shikast-e qīmat:* loss of value.

Listen, you plunderer of the precious commodity of my faithfulness. The value of my heart relied upon the asset of my faithfulness. Now it is gone, and my heart is worthless. This heart can now yield no sighs. The most precious commodity in a lover's heart is his fidelity. The beloved slept with the rival, thereby relinquishing any duty on the part of the lover to remain faithful. This is a matter of great desecration for the lover. Another explanation is that a breaking heart makes no sound. Why then does the beloved say that I did not hear any heart breaking?

کیا کس نے جگرداری کا دعویٰ؛ شکیبِ خاطرِ عاشق بھلا کیا

kīyā kis ne jigar dārī kā da'vā
shikeb-e ḳhāṭir-e 'āshiq bhalā kyā (22:11; #144)

Who has made the claim to be patient?
Why then should there be testing of the lover's patience?

jigar darī: patience and control; *shikeb*: patience; *ḳhāṭir*: courtesy.

O' my love, who claimed courage of patience? You must know that lovers and patience do not mix. Do not test my courage to bear pain by keeping me away from you. I never claimed patience.

یہ قاتل وعدۂ صبر آزما کیوں؛ یہ کافر فتنۂ طاقت رُبا کیا؟

yih qātil va'd'a(h)-e ṣabr āzmā kioñ
yih kāfir fitn'a(h)-e ṭāqat rubā kyā (22:12; #145)

Why is the murderer testing my patience?
Why is the disbeliever creating a commotion to take my strength away?

fitna(h): commotion; *ṭāqat rubā*: taking strength away.

O! Murderer, why do you make these promises that test my patience? O! Disbeliever (the beloved), why do you create these commotions that take my strength away. The ordeal of waiting kills me. The lover is pleading to the beloved not to make promises that raise hope and thus test his patience. The promise made by the beloved is to kill the lover.

بلائے جاں ہے، غالبؔ اُس کی ہر بات
عِبارت کیا، اِشارت کیا، ادا کیا!

balā'e jāñ hai, Ġhālib us kī har bāt
'ibārat kyā, ishārat kyā, adā kyā (22:13; #146)

Everything about her wreaks havoc, *Ġhālib*!
What to say of her expression, her hinting and her coquettishness?

balā'-e jāñ: heart wrecking; *'ibārat*: writing, expression; *ishārat*: hints; *adā*: coquettishness.

Whatever she does results in total havoc for me. Her every move has killer's instinct.

23

درخورِ قہر و غضب جب کوئی ہم سا نہ ہُوا   پھر غلط کیا ہے کہ ہم سا کوئی پیدا نہ ہُوا

dar ḳhor-e qahr-o-ġhaẓab jab ko'ī ham sā na(h) hu'ā
phir ġhalat kyā hai kih ham sā ko'ī paidā na(h) hu'ā (23:1; #147)

If there wasn't anyone like us, worthy of anger and punishment,
Then what's wrong with it that there was no one ever created like us?

dar ḳhor: worthy; *qahr-o-ġhaẓab*: anger and punishment.

When only humans are worthy of His punishment for bad deeds, then it is not presumptuous to say that no one is as exalted as human beings. We are the supreme creation of God. The concept of *ashraful-maḳhlūqāt* (supreme being of man) is presented here in a very clear context. He gets angry with only those who are close to Him and since He gets angry with us, we must be very close to Him. The question is raised—if we are the exalted creatures, then why such anger and punishment? The verse can also be interpreted to mean that as I am selected to bear the tyranny of the beloved, I must be special.

بندگی میں بھی وُہ آزادہ و خودبیں ہیں، کہ ہم   اُلٹے پھر آئے درِ کعبہ اگر وَا نہ ہُوا

bandagī meñ bhī vuh āzāda(h)-o-ḳhudbīñ haiñ, kih ham
ulṭe phir āe dar-e ka'ba(h) agar vā na(h) hu'ā (23:2; #148)

Even in servitude, we are so independent and self-centered that
We would turn back if the door to the *Ka'bā* were not open.

bandagī: submission, obedience; *ḳhudbīñ*: self-centered.

In obedience and worship of God, I chose not to give up my independence and self-respect. Visiting *Ka'ba,* if I would find the door closed, I would return rather than ask someone to open it. The doors to *Ka'ba* entrance inside the black cube are opened only on very special occasions to kings and royalty. The poet chooses not to seek favor in order to achieve entrance, but at the same time, he is not going to any other house of worship, either. He would rather be hurt than ask for a favor.

سب کو مقبول ہے دعویٰ تری یکتائی کا　　　رُوبرُو کوئی بُتِ آئینہ سیما نہ ہُوا

sab ko maqbūl hai da'vā terī yaktā'ī kā
rūbarū ko'ī but-e ā'īna(h) sīmā na(h) hu'ā (23:3; #149)

All acknowledge your declaration of singularity;
Face to face, no idol could see you in the mirror.

maqbūl: accepted; *da'vā:* claim; *yaktā'ī:* singularity; *rūbarū:* face to face; *but:* statue; *ā'īna(h):* mirror; *sīmā:* appearance.

Everyone accepts the declaration of Your oneness. No one has ever come face to face with You, for if they had, it would have challenged Your oneness. When they approach the mirror and come face to face, they see their own image and thus their own duality while Your oneness goes unchallenged. This means that God is everything and in everything. To see Him will mean a duality of His character. In the mirror, we see only our reflection, not that of God, though He is within us. Calling the observer an idol creates a special situation since his or her existence with God is mutually exclusive.

کم نہیں نازشِ ہمنامیٔ چشمِ خُوباں　　　تیرا بیمار، بُرا کیا ہے، گر اچھا نہ ہُوا

kam nahiñ nāzish-e hamnāmī' chashm-e ḳhūbāñ
terā bīmār, burā kyā hai gar achhā na(h) hu'ā (23:4; #150)

No small pride it is that I got to be called after the eyes of the beloved.
Your patient, what is wrong, if he did not get well?

nāzish: pride; *hamnāmī*: same name; *chashm-e ḳhūbāñ*: eyes of beloved.

It is no small pride that I was compared to your beautiful eyes. The half-open, intoxicating eyes of beloved are called feeble, as is the condition of the lover.

سینے کا داغ ہے وہ نالہ کہ لب تک نہ گیا   خاک کا رزق ہے وہ قطرہ کہ دریا نہ ہوا

sīne kā dāġh hai vuh nāla(h) kih lab tak na(h) gayā
ḳhāk kā rizq hai vuh qaṭra(h) kih daryā na(h) hu'ā (23:5; #151)

The sigh that did not make to the lips turned into a scar of the heart;
The drop that didn't merge with the ocean became the staple of sand.

rizq: staple; *qatra(h)*: drop.

Sighs not reaching the lips become the heart's dark spots. Sand sucks whatever drop of water that does not become the ocean. A sigh's destiny is that it be heard, and so it must complete its journey by reaching the lips. A drop must merge with the ocean to be an ocean or else sand absorbs it, wasting it. Unless taken to the final stage, all efforts come to naught. By absorbing sighs, the heart suffers more grief. Note that as sand absorbs water, it leaves a slight blemish at the surface. Also note that a fiery sigh withheld inside the heart scorches it.

نام کا میرے ہے جو دُکھ کہ کسی کو نہ مِلا   کام میں میرے ہے جو فتنہ کہ برپا نہ ہُوا

nām kā mere hai jo dukh kih kisī ko na(h) milā
kām meñ mere hai jo fitna(h) kih barpā na(h) hu'ā (23:6:152)

The pain assigned to me is the pain that was never given to anyone else;
The commotion in my life is such, the likes of which had never been raised before.

fitna(h): tumult, commotion.

The hurt I feel is uniquely harsh, and the tumult and commotion in my life has not been experienced in anyone else's life before me. I am singled out because I am dearer to Him than anyone else. I am the recipient of all of His favors.

ہر بُنِ مُو سے دمِ ذکر نہ ٹپکے خُوں ناب   حمزہ کا قصہ ہُوا، عشق کا چرچا نہ ہُوا

harbun-e mū se dam-e żikr na(h) ṭapke ḳhūnnāb
ḥamza(h) kā qiṣṣa(h) hu'ā, 'ishq kā charchā na(h) hu'ā (23:7; #153)

The blood would not drip from the root of every hair, listening to my story;
It appeared more like the tale of Hamzah, not the story of my love.

harbun-e mū: root of every hair; *dam*: time; *żikr*: discussion, story telling; *ḳhūnnāb*: pure blood; *ḥamza(h)*: legendary tale of Hamza, known for group telling (nothing to do with *Haẓrat* Hamza).

There was a discussion about my story. The listeners appeared very moved as if the only thing left was blood dripping from the root of every hair (a sign of extreme affliction). This exaggeration of people listening to my story, pretending that they are deeply moved, is a farce. They are actually bemused by it, as if they were listening to the colorful tales of Hamza, a legendary storyteller. People may show sympathy for your misfortune, but mostly they enjoy hearing about your suffering. Another simpler interpretation is that the talk about true love causes the root of every hair to bleed; if not, then this is merely a common story.

قطرے میں دجلہ دکھائی نہ دے اور جُزو میں کُل   کھیل لڑکوں کا ہُوا، دیدۂ بینا نہ ہُوا

qaṭre meñ dajla(h)h dikhā'ī na(h) de aur juzv meñ kul
khel laṛkoñ kā hu'ā, dida(h)' bīnā na(h) hu'ā (23:8; #154)

Not being able to see the river in the drop, or the whole in the part,
Then it is a mere child's play, not an eye with vision.

dajla(h): a famous river of Iraq, meant to indicate a river; *juz*: part; *kul*: whole; *dīd'ah-e bīnā*: eye of vision.

If you cannot see the river in a drop, or the entire being in its parts, then you are behaving childishly. It is certainly not what a visionary eye will see. It shows your immaturity. In the *Sufi* theme, the whole universe lies within each particle and a single drop contains the entire ocean.

تھی خبر گرم کہ غالب کے اُڑیں گے پُرزے
دیکھنے ہم بھی گئے تھے پہ تماشا نہ ہُوا

thī ḳhabar garm kih Ġhālib kih uṛeñ ge purze
dekhne ham bhī ga'e the pa(h) tamāshā na(h) hu'ā (23:9; #155)

The news was hot that *Ġhālib* would be reduced to pieces.
We too went to see, but there wasn't any such spectacle to see.

That *Ġhālib* would be insulted and shamed was big news. We, like so many others, were eager and went to see this spectacle! To our great disappointment, it did not happen. The rivals had created a situation that would have wrought the beloved's indignation towards *Ġhālib*, but the beloved ignored it all. This may also refer to attempts of his peers to ridicule his poetry that withstood the test of time.

24

اسدؔ ہم وہ جنوں جولاں گدائے بے سروپا ہیں　　کہ ہے سر پنجۂ مژگانِ آہو پشت خار اپنا

Asad ham vuh junūñ jaulāñ gadā e be sar-o-pā haiñ
kih hai sar panja(h)' mizhgān-e āhū pusht ḳhār apnā (24:1; #156)

Asad, we are those wanderers in madness, roguish paupers,
To whom the eyelids of the deer serve as the handy back-scratching claw.

junūñ jaulāñ: wanderer in madness; *be sar-o-pā:* a rogue, a rascal, ruffian, roguish; *mizhgāñ:* eyelids; *āhū:* deer; *pusht ḳhār*: a device to scratch back; *ḳhār:* thorn.

The frenzied lover running in the wilderness is leaving behind chasing deer. Unable to afford even a back-scratching claw, the eyelids of the deer are doing the job. Through exaggeration, a state of frenzy is illustrated. Running without a head or feet indicates a state of nonexistence. The deer's eyelids are in some way connected to the eyes of the beloved, as they are often compared to the eyes of deer.

25

پئے نذرِ کرم تحفہ ہے شرمِ نارسائی کا
بہ خوں غلتیدۂ صد رنگ دعویٰ پارسائی کا

pa'e nażr-e karam toḥfa(h) hāi sharm-e nārasā'ī kā
ba(h) ḳhūñ ġhaltīda(h)' ṣad rang da'vā pārsā'ī kā (25:1; #157)

Offering to the benevolent eye is my admission of shame for not reaching out.
Laced with blood in hundreds of colors is my claim of piety.

nāżr: offering; *karam*: God; *sharm-e nārasā'ī*: embarrassment for not reaching to God; *ġhaltida(h)*: laced; *ṣad*: hundred; *rang:* color; *pārasā'ī*: piety.

The only thing I can do to shield my embarrassment from the Almighty for not reaching out to Him is to admit not being able to bring my "piety" to Him. My piety is laced with blood in hundreds of colors, i.e., it is full of sins. He is Benevolent and Beneficent. He would forgive me my candidness. A straightforward admission to my sins is my best hope for forgiveness. Everyone appearing before Lord claims piety; my claim of piety is that it is laced with sins.

نہ ہو حسنِ تماشا دوست رسوا بے وفائی کا
بہ مہرِ صد نظر ثابت ہے دعویٰ پارسائی کا

na(h) ho ḥusn-e tamāshā dost rusvā bevafā'ī kā
ba(h) mohr-e ṣad naẕar s̈ābit hai da'vā pārasā'ī kā (25:2; #158)

The display of unabashed beauty does not bring disgrace of unfaithfulness,
As the lowering of hundreds of eyes proves her claim of chastity.

ḥusn-e tamāshā dost: exhibitionist beloved of beauty; *rusvā*: disgrace; *ba(h) mohr*: close.

It is not proper to question the beloved's faithfulness just because she proudly shows her beauty to all, like an exhibitionist. However, hundreds who look at her must lower their gaze in awe and do not catch a full glimpse of her, so her claim of modesty and piety remains intact. The poet is apparently protecting his beloved's flirtatious behavior, making sure her modesty is not questioned.

زکاتِ حسن دے، اے جلوۂ بینش، کہ مہر آسا
چراغِ خانۂ درویش ہو کاسہ گدائی کا

zakāt-e ḥusn de, ai jalva(h)' bīnish, kih mahr āsā
chirāġh-e ķhāna(h)' darvesh ho kāsa(h) gadā'ī kā (25:3; #159)

Give alms of beauty, O! Sparkle of my eye, for like the sun
The beggar's bowl would turn into a bright lamp in the home.

zakāt: charity (required giving by Islamic tenet); *jalv'a(h)-e bīnish*: sparkle of vision; *mahr āsā*: like sun; *charāġh-e ķhānāh*: lamp for house; *darvesh*: beggar; *kāsa(h)*: begging bowl.

O! Sparkles of my eye, my beloved, give me the charity of your beauty so that my begging bowl will light up like the sun. When I bring it home, it will illuminate the gloomy quarters of this beggar. The begging bowl is round like the sun. When she drops the alms of beauty into the bowl it lights up like the sun, illuminating the dark home of the lover.

نہ مارا جان کر بے جرم، غافل! تیری گردن پر
رہا مانندِ خونِ بے گنہ حق آشنائی کا

na(h) mārā jān kar bejurm, ġhāfil! terī gardan par
rahā mānind-e ḳhūn-e beguna(h) ḥaq āshnā'ī kā (25:4; #160)

O! Heedless one, you did not kill me, thinking of me as innocent, but now it is on your neck:
The innocent blood of the obligation of friendship.

You did not kill me for you believed that perhaps my crime was not harsh enough to deserve this sentence. You were afraid that if you were to kill me without proof of guilt, the blood would be on your neck. But because you did not kill me, you killed our friendship because it was my desire to get killed by you. I expected this from our friendship. O! Ignorant, now you owe me. Now the honor (blood) of my friendship rests on you (on your neck). It would have been better had you killed me rather than kill our friendship. Friendship required extending favors, the favor of being killed by you, my love. A lovely play on words.

تمنائے زباں محوِ سپاسِ بے زبانی ہے
مٹا جس سے تقاضا شکوۂ بے دست و پائی کا

tamannā'e zabāñ maḥv-e sipās-e be zabānī hai
miṭā jis se taqāẓā shikva(h)' be dast-o-pā'ī kā (25:5; #161)

Tongue's desire to speak is busy giving thanks for tonguelessness
That has wiped out my complaint of being helpless.

sipās: thankful; *taqāẓā*: reason; *be dast-o-pā'*: without hand or feet, helpless.

I wanted to express my desperation, but I could not utter a word. Seeing this she became kind. For this I must give thanks for my inability to say anything. It turned out to be the reason for my achieving the goal of attracting her kindness.

وہی اک بات ہے جو یاں نفس واں نکہتِ گل ہے
چمن کا جلوہ باعث ہے مری رنگیں نوائی کا

vohī ik bāt hai jo yāñ nafas vāñ nakhat-e gul hai
chaman kā jalva(h) bā'is hai merī rangīñ navā'ī kā (25:6; #162

It is the same thing that here is my breath and there is the scent of flowers.
The splendor of the garden is the cause of my colorful songs.

nafas: sighs; *nākhat-e gul*: scent of flowers.

My sighs and the smell of flowers have much in common. With the arrival of spring, we both begin our act. Both are colorful and both add to the beauty and splendor of the garden. The splendor of the garden makes me feel more romantic and is the cause of my sighs as I think more about my beloved.

دہانِ ہر بتِ پیغارہ جو زنجیرِ رسوائی
عدم تک بے وفا چرچا ہے تیری بے وفائی کا

dahān-e har but-e paiġhāra(h) jū zanjīr-e ruṣvā'ī
'adam tak bevafā charchā hai terī bevafā'ī kā (25:7; #163)

The mouth of every beauty is taunting me, creating a chain of embarrassment.
Infinitely, there is talk of your unfaithfulness, O! Unfaithful.

dahānā: mouth; *paiġhāra(h) jū*: one who taunts; *jū*: one who.

From every beauty I hear how unfaithful my beloved is and they taunt me for remaining your lover. Like the links in a chain (comparing the mouth to links), the news has gone far. How far? Until eternity! The mouth of the beloved is small (almost nonexistent). Any size chain will have an infinite number of links (mouths). Taking these two facts into account is like the calculus argument where, as "dx" approaches zero, the number of fractions becomes infinite. Comparing the mouth to a link of chain and then pointing to infinity is indeed very mathematical and genuinely imaginative. Also, there is a clever use of "nonexistence." The mouth of the beloved is so small it is almost nonexistent (a sign of beauty). Here the lover is making a subtle effort to persuade the beloved to give up her unfaithfulness to him.

نہ دے نامے کو اتنا طول غالبؔ مختصر لکھ دے
کہ حسرت سنج ہوں عرضِ ستم ہائے جدائی کا

na(h) de nāme ko itnā t̤ūl Ġhālib, muḳhtaṣir likh de
kih ḥasrat sanj huñ ʿarẓ-e sitam hā'e judā'ī kā (25:8; #164)

Drag it not, *Ghālib*; make your letter brief to say
That I am holding unfulfilled desires to tell of the tyranny of love's separation.

nāma(h): letter; *t̤ūl*: stretch, drag; *muḳhtaṣir*: brief; *ḥasrat sanj*: holding unfulfilled desires.

Do not prolong your letter, *Ġhālib*. Keep it brief. Just say that your desire to express the hardships of separation remains unfulfilled.

26

گر نہ اندوہِ شبِ فرقت بیاں ہو جائے گا   بے تکلف، داغِ مہ مُہرِ دہاں ہو جائے گا

gar na(h) andoh-e shab-e furqat bayāñ ho jāe gā
be takalluf dāġh-e mah mohr-e dahāñ ho jāe gā (26:1; #165)

Would not the pain of night of separation become evident
Spontaneously as the spot of moon would turn into a seal upon my lips?

andoh: pain; *be takalluf*: spontaneously.

In the moonlit night, my desire to meet her is as intense as the pain of not being able to. No matter how much I try to conceal it, my desire is apparent. If I keep my lips sealed, the seal is like the dark spots on the moon. Readily discernable to all, it tells the whole story. The spots on the moon are compared to sealed lips. A situation is created out of the moonlit night, the spots on the moon, and the seal on lips. Also in this verse, the beloved is called "moon" and the spots on the moon the marked heart by separation. If I could not express the feelings of my heart, (sealed by the branding of heart) then I would most likely not survive.

زہرہ گر ایسا ہی شامِ ہجر میں ہوتا ہے آب   پرتوِ مہتاب سیلِ خانماں ہو جائے گا

zahra(h) gar aisā hī shām-e hijr meñ hotā hai āb
partau-e mahtāb sail-e ḳhānmāñ ho jāe gā (26:2; #166)

If the spleen turns to water like this in the night of separation,
Then the moonshine will flood the possessions of my home.

zahra(h): spleen, the sign of courage; *partau-e mahtāb*: moonlight; *sail*: flood.

Being separated from you is so painful that it seems as though my spleen will turn to water (an expression of intense suffering). Separation on a moonlit night is unbearable, and the moonlight shining through my home intensifies the pain and destroys my home (heart). The moonshine coming indoors is like a flood taking away the assets of my home. If this flood took away my courage, then surely my heart will go as well. The use of "spleen turning into water" is colloquial in nature. This white moonlight gives a flowing, flooding effect.

لے تو لوں سوتے میں اُس کے پانْو کا بوسہ مگر   ایسی باتوں سے وہ کافر بدگماں ہو جائے گا

le to lūñ sote meñ us ke pāuñ kā bosa(h) magar
aisī bātoñ se vuh kāfir badgumāñ ho jāe gā (26:3; #167)

I would have kissed her feet, while she lay sleeping, but,
With this kind of act, that idol might become suspicious.

The beloved is sleeping and the lover is sitting by her side. He is thinking of kissing her feet (calling her an idol), but at the same time he is afraid that if she wakes up and finds out what he is doing, she would surely became upset and distrustful of him. The poet worries that the sleeping beauty would believe he was taking advantage of her if he were to kiss her feet. The dilemma arises because kissing her feet is an act of idolatry (an act of non-believers in God) and she wants the lover to stay a believer in her (to keep thinking of her as Goddess, not an idol). A simple verse made complicated by the use of word "idol."

دِل کو ہم صرفِ وفا سمجھے تھے، کیا معلوم تھا   یعنی یہ پہلے ہی نذرِ امتحاں ہو جائے گا

dil ko ham ṣarf-e vafā samjhe the, kyā maʿlūm thā
yaʿnī yih pahle hī nāżr-e imtiḥāñ ho jāe gā (26:4; #168)

My heart, I thought, would be consumed in faithfulness to her, but I did not know
That it would lose out in its first round of the test.

ṣarf: spend.

I thought my heart was resilient enough to bear the hardships of proving my love to her, but before I could do this, I lost my heart to her. The challenge was too great to keep my heart to myself so it could bear the hardships of love. She took my heart in the first encounter. What was supposed to be consumed in being faithful to her, I lost to her at first sight.

سب کے دل میں ہے جگہ تیری، جو تو راضی ہوا　　مجھ پہ گویا اک زمانہ مہرباں ہو جائے گا

sab ke dil meñ hai jaga(h) terī, jo tū rāẓī hu'ā
mujh pa(h) goyā ik zamāna(h) mahrbāñ ho jāe gā (26:5; #169)

In every heart, there is a place for You, and, if You are pleased
With me, the whole world will become kind to me as well.

You are in the heart of everyone, O! Lord. If You could be on my side, the whole world would become kind to me. Beseeching God, the poet asks for His benevolence and asserts that if He could bestow His kindness, so would the whole world.

گر نگاہِ گرم فرماتی رہی تعلیمِ ضبط　　شعلہ خس میں جیسے خوں رگ میں نہاں ہو جائے گا

gar nigāh-e garm farmātī rahī ta'līm-e ẓabṭ
sho'la(h) ḳhas meñ, jaise ḳhūñ rag meñ, nihāñ ho jāe gā (26:6; #170)

If the angry eye kept admonishing patience then,
Like flame in straw, the blood in veins would disappear as well.

nigāh-e garm: displeasure, anger; *nihāñ*: hidden.

If your angry eye keeps telling me to be patient and hold my fire of love, then the blood in my veins will dry out (become invisible) like a spark disappearing in dried straw. This would destroy me. See the shape of straw and the shape of veins; see how quickly sparks are consumed by straw. The drying of blood in the veins is also used to indicate extreme fear and distress. In fear, people turn yellow as blood drains out to vital organs; that is the connecting simile to the drying of blood.

باغ میں مجھ کو نہ لے جا ورنہ میرے حال پر   ہر گلِ تر ایک چشمِ خوں فشاں ہو جائے گا

bāġh meñ mujh ko na(h) lejā varna(h) mere ḥāl par
har gul-e tar ek chashm-e ḳhūñ fishāñ ho jāe gā (26:7; #171)

Take me not to the garden, or else, looking at my condition;
Every fresh rose would turn into a blood-shot eye.

gul-e tar: fresh red rose.

The poet does not want to spoil the joys of others with his pathetic presence. By invoking their sympathy, their joy will be spoiled. The flowers are called eyes and by turning red, shedding blood-tears, they look as if they have blood-shot eyes. As flowers cry, they create a sense of sadness that spoils the joys of the garden. Note the similarity between a blood-shot eye and blooming rose.

وائے گر میرا ترا انصاف محشر میں نہ ہو   اب تلک تو یہ توقع ہے کہ واں ہو جائے گا

vāe gar merā terā inṣāf maḥshar meñ na(h) ho
ab talak to yih tavaqoʿ hai kih vāñ ho jāe gā (26:8; #172)

Alas! What if on the Day of Judgment there is no justice rendered between us?
So far, I keep hoping that it will happen.

What if there is no justice granted us by the Lord on the Day of Judgment? So far, I am hoping and expecting that this will happen. The poet is expecting justice on the Day of Judgment but is wondering at the same time, expressing his doubts and fears that he will be left with his sufferings. In other words, just like the beloved, God would also be cruel and unjust. Pessimism is raising head here.

فائدہ کیا سوچ، آخر تُو بھی دانا ہے اسد
دوستی ناداں کی ہے جی کا زیاں ہو جائے گا

fā'ida(h) kyā soch, āḳhir tū bhī dānā hai Asad
dostī nādāñ kī hai jī kā ziyāñ ho jāe gā (26:9; #173)

After all, you are also intelligent, Asad, think, what is there to gain?
This is a friendship of a fool that will make you lose your life.

The innocence of the young beloved borders on being foolish. This is sure to cause you trouble, the poet admonishes himself. The adage that a cunning enemy is better than an innocent or ignorant friend applies here.

27

درد منت کشِ دوا نہ ہُوا   میں نہ اچھا ہُوا، بُرا نہ ہُوا

dard minnat kash-e davā na(h) hu'ā
maiñ na(h) achhā hu'ā, burā na(h) hu'ā (27:1; #174)

The pain not did not get indebted to medicine;
If I did not get well, it was just as well.

minnat kash: under obligation.

The pain did not accept the debt of medicine to be alleviated. If that meant that I did not get well, it was just as well. Having taken medicine, I may have gotten well, but then the burden and obligation of medicine would have been even more severe than the pain it cured. The concept of "self-exaltation" is presented here amicably. I would rather die than get cured if it means incurring a debt or obligation. The verse refers to higher meaning of taking obligations from others, even though they may mean well.

جمع کرتے ہو کیوں رقیبوں کو   اِک تماشا ہُوا، گِلا نہ ہُوا

jama` karte ho kioñ raqīboñ ko
ik tamāshā hu'ā, gilā na(h) hu'ā (27:2; #175)

Why are you gathering all the rivals?
Making a spectacle out of it, as if it were not a plaint.

The poet complains to the beloved about making a spectacle out of his plaint. Why gather these rivals to see me complain? Of course, they are here to throw jest at me. It was all right if you did not want to listen to my plaint, but such insults at the hands of rivals are not justified. The poet is obviously upset. He would have preferred that the discussion between him and the beloved take place in privacy.

ہم کہاں قسمت آزمانے جائیں   تو ہی جب خنجر آزما نہ ہوا

ham kahāñ qismat āzmāne jāeñ
tū hī jab ḳhanjar āzmā na(h) hu'ā (27:3; #176)

Where shall we go to try out our luck?
If you were not even trying out the dagger.

Where shall I go to test my luck if you, my beloved, are not ready to ply your dagger? The most fortunate thing that can happen to me is to be killed by your dagger. But if you aren't ready to do so, then where can I go to find such a fortunate reward? Nowhere!

کتنے شیریں ہیں تیرے لب کہ رقیب   گالیاں کھا کے بے مزا نہ ہوا

kitne shīrīñ haiñ tere lab kih raqīb
gālīyāñ khā kih be maza(h) na(h) hu'ā (27:4; #177)

How sweet are your lips, that the rival
Did not get sour at your rebukes.

The sweetness of your lips makes your rebukes palatable. The use of the word "bad taste" creates a unique structure. If your rebukes were sweet, what would your words of kindness be like? In addition, what would happen if you were ever to extend this kindness to me? An interesting arrangement is made from "eating rebuke" "palatable" and "lips." How could anything coming from the beloved's lips not be tasty? Obviously, the rival loved it!

ہے خبر گرم اُن کے آنے کی   آج ہی گھر میں بوریا نہ ہُوا

hai ḳhabar garm unke āne kī
āj hī ghar meñ boriyā na(h) hu'ā (27:5; #178)

The news is hot that of her arrival.
Just today, there is not even a rag in my house.

boriyā: tattered rug, rag.

It is ironic that a visit from her is imminent when there is not even a rag to offer her to sit upon. It is noteworthy that the poet has not been informed directly. He has just heard it from friends. Knowing deep in his heart that the news is not true, he worries about how he would welcome her, just to distract himself from his perpetual disappointment.

کیا وہ نمرود کی خدائی تھی؟   بندگی میں مرا بھلا نہ ہُوا

kyā vuh namrūd kī ḳhudā'ī thī
bandagī meñ merā bhlā nah hu'ā (27:6; #179)

What a declaration of Divinity by Namrud it was!
My devotion to others did not help me much either.

Namrud's declaration of being God did not help him much, nor did it help me to express my devotion to other human beings (in humility). They both proved to be the same—useless. Humility and declaring exaltation are beautifully matched.

جان دی، دی ہوئی اُسی کی تھی   حق تو یوں ہے کہ حق ادا نہ ہُوا

jān dī, dī hu'ī usī kī thī
ḥaq to yūñ hai kih ḥaq adā na(h) hu'ā (27:7; #180)

I returned my life, for He gave it anyway.
The fact is that the debt was still not repaid to Him.

ḥaq: God, reality, fact, truth.

Returning life did not absolve me of the obligation that He had bestowed by bringing me to life. His obligation remained even though the life He gave to me was gone. The play on words is the use of the same term for rights and God.

زخم گر دب گیا، لہو نہ تھما   کام گر رک گیا، روا نہ ہوا

zakhm gar dab gayā, lahū na(h) thamā
kām gar ruk gayā, ravā na(h) hu'ā (27:8:#181)

Though the wound got suppressed, the bleeding did not stop,
But the work once stopped, did not start again.

ravā: going, restarted.

Though the wound was suppressed, it kept bleeding. The same should have happened to other things in my life. They should have continued though they were halted, like the kindness of the beloved. Whatever was beneficial to me did not continue; what was not, remained.

رہزنی ہے کہ دلستانی ہے   لے کے دل، دلستاں روانہ ہوا

rahzanī hai kih dilsitānī hai
le ke dil, dilsatāñ ravāna(h) hu'ā (27:9; #182)

Is it a robbery or teasing hearts?
Usurping the heart, the heart-teaser has fled.

dilsatānī: teasing heart; *dilsatāñ*: heart tease.

Is it robbery or heart teasing? She picked up the heart and left. She came, grabbed the heart, and ran—that is more like robbery than stealing the heart, which would have required a few coquettish moves, a few heartwarming acts. None of this happened; she simply stole it. In the back of his mind, however, the lover is still very happy.

کچھ تو پڑھیے کہ لوگ کہتے ہیں
آج غالبؔ غزل سرا نہ ہُوا

kuchḥ to paṛhīye kih log kahte haiñ
āj Ġhālib ġhazal sarā na(h) hu'ā (27:10 #183)

Read something for people are muttering
That *Ġhālib* is not reciting his *ġhazals* today.

sarā: recitation.

Ġhālib is talking to himself in this verse saying, "Go on. Recite something or else the audience will feel cheated of being able to hear your eloquent poetry." It can also mean that since *Ġhālib* is not reciting today, let others perform, even though it will not be as good. Anecdotally, this verse was uttered when *Ġhālib* was asked to recite his poetry.

28

گلہ ہے شوق کو دل میں بھی تنگیٔ جا کا　　گہر میں محو ہُوا اِضطراب دریا کا

gila(h) hai shauq ko dil meñ bhī tangī' jā kā
gohar meñ meḥv hu'ā iẓṭirāb daryā kā (28:1; #184)

The desire complains of the tightness in the heart.
Lost in the pearl is the entire tumult of the sea?

gila(h): complaint; *shauq*: desire, love; *tangī*: narrowness; *iẓṭirāb*: restlessness

Whereas my heart is big, my desire for love is even bigger. Desire complains that the heart is too narrow. This also refers to the heart's feeling tight. Just as the tumultuousness of an ocean cannot be contained inside a pearl, our desires cannot be contained in the heart. The second line of the verse should be read with a question mark. Some have interpreted it as an affirmative statement saying that the tumult of the ocean can reside inside the pearl, but our desire for love cannot be contained in our heart. This does not appear appropriate.

یہ جانتا ہُوں کہ تُو اور پاسخِ مکتُوب!　　مگر ستمزدہ ہُوں ذَوقِ خامہ فرسا کا

yih jāntā hūñ kih tū aur pāsuḳh-e maktūb
magar sitamzada(h) hūñ zauq-e ḳhāmā farsā kā (28:2; #185)

I know well, if you would answer my letters!
But a victim I am of my own devotion as I continue to write.

pāsuḳh-e maktūb: answer to letter; *zauq-e ḳhāmā farsā*: devotion to writing.

I know well that you will not respond to my letters. This does not, however, discourage me from writing to you. That is because my devotion forces me to continue my vigilant writing without being discouraged by its outcome.

حناے پاے خزاں ہے بہار اگر ہے یہی   دوامِ کلفتِ خاطر ہے عیش دُنیا کا

ḥinā-e pāe ḳhizāñ hai bahār agar hai yahī
davām-e kulfat-e ḳhāt̤ir hai ʿaish dunyā kā (28:3; #186)

If there is spring then it is merely the *henna* for the feet of the fall season.
The luxuries of life are merely a source of sorrow in this world.

davām: world; *kulfat-e ḳhāt̤ir*: source of sadness.

The spring season is like *henna* (colorful decoration) of the feet of fall that disappears as the fall season takes over. This is analogous to how we lose the luxuries of life to sorrow and pain. Comfort is elusive; pain is reality. Calling the spring season *henna* to the feet of the fall season creates many interesting comparisons. *Henna* is a temporary color, meaning that fall is permanent; applying *henna* to the feet also prevents walking until it dries, meaning it freezes the permanence of the fall season. In brief, this verse talks about the permanence of sorrow. It is better to accept our permanent fate than to become enchanted by the temporary luxuries of life (spring season).

غمِ فراق میں تکلیفِ سیرِ باغ نہ دو   مجھے دماغ نہیں خندہ ہاے بےجا کا

ġham-e firāq meñ taklīf-e sair-e bāġh na(h) do
mujhe damāġh nahiñ ḳhanda(h) hāi bejā kā (28:4; #187)

Trouble me not to stroll in the garden in my sorrow of separation,
For I cannot tolerate any untimely irritating laughter.

damāġh nahīñ: cannot tolerate; *ḳhanda(h) hāi bejā*: untimely laughter.

I am utterly consumed by sorrow. Do not bother me by inviting me to walk in the garden. There I will see blooming flowers that appear as though they are laughing. This gesture is very inappropriate for me now; I cannot tolerate any gesture of happiness or anything that might remind me of my happy days. Also see, "*tujhe aṭkheliyāñ sujhī heñ ham bezār beṭhe haiñ.*"

ہنوز محرمیٔ حسن کو ترستا ہوں   کرے ہے ہر بُنِ مُو کام چشمِ بینا کا

hanoz maḥramī' ḥusn ko tarastā hūñ
kare hai harbun-e mū kām chashm-e bīnā kā (28:5; #188)

Still I long desperately for intimacy to the beauty.
The roots of my hair working like the inquisitive eye.

maḥram: informal intimate, close; *tarastā*: crying for, longing; *harbun*: root; *mū*: hair.

I have been aspiring to be close to her, to be intimate with her, so that I may satisfy my desire to see her beauty. In anticipation, the root of every hair on my body has turned into an eye so that I can absorb the spectacle of her beauty quickly. Two eyes would not be enough. Every strand of hair turning into an eye signifies desperate desire as well. Another interpretation makes this an ode to the Lord. Even if every hair on my body turns into an eye that understands reality, understanding You is not possible and I shall remain deprived of knowing the truth.

دل اُس کو پہلے ہی ناز و ادا سے دے بیٹھے   ہمیں دماغ کہاں حسن کے تقاضا کا

dil us ko, pahle hī nāz-o-adā se de baiṭhe
hameñ damāġh kahāñ ḥusn ke taqāẓā kā (28:6; #189)

Having given my heart to her before any display of coquetry and style.
How can I bear to let the beauty ask for it first?

nāz-o-adā: style and coquettishness; *damāġh kahāñ:* whither tolerance.

I gave my heart to her even before she unleashed her style and coquettishness on me. Normally, the beloved would ask for the heart and it would be offered to her, but I did not have the patience to succumb to her style.

نہ کہہ کہ گریہ بہ مقدارِ حسرتِ دل ہے   مری نگاہ میں ہے جمع و خرج دریا کا

na(h) kah kih girya(h) ba(h) miqdār-e ḥasrat-e dil hai
merī nigāh meñ hai jama̒-o-ķhirj daryā kā (28:7; #190)

Say not that the weeping is proportional to the anguish of the heart.
In my view, there is a river flowing continuously.

merī nigāh meñ: in my plan, in my view; *jama̒-o-ķhirj daryā kā*: continuous flow of river.

Do not challenge me by saying that weeping is proportional to the anguish in our hearts. My lamenting is far less compared to my desperation. If the flow of tears tells the depth of sorrow, then be prepared, for I am planning to let a river flow. The use of "crying," "river," "tears," all creates a very wet situation.

فلک کو دیکھ کے کرتا ہوں اُس کو یاد اسد
جفا میں اِس کی ہے انداز کارفرما کا

falak ko dekh ke kartā hūñ us ko yād Asad
jafā meñ is kī hai andāz kārfarmā kā (28:8; #191)

Looking to the sky reminds me of her, Asad.
In her tyranny, the style is the same as that of the Creator.

falak: sky; *jafā*: cruelty; *andāz*: style; *kārfarmā:* caretaker, Creator.

Both the sky (actually heaven, used here to connote fate) and the beloved are cruel and have the same unpredictable style of unleashing cruelty. There is no indication here that God is claimed to be behind both. The beloved simply has the same style and disposition, predictably cruel, as that of heaven. So, whenever I look at the sky I think of her.

29

قطرۂ مے بسکہ حیرت سے نفس پرور ہوا   خطِ جامِ مے سراسر رشتۂ گوہر ہوا

qaṭra(h)' mai baskih ḥairat se nafas parvar hu'ā
ḳhaṯ-e jām-e mai sarāsar, rishta(h)' gohar hu'ā (29:1; #192)

The drop of wine, totally stunned, held its breath,
As the meniscus of wine in the goblet became strewn with pearls all around.

ḥairat: surprise, stun; *nafas parvar*: holding breath, lazy; *ḳhaṯ-e jām*: measure mark on the glass, meniscus; *sarāsar*: completely.

When she raised the glass of wine to her lips, the drops took on her reflection, became stunned and frozen at the meniscus level in the glass, and were made to appear as a thread strewn with pearls. Stunning and freezing is an oft-repeated theme. The mirror, for example, is said to be in a stunned state, looking at the beauty of the beloved. This verse creates a very difficult visualization. The beloved has brought the glass to her lips. As she tilts the glass, a layer of wine remains on its side. In this layer of wine, her reflection appears and the droplets of wine appear frozen in surprise at her beauty. Looking at the glass from outside, it appears as though there were a string of pearls strewn inside the wine goblet. In addition, as she brings the glass to her lips, her moist breath enters the glass, fogging it, adding to the appearance of pearls. In his own explication of the verse, *Ġhālib* considers this verse to be of a complex imagination but not too exciting.

اعتبارِ عشق کی خانہ خرابی دیکھنا　　غیر نے کی آہ، لیکن وہ خفا مجھ پر ہوا

iʿtibār-e ʿishq kī ḳhana(h) ḳharābī dekhnā
ġhair ne kī āh, lekin vuh ḳhafā mujh par huʾā (29:2; #193)

See the devastation of my heart by her trust in my love.
The rival sighed, but she became upset with me.

ḳhana(h) ḳharābī: messing up of things (lit. destruction of home).

My beloved believes in my devotion to her to such an extent that whenever she hears a sigh, she immediately assumes that it must be me, even when it is the rival. Such attention and trust from the beloved will surely lead me to only one destiny—destruction of my plans to ever get her favors because she stays upset with me all the time. The incessant sighs she keeps hearing are those of the rival, yet she believes them to be mine. Sometimes it backfires to be believed in. We should keep in mind that the ultimate goal *is* to receive her wrath and thus this verse can be interpreted quite oppositely as well. "Look at the beauty of my devastation."

30

جب بہ تقریبِ سفر یار نے محمل باندھا
تپشِ شوق نے ہر ذرّے پہ اِک دِل باندھا

jab ba(h) taqrīb-e safar yār ne maḥmil bāndhā
tapish-e shauq ne har żarre pa(h) ik dil bāndhā (30:1; #194)

Whenever for the purpose of travel, she readied her carriage,
The throbbing passion tied a heart to every grain of sand.

taqrīb: occasion, purpose; *maḥmil bāndhā:* readied a carrier for riding camel (camel-litter) for travel; *tapish*: pulsation, palpitation, beating.

This verse describes the condition of the lover's heart as the beloved readies to leave him. The intensity of emotions ties every particle of sand to the heart. This means that every particle of sand takes on the heat of the lover's commotion and begins to look like the lover's heart. Now, as her carriage passes through the desert, she tramples a million hearts—millions of unfulfilled desires. The use of "to tie the carriage" as a sign of determination to leave and "to tie the heart" with no choice left are made to rhyme creating a very imaginative pursuit.

اہلِ بینش نے بہ حیرت کدۂ شوخیٔ ناز
جوہرِ آئینہ کو طوطیٔ بسمل باندھا

ahl-e bīnish ne ba(h) ḥairat kada(h)' shokh'ī-e nāz
johar-e ā'īna(h) ko ṭuṭī' bismil bāndhā (30:2; #195)

Stunned in the house of coquetry, those with insight
Called the green spots in the mirror the fluttering wounded parrots.

ahl-e bīnish: those having insight; *ḥairat kada(h)*: house of surprise (mirror); *bismil*: wounded; *ṭuṭī*: parrot; *johar-e ā'īna(h)*: green spots on mirror.

When the beloved looked into the mirror coquettishly, the entire atmosphere was stunned with her beauty. So much so that the green spots on the mirror began to flutter like wounded parrots. This comparison is extremely unique. In those days, applying a metal coating onto glass made mirrors. In damp weather, the metal would rust leaving green spots on the mirror. The parrot, also green, is compared to the spots on the mirror. This is a pure *Ġhālib*ian construction. As the beloved began looking into the mirror, the intensity of her beauty was such that even those green spots began fluttering. How else can a poet make the scene more dramatic? The scenario becomes more complicated when we realize that people teach parrots to talk by holding them in front of a mirror. In this verse, the mirror is speaking through the tongue of parrots, which are not there.

یاس و اُمّید نے یک عَربدہ مَیداں مانگا
عجزِ ہمّت نے طِلسمِ دلِ سائل باندھا

yās-o-ummīd ne yak ʽarbada(h) maidāñ māngā
ʽijz-e himmat ne ṭilism-e dil-e sā'il bāndhā (30:3; #196)

Despair and hope demanded an arena for fight as
The low esteem was casting a spell on the heart of the beggar.

ʽarbada(h): war; *maidāñ*: field; *ʽijz-e himmat*: low esteem; *ṭilism*: spell; *sā'il*: beggar.

Approaching the beloved stirs many doubts in my heart. Will she or will not she give in to me? There is always a debate raging in my heart about how she will react. My low esteem, however, creates a dilemma, a spell in my heart, of hope and disappointment. This beggar heart remains under the spell of this dilemma: The lover's heart is never sure, yet it keeps hoping that something good will happen. Despair and hope fight because of the spell cast on the lover's heart. The second line should be read first to make the meaning clear.

نہ بندھے تشنگیِ ذوق کے مضموں، غالب
گرچہ دِل کھول کے دریا کو بھی ساحل باندھا

na(h) bandhe tashnagī' żauq ke maẓmūñ, Ġhālib
garcheh dil khol kih daryā ko bhī sāḥil bāndhā (30:4; #197)

Not able to express details of my thirst of desire, *Ġhālib*;
Even though we tied the river with banks to our heart's content.

tashnagī' żauq:thirst of desire; *mazmuñ*: subject matter; *sāḥil*: bank of river; *bāndhe*: composed.

Despite my full efforts, I cannot write enough about my desire for her love. How strenuous were my efforts? If my expressions were a river, my desire was like its banks; no matter how much water hits the banks, they remain dry, deflecting all that the river offers them. The banks surround the river as the words encompass the thoughts of the poet.

31

میں اور بزمِ مے سے یوں تشنہ کام آؤں
گر میں نے کی تھی توبہ، ساقی کو کیا ہوا تھا

maiñ aur bazm-e mai se yūñ tashna(h) kām āu'ñ
gar maiñ ne kī thī tauba(h), sāqī ko kyā hu'ā thā (31:1; #198)

Would I ever come out of her assembly of wine thirsty?
If I had vowed to abstain, but then what happened to cupbearer?

tashna(h) kām: left thirsty.

I had vowed never to drink again but my vows were those of a drunkard, very fragile. However, in her assembly, the cupbearer took my vows seriously and did not offer me the wine. Coming out of the tavern, the poet faces his colleagues, who wonder how a drunkard became so pious, apparently a disgrace for drunkards. The poet now offers the excuse that something must have gone wrong with the cupbearer. Though I came out thirsty, it had nothing to do with me. I would have broken the vows readily, had the cupbearer offered me a drink. Here the wine is the kindness of beloved and "abstain" refers to the lover's resolve to resist temptation.

ہے ایک تیر جس میں دونوں چھدے پڑے ہیں
وہ دن گئے کہ اپنا دل سے جگر جدا تھا

hai ek tīr jis meñ donoñ chhide paṛe haiñ
vuh din gae kih apnā dil se jigar juda(h) thā (31:2; #199)

A single arrow it is in which both are left pierced;
Gone are the days when my heart was separate from my liver.

On one arrow are strung both a heart and a liver, which illustrates that the days when the heart and liver used to be separate are over. This means that both defenders of my courage are down together and thus cannot support each other. The vital organs are supposed to support each other, as is an oft-repeated theme in *Ġhālib*'s poetry. However, the arrow of her beauty was so potent that it dismantled all of my defenses at once. The heart is supposed to be the emotional component, whereas the liver signifies strong patience.

درماندگی میں غالبؔ کچھ بن پڑے تو جانوں
جب رِشتہ بے گِرہ تھا، ناخُن گِرہ کُشا تھا

darmāndgī meñ Ġhālib kuchh ban paṛe to jānuñ
jab rishta(h) be gira(h) thā, nāḳhun gira(h) kushā thā (31:3; #200)

I would be impressed if, in the desperation of sorrow, something works out *Ġhālib*.
When the thread had no knots, the nails were apt at undoing them.

darmāndgī: sorrow, desperation: *rishta(h)*: relations, connection, thread.

When I had the energy and ability to solve my problems, there were no problems to resolve. Now, with the ability and energy gone, problems abound. The poet reflecting on this irony challenges himself by saying, "Show what you can do now that you are desperate." When I had no knotty situations in my life, my nails were quick at undoing the knots. Now, when I need these nails, they are unable to undo the knots.

32

گھر ہمارا جو نہ روتے بھی تو ویراں ہوتا
بحر گر بحر نہ ہوتا تو بیاباں ہوتا

ghar hamārā jo na(h) rote bhī to vīrāñ hotā
baḥar gar baḥar na(h) hotā to bayābāñ hotā (32:1; #201)

Had I not been weeping, my house would still have been a ruin.
If the ocean had not been an ocean, it would have been a desert.

vīrāñ: desolate place, ruin; *baḥar*: ocean; *bayābāñ*: desert.

My home, had I not been weeping, would have been a place whose desolation matched that of the ocean. But had the ocean (of tears) not been there, the underneath would still have been a desolate place. This is a coincidental mention of the scientific and historic fact that the deserts of today were oceans of the past. The connection between crying and desolation is perhaps conjectural meaning that my tears have inundated the place, forcing everyone to move out of the neighborhood, but I stay there facing the desolation written in my fate. Even if I had not cried, this place would have been desolate anyway. It was fate.

تنگیٔ دل کا گلہ کیا یہ وہ کافر دل ہے
کہ اگر تنگ نہ ہوتا تو پریشاں ہوتا

tangī' dil kā gila(h) kyā yih vuh kāfir dil hai
kih agar tang na(h) hotā to pareshāñ hotā (32:2; #202)

Why to complain of the tightness of the heart? It is that disbeliever heart,
Which, if it were not sad, it would have been perturbed.

tangī: tight, hopeless, narrow; *gila(h)*: complaint; *pareshāñ:* perturbed, disressed, troubled.

Why complain of the narrowness of my disbelieving heart, for had it not been hopless (tight), it would have been perturbed. One way or the other it would suffer from something that eventually led to hurt and sorrow. Narrowness and being perturbed are two very different feelings. Narrowness of the heart refers to being sad due to the crowding of plaints. It is either sad or perturbed. In addition, the meaning of "*tang*" (tight) in the second line can be taken to mean hopelessness.

بعدِ یک عمرِ وَرَع بار تو دیتا بارے
کاش رِضواں ہی درِ یار کا درباں ہوتا

b'ad-e yak 'umr-e vara' bār to detā bāre
kāsh riẓvāñ hī dar-e yār kā darbāñ hotā (32:3; #203)

After a lifetime of abstinence, he should have given at least a chance.
I wish that the guard to heaven were her doorkeeper.

'umr-e vara': life of abstinence; *bār*: chance; *riẓvāñ*: guard to heaven.

The poet is at the beloved's door begging the doorkeeper to let him in. The guard is not budging. The poet is now wishing that the guard were the same person who guards the doors to heaven (St. Peter), because a lifetime of abstinence would have allowed the guard to let him in. Here, at the doorsteps of the beloved, even a lifetime of abstinence and praying will not let him in. It is easier to find entry to paradise than to enter her home.

33

نہ تھا کچھ تو خدا تھا، کچھ نہ ہوتا تو خدا ہوتا
ڈُبویا مُجھ کو ہونے نے، نہ ہوتا میں تو کیا ہوتا

na(h) thā kuchh to ḳhudā thā, kuchh na(h) hotā to ḳhudā hotā
ḍuboyā mujh ko hone ne, na(h) hotā maiñ to kyā hotā (ß3:1; #204)

When there was nothing, there was God; had there been nothing, God would still have been.
Drowned because I existed, how would it have mattered if I did not exist?

ḳhudā: God; *duboyā*: destroyed, sank, disgraced.

When there was nothing, there was God. Had nothing ever existed, God still would have. So, if I had not been created it would have had no impact whatsoever. However, bringing me into existence is akin to drowning me, or putting me through a lifetime of suffering. A remarkable rendition of one of the oldest questions in philosophy is portrayed here—why did God create us since He obviously did not need us? Moreover, having created us, why did He make human life a period of insurmountable suffering? What does God get out of seeing us suffer? The theme of this verse describes in its entirety the philosophy of *Ġhālib* about life and its Creator.

ہُوا جب غم سے یُوں بے حِس تو غم کیا سر کے کٹنے کا
نہ ہوتا گر جُدا تن سے تو زانو پر دھرا ہوتا

hu'vā jab ġham se yuñ beḥis to ġham kyā sar ke kaṭne kā
na(h) hotā gar juda(h) tan se to zānū par dharā hotā (ß3:2; #205)

**Having gone insensitive to pain, then why fear of decapitation?
Had it not been separated from the body, it would have been
resting on the knees.**

beḥis: refractory, numb, insensitive; *dharā:* lying, being put.

Why should I worry about decapitation if I am insensitive to even the most intense pain? If there were no decapitation, the head on my lap would have lost all feeling and control. This also means that even if my head had not been removed from my body, it would have been in my lap contemplating in great sorrow. When all feelings are gone, why worry about death. "Head on the knees" signifies contemplating in frustration.

ہوئی مُدّت کہ غالب مر گیا، پر یاد آتا ہے
وہ ہر اِک بات پر کہنا کہ یُوں ہوتا تو کیا ہوتا

*hu'ī muddat kih Ġhālib mar gayā, par yād ātā hai
vuh har ik bāt par kahnā kih yūñ hotā to kyā hotā (33:3; #206)*

**It has been a long time since *Ġhālib* died, but he does keep
coming to our thoughts.
His arguing at everything, "What would it have been, if it
were like this or like that?"**

It has been a long time since *Ġhālib* died, but he is still remembered for his arguments of "what if?" in everything. He was curious about things around him and ever hopeful for things to work out positively. His curiosity was part of his wishful thinking. We still remember the philosophic thoughts of *Ġhālib.*

34

یک ذرۂ زمیں نہیں بیکار باغ کا
یاں جادہ بھی فتیلہ ہے لالے کے داغ کا

yak żarra(h)' zamīñ nahiñ bekār bāġh kā
yāñ jāda(h) bhī fatīla(h) hai lale ke dāġh kā (34:1; #207)

Not a particle of earth is useless in the garden.
Here, even the walkway is the wick to tulips' spots.

jāda(h): path; *fatīla(h)*: wick; *lālā*: red flower (tulip).

Nothing in the garden is futile, even the worn-out walking path which serves as a wick to light up the lamps of red flowers. (Flowers bloom on both sides of the pathway). Calling the pathway a source of the flower's spots means growth of flowers and hints at how the lovers get their hearts branded in the spring season. No space is spared in the garden where there are no blooming flowers; even the worn-out walkways are filled with tulips on both sides. To compare the pathways with a wick is noteworthy; both are straight, narrow, and support energy and life. By calling the tulips lamps, the poet makes a comparison between the wick and the walkway—a dazzling description of the arrival of spring!

بے مے کسے ہے طاقتِ آشوبِ آگہی
کھینچا ہے عجزِ حوصلہ نے خطِ ایاغ کا

be mai kise hai ṯāqat-e āshob-e āgahī
kheñchā hai ʿajz-e ḥauṣle ne ḳhaṯ ayāġh kā (34:2; #208)

Without wine, who has the strength to bear the tumultuousness of awareness?
My low courage has taken to the shot-glass of wine.

āshob: tumultuousness; *āgahī*: awareness; *ḳhaṯ ayāġh*: glass of wine (shot glass).

The tumult of consciousness is so intense that its only resolve is to drink until you lose awareness. My low courage cannot bear this tumult and thus I must drink until I lose all consciousness. This way I will not be able to feel the pain of reality, of injustices, of losing friends to death, of man's existence coming to naught. By measuring the wine in a (shot) glass instead of simply using a wineglass is significant. We use the shot-glass to know how much to drink. The poet needs to drink enough to lose himself and he would rather know it from the measurement than from his own condition of deliriousness. He is afraid that in his drunken state he may not drink enough, so a measurement is in order. It is not to contain drinking. The lowself-esteem (small self-image) of the poet is juxtaposed with the small glass here. The second line may also be interpreted as Cupbearer has taken to using the measuring glass because of her miserly nature. We need an open tap of wine.

بلبل کے کاروبار پہ ہیں خندہ ہائے گل
کہتے ہیں جس کو عشق، خلل ہے دماغ کا

bulbul ke kārobār pa(h) haiñ ḳhanda(h) hāi gul
kahte haiñ jis ko ʿishq, ḳhalal hai damāġh kā (34:3; #209)

At the routine of the nightingale, the flowers are laughing.
What we call love, is but the derangement of the mind.

kārobār: routine, dealings; *ḳhalal:* defect.

The nightingale is in love with flowers and screams the condition of her heart. The flowers, on the other hand, are laughing at her naïveté. The blooming flowers are also called laughing flowers as their petals open. The nightingale knows she is not heard and even if she were, she would not care and would continue her lamentation. This shows that love is actually a mental derangement and not a normal, rational state. Lovers are disgraced as the world finds out about their lunacy and they become a laughing stock. This is one of the most widely quoted verses of *Ġhālib*.

تازہ نہیں ہے نشۂ فکرِ سخن مجھے
تریاکیِ قدیم ہوں دودِ چراغ کا

tāza(h) nahiñ hai nasha(h)' fikr-e suḳhan mujhe
tiryākī' qadīm huñ dūd-e chirāġh kā (34:4; #210)

The intoxication of creative writing is not new to me.
A chronic addict I am to smoke of lamp.

tiryākī: opium user; *dūd-e chirāġh*: smoke of lamp.

Creative expression is not new to me. I have been doing it for a very long time. I am the caretaker of the lamp of intellectualism because I am addicted to visionary thoughts. The poet refers to the lamp as the source of illumination. However, when smoking opium, soot comes as it does from the oil-lamp. Intoxication of creative writing is placed beautifully to create a highly imaginative atmosphere.

سو بار بندِ عشق سے آزاد ہم ہوئے
پر کیا کریں کہ دل ہی عدو ہے فراغ کا

sau bār band-e 'ishq se āzād ham hu'e
par kyā kareñ kih dil hī 'adū hai firāġh kā (34:5; #211)

**Hundreds of times, I freed myself from the bindings of love.
But what shall I do if my own heart is enemy to my freedom?**

ʿadū: enemy; *firāġh*: independence, freedom.

I managed to free myself from the bindings of love many times, but each time my own heart became my enemy and dragged me back into the same bondage. What can you do when your own heart is your enemy? There can be no freedom. Blaming everything on their heart is the common excuse of lovers.

بے خونِ دل ہے چشم میں موجِ نگہ غبار
یہ مے کدہ خراب ہے مے کے سُراغ کا

*bekḥūn-e dil hai chashm meñ mauj-e nigah ġhubār
yih mai kada(h) ḳharāb hai ma'i ke surāġh kā (34:6; #212)*

**Without blood in the heart, the vision is like a wave of dust storm.
This tavern is desperately searching for the wine.**

ġhubār: dust storm; *mai kada(h)*: tavern; *surāġh:* sign, lead.

If there is no blood left in the heart, the eyes cannot shed tears of blood. What then would be left in these eyes save for waves of dust (dusty eyes do not allow you to see)? Meaning, they will lose their vision. The same thing applies to the tavern, which, without wine, is a desolate place. What we need to do is make our eyes bloodshot again so, we can see, and fill the tavern with wine so that it can brighten up our world. Here the tavern is compared to the eye, and blood to wine. These days I no longer shed tears of blood and it makes me feel like the tide of my vision has dried to dust. It is like a desolate tavern with no liquor to serve.

باغِ شگفتہ تیرا بساطِ نشاطِ دل
ابرِ بہار خمکدہ کس کے دماغ کا

bāġh-e shagufta(h) terā bisāṭ-e nishāṭ-e dil
abr-e bahār ḳhumkadah kis kih damāġh kā (34:7; #213)

Your heart is filled with joy from the blooming of the garden.
Who cares about the clouds of spring or the tavern?

bisāṭ: cause; *nishāṭ-e dil*: joy of heart; *ḳhumkada(h)*: tavern.

My heart finds joy only through the blooming garden of your beauty. Drinking on cloudy spring days, a customary delight of lovers, could give no comparable pleasure. The use of the garden, blooming, joy, clouds, and tavern all form an intricate part of the theme connecting spring to drinking and to the display of the beloved's beauty. The sight of a fresh, blooming garden reminds the lover of the beloved and with that comes his ultimate joy.

35

وہ مری چینِ جبیں سے غمِ پنہاں سمجھا
رازِ مکتوب بہ بے ربطیٔ عنواں سمجھا

vuh merī chīn-e jabīñ se ġham-e pinhāñ samjhā
rāz-e maktūb ba be rabṯī' u'nvāñ samjhā (35:1; #214)

From the wrinkles on my forehead, she knew my hidden sorrow.
The content of my letter she understood from its badly scrawled address.

chīn: wrinkle; *jabīñ*: forehead; *pinhāñ*: hidden; *rāz*: secret; *maktūb*: letter; *be rabṯī*: haphazard, disorderly; *u'nvāñ*: title.

By reading the wrinkles on my forehead, she understood well the turmoil hidden inside—just as one can guess the contents of a letter by looking at its title, or opening it if it is written haphazardly. Comparing wrinkles on the forehead to the haphazard beginning of a letter also tells what is to come—a disjointed expression of feelings.

یک الف بیش نہیں صیقلِ آئینہ ہنوز
چاک کرتا ہوں میں جب سے کہ گریباں سمجھا

yak alif besh nahiñ ṣa'iqal-e āi'nah hanūz
chāk kartā hūñ maiñ jab se kih girībāñ samjhā (35:2; #215)

The polish of the mirror is not beyond its initial flaws.
I have been tearing it since I understood the purpose of my collar.

alif: first alphabet of *Urdū* (straight vertical line referring to imperfection in the polished steel mirror and also to mean beginning); *alif besh:* beyond beginning; *ṣaiqal*: polish; *garebāñ:* shirt collar.

Since I came to know what the shirt collar is for, I tear it. But the tear in my collar has not gone beyond the line shaped like the Urdu alphabet I (alif). It is still straight and contained (straight slit, not torn randomly). A comparison of this situation is made with the old-style steel mirrors where metal coatings were applied. At the time of application, straight ridges often appeared that were rubbed extensively to polish the mirror. The same applies here to my efforts in perfecting my love. I have, since learning the meaning of love, worked hard at it, but I am still in the beginning stage. The *alif* marking on the mirror of self has not yet been removed. I have yet to polish my expression, to take care of the straight line in the mirror and in my collar: I have ways to go before I reach lunacy. Note that both start with a straight line—a cut and a ridge—that resembles the first alphabet of *Urdū* and Persian.

شرحِ اسبابِ گرفتاریٔ خاطر مت پُوچھ
اِس قدر تنگ ہُوا دِل کہ مَیں زِنداں سمجھا

sharḥ-e asbāb-e giraftārī' ḳhaṯir mat puchh
is qadar tang hu'ā dil kih maiñ zindāñ samjhā (35:3; #216)

Ask me not to explain the reasons for getting love-arrested. The heart had become so narrow that I thought of it as a prison cell.

sharḥ: explanation, to open; *asbāb*: reason, cause.

Do not ask me to explain the reasons for my sorrow that comes from being love-arrested. My heart has tightened (saddened) to a point where it seems like a prison cell. Tightening of the heart is due to extreme grief. It is like a prison from which nothing can escape; in this case, not even the sighs of my heart. Comparing a saddened heart with a prison cell has many parallels: sighs trying to escape from the heart and the prisoners from the cell. Both are extremely perturbed. It was this locking in of sighs because of extreme sorrow that caused my heart to appear like a prison cell. Opening, tightness, arrest, and prison are used to juxtapose themes.

بدگمانی نے نہ چاہا اُسے سرگرمِ خرام
رُخ پہ ہر قطرہ عَرَق دیدۂ حَیراں سمجھا

badgumānī ne nā chāha use sargarm-e ḳhirām
ruḳh pe har qaṯrah a̓rq dīda(h)' ḥairāñ samjhā (35:4; #217)

My suspicion did not like her strolling around, as
Every drop of sweat on her face turned out to be the extract of stunned eyes.

a̓rq: extract.

She has decided to go for a stroll, but my heart does not want her to go. As she walks, sweat drops will appear on her face and I am suspicious that these will be more than just sweat drops. I imagine they will be hundreds of stunned eyes of rivals that are always vying to look at her. This would be intolerable to me. The poet does not want his beloved strolling around lest the rival sees her. Drops of sweat reflecting light, her brilliance, and the comparison to the extract of a stunned eye are noteworthy. Calling sweat drops the extract of stunned eyes is an original *Ġhālib* thought. The second line may also be interpreted a little differently. She hesitates taking a stroll lest the eyes of rivals make her sweat with embarrassment.

عجز سے اپنے یہ جانا کہ وہ بدخو ہوگا
نبضِ خس سے تپشِ شعلۂ سوزاں سمجھا

ājz se apne yih jānā kih vuh badḳhū ho gā
nabẓ-e ḳhas se tapish-e shola(h)ʾ sozañ samjhā (35:5; #218)

From my weakness, I realized why would she be ill tempered
As from the pulse of straw I appreciated the throbbing in the burning flames.

nabẓ-e ḳhas: pulse of straw; *tapish:* pulsation, beating, palpitation; *sozañ:* burning.

Knowing my weakness and humility (inferiority), I conclude that I deserve her admonishment and anger because she abhors weak souls. Just as it is the destiny of straw to catch fire and burn, I must also receive the unleashing of her wrath. Like the straw destined for destruction, so am I. The "pulse of straw" is used to exaggerate the weakness. Straw itself is flimsy; imagine how imperceptible would be its pulse. Her anger is the fire; the lover is the feeble straw.

سفرِ عشق میں کی ضعف نے راحت طلبی
ہر قدم سائے کو میں اپنے شبستاں سمجھا

safar-e ỉshq meñ kī ẓoʾf ne rāḥat ṯalabī
har qadam sāe ko meñ apne shabistāñ samjhā (35:6; #219)

In the journey of love, my fatigue begged to rest.
At every step, I thought of my own shadow as a night-time resting-place.

ẓoʾf: weakness; *sāe:* shadow; *shabistāñ*: night-time resting place.

In the long journey of love, my weariness is crying for rest. It is so bad that upon every step, my own shadow falling on the ground appears to be a bed to rest upon. To consider your own shadow a restingplace signifies an extreme state of delirium. The irony is that I cannot reach this restingplace because it is always running away from me. The long journey, no hope for rest, and a very tired body and soul are merged here into one example.

تھا گریزاں مژۂ یار سے دل تا دمِ مرگ
دفعِ پیکانِ قضا اِس قدر آساں سمجھا

tha gurezāñ miẓah' yār se dil ta dam-e marg
daf-e paikān-e qaẓa' is qadar āsāñ samjhā (35:7; #220)

My heart avoided beloved's eyelashes till death;
Warding off the call of destiny, I had thought of as easy.

gurezāñ: avoiding; *miẓah:* eyelashes; *yār*: beloved; *dam*: breath; *marg*: death; *daf*: warding off; *paikān*: call, tip of arrow; *qaẓa'*: destiny; *qadr*: worth *āsāñ*: easy.

I was avoiding facing my beloved's killer eyelashes thinking it was a smart way to avoid death, thus I waited until the time of death to face her eyelashes. What I did not realize was that her eyelashes *were* the messengers of death. Avoiding them only promised me a life of futility. I could not avoid the tip of her eyelashes: It was my destiny.

دِل دیا جان کے کیوں اُس کو وفادار اسدؔ
غلطی کی کہ جو کافر کو مُسلماں سمجھا

dil diyā jān kih kyoñ us ko vafādār, Asad
ghalaṯī kī kih jo kāfir ko musalmāñ samjhā (35:8; #221)

Why did you give your heart, thinking that she is faithful, Asad?
It was indeed a mistake to think of a disbeliever as Muslim.

I gave my heart to my beloved thinking that she would be faithful to me. What a mistake that was! It was a false thought that a disbeliever would begin thinking like a Muslim whose basic tenet is to uphold the belief of faithfulness. To expect this from a disbeliever is a mistake. By claiming to have given your heart to someone who would have been faithful raises an extremely delicate issue here. Once the beloved becomes faithful, all turmoil disappears and all pleasure of love goes with it. Thus, thinking that the heart was given to a Muslim is double jeopardy. The lover does not want her to be faithful. Two opposing meanings can be drawn here.

36

پھر مجھے دیدۂ تر یاد آیا   دل، جگر تشنۂ فریاد آیا

phir mujhe dīda(h)' tar yād āyā
dil, jigar tashnah' faryād, āyā (36:1; #222)

Then again, I remembered my eyes bedewed with tears,
As the heart with its compelling longings began to complain.

jigar tashnah: intense longing ; *faryād*: cry, complain.

Suddenly, I remembered the days of weeping and my heart cried in longing for the ecstasy of tears. The only way to satisfy my desire for this ecstasy was to cry without end; I realized it as soon as I remembered my feelings. Another meaning from this verse can be drawn from the bedewed eyes of the beloved inflicting great distress on the lover and making his heart tumultuous.

دم لیا تھا نہ قیامت نے ہنوز   پھر ترا وقتِ سفر یاد آیا

dam liya thā nā qiyāmat ne hanūz
phir tera vaqt-e safar yād āyā (36:2; #223)

The passing of the Doomsday had barely paused, when
I came to recall the time of your parting.

vaqt-e safar: time of travel, parting.

Your death was like the end of the world to me. I had barely survived this pain when I remembered again the moment of separation from you. Once again, all passion broke free. Those who have lost loved ones can take this verse to heart. *Ġhālib* probably wrote this verse with the death of his nephew, *Ārif*, in mind.

سادگی ہاے تمنا، یعنی　　پھر وہ نیرنگِ نظر یاد آیا

sādgī hāi tamanna, ya'nī
phir vuh nairang naẓar yād āyā (36:3; #224)

Such is the simplicity of my desire, Alas!
That beloved with bewitching glance came into my thoughts again.

sādgī: simplicity; *nairang*: magic, deception, trick, deceit, miracle.

Look at the simplicity of my desires. Despite my experience of her deceit, I continue to long for her faithfulness and kindness. What a simpleton I am? The sorcery of those eyes keeps on making me come back.

عذرِ واماندگی، اے حسرتِ دل!　　نالہ کرتا تھا، جگر یاد آیا

u'zr-e vāmāndgī, ay ḥasrat-e dil
nālah kartā thā, jigar yād āyā (36:4; #225)

Excuse my helplessness, O! Longings of the heart!
While sending plaints, the thought of my liver came to my mind.

vāmāndgī: helplessness; *ḥasrat*: longings.

O! Longings of my heart accept my excuse of helplessness. I was ready to adduce my plaint, when I considered my liver, which, I realized, could not weather my lamenting; so I stopped. The heart was, of course, disappointed because it longed to release comforting sighs; but the liver, which was damaged badly, got in the way of my wants. The liver is the organ of courage and the heart seat of the emotions. Unable to lose myself in intoxication because of a damaged liver, it was better to curtail lamenting for that which enhances pain and thus increases the need to drink.

زندگی یُوں بھی گزر ہی جاتی کیوں ترا راہگزر یاد آیا

zindagī yūñ bhī guzar hī jātī
kyoñ tera rāhguzar yād āyā (36:5; #226)

Somehow my life would have passed as it is.
Why did I come to remember the path you used to frequent?

My life, as bad as it was, would have been spent crying, lamenting. But then, remembering the path you used to take devastated me further. This reminded me of how I was thrown into these alleys and how I saw you walking hand in hand with strangers in these same alleys. That made the situation all the more intolerable.

کیا ہی رِضواں سے لڑائی ہوگی گھر ترا خُلد میں گر یاد آیا

kyā hī riẓvāñ se laṛāī hogī
ghar tera ḳhuld meñ gar yād āyā (36:6; #227)

What a spectacular fight this would be with the heaven's gatekeeper,
If the thought of your home ever came to my mind in heaven?

While in heaven, I would think of the luxuries of your abode, my beloved, and that would be problematic. Were I to mention this to the gatekeeper of paradise, he would surely quarrel with me, trying to prove me wrong, and if I decided to walk out of paradise toward your home, he would fight with me again, to impress upon me how stupid I am. A good fight with the gatekeeper of paradise is in the offing. An exquisitely *Ġhālib*ian satire!

آہ وُہ جُرأتِ فریاد کہاں دِل سے تنگ آ کے جگر یاد آیا

ah vuh jura't-e faryād kahāñ
dil se tang ā kih jigar yād āyā (36:7; #228)

Alas! Where is that courage to lament?
Getting tired of my heart, I thought of my liver.

With liver intact, I had the energy to lament, but now it is wasted; yet my heart keeps insisting on letting out the sighs. I long for my liver, so that I might quiet my heart by releasing my sighs.

پھر ترے کوچے کو جاتا ہے خیال   دل گم گشتہ ، مگر ، یاد آیا

phir tere kūche ko jātā hai ḳhayāl
dil-e gum gushta mager yād āyā (36:8; #229)

Then again the thought wanders towards your alley;
Perhaps the thought of my long-lost heart has come to me.

mager: used here to mean perhaps.

The thought of your alley suddenly comes to mind, this from thinking of my heart, which, most likely and assuredly, I lost there.

کوئی ویرانی سی ویرانی ہے!   دشت کو دیکھ کے گھر یاد آیا

koī virānī sī virānī hai
dasht ko dekh kih ghar yād āyā (36:9; #230)

What desolation is this desolation
That the sight of the desert reminded me of my home?

virān: ruin, desolate, dismal.

The poet is comparing the desolation of his home to the desert; however, by questioning the nature of desolation, a conflict arises. Which is more desolate? We must conclude that while in the desert, the poet thought of it as his home before coming to the realization that he was in a desert. We can still deduce that the desolation of the desert is nothing compared to his home; it reminds him of his home, which is more desolate yet.

مَیں نے مجنوں پہ لڑکپن میں اسدؔ
سنگ اُٹھایا تھا کہ سر یاد آیا

maiñ ne majnūñ pe laṛakpan meñ Asad
sang uṭhāyā thā kih sar yād āyā (36:10; #231)

In my boyhood, I had flung a stone at *Majnūn*, Asad
When suddenly I thought of my own head.

Once in my childhood, as I was about to throw a stone at *Majnooñ*, I stopped. It occurred to me that perhaps I would turn out just as crazy and that children might throw stones at me when I reach his age. I somehow received a portent of my fate.

37

ہوئی تاخیر تو کچھ باعثِ تاخیر بھی تھا   آپ آتے تھے، مگر کوئی عناں گیر بھی تھا

hu'ī tāḳhīr to kuchh bā'is-e tāḳhir bhī thā
āp āte the, magar ko'ī 'ināñgir bhī thā (37:1; #232)

If there was a delay, then for sure there must have been some reason;
You were coming to see me but was there someone who held you back?

tāḳhir: delay; *bā'is*: cause of; *'ināñgir*: someone holding back, one who holds the reins.

Although suspicious of the beloved's connection to the rival, the poet is politely offering to her a ready excuse that it was not her fault; some stranger may have held her back. However, all the while, he expresses his distrust of her. The tone is sarcastic.

تم سے بے جا ہے مجھے اپنی تباہی کا گلہ   اس میں کچھ شائبۂ خوبیٔ تقدیر بھی تھا

tum se bejā hai mujhe apnī tabāhī kā gila(h)
us meñ kuchh shā'iba(h)' ḳhubī' taqdīr bhī thā (37:2; #233)

Unwarranted is my plaint to you for my devastation.
In it there was some contribution of the goodness of my fate as well.

shā'iba(h): contribution.

My beloved, I cannot blame you for my devastation; it would not have happened had it not been written in my fate. There is an element of sarcasm and at the same time, acceptance of realization. The word "*kuchh*" (some) provides the key, meaning there was definitely more than just my fate. The beloved is not entirely blameless.

تو مجھے بھول گیا ہو تو پتا بتلا دوں؟ کبھی فتراک میں تیرے کوئی نخچیر بھی تھا

tū mujhe bhūl gayā ho to patā batlā duñ
kabhī fitrāk meñ tere ko'ī naḳhchīr bhī thā (37:3; #234)

Let me tell you my whereabouts, just in case you've forgotten me
That there was once a catch in the stirrup of your saddle.

fitrāk: straps of saddle, stirrup; *naḳhchir*: catch.

The beloved has forgotten all about the lover, who is reminding her of his whereabouts by reminiscing about how she used to catch him. Like a catch tied to the stirrups of a saddle, you dragged me and punished me and now you do not even know who I am? This is an attempt to embarrass her for her forgotten cruelty. There is no complaint here about the treatment received, merely a reminiscing of the times gone by; and a desire for the return of said times.

قید میں ہے ترے وحشی کو وہی زلف کی یاد ہاں کچھ اک رنج گرانباریٔ زنجیر بھی تھا

qaid meñ hai tere vaḥshī ko vuhī zulf kī yād
hāñ kuchh ik ranj-e girañbārī' zanjīr bhī thā (37:4; #235)

In the prison, your lunatic remembers those tresses well.
Yes, some sorrow of heaviness of chains was there, too.

girāñbārī: heaviness.

Imprisoned, I thought I would not be able to bear the weight of chains; however, remembering your tresses lightened the burden of these chains. The chains of your tresses were much heavier.

بجلی اک کوند گئی آنکھوں کے آگے تو کیا   بات کرتے کہ میں لب تشنۂ تقریر بھی تھا

bijlī ik kaund gā'ī āñkhoñ ke āge to kyā
bāt karte kih maiñ lab tashna(h)' taqrīr bhī thā (37:5; #236)

So what if a flash of lightning struck before my eyes?
You should have talked to me, for my lips were thirsty to say something.

kaund: struck; *tashna(h)-e taqrīr:* thirsty to talk, desperate to express.

The beloved appeared before the lover like a bolt of lightning, for she left as quickly as she came. There was not enough time to tell you how my lips were parched, lips that struggled to tell their story; you should have stayed a little longer to hear it. The time the beloved spent with the lover appears fleeting, as does the lightning. The fact implied is no matter how long she would have stayed, it still would not have been long enough. He would not have been able to say anything anyway.

یوسف اس کو کہوں اور کچھ نہ کہے، خیر ہوئی   گر بگڑ بیٹھے تو میں لائقِ تعزیر بھی تھا

yūsuf us ko kahūñ aur kuchh na(h) kahe, ḳhair huī'
gar bigaṛ baiṭhe to maiñ lā'iq-e ta'zīr bhī thā (37:6; #237)

Calling her Joseph and she said nothing, was just lucky.
Had she gotten annoyed, I would have well-deserved punishment.

ta'zīr: punishment.

Calling the beloved, Joseph (Yusuf) because of his legendary beauty may have backfired, but she did not notice and that saved my life. The Amir of Egypt had brought Joseph as his slave and she (my beloved) would not have liked being compared to a slave; rather, she is a slave driver. She may also have misconstrued I was degrading her beauty by comparing her to anyone, even if the comparison was to the most beautiful person, as the legend goes. However, since she did not notice, it was all right, but, if she had, I certainly would have deserved punishment for being so impolite. Here the poet is talking about comparing the beauty of the beloved to a male; consequently, the beloved may have been male as well.

دیکھ کر غیر کو ہو کیوں نہ کلیجا ٹھنڈا　　　نالہ کرتا تھا، وَلے طالبِ تاثیر بھی تھا

dekh kar ġhair ko ho kioñ na(h) ho kaleja ṭhanḍā
nāla(h) kartā thā, vale t̤ālib-e tās̤īr bhī thā (37:7; #238)

Why would it not give me satisfaction, seeing the rival
Making a plaint and hoping, too, that it would be effective?

kaleja ṭhanḍā karnā: to draw satisfaction; *t̤ālib-e tās̤īr:* desirous of effect.

It comforts me, cools my heart, to see the rival begging for his cries to be heard. His frustration gives me satisfaction that if I was not successful in my pleas, then at least neither was anyone else. The lover is not happy that the rival is lamenting; he is happy that someone will be joining him in his misery. Naturally, the lover is happy that the beloved is paying no attention to the rival. The rival's lament does not make the poet happy, yet the fact that the rival has joined him in his misery does. The beloved's not paying any attention to the rival is another source of satisfaction. There is also an expression of audacity hoping that the beloved is more inclined towards the lover.

پیشے میں عیب نہیں، رکھیے نہ فرہاد کو نام　　　ہم ہی آشفتہ سروں میں وُہ جوانمیر بھی تھا

peshe meñ ʿaib nahiñ, rakhiye na(h) farhād ko nām
ham hī āshufta(h) saroñ meñ vuh javāñmīr bhī thā (37:8; #239)

There's nothing wrong with the profession, so you shouldn't blame *Farhād*.
He was among us the lunatic, who died young.

nām rakhnā: to blame; *āshufta(h) sar*: mad (lover), lunatic; *javāñmīr*: died in youth.

Farhād, the lover of *Shīrīn*, should not be accused of giving his life in the name of his beloved by striking his head with an axe. Lovers do not need the help of any implements to give their life, but pardon him, for he was one of the mad lovers like us; he was from our fraternity. Calling loving a profession is unique, for professionals do have their codes of ethics. *Ġhālib* has repeatedly belittled *Farhād*; for example, in being tied to customs, for doing something for his beloved's husband, and so on. However, here *Ġhālib* is defending *Farhād* by claiming that he was too young to have learned the etiquette of the profession fully. However, he *was* amongst us; we must support him. Great respect is given here to the profession of loving. It does not matter what you do for a living (as *Farhād* dug channels), but if you belong to the profession of love, you are indeed the lucky one.

ہم تھے مرنے کو کھڑے، پاس نہ آیا، نہ سہی　　آخر اس شوخ کے ترکش میں کوئی تیر بھی تھا

ham the marne ko khaṛe, pās na(h) āyā, na(h) sahī
āḳhir us shoḳh ke tarkash meñ ko'ī tīr bhī thā (37:9; #240)

We were standing ready to die, but she did not come close, so be it;
After all, was there any arrow left in her quiver?

tarkash: quiver

We were ready to give our life, but she chose not to kill us with the arrow of her piercing glance; she did not even approach close enough to fire her arrow. I wonder if it was because she had already used them all up. It is all right if she used these arrows for someone else. She paid no regard to our gesture of offering our life. She did not care; so be it. The lover concludes that the reason she did not fire an arrow was because she had run out of them, not that she did not want to. This is clearly an audacious thought on behalf of the lover.

پکڑے جاتے ہیں فرشتوں کے لکھے پر ناحق   آدمی کوئی ہمارا دمِ تحریر بھی تھا

pakṛe jāte haiñ farishtoñ ke likhe par nāḥaq
ādmī ko'ī hamārā dam-e taḥrīr bhī thā (37:10; #241)

We are unjustifiably accused at the reporting of angels.
Was any witness of ours present there at the time of writing?

dam-e taḥrīr; time of writing.

Accusing angels of being untrustworthy, and demanding that there should have been a witness when good and bad deeds were written by angels on the left and right shoulders, provides indeed a rare and refreshing juxtaposition. Contesting the testimony of angels in the court of God is typically *Ġhālib*.

Note: According to *Qur'ān, Surah Qāf* (50:17), "Behold, two (guardian angels) appointed to learn (his doings), learn (and note them), one sitting on the right and one on the left."

ریختے کے تمہیں استاد نہیں ہو غالب
کہتے ہیں اگلے زمانے میں کوئی میر بھی تھا

rekhte ke tumhīñ ustād nahīñ ho Ġhālib
kahte haiñ agle zamāne meñ ko'ī mīr bhī thā (37:11; #242)

You are not the only master of *Urdū ġhazals*, O! *Ġhālib*.
The saying goes that in the era gone by, there was someone by the name of *Mīr* as well.

reḳhte: mixture of many, here it means the *Urdū* language, particularly *Urdū ġhazal*.

Whereas admitting to the greatness of *Mīr Taqī Mīr*, *Ġhālib* does not censure himself. *Ġhālib* repeatedly strokes his ego by comparing himself to classic masters.

38

لبِ خشک در تشنگی مُردگاں کا   زیارت کدہ ہُوں دِل آزردگاں کا

lab-e ḳhushk dar tashnagī murdagāñ kā
ziyārat kada(h) huñ dil āzurdgāñ kā (38:1; #243)

Parched lips of those who died thirsty,
A memorial I am of the forsaken hearts.

labe ḳhushk: dried, parched lip; *dar tashnagī murdagāñ*: those who died thirsty (of fulfilling their desire); *ziyārat kada(h):* memorial, where people would come to pay homage; *dil āzurdgāñ:* whose hearts are hurt, destroyed, lovers.

I am the "parched lips" of all those who have given their lives in the name of passion for the beloved, meaning the passion of all of those vanquished lovers has condensed into me. It is for this reason that all those with broken hearts pay me extreme respect and come to visit me as if I were the memorial of their forsaken hearts. I am the exalted one.

ہمہ نااُمیدی، ہمہ بدگمانی   مَیں دل ہُوں فریبِ وفا خوردگاں کا

hama(h) nā umīdī, hama(h) badgumānī
maiñ dil huñ fareb-e vafā ḳhurdgāñ kā (38:2; #244)

Always hopeless, always distrustful,
I am the heart of those stung by the deception of faithfulness.

hama(h): always; *badgumānī:* distrust; *fareb-e vafā ḳhurdgāñ:* deceived by faithfulness.

Always hopeless, always distrustful, that is I; it is indeed the life of those who live with the illusion of trust and faithfulness from their beloved. Hopelessness because, despite repeated attempts, I never succeeded in letting her know the truth of my heart, and distrustful because when I saw how my sincere devotion had been trampled, I knew that sincerity meant nothing in this world.

39

تُو دوست کِسی کا بھی، ستمگر! نہ ہُوا تھا
اَوروں پہ ہے وُہ ظُلم کہ مُجھ پر نہ ہُوا تھا

tū dost kisī kā bhī sitamgar! na(h) hu'ā thā
auroñ pa(h) hai vuh ẕulm kih mujh par na(h) hu'ā thā (39:1; #245)

You have never been a friend to anyone, O! Tyrant.
What cruelties have you unleashed on others that were not unleashed on me?

sitamgar: tyrant; *ẕulm*: cruelty.

You have never been a friend to anyone, O' tyrant, I know. But I have a complaint to make. Your cruelty to others is much more intense than what you have shown me and what I deserve, if you had only considered me as your friend. More cruelty to others is a favor to them. By showing less cruelty to me, you demonstrate that you are less friendly to me, though you are friend to no one.

چھوڑا مہِ نَخشَب کی طرح دستِ قضا نے
خورشید ہَنُوز اُس کے برابر نہ ہُوا تھا

choṛā mah-e nāḳhshab kī t̤arḥ dast-e qaẓā ne
ḳhurshīd hanoz us ke barābar na(h) hu'ā thā (39:2; #246)

The hand of destiny quit trying like the fabled moon of Nakhshab,
For the sun still wasn't an equal match to her.

mah-e nāḳhshab: a luminous appearance resembling the moon, produced from a well at the foot of mount Siyam in the town of Nakhshab in Turkistan by the juggler *Muqanna*' every night during a period of four months; it is also called *mah-e siyām*; *dast-e qazạ̄:* hand of destiny.

Just like the artificial moon could not endure the real moon and *Hakīm Nāḳhshab Muqanna*', who had made the artificial moon, gave up trying to make one, Nature also wanted to create a sun to match your brilliance but gave up in futility, leaving the sun as it was with its imperfections. My beloved's brilliance dazzles the sun. Comparing Nature's act to a juggler tells the frustration of Nature.

توفیق بہ اندازۂ ہمت ہے ازل سے
آنکھوں میں ہے وُہ قطرہ کہ گوہر نہ ہُوا تھا

taufīq ba(h) andāza(h)' himmat hai azal se
āñkhoñ meñ hai vuh qatṛa(h) kih gauhar na(h) hu'ā thā (39:3; #247)

From eternity, the ability is in proportion to courage.
In the eye is that drop which did not turn into pearl.

taufīq: ability; *andāza(h)-e himmat:* proportional to courage; *gauhar:* pearl.

Nature always bestows achievements in proportion to courage; there is a drop of water whose only hope is to turn into a pearl, and then there is the drop of water that aspires to be a tear in the lover's eye. Turning into a pearl is not easy, but that does not compare with the persuasion of the drop of water that turns into a tear in the lover's eye. A pearl cannot match a tear. The value of things depends on their destiny. A flower in the necklace of the beloved is no ordinary flower; a gem in the crown of a king is no ordinary gem. The effort of the journey makes all the difference in our destinies.

جب تک کہ نہ دیکھا تھا قدِ یار کا عالم
میں معتقدِ فتنۂ محشر نہ ہوا تھا

jab tak kih na(h) dekhā thā qad-e yār kā `ālam
maiñ mo`taqid-e fitna(h)' maḥshar na(h) hu'ā thā (39:4; #248)

Until I saw the grandeur of the stature of the beloved,
I did not believe in the commotion maker of the Day of Resurrection.

mo`taqid: believer; *fitna(h)*: tumult; *maḥshar*: Doomsday: Day of Resurrection.

Until I witnessed the grandeur of her stature, I was not convinced of the tumult of Doomsday; wherever she goes, she will wreak devastation. The trickery of words here refers to the beloved as a troublemaker as well as to the chaos she entails. The poet believes she is a "troublemaker" the likes of which will appear on the Day of Resurrection, as the anecdote goes. Now I believe that there will be true commotion on the Day of Resurrection.

میں سادہ دل، آزردگیِ یار سے خوش ہوں
یعنی سبقِ شوق مکرّر نہ ہوا تھا

maiñ sāda(h) dil, āzurdagī' yār se ḳhush huñ
ya`nī sabaq-e shauq mukarrar na(h) hu'ā thā (39:5; #249)

Naïve at heart, happy I am at her being angry,
As if a lesson to my desire had not been taught before.

sāda(h) dil: naive at heart; *āzurdagī*: anger; *mukarrar*: repeat, again.

I am happy that I will get another chance to please her now that she is angry with me. Unfortunately, in my naiveté, I do not understand that regardless of how I try, she will not be pleased with me. Another chance at redemption is simply deceiving myself, a waste of time. But I am happy that I had the opportunity.

دریاے معاصی تُنک آبی سے ہُوا خشک
میرا سرِ دامن بھی ابھی تر نہ ہُوا تھا

daryāe maʿāṣī tunuk ābī se hu'ā ḳhushk,
merā sar-e dāman bhī abhī tar na(h) hu'ā thā (39:6; #250)

Though the river of sins dried out for scarcity of water,
The edge of my garb had not even become wet.

maʿāṣī: sins; *tunuk ābī*: shortage of water.

My passion to commit sin was so great that despite imbibing all sins from the river of sin, my shirt-skirt barely got wet while the river dried up. Despite having committed all sins, my desire to sin did not relent. "Sins carried in lapel" is an oft-repeated theme.

جاری تھی اسدؔ داغِ جگر سے مری تحصیل
آتشکدہ جاگیرِ سمندر نہ ہُوا تھا

jārī thī Asad dāġh-e jigar se merī taḥṣīl
ātish kada(h) jāgīr-e samandar na(h) hu'ā thā (39:7; #251)

My taking of fire went on from the brandings in the heart, Asad.
The fireplace had not yet turned into an abode for the salamander.

taḥṣīl: acquisition; *ātish kada(h)*: fireplace; *samandar*: salamander, a lizard that lives in fire that had remained lit for at least a few centuries and it dies if taken out of fire, an anecdote (See Glossary).

A fireplace cannot be compared to my heart's burning. My heart has been burning longer than the fire that burned for centuries and produced salamanders.

40

شب کہ وُہ مجلس فروزِ خلوتِ ناموس تھا
رشتۂ ہر شمع خارِ کسوتِ فانوس تھا

shab kih vuh majlis furoz-e ḳhilvat-e nāmūs thā
rishta(h)’ har shamaʿ ḳhār-e kisvat-e fānūs thā (40:1; #252)

Last night in her private assembly, as she exposed her beauty,
The candlewick turned in a thorn in the apparel of chandelier.

nāmūs: sanctity, honor; *rishta(h)-e shamaʿ:* candle wick; *kisvat*: apparel, dress; *kisvat-e fānūs*: mesh wrapped around the glass lamp or chandelier.

Last night my beloved, in her private assembly, exposed her beauty. This dazzling display proved too much for the candle, which began to burn brightly with jealousy and wanted to take off her thorny garb—the chandelier—to match the dazzle of the barely clad beloved. Referring to the mesh around the chandelier a thorny garb is an intriguing comparison. As the candle burns, it heats up the glass, making it red-hot and consequently more uncomfortable. The chandelier in this instance was a thorn between the candle and the beloved because the candle was dying to bare herself as had the beloved, in jealousy. Calling the chandelier a garb of the candle was necessary because the beloved had removed her garb. The candlewick is also called the thorn of candle; thus as candle burns brightly, it removes that thorn also. Very complex visualization is in offing here.

مشہدِ عاشق سے کوسوں تک جو اُگتی ہے حنا
کس قدر یارب ہلاکِ حسرتِ پابوس تھا

mashad-e `āshiq se kosoñ tak jo ugtī hai ḥinā
kis qadar yārabb halāk-e ḥasrat-e pābos thā (40:2; #253)

Miles around, from the point of my martyrdom, grows *henna*.
How, O! Lord, was I a victim of my desire to kiss her feet?

mashad: point of martyrdom; *kosoñ*: miles (one *kose* is equal to two miles); *pābos*: to kiss feet.

Where the lover was murdered, *henna* grows all around, taking its nutrition from the lover's blood that seeped through the fields and his remains that turned into ashes. The only way the lover can reach the feet of his beloved is if the *henna* taking its nutrition from his dust reaches her and she applies it to her feet. Since included in the *henna* would be the molecule that came from the body and blood of the lover, the lover will reach her feet. The red color of *henna* and of blood in killing calls for further attention.

حاصلِ اُلفت نہ دیکھا جز شکستِ آرزو
دل بہ دل پیوستہ، گویا، یک لبِ افسوس تھا

ḥāṣil-e ulfat na(h) dekhā juz shikast-e ārzū
dil ba(h) dil pevasta(h), goyā, yak lab-e afsos thā (40:3; #254)

The outcome of love never saw anything but the shattering of desire;
The hearts when fused together appear as saddened lips.

juz: except; *shikast-e ārzū:* defeat of desire; *pevasta(h):* fused, merged; *lab-e afsos:* saddened lips.

Even if my love succeeds, the ultimate result will be loss of hope and more disappointment. Two hearts merged appear in shape like two lips fused in sorrow. Pressed lips in sadness and disappointment are compared here with fused hearts. Two hearts merge when they fall in love, but soon distrust and disappointment creeps in, ending it all in a loss of desire—lips of sadness leave nothing but despair.

کیا کہوں بیماریِ غم کی فراغت کا بیاں
جو کہ کھایا خُونِ دِل، بے مِنّتِ کیموس تھا

kyā kahūñ bīmārī' ġham kī farāġhat kā bayāñ
jo kih khayā ḳhūn-e dil, be minnat-e kamūs thā (40:4; #255)

What to say of the idleness of the illness of sorrow?
Whatever I eat turns into blood bypassing digestion.

farāġhat: leisure, rest, ease; *kamūs*: second stage of digestion.

What to say of the idleness of my suffering in sorrow; whatever I eat bypasses digestion and ends up converting directly into blood—as if I am not eating food but drinking blood. "Eating sorrow" and "eating one's heart out" are intended here. The sickness of sorrow has left me so incapacitated that my food bypasses digestion: it is like eating blood.

41

آئینہ دیکھ اپنا سا مُنہ لے کے رہ گئے
صاحب کو دِل نہ دینے پہ کتنا غُرور تھا

ā'īna(h) dekh apnā sā mun(h) le ke rah ga'e
ṣāḥib ko dil na(h) dene pa(h) kitnā ġhurūr thā (41:1; #256)

Looking into the mirror, you got embarrassed to see a face like your own.
Madam! How proud were you for not letting your heart go?

apnā sā muñh: face like your own (embarrassed, abashed); *ṣāḥib*: Mister (meaning Madam), used here sarcastically to address the beloved; *ġhurūr*: pride.

Looking into the mirror embarrassed you because you were so proud of never giving your heart to anyone. But after seeing yourself in the mirror, you had no choice but to fall in love with your image. Now you know how, we, the lovers, feel about you. Your vanity is shattered and you are embarrassed. You understand the meaning of giving your heart to a beautiful thing. A remarkable rendition of narcissism is presented here.

قاصد کو اپنے ہاتھ سے گردن نہ ماریے
اُس کی خطا نہیں ہے یہ میرا قصُور تھا

qāṣid ko apne hāth se gardan na(h) māriye
us kī ḳhaṭā nahiñ hai yih merā quṣūr thā (41:2; #257)

Slay not the messenger with your own hands.
It is not his mistake, it was my fault.

qāṣid: messenger.

The lover has sent a letter to his beloved that has enraged her. Now she wants to kill the messenger. The lover is pointing to himself, not the messenger, as the deserving target. The lover wants the pleasure of being killed by her and he is presenting this argument as if he is trying to protect the messenger.

42

عرضِ نیازِ عشق کے قابل نہیں رہا
جس دِل پہ ناز تھا مجھے، وُہ دِل نہیں رہا

ʿarẓ-e niyāz-e ʿishq ke qābil nahiñ rahā
jis dil pa(h) nāz thā mujhe, vuh dil nahiñ rahā (42:1; #258)

My supplications of love are no longer worthy of my beloved;
The heart, in which I took great pride, is there no more.

ʿarẓ-e niyāz: expression of offering, supplication to beloved; *nāz:* pride.

I can no longer chant the rhymes of love, for my heart, of which I was so proud, has lost the ability to do so. The offering of love—the tiresome rituals—I can no longer muster the energy to cope.

جاتا ہُوں داغِ حسرتِ ہستی لیے ہُوئے
ہُوں شمعِ کُشتہ، در خورِ محفل نہیں رہا

jatā hūñ dāġh-e ḥasrat-e hastī liye hu'e
huñ shamʿ-e kushta(h), dar ḳhor-e maḥfil nahiñ rahā (42:2; #259)

I am leaving taking with me the scars of life's unfulfilled desires.
Like an extinguished candle, I am gone, removed from the assembly.

shamʿ-e kushta(h): extinguished candle; *dar ḳhor*: sent out.

I am leaving this world with the sorrow of unfulfilled longings. I am like a burnt-out candle pulled from the candlestick. Comparing life to a burnt-out candle that is replaced expresses extreme dejection and loneliness: elements of being love-stricken and rejected. Note that at one time the burnt-out candle was in the candlestick. Thrown out of the candlestick, all hope is gone.

مرنے کی اے دِل اور ہی تدبیر کر کہ میں
شایانِ دست و بازُوے قاتل نہیں رہا

marne kī ai dil aur hī tadbīr kar kih maiñ
shāyān-e dast-o-bāzū-e qātil nahiñ rahā (42:3; #260)

Contrive some other means of dying, O! My heart!
I am no longer worthy of the arms and hand of the slayer.

tadbīr: workings, solution.

Giving my life to my love was my goal. Being killed by the beloved's hands would have been ideal. However, I am now too insignificant to be worthy of her attention; she will not waste her efforts to kill me. With new rivals coming in to offer their lives, I am no longer a desirable option for her. But I must prove my love and thus must find some alternate way to lose my life.

برُوے شش جہت درِ آئینہ باز ہے
یاں اِمتیازِ ناقص و کامل نہیں رہا

barrūe shash jahat dar-e ā'īna(h) bāz hai
yāñ imtiyāz-e nāqiṣ-o-kāmil nahiñ rahā (42:4; #261)

In the six directions there appear doors to mirror juggler.
The distinction between the flawless and the defective remains no more.

barrū: face to face; *shash jahat*: six directions (all around); *ā'īnah bāz*: mirror juggler; *dar*: door; *imtiyāz*: distinction; *nāqiṣ*: faulty;

kāmil: perfect.

I see mirrors of wisdom in all directions. The mirror juggler is God having provided evidence of reality all around. My intellect was like a mirror: unidirectional. As my vision improved, I could discern the superficiality of the difference between what is flawless and what is not. Now that I have reached this stage of perfection in my multi-directional vision, I no longer see things as defective. They all seem perfect. This verse points to the narrowness of human vision, wherein perfection is merely a creation of our bias rather than any absolute reality.

وا کر دیے ہیں شوق نے بندِ نقابِ حسن
غیر از نگاہ اب کوئی حائل نہیں رہا

vā kar diye haiñ shauq ne band-e niqāb-e ḥusn
ġhair az nigāh ab koī 'ḥā'il nahīñ rahā (42:5; #262)

Passion has opened the ribbons tying the veil of beauty. Except for my own sight, now there remains no obstacle in-between.

ḥā'il: interfering, in between.

My passion was so strong that the beloved was forced to drop her veil. Now only my sight remains in between for me to admire her. Beauty can only be appreciated unveiled, but the sight is keeping it from being seen, indicating imperfection of vision. Beauty can only be appreciated if we have the eye to appreciate it. Our desire can only take us to the beauty. It cannot make us appreciate it, value it, and enjoy it. The beauty behind the veil offers much to admire; exposed, we are less able to appreciate it as our own shortcomings are exposed.

گو میں رہا رہینِ ستم ہائے روزگار
لیکن ترے خیال سے غافل نہیں رہا

go maiñ rahā rahīn-e sitam hāi rozgār
lekin tere ḳhayāl se ġhāfil nahīñ rahā (42:6; #263)

Though I remained involved in, managing the tyrannies of living,
I was, however, never oblivious of your thought and memory.

rahīn: dedicated, engrossed.

Though I was deeply engrossed in handling the cruelties of everyday life, I was never oblivious to thinking of you. This was because the thought of you made the cruelties of life look simple, so I sailed through them. In addition, the thought of you was enough to give me joy and comfort to cope with the tribulations I faced. In both cases, it was good to think of you.

دل سے ہوائے کشتِ وفا مٹ گئی کہ واں
حاصل سوائے حسرتِ حاصل نہیں رہا

dil se havā-e kisht-e vafā miṭ ga'ī kih vāñ
ḥāṣil sivāe ḥasrat-e ḥāṣil nahīñ rahā (42:7; #264)

Uprooted from my heart is the desire to cultivate the crop of fidelity,
For nothing remains here except stifled desires.

havā: desire; *kisht*: crop.

The desire to make my devotion stronger has been erased from my heart. Nothing remains except my unfulfilled wishes. The despair of lost desire is so strong that all desire is gone. Here the poet has used the word *ḥāṣil* to mean both, the result and what comes of efforts. I gained nothing from cultivating the crop of fidelity—except for losing desire to find something in it.

بیدادِ عشق سے نہیں ڈرتا، مگر اسدؔ
جس دِل پہ ناز تھا مجھے، وُہ دِل نہیں رہا

bedād-e ʿishq se nahiñ dartā, magar Asad
jis dil pa(h) nāz thā mujhe, vuh dil nahiñ rahā (42:8; #265)

Not afraid of bearing the tyrannies of love, but then, Asad,
The heart in which I once took much pride, that heart is gone now.

I am not afraid of facing the hardships of love; it is just that the heart, in which I took so much pride for being able to bear this burden, is gone. Meaning, I have been through so much that there is no longer the desire to offer my love. The heart no longer provides the excitement needed to bear the burden. Note that at one time I was very proud of my heart, meaning, I was able to face the tyrannies like a brave lover. Helplessness of a dying soul is personified here.

43

رشک کہتا ہے کہ اُس کا غیر سے اِخلاص حَیف
عقل کہتی ہے کہ وُہ بے مہر کس کا آشنا

rashk kahtā hai kih us kā ġhair se iḳhlāṣ ḥaif
'aql kahtī hai kih vuh be mehr kis kā āshnā (43:1; #266)

Envy tells me that she is sincere to a stranger, Alas!
Wisdom tells, "Whose friend could that unaffectionate soul be?"

rashk: envy; *iḳhlāṣ*: sincerity; *be mehr:* unaffectionate; *āshnā:* friend.

My envious heart keeps thinking that maybe she is friendly and sincere to the stranger because she is oblivious to me. However, my wisdom tells me that this is not possible; how can she be kind to anyone, even if it is my enemy? This also reassures me that if she is not kind to me, it has little to do with me. It is because that is how she is, and I am no more distant from her than anyone else. Then, what is the place of wisdom in love? I remain envious, just in case she favors someone else.

ذرہ ذرہ ساغرِ مَے خانۂ نیرنگ ہے
گردشِ مجنوں بہ چشمکہاے لیلیٰ آشنا

ẓarra(h) żarra(h) sāġhar-e mai ḳhāna(h)' nairang hai
gardish-e majnūñ ba(h) chasmk hāe lailā āshnā (43:2; #267)

Every particle is a goblet in the enchanted tavern of mystery;
Wanderings of *Majnūn* driven by *Lailā*'s winks are well known.

mai ḳhān'a(h) nairang: tavern of mystery (mystery of universe);
chasmak: hinting with eye movements, winking.

Just like the wanderings of *Majnūn* that follow the command from the eyes of *Lailā*, every particle in the universe is like a goblet dancing at the command of the Almighty. Everything material, and how it expresses itself, operates under God's plan. In the tavern, the goblet revolves among the drinkers; the world rotates and *Majnūn* encircles the wilderness, all under their own influence. The universe operates under one law, the law of God. Everything is under His influence. Notice the use of the word, "rotation" in all comparisons; this is the basic physics of the balance of universe.

شوق ہے ساماں طرازِ نازشِ اربابِ عجز
ذرہ، صحرا دستگاہ و قطرہ، دریا آشنا

shauq hai sāmāñ ṭarāz-e nāzish-e arbāb-e ʿijz
ẓarra(h), ṣaḥrā dastgāh-o-qaṭra(h), daryā āshnā (43:3; #268)

Passion provides the means to be prideful to the humble one.
A particle with vastness of wilderness and a drop like an ocean is well known.

sāmāñ ṭarāz: provider of things; *dastgāh*: capability.

For us, the souls of humbleness, it is enough to take pride that we are full of passion for love; the kind of passion that endows each speck of dirt the vastness of the wilderness, and to each drop of water, the depth of the ocean. To the humble, passion for love exalts them: love merges the lover with the beloved.

مَیں اور اِک آفت کا ٹکڑا، وُہ دلِ وحشی کہ ہے
عافیت کا دُشمن اور آوارگی کا آشنا

maiñ āur ik āfat kā ṭukṛā, vuh dil-e vahshī kih hai
ʿāfiyat kā dushman aur āvārgī kā āshnā (43:4; #269)

I and that piece of disaster—my wild heart, which is,
Enemy to comfort and used to wandering.

ʿāfiyat: comfort, security; *āvārgī*: wandering.

I must put up with my lunatic heart, that likes to wander and does everything that takes away comfort and peace in my life. This part of me is out to destroy me.

شکوہ سنجِ رشکِ ہمدگر نہ رہنا چاہیے
میرا زانو مونس اور آئینہ تیرا آشنا

shikva(h) sanj-e rashk-e hamdigar na(h) rahnā chāhīye
merā zānū mūnis aur ā'īna(h) terā āshnā (43:5; #270)

We should not complain of jealousy to each other;
If I am engrossed onto my knee, then you are lost in the mirror too.

shikva(h) sanj: complainer; *hamdigar*: with each other; *mūnis*: friend, one with familiarity.

The lover and the beloved are complaining to each other in jealousy. The beloved, seeing the lover sitting with his head on his knees, believes that the lover is thinking about someone, perhaps another beloved. The lover responds that if this is the case, then tell me why you look into the mirror so frequently. Is there another lover who praises you so much that you have begun to admire yourself more? The lover also admonishes that friends should not grow jealous of each other and suspect each other's behavior.

کوہکن نقاشِ یک تمثالِ شیریں تھا، اسد
سنگ سے سر مار کر ہووے نہ پیدا آشنا

kohkan naqqāsh-e yak timṡāl-e shīriñ thā, Asad
sang se sar mār kar hove na(h) paidā āshnā (43:6; #271)

The mountain digger was merely a sculptor making a statue of *Shīrīn*, Asad,
But striking one's head on the stone would not produce a beloved?

kohkan: mountain digger, referring to *Farhād*; *naqqāsh:* sculptor; *timṡāl:* statue; *āshnā:* beloved.

Farhād was a sculptor who wanted to cut stone into *Shīrīn*'s image. When he hit his head on the stone, *Shīrīn* should have come running to him. Since she did not, this proved that the love of *Farhād* was superficial. The second line is a longing question. If love is real, its sacrifice melts the heart. *Farhād*'s efforts were in vain: he wanted to bring forth *Shīrīn*, but all he could do was to carve out her image. See the combination of words: sculptor, statue, sculpting, and producing the beloved.

44

ذکر اُس پری وش کا، اور پھر بیاں اپنا   بن گیا رقیب آخر تھا جو رازداں اپنا

żikr us parīvash kā, aur phir bayāñ apnā
ban gayā raqīb āḳhir, thā jo rāzdāñ apnā (44:1; #272)

The description of that nymph, in my impressive style;
He, who was my confidant, eventually turned into my rival.

parīvash: beautiful (fairy persona), nymph; *rāzdāñ:* secret keeper, confidant.

I told my confidant about my beloved who has stolen my heart: what she is like and the many ways she plays with my heart. My confidant listened to me and fell in love. Such was the emotive power of my description that just talking about my beloved made him fall in love with her.

مے وہ کیوں بہت پیتے بزمِ غیر میں یارب   آج ہی ہُوا منظور اُن کو اِمتحاں اپنا

mai vuh kioñ būhat pīte bazm-e ġhair meñ yārabb
āj hī hu'ā manẓūr un ko imteḥañ apnā (44:2; #273)

Why would she drink so much in the company of my rival, O! Lord?
And just today would she decide to test her resolve?

The beloved wanted to see how much could she drink. This would give the lover an opportunity to take advantage of her when she became tipsy. Unfortunately, she chose to do this in the company of the rival. What a pity! Suspicion rises in the mind of the lover. What did the rival do to her while she was drunk? Another explanation assumes that it is the lover whose patience is being tested as the beloved has taken to drinking with the rival.

منظر اک بلندی پر اور ہم بنا سکتے　　عرش سے اُدھر ہوتا، کاشکے مکاں اپنا

manzar ik balandī par āur ham banā sakte
'arsh se udhar hotā, kāsh kih, makāñ apnā (44:3; #274)

A vantage point of height, if I could have built for me,
Down below from heaven, if there were my home.

manzar: view; *bulandī:* height; *'arsh:* heaven.

To know who I was, I wanted to see my home (myself) from distance. The highest distance possible, of course, was heaven, but that proved useless as my home was at just about the same level. As I am part of heaven, part of God's abode, we are the same and inseparable.

دے وہ جس قدر ذلت ہم ہنسی میں ٹالیں گے　　بارے آشنا نکلا، اُن کا پاسباں اپنا

de vuh jis qadar żillat ham hañsī meñ ṭāleñ ge
bāre āshnā niklā, un kā pāsbañ, apnā (44:4; #275)

Whatever insult he doles out, I will take it in good humor;
The guard to her home turned out to be my old acquaintance.

żillat: disgrace; *bāre:* by chance*; āshnā:* friend; *pāsbāñ:* protector.

Visiting the beloved has often been a disaster. Berating by, and even fist fighting with, the guard at her home was not uncommon. Now these acts do not seem insulting or disgraceful to me, for the guard to her home turned out to be my old friend. Now it is not a disgrace if he beats me up. It is just a friendly brawl. The message, of course, is meant for the spectators.

درد دل لکھوں کب تک، جاؤں اُن کو دکھلا دوں
انگلیاں فگار اپنی، خامہ خونچکاں اپنا

درد دل لکھوں کب تک، جاؤں اُن کو دکھلا دوں   انگلیاں فگار اپنی، خامہ خونچکاں اپنا

dard-e dil likhuñ kab tak, jāuñ un ko dikhlā duñ
ungliyāñ figār apnī, ḳhama(h) ḳhūñchukāñ apnā (44:5; #276)

For how long shall I write about the anguish of the heart?
Instead, I should go and show her
My wounded fingers and the blood-dripping pen.

figār: wounded; *ḳhama(h)*: pen; *ḳhūñchukāñ*: dripping blood.

I have long been writing about the condition of my heart and I keep sending her my letters. Now the condition is such that my fingers are wounded and the pen has begun to drip blood. Perhaps I should go to her and show her my hands and my pen. She will then understand the whole story and I will not have to write about it any more.

گھستے گھستے مِٹ جاتا، آپ نے عبث بدلا   ننگِ سجدہ سے میرے، سنگِ آستاں اپنا

ghiste ghiste miṭ jātā, āpne abaṡ badlā
nañg-e sajda(h) se mere, sang-e āstāñ apnā (44:6; #277)

Being rubbed, it would have disappeared anyway; wastefully you replaced
The doorsill for my making the disgraceful supplications.

'abaṡ: unnecessarily; *nañg-e sajda(h):* disgrace of prostration; *sang-e āstāñ:* doorsill.

The lover supplicated at the beloved's threshold, and to show the world she despised his touching her threshold, she replaced the stone. The lover is making the humble suggestion that it was perhaps wasteful and unnecessary. His rubbing at the threshold with his forehead would have rubbed the stone off the threshold anyway. It would have been more appropriate to replace it then, not now.

تا کرے نہ غمازی، کر لیا ہے دشمن کو   دوست کی شکایت میں ہم نے ہمزباں اپنا

tā kare na(h) ġhammāzī, kar liyā hai dushman ko
dost kī shikāyat meñ ham ne hamzabāñ apnā (44:7; #278)

So he would not squeal, I have taken my enemy
To be my confidant in complaining about the beloved.

ġhammāzī: squealing.

The rival used to squeal to the beloved about lover's complaints. To stop this, the lover has cleverly made the rival his confidant. Elsewhere, the poet says, "*'āshiq hūñ pa(h) ma'shūq farebī hai merā kām.*" (A lover I am, but deceiving the beloved is my trade.)

ہم کہاں کے دانا تھے، کس ہنر میں یکتا تھے
بے سبب ہوا غالبؔ دشمن آسماں اپنا

ham kahāñ ke dānā the, kis hunar meñ yakta(h) the
be sabab hu'ā Ġhālib dushman āsmāñ apnā (44:8; #279)

What sagacity we had, and what skills had we mastered that
Without just cause, O! *Ġhālib*, the heaven turned our enemy?

I was neither a wise man nor a skilled artisan; why then did heaven turn against me? Heaven showing enmity to intelligence and talent is an oft-repeated plaint in *Urdū*, Persian, and Arabic poetry. Here the poet, while admitting his own excellence, questions if it was justified for heaven to wreak havoc on him. A hidden element of humbleness is also evident. The author has to excel to higher standards, which he has yet to achieve.

45

سرمۂ مفتِ نظر ہوں، مری قیمت یہ ہے   کہ رہے چشمِ خریدار پہ احساں میرا

surma(h)' muft-e naẕar hūñ, merī qīmat yih hai
kih rahe chashm-e ḳharīdār pa(h) iḥsāñ merā (45:1; #280)

I am like the antimony for eye given away, this is my value,
Just so the eyes of the customer would remain obliged to me.

What is my value? I am like the powdered antimony (used to decorate eyes) distributed free to the public. The only thing I get in return is that the eyes of the customer remain indebted to me. My verses are like the antimony that I distribute freely, hoping that those who read them enjoy them and feel indebted to me. Powdered antimony is historically used to improve vision; these verses are expected to improve luminary vision.

رخصتِ نالہ مجھے دے کہ مبادا ظالم   تیرے چہرے سے ہو ظاہر غمِ پنہاں میرا

ruḳhṣat-e nāla(h) mujhe de kih mubādā ẕālim
tere chahre se ho ẕāhir ġham-e pinhāñ merā (45:2; #281)

Permit me, at least, to air my sighs, O! Tyrant, lest
Your face reveals the evidence of my hidden suffering.

ruḳhṣat: to let go; *mubādā*: lest; *ẕālim:* cruel; *pinhāñ*: hidden.

O! My tyrant beloved, allow me to continue with my plaint, though I have been admonished not to. The lover is saying that if she does not let his plaint go out, his condition will worsen. This might cause her distress and she may begin to show feelings of guilt on her face. People looking at her face may figure out that the beloved is the reason for my suffering. This is a most audacious approach the lover is taking—assuming that the beloved cares about the lover, or the world.

46

غافل بہ وہمِ ناز خود آرا ہے ورنہ یاں
بے شانۂ صبا نہیں طُرّہ گیاہ کا

ġhāfil ba(h) vahm-e nāz ḳhud ārā hai varna(h) yāñ
be shāna(h)' ṣabā nahiñ ṯurra(h) gīyāh kā (46:1; #282)

The heedless are deceived in taking pride in self-being, or else here,
Even the grass does not rise to fluttering without the shoulder of the breeze.

shāna(h): shoulder; *ṯurra(h)*: style, parade; *gīyāh*: grass.

We are ignorant if we think that our salvation is a result of our doings and planning. The fact is that the planning of Providence gives us support. The humble blade of grass rises to flutter proudly only on the shoulders of the breeze. Without the breeze, it will fall; without support from God, we will never rise.

بزمِ قدح سے عیشِ تمنا نہ رکھ، کہ رنگ
صیدِ ز دام جستہ ہے اِس دامگاہ کا

bazm-e qadḥ se 'aish tamannā na(h) rakh, kih rang
ṣaid-e zavām jasta(h) hai is dām gāh kā (46:2; #283)

Do not long for the joy from drinking parties, for
Its gaiety is the catch that has already escaped the snare.

bazm-e qadḥ: gathering at the tavern; *rang:* color, happiness; *ṣaid-e zavām jasta(h):* catch that runs away after being caught; *dām gāh:* place of catching prey, meaning here, the tavern.

People think that the tavern where we go to drink brings us much happiness and joy. But joy and happiness are fleeting, like prey that escapes from the net spread here (in the tavern). And surely the prey that gets away learns not to be caught again. Drinking does not make us content; it just gives us a fleeting moment of joy. The use of the word "*rang*" or "color" has two meanings: first, the happiness; and the other, flushing of the face that occurs after drinking wine. This also fades quickly.

رحمت اگر قبول کرے، کیا بعید ہے
شرمندگی سے عذر نہ کرنا گناہ کا

raḥmat agar qubūl kare, kyā baʿīd hai
sharmindagī se ʿuzr na(h) karnā gunāh kā (46:3; #284)

God might accept, as it is not beyond possibility,
Our not offering apologies for sins, because of shame.

raḥmat: Lord; *baʿīd*: beyond; *ʿuzr:* excuse.

Buried in sins, the poet is so ashamed that he does not offer any excuse for his acts. He is hoping that God will accept his admission without any explanation and pardon him, accepting his untold repentance. And, the poet says, it is not beyond belief that God can do this. God can do anything, but to give God the benefit of the doubt is remarkable.

مقتل کو کس نشاط سے جاتا ہوں میں، کہ ہے
پُرگل خیالِ زخم سے دامن نگاہ کا

maqtal ko kis nishāṯ se jātā hūñ maiñ, kih hai
pur gul ḳhayāl-e zaḳhm se dāman nigāh kā (46:4; #285)

I am walking to the altar with such sheer ecstasy, that
The thought of wounds has filled the lap of my vision with flowers.

maqtal: altar for sacrifice.

The joy of being killed by her is obvious—the eye sees the wounds as flowers. Besides being honored, my murder will release me of my lifetime of suffering. I am walking to the altar with the joyful thought of red flowers (my wounds) in my vision. Red flowers blooming and carved wounds make a colorful simile in this verse.

جاں در ہوائے یک نگہ گرم ہے اسد
پروانہ ہے وکیل ترے دادخواہ کا

jāñ dar havāe yak nigah-e garm hai Asad
parvānāh hai vakil tere dādḳh(v)āh kā (46:5; #286)

Life is clinging to the hope of just one fiery glance, Asad;
The moth is the witness to your plaintiff.

havā: aspiration, hope; *vakil*: witness; *dādḳh(v)āh*: plaintiff, petitioner, claimant.

My life is waiting to receive just one warm glance from the beloved, and then I am ready to die. This plaintiff of yours has made the moth his witness to this event. The moth also gives its life to the warm eye of the candle (the flame). Who could be a more qualified witness to this act? Only a moth appreciates the suffering that leads to the desire to immolate oneself and to enjoy the pain of immolation. Only a moth can know what I have endured.

47

جور سے باز آئے، پر باز آئیں کیا   کہتے ہیں ہم تجھ کو منہ دکھلائیں کیا

jaur se bāz āe, par bāz ā'eñ kyā
kahte haiñ ham tujh ko muñh dikhlā'eñ kyā (47:1; #287)

Refrained from cruelty, but what refraining?
Saying, "I am too embarrased to show my face to you?"

jaur: cruelty, oppression; *bāz:* refrain.

Listening to the complaint of the lover, the beloved has stopped being cruel. In addition, realizing that she has been unfair, she is now too embarrassed to show her face to the lover. However, to the lover, not being able to see her is a much greater cruelty. The question therefore arises: is this refraining from cruelty? No matter what she does, she remains cruel.

رات دن گردش میں ہیں سات آسماں   ہو رہے گا کچھ نہ کچھ گھبرائیں کیا

rāt din gardish meñ haiñ sāt āsmāñ
ho rahe gā kuchh na(h) kuchh ghabrā'eñ kyā (47:2; #288)

Through days and nights, the seven heavens keep revolving;
Why should we worry, for something would eventually happen.

The seven heavens that comprise the universe are in continuous revolution, as the legend goes. Whatever happens in this world, be it good or ill, is a result of the rotation of the heavens. The poet observes that the continuous movement of the universe assures that everything is in a state of flux and change is imminent. Change must include the salvation of the lovers as well. The days of sorrow will soon be gone. The poet consoles himself—happy days are coming.

لاگ ہو تو اُس کو ہم سمجھیں لگاؤ   جب نہ ہو کچھ بھی تو دھوکا کھائیں کیا

lāg ho to us ko ham samjheñ lagāo
jab na(h) ho kuchh bhī to dhokā khā'eñ kyā (47:3; #289)

Enmity, if there were, I would think of it as affection,
But with no feelings at all, how would I deceive myself?

lāg: enmity; *lagā'o*: association, love.

Any association with the beloved, whether enmity or friendship, is what the poet wants, believing that someday things will work out. But when she does not have any feelings at all, it is difficult to build castles in the air. This theme is oft repeated. The lover wants the beloved to be cruel if she cannot be kind. A state of total obliviousness is quite unproductive.

ہو لیے کیوں نامہ بر کے ساتھ ساتھ   یارب اپنے خط کو ہم پہنچائیں کیا

ho liye kioñ nāma(h) bar kih sāth sāth
yārabb apne ḳhaṯ ko ham pahuñchā'eñ kyā (47:4; #290)

Why did I go along with my letter carrier;
O God! Is that how to deliver my letter to her?

Impatient, I accompanied the letter carrier to her house, fearing he might destroy or not even deliver my letter. However, I realized that it is below my dignity to carry my own letter. The poet is wondering whether she will accept the letter if she sees him. Temptations, tribulations, and impatience of a lover are eloquently delivered here.

موجِ خوں سر سے گزر ہی کیوں نہ جائے   آستانِ یار سے اٹھ جائیں کیا

mauj-e ḳhūñ sar se guzar hī kioñ na(h) jāe
āstān-e yār se uṭh jā'eñ kyā (47:5; #291)

Even if the tide of blood goes over the head,
Would we ever leave the doorstep of beloved?

The poet, having landed at her doorstep, finds it a disgrace to leave, come what may. No calamity, not even a tide of blood, would move him. The tide of blood refers also to whatever killing may go on there. But in everyday use, the tide of blood signifies extreme hardship and injustice.

عمر بھر دیکھا کیا مرنے کی راہ   مر گئے پر، دیکھیے دِکھلائیں کیا

'umr bhar dekhā kīyā marne kī rāh
mar ga'e par, dekhiye dikhlā'eñ kyā (47:6; #292)

Having waited all my life for death to arrive,
Now dead, let us see what would come out of it.

Death was considered a reprieve from the pain and sorrow of life. Not sure if even death will relieve it, the poet states pessimistically that we will see what good this will bring.

پوچھتے ہیں وہ کہ غالب کون ہے
کوئی بتلاؤ کہ ہم بتلائیں کیا

pūchhte haiñ vuh kih Ġhālib kaun hai
ko'ī batlā'o kih ham batlā'eñ kyā (47:7; #293)

They are asking me: "Who is *Ġhālib*?"
What shall I tell them, would someone advise me?

The inquiry about *Ġhālib* perplexes the poet. If *Ġhālib* were just one being, he would tell them. However, with so many personalities, so many talents, it is difficult to tell them just who he is. A lover, a poet, an intellectual, a failure, a man—or what? This can also be interpreted as the beloved asking obliviously, "Who is *Ġhālib*, about whom I hear so much?"

48

لطافت بے کثافت جلوہ پیدا کر نہیں سکتی   چمن زنگار ہے آئینۂ بادِ بہاری کا

laṯāfat be kaṡāfat jalva(h) pa'idā kar nahīñ saktī
chaman zangār hai āīna(h)' bād-e bahārī kā (48:1; #294)

Fineness without crudeness cannot manifest itself.
The garden is the coating of the mirror displaying images of a spring breeze.

kāṡāfat: crudeness; *zangār*: mirror coating.

Fineness is imperceptible without its opposite. Spirituality without materialism cannot exist. The spring breeze is pleasant, but it takes the expanse of the garden to make it felt: it is like glass becoming a mirror when a coating is applied to it. To see the pleasantries of nature, we must have a garden, which does what the coating does to the mirror—makes it visible and appreciable to us. The poet in this verse points to the necessity of having material to reflect and make perceptible the non-material elements of life. We need a painting to reflect the emotions of an artist; we need a poetic rendition to understand the mind of a poet.

حریفِ جوششِ دریا نہیں خودداریٔ ساحل   جہاں ساقی ہو تو، باطل ہے دعویٰ ہوشیاری کا

ḥarīf-e joshish-e daryā nahīñ ḳhuddārī' sāḥil
jahāñ sāqī ho tū, bāṯil hai da'vā hūshyārī kā (48:2; #295)

The self-respect of river bank cannot face the tides of the river.
When you are the cupbearer then the claim of sobriety is futile.

ḥarīf: opponent; *joshish*: tides; *ḳhuddārī*: self-respect; *sāḥil*: bank; *hūshyārī*: consciousness.

Riverbanks contain the river until the river rises and its tides smash the ego (the boundary) of the banks. The same is true when a beautiful cupbearer is serving wine: no attempt at restraint on me will survive. How can anyone claim consciousness in the presence of cupbearer? We must inundate ourselves, let the banks go and reach a state of unconsciousness—particularly, if you, beloved, are the cupbearer.

49

عشرتِ قطرہ ہے دریا میں فنا ہو جانا
درد کا حد سے گزرنا ہے دوا ہو جانا

ʿishrat-e qaṭra(h) hai daryā meñ fanā ho jānā,
dard kā ḥad se guzarnā hai davā ho jānā. (49:1; #296)

The ecstasy of a drop is to annihilate itself into ocean.
The pain going beyond bounds turns into its own panacea.

The *Sufi* concept of "extinction" is used to describe how ultimately pain is itself the remedy. A drop merging into an ocean loses its identity and becomes the ocean. The limit of all pain is death, and that surely relieves all pain: it is the cure for all suffering. To relieve pain, we must look to greater pain. This is an oft-repeated theme—greater pain absolves us from the need to seek remedy for minor ailments. However, at times *Ġhālib* talks about death not being the end of suffering either.

تجھ سے قسمت میں مری صورتِ قفلِ ابجد
تھا لکھا بات کے بنتے ہی جدا ہو جانا

tujh se qismat meñ merī, ṣūrat-e qufl-e abjad,
thā likhā bāt ke bante hī judā ho jānā. (49:2; #297)

From you, in my fate, in the appearance of an alpha lock,
It was written to separate just when things worked out.

qufl-e abjad: alpha lock ("abjad" comes from the letters in the order they are used in numerology associated with letters: abjd, hwz, huti, klmn); *bāt kā bannā*: things to work out.

It was in my fate to part from you just when things began to work out between us. It was like an alpha lock: when set properly, it parts its loop away from the body. See how things set properly and the code of the lock being set properly is matched. When we know the combination of the lock, it snaps open; when we knew the combination of the secret between us, we parted as well. Born with ill fate, things had to go wrong, and they always did. In how many ways *Ġhālib* comes up with unique construction is amply evident here.

دل ہوا کشمکشِ چارۂ زحمت میں تمام   مٹ گیا گھسنے میں اس عقدے کا وا ہو جانا

dil hu'ā kash-ma-kash-e chāra(h)' zaḥmat meñ tamām
miṭ gayā ghisne meñ is ʿuqde kā vā ho jānā (49:3 #298)

The heart got consumed in the struggle to resolve difficulties;
It got erased with rubbing, trying to open the knot.

kash-ma-kash: struggle; *chāra(h)*: resolution; *zaḥmat*: difficulty; *tamām*: finished; *u'qde*: mystery, knot; *vā*: open.

The heart was suffering from pain and sorrow and I tried to ward it off. Nothing worked, and in this incessant struggle, the heart was wasted; it became totally hopeless. It was as if I tried to untie a knot and the string disappeared because of rubbing, and this made it more difficult to undo. We kept practicing different things on the heart until it was wasted: only the knot remained. The word *u'qde* (knot) also means mystery. Before we could resolve the mystery of the misery of the heart, the heart was destroyed. Knot in the heart also means grief. We lost ourselves before we could rid our hearts of grief.

اب جفا سے بھی ہیں محروم ہم اللہ اللہ   اس قدر دشمنِ اربابِ وفا ہو جانا

ab jafā se bhī haiñ maḥrūm ham alla(h) alla(h)
is qadar dushman-e arbāb-e vafā ho jānā (49:4; #299)

Now we are deprived of cruelty also, God O! God!
Turning to such enmity for your true lovers?

jafā: cruelty; *maḥrūm*: deprived; *arbāb-e vafā*: true lovers.

The beloved decides to let go of her oppression and her cruelty to the lovers once she finds it gives them pleasure. Of course, there is no kindness involved, meaning that with cruelty gone, all relationships are over. A call for *any* relationship, even one of oppression, is requested. What then is real enmity: being cruel, or not being cruel?

ضعف سے گریہ مبدّل بہ دمِ سرد ہوا   باور آیا ہمیں پانی کا ہوا ہو جانا

ẓo'f se girya(h) mubaddal ba(h) dam-e sard hu'ā
bāvar āyā hameñ pānī kā havā ho jānā (49:5#300)

Weakness transformed my crying into cold breath
To make me realize how water turns into thin air.

ẓo'f: weakness; *girya(h)*: crying; *mubaddal*: transformed, changed; *bāvar*: to believe.

Weakness and inebriation made it difficult for me to even produce tears; all that came forth were cold sighs. Of course, tears were there, but they changed into vapor (air), like sublimation of ice into vapor. Such was the coldness of my existence. Only *Ġhālib* comes up with such subtle comparisons—true scientifically.

دل سے مٹنا تری انگشتِ حنائی کا خیال   ہو گیا گوشت سے ناخن کا جدا ہو جانا

dil se miṭnā terī angusht-e ḥina'ī kā ḳhayāl
ho gayā gosht se nāḳhūn kā judā ho jānā (49:6#301)

Removing the thought of your *henna*-tinted fingers from my mind
Is indeed like peeling the nails off from my fingers.

angusht-e ḥina'ī: finger tinted with *henna*

How will I ever forget those crimson, *henna*-tinted fingertips? To remove their thought is like removing the nails from my fingers. Note that *henna*-tinted fingers have a red color, which is how the fingers would appear if the nails were removed from them—a bit of play on words.

[Note: "Removing nails from flesh" is an idiom used to express extreme pain.]

ہے مجھے ابرِ بہاری کا برس کر کھلنا
روتے روتے غمِ فرقت میں فنا ہو جانا

hai mujhe abr-e bahārī kā baras kar khulnā
rote rote ġham-e furqat meñ fanā ho jānā (49:7; #302)

To me, the clearing of the sky after pouring from spring clouds
Is like becoming extinct, shedding tears continuously in the sorrow of separation.

Spring rain leaves shiny leaves, freshness in the air, a cool breeze, and a total clarity in the atmosphere. Reaching the stage of extinction from crying is the same stage of comfort and joy, freshness and crispness—as opposed to hurt and pain, which death takes away (clouds leaving).

گر نہیں نکہتِ گل کو ترے کوچے کی ہوس
کیوں ہے گردِ رہِ جولانِ صبا ہو جانا

gar nahīñ nakhat-e gul ko tere kūche kī havās
kioñ hai gard-e rah-e jaulān-e ṣabā ho jānā (49:8; #303)

If the aroma of flowers does not desire to reach your alley,
Why then, like the dust in the path is it sprinting like breeze?

nakhat: smell; *jaulān*: sprinting.

If the smell of flowers is not trying to reach your alley and to improve itself by merging with your body's smell, then why is it sticking to the breeze as dust? The breeze is sprinting towards the beloved's alley, the smell of flowers tagging along as the dust. If the smell of flowers does not want to reach her tresses to achieve perfection, then there is no reason to ride the coat tails of the breeze. Of course, the breeze wants to exalt itself!

تاکہ تجھ پر کھلے اعجازِ ہوائے صیقل　　دیکھ برسات میں سبز آئنے کا ہو جانا

tākih tujh par khule iʿjāz-e havā'e ṣaiqal
dekh barsāt meñ sabz ā'īne kā ho jānā (49:9; #304)

So it would reveal to you the miracle of the desire to be polished;
See how the mirror turns green in the rainy season.

iʿjaz: miracle; *havā*: desire; *ṣaiqal*: shine, polish; *havā*: desire, breeze, atmosphere; *barsāt*: rainy season; *ā'īna(h)*: mirror.

Mirror refers to an iron mirror made by applying a metal polish to the front side. When it becomes rusty, it appears green and therefore it requires rubbing and polishing again. Everything seeks perfection and wants to remove all spots and blemishes from its existence. In the rainy season, the appearance of green spots on mirrors is an excuse for the mirror to be polished again to reach a higher level of perfection. The desire for perfection is so intense that every heart is longing to be worked on to proves its mettle. The desire of the mirror is sincere and so the rust appears to satisfy its desire to get polished again. When the desire is sincere, things happen to lead us to their fulfillment. Notice the play on words: *havā* is also breeze; spring season spreading green grass and its humidity producing green rust spots on mirrors and greenery in the garden.

بخشے ہے جلوۂ گل، ذوقِ تماشا غالب
چشم کو چاہیے ہر رنگ میں وا ہو جانا

baḳhshe hai jalva(h)' gul żauq-e tamāshā Ġhālib
chashm ko chāhiye har rang meñ vā ho jānā (49:10; #305)

O! *Ġhālib*, the luster of flowers endows the taste to appreciate Nature;
The eye should always be open to see it.

jalva(h): splendor; *żauq*: taste; *tamāshā:* display; *chashm:* eye; *rang:* color, presentation; *vā:*open.

The bloom of spring brings many colors to our view, each one appearing different, but all part of a single display of Nature. Viewing this display gives us a chance to hone our taste to appreciate it. However, to do this, we must keep our eyes open, our vision broad. The second line also means that we should keep looking, regardless of our intent. The last two verses together form the non-traditional closing of this sonnet—they are entwined in their meaning also. The spring season brings a spectacular scene, giving our vision an opportunity to broaden itself. Look at the mirror (not into it); it turns green (with rust) just as the humid wind of the rainy season covers the landscape with a green coating (grass). How strong is the desire of the mirror to blend itself with the green landscape, even though it means that the mirror loses its own utility (since a rusted mirror no longer reflects)? Many meanings can be drawn from this simile, but the simplest one is that Nature blends things together and we should broaden our vision to that.

50

پھر ہُوا وقت کہ ہو بال کُشا موجِ شراب   دے بطِ مے کو دل و دستِ شنا موجِ شراب

phir hu'ā vaqt kih ho bālkushā mauj-e sharāb
de baṭ-e mai ko dil-o-dast-e shinā mauj-e sharāb (50:1; #306)

Time has come again for the wave of wine to take wings of flight;
Let the wave of wine give the duck-shaped decanter the strength to drift towards me.

bāl kushā honā: get wings ready to fly; *baṭ*: duck; *dil-o-dast-e shinā*: swimming heart and hand, courage and energy to swim.

It is spring, the time for wine to fly. The poet desires the duck-shaped decanter floating in the pool to come towards him. He is addressing the waves of wine inside the decanter to give the decanter heart and hand—meaning energy—to drift or sail towards him. The wave of wine inside the decanter is pushing it towards the poet. In a traditional drinking session while sitting around a pool, the wine is served in a decanter that floats in the pool. Whoever gets the decanter drinks from it and then places it back in the pool to let it drift to others.

پُوچھ مت وجہِ سیہ مستیِ اربابِ چمن   سایۂ تاک میں ہوتی ہے ہَوا موجِ شراب

pūchh mat vajh-e siyā(h) mastī' arbāb-e chaman
sāya(h)' tāk meñ hotī hai havā mauj-e sharāb (50:2; #307)

Ask not the reason for the deep intoxication of the dwellers of garden;
The breeze passing under the grape wine is turning into a wave of wine.

siya(h) mastī: intense ecstasy, deep ecstasy; *tāk*: grapevine.

Do not ask about the cause of the ecstasy of the garden dwellers. The breeze passing under the grapevine turns into a wave of wine and intoxicates them. The use of the phrase, "dark intoxication" to mean "deep intoxication" in the first line also refers to the darkening of leaves of a tree under wet and clouded skies. The whole garden is drunk because the breeze turned into wine as it passed under the grapevine. Joy, ecstasy, and intoxication come to everything in the garden as spring rains arrive.

جو ہُوا غرقۂ مے بختِ رسا رکھتا ہے   سر سے گزرے پہ بھی ہے بالِ ہُما موجِ شراب

jo hu'ā ġharqa(h)' mai baḳht-e rasā rakhtā hai
sar se guzre pa(h) bhī hai bāl-e humā mauj-e sharāb (50:3; #308)

He, who drowned in the wine is the fortunate one,
Even if the wave of wine goes over head, it proves to be the wing of *humā*.

ġharq'a(h)-e mai: drowned in wine, ecstatic; *baḳht-e rasā:* lucky; *bāl-e humā*: wing of "*humā*." Anecdote states that anyone coming under the shadow of the legendary bird *humā* gets lucky even to the extent of becoming an emperor.

Drowning generally means death unless it happens under the wave of wine; in this case, only those who have good fate get to drown themselves—meaning they are able to drink excessively. Tide going overhead also means calamity, but here it means even if very little wine is available, it is like going under the wings of the legendary bird *humā*. Anyone catching the shadow of *humā* becomes very lucky, and even emperor ship is not far for them. Drinking too much can prove fateful because we forget all our woes and feel like a king.

ہے یہ برسات وہ موسم کہ عجب کیا ہے اگر   موجِ ہستی کو کرے فیضِ ہوا موجِ شراب

hai yih barsāt vuh mausam kih ʿajab kyā hai agar
mauj-e hastī ko kare faiẓ-e havā mauj-e sharāb (50:4; #309)

The monsoon is that season that it should not surprise us if,
The beneficence of breeze turns the wave of life into wave of wine.

faiẓ-e havā: beneficence of air.

This the rainy season, the season when no one should be surprised if the beneficence of breeze turns our being into a wave of wine; we all become ecstatic and intoxicated. Ah! The cool intoxicating breeze of the rainy season! Note: The monsoon season is a season of great joy as the rains bring much-needed cooling-off from the long, hot summers in India.

چار موج اٹھتی ہے طوفانِ طرب سے ہر سو   موجِ گل، موجِ شفق، موجِ صبا، موجِ شراب

chār mauj uṭhtī hai ṭūfān-e ṭarab se har sū
mauj-e gul, mauj-e shafaq, mauj-e ṣabā, mauj-e sharāb (50:5; #310)

Four tides are rising out of the storm of joy from all directions:
The tide of flowers, the tide of twilight, the tide of breeze, and the tide of wine.

ṭarab: joy, cheerfulness; *har sū*: in all directions.

All around there is a scene of ecstasy and cheer. Flowers are blooming, the crimson twilight is sparkling after the rain, the breeze is cooling things off, and finally, the wine flowing—a heavenly scenario.

جس قدر رُوحِ نباتی ہے جگر تشنۂ ناز　　دے ہے تسکیں بہ دمِ آبِ بقا موجِ شراب

jis qadar rūḥ-e nabātī hai jigar tashna(h)' nāz
de hai taskīñ ba(h) dam-e āb-e baqā ma'uj-e sharāb (50:6; #311)

As much as the soul of plants is desperate to bloom,
The wave of wine gives consolation like the gulp of "water of life."

rūḥ-e nabātī: soul of plants; *jigar tashna(h)-e nāz*: dying to bloom;
dam-e āb-e baqā: gulp of "*āb-e ḥayāt*" (water of life).

The element of growth (the soul) in plants is there to make them grow and bloom quickly. Similarly, wine proves to be that promoting element (the soul) for humans. The tide of wine serves as a drink to console our souls giving us further desire for life, making us love life more and enjoy it more. The wine thus proves to be the "*āb-e ḥayāt*," the water of life. The tide of wine we are talking about here is the rain.

بسکہ دَوڑے ہے رگِ تاک میں خوں ہو ہو کر　　شہپرِ رنگ سے ہے بال کشا موجِ شراب

baskih doṛe hai rag-e tāk meñ ḳhūñ ho ho kar
shahpar-e rang se hai bāl kushā mauj-e sharāb (50:7; #312)

Turning into blood, it is running through the veins of the grapevine
Propelled by its color, the tide of wine has let its tresses down.

shahpar: aileron, propeller.

The wave of wine runs through the veins of the leaves of the grapevine like blood and flushes color into them. As the wave of color propels the leaves, they appear to be ready to fly. The vines are blooming with the color of wine; running of wine in the vein proves the flight, wherein the greenery and its color prove to be the propeller.

موجۂ گل سے چراغاں ہے گزرگاہِ خیال　　ہے تصوّر میں زبس جلوہ نما موجِ شراب

mauja(h)' gul se chirāġhāñ hai guzar gāh-e ḳhayāl
hai taṣavvur meñ zabas jalva(h) numā mauj-e sharāb (50:8; #313)

The wave of flowers is lighting up the path of my imagination,
While my imagination is radiant with the thought of the wave of wine.

mau'j-e gul: abundance of flowers (roses).

In our imagination, the wave of wine is displayed so intensely that it appears as if flowers are blooming all around. These displays of flowers are illuminating the alleys of my thoughts. The intense essence of wine makes one see blooming flowers all around. The flowers have such bright color that they are lighting up my imagination. This is a pure play on words. The redness of flowers and the brightness of flowers evoke the image of lamps—meaning that drinking wine has enlightened me and brightened my thinking.

نشے کے پردے میں ہے محوِ تماشائے دماغ　　بسکہ رکھتی ہے سرِ نشو و نما موجِ شراب

nashe ke parde meñ hai maḥv-e tamāshā-e damāġh
baskih rakhtī hai sar-e nashv-o-numā mauj-e sharāb (50:9; #314)

Behind the veil of intoxication, the wine is engrossed in monitoring my mind;
The tide of wine is working to make my mind grow and thrive.

parda(h): veil, curtain; *maḥv*: engrossed; *nashv-o-numā*: growth and grooming.

The tide of wine is so concerned about the growth of the mind that it has taken on a veil of ecstasy and then, reaching the mind, it is intently watching to assure that it grows and thrives. The intoxication of wine working to groom the mind should be seen in the context of the effects of inebriation. First it opens up the mind to many creative ideas, reduces inhibition, and makes one more expressive. Above all, it takes away the feeling of pain.

ایک عالم پہ ہیں طوفانیِ کیفیتِ فصل   موجۂ سبزۂ نوخیز سے تا موجِ شراب

ek ʿālam pa(h) haiñ ṯūfan'ī kaifīyat-e faṣl,
mauja(h)' sabza(h)' nauḳhez se ta mauj-e sharāb (50:10; #315)

At their peak are the stormy conditions of the crops;
From the waving fresh grass to the wave of wine.

ek ʿālam: extreme intensity (generally meaning all around); *ṯūfānī*: stirring up storms, *kaifīyat*: condition; *faṣl*: crop; stormy; *sabz'a(h)-e nauḳhez*: new growth of greenery.

From the lush fluttering new greenery to the wave (supply) of wine, every wave has stirred up a storm. There is greenery all around; drinking parties are going on everywhere and it appears that a storm of ecstasy and intoxication has come up, taken in the entire world.

شرحِ ہنگامۂ ہستی ہے، زہے موسمِ گل   رہبرِ قطرہ بہ دریا ہے، خوشا موجِ شراب

sharḥ-e hangāma(h)' hastī hai, zihe mausam-e gul
rahbar-e qaṯra(h) ba(h) daryā hai, ḳhushā mauj-e sharāb (50:11; #316)

Spring reveals the reason for the tumult of existence.
The wave of wine gladly showing the way to the drop to unite with the sea.

sharḥ: explanation; *zihe*: because of; *rahbar*: directing; *ḳhushā*: joyful.

How useful is the season of flowers? It explains the reality of the turmoil of existence. How joyful is the wave of wine? It directs the drops of water to the river. Blooming flowers point to life and at the same time, point to death—the fall season—providing many answers to how Nature has laid out its grand plan for us. For a drop of water, "ecstasy" is to merge with the river. For a man, it is to merge with the Almighty. How joyful is the inebriation that removes all inhibitions and allows a man to lose himself in Him. The lesson here is that nothing remains the same. Change is inevitable and the only reality is extinction. Wine makes us see what is not obvious.

ہوش اُڑتے ہیں مرے جلوۂ گل دیکھ، اسدؔ
پھر ہُوا وقت کہ ہو بال کُشا موجِ شراب

hosh uṛte haiñ mere, jalva(h)' gul dekh, Asad
phir hu'ā vaqt kih ho bāl kushā mauj-e sharāb (50:12; #317)

I am losing my senses, looking at the display of flowers, Asad.
Again it is time for the wave of wine to let its tresses down.

The display of flowers all around is making me intoxicated. It is time to open the locks of wine and let it flow.

51

افسوس کہ دنداں کا کیا رزق فلک نے
جن لوگوں کی تھی درخورِ عقدِ گہر انگشت

afsos kih dandāñ kā kīyā rizq falak ne
jin logoñ kī thī dar ḳhor-e ʿaqd-e gohar angusht (51:1:318)

Regret that the heaven provided the staple for teeth,
The fingers of those that deserved to play with strings of pearls.

dandāñ: teeth; *dar ḳhor:* suitable, proper; *ʿaqd-e gohar*: string of pearls; *angusht*: finger.

It is regretful that heaven has provided the staple of teeth, the fingers, to the rich. The same fingers that used to play with strings of pearls are now being bitten. Biting fingers represents shock and sorrow over loss of riches. To the great surprise and sorrow of the wealthy, riches can be lost. This expression of regret has an air of sarcasm.

کافی ہے نشانی تری، چھلّے کا نہ دینا
خالی مجھے دِکھلا کے بہ وقتِ سفر انگشت

kāfī hai nishānī terī, chhalle kā na(h) denā
ḳhālī mujhe dikhlā kih ba(h) vaqt-e safar angusht (51:2; #319)

It is enough as your souvenir, not giving me the band,
Merely displaying your finger to me at the time of leaving.

nishanī: charm, souvenir; *chhallā*: band worn on finger.

The poet asked the beloved for her ring as a souvenir, but she refused and instead showed her bare finger. Seeing that she is not wearing a ring and thus cannot give one, the poet is assuming that she would have given it to him if she had it. This is an audacious assumption. Another possibility is that she is telling the lover that she has already given it to someone else. However, the lover feels otherwise.

لکھتا ہوں اسد سوزشِ دل سے سخنِ گرم
تا رکھ نہ سکے کوئی مرے حرف پر انگشت

likhtā hūñ Asad sozish-e dil se suḳhan-e garm
tā rakh na(h) sake ko'ī mere ḥarf par angusht (51:3; #320)

I write warm words from the fire in my heart, Asad,
Lest someone would point a finger at my words.

I put my heart and soul into writing delectable warm stuff so no one can question any word of it. The use of warm words and touching hot stuff ("putting a finger") is a rather clever way to say, point a finger.

52

رہا گر کوئی تا قیامت سلامت
پھر اک روز مرنا ہے حضرت سلامت

rahā gar ko'ī tā qiyāmat salāmat
phir ik roz marnā hai ḥaẓrat salāmat (52:1; #321)

Even if someone survived until the Day of Resurrection,
Then Mr. Long-live, death is still imminent some day.

Even if someone lived until the Day of Resurrection, he would still die, as life cannot exist beyond that day. Death is inevitable whether it comes now or later. The poet is addressing *Haẓrat Khizr*, the legendary man who lives forever (see Glossary.) Addressing people with a salutation title carries an air of sarcasm here.

جگر کو مرے عشقِ خوننابہ مشرب
لکھے ہے: خداوندِ نعمت سلامت!

jigar ko mere, i'shq-e ḳhunnāba(h) mashrab
likhe hai: ḳhudāvand-e ni'mat salāmat (52:2; #322)

The passion of drinking blood is writing to my liver:
"That with God's blessing, you may live a long life."

ḳhunnāba(h): blood; *mashrab:* drinking, imbibing.

Drinking blood is synonymous with expression of extreme suffering, which is what the lover loves. This passion is hoping that the liver survives so that the lover can keep making it bleed over and over again. Liver is also a symbol of courage; the lover is wishing himself enough courage to continue to bear the hardships of love.

علی الرغمِ دشمن شہیدِ وفا ہوں
مبارک مبارک سلامت سلامت

'alī arraġhm-e dushman shahīd-e vafā hūñ
mubārak mubārak salāmat salāmat (52:3; #323)

Opposite to the nature of the rival, I am a martyr to my devotion.
Congratulation! Congratulation! Long live! Long live!

'alī arraġhm: opposite.

Unlike the rival, I gave my life in the path of faithfulness and deserve congratulations for passing the test. "Long-live," because martyrs never actually die. They live forever. The lover is congratulating himself loudly, hoping that the beloved may hear him.

نہیں گر سر و برگِ ادراکِ معنی
تماشائے نیرنگِ صورت سلامت

nahiñ gar sar-o-barg-e idrāk-e ma'nī
tamāshāe nairang-e ṣurat salāmat (52:4; #324)

If there is no way to comprehend the significance of things,
Then long live the display of deception of appearance.

sar-o-barg: resource; *idrāk:* perception, comprehension; *ma'nī*: significance; *tamāshā:* display; *ṣurat*: appearance.

It is not possible for me to reach the depth of understanding about the reality of the universe, because whatever is displayed is deceptive. I pray, however, that it continues. Taking an antithesis clue from

Sufism, *Ġhālib* calls for the love of material things (such as his corporeal lover) as the road to loving God: In man, I see the face of God. What we see around us is a reflection of what we cannot see. Therefore, loving what we can see makes us love what we should love. The beloved has been called a corporeal God and loving her brings pain and purity to my heart, and thus brings me closer to God. *Ġhālib* is recommending pursuit of material things for they represent what is beyond them.

53

مُند گئیں کھولتے ہی کھولتے آنکھیں غالِب
یار لائے مِری بالیں پہ اُسے، پر کس وقت

mund gai'ñ kholte hī kholte āñkheñ Ġhālib
yār lāe merī bālīñ pa(h) use, par kis vaqt (53:1; #325)

The eyes closed despite efforts to keep them open, *Ġhālib.*
Friends brought her to my bedside, but at what time?

mund: close; *bālīñ*: pillow, bed, couch.

Despite great efforts to stay alive, death arrived just when my friends managed, somehow, to bring her to visit me. It was too late.

54

آمدِ خط سے ہُوا ہے سرد جو بازارِ دوست   دودِ شمعِ کشتہ تھا شاید خطِ رُخسارِ دوست

āmad-e khat se hu'ā hai sard jo bāzār-e dost
dūd-e shama'-e kushta(h) thā shāyād khaṭ-e rukhsār-e dost (54:1; #326)

The arrival of down on the cheek has cooled off the assembly of the beloved.
The smoke of an extinguished candle was perhaps the streak on the cheek of the beloved.

khaṭ: hair line, the down on the cheek of a youth; *sard*: dull, dead; *dūd*: smoke; *shama'-e kushta(h)*: candle just put out; *shāyād*: perhaps; *rukhsār*: cheek.

As the beloved's face has begun to show hair, her assembly has cooled off as her lovers have run away. My beloved's face was like a bright candle; now put out, it shows the streak of smoke on her face and dulls her beauty. This is a derogatory verse. However, despite the loss of beauty, the poet still calls her a friend (a beloved) while those who were untrue lovers have run away, for they were only interested in physical beauty and not the inner self. This verse may well point to the Persian poetry tradition of addressing young Turkish boys as beloved.

اے دلِ ناعاقبت اندیش ضبطِ شوق کر   کون لا سکتا ہے تابِ جلوۂ دیدارِ دوست

ai dil-e nā 'āqibat andesh ẓabṭ-e shauq kar
kaun lā saktā hai tāb-e jalvah' didār-e dost (54:2; #327)

O! Imprudent Heart, control your desire.
Who can muster the strength to see the radiant display of beloved?

nā ʿāqibat andesh: not concerned with future, imprudent.

The heart desires to see her but the mind is warning of the consequences. Reference is made to Moses asking for God's display.

خانہ ویراں سازیِ حیرت تماشا کیجیے   صورتِ نقشِ قدم ہوں رفتۂ رفتارِ دوست

ḳhāna(h) vīrāñ sazī' ḥairat tamāshā kijīye
ṣurat-e naqsh-e qadam hūñ raftah' raftār-e dost (54:3; #328)

See, how becoming stunned destroys home.
Enamored by the swiftness of the beloved, I am like her footprint.

ḳhana(h) virāñ sazī: to destroy home; *tamāshā kijiye*: to see; *raft'ah*: used here to mean *farīfta*(*h*), in love, enamored.

I am dazzled by my beloved's gait; I love it. I feel like the footprint she has left behind and this feeling will destroy my heart (house). A footprint is like motion frozen in time. Looking at her, I am frozen, stunned. A footprints soon withers away, as I would, having fallen in love. My beloved just passed by me and dazzled me with her speed, but her footprints remain there frozen in the dust like a stunned face. Stunned by her, I will become oblivious to everything and that will destroy my house (heart), as I will stop caring for it. Note that footprints are also impermanent and they show the speed of movement. Here *Ġhālib* makes some very lofty, yet down to earth comparisons.

عشق میں بیدادِ رشکِ غیر نے مارا مجھے   کشتۂ دشمن ہوں آخر گرچہ تھا بیمارِ دوست

ʿishq meñ bedād-e rashk-e ġhair ne mārā mujhe
kushta(h)' dushman hūñ āḳhir, garchi(h) thā bīmār-e dost (54:4; #329)

In love, the tyranny of jealousy to the rival has killed me.
Finally, a victim of enemy, though I was lovesick for the beloved.

kushta(h): victim, killed by; *bīmār-e dost*: lover, lovesick.

I am lovesick for her and would have given my life in the name of my beloved; however, as my beloved became kinder to my rival, the jealousy proved too much and took my life. I was supposed to sacrifice my life to her; instead, I ended up as a victim of my rival—that hurts!

چشمِ ما روشن کہ اُس بے درد کا دِل شاد ہے   دیدۂ پُر خُوں ہمارا ساغرِ سرشارِ دوست

chashm-e mā roshan kih us bedard kā dil shād hai
đida(h)' pur ḳhūñ hamārā, sāġhar-e sarshār-e dost (54:5; #330)

I am happy that the heart of that callous beloved is full of joy.
My bloodshot eyes are goblets filled with wine for my beloved.

chashm-e mā roshan: my eyes are brightened, I am happy; *sarshār*: filled.

My eyes filled with blood are like goblets filled with wine for my beloved to drink from. If giving me sorrow to cry blood-tears makes her happy, then I am happy as well. The second line should be read first. The beauty of this verse comes from using the idiom, "brightened eyes," to indicate happiness and then to list blood-shot eyes as wine goblets. Note: the shape of the eyes is often compared to a wineglass.

غیر یُوں کرتا ہے میری پُرسش اُس کے ہجر میں   ق   بے تکلّف دوست ہو جیسے کوئی غم خوارِ دوست

ġhair yūñ kartā hai merī pursish us ke hijr meñ
be takalluf dost ho jaise ko'ī ġhamḳh(v)ār-e dost (54:6; #331)

In my woes of separation, the stranger is consoling me, as if
He were an intimate friend, sharing sorrow with another friend.

The stranger has come to console the lover. The lover knows that the stranger is the rival and it irritates him that the rival is consoling him as if he were a close friend. There is a sense of jealousy here since the rival is talking about the beloved being unkind to the lover; the rival is acting as if he were a more intimate friend of the lover's beloved. The rival is trying to be intimate with the lover while portraying his intimacy with the beloved.

تاکہ مَیں جانوں کہ ہے اِس کی رسائی واں تلک　　مُجھ کو دیتا ہے پیامِ وعدۂ دیدارِ دوست

tākih maiñ jānūñ kih hai is kī rasāī' vāñ talak
mujh ko detā hai payām-e va'da(h)' dīdār-e dost (54:7; #332)

Just so I would think that that he has access to her,
He is extending the beloved's invitation of promise to meet me.

The rival has brought a message to the lover that the beloved wants to see him. The envious lover concludes that the only reason the rival is extending this invitation is to flaunt that he has access to her. If the message is correct, then I am shattered because of envy that she talked to the rival. If this is how she wants to meet me—through someone else—it is hardly what I had in mind. If the message is incorrect, then I am shattered because the rival is rubbing it in.

جب کہ مَیں کرتا ہُوں اپنا شکوۂ ضعفِ دماغ　　سر کرے ہے وُہ حدیثِ زُلفِ عنبر بارِ دوست

jab kih maiñ kartā hūñ apnā shikvah' ẓo'f-e damāġh
sar kare hai vuh ḥadīs-e zulf-e 'añmbar bār-e dost (54:8; #333)

Whenever I complain of the inebriation of my mind,
He brings into discussion her tresses exuding an amber aroma.

sar karnā: to begin; *ḥadīs*: statement.

Strong aromatics are often used to stimulate the mind and to bring people out of amnesia. As the poet mentions his mental inebriation, the rival talks about the amber aroma of the beloved's tresses. Apparently, the intent is to help the poet come out of his amnesia, but the rival also inflicts deeper wounds by telling the poet that he has been close to her tresses, he has also smelled the scent of her hair.

چپکے چپکے مجھ کو روتے دیکھ پاتا ہے اگر   ہنس کے کرتا ہے بیانِ شوخیِ گفتارِ دوست

chupke chupke mujh ko rote dekh pātā hai āgar
hañs kih kartā hai bayān-e shoḳhī' guftār-e dost (54:9; #334)

If ever he finds me crying quietly,
Laughingly he talks about the beloved's witty conversation.

The rival finding the lover crying in desperation tries to console him, talking about how the beloved talks coquettishly. The attempt is to soothe the lover but the effect is the opposite. The feeling of envy over how the rival knows about her witty conversation makes things worse. Crying quietly is contrasted to the laughing of the rival.

مہربانیہاے دشمن کی شکایت کیجیے؟   یا بیاں کیجے سپاسِ لذتِ آزارِ دوست؟

mahrbānī hāi dushman kī shikāyat kijīye
yā bayāñ kīje sipās-e lażżat-e āzār-e dost (54:10; #335)

Should I complain of the extreme kindness of the rival
Or express gratitude for the pleasure from beloved's tormenting?

mahrbānī hāi: extreme kindness; *sipās*: gratitude; *āzār*: hurt, torment.

Should I complain of the rival's kindness that hurts or be grateful for the torment inflicted by the beloved? Actually, I must thank them both, for the intent is the same in both instances. In one case, by being cruel to me (the beloved), and in another, by faking sympathy to me (by the rival).

یہ غزل اپنی، مجھے جی سے پسند آئی ہے آپ
ہے ردیفِ شعر میں غالبؔ زبس تکرارِ دوست

yih ġhazal apnī, mujhe jī se pasand āʾī hai āp
hai radīf-e shiʿr meñ Ġhālib zabas takrār-e dost (54:11; #336)

I myself like to take this *ġhazal* to my heart;
For in its *each verse*, *Ġhālib*, it repeats the word, beloved.

radīf-e shiʿr: the ending repetitive word of verse.

A *ġhazal* where the word "beloved" is oft repeated must be good to read and write. Friend is the beloved and to talk about her in every verse can only be pleasurable. (*radīf*-refrain) is the repetitive part of the ending of the second line of each verse; in the first verse, it is repeated in both lines.

55

گلشن میں بند و بست بہ رنگِ دِگر ہے آج
قمری کا طوق حلقۂ بیرونِ در ہے آج

gulshan meñ band-o-bast ba(h) rang-e digar hai āj
qumrī kā ṯauq ḥalqa(h)' berūn-e dar hai āj (55:1; #337)

Today the arrangements take a different turn in the garden;
The ring on the turtledove's neck is the latch on the outside of gate today.

barang-e digar: of different shade; *qumrī*: a type of partridge with a ring around neck, turtledove; *ḥalqa(h) berūn-e dar*: latch on outside door.

The beloved's arrival is imminent and special arrangements are being made to welcome her. So special are the arrangements that even the turtledove has been removed from the garden, lest it embarrass the beloved by gazing at her beauty. Turtledove gazes at moon, the legend goes. Comparing the ring around the neck of the turtledove to the door latch also means that the entrance to the garden has been closed for ordinary souls like the lover. This verse shows how unique is *Ġhālib*'s imagination.

آتا ہے ایک پارۂ دِل ہر فغاں کے ساتھ
تارِ نفس کمندِ شکارِ اثر ہے آج

ātā hai ek pāra(h)' dil har fuġhāñ ke sāth
tār-e nafas kamand-e shikār-e aṡar hai āj (55:2; #338)

With every wail comes out a piece of the heart as well;
The line of breath is throwing a noose to capture the impact today.

pāra(h): pieces; *fuġhāñ*: sigh; *tār-e nafis*: line of breath; *kamand*: noose.

My lamentation has becomes more effective as I put my heart into it. My breath, carrying my sighs, is like a noose thrown to catch the prey. The noose is carrying with it pieces of my heart as bait. The prey is the attention of beloved. The line of breath and the noose are remarkably juxtaposed. It is another example where *Ġhālib* creates a physical and metaphoric situation simultaneously.

اَے عافیت کنارہ کر، اے انتظام چل
سیلاب گریہ درپئے دِیوار و دَر ہے آج

ai ʿāfiyat kināra(h) kar, ai intiẕām chal,
sailāb-e giryah darpaʾe divār-o-dar hai āj (55:3; #339)

O! Security, move on, arrangements move over;
The flood of tears is out to demolish the doors and walls today.

kināra(h) kar: move on, get on the side.

What security and what arrangement can protect the life and home while the house is about to fall down under the flood of tears? It is useless to think of saving anything in their path. The lover has decided to let his tears flow in abundance.

56

لو ہم مریضِ عشق کے بیماردار ہیں
اچھا اگر نہ ہو تو مسیحا کا کیا علاج!

lo ham marīẓ-e `ishq ke bīmār dār haiñ
achhā agar na(h) ho to masīḥā kā kyā `ilāj (56:1; #340)

So I am attending the patient of love.
If he does not get well, what should we then do to the healer?

masīḥā: The healer, Jesus.

I believe there is no treatment possible for the lovesick, but if you insist, we will attend to the patient and call in the healer. However, if that does not work, then what shall we do to the healer? If we say that the treatment did not work, then it will bring much embarrassment to the healer and that would not be fair because we know that the treatment was good. Here the healer is Jesus, whose treatment never fails except now this will bring a bad name to Jesus. "What to do with the healer?" has a tone of irritation. The insistence that we should try to treat the lovesick would result only in having a failed healer on our hands.

57

نفس نہ انجمنِ آرزو سے باہر کھینچ
اگر شراب نہیں، انتظارِ ساغر کھینچ

nafas na(h) anjuman-e ārzū se bāhar khainch
agar sharāb nahiñ, intiẓār-e sāġhar khainch (57:1; #341)

Breathe not outside the assembly of desire.
If there is no wine then go on waiting for the goblet.

intiẓār khainch: to wait.

With each breath, you must breathe optimism; breathe only in the company of hope and desire. If you are out of wine, just wait, the goblet will come your way sooner or later. Be steady and hopeful. Here we have an optimistic admonition of *Ġhālib.*

کمالِ گرمیِ سعیِ تلاشِ دید نہ پوچھ
بہ رنگِ خار مرے آئینے سے جوہر کھینچ

kamāl-e garmī' saī'-e talāsh-e dīd na(h) pūchh
ba(h) rang-e ḳhār mere ā'īne se johar khainch (57:2; #342)

Ask not of the success of efforts to find an appreciating eye.
Remove the lines from my mirror, as if they were thorns.

johar: lines in the steel mirror, substance, talent. (See Glossary)

Trying to find someone who would appreciate my talents, I have become disgusted. All I can ask of you, my friend, is to take out the talent from (the mirror of) my personality, as you would remove the lines from a poorly polished mirror. Now that there is no one I can find to appreciate my talents, it is better to destroy them. I can then rest. The lines in the mirrors are a favorite expression of *Ġhālib*. The lines in steel mirrors can be removed by polishing. Here, it means that people should make a greater effort to understand him. Calling the lines "thorns" signifies their undesirable placement. Another meaning of this verse refers to efforts to see the beloved; in the mirror of my desperation, you will find thorns that I need to remove.

تجھے بہانۂ راحت ہے انتظار اے دل
کیا ہے کس نے اشارہ کہ نازِ بستر کھینچ

tujhe bahāna(h)' rāḥat hai intiẓār ai dil,
kīyā hai kis ne ishāra(h) kih nāz-e bistar khainch (57:3; #343)

You are waiting merely as an excuse for resting, O! Heart.
Who has instructed you to be pampered in bed?

Comfortably lying in bed waiting for her to come is not appropriate. Love requires effort, not comfort. The lover is waiting in comfort for something to happen. The poet finds it rather improper, for it is not in the character of the lover. Nothing comes without effort, especially the beloved. The tone is something like, "Who told you to rest?"

تری طرف ہے، بہ حسرت، نظارۂ نرگس
بہ کوریٔ دل و چشمِ رقیب ساغر کھینچ

terī ṭaraf hai, ba(h) ḥasrat, naẓāra(h)' nargis
ba(h) korī' dil-o-chashm-e raqīb sāġhar khainch (57:4; #344)

The narcissus is looking towards you, gazing with envy.
Devoid of heart and eye is the rival, so drink the cup.

nargis: the narcissus, jonquil; *kor'ī*: devoid.

The narcissus and I are both mesmerized by you and therefore I consider narcissus to be my rival. "Rival without heart or eye" is a Persian idiom used to cast a spell—may God protect you from the evil eye. May God protect you—I drink to that. Rivalry with the narcissus is invoked here only to inject the use of an archaic idiom.

بہ نیم غمزہ ادا کر حقِ ودیعتِ ناز
نیامِ پردۂ زخمِ جگر سے خنجر کھینچ

ba(h) nīm ġhamza(h) adā kar ḥaq-e vadia't-e nāz
niyām-e parda(h)' zaḳhm-e jigar se ḳhanjar khainch (57:5; #345)

With a half-amorous glance, pay back the obligations of trust confided in you by coquetry.
Take the dagger out from the casing of the veil of heart's wound.

ġhamza(h): amorous glance, coquetry; *vadia't*: vested, property in trust.

Return the dagger to the beloved by taking it out of its sleeve, which is your heart (it's a veil because the dagger is hidden in there). Her dagger of coquetry was her property in trust to you. For keeping it as long as you did, you deserve to be stabbed in the heart with a half-amorous glance. That is your punishment; that is your reward.

مرے قدح میں ہے صہبائے آتشِ پنہاں
بہ روئے سفرہ کبابِ دلِ سمندر کھینچ

mere qadḥ meñ hai ṣahbā-e ātish-e pinhāñ
ba(h) rūe sufrah kabāb-e dil-e samandar khainch (57:6; #346)

In my bowl there is the wine of hidden fire.
For my meal serving, give me kabobs made of heart of salamander.

qadḥ: bowl; *ṣahbā:* wine; *ātish-e pinhāñ*: hidden fire; *sufrah*: dinner table setting; *samandar:* salamander, a lizard that comes to life if fire remains lit for at least a few centuries, an anecdote.

The goblet of my heart is filled with the fire of love and that is what I drink with my meal. For my dinner table, I want the kabobs made from the heart of salamander (an anecdotal lizard that appears out of fire after the fire has been lit for centuries). This means that to match the fiery drink, I should eat something exotic—in this case, that which represents centuries of the burning flame. The heart of the lover has been burning for a long time, which has provided a vintage wine that must be accompanied by something equally exotic, like the kabobs made from the heart of the salamander. Notice the arrangement of heart to heart. Another hint here belittles the salamander as it is compared to lover's heat of anguish.

58

حسن غمزے کی کشاکش سے چھٹا میرے بعد   بارے، آرام سے ہیں اہلِ جفا میرے بعد

ḥusn ġhamze kī kashākash se chhuṭā mere baʿd
bāre ārām se haiñ ahl-e jafā mere baʿd (58:1; #347)

Freed of the constant strife of coquetry is the beauty after my death.
Finally, the oppressors are at ease, after my death.

ġhamza(h): coquettishness; *kashākash*: constant strife; *ahl-e jafā*: oppressors, beloveds.

Concerted efforts were incumbent upon the beloved to show her coquettishness. With my death, these efforts are no longer needed. Lover's death must have comforted the oppressor beloved. The cruelty of the beloved is coquettishness. The use of the plural form for beloved is meant to address all beloveds of the world. Now they all can rest. I am dying as a legend, as a symbolic lover. There is also an air of self-pride in this expression.

منصبِ شیفتگی کے کوئی قابل نہ رہا   ہوئی معزولیٔ انداز و ادا میرے بعد

manṣab-e sheftagī ke ko'ī qābil na(h) rahā
hu'ī maʿzūlī' andāz-o-adā mere baʿd (58:2; #348)

No one remained worthy to fill the ranks of mad lovers.
The style and coquetry have been dethroned, after my death.

manṣab: position; *sheftagī*: madness in love; *maʿzūl*: dethroned.

Repeating a similar theme as in the verse before, the poet claims that after his death, no one can fill his shoes as a lover. This makes the coquettishness of the beloved unnecessary, for there is no one qualified left on whom to practice. See the connection between position (status) and being dethroned.

شمع بجھتی ہے تو اُس میں سے دھُواں اُٹھتا ہے   شعلۂ عشق سیہ پوش ہُوا میرے بعد

shamaʿ bujhtī hai to us meñ se dhūāñ uṭhtā hai
sho'la(h)' 'ishq sīyāh posh hu'ā mere ba'd (58:3; #349)

A streak of smoke billows out when a candle is extinguished.
The flame of love has taken a black mourning garb, after my death.

sīyāh: black, dark; *posh*: garb, attire.

When the flame of the candle is put out, the candle bemoans the loss by letting out smoke. After the smoke of the candle dissipates, it can be lit again; but with my death, the flame of love shall never be lit again. It shall remain in perpetual darkness. *Ġhālib* considers his love incomparable and claims that after his death, no one will be able to love as passionately and truly as he did. Therefore, the flame of love takes on a black garb; that is, it extinguished itself, after the death of the poet. Many plays on words are involved here: candle, flame, smoke, black garb, extinguishing, and death.

خوں ہے دل خاک میں احوالِ بتاں پر، یعنی   اُن کے ناخن ہُوئے محتاجِ حنا میرے بعد

ḳhūñ hai dil ḳhāk meñ, aḥvāl-e butāñ par; ya'nī
un ke nāḳhūñ hu'e moḥtāj-e ḥinā mere ba'd (58:4; #350)

My heart bleeds in the grave, at the consternation of the beloved, as
Her nails now go begging for *henna*, after my death.

When I was alive, my blood would serve to color her nails (like *henna*). In death, I feel sorry to see her searching for *henna*, and it hurts more, making my heart bleed as I lay in the grave. The bleeding of the heart and the color of *henna* are compared here in a play of words.

درخورِ عرض نہیں جوہرِ بیداد کو جا   نگہِ ناز ہے سرمے سے خفا میرے بعد

dar ḳhur-e ʿarẓ nahiñ jauhar-e bedād ko jā
nigah-e nāz hai surme se ḳhafā mere baʿd (58:5; #351)

No one worthy of facing her talent for cruelty is left behind.
The prideful eye is deprived of antimony, after my death.

dar ḳhur-e ʿarẓ: worth presenting; *ʿarẓ*: expression; *jauhar*: real matter, talent; *bedād*: cruelty.

My beloved needed a medium to bring out her talent for cruelty, and I was that medium. With my death, she has no one left to unleash her cruelty, which means that now it is futile for her to decorate her eyes with antimony. The word used for antimony also means "talent." Therefore, taking out her talent has a double meaning—no talent left in her cruelty, and no talent left in her eyes.

ہے جنوں اہلِ جنوں کے لیے آغوشِ وداع   چاک ہوتا ہے گریباں سے جدا میرے بعد

hai junūñ āhl-e junūñ ke liye āġhosh-e vadāʿ,
chāk hotā hai girebāñ se judā mere baʿd (58:6; #352)

The frenzy is bidding farewell to lunatics.
The slit is separating from the collar, after my death.

Frenzied lovers need a slit in the collar to tear it. After my death, I no longer see the slit—meaning that the lovers are no longer able to express their feelings. I was the symbol of frenzy, and after my death it is gone as a trait of lovers (the lunatics). The tradition of lunacy ends after my death.

کون ہوتا ہے حریفِ مئے مرد افگنِ عشق   ہے مکرر لبِ ساقی میں صلا میرے بعد

kaun hotā hai ḥarīf-e mai mard afgan-e ʿishq
hai mukarrar lab-e sāqī meñ ṣalā mere baʿd (58:7: 353)

**"Who dares to taste the heady wine of love that knocks men out?"
Repeated is the call on the lips of the cupbearer, after my death.**

mai mard afgan: wine that will knock men out; *ṣalā*: call to come (for food or wine).

The beloved is daring all men with the potent wine of love, but there are no takers now that I am dead. The beloved is calling in two different tones. First, to ask if there are any takers and secondly, when no one appears, mumbling as if to say, "Who would come?" disappointedly. An extremely keen observation of human behavior is presented here. Making a call and then mumbling to oneself shows hope and disappointment at the same time. It is verses like this that elevate *Ġhālib*'s diction above all other poets of *Urdū*.

غم سے مرتا ہوں کہ اِتنا نہیں دُنیا میں کوئی
کہ کرے تعزیتِ مہر و وفا میرے بعد

ġham se martā huñ kih itnā nahiñ dunyā meñ ko'ī
kih kare ta'ziyat-e mahr-o-vafā mere ba'd (58:8; #354)

**I am dying of sorrow that there is no one left in this world
Who would condole at the death of love and faithfulness, after my death.**

ta'ziyat: condolence.

The poet is concerned that after he dies, no one will care for the values of love and faithfulness. This thought is killing him. He is dying of sorrow that there is not anyone in the world who would offer condolences to love and faithfulness after his death. He is dying of worry: who will show concern about the extinct qualities of faithfulness? I am the only living legend who places any value on these virtues. After my death, the lack of faithfulness will become a norm for society, and lovers will no longer be sincere.

آئے ہے بیکسیِ عشق پہ رونا غالبؔ
کس کے گھر جائے گا سیلابِ بلا میرے بعد

ā'e hai bekasī' 'ishq pa(h) ronā Ġhālib
kis ke ghar jāe gā sailāb-e balā mere ba'd (58:9; #355)

Tears exuding at the helplessness of love, O! *Ġhālib*.
To whose abode would this destructive flood go, after my death?

bekasī: helplessness; *balā*: catastrophe.

While alive, I was holding the catastrophic flood, namely love. After my death, the floodgates will open and this flood will inundate many homes—I wonder which ones? The flood will visit many homes in search of someone to uphold its vanity. This helplessness of love is indeed hurtful to me and makes me cry. After my death, the beloved will not find another lover like me, although she will try. Note the flow of tears in crying and the flooding.

59

بلا سے، ہیں جو بہ پیشِ نظر در و دیوار   نگاہِ شوق کو ہیں بال و پر در و دیوار

balā se, haiñ jo ba(h) pesh-e naẕar dar-o-đīvār
nigāh-e shauq ko haiñ bāl-o-par dar-o-divār(59:1; #356)

To hell with it if the walls and doors are blocking my view.
To the sight of lovers, feathers and wings are these doors and walls.

If doors and walls block my access to the beloved, I am not bothered, for it gives me greater desire to see her and makes me more determined and persistent. Every hurdle makes my resolve stronger. The walls and doors give me feathers and wings.

وفورِ اشک نے کاشانے کا کیا یہ رنگ   کہ ہو گئے مرے دیوار و در، در و دیوار

vufūr-e ashk ne kāshāne kā kīyā yih rang
kih ho ga'e mere đīvār-o-dar, dar-o-đīvār (59:2; #357)

The abundance of tears has done this to my home
That the walls and doors have turned into doors and walls.

vufūr: excess, abundance; *kāshānā*: home; *rang*: condition, colour.

Turning everything upside down, the flow of tears has brought enough soil to block the doors (turning them into walls) and make cracks in walls (and turned them into doors). Careful reading of the order of walls and doors is needed to decipher the meaning.

بلا سے ہیں جو یہ پیشِ نظر در و دیوار
نگاہِ شوق کو ہیں بال و پر در و دیوار

نہیں ہے سایہ، کہ سُن کر نویدِ مقدمِ یار　　گئے ہیں چند قدم پیشتر در و دیوار

nahiñ hai sāyā(h), kih sun kar navīd-e maqdam-e yār
ga'e haiñ chand qadam peshtar dar-o-divār (59:3; #358)

It is not the shadow; upon hearing the good news of the arrival of the beloved,
The doors and walls have stepped forward a few steps.

navīd: good news; *maqdam*: arrival.

The shadow of the door and wall of my home is not a shadow. It is actually the doors and walls leaning forward to welcome the beloved. When walls and doors are so eager upon hearing the news of her arrival, just think how my heart will express my respect and excitement.

ہُوئی ہے کس قدر ارزانیٔ مے جلوہ　　کہ مست ہے ترے کُوچے میں ہر در و دیوار

hu'ī hai kis qadar arzānī' mai jalva(h)
kih mast hai tere kūche meñ har dar-o-divār (59:4; #359)

How abundant it has become, the wine of your display
That every door and wall is lurching intoxicated in your alley.

arzānī: abundance.

As the beloved walks through her alley, the walls and doors are catching a glimpse and getting intoxicated with ecstasy. Just about everybody in your alley is drunk. If the doors and walls are feeling this way, imagine how humans would feel—this the question raised here.

جو ہے تجھے سرِ سودائے اِنتظار، تو آ　　کہ ہیں دُکانِ مَتاعِ نظر دَر و دیوار

jo hai tujhe sar-e saudā-e intiẓār, to ā
kih haiñ dukān-e matā'-e naẓar dar-o-divār (59:5; #360)

If you are ready to buy the goods of waiting, come!
The doors and walls have become the shops of the commodity of lovers' glances.

matā̑: commodity, goods.

Open eyes are called the commodity or goods of waiting. Thousands of eyes are glued to your door and walls, impatiently hoping to catch a glimpse of you. It is as if a shop of eyes has been neatly arranged. If the beloved wants to make a purchase of this commodity, she should come out and see what awaits her. It will also be an opportunity for us, the lovers, who will then get to see her as well.

ہجومِ گریہ کا سامان کب کیا میں نے　　کہ گر پڑے نہ مرے پاؤں پر در و دیوار

hujūm-e girya(h) kā sāmān kab kīyā maiñ ne
kih gir paṛe na(h) mere pāuñ par dar-o-dīvār (59:6; #361)

When did I ever plan to cry profusely
That the doors and walls have fallen on my feet?

Afraid of being washed away by the flow of my tears, the doors and walls have bowed down to my feet, begging me not to cry. Bowing to one's feet is an expression of humility.

وہ آ رہا مرے ہمسائے میں، تو سائے سے　　ہوئے فدا در و دیوار پر در و دیوار

vuh ārahā mere hamsāe meñ, to sā'e se
hu'e fidā dar-o-dīvār par dar-o-dīvār (59:7; #362)

As she is arriving to visit my neighbor, so through their shadow
My doors and walls are falling in love with the neighbor's doors and walls.

My beloved is coming to visit my neighbor. Knowing this, the doors and walls of my home have gone crazy with excitement. The only way they can acknowledge her presence is to let their shadow fall on the walls and door next door so that she will pass through the shadow. This is how my doors and walls express their adoration and love. The *Urdū* word used for neighbor rhymes with shadow and that is the main play of words in this verse.

نظر میں کھٹکے ہے بن تیرے، گھر کی آبادی   ہمیشہ روتے ہیں ہم دیکھ کر در و دیوار

naẓar meñ khaṭke hai bin tere, ghar kī ābādī
hamesha(h) rote haiñ ham dekh kar dar-o-dīvār (59:8; #363)

Without you, the habitation of my home stings my eyes.
I am always in tears when I look at the doors and walls.

It bothers the lover to see his home appear inhabited if the beloved is not there. The habitation or liveliness of home appears intolerable to him. When I look at the doors and walls, I feel like crying. As I begin to cry, the doors and walls will be washed away. This home will be a deserted place—which, basically, is what I want anyway, if you are not here.

نہ پوچھ بے خودیٔ عیشِ مقدمِ سیلاب   کہ ناچتے ہیں پڑے، سر بسر، در و دیوار

na(h) pūchh be ḳhudī' 'aish-e maqdam-e sailāb
kih nāchte haiñ paṛe, sar basar, dar-o-dīvār (59:9; #364)

Ask not about the ecstasy of love at the arrival of flood
That the doors and walls appear dancing with joy, head to head.

maqdam: coming; *sar basar*: head to head.

The doors and walls are joyful that the flood will destroy them, and they dance to show their ecstasy. The doors and walls dance head-to-head as they float, stuck to each other.

نہ کہہ کسی سے، کہ غالبؔ نہیں زمانے میں
حریفِ رازِ محبّت، مگر دَر و دیوار

na(h) kah kisī se, kih Ġhālib nahiñ zamāne meñ
ḥarif-e rāz-e muḥabbat, magar dar-o-dīvār (59:10; #365)

Tell no one now that *Ġhālib* is no longer in this world
Except the doors and walls, who would keep the secrets of your love.

In these times, tell no one, except the doors and walls, your secrets of love. *Ġhālib*, claiming to be a good secret-keeper, warns lovers not to give away their secrets to others. Talking to walls and doors is also a sign of lunacy. It is better to be considered a lunatic rather than risk letting the whole world know your secrets.

60

گھر جب بنا لیا ترے در پر کہے بغیر   جانے گا اب بھی تو نہ مرا گھر، کہے بغیر

ghar jab banā liyā tere dar par kahe baġhair
jāne gā ab bhī tū na(h) merā ghar, kahe baġhair (60:1; #366)

Now that I have built my home at your doorstep without telling you,
Would you still not know of this until I point it out to you?

Though I have built my home right at your doorstep, you still ignore it as you pass by it every day. I must point this out to you so you do not use the same old excuse for not coming to my home. Wishful thinking is expressed here.

کہتے ہیں، جب رہی نہ مجھے طاقتِ سخن   جانوں کسی کے دل کی میں کیوں کر کہے بغیر

kahte haiñ, jab rahī na(h) mujhe ṭāqat-e suḳhan
jānūñ kisī kih dil kī maiñ kioñ kar kahe baġhair (60:2; #367)

Telling me, after I had lost the ability to speak,
"How will I know your heart's condition without being told?"

When the poet had energy and used to tell her about his heart's condition, she ignored him. Now, knowing well that he cannot speak, having lost his power of speech due to weakness, she is acting cruel by saying that she will not know unless he tells her.

کام اس سے آپڑا ہے کہ جس کا جہان میں   لیوے نہ کوئی نام ستمگر کہے بغیر

kām us se āpaṛā hai kih jis kā jahān meñ
leve na(h) ko'ī nām sitamgar kahe baġhair (60:3; #368)

**I must now deal in this world with the one, whose
Name no one takes without calling her a tyrant.**

Fate has brought me to deal with her, the beloved, whose reputation is that of a tyrant. How can I have any hope of ever working things out with her? What hope do I have of achieving my goal?

جی میں ہی کچھ نہیں ہے ہمارے، وگرنہ ہم   سر جائے یا رہے، نہ رہیں پر کہے بغیر

*jī meñ hī kuchh nahiñ hai hamāre, vagarna(h) ham
sar jāe yā rahe, na(h) raheñ par kahe baġhair (60:4; #369)*

**There is not much left to say in my heart, or else, I would not
Have hesitated to say it, whether my head stays or goes.**

I am quiet because I do not have much to say; take it not as cowardice. I am not afraid. If I had anything to say, I would have said it, even if it had meant losing my head. The lover is claiming bravery while, at the same time, expressing a feeling of hollowness that comes from hopelessness.

چھوڑوں گا میں نہ اس بت کافر کا پوجنا   چھوڑے نہ خلق گو مجھے کافر کہے بغیر

*chhoṛūñ gā maiñ na(h) us but-e kāfir kā pūjnā
chhoṛe na(h) ḳhalq go mujhe kāfir kahe baġhair (60:5; #370)*

**I would not quit worshipping that infidel idol,
Even if the world would not let go without calling me an
idolater.**

The beloved is addressed as idol of infidels. I shall continue to supplicate even if it means I get labeled as an idolater. Such is my devotion and belief in her. The classic themes of idols, supplication, and the beloved as disbeliever are invoked here.

مقصد ہے ناز و غمزہ، ولے گفتگو میں کام　　چلتا نہیں ہے دشنہ و خنجر کہے بغیر

maqṣad hai nāz-o-ġhamza(h), vale guftagū meñ kām
chaltā nahiñ hai dashna(h)-o-ḳhanjar kahe baġhair (60:6; #371)

Whereas the purpose is to talk about her coquetry and amorous glances,
It does not work without bringing in the discussion of knives and daggers.

Stereotypically, whenever we talk about her, we use similes; an amorous glance is a dagger, for example. Perhaps there is much truth to it. I really want to talk about her coquetry and amorous glances, but look what I ended up saying: daggers and knives. A Freudian slip, perhaps.

ہر چند ہو مشاہدۂ حق کی گفتگو　　بنتی نہیں ہے بادہ و ساغر کہے بغیر

har chand ho mushāhidah' ḥaq kī guftagū
banti nahiñ hai bāda(h)-o-sāġhar kahe baġhair (60:7; #372)

Although talking about witnessing God,
It does not work without invoking discussion of wine and goblet.

Though we intend to talk about God's many virtues and power, when we begin talking about Him, we invariably invoke the discussion of wine and glass. Perhaps that is what brings us into a state of losing ourselves unto Him. We must be drunk to make any sense of what is totally indecipherable.

بہرا ہوں میں تو چاہیے دونا ہو التفات　　سنتا نہیں ہوں بات مکرر کہے بغیر

bahrā hūñ maiñ to chāhiye dūnā ho iltifāt
suntā nahiñ hūñ bāt mukarrar kahe baġhair (60:8; #373)

If I am deaf, then the kindness should be doubled for me,
For I cannot understand anything unless it is repeated to me.

iltifāt: kindness; *mukarrar*: repeated.

Irritated with *Ġhālib*, she snaps, "Are you deaf?" to which *Ġhālib* says "Yes. That's why I need your attention more. Repeat everything at least twice to make me understand." This allows the poet to hear her voice twice, even though what she says is unpleasant.

غالب نہ کر حضور میں تو بار بار عرض
ظاہر ہے تیرا حال سب اُن پر کہے بغیر

Ġhālib na(h) kar ḥuẓūr meñ tū bār bār ʿarẓ
ẓāhir hai terā ḥāl sab un par kahe baġhair (60:9; #374)

***Ġhālib*, do not repeat your petitions to his Lordship.**
Your condition is obviously known to him, without telling.

Here the Lordship is the King *Bahadur Shāh Zafar*, the last *Muġhal* Emperor if India, who knew all the woes of the poet but could do very little, being a defunct King. If we consider his Lordship to be God instead of the King, we can extract a more beautiful meaning.

61

کیوں جل گیا نہ تابِ رُخِ یار دیکھ کر   جلتا ہُوں اپنی طاقتِ دِیدار دیکھ کر

kioñ jal gayā na(h) tāb-e ruḳh-e yār dekh kar
jaltā huñ apnī ṯāqat-e dīdār dekh kar (61:1; #375)

Why didn't I burn looking at the brilliance of the beloved's face?
Burn, I do now looking at the strength of my vision.

The beloved has a brilliant, shining face that can easily burn anyone. When I looked at her, mustering all the strength I had I was saved from being scorched. Now I regret my strength, for it would have been more pleasurable had I been burned by her display! My strength kept me from a divine experience. Play of words: brilliance, burning, and to burn (sulking).

آتش پرست کہتے ہیں اہلِ جہاں مجھے   سرگرمِ نالہ ہائے شرر بار دیکھ کر

ātish parast kahte haiñ ahl-e jahāñ mujhe
sargarm-e nāla(h) hāi sharar bār dekh kar (61:2; #376).

Dwellers of the world call me fire worshipper,
Finding me busy sending plaints that spew fire.

My sighs are so fiery that people see this as fire coming out. They think that I am a fire worshipper–why else would I keep so much fire inside my house (my chest)? They also think of my continuous sighs keeping the fire alive as a religious symbol.

کیا آبروے عشق جہاں عام ہو جفا   رُکتا ہُوں، تم کو بے سبب آزار دیکھ کر

kyā ābrūe ʿishq jahāñ ʿām ho jafā
ruktā hūñ, tum ko besabab āzār dekh kar (61:3; #377).

What sanctity of love is left when cruelty has become so common?
I hesitate when I see you awarding pain without reason.

ābrū: sanctity; *besabab āzār:* pain without reason.

How can the sanctity of love be maintained if you dispense cruelty to everyone? I am hesitant to come close to you as I see you rewarding those who do not deserve to be hurt with sorrow and the pain of your love. Your flirtations tell me that you do not understand who the real lovers are.

آتا ہے میرے قتل کو، پر جوشِ رشک سے   مرتا ہُوں اُس کے ہاتھ میں تلوار دیکھ کر

ātā hai mere qatl ko, par josh-e rashk se
martā hūñ us ke hāth meñ talvār dekh kar (61:4; #378).

Though coming to behead me, but the intensity of jealousy
Is killing me to see the sword held in her hand.

To see her holding the sword is enough to make the lover jealous of the sword, as it is so close to her body. Before she can kill, the lover wants to die of jealousy. Play of words: beheading and dying of envy.

ثابت ہُوا ہے گردنِ مینا پہ خونِ خلق   لرزے ہے موجِ مے تری رفتار دیکھ کر

ṡābit hu'ā hai gardan-e mīnā pa(h) ḳhūn-e ḳhalq
larze hai mauj-e mai terī raftār dekh kar (61:5; #379).

The blood of people has been proven on the neck of the decanter.
The wave of wine is trembling, looking at your intoxicating gait.

The beloved drank, got tipsy and her gait became so intoxicating to others that it killed all those around her. The blood of these innocent people is, therefore, on the neck of the decanter for that is what started it all. If there were no decanter, there would be no wine and she would not drink and thus she would not walk like this and kill people. Now, the wine is afraid, trembling in the bottle, for getting the decanter in trouble. A subtle play of words comes from comparing the neck of decanter to beloved's waist as she walks coquettishly.

واحسرتا کہ یار نے کھینچا ستم سے ہاتھ   ہم کو حریصِ لذتِ آزار دیکھ کر

vā ḥasratā kih yār ne khainchā sitam se hāth
ham ko ḥarīṣ-e lażżat-e āzār dekh kar (61:6; #380).

How sad that the beloved has pulled back on dispensing cruelty,
Seeing my avarice for relishing the pleasures of affliction!

vā ḥasratā: statement of extreme sorrow; *ḥarīṣ:* avaricious.

When she saw that I enjoyed suffering, she stopped her cruelty. How sad is it, questions the lover? By taking away her cruelty, she has become more impossible and painful to me; this has increased my pain, and thus, my joy.

بک جاتے ہیں ہم آپ متاعِ سخن کے ساتھ   لیکن عیارِ طبعِ خریدار دیکھ کر

bik jāte haiñ ham āp matāʻ-e suḳhan kih sāth
lekin ʻayār-e t̤abaʻ-e ḳharidār dekh kar (61:7; #381).

We sell ourselves along with our poetic wares,
But only after judging the standard of taste of the buyer.

ʻayār: standard, touch; *t̤abaʻ:* nature, temperament, taste.

When people buy my poetry (read my poetry) they get a part of me as well, but only if they are able to appreciate it. To be sold to someone means to appreciate him.

زُنّار باندھ، سُبحۂ صد دانہ توڑ ڈال   رَہرَو چلے ہے، راہ کو ہموار دیکھ کر

zunnār bāndh, subḥ' ṣad dāna(h) toṛ ḍāl
rahro chale hai, rāh ko hamvār dekh kar (61:8; #382).

Take the holy black string; break the rosary of a hundred beads,
Because the leader takes the path that appears smooth.

zunnār: black thread worn around neck by Hindus; *subḥ ṣad dāna(h)*: rosary with a hundred beads.

Plying the rosary through the fingers, the fingers ride the crest of beads as if it were a non-uniform path. Once the beads are removed (in this case, broken), that leaves only a smooth thread (like the black holy string used by idolaters, Hindus) worn around the neck. Why not just remove the beads and roll the fingers past a smooth thread, advises the poet, since the purpose of the beloved is not to recite any holy chant but to count the number of lovers she has killed. Since the number is infinite, it will be an insurmountable task to recite the rosary. It would be easier if she had a smooth thread. This suggestion is compared to what the leaders do as they take the road of least resistance. She is indeed a beloved that leads all other beloveds. Note the use of rosary, the black thread used by idolaters, and the beloved (idol) all in one continuum.

اِن آبلوں سے پانوؐں کے گھبرا گیا تھا مَیں   جی خوش ہُوا ہے راہ کو پُرخار دیکھ کر

in āblon̄ se pāun̄ ke ghabrā gayā thā main̄
jī ḳhush hu'ā hai rāh ko pur ḳhār dekh kar (61:9; #383).

These blisters on my feet had begun to bother me.
Now I am delighted to see a path full of thorns.

The thorns on the road will puncture my blisters to exude the water, relieve the pain of blisters, and make it easy for me to walk. Using a painful solution to resolve a painful problem is how the lover expresses his frustrations. He is, however, not giving up wandering.

کیا بدگماں ہے مجھ سے کہ آئینے میں مرے   طوطی کا عکس سمجھے ہے، زنگار دیکھ کر

kyā badgumāñ hai mujh se kih ā'īne meñ mere
ṭūṭī kā ʿaks samjhe hai, zangār dekh kar (61:10; #384).

How distrusting with me that looking in my mirror,
Finding the rust spots, she considers them reflections of parrots?

I was holding a steel mirror in my hand. It was rusted, with green spots. She came from behind, saw me looking into mirror, and mistook the green rust spots for the reflection of a parrot. She became distrustful of me because she thought that I was trying to teach my pet parrot to talk. She thinks that if I am so devoted to a parrot, then it means that I do not have time to love her. She expects the lover to be thinking only of her—even in idleness—and no one else, not even a bird.

گرنی تھی ہم پہ برقِ تجلی، نہ طور پر   دیتے ہیں بادہ ظرفِ قدح خوار دیکھ کر

girnī thī ham pa(h) barq-e tajallī, na(h) ṭūr par
dete haiñ bāda(h) ẓarf-e qadaḥ ḳh(v)ār dekh kar (61:11; #385).

The lightning of manifestation should have struck me, not the mount Sinai.
The wine is given to drinkers in proportion to their capacity.

tajallī: display, manifestation, referring to lightning striking Moses; *ẓarf*: ability, forebearance, capacity.

The manifestation of God on the mount Sinai, shattered it and Moses passed out. This display was too much the mountain could not take it. Show the display to me, not to Moses. The wine should be dispensed to drinkers only as much as they can hold. I am ready to see your display, all of it. I can hold all the wine and all the display, the poet has challenged Moses.

سر پھوڑنا وہ غالبِ شوریدہ حال کا
یاد آگیا مجھے تری دیوار دیکھ کر

sar phoṛnā vuh Ġhālib-e shorida(h) ḥāl kā
yād āgayā mujhe terī divār dekh kar (61:12; #386).

The striking of head, of that lunatic *Ġhālib*,
I just remembered when I saw your wall.

shorida(h) ḥāl: lunatic.

Ġhālib used to hit his head against your wall in agony. Though it is just a wall, the most significant thing about it is "how" *Ġhālib* used to hit it in agony. What the observer is recalling is not that this is *the* wall *Ġhālib* used to hit, but the agony he went through when hitting the wall. The wall is serving as a reminder, not a landmark.

62

لرزتا ہے مرا دل زحمتِ مہرِ درخشاں پر
میں ہوں وہ قطرۂ شبنم کہ ہو خارِ بیاباں پر

laraztā hai merā dil zaḥmat-e mahr-e daraḳhshāñ par
maiñ hūñ vuh qaṭra(h)' shabnam kih ho ḳhār-e bayābāñ par
(62:1; #387)

My heart trembles at the inconvenience caused to the bright sun;
I am that drop of dew that is hanging onto the tip of a thorn in the wilderness.

laraztā: shivers, trembles.

It appears unnecessary for the sun to go to so much effort just to evaporate a humble drop of dew. Moreover, not just any drop—the drop hanging onto the tip of the thorn, which is already shaky and ready to fall. My heart, so humble and barely hanging on to life, wonders what would happen if the beloved paid any attention to this humble creature. The poet suspects that she might pay attention to him, but knows that if she does, it will decimate him. He is shivering at the prospect. The images of the shivering of the dew and the warmth and brightness of sun are remarkable.

نہ چھوڑی حضرتِ یوسف نے یاں بھی خانہ آرائی
سفیدی دیدۂ یعقوب کی پھرتی ہے زنداں پر

na(h) choṛī ḥaẓrat-e yūsuf ne yāñ bhī ḳhana(h) ārā'ī
safaidī dīda(h)' ya'qūb kī phirtī hai zindāñ par (62:2; #388)

Honorable Joseph did not let go illuminating the home even here;
As Jacob's sclera of his eye kept wandering on the walls of the prison cell.

safaidī: whitewash; *safaidī dīda(h)*: sclera of eye; *phirtī:* wanders.

Joseph, the beautiful son of Jacob, would brighten any room wherever he is, even if it happens to be a prison cell. His loving father, Jacob, must have been watching him in the prison from a distance, as the walls of the prison cell have brightened from Jacob's wandering eyes. The sclera of the eye, which is white, appears to be giving a whitewash to the walls of the prison cell. Crying for Joseph, Jacobs's eyes had also turned white, blinded, crying for Joseph. Beauty, regardless of where it goes, creates the means of adorning itself, for its admirers are always present. This is a very difficult comparison: the eyes of Jacob wandering at the prison walls to keep an eye on his son and the white of eyes (sclera) producing a whitewash of walls.

فنا تعلیم درسِ بے خودی، ہوں اُس زمانے سے
کہ مجنوں لام اَلِف لکھتا تھا دیوارِ دبستاں پر

fanā ta'līm-e dars-e be ḳhudī, hūñ us zamāne se
kih majnūñ lām alif likhtā thā dīvār-e dabistāñ par (62:3; #389)

I have been a devotee to the lessons in rapture before the time
When *Majnūn* used to write only alphabets on the walls of the school.

fanā: devoted.

I have been devoted to the virtues of rapture and ecstasy for a long time, even when *Majnūn*, so well known for his ecstasy, was merely a student learning this art. This means that *Majnūn* may be famous for his lunacy, but I have appreciated this condition longer than any other lover. In many verses, *Ġhālib* has compared himself to *Majnūn* and concluded that he is better than *Majnūn*. See glossary: *Majnūn*.

فراغت کس قدر رہتی مجھے تشویشِ مرہم سے
بہم گر صلح کرتے پارہ ہائے دل نمکداں پر

farāġhat kis qadar rahtī mujhe tashvīsh-e marham se
baham gar ṣulḥ karte pāra(h) hāi dil namakdāñ par (62:4; #390)

How free would I have been of the anxiety to search for the treatment,
Had there been a truce among my heart's pieces on the salt shaker?

pāra(h) hāi dil: pieces of heart.

My heart was broken into many pieces, and each piece was fighting to get more salt rubbed onto it. This infighting became too much to handle and I took away the saltshaker. Now I have to go around looking for the treatment of my heart's woes—meaning, to find something else to hurt my heart. This is a very difficult task. It would have been so much better if the pieces of my heart had agreed to share the salt; I would have been spared having to look around for other means of hurting myself. Taking away the saltshaker took away the joy of pain.

نہیں اقلیمِ الفت میں کوئی طومارِ ناز ایسا
کہ پشتِ چشم سے، جس کے نہ ہووے مُہر عنواں پر

nahiñ iqlīm-e ulfat meñ ko'ī ṭūmār-e nāz aisā
kih pusht-e chashm se, jis ke na(h) hove mohar 'unvāñ par (62:5; #391)

In the kingdom of love, there is no decree of coquetry that
Has not been sealed on its opening from the back of the eyes.

ṭūmār: decree, book, office, heading; *pusht-e chashm*: the back of eye, to show obliviousness; *mohar*: stamp.

In the world of love, there is not any book on coquetry on the face of which my beloved has not put her seal of style. If there is any style in the world, it is in the eyes of my beloved. Note the similarity between a stamp and the shape of an eye. The use of the construction "back of the eyes" also means obliviousness of the beloved, but here it is meant to signify her style. Wherever there is something written about love, there is a mention of the style of my beloved, her unfaithfulness. The word used to describe decree also means a book or register. This will now mean that in the world of love, there has never been a book written where the title did not contain the word unfaithfulness. Another interpretation is that in the world of lovers, there is no lover whose heart has not been sealed with beloved's obliviousness (sealing of heart also connotes sadness). This is one of the most complicated verses to interpret.

مجھے اب، دیکھ کر ابرِ شفق آلودہ، یاد آیا
کہ فُرقت میں تری، آتش برستی تھی گلستاں پر

mujhe ab, dekh kar abr-e shafaq ālūda(h) yād āyā
kih furqat meñ terī, ātish barastī thī gulistāñ par (62:6; #392)

Now seeing the red lining of clouds has reminded me
How a fire used to rain on this garden waiting for you in separation.

abr: cloud; *shafaq:* red lining of sky, orange dusk; *ālūda(h)*: mixed, laced; *yād*: remembrance; *furqat*: separation, disunion (of lovers); *ātish*: fire.

Waiting and longing for you was like a rain of fire falling on the garden (my heart). The longing is gone after reunion with you, but I still remember the pain when I see the pink clouds in the sky after the rain, and it reminds me of the fire of separation I had suffered before reunion with you. A lover's wound remains—though it may subside, it reappears now and then. The lover remembers how it used to hurt but does not remember much about the joy of reunion.

بجز پروازِ شوقِ ناز کیا باقی رہا ہوگا
قیامت اِک ہوائے تند ہے خاکِ شہیداں پر

bajuz parvāz-e shauq-e nāz kyā bāqī rahā hogā
qiyāmat ik havā'e tund hai ḳhāk-e shahidāñ par (62:7; #393)

Except for the desire to please the beloved, what else would have remained?
The Resurrection is merely a strong wind blowing away the ashes of martyrs.

bajuz: except; *parvāz-e shauq-e nāz*: desire to go to any lengths to please the beloved; *qiyāmat*: Resurrection, Doomsday; *shahīd*: martyr;

The martyrs of your love have one thing left in them—their intense desire to please you. The Resurrection is merely a strong wind on the graves of your martyred lovers blowing away the dust of their ashes; but the ashes are already flying high to reach your alley, to please you. The Resurrection is supposed to put life back into the dead, raising them, but these lovers of yours are beyond this reward; they are already flying high, attempting to please you. They are beyond the stage where the Resurrection can raise them to heaven. This verse is indeed one of the loftiest creations of imagination by *Ġhālib*.

نہ لڑ ناصح سے غالب، کیا ہُوا گر اُس نے شدّت کی؛
ہمارا بھی تو آخر زور چلتا ہے گریباں پر!

na(h) laṛ nāṣiḥ se Ġhālib, kyā hu'ā gar usne shiddat kī
hamārā bhī to āḳhir zor chaltā hai garebāñ par (62:8; #394)

Fight not with preacher, *Ġhālib.* So what if he's been harsh?
After all, I do retain the control over my collar.

The preacher had been rude and harsh and the poet wants to confront him, but then he pauses and ponders the futility of this approach. He suggests that instead of wasting energy on fighting with the preacher, why not tear his own collar, and take out the frustration? It is much easier this way to show the preacher how vain his advice has been—to show him that insanity sustains.

63

ہے بسکہ ہر اک اُن کے اشارے میں نشاں اَور   کرتے ہیں مُحبّت تو گزرتا ہے گماں اَور

hai baski(h) har ik un ke ishāre meñ nishāñ āur
karte haiñ muḥabbat to guzartā hai gumāñ aur (63:1; #395)

Whereas in all of her gestures there are other meanings hidden.
When she loves me, it makes me suspect something else.

baski(h): whereas; *ishāre*: indicators, gestures; *nishāñ*: meaning.

Distrustful of her double face, the poet is suspicious of her. It may just be an enticement to unleash the cruelty of coquettishness. He is not sure that her expression of love does not have another motive. What she says and means are two different things.

یارب وُہ نہ سمجھے ہیں، نہ سمجھیں گے مری بات   دے اَور دِل اُن کو، جو نہ دے مُجھ کو زباں اَور

yārabb vuh na(h) sanjhe haiñ, na(h) sanjheñ ge merī bāt
de āur dil un ko, jo na(h) de mujh ko zabāñ aur (63:2; #396)

O! Lord, she has never, nor will she ever, understand my words.
Give her another heart, if not another tongue to me.

Trying to get his point—and his plea—across, the poet throws in the towel and asks for God's help in either giving her another heart (that will be more attentive or sympathetic), or else giving him some other means of expression (so that he will get to her heart). The simplicity and beauty with which *Ġhālib* expresses his most complex dilemma needs no other tongue.

ابرو سے ہے کیا اس نگہِ ناز کو پیوند
ہے تیر مقرر مگر اس کی ہے کماں اور

abrū se hai kyā us nigāh-e nāz ko pevand
hai tīr muqarrar magar is kī hai kamāñ aur (63:3; #397)

What connection there is between the beloved's glance and eyebrows?
Undoubtedly it's an arrow but its bow is somewhere else.

pevand: patch, connection; *muqarrar*: undoubtedly.

The connection between her amorous glances and eyebrows is a classic one—the arrow and bow. Here the poet splits the cliché and leaves the reader wondering where the bow is. It is certain that the arrow will be fired but the direction of the arrow will depend which way the bow is aimed. Who will get killed today, is the question raised by the poet, dismayed at it not being pointed towards him.

تم شہر میں ہو تو ہمیں کیا غم، جب اٹھیں گے
لے آئیں گے بازار سے، جا کر دل و جاں اور

tum shahar meñ ho to hameñ kyā ġham, jab uṭheñ ge
le āe'ñ ge bāzār se jā kar dil-o-jāñ aur (63:4; #398)

When you are in town, why should I worry, for whenever I would get up,
I would fetch some more hearts and lives from the market.

This is one of the most often quoted verses of *Ġhālib* but most people miss out the very fine point made here. The beloved has arrived in town and there is commotion among the lovers. They all know that they will lose their hearts and lives to her, as no one can resist her. In anticipation of this, the lovers have begun selling their hearts and lives causing the price of these "commodities" to drop. The poet is being sarcastic to the beloved. The poet is comparing his resolve with that of other, ordinary lovers who cannot withstand the rigors of loving.

ہر چند سبک دست ہوئے بت شکنی میں   ہم ہیں تو ابھی راہ میں ہے سنگِ گراں اور

har chand subuk dast hu'e but shikanī meñ
ham haiñ to abhī rāh meñ hai sang-e girāñ aur (63:5; #399)

Though we became dextrous shattering the idols,
More heavy stones shall remain in our path, as long we ourselves exist.

subuk dast: agile, quick, light-handed, dextrous; *but shikanī*: breaking idols; *girāñ*: heavy.

Whereas we have easily shattered many idols (our weaknesses), heavier stones remain in our path, our ego. Another interpretation of this verse: as long I am alive, I will keep attracting more idols (sins) in my path, because that is in the nature of man.

ہے خونِ جگر جوش میں، دل کھول کے روتا   ہوتے جو کئی دیدۂ خوں نابہ فشاں اور

hai ḳhūn-e jigar josh meñ, dil khol ke rotā
hote jo ka'ī dīda(h)' ḳhunnāba(h) fishāñ aur (63:6; #400)

The blood in the liver is boiling. I would have cried to the heart's content
If only there were a few more blood-crying eyes.

dīda(h)-e ḳhunnāba(h) fishāñ: blood crying eyes.

The pain and suffering have hurt the liver badly. The blood surging wildly in the liver has created a great tension in there. To express my sorrow and relieve the tension, I must cry tears of blood. However, with only two eyes, it is not possible to let it all go.

مرتا ہوں اِس آواز پہ، ہر چند سر اُڑ جائے
جلاد کو لیکن وہ کہے جائیں کہ "ہاں اور"

martā hūñ is āvāz pa(h), har chand sar uṛ jāe
jallād ko lekin vuh kahe jāe'ñ kih hāñ āur (63:7; #401)

Dying for that voice, even though my head might roll,
If she would keep telling the executioner, "Yes more!"

Even at the time of his execution, the lover is delighted to hear the beloved's voice, albeit this may just be the instruction to the executioner to strike again and again. Whereas death resolves all relationships, for the lover, death is the reward. To hear her voice at the time of death is the ultimate reward. Notice the use of the word "dying" at the time of execution.

لوگوں کو ہے خورشیدِ جہاں تاب کا دھوکا
ہر روز دِکھاتا ہُوں مَیں اِک داغِ نہاں اَور

logoñ ko hai ḳhurshid-e jahāñ tāb kā dhokā
har roz dikhātā hūñ maiñ ik dāġh-e nihāñ aur (63:8; #402)

People mistakenly take it as bright world-illuminating sun,
Every day when I show them more of my hidden brandings.

The spots of lost love in my heart are so intense with heat and glow so brightly that onlookers mistake them for the sun.

لیتا، نہ اگر دِل تمھیں دیتا، کوئی دَم چین
کرتا، جو نہ مرتا، کوئی دن آہ و فغاں اَور

letā, na(h) agar dil tumhaiñ detā, ko'ī dam chain
kartā, jo na(h) martā, ko'ī din āh-o-fuġhāñ aur (63:9; #403)

I would have found a moment of peace, had I not given my heart to you;
I would have lamented a little longer, had I not died.

If I had not given my heart to you, there might have been some moments of peace in my life. The poet says he has never had a day of peace since giving his heart. If I had not died, then I would have continued lamenting. The reading order is 1-3 in both lines. Elsewhere, *Ġhālib* writes: "*agar aur jīte rahte yahī intizār hotā*" (had I lived longer, the wait would have still have been the same).

پاتے نہیں جب راہ تو چڑھ جاتے ہیں نالے   رکتی ہے مری طبع تو ہوتی ہے رواں اور

pāte nahiñ jab rāh to chaṛh jāte haiñ nāle
ruktī hai merī t̤abaʿ to hotī hai ravāñ āur (63:10; #404)

Not finding a vent, the sighs strengthen.
When my expressions are stifled, they turn more fluent.

Obstacles blocking the flow of water in a river raise the level of the water and make it flow faster (broadening its expanse and increasing its flow rate). The flow of sighs and the expression of ideas are all enhanced when hindered in any way. What obstructs the expression is the sorrow; it therefore makes the speech more potent.

ہیں اور بھی دنیا میں سخنور بہت اچھے
کہتے ہیں کہ غالب کا ہے انداز بیاں اور

haiñ āur bhī dunyā meñ suḳhanvar bahut achhe
kahte haiñ kih Ġhālib kā hai andāz-e bayāñ āur (63:11; #405)

There are indeed other eloquent poets in this world as well,
But it is said that *Ġhālib*'s style of diction is something else.

Self-praise through the mouth of others is what *Ġhālib* suggests here. Even in self-praise, indeed his style is something else.

64

صفائے حیرتِ آئینہ ہے سامانِ زنگ آخر   تغیرِ آبِ بر جا ماندہ کا پاتا ہے رنگ آخر

ṣafāe ḥairat-e ā'īna(h) hai sāmān-e zang āḳhir
taġhaiyur āb-e bar jā mānda(h) kā pātā hai rang āḳhir (64:1; #406)

The stunning sparkle of mirror causes it to rust.
Change finally appears in the color of water in stagnancy.

ṣafā: cleanliness, spark; *taġhaiyur*: change; *āb-e bar jā mānda(h)*: stagnant water.

Shining of a mirror is called a frozen or stunned state. In its sparkling state, the mirror appears stunned or stagnant. As a result, the mirror becomes rusted (here we are talking about iron mirrors). A similar situation exists in a pond of water that is stagnant, for algae grows in it and changes the color to green. In addition, bacteria begin to grow in it, a fact that perhaps *Ġhālib* did not realize when writing this verse. Note: flowing water is always drinkable since bacteria do not multiply in it. Any stagnancy in our thoughts creates the deterioration of ideas.

نہ کی سامانِ عیش و جاہ نے تدبیر وحشت کی   ہوا جامِ زمرد بھی مجھے داغِ پلنگ آخر

na(h) kī sāmān-e aish-o-jā(h) ne tadbīr vaḥshat kī
hu'ā jām-e zamurrud bhī mujhe dāġh-e palang āḳhir (64:2; #407)

No provisions of comfort and luxury could resolve my lunacy.
The bowl of emerald, too, only reminded me of leopard spots.

palang: a leopard, a panther.

No luxuries of life could dissuade me from the path of lunacy. Even the bowl studded with emerald, given to me for drinking wine, reminds me of the spots on the leopard, which, in turn, is a reminder of the wilderness. No material things can change my resolve. I do not see any value in the emerald bowl except that it reminds me of wilderness. Reference is made here to the bowl of King Jamshed (See Glossary).

65

جنوں کی دستگیری کس سے ہو، گر ہو نہ عریانی
گریباں چاک کا حق ہو گیا ہے میری گردن پر

junūñ kī dastgirī kis se ho, gar ho na(h) ʿuryānī
garebāñ chāk kā ḥaq ho gayā hai merī gardan par (65:1; #408)

How can we express lunacy, if not through nakedness?
The slit of the collar has earned an obligation on my neck.

dastgirī: expression.

The expression of lunacy can only be made after exposing oneself. This shows our poverty and insensibility. My torn collar has exposed my body and therefore my lunacy. I am thankful to the slit in my collar now that I no longer have anything to hide. Owing an obligation to the collar is described as a favor to the neck; meaning that something of extreme value was received. See how collar, neck, nakedness, and tear all rhyme well to express the tumult of lunacy.

بہ رنگِ کاغذِ آتش زدہ، نیرنگِ بیتابی
ہزار آئینہ دِل باندھے ہے بالِ یک تپیدن پر

ba(h) rang-e kāġhaz-e ātishzada(h), nairang-e betābī
hazār āʾīna(h) dil bāndhe hai bāl-e yak tapīdan par (65:2; #409)

Like the condition of scorched paper, the magic of tumultuousness is
Tying thousands of mirrors of heart on the rising wings.

nairang-e betābī: magic of tumultuousness; *bāl:* wings, arms; *tapīdan:* restlessness, rising.

When paper burns it curls into ashes and begins drifting, rising up into the air becoming very light. The words written upon it appear like shiny spots. This observation is made as a basis to express the tumultuousness of a scorched soul. The condition of my heart is that of burned paper; tossing, turning, curling. The shiny spots on the papery ashes are the mirrors of heart that cause the wings (meant here as hope) to rise. It seems as if the shiny spots are helping the burned paper fly. Note that the word used to indicate rising also means restlessness. Thus we can say that hearts are tied to the wings of restlessness. My intensity of tumultuousness is evident as thousands of mirrors reflect my devastated desires. The primary meaning here is that although in a state of complete despair, hope arises out of the ashes (like burned paper taking wing). See also "tying hearts on my sleeve" (Othello).

فلک سے ہم کو عیشِ رفتہ کا کیا کیا تقاضا ہے
متاعِ بُردہ کو سمجھے ہوئے ہیں قرض رہزن پر

falak se ham ko aish-e rafta(h) kā kyā kyā taqāẓā hai
matā'-e burda(h) ko samjhe hu'e haiñ qarẓ rahzan par (65:3; #410)

How we insist upon heaven to return our luxuries from the bygone times.
We think that the goods stolen were merely borrowed by the robber.

'aish-e rafta(h): luxuries of times bygone; *matā'-e burda(h)*: robbed belongings; *rahzan*: robber.

The heavens have robbed us of past luxurious times and we are praying for their return. It is as if we think the robber has merely borrowed our belongings and hope that he will soon return them. How foolish!

ہم اور وُہ بے سبب رنج، آشنا دشمن، کہ رکھتا ہے
شعاعِ مہر سے تُہمت نگہ کی، چشمِ رَوزن پر

ham aur vuh be sabab ranj, āshnā dushman, kih rakhtā hai
shuʿā-e mahr se tohmat nigāh kī, chashm-e rauzan par (65:4; #411)

Getting upset with me for no reason, the enemy of lovers, she Blames me for the rays of the sun as if they were my glance entering the window.

be sabab ranj: getting upset without reason; *āshnā dushman*: enemy of friend; *rauzan:* small window.

I am involved with such a suspicious and paranoid beloved that she gets upset when she sees a ray of sun shining through her window. She thinks of it as a beam of vision coming from my eyes, watching her through the window. She really thinks that the sun shining through her window is me looking at her. Repeatedly, *Ġhālib* has described vision as if it were a beam, a string, coming out of eye. Fact is that it is the light entering the eye that causes vision to appear.

فنا کو سونپ، گر مُشتاق ہے اپنی حقیقت کا
فُروغِ طالعِ خاشاک ہے مَوقُوف گلخن پر

fanā ko sauñp, gar mushtāq hai apnī ḥaqīqat kā
furoġh-e ṯāliʿ-e ḳhāshāk hai mauqūf gulḳhan par (65:5; #412)

Give yourself unto extinction, if you aspire to know your reality. The good fortune of waste is dependent on the furnace.

fanā: extinction; *mushtāq*: dependent on; *furoġh-e ṯāliʿ:* good fortune; *ḳhāshāk*: garbage, refuse, *mauqūf*: contingent; *gulḳhan:* waste-bin, furnace, stove.

Give yourself up to extinction in the name of the beloved (or God) if you aspire to understand the reality about yourself. The refuse has the good fortune to burn in the fire of furnace (incinerator), reaching its destiny. Likewise, you must also reach your destiny by burning yourself in the fire of love. The refuse keeps getting shoved around until it reaches the furnace; so are we until we offer ourselves into extinction. Notice how the burning of refuse and giving yourself into extinction are compared here. Also, comparing self to refuse is done to show how humble a human soul is.

اسدؔ بسمل ہے کس انداز کا، قاتل سے کہتا ہے
"تو مشقِ ناز کر، خونِ دو عالم میری گردن پر"

Asad bismil hai kis andāz kā, qātil se kehtā hai
"*tū mashq-e nāz kar, ḳhūn-e do ʿālam merī gardan par*" *(65:6; #413)*

What kind of a wounded man is Asad, telling the killer,
"Keep practicing your coquetry, the blood of two worlds is on my neck."

The beloved has wounded Asad, who, while bleeding is encouraging the beloved to continue killing others with her coquetry. He assures her that he is willing to take the responsibility of these murders by taking their blood on his own neck. This is possible because she is doing it not of her own volition, but at the suggestion of Asad. (In English law, the one who plots the murder is subject to first-degree murder charges.). Since these murders would have been committed at Asad's invitation, the beloved would not be responsible for them. There is another explanation of how she will be proven innocent later. The beloved will not be responsible for these murders because she will only be using her amorous glances to kill. Since amorous glances are not considered a weapon, legally, she cannot be convicted. The most significant aspect of this verse is the use of the word "what" that expresses surprise at what type of man Asad is who would suggest such to his beloved? Why is he encouraging the beloved to entice others? It is an attempt to please her because killing one lover does not satisfy her ego. At the same time, it is not normal behavior for the lover to suggest that his beloved entice others.

66

ستم کش مصلحت سے ہوں کہ خوباں تجھ پہ عاشق ہیں
تکلف برطرف، مل جائے گا تجھ سا رقیب آخر

sitam kash maṣlaḥat se hūñ kih ḳhūbāñ tujh pa(h) ʿāshiq haiñ
takalluf barṯaraf mil jāe gā tujh sā raqīb āḳhir (66:1; #414)

Enduring the cruelty though beauties are in love with you is for a reason.
Suffering aside, I am hoping to find a rival like you, finally.

sitam kash: bearing cruelty; *maṣlaḥat*: reason; *ḳhūbāñ*: beauty, beloved; *takalluf barṯaraf*: suffering aside.

I am enduring the torment of watching the beloved flirt with a new, handsome (beautiful; see below why this is an argument) lover joining the ranks. Sooner or later he (she) will also be a target of the beloved's torment and end up singing sighs of separation. I know I will soon have a rival who is just as good-looking (beautiful) as you. There is a difficulty in interpreting this verse. The word "beauties" refers to women. If another woman is in love with the beloved, then lesbianism on the part of the beloved is claimed here. Moreover, when the beloved rejects her new lover, the poet is ready to usurp her. If we assume that the new lover is a man, then by the same argument, the lover is assumed a homosexual as the lover usurps another male. Most commentators avoid this delineation and interpret the verse as the turning over of the rival to the lover. There is no difficulty here if we read between the lines and assume the fact of Turkish slave boys being the beloved in the Persian courts. The tone of *Urdū* poetry in addressing beloved as male is best exemplified in this verse.

67

لازم تھا کہ دیکھو مرا رستہ کوئی دن اور
تنہا گئے کیوں اب رہو تنہا کوئی دن اور

lāzim thā kih dekho merā rastā ko'ī din aur
tanhā gae kioñ, ab raho tanhā ko'ī din aur (67:1; #415)

It was required that you wait for me for a few days more.
Why did you go alone? Now live alone, for a few days more!

Written in the memory of his wife's nephew, *Ārif*, who died prematurely, *Ġhālib* mourns his death. You should have waited for me to go along with you. Now that you have gone alone, wait a few days until I join you. The tone is of loving sarcasm here.

مٹ جائے گا سر گر ترا پتھر نہ گھسے گا
ہوں در پہ ترے ناصیہ فرسا کوئی دن اور

miṭ jāe gā sar, gar terā patthar na(h) ghise gā
hūñ dar pa(h) tere nāṣiya(h) farsā ko'ī din aur (67:2; #416)

My forehead will get rubbed off, if not your tombstone.
At your doorstep, I am rubbing my forehead for a few days more.

nāṣiya(h) farsā: one who rubs his forehead.

As I rub my forehead onto your tombstone, either the stone or my head will disappear. This means that it will wear off the tombstone and I will merge with you or I will lose my forehead and die—either way I shall join you.

آئے ہو کل، اور آج ہی کہتے ہو کہ جاؤں　　مانا کہ ہمیشہ نہیں، اچھا، کوئی دن اور

āi ho kal, āur āj hī kahte ho kih jā'uñ
mānā kih hamesha(h) nahiñ, achhā, ko'ī din aur (67:3; #417)

You just came yesterday and insist on leaving today;
I know that it is not forever, but you should have stayed a few days more.

You are so young to be insisting on leaving the world. I understand you cannot stay in this world forever, but you should have stayed at least a few more days.

جاتے ہوئے کہتے ہو قیامت کو ملیں گے　　کیا خوب، قیامت کا ہے گویا کوئی دن اور

jāte hue' kahte ho qiyāmat ko mileñ ge
kyā ķhūb, qiyāmat kā hai goyā ko'ī din aur (67:4; #418)

Leaving me, you ṣay that we shall meet on the Day of Resurrection.
How nice! Is this a day other than the Doomsday?

The day of your death is Doomsday for me; for you to say that I will see you on the Day of Resurrection is redundant, for today is that day. In *Urdū* poetry, Doomsday is akin to ultimate chaos.

ہاں اے فلکِ پیر، جواں تھا ابھی عارف　　کیا تیرا بگڑتا جو نہ مرتا کوئی دن اور

hāñ ai falak-e pīr, javāñ thā abhī 'ārif
kyā terā bigaṛtā jo na(h) martā ko'ī din aur (67:5; #419)

Yes, O! Old-man-heaven? *Ārif* was still young.
What would it have mattered to you, if he hadn't died for a few days more?

falak: heaven; *pīr*: old man.

Questioning the heavens about the wisdom of the death of *Ārif*, the poet pleads to know how it would have mattered had *Ārif* lived a little longer.

تم ماہِ شبِ چار دہم تھے مرے گھر کے   پھر کیوں نہ رہا گھر کا وہ نقشا کوئی دن اور

tum māh-e shab-e chār dahum the mere ghar ke
phir kioñ na(h) rahā ghar kā vuh naqshā ko'ī din aur (67:6; #420)

You were the moon of the 14th night in my home.
Then why didn't my home's aura stay the same for a few days more?

māh-e shab-e chār dahum: full moon (moon of the fourteenth night).

You were like the full moon brightening up my home, then suddenly you were gone and my home was thrust into darkness. Unlike the moon that recedes slowly, you disappeared suddenly.

تم کون سے تھے ایسے کھرے داد و ستد کے!   کرتا مَلَکُ الموت تقاضا کوئی دن اور

tum kaun se the aise khare dād-o-sitad ke
kartā malakulmaut taqāẓā ko'ī din aur (67:7; #421)

You were not so straightforward in your wheeling-dealings.
To the angel of death, you could have negotiated for a few days more.

khare: straightforward; *dād-o-sitad:* wheeling-dealing; *malakulmaut:* the angel of death.

You were not straightforward enough to say yes to the angel of death upon his asking. You should have talked the angel of death out of his duty for a few more days.

مجھ سے تمھیں نفرت سہی، نیّر سے لڑائی   بچّوں کا بھی دیکھا نہ تماشا کوئی دن اور

mujh se tumheñ nafrat sahī, naiyyar se laṛā'ī
bachchoñ kā bhī dekhā na(h) tamāshā ko'ī din aur (67:8; #422)

It is fine that you hated me and fought with Nayyar,
But you didn't even see the children playing for a few days more.

naiyyar: Ziauddin Ahmad Nayyar, brother-in-law of *Ġhālib* and a master of Persian poetry.

There was no excuse for you to leave because you may have hated me or had a fight with Nayyar. However, what was the fault of your children? You should have waited to see them play for a few more days. The first line does not mean this verbatim. It is simply given as an example of possible situations. *Ġhālib* does not mean that he was hated by *Ārif*.

گزری نہ، بہ ہر حال، یہ مُدّت خُوش و ناخُوش   کرنا تھا جواں مرگ! گزارا کوئی دن اور

guzrī na(h), bahar ḥāl, yih muddat ḳhūsh-o-nāḳhūsh
karṇā thā javāñ marg! guzārā ko'ī din aur (67:9; #423)

Did you not live through the moments of joy and sorrow at times somehow,
O' you who died early, you could have lived like this for a few days more!

javāñ marg: one who died in youth; *guzārā*: to bear with, to have lived on.

There were many joys and sorrows in your life, but somehow things worked out. Dying early and giving us this sorrow was not necessary. You could have easily spent some more days like that.

نادان ہو جو کہتے ہو کہ کیوں جیتے ہیں غالب
قسمت میں ہے مرنے کی تمنا کوئی دن اور

nādāñ ho jo kehte ho kih kioñ jīte haiñ Ġhālib
qismat meñ hai marne kī tamannā ko'ī din aur (67:10; #424)

Ignorant you are questioning why does *Ġhālib* continue to live?
It is in my fate to continue to pray for death for a few days more.

After suffering through horrendous experiences, people may wonder why *Ġhālib* did not die of this sorrow. Little do they know that *Ġhālib* suffers a greater pain waiting for his death now.

68

فارغ مجھے نہ جان کہ مانندِ صبح و مہر
ہے داغِ عشق زینتِ جیبِ کفن ہنوز

fāriġh mujhe na(h) jān kih mānind-e ṣubḥ-o-mahr
hai dāġh-e ʿishq zīnat-e jeb-e kafan hanoz (68:1; #425)

Think of me not as freed, for like the sun and morning,
The scar of love still adorns the collar of my shroud.

fāriġh: free of; *jeb*: collar.

Even after my death, I am not free from the matters of life and love. Like the connection between the sun and dawn (as they cannot be separated), the scar of love continues to decorate the collar of my shroud. Shroud and morning are both white and the sun is compared to the burning scar. This means that even with life gone, the scars of love continue to shine.

ہے نازِ مفلساں زرِ از دست رفتہ پر
ہوں گل فروشِ شوخیٔ داغِ کہن ہنوز

hai nāz-e muflisāñ zar-e az dast rafta(h) par
hūñ gul farosh-e shoḳhī' dāġh-e kohan hanoz (68:2; #426)

Like a destitute man taking pride in the wealth gone from his hand,
I am still a flower-vendor of the coquetry of my chronic scars.

muflisāñ: poor; *zar*: wealth; *dast rafta(h)*:gone from hand; *dāġh-e kohan:* chronic scars.

Like a destitute man displaying pride in his lost wealth, or a flower-vendor talking about the good flowers he has sold, I too am showing the sparkle of my chronic wounds like a flower-vendor. My assets were the wounds given to me by my beloved, but they are now gone for she no longer hurts me. I am filled with pride talking about the pleasures of the good old days, telling everyone how good it used to be, while showing them the chronic scars in my heart.

مے خانۂ جگر میں یہاں خاک بھی نہیں
خمیازہ کھینچے ہے بُتِ بیداد فن ہنوز

mai ķhāna(h)' jigar meñ yahāñ ķhāk bhī nahiñ
ķhamyāza(h) khinche hai but-e bedād fan hanoz (68:3; #427)

In the tavern of liver, there is not even dust left.
The idol, bent on tyranny, however, is still stretching in hangover.

ķhāk bhī nahiñ: not even dust left; *ķhamyāza(h) khainch*: to stretch, yawn; *but-e bedād fan*: an idol bent on tyranny.

In the tavern of my liver, even the dust is gone which means that not a drop of blood is left. Even so, that tyrannical idol is yawning in a hangover, asking for more wine, which is my blood. I have given all my blood without sparing a drop. There is nothing left to give her. "Not even dust left," means also that nothing is left. It is all dried out.

69

حریفِ مطلبِ مُشکل نہیں فُسُونِ نیاز
دُعا قبول ہو یارب، کہ عُمرِ خِضر دراز

ḥarīf-e maṯlab-e mushkil nahiñ fusūn-e niyāz
du'ā qubūl ho yārabb, kih u'mr-e Ḳhiẓr darāz (69:1; #428)

The chants of humility no longer resolve my problems;
May the prayers be accepted, O! Lord that *Khizr* lives a long life!

ḥarīf: opponent; *fusūn-e niyāz*: chant of humility, offerings; *'umr-e Ḳhiẓr darāz:* may *Ḳhiẓr* have long life (*a fait accompli*).

My humble prayers were not strong enough to resolve the predicament I am in. Let us pray for a long life for *Haẓrat Ḳhiẓr* (legend: *Ḳhiẓr* lives forever), for that is something that is already achieved. By praying for that, at least one of my prayers will be answered. This illustrates an extreme situation of hopelessness; all other aspirations have gone to waste regardless of the efforts made. *Ġhālib* has frequently used the story of *Ḳhiẓr* to express many thoughts (see Glossary).

نہ ہو، بہ ہرزہ، بیاباں نُوردِ وہمِ وُجُود
ہنُوز تیرے تصوّر میں ہے نشیب و فراز

na(h) ho, ba(h) hirza(h), bayābāñ navard-e vahm-e vujūd
hanūz tere taṣavvur meñ hai nasheb-o-farāz (69:2; #429)

Wander not aimlessly in the wilderness of doubts about your existence.
Many peaks and valleys are yet to come in your thoughts.

ba(h) hirza(h): futile; *bayābāñ*: desert, wilderness; *navard*: wander; *vahm*: imagination, doubts; *vujūd*: existence; *hanūz*: yet; *taṣavvur*: imagination, fancy; *nasheb-o-farāz*: rise and fall, peaks and valleys.

Do not wander in futility trying to decipher the sources of your existence. There are many ups and downs in your thinking to come. Like the wandering dust of desire that goes nowhere, do not waste your time deciphering doubts about existence. There remain many stages of learning before you can even begin to understand it all and you are just a beginner.

وصال جلوہ تماشا ہے، پر دماغ کہاں
کہ دیجے آئنۂ انتظار کو پرواز

viṣāl jalva(h) tamāshā hai, par damāġh kahāñ
kih dīje ā'īna(h)' intiẓār ko parvāz (69:3; #430)

Union with beloved brings dazzling display but where is the resolve
To give polish to the mirror of waiting?

jalva(h) tamāshā: display of dazzling beauty; *parvāz*: polish.

Undoubtedly, union with the beloved will prove a thing of beauty never seen before, but waiting for the moment to arrive is intolerable. Polishing the crystal ball to see what is in our future is too frustrating. Elsewhere *Ġhālib* writes, "Who lives long enough to win your tresses?"

ہر ایک ذرۂ عاشق ہے آفتاب پرست
گئی نہ خاک ہوئے پر ہوائے جلوۂ ناز

har ek żarra(h)' `āshiq hai āftāb parast
ga'ī na(h) ḳhāk hu'e par havāe jalva(h) nāz (69:4; #431)

Every particle of lover's ashes is worshipping the sun;
Though reduced to dust, the desire to see the display of beauty remained.

āftāb parast: sun worshipper; *havāe jalva(h) nāz*: desire to see display of her grace.

Dead and reduced to ashes, each particle of the lover's dust is still worshipping the sun, drawing its sparkle from its light. In Sufi teachings, dust particles are still desirous of merging with the whole. In corporeal terms, the dust is still crying for the display of the beloved to make it shine more. To become illuminated is the reason for the particles to float around randomly. Note that an object shines only when light falls on it. The light on a particle would fall if it faces a bright object, like the face of beloved.

نہ پوچھ وسعتِ مےخانۂ جنوں غالب
جہاں یہ کاسۂ گردوں ہے ایک خاک انداز

na(h) pūchh vus̀at-e ma'i ḳhāna(h)' junūñ Ġhālib
jahāñ yih kāsa(h)' gardūñ hai ek ḳhāk andāz (69:5; #432)

Ask not about the expanse of the tavern of lunacy, *Ġhālib*.
Compared to this, the bowl of heaven is merely a dustbin.

kāsa(h) gardūñ: bowl of heaven; *ḳhāk andāz*: dust bag.

The size of the tavern of frenzy can be judged by comparing it with heaven. Shaped like a bowl, heaven is so small that we could only collect in it the dust of the tavern to throw away. Comparing the bowl of heaven to a bowl of wine and then using it to collect dust, to which we will all be reduced eventually, is a remarkable thought. Heaven may be a place for the dust of humans, yet it does not compare to what the bowl of wine is to me.

70

وسعتِ سعیِ کرم دیکھ کہ سرتا سرِ خاک
گزرے ہے آبلہ پا ابرِ گہربار ہنوز

vusʿat-e saʿī-e karam, dekh kih sar tā sar-e ḳhāk
guzre hai ābla(h) pā abr-e gohar bār hanūz (70:1; #433)

Look at the expanse of His benevolence, that all around the world,
The wandering clouds with blistered feet are showering pearls.

vusʿat: expanse, grandiose; *saʿī*: endeavor; *karam*: kindness, benevolence; *sar ta sar-e ḳhāk*: entire earth; *ābla(h) pā*: feet with water blisters; *gohar bār*: pearl giving; *hanūz*: yet.

Look at the boundless endeavor and benevolence of the Almighty—the clouds wandering into the distance. Blisters on their feet (filled with water), they shower us with pearls (raindrops) for the benefit of the entire earth. Wandering clouds with water blisters on their feet is indeed a remarkable comparison to the wandering of lovers.

یک قلم کاغذِ آتش زدہ ہے صفحۂ دشت
نقشِ پا میں ہے تبِ گرمیٔ رفتار ہنوز

yak qalam kāġhaż-e ātish zada(h) hai ṣafa(ḥ)' dasht
naqsh-e pā meñ hai tab-e garmī' raftār hanūz (70:2; #434)

The pages of wilderness are like paper burned through.
In the footprints there is still the strength of heady pace.

yak qalam: throughout, altogether; *kāġhaz*: paper.

Like the dark spots on paper as it burns, you can see the burning footmarks, the tracks in the desert, which I traversed with great speed, and still have the energy for wandering. The delicate comparison made here requires understanding of how paper burns. It creates patches shaped like random footmarks. The mention of agility and speed signifies a desperate run to find the beloved. The desert is the burnt paper with the footmarks. Pen, paper, marks, heat, and fire are all remarkably aligned.

71

کیوں کر اُس بُت سے رکھوں جان عزیز
کیا نہیں ہے مجھے ایمان عزیز

kioñ kar us but se rakhūñ jān ʿazīz
kyā nahīñ hai mujhe imān ʿazīz (71:1; #435)

How can I keep my life saved from that idol?
Is not my belief dear to me?

If I keep myself protected from her torments, she will certainly take away my belief; meaning, that if I came to believe in that idol, I would become an idolater, which is against the belief of "believers." That is a superficial meaning. It really means that my true faith and belief is to give my life to her. How then can I even think of keeping my life safe from her?

دل سے نکلا، پہ نہ نکلا دل سے
ہے ترے تیر کا پیکان عزیز

dil se niklā, pa(h) na(h) niklā dil se
hai tere tīr kā paikān ʿaziz (71:2; #436)

It came out of my heart, but it did not leave my heart.
The tip of your arrow is most dear to me.

paikān: tip.

The arrow of your amorous glance pierced right through my heart. The sweet agony keeps reminding me of you. It is as if the tip of the arrow were still in my heart. I continue to cherish this thought. When the arrow enters the heart, the greatest damage and hence the pain is caused by its piercing tip.

تاب لائے ہی بنے گی غالب
واقعہ سخت ہے اور جان عزیز

tāb lāe hī bane gī Ġhālib
vāq'iah saḳht hai āur jān 'aziz (71:3; #437)

Tolerate, you must somehow, *Ġhālib* !
The incident is indeed unbearable but then life is dear, too.

tāb: tolerate.

The incident is difficult to bear and it seems that the only solution is to die, but then life is also dear to me. I must, therefore, persevere rather than give up. Live with courage; that is the message here. The incident, of course, is falling in love.

72

نہ گلِ نغمہ ہوں، نہ پردۂ ساز　　میں ہوں اپنی شکست کی آواز

na(h) gul-e nāġhma(h) huñ, na(h) parda(h)' sāz
maiñ hūñ apnī shikast kī āvāz (72:1; #438)

I am neither a pleasant melody nor I am the musical chord.
I am the sound of my own broken-self.

gul-e nāġhma(h): happy song, pleasant song; *parda(h) sāz*: a musical note, a chord.

I am neither a pleasant melody nor I am an organized sound of a musical instrument. I am merely a sound of my own breaking. The sound of things breaking is not a pleasant one; there is no rhythm in it. A pleasant melody is made up of the musical chords. I am neither. Picasso depicted the same thought in his painting *Scream*. If you think of me as sound, I have no rhythm and no one likes hearing me for I am unpleasant. I am just a broken man expressing abrupt thoughts. Mostly, this verse is misinterpreted as: I no longer rejoice in the festivities.

تو اور آرائشِ خمِ کاکل

میں اور اندیشہ ہائے دور و دراز

تُو اور آرائشِ خمِ کاکل   مَیں اور اندیشہ ہائے دُور دراز

tū āur ārāi'sh-e ḳham-e kākul
maiñ aur andesha(h) hāi dūr darāz (72:2; #439)

There is you and your adorning the curls of your tresses?
Here am I and my apprehensions of the distant future!

ārāi'sh: adorning, applying make up; *ḳham*: curves, curls; *kākul*: tresses; *dūr*: remote, far; *andesha(h)*: fear of something happening.

While my beloved is engrossed in adorning the curls in her tresses, I am lost in the fear of the distant future, a time when my beloved will lose her beauty. Will I still be able to experience sheer joy upon looking at her playing with her tresses? An extremely meaningful verse, it does not refer to fearing the loss of beauty; it refers to whether I will still enjoy her company then. The use of the word "fear" here means fear of something happening that is not supposed to happen. The beloved would lose her beauty and one cannot be fearful of it. Whether I would continue to enjoy looking at her is the fear here, because the joy of the present is over-riding. The poet is not able to relish the moment for the "fear" of losing it in the future. Many interpreters leave "fear" unexplained.

لافِ تمکیں، فریبِ سادہ دِلی   ہم ہیں اور رازہائے سینہ گداز

lāf-e tamkīñ, fareb-e sāda(h) dilī
ham haiñ aur rāz hāi sīna(h) gudāz (72:3; #440)

Boasting of self-control is a deception of foolish hearts.
For here we are with our chest full of secrets that melt hearts.

lāf: boasting; *tamkīñ*: control; *fareb*: deception; *sada(h)*: simple; *sīna(h)*: chest.

My boasting that I can hide my feelings is indeed foolish. The secret buried in my chest, that I am in love, will come out anyway. People will come to know sooner or later. How long can I hide it?

ہوں گرفتارِ اُلفتِ صیّاد   ورنہ باقی ہے طاقتِ پرواز

huñ giraftār-e ulfat-e ṣaiyyād
varna(h) bāqī hai ṭāqat-e parvāz (72:4; #441)

I am caught in the love of the bird catcher;
Otherwise, I do have the strength to fly away.

ṣaiyyād: bird catcher, hunter, fowler; *parvāz*: flight.

I am strong enough to break the strings of the snare and free myself, but my love for the beloved keeps me enticed and in bondage to her. We all have the strength to get out of the things that keep us tied down, but our love for them, particularly the love of material things, keeps us tied to them. The tone of the verse is apologetic. The beloved is addressed as a bird catcher or fowler to make the use of "fly," in the verse.

وُہ بھی دِن ہو کہ اُس ستمگر سے   ناز کھینچوں بجائے حسرتِ ناز

vuh bhī din ho kih us sitamgar se
nāz khainchūñ bajāe ḥasrat-e nāz (72:5; #442)

I hope the day will come when from that tormentor;
I shall get coquetry rather than just hoping for it desperately.

The poet is hoping that someday he will receive her coquetry instead of simply longing for it.

نہیں دل میں مرے وہ قطرۂ خوں   جس سے مژگاں ہُوئی نہ ہو گل باز

nahiñ dil meñ mere vuh qaṭra(h)' ḳhūñ
jis se mizhgāñ hu'ī na(h) ho gul bāz (72:6; #443)

Not present in my heart is that drop of blood,
With which my eyelashes have not played the game of tossing flowers.

gul bāz: one who plays with flowers.

Crying tears of blood, the eyelashes think of them as flowers and play with them. I have already shed my last drop of blood. Flowers are red like blood, and blood as it flows out is referred to as the eyelashes playing with flowers, tossing them around as they flutter.

اے ترا غمزہ، یک قلم انگیز   اے ترا ظلم، سربسر انداز

ai terā ġhamza(h), yak qalam angez
ai terā zulm, sar basar andāz (72:7; #444)

O! Your amorous glances altogether exciting.
O! Your cruelty altogether full of style!

yak qalam: all together; *angez*: exciting; *sar basar:* from head to toe.

O' Beloved, I have to bear it all: your exciting amorous glances and your cruelty, full of pride, coquetry and style.

تو ہوا جلوہ گر، مبارک ہو   ریزشِ سجدۂ جبینِ نیاز

tū hu'ā jalva(h) gar, mubārak ho
rezish-e sajda(h)' jabīn-e niyāz (72:8; #445)

You have displayed your beauty. Congratulations to
The forehead that fell into supplication in humbleness.

rezish: to fall.

It is the fortune of my forehead that it got a chance to thank you by supplicating to your beauty when it was displayed.

مجھ کو پوچھا تو کچھ غضب نہ ہوا　　میں غریب اور تو غریب نواز

mujh ko pūchhā to kuchh ġhaẓab na(h) hu'ā
maiñ ġharīb aur tū ġharīb navāz (72:9; #446)

If you inquired about me, it was no big event.
I am a poor wayfarer and you are the caretaker of the poor.

ġhaẓab: anger, wrath, rage, indignation.

Because you normally take care of people, it was no big event or favor when you asked how I was doing.

اسد اللہ خاں تمام ہوا
اے دریغا! وہ رندِ شاہد باز

Asad Ulla(h) Ḳhāñ tamām hu'ā
ai direġhā! vuh rind-e shāhid bāz (72:10; #447)

***Asad Ullah Ḳhān* has passed away.**
Alas! That wine addict and womanizer!

direġhā: alas; *rind:* drunkard*;* *shāhid bāz*: whoremonger, womanizer.

Now that *Asad Ullah Ḳhān* (presented very formally to address himself) is gone, who will fill his shoes? *Ġhālib* was a drunkard who chased women. Many interpreters have diluted the choice of words made in the second line whereby the poet is labeled merely a lover of beautiful women; in real meaning *Ġhālib* is insulting himself.

73

مژدہ، اے ذوقِ اسیری کہ نظر آتا ہے
دامِ خالی قفسِ مرغِ گرفتار کے پاس

muzhda(h), ai żauq-e asīrī kih naẓar ātā hai
dām ḳhālī qafas-e murġh-e giraftār ke pās (73:1; #448)

Felicitations! O! Longing for captivity, it appears that
The net is empty near the cage of the bait-bird.

muzhda(h): good news; *żauq-e asīrī*: desire to be caught; *dām*: net, snare; *murġh-e giraftār*: bait bird.

It is good that the net of the beloved is empty as she is enticing you. By using the bait of a captive bird, she shows that if others can survive, so can you. There is a possibility of receiving much kindness from her being the first lover. This is one of those verses that create an unusual melancholic feeling in the reader's heart, everytime it is recited.

جگرِ تشنۂ آزار تسلی نہ ہوا
جوئے خوں ہم نے بہائی بنِ ہر خار کے پاس

jigar-e tashna(h)' āzār tasallī na(h) hu'ā
jūe ḳhūñ ham ne bahā'ī bun-e har ḳhār ke pās (73:2; #449)

The liver thirsty for more torment was not satisfied,
Though we let out a river of blood at the root of every thorny bush.

jigar-e tashna(h) āzār: liver thirsty for more pain; *bun-e har ḳhār*: root of every thorny bush.

The poet's liver was crying for more torment. It was wandering around seeking to get entangled in thorny bushes so that it could bleed into their roots. This means that the liver wanted to get bruised by the thorny bushes so that it would bleed profusely. However, this, too, wasn't sufficient. The liver wished to be satisfied with its desire for torment. What more can be asked and what more can be had?

مُند گئیں کھولتے ہی کھولتے آنکھیں ہے ہے
خُوب وقت آئے تُم اِس عاشقِ بیمار کے پاس

mund ga'iñ kholte hī kholte āñkheñ hai hai
ḳhūb vaqt āe tum is ʿāshiq-e bīmār ke pās (73:3; #450)

The eyes closed despite much effort to keep them open. Alas! Alas!
What good time you chose to come to see your sick lover.

mund: closed.

Weakness of age and the hardship of torment had left the poet with little energy. It was difficult to even keep his eyes open when the beloved arrived. He moaned, "You should have come sooner."

مَیں بھی رُک رُک کے نہ مرتا، جو زباں کے بدلے
دشنہ اک تیز سا ہوتا مرے غمخوار کے پاس

maiñ bhī ruk ruk ke na(h) martā, jo zabāñ ke badle
dashna(h) ik tez sā hotā mere ġhamḳh(v)ār ke pās (73:4; #451)

I would not have died so slowly, if, instead of that sharp tongue,
There had been a sharp dagger held by my consoler.

zabāñ: (harsh) tongue; *dashna(h)*: dagger; *ġhamḳh(v)ār*: consoler.

At the time of death, my friends, who are supposed to share my grief, are telling me how foolish it was of me to reach this pathetic stage. This is very painful to me, like death itself. I wish they had a sharp dagger instead of a sharp tongue with which to kill me with one sharp blow, to relieve me of the pain, proving that they have indeed come to alleviate my pain.

دہنِ شیر میں جا بیٹھیے لیکن اَے دِل
نہ کھڑے ہُوجیے خُوبانِ دِل آزار کے پاس

dahn-e sher meñ jā baiṭhiye lekin āe dil
na(h) khaṛe hūjiye ḳhūbān-e dil āzār ke pās (73:5; #452)

Go sit in the mouth of a lion, but O! Heart!
Stand not close to the beauties that devastate heart.

Sitting in the mouth of a lion will cause sudden death; the beloved, though, will kill you slowly with much more torment. A straightforward lesson is given to novice lovers.

دیکھ کر تجھ کو، چمن بسکہ نمُو کرتا ہے
خود بخود پہنچے ہے گل گوشۂ دستار کے پاس

dekh kar tujh ko, chaman baske numū kartā hai
ḳhud baḳhud pahuñche hai gul gosha(h)' dastār ke pās (73:6; #453)

Looking at you, the garden just begins to sprout.
Of their own accord, the flowers reach to touch the edge of your turban.

numū karnā: to grow; *gosha(h)*: edge; *dastār*: turban.

The sight of the beloved provides much freshness to the garden which begins to grow so fast that the flowers reach the height of the turban;

meaning that the plants that bear flowers have suddenly grown from a bush to the height of a tree.

مر گیا پھوڑ کے سر غالبِ وحشی ہے ہے!
بیٹھنا اُس کا وہ آ کر تری دیوار کے پاس

mar gayā phoṛ ke sar Ġhālib-e vaḥshī, hai hai
baiṭhnā us kā vuh ākar terī divār ke pās (73:7; #454)

He killed himself by smashing his head, that lunatic *Ġhālib*, Alas! Alas!
How he used to come and sit by your wall.

Remembering how *Ġhālib* used to come and sit by the wall of the beloved's house has deep meaning here. "Come and sit," makes it expressive whereas without "coming" it would just mean someone sitting. *Ġhālib* used to come and sit there, hoping to hear a word or two from the beloved or to catch a glimpse of her. Totally frustrated he finally banged his head against the wall and killed himself.

74

نہ لیوے گر خسِ جوہر طراوت سبزۂ خط سے
لگا دے خانۂ آئینہ میں رُوئے نگار آتش

na(h) leve gar ḳhas-e johar ṯarāvat sabza(h)'-e ḳhaṯ se
lagā de ḳhana(h)' ā'ina(h) meñ rū'e nigār ātish (74:1; #455)

If the straws of the mirror not imbibe the moisture from the greenery of down on the face,
The blazing countenance of my beloved's face would have put the house of mirror on fire.

ḳhas: grass, straw; *ṯarāvat:* wetness, moisture; *sabza(h)'-e ḳhaṯ*: the green tinge of hair (down) growing on the face of a youth; *ḳhaṯ*: first growth of moustache and beard in a youth, down on the face of youth; *rū'e nigār*: face of beloved; *johar*: mirror coating that appears as lines in iron mirrors and in this verse, these lines are called the straw.

The face of my beloved is so fiery that if she looks into the mirror the shiny coating of the mirror will be set on fire. However, because of the greening of the face (which illustrates a cooling effect), the straw in the mirror has been saved because the straw of the mirror has taken moisture from the face. The source of moisture is the greenish tinge (like green grass) appearing on beloved's youthful face because of the arrival of down. The straws of the mirror are the lines in the mirror that are left when the mirror is coated. If the beloved had not lost her attractiveness, this would have destroyed the universe (house of mirrors). The beloved here could well be a male (see Glossary: male beloved). This verse is full of plays on words. Straw, greenery, moisture, fire, mirror, and shine are all present here in a very complex portrayal of the beloved.

فروغِ حسن سے ہوتی ہے حلِ مشکلِ عاشق
نہ نکلے شمع کے پا سے، نکالے گر نہ خار آتش

furoġh-e ḥusn se hotī hai ḥall-e mushkil-e ʿāshiq
na(h) nikle shamaʿ ke pā se, nikāle gar na(h) ḳhār ātish (74:2; #456)

The luminous splendor of her beauty resolves the difficulties of the lovers.
It would not come out of the feet of the candle if the flame did not remove the thorn.

furoġh: brightness, splendor, illumination; *ḳhār*: wick, thorn.

The bright splendor of beauty resolves many difficulties of lovers; it removes the thorn of desperation from their hearts. A candle cannot produce a flame without the wick, which is called a thorn in the candle. The candle and the wick both burn which removes the thorn (wick) when the candle melts completely. The foot of the candle is the rosette of wax remaining after the candle has burnt down. Witnessing the splendor of beauty removes the thorn from the heart of lovers. They melt just as a molten candle that carries no thorn.

75

جادۂ رہ خور کو وقتِ شام ہے تارِ شعاع
چرخ وا کرتا ہے ماہِ نو سے آغوشِ وداع

jāda(h)' rah ḳhor ko vaqt-e shām hai tār-e shuaʿ
charḳh vā kartā hai māh-e nau se āġhosh-e vidāʿ (75:1; #457)

A ray of lights marks the track that the sun treks at dusk
As the sky opens its arms with the display of the crescent to bid it farewell.

jāda(h): path; *ḳhor*: sun; *charḳh*: heaven; *vā karnā*: to open; *vidāʿ*: farewell.

A ray of evening sun delineates the path the sun would take to set. At the same time, the crescent appears in the sky with its curved shape as if heaven were extending its open arms to bid farewell to the sun. The poet is moved by the scene of a sunset.

76

رُخِ نگار سے ہے سوزِ جاودانیِ شمع
ہوئی ہے آتشِ گُل، آبِ زندگانیِ شمع

rukh-e nigār se hai soz-e jāvedānī' shamà
hu'ī hai ātish-e gul, āb-e zindigānī' shamà (76:1; #458)

The radiant face of beloved gives to the candle a perennial burning.
The pink fire of her cheeks gives the water of life to the candle.

rukh: face; *nigār*: beloved; *soz*: burning; *jāvidānī:* perpetual, perennial; *ātish-e gul*: pink complexion of the beloved, fire of flowers.

The candle burns, out of jealousy, after having seen my beloved's beautiful face. The pink cheeks of my beloved have thus given the candle the gift of life—since a candle must burn to stay alive. See the simultaneous use of burning, candle, fiery cheeks, and water for life.

زبانِ اہلِ زباں میں ہے مرگ خاموشی
یہ بات بزم میں روشن ہوئی زبانیِ شمع

zabān-e ahl-e zabāñ meñ hai marg khāmoshī
yih bāt bazm meñ roshan hu'ī zabānī' shamà (76:2; #459)

In the usage of the masters of language, death is silence.
This became illuminated in the assembly through the tongue of the candle.

Those who call death "silence" have learned it by looking at a candle. A candle is considered "silenced" when put out and "alive" when lit, for its light keeps assembly alive. Notices that a candle flame, which is called a tongue here, is shaped like a tongue.

کرے ہے صرف بہ ایمائے شعلہ، قصّہ تمام
بطرزِ اہلِ فنا ہے فسانہ خوانیٔ شمع

kare hai ṣirf ba(h) īmāʾe shoʿla(h), qiṣṣa(h) tamām
baṭarz-e ahl-e fanā hai fasānā(h) ḳh(v)ānīʾ shamaʿ (76:3; #460)

The candle, just at the hint of flame, ends the story.
Which is like the story of self-annihilators, as the candle relates it.

īmāʾ: belief, faith; *shoʿla(h):* flame; *qiṣṣa(h):* tale; *tamām*: end; *ṭarz*: manner; *fasāna(h):* romance, tale; *shamaʿ*: candle.

Through the tongue of the flame the candle concludes its story by illustrating that it is being burnt and destroyed. The flame represents sadness and its shape is that of a tongue. The candle is using the flame, which, in turn, is the cause of her destruction, to tell her story. Just like the lovers who burn themselves in the fire of love, the candle's life is sacrificial to its flame. This is a very delicate concept indeed.

غم اُس کو حسرتِ پروانہ کا ہے اے شعلہ!
ترے لرزنے سے ظاہر ہے ناتوانیٔ شمع

ġham us ko ḥasrat-e parvāna(h) kā hai ai shoʿla(h)
tere larazne se ẓāhir hai nātavānīʾ shamaʿ (76:4; #461)

Bearing the grief of the unfulfilled longings of the moth,
O! Flame,
The weakness of the candle is revealed from your flickering.

laraznā: flickering.

The flickering of the candle flame displays its weakness because of the sorrow it feels—the sorrow comes from knowing the desperate desire of the moth to immolate itself in the flame.

ترے خیال سے رُوح اہتزاز کرتی ہے
بہ جلوہ ریزیٔ باد و بہ پرفشانیٔ شمع

tere ḳhayāl se rūḥ ihtizāz kartī hai
ba(h) jalva(h) rezī' bād-o ba(h) purfishānī' shamaʿ (76:5; #462)

The soul begins to swirl in ecstasy with your thought,
Like the blowing wind swirling the flame of candle.

ihtizāz: movement as in ecstasy (swirling in ecstasy); *jalva(h) rezī bād*: wind blowing; *purfishānī shamaʿ*: swirling of flame of candle.

Just as your thought gives me the energy to swirl with joy, the wind does the same to the flame; it shoots the flame. The blowing winds flickering the flame of the candle is what your thought does to my soul.

نشاطِ داغِ غمِ عشق کی بہار نہ پوچھ
شگفتگی ہے شہیدِ گلِ خزانیٔ شمع

nishāṯ-e dāġh-e ġham-e ʿishq kī bahār na(h) pūchh
shuguftagī hai shahid-e gul-e ḳhizānī' shamaʿ (76:6; #463)

Ask not about the blooming ecstasy of the scars of love's grief,
As it envies the freshness of the rosette of a burnt-out candle.

shuguftagī: freshness; *gul-e ḳhizānī-e shamaʿ*: the autumn flower of candle; meaning the rosette of wax remaining after the candle burns out completely.

The freshness of my branded heart is envious of the freshness of the rosette of wax left behind after the candle burns out—meaning to show how dried out or desperate is lover's heart. This brings great joy to the lover. The delicate description in this verse comes from an unusual play of words: spring season (excessive joy), autumn flower of candle (to indicate dryness), and a comparison of heart's freshness (moisture) to that of a burnt-out candle.

جلے ہے دیکھ کے بالینِ یار پر مجھ کو
نہ کیوں ہو دِل پہ مرے داغِ بدگمانیٔ شمع

jale hai dekh ke bālīn-e yār par mujh ko
na(h) kioñ ho dil pa(h) mere dāġh-e badgumānī' shamà (76:7; #464)

It burns with jealousy, finding me by her bedside.
Why would not my heart bear the scar of suspicion for the candle?

bālīñ: by the headrest of bed.

The lover is standing by the beloved's bedside and this causes the candle to become jealous, which hurts the poet. Why should it hurt? Because ultimately the fate of the poet is the same as that of the candle: it is uncomfortable to burn and to see those sharing the same fate being distrustful.

77

بیمِ رقیب سے نہیں کرتے وِداعِ ہوش
مجبُور، یاں تلک ہُوئے اے اِختیار حَیف

bīm-e raqīb se nahiñ karte vidā̀-e hosh
majbūr, yāñ talak hu'e ai ikhtiyār ḥaif (77:1; #465)

For the fear of the rival, I do not let my senses go.
O! Self control, what shame it is that we are so constrained?

bīm-e raqīb: fear of rival; *vidā̀-e hosh*: bidding farewell to senses; *ikhtiyār:* control.

I wanted to lose my senses and become a lunatic, but I did not for fear of my rival. That indicates how much control I have left over myself. The fear of the rival can be for two reasons. First, if I lose my sanity, the rival may take advantage of the beloved. Secondly, it will cause embarrassment to my beloved because my rival and others would know how much I love her.

جلتا ہے دِل کہ کیوں نہ ہم اِک بار جل گئے
اَے ناتمامئ نَفَسِ شُعلہ بار حَیف

jaltā hai dil kih kioñ na(h) ham ik bār jal gae
ai nā tamāmī' nafas-e sho'la(h) bār ḥaif (77:2; #466)

My heart sulks why didn't I just get burned once,
O! The incompleteness of the flame-spewing breath; Alas!

My breath spews fire and thus with each breath it burns my heart (sulks). The intensity of fire is not enough to destroy me once, to relieve the pain of slow burning forever.

78

زخم پر چھڑکیں کہاں طفلانِ بے پروا نمک   کیا مزہ ہوتا اگر پتھر میں بھی ہوتا نمک

zaḳhm par chhiṛkeñ kahāñ ṭiflān-e be parvā namak
kyā maza(h) hotā agar patthar meñ bhī hotā namak (78:1; #467)

Why would the careless children sprinkle salt onto my wounds?
What pleasure this would be, had there been salt in stones, as well.

Playful, heedless children are throwing stones at the lover, but what the lover wants is salt to rub into his present wounds —not new wounds, for he already has enough. He is wishing that there were salt in the stones thrown at him to enhance his pleasure. He has no hope that the children will have been thoughtful enough to bring him salt.

گردِ راہِ یار ہے سامانِ نازِ زخمِ دل   ورنہ ہوتا ہے جہاں میں کس قدر پیدا نمک

gard-e rāh-e yār hai sāmān-e nāz-e zaḳhm-e dil
varna(h) hotā hai jahāñ meñ kis qadar paidā namak (78:2; #468)

The dust of the beloved's alley is a means of pride for the heart's wounds.
Or else from where on earth would come so much salt?

For the wounded heart, it is a matter of pride that it has access to the dust of the beloved's alley. This dust, when filled into wounds, brings extreme pain and takes away any hope of healing. There is not enough salt anywhere else in the world to bring the same pain and same comfort. The dust of the beloved's alley is more potent. A careful interpretation is required here. The poet is saying that the potency of the dust of the beloved's alley is so strong that there is not enough salt in the world to match it. Another noteworthy point is that filling wounds with dust makes it difficult for the wound to heal.

مجھ کو ارزانی رہے، تجھ کو مُبارک ہو جیو نالۂ بلبل کا درد اور خندۂ گل کا نمک

mujh ko arzānī rahe, tujh ko mubārak ho jīo
nāla(h)-e bulbul kā dard āur ḳhanda(h)' gul kā namak (78:3; #469)

May I keep getting it abundantly? May you go on living!
The pain of the nightingale's cry and the salt in the laughter of flowers.

arzānī rahe: keep getting freely; *ḳhanda(h)-e gul*: blooming of flowers (laughter of flowers).

The four parts of the verse need to be reconnected transversely. "May I keep getting the pain of the nightingale's cry" and "may you (the beloved) go on living with salt in your laughter." Why does the nightingale cry at the blooming of flowers? It is because she knows that the association is temporary; soon the spring will be gone and she will no longer see the flowers. Your laughter sprinkles salt onto my wounds. May you live long to continue doing so! The blooming of flowers is called the laughter of flowers. The poet wishes to have more pain like the nightingale to which the laughter (blooming) of the flowers acts as salt. Like the nightingale, the poet also knows that he may not hear the laughter of the beloved for long.

شورِ جولاں تھا کنارِ بحر پر کس کا کہ آج گردِ ساحل ہے بہ زخمِ موجۂ دریا نمک

shor-e jaulāñ thā kanār-e baḥar par kis kā kih āj
gard-e sāḥil hai ba(h) zaḳhm-e mauja(h)' daryā namak (78:4; #470)

Who had created the noise of a galloping horse on the seashore today
That the sand of the ocean beach has become the salt to the wounds of the waves?

shor-e jaulāñ: noise of running horses; *kanār*: shore; *gard*: dust; *sāḥil*: beach; *zaḳhm*: wound; *mauj*: wave; *daryā*: river, here taken as ocean because of the salt comparison.

My beloved comes crashing in. Her horse has kicked the sand on the beach, which proved to be salt on the wounds of the ocean's tides. The ocean is made to feel jealous and hurt when it sees the agility of the beloved on the running horse. This is an unusual comparison of the agility of the beloved and the agility of the ocean waves. Note that the ocean water is already salty; sprinkling salt onto its wounds is a remarkable extension of thought in the virtual context. The opening of waves is also compared to an open wound. As the waves roll over, it appears to be the lips of a wound parting.

داد دیتا ہے مرے زخمِ جگر کی واہ واہ یاد کرتا ہے مجھے، دیکھے ہے وُہ جس جا نمک

dād detā hai mere zaḳhm-e jigar kī, vāh vāh
yād kartā hai mujhe, dekhe hai vuh jis jā namak (78:5; #471)

Bravo! she admires the wounds of my liver,
As she calls me wherever she sees salt.

My beloved knows that no amount of salt is enough for my wounds, so whenever she comes across any pile of salt, she thinks of me and calls me to come satisfy my hunger for more pain. The beloved is praising the voracity of my wounds. We can also write it as "she comes to think of me" whenever she sees salt.

چھوڑ کر جانا تنِ مجروحِ عاشق حیف ہے دِل طلب کرتا ہے زخم اور مانگے ہیں اعضا نمک

chhoṛ kar jānā tan-e majrūḥ-e ʿāshiq ḥaif hai
dil ṭalab kartā hai zaḳhm aur mānge haiñ āʿẓā namak (78:6; #472)

It would be regrettable to leave the smitten body of the lover alone.
As the heart demands wounds while the other body organs ask for salt.

tan-e majrūḥ: wounded body; *aʿẓā*: body parts.

The beloved has wounded the lover, but now the wounds demand salt to increase the pain. The body has been wounded so the heart now demands to be wounded, too. This means that no pain the beloved has given is enough; more is needed.

غیر کی مِنّت نہ کھینچوں گا پئے توفیرِ درد　　زخم مثلِ خندۂ قاتل ہے سَر تا پا نمک

ġhair kī minnat na(h) khechūñ gā paī' taufīr dard
zaḳhm misl-e ḳhanda(h)' qātil hai sar tā pā namak (78:7; #473)

I shall not take the obligation of any stranger to enhance my pain.
My wounds like the grin of the slayer are completely filled with salt.

ġhair: stranger; *minnat khenchnā*: to not take an obligation; *taufīr*: to increase, enhance; *ḳhanda(h)*: smile; *qātil*: killer.

I shall not ask any stranger to help me enhance the pain of my wound (which resembles the parted lips of her smile). It is filled with salt and it is not possible to make it any more painful. A stranger can enhance my pain by laughing at me, but that is not necessary for my wound is the butt of the beloved's jokes. This alone provides me with perpetual pain. Notice how *Ġhālib* compares the opening of a wound to laughter.

یاد ہیں غالب تجھے وہ دن کہ وجدِ ذوق میں
زخم سے گرتا تو مَیں پلکوں سے چُنتا تھا نمک

yād haiñ Ġhālib tujhe vuh din kih vajd-e żauq meñ
zaḳhm se girtā to maiñ palkoñ se chuntā thā namak (78:8; #474)

O! *Ġhālib* ! Do you remember those days of ecstasy of desire
When you used to pick up the salt falling off your wounds with your eyelashes?

By pointing to an anecdote that warns those who waste salt have to pick it up with their eyelashes on the Day of Judgment, *Ġhālib* describes his desire to not lose a single grain of salt, for it is needed to keep wounds fresh. Ironically, however, he is not doing it to be spared punishment on the Day of Judgment.

79

آہ کو چاہیے اک عمر اثر ہوتے تک　　کون جیتا ہے تری زلف کے سر ہوتے تک

āh ko chāhiye ik ʿumr as̱ar hote tak
kaun jītā hai teri zulf ke sar hote tak (79:1; #475)

It takes a lifetime for the sighs to have any effect.
Who would ever live long enough to win your tresses?

Sighs unheeded will take a lifetime to be heard. I will be long gone before I could woo and win your love. "To win tresses," means to win the beloved and "to unwind them." The lover can only see her unwinding her tresses when he is close to her, and it will take a lifetime to reach that stage. The beloved would never let the poet come so close and would never let him win her heart. Some have interpreted this to mean union with the beloved.

دام ہر موج میں ہے حلقۂ صد کام نہنگ　　دیکھیں کیا گزرے ہے قطرے پہ گہر ہوتے تک

dām har mauj meñ hai ḥalqa(h)ʾ ṣad kām-e nahang
dekheiñ kyā guzre hai qaṭre pa(h) gohar hote tak (79:2; #476)

The gaping mouths of a hundred crocodiles make the rings of snares of every wave.
See what a drop goes through before turning into a pearl.

kām-e nahang: throat of crocodile.

Crocodiles with open mouths are the snares spread all around us. They are the hazards and challenges of life at every step and it is a miracle that we come out unscathed. Still, we should accept these challenges and keep trekking past them. The destiny of a drop is to turn into a pearl and not return to the coast to be absorbed by the sand and lost forever. We all have goals in life, which require facing extreme hardship to accomplish. We must not complain and we must not turn away from hardships—just like a drop that goes through an ordeal to turn into pearl.

عاشقی صبر طلب اور تمنا بیتاب　　دل کا کیا رنگ کروں خونِ جگر ہوتے تک

ʿāshiqī ṣabr ṭalab āur tamannā betāb
dil kā kyā rang karūñ ḳhūn-e jigar hote tak (79:3; #477)

Love demands patience while the desire remains impatient.
What shall I do with my heart until the liver rend asunder?

dil kā kyā rang karūñ: how shall I color my heart; difficult to translate, it means how shall I handle my heart, how shall I let my heart bleed in the meantime.

Desire's place is in the heart and patience dwells in the liver. Desire tests the patience, making the liver bleed until it is destroyed and then desire takes over. Here the poet wants to know how to handle his heart until patience gives in. Until my liver (patience) bleeds away, how shall I console my heart? Once the liver is gone, I can go ahead with the expression of my desires unabashedly. Note comparing "coloring the heart" with the bleeding of the liver. Here "coloring the heart," means consoling the heart.

ہم نے مانا کہ تغافل نہ کرو گے لیکن　　خاک ہو جائیں گے ہم، تم کو خبر ہوتے تک

ham ne mānā kih taġhāful na(h) karo ge lekin
ḳhāk ho jāeñ ge ham, tum ko ḳhabar hote tak (79:4; #478)

I admit that you will never become indifferent to me, but
I will long be reduced to dust before you come to know of me.

The lover accepts the beloved's promise that she will not ignore him, and yet he is concerned at the same time that unless she first comes to know him, how will she pay any attention to him? Before you come to know who I am, I will be long dead. Here the lover is giving the beloved the benefit of doubt. He accepts that the beloved is not cruel and it is not her fault that she cannot give him any attention. If she does not know who I am, how can she be expected to be attentive to me?

پرتوِ خور سے ہے شبنم کو فنا کی تعلیم   میں بھی ہوں ایک عنایت کی نظر ہوتے تک

partau-e ķhūr se hai shabnam ko fanā kī ta'līm
maiñ bhī hūñ ek 'ināyat kī naẓar hote tak (79:5; #479)

The radiance of the sun teaches the dew, imminence of its extinction.
I, too, shall live only until the gaze of kindness turns towards me.

partau-e ķhūr: radiance of sun.

The dew evaporates into thin air when the rays of sun strike it. This will be the fate of my existence. When she looks at me or when the Lord bestows His kindness on me, I shall then merge with Him, go into extinction, *fanā*, a philosophic rendition of the impermanence of things.

یک نظر بیش نہیں فرصتِ ہستی غافل   گرمیِ بزم ہے اک رقصِ شرر ہوتے تک

yak naẓar besh nahiñ furṣat-e hastī, ġhāfil
garmī' bazm hai ik raqṣ-e sharar hote tak (79:6; #480)

Life's existence does not last beyond the wink of an eye, O! Ignorant!
The life of assembly lasts only for the duration of the dance of the spark.

besh: more; ***furṣat***: time; ***ġhāfil***: ignorant; ***sharar***: spark.

Life, as we see it, is no more than a quick wink of Nature. How ignorant we are that we judge it by our sense of time. What is a hundred years when the Universe has been in existence for billions of years? To us, the warmth of company lasts for days, months, and years, yet it is no more than the lifetime of a spark rising from the flames and disappearing into thin air.

غم ہستی کا اسدؔ کس سے ہو جز مرگ علاج
شمع ہر رنگ میں جلتی ہے سحر ہوتے تک

ġham-e hastī kā Asad kis se ho juz marg ʿilāj
shamaʿ har rang meñ jaltī hai saḥar hote tak (79:7; #481)

O! Asad! What can relieve the grief of life except death?
The candle burns, as it must, till the break of dawn.

Death brings to an end to all the miseries of life just as dawn ends the burning misery of the candle (the candle's pain). Notice the comparison and the use of "it must." We must, while alive, suffer through agony, an oft-repeated theme where *Ġhālib* compares many characteristics of a candle to the lover's life. This verse is a rather melancholic arrangement describing man's helplessness.

80

گر تجھ کو ہے یقینِ اِجابت دُعا نہ مانگ
یعنی بغیر یک دلِ بے مُدّعا نہ مانگ

gar tujh ko hai yaqīn-e ijābat du'ā na(h) māng
ya'nī baġhair yak dil-e be mudda'ā na(h) māng (80:1; #482)

If you are confident of acceptance, then pray for nothing
Except for a heart that is free from desire, ask nothing.

ijābat: to be accepted; *baġhair yak*: without one; *dil-e be mudda'ā*: a heart without desire.

If you are sure that your prayers will be heeded, do not waste your efforts asking for small things. The thing to ask for is a heart that knows no desire. It is only after you are blessed with such a heart that you will no longer need anything else. No matter what you ask for and what you receive, there shall always remain something else to ask for and receive.

آتا ہے داغِ حسرتِ دل کا شُمار یاد
مجھ سے مرے گنہ کا حساب اے خُدا نہ مانگ

ātā hai dāġh-e ḥasrat-e dil kā shumār yād
mujh se mere guna(h) kā ḥisāb ai ḳhudā na(h) māng (80:2; #483)

I come to think of the count of wounds of desperations in my heart.
Ask me not, O! Lord, the account of my sins,

Accounting to God for my long list of sins, I cannot help but recall all the wounds given to me by God during my life. All right, so I drank, but did I get the bliss of union with the beloved? Wasn't this a sufficient punishment for my drinking? The tone of this verse is "do not ask me to open my mouth!" I have committed just as many sins as there are brandings on my heart due to lost hopes—they should balance out.

81

ہے کس قدر ہلاکِ فریبِ وفائے گل　　بلبل کے کاروبار پہ ہیں خندہ ہائے گل

hai kis qadar halāk-e fareb-e vafāe gul
bulbul ke kārobār pa(h) haiñ k̤handa(h) hāi gul (81:1; #484)

How terribly victimized by flower's deception of faithfulness;
The flowers are laughing at the dealings of the nightingale.

halāk: killed, victim.

Flowers that say they love her and are faithful to her deceive the nightingale. In reality, the blooming of flowers is not a sign of welcome to the nightingale. Rather, they are laughing at the nightingale for being gullible. The beloved does not smile to welcome you, instead, she is jeering in jest.

آزادیِ نسیم مبارک کہ ہر طرف　　ٹوٹے پڑے ہیں حلقۂ دامِ ہوائے گل

āzādī' nasīm mubārak kih har t̤araf
t̤ūt̤e par̤e haiñ ḥalqa(h)' dām-e havā-e gul (81:2; #485)

Congratulations! O! Breeze on your freedom, for now all around,
Left broken are the snare-loops of the flowers' desire.

nasīm: breeze; *havāe gul:* desire for flowers.

Breeze should be free to roam around, wafting away the smell of garden flowers. But the flowers do not want their scent to reach the lover, who may be saddened as it will remind him of his beloved. Thus, the breeze is restrained where it can go. As long as there was spring, the breeze was caught in a snare. With spring gone, flowers having withered away, the breeze is now free to roam anywhere. Congratulations! More commonly, this verse is interpreted as follows: "the snare-loops of the flowers' desire" is taken as the scent hidden in flower buds; with the arrival of spring season, the buds have opened (scattering of loops) and thus the snare for the flowers' scent is gone and the scent released into air. The breeze was waiting for this moment and now it can begin to waft the smell all around freely. This verse is an eloquent example of how *Ġhālib* has kept interpreters busy figuring out what he might have meant. Who is caught in the snare—the breeze or the scent of flowers? Who is desirous—the breeze or the flowers?

جو تھا سو موجِ رنگ کے دھوکے میں مر گیا   اے وائے نالۂ لبِ خونیں نوائے گل

jo thā so mauj-e rang ke dhoke meñ mar gayā
ai vāe nāla(h)' lab-e ḳhūniñ navāe gul (81:3; #486)

The one that lasted got killed by the deception of the wave of color.
Alas! The laments of the lips of these flowers now raise blood-filled sighs.

mauj-e rang: wave of color; *dhoke meñ mar gayā*: got killed by deception; *lab-e ḳhūnī navā*: lips raising blood-filled sighs.

The hardy flowers were deceived into thinking that they were immortal. Now they too are lamenting over their demise, raising blood-filled sighs. Those of us who believe that the joys of life are everlasting have a surprise waiting for them. Reality will soon take its toll on us.

خوش حال اُس حریفِ سیہ مست کا کہ جو   رکھتا ہو مثلِ سایۂ گل، سر بہ پائے گل

ḳhush ḥāl us ḥarīf-e siyā(h) mast kā kih jo
rakhtā ho miśl-e sāya(h)' gul, sar ba(h) pāe gul (81:4; #487)

Fortunate is the one who stays extremely intoxicated,
Keeping his head at the feet of flowers like their shadow.

ḥarīf in the same profession, fighting opponent; *siyā(h):* black; *siyā(h) mast:* extremely ecstatic, intoxicated.

Here flower means the beloved. How fortunate is the lover, who, in his deep ecstasy of love, places his head at the feet of the flowers, the beloved. Fortunate is he who follows the beloved so closely that he is like her shadow. A shadow is dark and so shadow refers to "black ecstasy," meaning extreme ecstasy. The shadow of the beloved is intoxicating.

ایجاد کرتی ہے اسے تیرے لیے بہار　　میرا رقیب ہے نفَسِ عطر سائے گل

ijād kartī hai ise tere liye bahār
merā raqīb hai nafas-e ʿiṭr sāe gul (81:5; #488)

It is for you that the spring creates all of this.
My rival is the fragrant breath of flowers.

nafas-e ʿitr sāe gul: fragrant breath of flowers.

My rival is the fragrance of flowers because it reaches you, but I cannot. It is in the spring that flowers bloom and spread their essence to you. This only makes me feel jealous. Here the poet is complaining to spring for bringing jealousy.

شرمندہ رکھتے ہیں مجھے بادِ بہار سے　　مینائے بے شراب و دلِ بے ہوائے گل

sharminda(h) rakhte haiñ mujhe bād-e bahār se
mīnāe be sharāb-o-dil-e be havāe gul (81:6; #489)

They keep embarrassing me facing the breeze of spring;
A decanter without wine and a heart without desire for flowers.

havā: desire.

My decanter is empty and my heart free of the desire for flowers. Because of this, I am embarrassed for the spring breeze ushers in the season to enjoy both. There is no wine and no desire to see the flowers. The coming of spring should excite the desire to see the garden and to drink, but I am embarrassed to face the breeze because I lack both. The lover has reached that stage of frustration where no desire is left.

سطوت سے تیرے جلوۂ حسنِ غیور کی   خوں ہے مری نگاہ میں رنگِ ادائے گل

siṭvat se tere jalva(h)' ḥusn-e ġhayūr kī
ḳhūñ hai merī nigāh meñ rang-e adāe gul (81:7; #490)

Compared to the reverence of display of your awe-inspiring beauty,
The coquetry of flowers is merely a bloody situation in my view.

siṭvat: awe, reverence; *ġhayūr*: self respecting.

In awe of your beauty that keeps me from looking at anyone else, I consider the colorful display of flowers to be merely a bloody situation, meaning that I pay no attention to it. The only thing of importance to me is your display of admirable beauty. I do not admire the flowers; my admiration is only for you.

تیرے ہی جلوے کا ہے یہ دھوکا کہ آج تک   بے اختیار دوڑے ہے گل در قفائے گل

tere hī jalve kā hai yih dhokā kih āj tak
be iḳhtiyār dauṛe hai gul dar qafāe gul (81:8; #491)

It is the deception of the display of your beauty that still today,
The flowers are running uncontrolled, back to back.

gul dar qafāe gul: flower behind flower.

It is the deception of your display that causes flowers to line up hoping to catch a glimpse of you. Two things make this verse difficult to explain. "The deception of display" is used here to mean a façade. The use of "till today" apparently means "even today." Now the meaning comes out as follows: the beauty of the beloved is a tarnished façade of beauty that continues to attract flowers (lovers) even today, long after the beauty is gone. More commonly and wrongly, this verse is interpreted as: flowers are growing rapidly to look at you.

غالب مجھے ہے اُس سے ہم آغوشی آرزو
جس کا خیال ہے گُلِ جیبِ قبائے گل

Ġhālib mujhe hai us se ham āġhoshī ārzū
jis kā ḳhayāl hai gul-e jeb-e qabāe gul (81:9; #492)

Ġhālib, I am longing to embrace her in my arms, the one,
Whose thought is like the flower decorating the pocket of a flower gown.

āġhosh: in the arms; *jeb*: pocket, collar; *qabā*: long gown.

Beautiful is the thought of her in my arms. It can be compared to decorating a gown of flowers *with* flowers. Gowns are decorated with embroidered flowers or real flowers (as a brooch). Here the gown itself is made of flowers and a more attractive flower is needed to decorate its pockets. The most beautiful of the beautiful thoughts is what is meant here.

82

غم نہیں ہوتا ہے آزادوں کو بیش از یک نفس
برق سے کرتے ہیں روشن شمعِ ماتم خانہ ہم

ġham nahiñ hotā hai āzādoñ ko besh az yak nafas
barq se karte haiñ roshan shamà-e mātam ķhana(h) ham (82:1; #493)

The free do not get bereaved for more than a fleeting moment.
We light candles from the bolt of lightning in our dark homes.

ġham: sorrow; *āzād*: free; *besh az yak nafas*: more than a breath, fleeting moment; *roshan*: illuminated; *yak*: one; *nafas*: soul; *shamà*: candle; *mātam ķhana(h)*: dark homes, homes in mourning.

Free souls cannot be saddened or restrained by the chains of sorrow even for a moment. Instead, we use a momentary spark of lightning to light candles for our dark homes. The pain, when it comes to us, is like a flash of light, disappearing in a moment as we move on. The world is full of sorrow, but it impedes only those who are unable to bear the losses, who cannot move on.

محفلیں برہم کرے ہے گنجفہ بازِ خیال
ہیں ورق گردانیٔ نیرنگِ یک بت خانہ ہم

maḥfileñ barham kare hai ganjfa(h) bāz-e ķhayāl
haiñ varq gardānī' nairang-e yak but ķhana(h) ham (82:2: 494)

The card-player of imagination is creating the gatherings,
As I keep flipping the pages of the magical book in the house of idols.

ganjfa(h): a type of playing card game wherein 56 round cards are dealt among 8 players; *varq gardānī'*: shuffling card, flipping pages; *naịrang*: magic, mystery, strange; *but ḳhana(h):* house of idols (of longings).

Like the player of *ganjfa* (playing cards) who keeps flipping the cards, I keep flipping the pages of my memory that is filled with strange deceptions of my imagination, memories of the assembly of the idol, my beloved. With each flip, a show of events comes to mind, and then disappears, only to be replaced with another. This way I see assemblies put together and destroyed. This is the plan of man's life as well. Deeper meaning to the verse becomes evident as we see the pageantry of civilizations turning over as if this were a page of a book of mystery.

باوجودِ یک جہاں ہنگامہ، پیدائی نہیں
ہیں چراغانِ شبستانِ دلِ پروانہ ہم

bāvajūd-e yak jahāñ hangāma(h), paidāī' nahiñ
haiñ charāġhān-e shabistān-e dil-e parvāna(h) ham (82:3; #495)

Despite the tumult all around, there is no real existence,
As we are merely the lit up lamps in the bedchamber of a moth's heart.

bāvajūd: despite; *jahāñ hangāma(h):* too much tumult and uproar; *paidāī'*: existence *shabistān:* secluded private quarters, sleeping place; *parvānā(h):* moth;.

My existence is full of tumult and uproar, and just as impermanent as a moth burning over a flame in a flash, illuminating its secluded heart momentarily. Our existence is no more permanent than this flash of light. This analogy expounds on the lover's anguish, his desire to immolate himself and the helplessness over his heart's desires.

ضعف سے ہے، نے قناعت سے، یہ ترکِ جستجو
ہیں وبالِ تکیہ گاہِ ہمتِ مردانہ ہم

ẓoʿf se hai, ne qanāʿt se yih tark-e justujū
haiñ vabāl-e takyā(h) gāh-e himmat-e mardānā(h) ham (82:4; #496)

This giving up of struggle is from weakness, not from contentment;
A disgrace we are to the abode of manly courage.

ẓoʿf: weakness; *qanāʿt*: contentment; *tark*: give up; *justujū*: struggle; *vabāl*: disgrace, liability; *takyā(h) gāh*: place to rest against, an abode.

Giving up the struggle is a result of our weakness, not a sign of contentment. We are a disgrace to manly courage and to hide it we call it our lack of interest, our content disposition. We have become awkward and in order to hide it we say that we are content. Manly courage requires that we control our urges; instead, we keep running after our elusive dreams. This running around has tired us and now we stand disgraced before the tasks at hand. To hide our embarrassment we say that we are content.

دائم الحبس اِس میں ہیں لاکھوں تمنائیں اسدؔ
جانتے ہیں سینۂ پُرخوں کو زنداں خانہ ہم

dā'im alḥabs is meñ haiñ lākhoñ tamannāeñ, Asad
jānte haiñ sīna(h)' pur ḳhūñ ko zindāñ ḳhāna(h) ham (82:5; #497)

In it are sentenced to life, millions of desires, Asad;
We consider our chest full of blood as a prisoner's cell.

dā'im alḥabas: life sentence.

My chest was full of unfulfilled desires locked up for a lifetime. Bled to deaṯh, these desires now fill my chest as if it were a prison cell filled with blood.

83

بہ نالہ حاصلِ دل بستگی فراہم کر
متاعِ خانۂ زنجیر، جز صدا معلوم!

ba(h) nāla(h) ḥāṣil-e dil bastagī farāham kar
matā̒-e ḳhāna(h)' zanjīr, juz ṣadā, ma̒lūm (83:1; #498)

Bring out the laments that please the heart;
The entire worth of the chains is nothing but its rattling sound.

dil bastagī: connection to heart, to please heart; *matā̒*: asset, worth.

O! Lovers, you should continue sending the sighs and laments that so please your beloved. However, you must also know that these plaints are like chains (as they are continuous), and a chain is only worth its rattling sound, the kind of sound that is easily ignored. Like a rattling chain, your plaints will be ignored but their sound will please her.

84

مجھ کو دیارِ غیر میں مارا وطن سے دور
رکھ لی مرے خدا نے مری بیکسی کی شرم

mujh ko diyār-e ġhair meñ mārā vaṭan se dūr
rakh lī mere ḳhudā ne merī bekasī kī sharm (84:1; #499)

Having killed me in a foreign land, far away from home,
My God has saved me from the disgrace of destitution.

bekasī: hopelessness, loneliness, destitution.

I died in a foreign country, away from home, and I thank the Lord for that. If I had died in my home, I would have been left without shroud or burial and that would have been very embarrassing. Away from home, though, no one knows me and so I would not be embarrassed if that happened here. Note that the poet is thanking God for not letting people know how unappreciated he was at home. It is a lament of the treatment his peers gave him; it is an admission that no one appreciated him at home.

وہ حلقہ ہائے زلف کمیں میں ہیں اے خدا
رکھ لیجو میرے دعویٔ وارستگی کی شرم

vuh ḥalqa(h) hāi zulf kamīñ meñ haiñ ai ḳhudā
rakh lījo mere da'v'ī vārastagī kī sharm (84:2; #500)

Those ringlets of tresses are waiting in ambush, O! Lord!
Save me from the embarrassment of my claim to freedom.

kamiñ: ambush, look out; *vārastagī:* freedom.

The beloved is all set to snare. Her tresses are curled and well adorned. I declared that no one could catch me and that I was a free man. Now I am about to be embarrassed. Please help, God.

85

لوں وام بختِ خفتہ سے یک خوابِ خوش ولے
غالب یہ خوف ہے کہ کہاں سے ادا کروں

lūñ vām baḳht-e ḳhufta(h) se yak ḳh(v)āb-e ḳhūsh vale
Ġhālib yih ḳhauf hai kih kahāñ se adā karūñ (85:1; #501)

I might borrow from my sleeping fate, a night of carefree sleep
***Ġhālib*, but I fear, from where would I repay the debt?**

vām: loan, borrowing; *baḳht-e ḳhufta(h):* sleeping fortune; *ḳh(v)āb-e ḳhūsh*: carefree sleep, deep sleep without fear of interruption; *adā:* payment of debt.

If I borrow a night of beautiful dreams from my sleeping fortune, I am afraid I will not be able to pay back the debt. My bad fortune of not being close to my beloved has stolen my sleep. If I press my fortune and borrow a night of sleep, I will never be able to pay it back. Paying back requires that I do not sleep when I am able to. Since I will never get close to my beloved, and will never have the peace of mind to sleep, it is out of the question that I will ever be able to repay the debt. The poet uses his pen name, *Ġhālib,* meaning inundated (with fear). In addition, the poet wanting to borrow from his sleeping fortune is a good play on words.

86

وہ فراق اور وہ وصال کہاں
وہ شب و روز و ماہ و سال کہاں

vuh firāq āur vuh viṣāl kahāñ
vuh shab-o-roz-o-māh-o-sāl kahāñ (86:1; #502)

Where is that separation and that union now?
Where are those days and nights and months and years?

Where have those times gone when I was in love and would suffer both from the pain of our separation as well as the joy of reunion? Where have those nights and days gone? Where have those months and years gone?

فرصتِ کاروبارِ شوق کسے
ذوقِ نظارۂ جمال کہاں

furṣat-e kārobār-e shauq kise
żauq-e naẕẕāra(h)' jamāl kahāñ (86:2; #503)

Who now has time to engage in the transactions of love?
Where is the yearning for the sight of the display of beauty?

Now my situation is such that I hardly find time to do things that satisfy my desire, so much so that I have even lost the taste (actually longing) to see her beauty. I no longer enjoy looking at her. The poet is concerned that by not being able to nurture the desire, he is losing his urge for it.

دل تو دل وُہ دماغ بھی نہ رہا
شورِ سودائے خطّ و خال کہاں

dil to dil vuh damāġh bhī na(h) rahā
shor-e saudāe ḳhaṯ-o-ḳhāl kahāñ (86:3; #504)

What to speak of the heart? Even the mind is gone!
Where is that passionate craving for her curvaceous figure?

shor: passion, emotion, fervour; *saudā:* transaction, barter, trade, connection; *ḳhaṯ-o-ḳhāl:* lines and beauty mole, curvaceous figure.

I used to fantasize about her beautiful features, her mole, and her curves. My heart has been gone a long time now; it seems that now my mind cannot bring those pleasures of imagination back.

تھی وہ اِک شخص کے تصوّر سے
اب وہ رعنائیِ خیال کہاں

thī vuh ik shaḳhṣ ke taṣavvur se
ab vuh ra'nāī' ḳhayāl kahāñ (86:4; #505)

Once inspired by the thought of a person,
Where has that beauty of thought gone now?

ra'nāī' ḳhayāl: beauty, tenderness, loveliness of thoughts.

Calling the beloved "a person" and not just "beloved" is significant here. Since the purpose is to state that all feelings are gone for that beloved, she becomes a "person" instead of a "beloved." All the beautiful thoughts that used to come to my mind that were associated with her are now gone.

ایسا آساں نہیں لہو رونا
دل میں طاقت جگر میں حال کہاں

aisā āsāñ nahiñ lahū ronā
dil meñ ṭāqat jigar meñ ḥāl kahāñ (86:5; #506)

It is not easy to shed blood-tears;
Where is the strength of heart and where is the steadfastness of my liver?

To cry blood-tears illustrates a great depth of grief and anguish. The heart is the bastion of emotion while the liver is the provider of courage. With both emotional strength and the courage to face grief gone, shedding tears of blood, that is experiencing the joys of grief, is no longer possible.

ہم سے چھوٹا قمار خانۂ عشق
واں جو جاویں، گرہ میں مال کہاں

ham se chhūṭā qimār ḳhāna(h)' ʿishq
vāñ jo jāveñ, girah meñ māl kahāñ (86:6; #507)

We stopped frequenting the gambling den of love,
But to return there, where is the wager in our pockets?

qimār ḳhānā(h): gambling den; *girah:* money kept in a cloth knot, generally in the lapel of skirt; *māl:* money.

To go to the gambling den of love, one needs something to place a bet with. We have neither the currency of heart nor the coins that are really scars (spots) in the heart (the scar's shape is compared to the *ashrafī*, the currency of time). These are the wagers a lover must take to the den of love to gamble. With none of these things left, how can we enter the den?

فکرِ دُنیا میں سر کھپاتا ہوں
میں کہاں اور یہ وبال کہاں

fikr-e dunyā meñ sar khapātā hūñ
maiñ kahāñ āur yih vabāl kahāñ (86:7; #508)

Wasting my mind away on the worries about the world,
Who am I to get involved with these curses?

vabāl: curse, divine vengeance, ruin.

I have become engrossed in the day-to-day affairs of the world where I am now fully occupied. This is indeed a curse because it is not my style to involve myself with material things. However, once involved, I cannot get out of it.

مضمحل ہو گئے قویٰ غالب
وہ عناصر میں اعتدال کہاں

muẓmaḥil ho gaʾe qavā Ġhālib
vuh ʿanāṣir meñ iʿtidāl kahāñ (86:8; #509)

O! *Ġhālib*, the strength of body has taken to emaciation!
Where has the balance in the elements of the body vanished?

muẓmaḥil: weak, old, lethargic; *qavā:* plural of strength; *ʿanāṣir*: elements of body; *iʿtidāl:* moderation, balance.

Bodily strength has given in to weakness and age and now the balance of the body's elements—agility, thinking, and desire—is gone. In old age, we can only lament this loss. In traditional Chinese medicine, this amounts to an imbalance of *yang* and *yin*. In physiological terms, *Ġhālib* is saying that our body chemistry is out of balance now.

87

کی وفا ہم سے تو غیر اس کو جفا کہتے ہیں   ہوتی آئی ہے کہ اچھوں کو برا کہتے ہیں

kī vafā ham se to ġhair is ko jafā kahte haiñ
hotī ā'ī hai kih achhoñ ko burā kahte haiñ (87:1; #510)

An act of faithfulness towards me causes rivals to decry oppression.
Maligning good as bad has been going around for a long time.

Rivals believe her faithfulness to me is oppressive to them. The poet is afraid that she might pay attention to it and is trying to persuade her that calling good things bad is what the world is all about. Pay no attention to it.

آج ہم اپنی پریشانیٔ خاطر اُن سے   کہنے جاتے تو ہیں پر دیکھیے کیا کہتے ہیں

āj ham apnī pareshānī' ḳhāṯir un se
kahne jāte to haiñ par dekhiye kyā kahte haiñ (87:2; #511)

Today, for the sake of our heart's distress,
I am going to say it to her but let us see what may I end up saying.

pareshān'ī ḳhāṯir: for the sake of distress of heart.

The distress of the heart is too much to handle so I have decided to confess to her the condition of my heart. However, let us see what comes out of my mouth once I actually face her. Alternately it also means let us see what she might say after hearing my woes.

اگلے وقتوں کے ہیں یہ لوگ، انہیں کچھ نہ کہو   جو مے و نغمہ کو اندوہ رُبا کہتے ہیں

agle vaqtoñ ke haiñ yih log inheñ kuchh na(h) kaho
jo mai-o-naġhma(h) ko ando(h) rubā kahte haiñ (87:3: 512)

Say nothing to them for they are the folks from a bygone period,
Those who call wine and song sorrow-relievers.

agle: past (sometimes used for future also); *ando(h) rubā:* sorrow relieving.

Foolish are they who think that wine and song reduce pain. They actually increase the pain. What shall we say to such naïve people? They are from a bygone era, meaning they have reached senility. This verse has often been interpreted as these people have different values, old style values. The fact is that this verse serves to ridicule them.

دل میں آ جائے ہے، ہوتی ہے جو فُرصت غش سے   اور پھر کون سے نالے کو رَسا کہتے ہیں

dil meñ ājāe hai, hotī hai jo furṣat ġhash se
aur phir kaun se nāle ko rasā kahte haiñ (87:4; #513)

She slips into my heart, the moment I get respite from unconsciousness.
And then to which plaint would you call reaching out?

People say that my lamenting is futile. That is wrong. As I begin my lament, I pass out. The moment I return to consciousness, the lament returns to my heart along with thoughts of her. If this is not the effect of my plaint, then what is "effective"? The poet asserts that if she comes into his imagination then his plaint has been heard. The poet is happy to think of her between periods of unconsciousness.

ہے پرے سرحدِ ادراک سے اپنا مسجود   قبلے کو اہلِ نظر قبلہ نما کہتے ہیں

hai pare sarḥad-e idrāk se apnā masjūd
qible ko ahl-e naẓar qibla(h) numā kahte haiñ (87:5; #514)

Beyond the bounds of wisdom is the one to Whom we supplicate.
Those with vision, call *Kaʿbā* merely a pointer to the direction of our prayers.

idrāk: wisdom; *masjūd*: one bowed (supplicated) to; *qibla(h): Kaʿbā* towards which Muslims face while praying.

I do not bow to *Kaʿbā*, instead, I bow to the Creator whose existence is beyond the grasp of human wisdom. The *Kaʿbā* is merely a legendary icon directing us to bow.

پائے افگار پہ جب سے تجھے رحم آیا ہے   خارِ رہ کو ترے ہم مہرِ گیا کہتے ہیں

pāe afgār pa(h) jab se tujhe raḥm āyā hai
ḳhār-e rah ko tere ham mahr gayā kahte haiñ (87:6; #515)

Since you have shown kindness toward my wounded feet,
We call the thorns in the path to your alley, the herb of grace.

pāe afgār: wounded feet; *mahr gayā*: a plant root, the possession of which brings good fortune and makes the beloved kinder (an anecdote), herb of grace.

Upon seeing the wounds of my bleeding feet, the beloved expressed sympathy. In response, the poet replied that the thorns in your alley are actually the "herb of grace" to me. These thorns bring good fortune because they brought you who gave attention to me.

اک شرر دل میں ہے اُس سے کوئی گھبرائے گا کیا   آگ مطلوب ہے ہم کو جو ہوا کہتے ہیں

ik sharar dil meñ hai us se ko'ī ghabrāe gā kyā
āg maṯlūb hai ham ko jo havā kahte haiñ (87:7; #516)

A spark there is in the heart; why should anyone be worried about it?
In reality, we want to fan this fire when we ask for air.

sharar: fire; *ghabrānā*: to be worried; *maṯlūb*: desired.

There is fire in my heart but I shall not be worried for it is my destiny that it burns. I am not trying to put out the fire as I gasp for air. Instead I am trying to fan the fire further. The burning in my heart given by my beloved is my destiny. Even though I ask her to extinguish the fire with her kindness, I know it will only flare it more.

دیکھیے لاتی ہے اُس شوخ کی نخوت کیا رنگ   اُس کی ہر بات پہ ہم نامِ خدا کہتے ہیں

dekhīye lātī hai us shoḳh kī nāḳhvat kyā rang
us kī har bāt par ham nām-e ḳhudā kahte haiñ (87:8; #517)

Let us see what would her haughtiness lead to
As we keep asking for God's blessing for everything she says.

nām-e ḳhudā: name of God, Gold bless you; *nāḳhvat:* haughtiness.

Praising her incessantly, asking for God's blessings for whatever she says is making her haughtier, the poet is wondering how far this haughtiness will go. Notice that she is already haughty. It is the excessive praise of the lover that makes it worse. The poet is giving her the benefit of doubt.

وحشت و شیفتہ اب مرثیہ کہویں شاید
مر گیا غالبِ آشفتہ نوا، کہتے ہیں

Vaḥshat-o-Sheftā(h) ab marsīya(h) kahveñ shāyad
mar gayā Ġhālib-e āshufta(h) navā, kahte haiñ (87:9; #518)

***Vehshat* and *Shefta* would probably chant elegies.**
It is rumored that *Ġhālib*, the singer of sad songs has passed away.

Vaḥshat-o-Sheftā(h): names of two famous poets of *Ġhālib*'s time; *āshufta(h) navā*: singing sad songs.

Now that *Ġhālib*, the poet who used to write sad poetry, is gone, his friends *Nawab Sheftā(h)* and *Vaḥshat* would probably write a good elegy for him.

88

آبرو کیا خاک اُس گُل کی کہ گلشن میں نہیں   ہے گریباں ننگِ پیراہن جو دامن میں نہیں

ābrū kyā ḳhāk us gul kī kih gulshan meñ nahiñ
hai garebāñ nang-e pairāhan jo dāman meñ nahiñ (88:1; #519)

What honor there is for the flower, which is not present in the garden;
A collar is a disgrace to the attire, if it is not torn down to the lap.

ābrū: honor; *ḳhāk:* dust; *nang-e pairāhan*: disgrace to attire.

The right place for a flower is in the garden. The right collar is the one that goes all the way down to the lap of the skirt. That is their zenith, otherwise both are disgraceful. Also, note that the petals of a flower appear as slits and thus some comparison is made between a full blooming flower and the slit of a collar.

ضعف سے اے گریہ کچھ باقی مرے تن میں نہیں   رنگ ہو کر اُڑ گیا، جو خوں کہ دامن میں نہیں

ẓo'f se ae girya(h) kuchh bāqī mere tan meñ nahiñ
rang ho kar uṛ gayā, jo ḳhūñ kih dāman meñ nahiñ (88:2; #520)

From feebleness, O! weeping, there is not much left in my body.
Having stained, it has faded away, the blood that is not in my skirt.

Weakness and infirmity have sapped the energy to cry. It has been so long since I cried that my bloodstained skirt has faded.

ہو گئے ہیں جمع اجزائے نگاہِ آفتاب   ذرّے اُس کے گھر کی دیواروں کے روزن میں نہیں

ho ga'e haiñ jamaʿ ajzā'e nigāh-e āftāb
żarre us ke ghar kī dīvāroñ ke rauzan meñ nahiñ (88:3; #521)

The elements of the sight of sun have gathered here;
These are not the particles of dust floating in the window of her home.

ajzā: components, elements; *rauzan*: small openings in the wall to let the light in.

Sunlight shining through dark openings in the wall illuminates floating particles; the poet says that these are not particles, but elements of the sight of the sun, which are trying to steal a glimpse of the beloved. The sun does not have the courage to face her because she will outshine the sun. As a result, the sun is sending its vision to her window to appear like floating particles there.

کیا کہوں تاریکیِ زندانِ غم اندھیر ہے   پنبہ نورِ صبح سے کم جس کے روزن میں نہیں

kyā kahūñ tārikī' zindān-e ġham, andher hai
pañba(h) nūr-e ṣubḥ se kam jis ke rauzan meñ nahiñ (88:4; #522)

How can I describe the intensity of darkness in the prison of sorrow?
The cotton wool stuffed in its windows appears no less than the light of dawn.

pañba(h): cotton wool.

How dark is the darkness in the prison of my sorrow? If the white of cotton wool were stuffed in my window, it would appear no less than the light of dawn. (Too much darkness often yields a flash of light in the eyes). The white cotton wool in complete darkness is seen as a shining spot.

رونقِ ہستی ہے عشقِ خانہ ویراں ساز سے   انجمن بے شمع ہے، گر برق خرمن میں نہیں

raunaq-e hastī hai ʿishq-e ḳhāna(h) vīrāñ sāz se
anjuman be shamaʿ hai, gar barq ḳhirman meñ nahīñ (88:5; #523)

The sprightliness of life comes from the love that desolates. An assembly is without a candle if there is no lightning in the gathered harvest.

ḳhāna(h) vīrāñ sāz: destroyer of home; *barq ḳhirman*: lightning of harvest (threshing hard produces sparks that often burn the crop) the lightning striking the crop.

The zest of life comes from our devotion to things, people, and places. How badly we want to achieve something is judged by what we are willing to give up for it. It is only when we are ready to give our life (destroy our home) for someone or something that real love appears. Without the spark of love that may burn us, as the lightning burns stored harvest, our lives will be like an assembly without a candle—dark and deserted. From the tales of *Farhād* to Edmund Hillary reaching the top of Mount Everest, we hear about people risking their lives to achieve life's greatest dreams. It is only when we risk lightning for our harvest of existence that we achieve the ultimate. This verse is indeed a divine example of *Ġhālib*'s magical thoughts.

زخم سلوانے سے مجھ پر چارہ جوئی کا ہے طعن   غیر سمجھا ہے کہ لذت زخمِ سوزن میں نہیں

zaḳhm silvāne se mujh par chāra(h) jūʾī kā hai taʿn
ġhair samjhā hai kih lażżat zaḳhm-e sozan meñ nahīñ (88:6; #524)

Getting my wounds stitched brings the taunt of seeking remedy. The rival thinks there's is no delight in the wounds caused by the stitching needle.

As I was having my wounds stitched, the rival taunted me by saying that real lovers do not want their wounds stitched and healed. However, what he does not know is that the needle, as it passes through wounds, creates its own wounds. I was not going to give up experiencing this extraordinary pleasure. They do not know that I am having my wounds stitched in order for them to be deepened, not healed. No stitching can close my wounds.

بسکہ ہیں ہم اِک بہارِ ناز کے مارے ہوئے جلوۂ گل کے سوا گرد اپنے مدفن میں نہیں

baskih haiñ ham ik bahār-e nāz ke māre hu'e
jalva(h)' gul kih sivā gard apne madfin meñ nahiñ (88:7; #525)

Whereas we are the victims of the blossoming coyness,
Except for the display of flowers, there is nothing in my grave.

bahār-e nāz: blossoming coyness; *madfan:* grave.

A victim of her beauty and coquetry, upon reaching my grave I find that there is no dust in it (nothing in it), just flowers all around as if it were spring. By being killed by her, the dust inside the grave has turned to flowers. (Note: Muslims are buried without a coffin.) Flowers are comforting; dust is not. Killed by the display of her coquetry, I am at peace lying in the bed of flowers instead of dust. The play on words here involves calling the display of beauty the "spring of beauty."

قطرہ قطرہ اک ہیولیٰ ہے نئے ناسور کا خوں بھی ذوقِ درد سے فارغ مرے تن میں نہیں

qaṭra(h) qaṭra(h) ik hayūlā hai nai' nāsūr kā
ḳhūñ bhī żauq-e dard se fārigh mere tan meñ nahiñ (88:8; #526)

Every drop is the matter that creates new chronic wounds;
Even the blood in my body is not free from the desire for pain.

hayūlā: constituent matter of being; *nāsūr:* chronic non-healing wound; *fārigh*: free of, without.

All over my body there are non-healing, chronic wounds that keep dripping blood. Despite this, other body organs, including blood itself, desire greater pain. It is in this way that every drop of blood is ready to turn itself into a wound that will never heal. My blood wants increased pain to enhance my ecstasy. Every drop of blood provides a substance or matter that makes wounds. This means that the entire body offers itself to be the target of wounds.

لے گئی ساقی کی نخوت قلزم آشامی مری   موجِ مے کی آج رگ مینا کی گردن میں نہیں

le ga'ī sāqī kī nāḳhvat qulzum āshāmī merī
mauj-e ma'i kī āj rag mīnā kī gardan meñ nahiñ (88:9; #527)

My ability to drink oceans took away the haughtiness of cupbearer; Today the vein of the tide of wine is no longer in the neck of the decanter.

nāḳhvat: haughtiness; *qulzum āshāmī:* to drink oceans, meaning the ability to drink beyond limits.

The cupbearer challenged me by saying that no one can drink her strong wine (meaning to survive her coquetry). To her great chagrin, I finished every drop. The neck of the decanter bowed in shame as if it did not have the jugular vein left in it that would keep its head straight (The stiff neck gone). With the wine gone, the jugular vein of the decanter was drained so the neck of the decanter drooped in shame for it had caused embarrassment to the cupbearer. Note that the vein-shaped neck of the decanter, which was filled with wine when the decanter was full, appeared as if the wine were rocking with the waves.

ہو فشارِ ضعف میں کیا ناتوانی کی نمود   قد کے جھکنے کی بھی گنجائش مرے تن میں نہیں

ho fishār-e zo'f meñ kyā nātavānī kī namūd
qad ke jhukne kī bhī gunjāi'sh mere tan meñ nahiñ (88:10; #528)

What show of feebleness it would be as weakness squeezes from all sides,
Leaving no room in my body to even to take a hunched posture.

fishār: squeezed from all sides; *namūd*: display, show.

My feebleness squeezes me from all sides so much so that I do not crouch as weak, old people do when they are old and frail. When weakness strikes bones and muscles, people lose their strength and take a crouched, hunchbacked posture. In the case of the poet, the weakness is so intense that the muscles have shrunk, squeezing the body, keeping it from crouching, keeping the poet upright, unable to show his weakness.

تھی وطن میں شان کیا غالب کہ ہو غربت میں قدر
بے تکلف، ہوں وہ مشتِ خس کہ گلخن میں نہیں

thī vaṭan meñ shān kyā Ġhālib kih ho ġhurbat meñ qadr
be takalluf, hūñ vuh musht-e ḳhas kih gulḳhan meñ nahiñ (88:11; #529)

What dignity was there at home, *Ġhālib*, that there would be any respect, away from home?
Frankly speaking, I am that fistful of garden-waste that is not in the dustbin.

vaṭan: native country; *shān*: dignity; *ġhurbat*: poverty, foreign land; *qadr*: worth, value; *be taklluf*: informal; *musht*: handful; *ḳhas:* garden-waste; *gulḳhan*: garbage incinerator, dust-bin.

I did not receive much respect in my own home so why should I expect to get any away from home? At home I was left in one place, like the garden-waste waiting in its container to be burned. Away from home, though, I've been kicked around, meaning that even the garden-waste is insulted when it is not at home. This *ġhazal* was written by *Ġhālib* in Bandah on the way to Calcutta to plead for his case of pension. *Ġhālib*'s original handwriting for this *ġhazal* is preserved at the Punjab University Library in Lahore, Pakistan.

89

عہدے سے مدحِ ناز کے، باہر نہ آسکا
گر اِک ادا ہو تو اُسے اپنی قضا کہوں

ʿohde se madḥ-e nāz ke, bāhar na(h) āsakā
gar ik adā ho to use apnī qaẓā kahūñ (89:1; #530)

**I could not fulfill my obligation to offer an ode to her coyness.
Had there been just one coquettish style, I would have called it my death.**

ʿohde se bāhar āsakā: was able to discharge responsibility; *ʿohda(h):* responsibility; *madaḥ-e nāz:* praise, ode to coquetry; *qaẓā:* death.

I failed to express praise for her style and coquetry when given the honor of an audience with her. There were so many things that needed praise, each one requiring me to lay down my life just as a token of my expression of praise. Had there been just one thing to praise, and since I had only one life to give, I would have fulfilled my obligation. Since I cannot die more than once, I could not fulfill the honor given to me to express my ode.

حلقے ہیں چشم ہاے کشادہ بہ سُوے دِل
ہر تارِ زُلف کو نگہِ سُرمہ سا کہوں

ḥalqe haiñ chashm hāi kushāda(h) ba(h) sūe dil
har tār-e zulf ko nigah-e surma(h) sā kahūñ (89:2; #531)

**The snares of wide eyes are gazing towards my heart;
Each strand of her tresses, I would call, an eye adorned with antimony.**

nigāh-e surma(h) sā: eyes decorated (adorned) with black antimony.

The braided knots in the beloved's tresses can be called wide (big) eyes looking into my heart. The braided knots are black and appear to be eyes, but not just any eyes. These are decorated with antimony powder and are made to seem more attractive. The net also has an opening resembling braids. All these points confirm that the beloved is ready to take the lover into captivity.

میں اور صد ہزار نوائے جگر خراش
تو اور ایک وہ نہ شنیدن کہ کیا کہوں

maiñ āur ṣad hazār navā'e jigar ḳharāsh
tū āur ek vuh na(h) shunidan kih kyā kahūñ (89:3; #532)

I and my millions of liver-rending sighs;
You, the one not listening, so what can I say?

ḳharāsh: rending; *na(h) shunidan*: not listening.

What shall I say of your obliviousness that you refuse to listen to my laments, each one being strong enough to tear my liver apart? Note that the liver is home to courage. This means that these sighs are causing much damage to the liver and the beloved's indifference will destroy my courage.

ظالم مرے گماں سے مجھے منفعل نہ چاہ
ہے ہے! خدا نہ کردہ، تجھے بیوفا کہوں

z̤ālim mere gumāñ se mujhe munfaʿil na(h) chāh
hai hai! ḳhudā na(h) karda(h), tujhe bevafā kahūñ (89:4; #533)

O! Tyrant, embarrass me not in front of my doubts.
Alas! Alas! God forbid if I would ever call you unfaithful.

munfa'il: embarrassed.

My doubt was suspicious of you, my cruel beloved. As my doubts are being proven correct, I am embarrassed and beg you, my beloved, to save me from this embarrassment. Be faithful to me because I would rather not call you unfaithful, at the behest of my doubt. *Ġhālib* creates a triad here. "Himself," "the doubt" and the "beloved." He is asking for the faithfulness of the beloved to come out of an embarrassing situation. What a way to coerce her!

90

مہرباں ہو کے بُلا لو مجھے ، چاہو جس وقت
مَیں گیا وقت نہیں ہُوں کہ پھر آ بھی نہ سکُوں

mahrbāñ ho ke bulā lo mujhe, chāho jis vaqt
maiñ gayā vaqt nahiñ hūñ kih phir ā bhī na(h) sakūñ (90:1; #534)

Turning kind towards me, call me back any time you want;
I am not like the time bygone that cannot be recalled.

O! Beloved, you were harsh to me so I took refuge from your assembly. Now you think that I will not return. Be kind to me and call me back. I am not like time that has passed and cannot be recalled. I can come back whenever you want.

ضُعف میں طعنۂ اغیار کا شکوہ کیا ہَے
بات کچھ سر تو نہیں ہَے کہ اُٹھا بھی نہ سکُوں

ẓo'f meñ t̤ana'(h)' aġhyār kā shikva(h) kyā hai
bāt kuchh sar to nahiñ hai kih uṭṭhā bhī na(h) sakūñ (90:2; #535)

In my feebleness, why should I complain of taunting rivals?
Their talk is not like my head that I am unable to lift.

t̤a'na(h): taunt.

I have become weak and strangers taunt me for my feebleness. They challenge me to show how I can continue to claim to be a lover. These taunts are mere words, though, and I can easily tolerate them. These are not like my head that I am unable to lift. While admitting to weakness, the poet remains strong by confronting those ridiculing gestures.

زہر ملتا ہی نہیں مجھ کو، ستمگر! ورنہ
کیا قسم ہے ترے ملنے کی کہ کھا بھی نہ سکوں؟

zahar miltā hī nahiñ mujh ko, sitamgar! varna(h)
kyā qasam hai tere milne kī kih khā bhī na(h) sakūñ (90:3; #536)

The poison is not available to me, O! Tyrant, otherwise,
What oath there is that I would not take except not meeting you?

qasam milne kī; oath to meet.

If poison were available, I would readily take it. This would be easier than taking an oath to never meet you again.

NOTE: The three verses of this *ġhazal* show a masterpiece play on words. In the first verse, the poet uses the rhetoric of coming and going. In the second, lifting and bearing, and in the third he talks about taking by mouth (eating) both poison and an oath. (Taking an oath is expressed as "eating oath" in *Urdū*).

91

ہم سے کھُل جاؤ بہ وقتِ مے پرستی ایک دن
ورنہ ہم چھیڑیں گے رکھ کر عُذرِ مستی ایک دِن

ham se khul jā'o ba(h) vaqt-e mai parastī ek din
varna(h) ham chheṛeñ ge rakh kar ʿużr-e mastī ek din (91:1; #537)

Be intimate with me, while drinking one day,
Or else one day, I will tease you under the guise of being drunk.

khul jā'o: open up, be intimate; *mai parastī:* drinking wine.

The poet invites the beloved to become intimate with him during the drinking session. If she does not, he threatens to make a move under the pretense of being drunk. Asking for intimacy and then threatening to be intimate whether she complies or not during the drinking session is a smart trick. If she is not affectionate with me, I may drink out of frustration and thus end up being disrespectful to her. This is why it is better for her to take the initiative to keep things under control.

غرّۂ اَوجِ بنائے عالَمِ اِمکاں نہ ہو
اِس بُلندی کے نصیبوں میں ہے پستی ایک دِن

ġharra(h)' āuj-e bināe' ʿālam-e imkāñ na(h) ho
is bulandī ke nāṣīboñ meñ hai pastī ek din (91:2; #538)

Take no pride in the lofty foundations of the world's existence;
In the fate of these heights is the downfall one day.

ġharra(h): pride; *āuj:* zenith, summit; *bīnā:* foundation; *pastī:* humility, down fall.

The grandeur of material things in this world is deceptive because one day this will all come to naught. We see fortunes changing hands every day. How true!

قرض کی پیتے تھے مے لیکن سمجھتے تھے کہ ہاں
رنگ لاوے گی ہماری فاقہ مستی ایک دِن

qarẓ kī pīte the mai lekin samajhte the kih hāñ
rang lāve gī hamārī fāqa(h) mastī ek din (91:3; #539)

Drinking wine on borrowed money but thinking that yes!
Our intoxication in poverty would bring disaster one day.

rang lāve gī: would make something happen; *fāqa(h) mastī:* intoxication in starvation (poverty).

I used to drink on borrowed money and knew that it would get me into trouble one day. The use of the word "*lekin*" (but) in the first line makes "something coming out of this," unbelievable. An anecdote says that *Ġhālib* read this verse in court while defending a suit for the payment of his debts. The judge decreed against *Ġhālib* and then went on to pay the debt and fine from his own pocket. The judge was Mufti Sadruddin Azurda(h), an admirer of *Ġhālib* and a well-known poet himself.

نغمہ ہاے غم کو بھی اَے دِل غنیمت جانیے
بے صدا ہو جاے گا یہ سازِ ہستی ایک دِن

naġhma(h) hā'i ġham ko bhī ai dil ġhanīmat jāniye
be ṣadā ho jāe gā yih sāz-e hastī ek din (91:4; #540)

O! Heart! Consider even the songs of sorrow to be a blessing;
For one day this instrument of existence will become soundless.

nāġhma(h) hā'i ġham: the song of sorrow; *ġhanīmat*: blessing, enough; *be ṣadā:* without sound.

If hearing songs of happiness is not our fate, then we should consider the melodies of sorrow as blessings (enough), for one day this instrument of existence—our being—will cease making any sound at all. We will all die and then there will be no songs of any type left to sing. Whatever this life hands you, consider it a blessing from God. The way *Ġhālib* has expressed the reality of life and death in this verse cannot be replicated.

ڈھول دھپّا اُس سراپا ناز کا شیوہ نہیں
ہم ہی کر بیٹھے تھے غالبؔ پیش دستی ایک دن

dhūl ḍhappā us sarāpā nāz kā sheva(h) nahiñ
ham hī kar baiṭhe the Ġhālib peshdastī ek din (91:5: 541)

Getting into a brawl is not the style of that altogether coy beloved;
It was I who had started it, *Ġhālib*, one day.

dhūl dhappā; brawl; *sarāpā nāz*: coquettish head to toe; *sheva(h):* style; *peshdastī:* forestalling, getting ahead of, anticipation.

One should not complain about the behavior of the beloved. It is not her style; it was a reaction to what I did. Saying "I started it all" is an excuse for the beloved's behavior. In the back of his mind, the poet is happy. At least some contact was made with her and, now that they know that I started it, it is a matter of great pride for me. This is indeed an example of pure *Ġhālib* wit.

92

ہم پر جفا سے ترکِ وفا کا گماں نہیں   اِک چھیڑ ہے وگرنہ مُرادِ امتحاں نہیں

ham par jafā se tark-e vafā kā gumāñ nahiñ
ik chheṛ hai vagarna(h) murād imteḥāñ nahiñ (92:1; #542)

Tyranny towards me is not for assuming I have turned unfaithful;
It is merely a teasing; otherwise testing me is not her intent.

My beloved is tyrannical towards me because she knows I take it gladly and would never turn against her. She is just teasing me and not testing my resolve, about which she is already convinced. This is just another way that the poet is trying to justify the beloved's oppressive behavior.

کس مُنہ سے شکر کیجیے اِس لُطفِ خاص کا   پُرسش ہے اور پاے سخن درمیاں نہیں

kis muñh se shukr kījiye is luṭf-e ḳhāṣ kā
pursish hai āur pāe suḳhan darmiyāñ nahiñ (92:2; #543)

How can I possibly thank her for her special favor:
Her asking about my condition without even exchanging any words?

pāe suḳhan; feet of talk; *darmiyāñ:* in-between.

The beloved is asking the lover how he is with gestures only. It is indeed an indication of extraordinary attention that is not extended to others. In the first line, the use of "with what face" *(kis muñh se)* extends the gestures in the second line.

ہم کو ستم عزیز، ستمگر کو ہم عزیز   نامہرباں نہیں ہے اگر مہرباں نہیں

ham ko sitam ʿaziz, sitamgar ko ham ʿaziz
nā mahrbāñ nahiñ hai āgar mahrbāñ nahiñ (92:3; #544)

Torture is dear to me, and I to the torturer.
Unkind she is not, if she is not kind.

sitam: torture; *ʿazīz:* dear; *mahrbāñ*: kind.

I love to be tortured and she likes to torture. In this way we are both dear to each other. In reality, she is being kind to me by not being kind because that is what I want—her unkindness and torture. In a way, she is too kind to me.

بوسہ نہیں، نہ دیجیے دشنام ہی سہی   آخر زباں تو رکھتے ہو تم گر دہاں نہیں

bosa(h) nahiñ, na(h) dījiye dushnām hī sahī
āḳhir zabāñ to rakhte ho tum gar dahāñ nahīñ (92:4; #545)

If not a kiss, never mind, give me a rebuke instead;
After all, you do have tongue, if not a mouth.

The lover accepts the excuse that the beloved does not have a mouth for kissing. She is supposed to have a small, non-existent mouth. He sarcastically expresses that she surely has a tongue (tongue-lasher), with which to give him a rebuke instead. Getting anything from the beloved is a gift. Only *Ġhālib* can be saracastic at the same time he appears thankful.

ہر چند جاں گدازیٔ قہر و عتاب ہے   ق   ہر چند پشت گرمیٔ تاب و تواں نہیں

har chand jāñ gudāzī' qahr-o-ʿitāb hai
har chand pusht garmī' tāb-o-tavāñ nahiñ (92:5; #546)

Whereas baneful is cruelty and tyranny;
Whereas there is no strength and tolerance left to endure.

har chand; whereas; *jāñ gudāz:* baneful; *pusht garmī:* support, help, assistance.

While it is regretful that she continues her cruelty and tyranny, it is more woeful that I do not have the strength and energy to bear it. Read this verse in continuation with the next verse. The two verses joined here make a "*qit'a*" (a quatrain).

جاں مُطرِبِ ترانۂ ھَل مِن مَزِید ہے　　لب پردہ سنجِ زمزمۂ الاماں نہیں

jāñ muṭrib-e tarāna(h)' halle min mazzīd hai
lab parda(h) sanj-e zamzamah' alāmāñ nahiñ (92:6; #547)

The soul is still singing the tune: "Is there more?"
The singing lips are not chanting the ballad to beseech reprieve.

muṭrib: singer; *hal min mazzīd:* is there more?, taken from the Qur'ān ("The day when We will ask the hell, "Are you filled," the hell will respond, "Is there more?"); *alāmāñ:* refuge, reprieve; *zamzama(h):* chanting; *parda(h) sanj:* someone using the curtain of musical instrument, a musician, a singer.

These two verses form a quatrain. While the cruelty of the beloved kills and we no longer have the tolerance and strength to bear it, even then the soul sings a ballad. This means that the lover wants more and more anger and cruelty from the beloved. All this time, the lips belie no characteristic of asking for a reprieve or kindness. Making reference to the quote from the *Qur'an*, "asking for more," from God places the beloved at a high level of reverence.

خنجر سے چیر سینہ اگر دل نہ ہو دو نیم　　دل میں چھری چبھو، مژہ گر خوں چکاں نہیں

ḳhanjar se chīr sīna(h) agar dil na(h) ho do nīm
dil meñ chhurī chubho, mizha(h) gar ḳhūñ chakāñ nahiñ (92:7; #548)

Rip your chest with a dagger, if your heart is not already split into two halves.
Stab your heart with a knife, if your eyelashes are not yet dripping blood.

nīm: half; *k̤hanjar*: dagger; *chakāñ*: dripping.

Rip your chest with a dagger if your heart is not already ripped in two. Pierce your heart with a knife if your eyelashes are not yet dripping blood. The poet is advising novice lovers how to reach the zenith of their love. Until it hurts, it is not felt.

ہے ننگِ سینہ دل اگر آتش کدہ نہ ہو　　ہے عارِ دل نفس اگر آذر فشاں نہیں

hai nang-e sīna(h) dil agar ātishkada(h) na(h) ho
hai ʿār-e dil nafas agar āżar fishāñ nahiñ (92:8; #549)

It is an embarrassment to the chest if the heart is not a fire-temple;
It is shameful to the heart, if the breath does not spew fire.

ātishkada(h); fire-temple; *āżar fishāñ:* blowing fire; *nang:* shame, embarrassment; *ʿār:* shame.

A heart not burning in the fire of love is an embarrassment to the chest (its keeper); a breath not blowing fire is a shame. We must be burning and hurting to prove our worth as lovers.

نقصاں نہیں جنوں میں، بلا سے ہو گھر خراب　　سو گز زمیں کے بدلے بیاباں گراں نہیں

nuqṣāñ nahiñ junūñ meñ, balā se ho ghar k̤harāb
sau gaz zamīñ ke badle bayābāñ girāñ nahiñ (92:9; #550)

Nothing is lost being in frenzy, so what if my home is ruined?
In lieu of a hundred yards of land, the wilderness is not a bad bargain.

If the lover takes to the wilderness, his home would turn to ruin as no one would be left to care for his house. Choosing between the ruins, the lover chooses wilderness for there is more land to wander.

کہتے ہو کیا لکھا ہے تری سرنوشت میں   گویا جبیں پہ سجدۂ بت کا نشاں نہیں

kahte ho kyā likhā hai terī sar navisht meñ
goyā jabīñ pa(h) sajda(h)' but kā nishāñ nahiñ (92:10; #551)

Questioning me about what is written in my life's story,
As if you do not see the mark on my forehead from supplicating before the idol.

sajda(h): supplication; *jabīñ*: the forehead; *sar navisht*: full story.

You ask me to tell you the story of my life. Can you not see the mark on my forehead that comes from supplicating before the idol that is you? That is what I have been doing all my life.

پاتا ہوں اس سے داد کچھ اپنے کلام کی   روح القدس اگرچہ مرا ہمزباں نہیں

pātā hūñ us se dād kuchh apne kalām kī
rūḥ-ul-quds agarchi(h) merā hamzabāñ nahīñ (92:11; #552)

I do get some praise from him of my poetry,
Even though Gabriel does not speak the same language as I do.

rūḥ-ul-quds: the angel of revelation, Gabriel

The archangel Gabriel understands only some of my poetry as we speak different languages. Even so, he keeps inspiring me to experience sublime thought. This is how appreciative he is. A deep reference is made here to revelations given by Gabriel to prophets. Elsewhere *Ġhālib* writes: "I get these thoughts from the unknown world." He laments the inability of his peers to understand him.

جاں ہے بہائے بوسہ ولے کیوں کہے ابھی
غالب کو جانتا ہے کہ وہ نیم جاں نہیں

jāñ hai bahāe bosa(h) vale kioñ kahe abhī
Ġhālib ko jāntā hai kih vuh nīm jāñ nahiñ (92:12; #553)

Life is the price of one kiss, but why should she declare it yet?
She knows that *Ġhālib* is not half-dead.

bahā: price; *vale:* but; *nīm jāñ:* half-dead.

The beloved demands the lover's life for the price of a kiss, but she is not revealing this to *Ġhālib* until he is half dead. Since the price of a kiss is full life, reaching the stage of being half dead would disqualify *Ġhālib*. That is why she is not telling and waiting until *Ġhālib* reaches that stage.

93

مانعِ دشت نوردی کوئی تدبیر نہیں
ایک چکر ہے مرے پانو میں، زنجیر نہیں

mānaʿ-e dasht navardī koʾī tadbīr nahiñ
ek chakkar hai mere pāuñ meñ, zanjīr nahiñ (93:1; #554)

No convincing can prevent me from wandering in the desert;
There is a whirling in my feet, not a chain.

mānaʿ: prohibiting; *dasht navardī:* wandering in the desert; *tadbīr;* solution; *pāuñ meñ chakkar:* whirling in feet, lust for wandering.

Nothing can stop me from wandering in the desert. My feet are addicted to wandering and no chain can tie me down, for it is the chain itself that has turned into a whirlpool, taking me around. Note the use of whirlpool and chain with its round links. If the chain itself is causing me to roam, what then can stop me?

شوق اُس دشت میں دوڑائے ہے مجھ کو کہ جہاں
جادہ غیر از نگہِ دیدۂ تصویر نہیں

shauq us dasht meñ doṛāe hai mujh ko kih jahāñ
jāda(h) ġhair az nigah-e dīda(h)ʾ taṣvīr nahiñ (93:2; #555)

The desire is making me run to that desert where
The tracks are no more than the vision in the eye of a painting.

shauq: desire, interest;; *dasht:* desert; *jāda(h):* path; *nigāh*: glance; *dīda(h):* the eye; *taṣvīr:* painting.

My passion for wandering brought me to a desert where the tracks are nonexistent just as vision is nonexistent in the eye of a painting. Since the eyes of the painting are an artist's creation, they can have no sight. (In many places *Ġhālib* talks about vision as if it were a straight line coming out from the eyes. Note also the comparison made here with the shape of tracks). But why are there no signs or tracks of wandering in the desert? It is because there is great turmoil in the desert. There the wind blows hard, there is flying sand, and all of this creates the scenario of an unbearable abode—a place where *Ġhālib's* desire forces him to go, where no ordinary lovers can survive.

حسرتِ لذتِ آزار رہی جاتی ہے
جادۂ راہِ وفا، جز دمِ شمشیر نہیں

ḥasrat-e lażżat-e āzār rahī jātī hai
jāda(h)' rāh-e vafā, juz dam-e shamshīr nahiñ (93:3; #556)

The longings for the delight of pain stay unfulfilled;
The path to fidelity is nothing but the edge of a sharp sword.

dam-e shamshīr: edge of sword.

The passion for the delight of love proves fleeting since the path to fidelity goes along the edge of the sword. To love is to sacrifice your life and that takes away the prospect of ever enjoying the delights of pain. If we give our life in the first instance, how can we go on to enjoy the fruits of love?

رنجِ نومیدیٔ جاوید! گوارا رہیو
خوش ہوں گر نالہ زبونی کشِ تاثیر نہیں

ranj-e naumidī' jāved! gavārā rahīyo
ḳhush hūñ gar nāla(h) zabūnī kash-e tāsīr nahiñ (93:4; #557)

Long live, the sorrow of disappointment! Keep tolerating!
I am glad that my plaint is not disgraced by its strife for effect.

jāved: long-live; *gavārā:* tolerate; *zabūnī:* disgrace; *tāsīr:* effective.

My plaint does not beg to be heard and thus does not suffer humiliation. I would rather have perpetual sorrow than bear the burden of having to be heard.

سر کھجاتا ہے، جہاں زخمِ سر اچھا ہو جائے
لذتِ سنگ بہ اندازۂ تقریر نہیں

sar khujātā hai, jahāñ zaḳhm-e sar achhā ho jāe
lażżat-e sang ba(h) andāzah' taqrīr nahiñ (93:5; #558)

Scratching the head, as the wounds of the head heal,
The delight from stones defies the expression of speech.

khujātā: scratching; *ba(h) andāza(h):* according to estimate; *taqrīr:* expression.

As the wounds caused by stoning begin to heal, the head becomes desirous of a new round of stoning. Note that as wounds heal, they become pruritic. Scratching the head also expresses desire or wonder about what to do. The sheer delight of being stoned to create fresh wounds cannot be explained in words, the poet says. Scratching the head can mean many things here, including getting stoned again.

جب کرم رخصتِ بیباکی و گستاخی دے
کوئی تقصیر بجز خجلتِ تقصیر نہیں

jab karam ruḳhṣat-e bebākī-o-gustāḳhī de
ko'ī taqṣīr bajuz ḳhajlat-e taqṣīr nahiñ (93:6; #559)

When her kindness allows me to be bold and forward,
Then there is no excuse but to call excuses shameful.

ruḳhṣat: permission; *bebākī:* boldness; *gustāḳhī:* impoliteness; *taqṣīr:* excuse; *ḳhajlat;* shame.

In her kindness, she has allowed me to be close to her and thus allowed me to take advantage of her. At this moment, any excuse to not take advantage cannot be accepted for it will be shameful under the circumstances to offer any excuse. Here is a quote from Zorba the Greek: "Let me tell you my son, what is sin. When a woman asks you to bed and you say no, that's sin."

غالبؔ اپنا یہ عقیدہ ہے بقولِ ناسخؔ
آپ بے بہرہ ہے، جو معتقدِ میرؔ نہیں

Ġhālib apnā yih ʿaqīda(h) hai baqaul-e nāsiḳh
āp be bahra(h) hai, jo moʿtaqid-e mīr nahiñ (93:7; #560)

Ġhālib*, this is my belief, as also said by *Nasiḳh:
"He is himself unaware, who is not a believer in *Mīr*."

ʿaqīda(h): belief; *be bahra(h):* unaware.

Mīr Taqī Mīr was the icon of *Urdū ġhazal* before the time of *Ġhālib*. *Nasiḳh* was *Ġhālib*'s contemporary.

94

مت مردمکِ دیدہ میں سمجھو یہ نگاہیں
ہیں جمع سُوَیدائے دلِ چشم میں آہیں

mat mardomak-e dīda(h) meñ samjho yih nigāheñ
haiñ jamaʿ suvaidāe dil-e chashm meñ āheñ (94:1; #561)

Think not that the vision is in the sclera of the eye.
These are the sighs that have congregated in the dark spot of the heart of eye.

mardomak-e dīda(h): sclera, white part of eye.

The iris of the eye is the heart of the eye and is made up of sighs that burn the heart. The vision of the eyes is not in the sclera but in its dark spot. Displaying a good understanding of the anatomy of the eye, the poet plays with the exhaling of sighs and coming out of vision (or sight), one from the heart and the other from the iris (the black heart of the eye). The heart (of the lover and of the eye) is black in both cases. He emphasizes that sight does not come from the sclera, the white part. Frequently, *Ġhālib* talks about sight as if it were a thread or wire. Anatomically speaking, light goes into the eye while nothing comes out of it.

95

برشکالِ گریۂ عاشق ہے، دیکھا چاہیے
کھل گئی مانندِ گُل سَو جا سے دیوارِ چمن

bar shikāl-e girya(h)ʾ ʿāshiq hai, dekhā chāhiye
khil gaʾī mānind-e gul sau jā se dīvār-e chaman (95:1; #562)

The downpour of the lover's crying needs appreciation,
As the flowers are blooming at hundreds of places in the walls of the garden.

bar shikāl; rainy season; *sau jā:* hundreds of places.

The downpour of tears has made flowers bloom all over the walls of the garden. It can also mean that the tears of lovers have created many cracks in the wall. For the first meaning, if the tears of lovers can make flowers bloom over the walls of the garden, imagine what they can do to the garden, a place more conducive to the growth of flowers. In the second explanation, we can alter the meaning by using "open" instead of "blooming" in the second line, which will then mean that the walls of the garden have opened up like flowers because of the flow of tears. Now, as the flooding reaches the garden, let us see what it would do to the garden.

اُلفتِ گُل سے غلط ہے دعویٔ وارستگی
سرو ہے با وصفِ آزادی گرفتارِ چمن

ulfat-e gul se ġhalaṯ hai daʿvaīʾ vārastagī
sarv hai bā vasf-e āzādī giraftār-e chaman (95:2; #563)

**Wrong it is to claim independence from the love of flowers.
The Cypress tree though independent remains enslaved to the garden.**

vārastagī; freedom; *da'vaī:* claim; *ulfat*: love.

No matter how much distance we put between worldly things and ourselves we nevertheless get entangled in them. To live in the garden and not fall in love with flowers is impossible. The cypress tree with its tall stature claims independence but remains grounded in the garden. Some of us are more attached to things than others, but all of us remain enslaved to our worldly desires and needs. How true!

96

عشق تاثیر سے نومید نہیں
جاں سپاری شجرِ بید نہیں

'ishq tāṡīr se naumīd nahiñ
jāñ sipārī shajar-e baid nahiñ (96:1; #564)

Love is not forlorn of the hope of being effective.
Giving one's life for someone is no fruitless tree of willow.

baid: willow; *jāñ sipārī*: to offer life.

I am hopeful of the result of my love. Sacrificing oneself for someone is not like the willow tree that does not bear fruit. It will someday bring success.

سلطنت دست بہ دست آئی ہے
جامِ مے خاتمِ جمشید نہیں

سلطنت دست بہ دست آئی ہے
جامِ مے خاتمِ جمشید نہیں

salṭanat dast ba(h) dast ā'ī hai
jām-e mai ḳhātam-e jamshed nahiñ (96:2; #565)

The kingdoms are handed down through generations.
The goblet of wine is not the seal of Emperor Jamshed.

salṭanat: kingdom; *dast ba(h) dast*: hand to hand; *jām*: goblet; *mai:* wine; *ḳhātam:* ring with owner's name engraved, seal; *jamshed:* Emperor of Persia who, according to the legend, invented wine. In addition, the goblet of Jamshed would reveal the present and future.

Kingdoms come through inheritance, but a goblet of wine comes to the hands of the fortunate ones only. King Jamshed received the inheritance ring, but its value is less than the goblet of wine in the hands of drinkers. Here the goblet of wine means the kindness of the beloved (for she fills the glass) and something that is earned through hard labor. The reference to Persian King Jamshed is made here because he is credited with inventing wine.

ہے تجلی تری سامانِ وجود
ذرہ بے پرتوِ خورشید نہیں

hai tajallī terī sāmān-e vūjūd
żarra(h) be partau-e ḳhūrshīd nahiñ (96:3; #566)

Your manifestation is the reason for all existence.
A speck is nonexistent without the radiance of the sun.

tajallī: dazzle; *sāmān:* cause; *vūjūd:* existence*; żarra(h):* speck; *be:* without, void of; *partau*: shine; *ḳhūrshīd*: sun.

It is the sparkle of God that brings me into existence. Like a speck of dirt, which does not exist until the bright light of the sun, illuminates it. This phrase gives a nod to Buddhist teachings of existence that ask, "Does the speck of dirt exist if there is no light to show it to us?"

رازِ معشوق نہ رُسوا ہو جاے
ورنہ مر جانے میں کچھ بھید نہیں

rāz-e ma'shūq na(h) rusvā ho jāe
varna(h) mar jāne meñ kuchh bhed nahiñ (96:4; #567)

Lest the secret of the beloved would bring disgrace,
Otherwise there is no hidden reason for me not dying.

rāz; secret; *ma'shūq:* beloved; *rusvā:* disgrace, defamation; *bhed:* secret.

Suffering the pain of love, it would be better to die and relieve my suffering. I would have no problem dying except for one thing. If I die, the whole world will know that I could not bear the hardships of love. It will be a disgrace to the beloved to have such a feeble lover, and it would be a disgrace to me for being one. That is why I continue to live; there is no other reason.

گردشِ رنگِ طرب سے ڈر ہے
غمِ محرومیٔ جاوید نہیں

gardish-e rang-e ṭarab se ḍar hai
ġham-e maḥrūmī' jāved nahiñ (96:5; #568)

I am afraid of the changing state of joy,
No fear there is for the despairs of life.

gardish: rotation; *rang*: color, state; *ṭarab*: joy, cheer; *jāved:* living long.

I am not concerned with the sorrows of life for they are permanent and we can learn to live with them. It is the joy and celebrations that I fear because they soon come to naught.

کہتے ہیں، جیتے ہیں اُمّید پہ لوگ
ہم کو جینے کی بھی اُمّید نہیں

kahte haiñ, jīte haiñ ummīd pa(h) log
ham ko jīne kī bhī ummīd nahiñ (96:6; #569)

There is a saying that people live on hope,
But we do not even have any hope of living.

Hope gives life, but in my case there is little chance of living, so what does the hope support? Living souls make great plans, achieve much, and stay busy with matters of life—they live on hope. In my case, life is no longer a viable option. The poet is saying simply: people live on hope and I have no hope of living.

97

جہاں تیرا نقشِ قدم دیکھتے ہیں
خیاباں خیاباں اِرم دیکھتے ہیں

jahāñ terā naqsh-e qadam dekhte haiñ
ḳhiyābān, khiyābāñ iram dekhte haiñ (97:1; #570)

Wherever we see the impressions of your feet,
A bed of blooming flowers in the heaven we see.

ḳhiyābān: bed of flowers; *iram:* name of an old city, a simile to heaven, the fabulous garden said to have been built by Shaddad bin ʹAd in emulation of the garden of paradise, paradise.

The footsteps of the beloved are akin to flower-beds (repeated twice to mean extensive spread) in the heavens. If her footsteps cause flowers to bloom in heaven, imagine what the rest of her body would do! A simple exaggeration of beauty is presented here.

دلِ آشفتگاں خالِ کنجِ دہن کے
سُویدا میں سیرِ عدم دیکھتے ہیں

dil āshuftagāñ ḳhāl-e kunj-e dahan ke
suvaidā meñ sair-e ʿadm dekhte haiñ (97:2; #571)

The hearts distressed by the mole at the end of mouth,
I see this black spot as a stroll in the nonexistent world.

dil āshuftagān: distressed heart; *khāl kunj-e dahan*: mole at the end of mouth; *suvaidā:* black spot (as the mole or as in heart); *ʿadm;* nonexistent.

The beloved has a very small mouth beside which is a tiny black mole. The spots in the hearts of lovers are also black. The heartbroken lovers (with black spots in their hearts) fall in love with that almost nonexistent mole. Enjoying the sight of this mole is like roaming (floating) through a nonexistent world. Besides extreme exaggeration, the theme of strolling in the nonexistent world also means that we dream of one day getting close to it.

ترے سرو قامت سے اک قدِ آدم
قیامت کے فتنے کو کم دیکھتے ہیں

tere sarv qāmat se ik qadd-e ādam
qiyāmat ke fitne ko kam dekhte haiñ (97:3; #572)

By the height of a person with your cypress-like stature,
The havoc-wreaker of the Doomsday, we see him cut short.

sarv qāmat: of the stature of cypress tree (meaning tall); *qadd-e ādam*: height of a man; *qiyāmat kih fitne:* havoc wreaker of the Doomsday.

We rarely come across anyone with the stature of a cypress tree. It is so attractive that it wreaks havoc on the heart of lovers. Alternate interpretations include a comparison with the Doomsday troublemaker, a mythical person. It is said that the beloved is hewn of this "troublemaker," making him (the troublemaker shorter than a man's height because the beloved has been taken from him. Briefly, your stature stirs the lovers into frenzy, the likes of which can only be seen on the Doomsday.

تماشا کر اے محوِ آئینہ داری
تجھے کس تمنا سے ہم دیکھتے ہیں

تماشا! کہ اے محوِ آئینہ داری
تجھے کس تمنّا سے ہم دیکھتے ہیں

tamāshā! kih ai maḥv-e āʾīna(h) dārī
tujhe kis tamannā se ham dekhte haiñ (97:4; #573)

What spectacle! That you are looking into mirror intently.
Imagine with what longings do we look at you?

tamāshā: spectacle; *maḥv:* engrossed; *āʾīna(h)*: mirror; *tamannā:* desire.

What a tremendous spectacle it is when you are engrossed in admiring yourself in the mirror. Can you imagine what desires this (your looking into the mirror) evokes in me? If you are so stunned by yourself, imagine my desire and how I must feel for you.

سُراغِ تَفِ نالہ لے داغِ دل سے
کہ شَب رَو کا نقشِ قَدم دیکھتے ہیں

surāġh-e taf-e nāla(h) le dāġh-e dil se
kih shabro kā naqsh-e qadam dekhte haiñ (97:5; #574)

Trace the direction of plaint from the scar in my heart,
Just like following the footprints of the night robber.

surāġh: clue, tracking; *taf:* direction; *shabro:* night time burglar.

Track the source of my plaint from the branding of my heart like you would track the night-time burglar from the impressions of his feet on the ground. If my plaint is heated, do not be surprised, for the branding of my heart is also hot. The comparison with a night burglar is made to accentuate the feeling of being robbed by love.

بنا کر فقیروں کا ہم بھیس غالب
تماشائے اہل کرم دیکھتے ہیں

banā kar faqīroñ kā ham bhes Ġhālib
tamāshāe ahl-e karam dekhte haiñ (97:6; #575)

Donning the garb of beggars, *Ġhālib*,
We witness the display of generosity of the kind ones.

Taking on the garb and actions of beggars, *Ġhālib* wants to see how the generous people behave with beggars, to test their repute. The verse does not infer that *Ġhālib* is a beggar, and is begging for the kindness of God. This is wrongly interpreted. It is merely a suspicious taunt at those "rich people" who vie for the reputation of being kind.

98

ملتی ہے خوئے یار سے نار التہاب میں   کافر ہوں، گر نہ ملتی ہو راحت عذاب میں

miltī hai ḳhūe yār se nār iltihāb meñ
kāfir hūñ, gar na(h) miltī ho rāḥat ʿażāb meñ (98:1; #576)

The roar of fire mimics the style of the beloved;
Disbeliever I would be if I did not find comfort in calamity.

miltī: resembles, getting; *ḳhue yār*: beloved's habits, style; *nār:* fire; *iltihāb:* roaring of flames.

The roaring flames of hell's fire resemble the fire of love I am used to getting from my beloved. The nature and intensity of this fire is very comforting because it reminds me of my beloved. If it were not, it would be akin to being a disbeliever. A comparison is being made between the beloved's style and the roaring of flames, not the fire. Leaping flames go up and down like the mood of the beloved. The flames of hell's fire are trying to mimic the beloved's fiery disposition, not otherwise. The flames of hell are compared to the beloved's mood; the beloved's mood is not labeled hellish. Another fine point is being made by stating that if I did not believe in it, it would be akin to being a "disbeliever," who ultimately ends up in the hell. It is a comforting feeling to the lover.

کب سے ہوں، کیا بتاؤں، جہانِ خراب میں   شب ہائے ہجر کو بھی رکھوں گر حساب میں

kab se hūñ kyā batāuñ, jahān-e kharāb meñ
shab hāi hijr ko bhī rakhūñ gar ḥisāb meñ (98:2; #577)

How long, shall I say I have been living in this terrible world;
If I take into account the nights of separation also?

jahān-e ḳharāb; terrible world; *hijr*: separation; *ḥisāb:* calculation, account.

It is difficult to judge how long I have been living in this terrible world for it depends on whether I include the nights of separation or not. Since these nights never end, it will be tantamount to living forever. By calling the world a terrible place, the poet points out how living in this world prolongs the agony infinitely. This verse is one of *Ġhālib*'s masterpieces, wherein he condenses a thousand words into two lines.

تا پھر نہ انتظار میں نیند آئے عمر بھر　　آنے کا عہد کر گئے آئے جو خواب میں

tā phir na(h) intiẓār meñ nīnd āe ʿumr bhar
āne kā ʿahd kar ga'e ā'e jo ḳh(v)āb meñ (98:3; #578)

So I would never sleep again in my life, waiting for her,
She promised to return as she appeared in my dreams.

She came into my dreams only to promise to be back soon. Of course, she will not return, but the flimsy hope she has raised is enough to keep me awake for the rest of my life. If her promise meant that she would come in my dreams, then I shall never see her, as I can no longer sleep. Coming into dreams was a deliberate effort to take away the brief moments of comfortable sleep—now that I can no longer sleep. "How can my lover sleep in comfort?" she must wonder.

قاصد کے آتے آتے خط اک اور لکھ رکھوں　　میں جانتا ہوں جو وہ لکھیں گے جواب میں

qāṣid ke āte āte ḳhaṯ ik āur likh rakhūñ
maiñ jāntā hūñ jo vuh likheñ ge javāb meñ (98:4; #579).

Let me keep ready another letter until the messenger returns,
For I know how would she respond to my letter.

qāṣid: letter carrier, messenger.

The lover has sent a letter to his beloved describing the condition of his heart. While he waits for an answer, he wants to write another letter for he suspects the answer that will come. Some interpreters of this verse have assumed that there would be no answer. If that were the case, why then would the carrier return? The poet believes that she will write a response but this response cannot be any different from what has been said before—a plain "no."

مجھ تک کب اُن کی بزم میں آتا تھا دَورِ جام
ساقی نے کچھ مِلا نہ دیا ہو شراب میں

mujh tak kab un kī bazm meñ ātā thā daur-e jām
sāqī ne kuchh milā na(h) diyā ho sharāb meñ (98:5; #580)

When, in her assembly did the goblet ever get around to me?
Might it not be that the cupbearer has mixed something in the wine?

It has never happened that, in her company, the wine decanter reached me. However, today it has reached me and I fear that it happened because there is something wrong with the wine; something may have been mixed in it. Most interpret it to be poison, but if that were the case, then those who had had it before the turn of the lover would have died and the decanter would not have been passed around. What the cupbearer has done is mix something to make wine stout so that others were unable to imbibe. This allowed enough in the decanter to go all the way around to the end of the line. The wine here is the challenge of the cupbearer and since she has raised the bar, others have given up leaving me to cross it.

جو مُنکرِ وفا ہو، فریب اُس پہ کیا چلے
کیوں بدگماں ہُوں دوست سے دشمن کے باب میں

jo munkir-e vafā ho, fareb us pa(h) kyā chale
kioñ badgumāñ hūñ dost se dushman kih bāb meñ (98:6; #581)

How can one be deceived who reneges on loyalty?
Why then should I be suspicious of my beloved regarding the rival?

munkir: one who denies; *fareb:* spell, deception; *badgumān*: suspicious.

Because she does not believe in loyalty, she cannot be put under any spell that would make her believe in the offerings of the rival. Why, then, should I be suspicious that she may have fallen to the claim of loyalty made by my rival? The claim of my rival is superfluous. The lover knows that the rival has succeeded and he is consoling his heart by saying that since she does not believe in faithfulness she would not accept the claims of faithfulness of the rival.

میں مضطرب ہوں وصل میں خوفِ رقیب سے   ڈالا ہے تم کو وہم نے کس پیچ و تاب میں

maiñ muẕṯarib hūñ viṣl meñ ḳhauf-e raqīb se
ḍālā hai tum ko vaham ne kis pech-o-tāb meñ (98:7; #582)

I am worried at the time of the union from the fear of the rival?
In what dilemma has the suspicion put you into?

muztarib: impatient, perturbed; *viṣl:* union, consummation; *raqīb*: beloved's lover; *vahm:* imagination; *pech-o-tāb:* perplex, dilemma.

At the time of union, the beloved becomes perplexed by the condition of the poet who is nervous and appears perturbed. This makes the beloved think that perhaps the lover is afraid of his rival. To this notion, the lover clarifies that his ecstasy is what makes him appear to be nervous. There is a very fine expression here of the stereotyped lover being weak, frightened, and docile.

میں اور حظِ وصل، خدا ساز بات ہے   جاں نذر دینی بھول گیا اضطراب میں

maiñ āur ḥaẕẕ-e vaṣl, ḳhudā sāz bāt hai
jāñ nażr denī bhūl gayā iẕṯirāb meñ (98:8; #583)

I, and the joy of union with her, it must be God's granting.
I got so excited that I forgot to sacrifice my life.

It was not my fate to unite with the beloved. This union must have been through God's special blessing. Ideally, I should have died of happiness, but that did not happen for I was too stunned to remember to die (that is, to give my life).

ہے تیوری چڑھی ہوئی اندر نقاب کے   ہے اک شکن پڑی ہوئی طرفِ نقاب میں

hai tevrī chaṛhī hu'ī andar niqāb ke
hai ik shikan paṛī hu'ī ṭarf-e niqāb meñ (98:9; #584)

A scowl there is inside the veil.
A crease fold there is on the outside of veil.

tevrī: scowl.

When the lover asked to see her face, she got upset and scowled. This caused her to show a crease in her veil that made it abundantly clear to the lover the inappropriateness of the time to ask for her kindness.

لاکھوں لگاؤ، ایک چرانا نگاہ کا   لاکھوں بناؤ، ایک بگڑنا عتاب میں

lākhoñ lagā'o, ek churānā nigāh kā
lākhoñ banā'o, ek bigaṛnā ʿitāb meñ (98:10; #585)

Millions of blandishments, and one glance of her coy eye;
Millions of adornments against one angry gesture.

Millions of her favors are indeed desirable, but a stolen glance of her coy eyes is more pleasurable. The millions of ways she adorns herself are soothing to see, but to witness her getting upset in anger is something else. To a lover, a stolen glance or her blowing up in anger is more precious than her favors and beauty.

وہ نالہ دل میں خس کے برابر جگہ نہ پائے   ق   جس نالے سے شگاف پڑے آفتاب میں

vuh nāla(h) dil meñ ḳhas ke barābar jaga(h) na(h) pāe
jis nāle se shigāf paṛe āftāb meñ (98:11; #586)

A plaint that does not find a place equivalent to that of a straw in the heart,
Is that plaint which rents asunder a crack in the sun.

ḳhas: straw; *shigāf*: crack.

A plaint, no matter how sincere, would not melt her heart and would have no effect on her. It may rend the sun, but it would get less room in her heart than would a piece of straw. The lover may shake the Universe with his plaint, but not her heart. The plaint tearing the sun apart shows the heat of plaints. The use of straw to signify a small room is made in the first line to bring in the heat that can burn the sun in the second line. Straw, fire, heat, and sun are all part of this very warm verse.

وہ سحر مدعا طلبی میں نہ کام آئے   جس سحر سے سفینہ رواں ہو سراب میں

vuh saḥr mudda'ā ṭalabī meñ na(h) kām āe
jis saḥr se safīna(h) ravāñ ho sarāb meñ (98:12; #587)

A magic that proves futile in achieving the fulfillment of my desires is
That spell which allows the rowing of boats in a mirage.

saḥr: magic; *mudda'ā ṭalabī*: achieving goals; *sarāb,* mirage.

Magic that performs such impossible things as rowing a boat in a desert mirage is of no use when it comes to achieving my heart's desires. There may be miracles in the world, but they cannot help me win her heart.

غالبؔ چھُٹی شراب پر اَب بھی کبھی کبھی
پیتا ہُوں روزِ ابر و شبِ ماہتاب میں

Ġhālib chhuṭī sharāb par ab bhī kabhī kabhī
pītā huñ roz-e abr-o-shab-e māhtāb meñ (98:13; #588)

***Ġhālib*, though I have renounced wine, yet still once in a while,**
I do drink on cloudy days and moonlit nights.

Drinking wine on cloudy days and moonlit nights is irresistible, even though I have given up drinking. However, all nights become moonlit nights when I think of her (face) and all days appear cloudy (comforting) when I fancy her kindness. Therefore, the imbibing goes on day and night.

99

کل کے لیے کر آج نہ خسّت شراب میں   یہ سوءِ ظن ہے ساقیِ کوثر کے باب میں

kal ke liye kar āj na(h) ḳhissat sharāb meñ
yih sū'ī ẕann hai sāqī' kauṡar ke bāb meñ (99:1; #589)

For the sake of tomorrow, be not a miser today in giving wine;
That is disrespectful to the cupbearer of Paradise.

ḳhissat: miserly; *sū'ī ẕann*: dishonoring; *kauṡar:* a legendary river in paradise.

For the sake of tomorrow, we should not lessen our drinking today. If tomorrow is the Day of Judgement and we believe that those who do not drink will get the wine of paradise, we are disrespecting the cupbearer of Paradise for we are saying that the cupbearer is discriminating and gives the wine only to those who do not drink. If tomorrow is the day of Judgement, the day we face God, then this argument is disrespectful to God, in whom alone resides the judgement concerning who does and who does not get the wine. He is indeed the cupbearer of Paradise. This is a typical argument by a drunkard who is justifying his next glass of wine.

ہیں آج کیوں ذلیل، کہ کل تک نہ تھی پسند   گستاخیِ فرشتہ ہماری جناب میں

ḥaiñ āj kioñ żalīl, kih kal tak na(h) thī pasand
gustāḳhī' farishta(h) hamārī janāb meñ (99:2; #590)

Why are we contemptible today, when only until yesterday, it was deplored,
The disrespect of angels in our honor?

żalīl; shameless; *gustākhī*: disrespect; *farishta(h)*: angel; *hamārī janāb meñ:* in my honor.

On the Day of Creation God told the angels to bow down to Adam. Such was the respect accorded to humans when it all began. The poet asks, "Why then have we as a race become so despicable and base?" He concludes that this, of course, is all our own doing. The poet is asking us to reflect on how mankind has deteriorated.

جاں کیوں نکلنے لگتی ہے تن سے دمِ سماع　　گر وہ صدا سمائی ہے چنگ و رباب میں

jāñ kioñ nikalne lagtī hai tan se dam-e samā'
gar vuh ṣadā samā'ī hai chang-o rabāb meñ (99:3; #591)

Why does the soul appear to fly from the body as the melody begins to play?
As if His voice is contained in the notes of *chang* and *rabāb*.

samā': listening to music; *ṣadā;* voice; *chang:* a stringed musical instrument; *rabāb:* a type of violin.

Why do lovers nearly die of ecstasy when they hear musical melodies? Do these musical instruments have in them the voice of the Lord? It is because of the desire to merge with the Lord that lovers want to end their life. The connection between the notes played on a musical instrument and the condition of a resonating heart is described here.

رَو میں ہے رخشِ عمر، کہاں دیکھیے تھمے　　نے ہاتھ باگ پر ہے نہ پا ہے رکاب میں

rau meñ hai rakhsh-e 'umr, kahān dekhiye thame
ne hāth bāg par hai na(h) pā hai rakāb meñ (99:4; #592)

Galloping fast is the steed of age, let's see where will it come to halt,
As neither the reins are in hand nor are the feet in the stirrups.

rau: swing; *rakhsh*: horse (perhaps referring to the fast horse of Rustam, a hero); *'umr:* age; *thame:* stay; *bāg*: leash; *rakāb:* saddle foot hold, stirrup.

The steed of time (age) is galloping. I do not know where and when it will stop, as I have no control over it. Life is like riding a horse without reins or stirrups. This is a lament on the downfall of the *Muġhal*s. The poets fearing that they will go down in history as failures.

اُتنا ہی مجھ کو اپنی حقیقت سے بُعد ہے   جتنا کہ وہمِ غیر سے ہوں پیچ و تاب میں

utnā hī mujh ko apnī ḥaqīqat se bo'd hai
jitnā kih vahm-e ġhair se huñ pech-o-tāb meñ (99:5; #593)

I am only that far removed from my reality, as much as I twist and turn at the mystery of the unknown.

ḥaqīqat: truth, reality; *bo'd:* distance; *vahm:* imagination, suspicion; *ġhair:* stranger, unknown; *pech-o-tāb:* perturbed, perplexed.

My perception of existence is just as flimsy and fragile as my not knowing about the existence of the unknown (God). I am upset that I cannot understand how and why God can exist. My own existence can only come if God exists. That explains why I do not know what to believe—whether I exist or not? The more I try to understand God, the farther away I get from my own reality.

اصلِ شہود و شاہد و مشہود ایک ہے   حیراں ہوں پھر مشاہدہ ہے کس حساب میں

aṣl-e shahūd-o shāhid-o-mashhūd ek hai
ḥairāñ hūñ phir mushāhida(h) hai kis ḥisāb meñ (99:6; #594)

In reality, the observing, the observer, and the observed are the same;
I am perplexed as to what to make out of the observation.

shahūd: observing; *shāhid*: observer; *mashhūd*: what is observed; *mushāhida(h)*: observation.

What is observed when the observed and the observer are the same? The meaning of observation cannot be a reality for it requires a duality to observe each other. When we are all one, we cannot reflect upon ourselves. The Universe and its Creator are the same and that includes us as well, so how can we see Him? At the same time, though, how can we not see Him as we see ourselves? *Ġhālib* describes here eloquently the most difficult concept of philosophy concerning existence and our observation of it. How can you see it, if you are a part of it?

ہے مشتمل نمودِ صُوَر پر وجودِ بحر　　یاں کیا دھرا ہے قطرہ و موج و حباب میں

hai mushtamil namūd-e ṣūr par vajūd-e baḥar
yāñ kyā dharā hai qaṯra(h)-o-mauj-o-ḥabāb meñ (99:7; #595)

The existence of the ocean depends on its appearance in many forms.
What otherwise makes the drops, the waves and the bubbles anyway?

mushtamil: consist of; *numūd:* appearance; *sūr:* image; *vajūd*: existence; appearance; *dharā*: left; *habāb:* bubble.

The existence of the ocean is manifested by the many images it creates. Its components, taken separately, do not have the grandiose character of an ocean. On the other hand, what appears to be the ocean is merely a collection of drops, waves and bubbles that we call the ocean.

شرم اِک ادائے ناز ہے، اپنے ہی سے سہی　　ہیں کتنے بے حجاب کہ ہیں یوں حجاب میں

sharm ik adāe nāz hai, apne hī se saḥī
haiñ kitne be ḥijāb kih haiñ yuñ ḥijāb meñ (99:8; #596)

Coyness is the style of the beloved even with herself.
How immodest of you to put on a veil around you like this.

Modesty is your style, which requires you to put a veil between you and yourself. Just putting a veil between us and not between yourself is a sign of not being modest enough as you expose yourself inside that veil. Being bashful with yourself is a coquettish style, but by putting on a veil, you have locked yourself with you. How immodest of you!

آرائشِ جمال سے فارغ نہیں ہنوز   پیشِ نظر ہے آئنہ دائم نقاب میں

ārā'ish-e jamāl se fāriġh nahiñ hanūz
pesh-e naẓar hai ā'īna(h) dā'im niqāb meñ (99:9; #597)

Still not done with adorning the beauty,
Behind the veil, she is looking into mirror.

ārā'ish: adorning; *dā'im*: always, perpetually.

Behind the veil, the beloved is perpetually adorning herself in front of the mirror and is not yet ready to lift the veil, allowing the world to see her perfect beauty. Nature continues to perfect the Universe behind the veil of illusions. Addressing God, the poet tells us that whatever is around us is just a veil as You work on perfecting the Universe.

ہے غیبِ غیب جس کو سمجھتے ہیں ہم شہود   ہیں خواب میں ہنوز جو جاگے ہیں خواب میں

hai ġhaib-e ġhaib jis ko samajhte haiñ ham shahūd
haiñ ḳh(v)āb meñ hanoz jo jāge haiñ ḳh(v)āb meñ (99:10; #598).

A mysterious mystery it is what we believe to be an evidence;
They are still dreaming who have been awakened in their dreams.

ḳh(v)āb: dream; *ġhaib*: unknown mystery; *shahūd:* witness; *hanoz:* yet, still.

At times, during our dreams, we see ourselves coming from a dream and whatever we are dreaming seems real. It is exactly the same when we begin to take the evidence of Nature that assures us that these are the signs of existence. The nonexistent is the most unfathomable of the unknown. This means that we fool ourselves into believing that we are able to understand the things around us, which, in reality, do not even exist. It is all a dream. To stretch the observation, we can include the observation of déjà vu here as well.

غالبؔ ندیم دوست سے آتی ہے بوئے دوست
مشغولِ حق ہوں بندگیٔ بوتراب میں

Ġhālib nadīm-e dost se ātī hai būe dost
mashġhūl-e ḥaq huñ bandagī' būturāb meñ (99:11; #599)

Ġhālib, the scent of the beloved radiates from the beloved's companion.
I am busy serving the Lord offering devotion to *Haẓrat Alī*.

nadīm-e dost: friend of friend; *būturāb*: drenched in dust (here meaning, *Haẓrat Alī*. Prophet Muhammad once addressed his son-in-law, *Haẓrat Alī* "*Būturāb*," and thus it became his nickname.)

By adoring *Haẓrat Alī*, the poet can smell God in him, the son-in-law of Prophet Mohammad.

100

حیراں ہوں، دل کو روؤں کہ پیٹوں جگر کو میں   مقدور ہو تو ساتھ رکھوں نوحہ گر کو میں

ḥairāñ huñ, dil ko ro'uñ kih pīṭuñ jigar ko maiñ
maqdūr ho to sāth rakhuñ nauḥagar ko maiñ (100:1; #600)

Perplexed am I if I should cry for my heart or lament for my liver;
I would keep a professional crier with me, if I could afford one.

Both heart and liver have been damaged. To lament for both is not possible for me alone. It would be better if I could afford to hire a professional crier. This is a splendid example of *Ġhālib*'s professional wit.

چھوڑا نہ رشک نے کہ ترے گھر کا نام لوں   ہر اک سے پوچھتا ہوں کہ جاؤں کدھر کو میں

choṛā na(h) rashk ne kih tere ghar kā nām luñ
har ik se pūchhtā huñ kih jāuñ kidhar ko maiñ (100:2; #601)

Jealousy prevented me from identifying your home.
"Which way to go?" I kept asking everyone whom I came across.

Desperate from love, I ran away to wander and now I am lost. I keep asking everyone, "Where should I go?" They, in turn, ask, "Where do you want to go?" Of course, I want to go to my beloved's home, but I keep quiet for I do not want them to know where she lives. If I tell them, they will probably get there first, fall in love with her, and become my rivals. They will all run to her home because after they see my condition they will be convinced of the power of her beauty that has turned me into a lunatic. My jealousy, therefore, kept me from telling others where the beloved lives.

جانا پڑا رقیب کے در پر ہزار بار   اے کاش جانتا نہ ترے رہگزر کو میں

jānā paṛā raqīb ke dar par hazār bār
ae kāsh jāntā na(h) tere rahguzar ko maiñ (100:3; #602)

I ended up going to the rival's door a thousand times;
I wish I had not known the path traversed by you.

raqīb: rival; *dar*: door; *hazār bār:* thousands of times; *kāsh:* wish I had; *rahguzar:* path taken.

Lamenting a thousand times the inevitability of visiting a rival's doorstep, the poet wishes that he had not discovered the path that the beloved takes in front of the rival's abode. Whereas the beloved is always close to the rival and visiting him often, to get to see her the poet must sit at the rival's door—an extremely denigrating situation. Here, knowing her path also means falling in love with the beloved. A very complicated verse, it can mean loving her means putting up with a rival. The lover sits at the rival's doorsteps to see her coming out. He also hangs around the rival's alley to see her pass through there, either intentionally or routinely. If I had not fallen in love with you, I would not have been disgraced enough to go to the rival's home to catch a glimpse of your coming out.

ہے کیا جو کس کے باندھیے میری بلا ڈرے   کیا جانتا نہیں ہوں تمھاری کمر کو میں

hai kyā jo kas ke bāndhīye, merī balā ḍare
kyā jāntā nahiñ hūñ tumhārī kamar ko maiñ (100:4; #603)

What is there that you would tie down tightly, who cares?
As if I do not know the reality about your waist.

kas ke bāndhīye: to tie down (a belt or a string around waist); *kamar*: waist.

Next to the small mouth of the beloved is her waist that also nearly does not exist. The beloved challenges him by saying that she is tying her waist to kill him. This is an idiom for getting ready to fight. The poet answers that he is not afraid, (my calamities would be afraid, not me) for I know you do not have a waist that you can tie tightly in order to get ready to fight.

لو وُہ بھی کہتے ہیں کہ یہ بے ننگ و نام ہے　　یہ جانتا اگر تو لُٹاتا نہ گھر کو مَیں

lo vuh bhī kahte haiñ kih yih be nāng-o-nām hai
yih jāntā āgar to luṭātā na(h) ghar ko maiñ (100:5; #604)

See, even she is calling me poor and destitute.
Had I known, I would not have let my home be looted.

nāng-o-nām: honor and reputation

Sacrificing all that I had in the pursuit of the beloved, I never hear from anyone but the beloved that I am destitute, not worth associating with. I was ready to take the taunts of others, but when the beloved taunts me like this, I wonder if it was worth losing everything for her.

چلتا ہُوں تھوڑی دُور ہر اک تیز رَو کے ساتھ　　پہچانتا نہیں ہُوں ابھی راہبر کو مَیں

chaltā huñ thoṛī dūr har ik tez rau ke sāth
pahchāntā nahiñ hūñ abhī rāhbar ko maiñ (100:6; #605)

Walking alongside for a short distance with every swift traveler,
I still do not recognize the leader.

Disillusioned about the course of my destiny, I tag along with anyone who goes fast, only to find someone else going faster. I still do not recognize the leader who can lead me to my destiny. We see examples of this everyday in people chasing money only to find they are too old to enjoy it. They did not realize that the goal was happiness and that money was just a means to it, perhaps the least important one.

خواہش کو احمقوں نے پرستش دیا قرار   کیا پُوجتا ہُوں اُس بُتِ بیداد گر کو میں

ḳh(v)āhish ko aḥmaqoñ ne parastish diyā qarār
kyā pūjtā hūñ us but-e bedād gar ko maiñ (100:7; #606)

The fools declared desire to be devotion.
Do I indeed worship that cruel idol?

āḥmaq: fool; *parastish:* worship, devotion; *qarār:* declaration; *pūjtā;* worship; *bedād gar*: cruel person.

I am in love and hold the desire for my beloved in my heart. My devotion is so intense that it appears to fools that I am worshipping her. I want to clarify that I am not. The fact is that I do not know where the desire (devotion) ends and where the worship begins.

پھر بیخودی میں بھُول گیا راہِ کُوئے یار   جاتا وگرنہ ایک دِن اپنی خبر کو مَیں

phir beḳhudī meñ bhūl gayā rāh-e kūe yār
jātā vagarna(h) ek din apnī ḳhabar ko maiñ (100:8; #607)

I forgot again, in my ecstasy, the path to the beloved's lane;
Otherwise, I certainly would have gone there to find myself one day.

be ḳhud: in ecstasy; *bhūl:* forgetfulness; *ḳhabar:* whereabouts.

In delirium, I forgot again the path to your alley where I had lost myself or else I might have gone there again to find myself. Since it was my fate to lose myself in your alley, I am not concerned about it. Let it be what it is. The use of "some day" or "one day" indicates obliviousness on the part of the poet. He is not too eager to rediscover himself. Also, note the use of the word, "again" in the first line, meaning that this has happened before as well.

اپنے پہ کر رہا ہوں قیاس اہلِ دہر کا — سمجھا ہوں دل پذیر متاعِ ہنر کو میں

apne pa(h) kar rahā huñ qiyās āhl-e dahar kā
samjhā huñ dil pażīr, matā̒-e hunar ko maiñ (100:9; #608)

I assume that others in this terrible world are like me as well,
As I consider it appealing to the heart, the goods of skills?

qiyās: guess; *āhl-e dahar:* those living in this world; *dil pażīr*: settling in heart; *matā̒-e hunar:* goods of skills.

Knowledge, wisdom, and diction are the valuable skills that are buried in my heart and I value them greatly. Foolishly, I believed that the rest of the world would also appreciate these things. He concludes, however, that such is not the case.

غالب خدا کرے کہ سوارِ سمندِ ناز
دیکھوں علی بہادرِ عالی گہر کو میں

Ġhālib ḳhudā kare kih savār-e samand-e nāz
dekhuñ Ālī Bahādur-e ʿālī Gohar ko maiñ (100:10; #609)

***Ġhālib*, may Lord allow, that he alights on the steed of pride,**
For me to see *Alī Bahadur*, of great hidden virtue.

samand: horse, steed; *nāz:* pride; *ʿālī*: high; *gohar*: pearl, hidden virtue.

This is part of the ode that was written for Nawab *Alī* Bahadur who was related to *Ġhālib.* It was in his home that *Ġhālib* stayed while en route to Calcutta to plead his pension case. The Nawab was indeed a very generous man. *Ġhālib* is wishing him prosperity in getting a good reputation. "Riding the horse of pride" is what he is wishing the Nawab.

101

ذکر میرا بہ بدی بھی اُسے منظور نہیں غیر کی بات بگڑ جاے تو کچھ دُور نہیں

żikr merā ba(h) badī bhī use manz̤ūr nahīñ
ġhair kī bāt bigaṛ jāe to kuchh dūr nahīñ (101:1; #610)

She is intolerant of hearing about me even derogatorily;
It would not be far-fetched if it backfires for the rival.

żikr: discussion; *ba(h) badī*: in bad words, derogatorily.

The beloved hates me so much that she cannot bear hearing my name even if it is spoken in a derogatory manner. The rival is trying to get the lover into trouble, but this may, in turn, get him into trouble if he does not stop. Hearing the rival speak what she does not want to hear may turn her against the rival. The lover illustrates a sublime trick to dissuade the rival into not smearing his name in front of the beloved.

وعدۂ سیرِ گلستاں ہے، خوشا طالعِ شوق مژدۂ قتل مقدر ہے جو مذکور نہیں

va'da(h)' sair-e gulistāñ hai, ḳhushā tāli'-e shauq
muz̤hda(h)' qatl muqaddar hai jo mażkūr nahīñ (101:2; #611)

The invitation to stroll in the garden is indeed a happy fortune;
However, the good news of murdering me is what is not mentioned here.

ḳhushā ṭāli'; happy fortune; *mażkūr:* mentioned; *muz̤hda(h):* good news.

The beloved has invited the lover, to his great fortune, for a stroll in the garden. However, the lover wishfully suspects that the beloved has some other plans. She plans to murder the lover in the garden and decorate it red with his blood. The lover gleefully agrees to that.

شاہدِ ہستیِ مُطلق کی کمر ہے عالَم لوگ کہتے ہیں کہ ہے، پر ہمیں منظور نہیں

shāhid-e hastī' muṯliq kī kamar hai 'ālam
log kahte haiñ kih hai, par hameñ manẕūr nahīñ (101:3; #612)

The Universe is like the waist of the Absolute Being,
Though people assert that it is, but it is not acceptable to me.

hastī: existence; *kamar:* waist; *'ālam*: universe; *manzūr:* acceptable; *shāhid*: evident; *muṯliq:* absolute.

The Universe like the waist of the Creator (meaning a symbol of His creation), and like my beloved's waist, it does not exist, despite what others say. In reality, it does not exist. Creativity of thought and syllogism of this verse are remarkable. The ultimate beauty of the beloved resides in her having such a tiny waist that it practically does not exist. Others regard the Universe as the ultimate expression of the beauty of Nature; therefore, it also does not exist. Nothing exists regardless of how beautiful it may appear. Only *Ġhālib* can dig this deep and get away with it.

قطرہ اپنا بھی حقیقت میں ہے دریا لیکن ہم کو تقلیدِ تُنک ظرفیِ منصور نہیں

qaṯra(h) apnā bhī ḥaqīqat meñ hai daryā lekin
ham ko taqlīd-e tunuk ẕarfī' Manṣūr nahiñ (101:4; #613)

My drop too, is, in reality, an ocean, but
Following the trend of *Manṣūr's* lowly act is not acceptable to us.

tunuk ẕarfi; lack of courage, weakness; *taqlīd:* following; *Manṣūr*: Mansoor Hussain, who declared "*ānal ḥaq*" meaning, I am God and was put to death.

The essence of my persona has merged with the ocean (the Creator) and has achieved the state of nonexistence that requires arduous efforts to reach. I cannot follow *Manṣūr* (see Glossary), the weak soul, who declared himself God. It is more difficult to merge yourself with Him than to declare to be Him.

حسرت، اے ذوقِ خرابی کہ وہ طاقت نہ رہی   عشقِ پُر عربدہ کی گوں تنِ رنجور نہیں

ḥasrat, ai żauq-e ḳharābī kih vuh ṭāqat na(h) rahī
'ishq-e pur 'arbada(h) kī goñ tan-e ranjūr nahīñ (101:5; #614)

Pity, O! Desire for destruction, for that strength is gone.
The weak body no longer has the vigor to face a love battle.

'ishq-e pur 'arbada(h): fighting love; *goñ*: able; *tan-e ranjūr*: weak body.

The battle of love, ideally, should have been fought until my death. Alas! My weakness precluded me from engaging in the battle, thus reducing my chances of being totally annihilated.

میں جو کہتا ہوں کہ ہم لیں گے قیامت میں تمہیں   کس رعونت سے وہ کہتے ہیں کہ ہم حور نہیں

maiñ jo kehtā hūñ kih ham leñ ge qiyāmat meñ tumheñ
kis ra'unat se vuh kehte haiñ kih ham ḥūr nahīñ (101:6; #615)

When I declare, "I will get you on the Day of Judgment,"
With what haughtiness she says, "I am not a nymph."

ra'unat: haughtiness.

Desperate since he is not able to claim her in this world, the lover declares that on the Day of Judgment he will be rewarded with Paradise in return for all his sufferings in this world. The nymphs in Paradise will be awarded to him, but he will ask for the beloved instead and shall be granted this wish. The beloved retorts, "You may get nymphs, but not me! I am not a nymph." What a show of haughtiness!

ظلم کر ظلم، اگر لطف دریغ آتا ہو   تو تغافل میں کسی رنگ سے معذور نہیں

ẕulm kar ẕulm, āgar luṯf dariġh ātā ho
tū taġhāful meñ kisī rang se ma'żūr nahīñ (101:7; #616)

Cruel be cruel if you are not inclined to be kind to me.
Not pardonable to me is your ignoring me in any way.

dariġh: disinclined; *ma'żūr:* pardonable.

The lover wants to maintain a connection with the beloved. If it cannot be her kindness, then let it be her cruelty, but ignoring the lover altogether is not acceptable. Elsewhere *Ġhālib* writes,"Break not the connection with me, if nothing else then let it be enmity."

صاف دُردی کشِ پیمانۂ جم ہیں ہم لوگ   وائے وہ بادہ کہ افشردۂ انگور نہیں

ṣāf durdī kash-e paimāna(h)' jam haiñ ham log
vāe vuh bāda(h) kih afshurḋa(h)-e angūr nahīñ (101:8; #617)

Clarified wine of Jamshed's goblet is what we desire.
Sorry, but not just any poor grape wine will do.

sāf durdī kash: wine with precipitate removed; *jam:* King Jamshed, the purported inventor of wine (See Glossary: Jamshed); *bāda(h):* wine; *afshurda(h)-e angūr*: expressed from grapes.

We, the drinkers, are followers of King Jamshed. Like him, we drink only the finest wines with the precipitate removed (clarified—the expensive kind). If the wine expressed from grapes were not available, then we would simply lament it and refrain from drinking any cheap wine. This verse gives a good indication of *Ġhālib's* life and how with the first penny he acquired, he would buy the best wines. His favorite was pink wine with which he would mix equal parts of rose water, to prolong the drinking. Also, note that red and pink wines go bad more often than do white wines. These wines must be tasted before imbibing, regardless of their vintage status. This verse expresses the aristocratic nature of a classy drinker.

ہوں ظہوری کے مقابل میں خفائی غالب
میرے دعوے پہ یہ حجت ہے کہ مشہور نہیں

hūñ ẓuhūrī ke muqābil meñ ḳhifāī' Ġhālib
mere da've pah yih ḥujjat hai kih mashhūr nahīñ (101:9; #618)

Ẓuhūrī and I are of equal rank, O! _Ġhālib_; though I remain unacknowledged.
The argument against my claim is that I am just not famous.

Ẓuhūrī: a poet who remained unacknowledged during his time but became famous later during the era of *Ġhalib*. The word "*ẓuhūrī* " also means something which is apparent to us; *ḳhifāī:* unacknowledged; *ḥujjat:* argument; *da'vā:* claim.

Playing with words, *Ġhālib* says, I am *Ẓuhūrī* (the poet and also a word meaning "apparent"), a good poet who wasted his life away without being recognized. The argument is supported by the thesis that he is not famous, though he is good. People say I am no good because I not famous. It is a circular paradigm.

102

نالہ، جز حسنِ طلب، اے ستم ایجاد، نہیں   ہے تقاضائے جفا، شکوۂ بیداد نہیں

nāla(h), juz ḥusn-e ṭalab ai siṭam ijād, nahīñ
hai taqāẓāe jafā, shikva(h)' bedād nahīñ (102:1; #619)

O! Creative oppressor, the plaint is nothing except asking gently.
It is insisting on oppression, not complaining of cruelty.

nāla(h): loud lament; *juz*: except; *ḥusn-e ṭalab*: asking with class, gently; *siṭam ijād:* discoverer of new cruelties; *bedād*: cruelty, oppression;

The beloved is always discovering new ways to torture the lover. The lover complains and the beloved gets upset. The lover says that these plaints are a subtle way of asking for more oppression and it seems to work. The beloved is getting upset with the lover and thus torments him more with her anger. These plaints are by no means an expression of complaint against your cruelty. By calling the beloved cruel, the poet asserts his right to masochism. Thinking of the beloved as someone who discovers new ways of cruelty is unique.

عشق و مزدوریِ عشرت گہِ خسرو، کیا خوب   ہم کو تسلیم نکو نامیِ فرہاد نہیں

'ishq-o mazdūrī' 'ishrat ga(h)-e ḳhusro, kyā ḳhūb
ham ko taslīm niko nāmī' farhād nahīñ (102:2; #620)

How nice it is to toil in love for the luxurious abode of *Ḳhusrao*!
We concede not to the good fame of *Farhād*.

'ishrat ga(h): place of luxury, palace; *Ḳhusrao:* The Persian King, the husband of *Shīrīn*, the beauty with whom *Farhād*, the legendary lover

from Persia, fell in love. *Farhād* was told to dig a channel of milk to *Ḳhusrao*'s palace if he wanted *Shīrīn*. He did it and then killed himself with the spade he dug the canal with when he was told of *Shīrīn*'s death, in an attempt to fool him; *taslīm*: to accept; *niko*: good, beautiful, a good thing.

Farhād was a great lover who earned a tremendous reputation, but we cannot appreciate his naivete in working to bring comfort to his rival. For *Shīrīn*, yes, but for her husband, no. *Farhād* was a great lover, but not a judicious one. The criticism here belittles *Farhād*. (See Glossary)

کم نہیں وُہ بھی خرابی میں پہ وُسعت معلُوم　　دشت میں ہے مجھے وُہ عَیش کہ گھر یاد نہیں

kam nahiñ vuh bhī ḳharābī meñ pa(h)' vusa't ma'lūm
dasht meñ hai mujhe vuh 'aish kih ghar yād nahīñ (102:3; #621)

That too is not any less desolate, except for its expanse.
I have such luxury in the wilderness that I forgot about my home.

"That" refers to home. The poet says, in a slightly awkward way, that both his home and the wilderness are equally desolate places, the difference being only in the size. I have no need to think of my home, as I am very much at home in the wilderness. The "luxury" in the wilderness is the lack of it.

اہلِ بِینِش کو ہے طُوفانِ حوادث مکتب　　لطمۂ مَوج کم از سِیلیِٔ اُستاد نہیں

ahl-e bīnish ko hai ṯūfān-e ḥavādis̤ maktab
laṯm'a(h)' mauj kam az sīlī' ustād nahīñ (102:4; #622)

To the wise, the streak of accidents is a school of experience;
The whipping of waves is no less than the slaps of the teacher.

ahl-e bīnish: wise people; *ḥavādis̤*: accidents; *laṯma(h):* whip; *sīl'ī:* slap.

By using an oft-repeated theme that teaches that mishaps are learning opportunities, *Ġhālib* calls a deluge of accidents a school where we learn by harsh experiences. Referring to accidents as a school reduces the feeling of misery, the same goes for the hurt inflicted by slap of a teacher who is always affectionate. When God doles hardship out to us, He is simply teaching us a lesson because He loves us.

وائے محرومیِ تسلیم و بداحالیِ وفا   جانتا ہے کہ ہمیں طاقتِ فریاد نہیں

vāe maḥrūmī' taslīm-o-badā ḥāl-e vafā
jāntā hai kih hameñ ṯāqat-e faryād nahiñ (102:5; #623)

Alas! How unfortunate it is not getting my pathetic state of faithfulness recognized.
She thinks I no longer have the energy left to lament.

vāe: Alas!; *maḥrūmī:* misfortune, deprivation; *taslīm:* acceptance; *bad ḥālī*: bad condition;

I do not wail because I know she does not like it, but now I have given her reason to think that I am too weak to wail. Had she considered my quietness as being a sign of patience and control, she might have someday shown her favors. Instead, she has begun to think that I have nothing to say about her mistreating me.

رنگِ تمکینِ گل و لالہ پریشاں کیوں ہے   گر چراغانِ سرِ رہگزرِ باد نہیں

rang-e tamkīn-e gul-o-lāla(h) pareshāñ kioñ hai
gar charāġhān-e sar-e rahguzar-e bād nahīñ (102:6; #624)

Why has the abiding color of the tulips and roses faded away,
If they are not the lamps left lit in the path of the wind?

tamkīn: patience; *charāġhañ sar-e rahguzar bād:* lamps lit in the face of wind.

Why are the flowers so pale? Is it because they are like glowing lamps in the face of a gusting wind? The wind makes them turn bright, and then they flicker and are extinguished by the head-on wind. The flowers bloom only to see their petals whither away, their stems dry out, and their once beautiful blooms fall. Happiness and beauty are indeed impermanent.

صبدِ گل کے تلے بند کرے ہے گلچیں   مژدہ! اَے مرغ، کہ گلزار میں صیاد نہیں

sabad-e gul ke tale band kare hai gulchīñ
muzhda(h)! ai murġh, kih gulzār meñ ṣaiyād nahiñ (102:7; #625)

Under the flower-basket, the flower-picker is tucking you.
It is good news! O! Nightingale, since the captor is not in the garden.

ṣabad-e gul: flower-basket; *gulchīñ*: flower-picker; *muzhda(h)!*: Good news!; *murġh*: bird, meaning here nightingale.

Being caught by the flower-picker and placed under the basket with freshly collected flowers is good since the captor, who comes to the garden to catch nightingales, is nowhere to be seen. A comparison of the two captors—the regular catcher and the flower-picker—is made here. The fact that the flower-picker and not the professional captor caught you reflects a limit of choices. In this case, at least we are caught under the basket with flowers around us and we are still left in the garden. In the other case, we would have been taken from the garden and God knows where we might end up. Apparently, this is a very complex thought, but the meaning is straightforward. We have little choice in how the world treats us. We must be thankful for wherever we end up because it may be a blessing in disguise. Another subtle interpretation here is that the captor has taken a different approach to capture the nightingale. He has taken on the guise of a flower-picker to deceive the nightingale.

نفی سے کرتی ہے اِثبات تَراوِش گویا　　دی ہے جائے دَہَن اُس کو، دمِ ایجاد نہیں

nafi se kartī hai is̈bāt tarāvish goyā
dī hai jā'e dahan us ko, dam-e ījād nahīñ (102:8; #626)

The denial brings out the positive evidence or else
A mouth was not given to her at the time of creation.

nafī: denial; *isbāt:* affirmation; *tarāwish:* dripping, coming out, become evident.

"No, no!" is how she begins and that utterance tells us that yes, she does have a mouth. The beloved has a small mouth, almost nonexistent, which is a customary sign of beauty. To get to know existence from nonexistence and to know yes from no is a remarkable juxtaposition here.

کم نہیں جلوہ گری میں ترے کُوچے سے بہشت　　یہی نقشہ ہے، ولے اِس قدر آباد نہیں

kam nahiñ jalva(h) garī meñ tere kūche se bahisht
yahī naqsha(h) hai, vale is qadar ābād nahīñ (102:9; #627)

The Paradise is no less than your alley in its dazzle.
The layout is the same, but it is but not as crowded.

kam: less; *jalva(h)*: display, show; *kūcha(h)*:alley; *bahish*t: Eden, heaven; *naqsha(h):* design, layout; ; *vale:* but; *is qadr:* so much; *ābād:* populated.

While Paradise is no less dazzling than your alley, it is not as crowded, even though the scene is the same. This means that fewer people wish to go to Paradise because they find you and your alley are more attractive, despite a great similarity between the two. Note that Paradise is compared to the beloved's alley, not vice versa.

کرتے کس منہ سے ہو غربت کی شکایت غالبؔ
تم کو بے مہریٔ یارانِ وطن یاد نہیں؟

karte kis muñh se ho ġhurbat kī shikāyat Ġhālib
tum ko be mahrī' yārān-e vaṯan yād nahīñ (102:10; #628)

With what face can you complain of the woes of being in exile, *Ġhālib*?
Do you not remember the indifference of your compatriots at home?

Much discomfort comes from staying in an alien abode, but you must not complain about it. Do you remember how your friends treated you in your own homeland? Your friends paid you hardly any attention, so if strangers do not respect you, what is the complaint? The use of "with what face?" connotes,"how can you?"

103

دونوں جہان دے کے وُہ سمجھے یہ خوش رہا
یاں آ پڑی یہ شرم کہ تکرار کیا کریں

donoñ jahān de ke vuh samjhe yih ḳhush rahā
yāñ āpaṛī yih sharm kih takrār kyā kareñ (103:1; #629)

Having given both worlds to me, He thinks that I am happy.
Here wrought upon me is the modesty what to argue.

jahān: the world; *samjhe:* understood; *ḳhush:* happy; *āpaṛī*: wrought upon; *sharm*: embarrassment, modesty; *takrār:* argument.

God's gifts to this world, the hereafter, and us are great and He believes that He has made us happy by bestowing these upon us. The dilemma we face is that the connection between the two is not suitable for us. Sins committed in this world shall bring punishment in the hereafter and that fear keeps us from enjoying this world. The hesitation comes from knowing that God thinks that He has done us a favor, but we think that this is not fair or even adequate. Some have interpreted this verse by considering the beloved to be the giver. She believes that I am happy, having given to me the two best things—the real world (by letting me come close to her), and the imaginative world (by letting me fantasize about her.) The fact is that I am embarrassed to argue with her that I do not want just that, but her mind and soul as well. I do not want to embarrass her by telling her how wrong she is.

تھک تھک کے ہر مقام پہ دو چار رہ گئے
تیرا پتا نہ پائیں تو ناچار کیا کریں

thak thak ke har muqām pe do chār rah ga'e
terā patā na(h) pāeñ to nāchār kyā kareñ (103:2; #630)

At every stage, in weariness, a few dropped out.
What would the helpless do if they could not find Your clue?

nāchār: helpless, destitute.

To find the Lord and inner happiness, we go places, and give our efforts in desperation, as we get disillusioned. Not knowing where to go, the clueless are indeed perplexed. Most of us do not know what we want in life but keep struggling fruitlessly, tiring ourselves out to reach some great unknown.

کیا شمع کے نہیں ہیں ہوا خواہ اہلِ بزم
ہو غم ہی جاں گداز تو غمخوار کیا کریں

kyā shama' ke nahiñ haiñ havā ḳh(v)āh āhl-e bazm
ho ġham hī jāñ gudāz to ġhamḳhuār kyā kareñ (103:3; #631)

Are the compatriots in the assembly not wishing to air the candle?
If the sorrow is itself soul melting, then what could the consoling friends do?

shama': candle; *havā ḳh(v)āh:* well-wisher, sympathizer, fanning; *bazm:* company (at a feast or entertainment); *ġhamḳhuār:* consoling friends; *jān:* life.

The pain of candle is known to all, yet no one can keep it from melting, for this is the destiny of candle. Similarly, our pain is such that no one can alleviate it. Another meaning is given by considering the fanning of flame by those pretending to be consolers. Do the lovers want to air or "fan" the candle making it burn brighter and, analogously, causing more suffering by enhancing the pain of burning? This is akin to our suffering when friends who know they cannot bring any relief to us continue to talk about the beloved and simply make it worse. This being the case, what could the friends do who want to console me? If the fate of my love is such that it would take my life, then no one can help me.

104

ہوگئی ہے غیر کی شیریں بیانی کارگر
عشق کا اُس کو گماں ہم بے زبانوں پر نہیں

hoga'ī hai ġhair kī shīrīñ bayānī kārgar
'ishq kā us ko gumāñ ham be zabānoñ par nahīñ (104:1; #632)

The sweet-talking of the rival has proved effective;
She no longer believes in love of us, the tongue-less.

kārgar: effective; *shīrīñ bayānī*: sweet talk; *be zabān:* tongueless, speechless.

The rival, talking fast and sweet, convinced the beloved of his love for her, though, in reality, it is a façade. Real lovers choose not to talk about themselves and have thus been ignored by the beloved. The situation points not only to a love triangle but also to how things often end up in a mess. The rival is portrayed as a deceptive man here.

105

قیامت ہے کہ سُن لیلیٰ کا دشتِ قیس میں آنا
تعجب سے وہ بولا: یُوں بھی ہوتا ہے زمانے میں؟

qiyāmat hai kih sun Lailā kā dasht-e Qais meñ ānā
ta'jub se vuh bolā: yūñ bhī hotā hai zamāne meñ (105:1; #633)

It was disastrous to tell of *Lailā* coming to meet *Qais* in the wilderness as
She retorted surprisingly, "That's how it happens in the world?"

To entice her, the lover told the beloved the legend of *Lailā* coming to meet her lover, *Qais*, in the wilderness. He had hoped that she will take a hint from the story. Instead, she shrugged it off by saying,"So, is that how things happen in the world?" cooling the lover.

دلِ نازک پہ اُس کے رحم آتا ہے مجھے غالبؔ
نہ کر سرگرم اُس کافر کو اُلفت آزمانے میں

dil-e nāzuk pa(h) us ke raḥm ātā hai mujhe Ġhālib
na(h) kar sargarm us kāfir ko ulfat āzmāne meñ (105:2; #634)

I feel pity at her tender heart, *Ġhālib.*
Excite not that idol into testing the affection.

ulfat: affection; *sargarm*: excited, busy.

Ġhālib! Do not try to test her affection. She has a very tender and fragile heart and it would be severely perturbed by any emotional upsurge. She may not be able to bear the exertion. Both sides can be tested in this situation. Test her affection for me and let her do things to test my affection for her. This verse is split equally, according to whichever way one wants to interpret it. In both instances, there is a plea not to inconvenience the beloved.

106

دِل لگا کر لگ گیا اُن کو بھی تنہا بیٹھنا
بارے اپنی بیکسی کی ہم نے پائی داد یاں

dil lagā kar lag gayā un ko bhī tanhā baiṭhnā
bāre apnī bekasī kī ham ne pā'ī dād yāñ (106:1; #635)

Having lost her heart to someone, she also craves to sit alone.
At last, we got an appreciation of our helplessness.

bāre: in short; *bekasī:* helpless; *dād:* praise, appreciation.

The beloved, having fallen in love, sits alone appearing helpless. Now she can appreciate how I feel and what I go through. Note that the person with whom the beloved has fallen in love is not the lover. This creates a melancholic situation.

ہیں زوال آمادہ اجزا آفرینش کے تمام
مہرِ گردوں ہے چراغِ رہگزارِ باد یاں

haiñ zavāl āmāda(h) ajzā āfrīnish ke tamām
mahar-e gardūñ hai charāġh-e rahguzār-e bād yāñ (106:2; #636)

Destined to decline are all elements of Nature;
Here the sun is like a lamp in the path swept by a tempest.

zavāl āmāda(h): going into decline; *ajzā:* component, elements; *tamām:* entire *charāġh*: lamp; *rāh guzar:* path.

All elements of nature are continually in decline. Look at the sun; it is like a lamp, lighting the path of the wind. It brightens and then disappears into oblivion at dusk. Here *Ġhālib* states the theory of physics that says since creation, all physical elements are in a state of continuous decline or degradation. This leads to the Universe collapsing back into a hole. *Ġhālib*'s declaration was proven a hundred years later by the theory of physics, particularly the Theory of Armageddon.

107

یہ ہم جو ہجر میں دیوار و در کو دیکھتے ہیں
کبھی صبا کو کبھی نامہ بر کو دیکھتے ہیں

yih ham jo hijr meñ dīvār-o-dar ko dekhte haiñ
kabhī ṣabā ko kabhī nāma(h) bar ko dekhte haiñ (107:1; #637)

This staring at the walls and doors that I do in separation is
Looking for the breeze at times and for the letter carrier at other times.

The lover is waiting to hear from the beloved. The message may arrive through the breeze coming over the wall (her scent if she is coming) or it might be announced by a knock from the letter carrier on the door announcing the arrival of her letter. The impatience of a lover waiting for word from his beloved is exquisitely described.

وہ آئے گھر میں ہمارے، خُدا کی قُدرت ہے
کبھی ہم اُن کو کبھی اپنے گھر کو دیکھتے ہیں

vuh āe ghar meñ hamāre ḳhudā kī qudrat hai
kabhī ham un ko kabhī apne ghar ko dekhte haiñ (107:2; #638)

Her coming to my home is indeed a miracle of God.
Repeatedly I look at her and then I look at my home.

The arrival of the beloved brings stunned surprise. The lover looks around in an effort to assure himself that he is indeed in his own home. In a state of complete disbelief, he calls this a miracle of God. Looking at her and then looking at his home is a remarkable expression of human nature. He is thinking,"Is this house worth her presence?"

نظر لگے نہ کہیں اُس کے دست و بازو کو
یہ لوگ کیوں مرے زخمِ جگر کو دیکھتے ہیں

naẓar lage na(h) kahīñ us ke dast-o-bāzū ko
yih log kioñ mere zaḳhm-e jigar ko dekhte haiñ (107:3; #639)

May her hand and arm be protected from the evil eye?
Why are these people looking so keenly at my heart's wound?

The deep, sharp wound carved into my heart is praise for the craftsmanship of its creator. People see it and in their hearts, they must be saying "O! What craftsmanship!" I hope this does not bring evil to the hands and arms of my beloved who created these wounds. In the expression,"Why are these people…" there is subtle innocence and a hidden prayer.

ترے جواہرِ طرفِ کُلہ کو کیا دیکھیں
ہم اَوجِ طالعِ لعل و گُہر کو دیکھتے ہیں

tere javāhir-e ṯarf-e kula(h) ko kyā dekheñ
ham āuj-e ṯāleʻ-e laʻl-o-gohar ko dekhte haiñ (107:4; #640)

Why should we look at the bejewelled brooch in your headdress?
We are merely appreciating the high fortune of the rubies and pearls.

javāhir-e ṯarf-e kulā(h): end of cap embroidered with jewels; *āuj*: height; *ṯāleʻ:* fortune; *laʻl-o-gohar*: jewels, rubies and pearl.

The beloved has decorated her head cover with a jeweled brooch. The lover denies that the brooch enhances her beauty or attracts attention. The reason behind looking at the brooch is to admire the great fortune of the jewels that have reached the zenith of their destiny, that of being placed on her head.

108

نہیں کہ مجھ کو قیامت کا اعتقاد نہیں
شبِ فراق سے روزِ جزا زیاد نہیں

nahiñ kih mujh ko qiyāmat kā i̊tiqād nahiñ
shab-e firāq se roz-e jazā ziyād nahīñ (108:1; #641)

No, it is not that I deny belief in the Doomsday.
But the Day of Retribution cannot be worse than the night of separation.

qiyāmat: Doomsday; *shab-e firāq:* night of separation; *roz-e jazā:* Day of Judgment, Retribution; *ziād:* more.

The lover tells his peers that Doomsday is nothing compared to a night of separation. The poet believes that the Day of Judgment will be frightfully terrible, but it cannot be worse than a night of separation. He says that for most people, the calamities of Doomsday will come only once. Lovers go through them every night.

کوئی کہے کہ شبِ مہ میں کیا بُرائی ہے
بلا سے، آج اگر دن کو ابر و باد نہیں

ko'ī kahe kih shab-e mah meñ kyā burā'ī hai
balā se, āj āgar din ko abr-o-bād nahīñ (108:2; #642)

Would someone tell me what is wrong with moonlit nights?
Who cares if there are no clouds or breeze in the day?

balā se: who cares; *ābr:* cloud; *bād:* breeze.

What is wrong with drinking on moonlit nights? Therefore, what if there are no clouds or breeze during the day (another reason to drink), since I drink only when it is cloudy or the moon is shining. If there were no clouds during the day, I would still drink, for the moonlit night is just around the corner.

جو آؤں سامنے اُن کے تو مرحبا نہ کہیں
جو جاؤں واں سے کہیں کو تو خیر باد نہیں

jo āu'ñ sāmne un ke to marḥabā na(h) kaheñ
jo jāūñ vāñ se kahīñ ko to ḳhair bād nahīñ (108:3; #643)

No welcome is offered to me when I come face-to-face with her,
Nor any good-byes when I leave her assembly to go elsewhere.

marḥabā: welcome; *ḳhair bād*: good-bye.

The customary, stereotypical indifference shown by the beloved brings neither a welcome nor a goodbye. What is more hurtful is that she shows no concern about when I come and when I leave.

کبھی جو یاد بھی آتا ہوں مَیں تو کہتے ہَیں
کہ آج بزم میں کچھ فِتنہ و فساد نہیں؟!

kabhī jo yād bhī ātā hūñ meñ to kahte haiñ
kih āj bazm meñ kuchh fitna(h)-o-fasād nahīñ (108:4; #644)

Even if she ever thinks of me, she says,
"There is not much havoc and rowdiness in my assembly today?"

The beloved does not notice me when things are peaceful in her assembly. When things get rowdy, though, she knows that I am present and wants to verify the fact. What a reputation I have earned!

علاوہ عید کے ملتی ہے اور دن بھی شراب
گدائے کوچۂ مے خانہ نامراد نہیں

'alāva(h) 'īd ke miltī hai āur din bhī sharāb
gadāe kūchah' mai ḳhānah nāmurād nahīñ (108:5; #645)

Besides the Eid day, the wine is available on other days as well.
The beggar in the alley of the tavern is never disappointed.

nāmurād: unfortunate, disappointed.

For some, the wine is something reserved for celebrations on special days like the day of Eid. The drinkers in the tavern, in the alley of beloved, are never disappointed. They get the wine of her beauty and celebrate every day.

جہاں میں ہو غم و شادی بہم، ہمیں کیا کام!
دیا ہے ہم کو خدا نے وہ دل کہ شاد نہیں

jahāñ meñ ho ġham-o-shādī baham hameñ kyā kām
diyā hai ham ko ḳhudā ne vuh dil kih shād nahīñ (108:6; #646)

What does it have to do with me, if there is joy and grief together in the world?
God has bestowed upon me a heart that cannot rejoice.

shād: delighted; *bāham*: together.

In this world, happiness and sorrow go hand in hand. It has nothing to do with me since God has given me a heart filled with neither sorrow nor happiness. This can also be taken to mean that God has given me a heart that cannot feel happiness so I am always sorrowful.

تم اُن کے وعدے کا ذکر اُن سے کیوں کرو غالب
یہ کیا کہ تم کہو اور وُہ کہیں کہ یاد نہیں

tum un ke va'de kā żikr un se kioñ karo Ġhālib
yih kyā kih tum kaho āur vuh kahaiñ kih yād nahīñ (108:7; #647)

Why should you bring into the discussion, her making promises, *Ġhālib*?
Might it be that you remind and she retorts that, "I do not remember."

The beloved made promises that remain unfulfilled and the lover suggests that she should not be reminded of them. If the lover mentions these promises, she will deny that she ever made them. She will insist that she does not remember anything like that. It is better, therefore, to leave things as they are. At least she made the promises and might later remember them. This gives the lover hope that they will be fulfilled someday. If she boldly contests that she does not remember anything, then all hope will be lost.

109

تیرے توسن کو صبا باندھتے ہیں
ہم بھی مضموں کی ہوا باندھتے ہیں

tere tausan ko ṣabā bāndhte haiñ
ham bhī maẓmūñ kī havā bāndhte haiñ (109:1; #648)

Offering odes to your agile horse, we call it wind;
We merely put hot air in our expressions.

tausan: a young unbroken horse, a high-blooded steed; *havā bāndhnā:* to express falsely.

Poet compares the beloved's horse to the wind and admits exaggerating by saying that the expression is merely "hot air." The play of words comes from calling her horse wind and calling the expression merely "hot air."

آہ کا کس نے اثر دیکھا ہے
ہم بھی اک اپنی ہوا باندھتے ہیں

āh kā kis ne āsar dekhā hai
ham bhī ik āpnī havā bāndhte haiñ (109:2; #649)

Who has seen a sigh ever work?
Yet, we just keep trying to push ourselves.

havā bāndhnā: to exaggerate; here it is used to state that we promote or push ourselves.

We know how ineffective are our plaints. The noise serves to impress others and perhaps her. We keep trying, knowing well that nothing will work.

تیری فرصت کے مقابل اے عمر
برق کو پا بہ حنا باندھتے ہیں

terī furṣat ke muqābil ai ʻumr
barq ko pā ba(h) ḥinā bāndhte haiñ (109:3; #650)

Compared to your duration of existence, O! Life,
We are merely applying henna to the feet of lightning.

furṣat: duration of time; *pā ba(h) ḥinā: henna* tinted feet.

When *henna* is applied to the feet, one has to wait for it to dry before walking. The duration of lightning is considered long in this instance, as if it had *henna* applied on its feet and was rendered unable to move quickly. The short duration of life can be compared to lightning that had *henna* applied to its feet, or, the duration of lightning appears longer than that of life. Even though *Ġhālib* uses some degree of exaggeration here, the reality is that his comparison is not far off. If we take the duration of the existence of the Universe (5 Billion years) and the duration of our life (say 70 years), it would be a fair comparison. Most of us would not be able to comprehend how humble and insignificant our existence is unless we look at this comparison, which *Ġhālib* presents here quite craftily.

قید ہستی سے رہائی معلوم
اشک کو بے سروپا باندھتے ہیں

qaid-e hastī se rihāī' maʻlūm
ashk ko be sar-o-pā bāndhte haiñ (109:4; #651)

Reprieve from the bondage of existence, I know!
Yet we continually shed tears senselessly.

be sar-o-pā: without head or feet, making no sense.

To free us from the bondage of existence is an elusive goal. Tears with no head or feet are ready to roll, but we keep them tied down in our verses. "Without head or feet" translates as making no sense. This means that knowing well that a reprieve from bondage is not possible; we foolishly shed tears and lament about it in our verses.

نشۂ رنگ سے ہے واشُدِ گل
مست کب بندِ قبا باندھتے ہیں

nasha(h)' rang se hai vā shud-e gul
mast kab band-e qabā bāndhte haiñ (109:5; #652)

The intoxication of color makes flowers bloom.
When do the intoxicated ones tie their tunic?

qabā: long garment open in front worn by men, a kind of tunic or cloak; *vā shud-e gul*: opening (blooming) of flowers.

Flowers are intoxicated by their own color and begin blooming, allowing their petals to open. The intoxicated ones are like flowers who let their tunic come open as they roam around. This verse creates the scenario of a colorful garden where everything is in ecstatic intoxication and swirling wildly in a whirling dervish dance.

غلطی ہائے مضامیں مت پوچھ
لوگ نالے کو رسا باندھتے ہیں

ġhalatī hāi maẓāmīn mat pūchh
log nāle ko rasā bāndhte haiñ (109:6; #653)

Ask not about the mistakes in our expression.
People construe a plaint as if it were bound to get there.

nāle: plaints; *rasā:* arriving, attaining, capable; *bāndhnā*: to bind.

It is an oxymoron to use the world "plaint" and "arriving" in the same expression, as many do, the poet complains. An exquisite play on words comes from the colloquial use of "arriving" and "expression," which also means to, "to bind." So when they say plaints arrive, they are also saying, to be held back.

اہلِ تدبیر کی واماندگیاں!
آبلوں پر بھی حنا باندھتے ہیں

ahl-e tadbīr kī vāmāndgiyāñ
ābloñ par bhī ḥinā bāndhte haiñ (109:7; #654)

O! The futility of those with sagacity?
They apply henna even on the blisters.

āhl: qualified; *tadbīr*: effort; *vāmāndgiyāñ:* futility.

Those who suggest plastering my feet with *henna* to heal my blisters suggest a futile effort. How pointless! If blisters could not keep me from wandering, how can a bandage of *henna* keep me restrained? Women apply *henna* to their feet to color them and they cannot walk while the *henna* dries.

سادہ پُرکار ہیں خوباں، غالب
ہم سے پیمانِ وفا باندھتے ہیں

sāda(h) purkār haiñ ḳhūbāñ, Ġhālib
ham se paimān-e vafā bāndhte haiñ (109:8; #655)

Simple and cunning is the beloved, O! *Ġhālib*,
Making a pact of faithfulness with me.

purkār: clever, cunning; *ḳhūbāñ*: beloved, excellent.

My beloved vows to be faithful to me and assumes that I will believe her—that is her simplicity, her naiveté. She is cunning, for she intends to deceive me. One single act displaying two different intents based on who is interpreting—the lover or the beloved.

110

زمانہ سخت کم آزار ہے، بہ جانِ اسد　　وگرنہ ہم تو توقّع زیادہ رکھتے ہیں

zamāna(h) saḳht kam āzār hai, ba(h) jāne Asad
vagarna(h) ham to tuvaqqu' ziyāda(h) rakhte haiñ (110:1; #656)

The world hardly brings any woes to the life of Asad,
Or else, we have had much higher expectations.

saḳht kam āzār: hardly giving any woes.

The lover asserts that the world does not give him enough woes. On the other hand, perhaps he thinks that his expectations are too high. The lover wants the beloved to know that whatever scorn she doles out is not enough; he is capable of taking a lot more.

111

دائم پڑا ہُوا ترے دَر پر نہیں ہوں مَیں
خاک اَیسی زندگی پہ کہ پتھر نہیں ہوں مَیں

dā'im paṛā hu'ā tere dar par nahiñ hūñ maiñ
ḳhāk aisī zindagī pa(h) ke patthar nahiñ hūñ maiñ (111:1; #657)

Lying perpetually at your doorsteps, I am not?
Shame on a life like this for I am not a stone.

dā'im: permanent; *ḳhāk:* dust; *zindagī:* life; *patthar:* stone.

How can you not see that I am lying on your doorstep for a long time? You disgrace me by treating me like a stone in your threshold. Know that I am not a stone that should be treated like this. If we read the first line without a question mark then it would show the desire of the lover to *be* the stone of her threshold.

کیوں گردشِ مُدام سے گھبرا نہ جاے دِل
اِنسان ہُوں، پیالہ و ساغر نہیں ہوں مَیں

kioñ gardish-e mudām se ghabrā na(h) jāe dil
insān hūñ, piyāla(h)-o-sāghar nahiñ hūñ meñ (111:2; #658)

Why would not my heart get distraught from circulating perpetually?
After all, I am a human being, not a goblet or decanter.

gardish-e mudām: encircling perpetually, wandering.

The wine goblet and decanter keep circulating for drinkers to take their share. Like the goblet and decanter, I am also going around, wandering.

From the circulation of the wine, at least some draw pleasure. What does anyone, including myself, get out of my wanderings? This verse refers to self-pity derived from being pushed around. It is also a desperate protest to the world for not being kind to him.

یارب زمانہ مجھ کو مٹاتا ہے کس لیے
لوحِ جہاں پہ حرفِ مکرر نہیں ہوں میں

yārab zamāna(h) mujh ko miṭātā hai kis liye
lauḥ-e jahāñ pa(h) ḥarf-e mukarrar nahiñ hūñ maiñ (111:3; #659)

O! Lord, why does the world keep erasing me?
I am not a letter written by mistake twice on the slate of the world.

lauḥ: slate; *ḥarf-e mukarrar:* repeated letter.

The events around me seem to be aimed at destroying me. It is as though I am accepted as a letter written twice by mistake on the slate of this world that needs to be erased. Erasing is used to describe destruction. I am not a redundant being, regardless of how the world treats me.

حد چاہیے سزا میں عقوبت کے واسطے
آخر گنہگار ہوں، کافر نہیں ہوں میں

ḥad chāhiye sazā meñ ʿuqūbat ke vāsṭe
āḳhir gunāhgār hūñ kāfir nahiñ hūñ meñ (111:4; #660)

A limit there must be to the harshness of punishment;
After all, I am only a sinner not an infidel.

ʿuqūbat: harshness.

The believers are supposed to be punished for their sins with commutable sentences, but not the infidels (in this case anyone prostrating before an idol—the beloved). The poet asserts that he is a sinner, not an infidel; therefore, the sentence should be of limited duration and not continued in perpetuity. A subtle hint is also made towards the beloved who is often called an idol. The poet asserts that he is not an idolater, just an ordinary sinner.

کس واسطے عزیز نہیں جانتے مجھے
لعل و زُمُرُّد و زر و گوہر نہیں ہوں مَیں

kis vāsṯe ʿazīz nahiñ jānte mujhe
laʿl-o zumurrud-o-zar-o-gohar nahiñ hūñ meñ (111:5; #661)

For what reasons do you not keep me dear to you,
I am neither a ruby, nor an emerald, gold or pearl?

This and the next two verses form an ode to Prophet Mohammed pbuh. I am neither a precious stone, nor gold, or pearl. I have no material characteristics, so why am I not dear to you, O! Prophet Mohammed pbuh? (Those who shun material things are dearer to the Prophet.)

رکھتے ہو تُم قدم مری آنکھوں سے کیوں دریغ
رُتبے میں مہر و ماہ سے کمتر نہیں ہوں مَیں

rakhte ho tum qadam merī ānkhoñ se kioñ direġh
rutbe meñ mahr-o-māh se kamtar nahiñ hūñ meñ (111:6; #662)

Why do you refuse to place your foot on my eyes?
No less am I than the moon and sun in my status!

direġh: denial, refusal.

In the night of the Journey, Mohammed pbuh traveled to heaven and perhaps touched the moon and sun. I am no less than the moon and sun. Why then do you not find my eyes worthy of your feet?

کرتے ہو مجھ کو منعِ قدم بوس کس لیے
کیا آسمان کے بھی برابر نہیں ہوں میں

karte ho mujh ko mana`-e qadam bos kis liye
kyā āsmān ke bhī barābar nahiñ hūñ meñ (111:7; #663)

Why do you forbid me to kiss your feet?
Am I not even equal to heavens?

In the Night of the Journey, Prophet Mohammed pbuh placed his foot upon heaven and thereby let the heavens kiss his feet. The poet complains that perhaps he is not equivalent to the heavens and that is why he has not been given the honor of kissing the Prophet's feet. In this and the previous verse, the poet invokes the grand status given to man by God, well above material things. He then questions why he is not allowed to come close to the prophet.

غالبؔ وظیفہ خوار ہو، دو شاہ کو دُعا
وُہ دِن گئے کہ کہتے تھے نوکر نہیں ہوں مَیں

Ġhālib vaẕīfa(h) kh(v)ār ho, do shāh ko du`ā
vuh din ga'e kih kahte the naukar nahiñ hūñ meñ (111:8: 664)

***Ġhālib*, pray for the King, for you are his pensioner.**
Gone are the days of saying, "I am not a servant to anyone."

vaẕīfa(h): stipend; *kh(v)ār:* consuming, taking.

Ġhālib entered the employment of King *Bahadur Shāh Zafir* on July 4th, 1850. This verse was written in a letter to *Nawab Kalb Alī Ḳhān* of *Rāmpūr* in 1866. It informs him of the resumption of his pension from the King.

112

سب کہاں، کچھ لالہ و گل میں نمایاں ہو گئیں   خاک میں، کیا صورتیں ہوں گی کہ پنہاں ہو گئیں

sab kahāñ, kuchh lāla(h)-o-gul meñ numāyāñ ho gaī'ñ
ḳhak meñ, kyā ṣūrateñ hoñgī kih pinhāñ ho gaī'ñ (112:1; # 665)

Not all, only a few have become evident as tulips and roses;
What images may lie in the dirt that remain hidden from us?

numāyāñ: evident; *ṣurat:* figure; *pinhāñ:* hidden.

The beauty of tulips and roses illustrates the attractive objects earth produces. Beneath the earth, there are countless hidden and beautiful possibilities that have not yet become evident to us. This verse refers to the many faces of dust and dirt and not the faces of buried ones, as often interpreted. One way we know that dirt exists is from its characteristic of supporting flowers and greenery, but there may be many more forms of it that remain hidden from us. We cannot know the many ways God can reveal Himself. Our ability to see things limits us from knowing the reality. A bat cannot see flowers. Does that mean that bat's worldview is at fault? There are hundreds of ways that God reveals Himself to us but we are not capable of appreciating them.

یاد تھیں ہم کو بھی رنگا رنگ بزم آرائیاں   لیکن اب نقش و نگار طاق نسیاں ہو گئیں

yād thīñ ham ko bhī rangā rang bazm ārāī'yāñ
lekin ab naqsh-o-nigār-e ṭāq-e nisyāñ ho gaī'ñ (112:2; #666)

We too had remembered the colorful embellishments of her assembly,
But now they have become the decorative carvings of the cupola of amnesia.

ārā: embellishing; *naqsh*: picture; *nigār:* painting; *ṭāq*: cupola; *nisyāñ:* oblivion.

The memories of colorful and riotous festivities with you, O' Beloved, were once very much a part of my memory, but now not even the memory of memory remains. Like an adornment of the cupola of amnesia, your memory is gone and whatever tracks are left do not tell me where they came from. The use of "cupola of amnesia" is a typical *Ġhālib*ian construction. It is equivalent to the niche of oblivion though more melancholic. The poet refers to how in old age we relish the memories of youth.

تھیں بَناتُ النّعشِ گردُوں دِن کو پردے میں نہاں　　شب کو اِن کے جی میں کیا آئی کہ عُریاں ہو گئیں

thī'ñ banāt-unna'sh-e gardūñ din ko parde meñ nihāñ
shab ko in ke jī meñ kyā ā'ī kih 'uryāñ ho gaī'ñ (112:3; #667)

Hiding behind the veil of daylight were the daughters of the dead in the sky.
In the night, what came to their mind that they bared themselves?

banāt-unna'sh gardūñ: the three stars in the tail of the constellation of the Bear, which has seven stars—an old Persian expression, literally meaning daughters of the dead in the sky because of their appearance as pall bearers. Of the seven northern stars, four are in the arrangement of coffin and three hanging. This is also called the constellation of women.

Watching the constellation of women—the seven northern stars—the poet admires how they become visible in the night. Calling the constellation "daughters of the dead" and referring to their veil and being naked, all at one time, is a new way of looking at the constellation.

قَید میں یعقوب نے لی، گو، نہ یُوسُف کی خبر　　لیکن آنکھیں رَوزنِ دِیوارِ زِنداں ہو گئیں

qaid meñ ya'qūb ne lī, go, na(h) yūsuf kī ḳhabar
lekin āñkheñ rauzan-e dīvār-e zindāñ ho gaī'ñ (112:4; #668)

Though Jacob did not inquire about Joseph in the prison
But his eyes turned into casement windows of the prison walls.

rauzan: casement window.

Though apparently Jacob maintained no contact with his son Joseph while in prison, he remained, however, attuned to Joseph's thoughts, so much so that Jacob's eyes assumed the appearance of the casement windows of the prison cell. Comparing eyes to casement windows has two meanings. First, incessant crying caused Jacob's eyes to turn "white," resembling a window through which light floods in; and secondly, the flow of tears was so forceful that it had broken open a window in the wall of the prison. This verse is a remarkable example of Ghalib at his most extremely imaginative.

سب رقیبوں سے ہوں ناخوش پر زنانِ مصر سے　　ہے زلیخا خوش کہ محوِ ماہِ کنعاں ہو گئیں

sab raqīboñ se hūñ na(h) ḳhush par zanān-e miṣr se
hai zulaiḳhā ḳhush kih maḥv-e māh-e kan'āñ ho gaī'ñ (112:5; #669)

Unhappy with all rivals except the women of Egypt;
Zulekha is happy that they were stunned looking at Joseph.

raqīb: rival; *zanān-e miṣr*: This refers to the women of Egypt who used to tease Zulekha (the wife of the chief of Egypt) that she had fallen in love with a slave, Joseph. As the story goes, Zulekha arranged a meeting of these women with Joseph, who had turned away from her; but the news got out. Once these women saw Joseph, they bit their fingers in disbelief of his "beauty" and started to call him an angel and gave up their criticism of Zulekha. Indeed, he was worth falling for. So what if he was a slave? *māh-e kan'āñ:* moon of Canaan; *Joseph*: Yousuf.

Zulekha was very unhappy with her rival women and particularly the women of Egypt who would tease her for falling in love with a slave.

When these women saw the slave, they became stunned in disbelief and stopped teasing Zulekha. This is a rather tricky verse.

جوئے خوں آنکھوں سے بہنے دو کہ ہے شامِ فراق   میں یہ سمجھوں گا کہ شمعیں دو فروزاں ہو گئیں

jūe ḳhūñ ānkhoñ se bahne do kih hai shām-e firāq
maiñ yih samjhūñ gā kih shamaʿeñ do furozāñ ho gaīʾñ (112:6; #670)

Let the river of blood flow from the eyes for 'tis the night of separation;
So I shall think that two candles have been lit.

jū-e ḳhūñ: river of blood; *shab-e firāq:* night of separation; *furozāñ*: lit.

Bleeding eyes are compared to bright lamps here. In the night of separation, the poet wants to let the eyes flow blood to brighten up the dark room. The darkness of the room represents the gloominess of the mind that crying is supposed to lighten (lift the burden).

ان پری زادوں سے لیں گے خلد میں ہم انتقام   قدرتِ حق سے یہی حوریں اگر واں ہو گئیں

in parī zādoñ se leñge ḳhuld meñ ham intiqām
qudrat-e ḥaq se yahī ḥūreñ āgar vāñ ho gaīʾñ (112:7; #671)

We will take revenge from these fairies in Paradise,
If by the grace of God, they turn into *houris* there.

parī zādoñ: offspring of fairies; *ḳhuld:* paradise; *ḥūr:* houris, nymphs.

The poet makes several assumptions here. First, that he will go to Paradise, despite his sins. Second, he believes that his beloved will also find a place in Paradise, despite her cruelty to mankind. Third, he assumes the beloved in the form of a houri will be assigned to him. And finally, he thinks he can be stern with her as his servant houri to take revenge for her excesses in this world. The poet is actually trying to frighten the beloved into submission in this world, relaying what is about to come if she does not give in. This verse typifies *Ġhalib*'s sense of humor.

نیند اُس کی ہے، دماغ اُس کا ہے، راتیں اُس کی ہیں   تیری زُلفیں جس کے بازو پر پریشاں ہو گئیں

nīnd us kī hai, dimāġh us kā hai, rāteñ us kī haiñ
terī zulfeñ jis ke bāzū par pareshāñ ho gaī'ñ (112:8; #672)

The sleep is his, the happiness is his, and the nights belong to him,
On whose shoulders did your tresses spread wantonly.

dimāġh: happiness; *pareshāñ*: spread in wanton.

He, who makes love to you, has the luxury of sleeping peacefully; has the ultimate joy of mind and to whom the whole night belongs. (Tresses scattered on the lover's shoulder must signify a rather intimate moment.)

مَیں چمن میں کیا گیا، گویا دبستاں کھُل گیا   بُلبلیں سُن کر مرے نالے غزل خواں ہو گئیں

maiñ chaman meñ kyā gayā, goyā dabistāñ khul gayā
bulbuleñ sun kar mere nāle ġhazal ḳh(v)āñ ho gaī'ñ (112:9; #673)

As I entered the garden, it appeared as if a school had opened, wherein
The nightingales began reciting love sonnets hearing my laments.

chaman: flower garden; *goyā:* as if; *dabistāñ*: school (here a place of literary contest); *bulbuleñ:* nightingales; *nāle*: laments; *ġhazal ḳh(v)āñ:* reciting ghazals.

As I entered the garden and began lamenting, the nightingales began reciting poetic verses as if to contest the quality and impressive clarity of my lamenting. This must be viewed in the classical structure of Urdu poetry, where nightingales only lament (not recite verses), but my lamenting was so good that they had to resort to reciting ghazals as if this were a school of learning. All of this happened because my laments touched them so deeply that they had to recite verses to express their own hurt.

جو مری کوتاہیِ قسمت سے مژگاں ہو گئیں وہ نگاہیں کیوں ہوئی جاتی ہیں یارب دل کے پار

vuh nigāheñ kioñ hū'ī jātī haiñ yārabb dil ke pār
jo merī kotāhī' qismat se mizhgāñ ho gaī'ñ (112:10; #674)

Those glances, O! Lord, why do they keep piercing through my heart,
That were blocked by her eyelashes, through my bad luck?

nigāh: glance; *kotāhī-e qismat:* shortcoming of fortune; *mizhgāñ:* eye lashes.

Those glances of hers pierce my heart even though they were arrested by her eyelashes and did not go farther because of my ill fortune. When she looked at me, her eyelashes turned toward me, but unfortunately her glance did not cross the boundary of her eyelashes, yet these restrained glances proved enough to rend my heart even if they did not reach me fully. Imagine what would happen if those glances had not been not arrested by her eyelashes. To understand this verse, one must visualize the ambivalence of the beloved while looking at her lover.

میری آہیں بخیۂ چاکِ گریباں ہو گئیں بسکہ روکا میں نے اور سینے میں ابھریں پے بہ پے

baskih rokā meñ ne āur sīne meñ ubhrīñ pae ba(h) pae
merī āheñ baḳhya(h)' chāk-e garebāñ ho gaī'ñ (112:11; #675)

Though I tried stifling them in my chest, they kept coming one after the other.
My sighs turned out to be the stitches for the slit of my collar.

baḳhya(h): stitch.

As I crushed my sighs, they kept bouncing back in my chest and served to return me to sanity. When I was insane, I used to rip my shirt collar to vent my sighs, but now those rips have been stitched back as I learned to suppress my feelings. The chest moving up and down as it filled with sighs resembles the motion of a needle going up and down stitching. As I stifled my sighs, sanity returned to me and I stopped tearing at my collar. The chest moving up and down to hold these sighs was like the needle of a sewing machine that repaired my torn collar. This is indeed a unique construction of thought.

واں گیا بھی میں تو اُن کی گالیوں کا کیا جواب   یاد تھیں جتنی دُعائیں صَرفِ درباں ہو گئیں

vāñ gayā bhī maiñ to un kī gāliyoñ kā kyā javāb
yād thīñ jitnī du'āeñ ṣarf-e darbāñ ho gaīñ (112:12; #676)

Even if I got in there, how would I respond to her abuses? Whatever felicitations I had memorized were used on the door-keeper.

gālī: abuses; *ṣarf*: spent; *darbāñ*: doorkeeper; *du'āeñ:* good wishes, felicitations.

To reach the beloved, the poet has to get past the doorkeeper to her house. The doorkeeper would not let him in, so to appease him he used all the good-willed statements he had memorized for the beloved. Now, face to face with the beloved, he has no more felicitations left for her. Curiosity remains as to why he couldn't repeat his felicitations. The answer comes from the idea of "spending" his felicitations, as if these were a physical commodity. To use the same wish for the beloved as used for the doorkeeper would be degrading. Another example of *Ġhalib*'s wit.

جاں فزا ہے بادہ، جس کے ہاتھ میں جام آگیا   سب لکیریں ہاتھ کی گویا رگِ جاں ہو گئیں

jāñ fizā hai bāda(h), jis ke hāth meñ jām āgayā
sab lakīreñ hāth kī goyā rag-e jāñ ho gaī'ñ (112:13; #677)

Wine is life giving; into whose hand the goblet comes,
All the lines of the palm seem to become the jugular vein.

jāñ: life; *fizā:* atmosphere; *lakīreñ*: lines; *rag-e jāñ*: artery of life, jugular.

He who gets to hold the goblet of wine becomes infused with new life as if the lines of the palm have turned into arteries, imbibing life out of the goblet and into the body of the person holding the goblet. There is a subtle reference to the red color of wine and its reflection onto the lines of the palm, making them appear reddish like arteries. Getting hold of the goblet is also akin to coming into good fortune.

ہم مُوَحِّد ہیں، ہمارا کیش ہے ترکِ رُسُوم   ملّتیں جب مٹ گئیں اَجزائے ایماں ہو گئیں

ham mu(v)aḥḥid haiñ, hamārā kaish hai tark-e rusūm
millateñ jab miṭ gaī'ñ ajzāe imāñ ho gaī'ñ (112:14; #678)

We are monotheists and our belief is to shatter the traditions;
When the creed and dogma are decimated, they become part of faiths.

mu(v)aḥḥid: monotheists; *kaish*: style; *tark:* discard. *rasūm:* traditions and rituals; *millateñ:* nations (used here to state creed and dogma); *miṭ:* destroy; *ajzā:* part; *imān*: belief.

A monotheist, I discard traditions of religion. It is through this destruction of traditions that we locate our true religion of monotheism. The discussion of the decimation of nations (*millateñ*) refers to differences in culture bred by our beliefs in different religions—they must be removed to strengthen the unity of people, the fundamental dictum of monotheism.

رنج سے خُوگر ہُوا اِنساں تو مِٹ جاتا ہے رنج　　　مُشکلیں مُجھ پر پڑیں اِتنی کہ آساں ہو گئیں

ranj se ḳhūgar hu'ā insāñ to miṭ jātā hai ranj
mushkileñ mujh par paṛīñ itnī kih āsāñ ho gaīñ (112:15; #679)

When man becomes used to sorrow, the pain of sorrow is alleviated.
So many hardships have fallen on me that they have become easier to endure.

ḳhūgar: habitual.

Repeated exposure to pain reduces the sensation of pain. Continuous suffering from sorrow reduces its impact. The same happens to us as we encounter difficulties in life. Sustaining ourselves through difficulties, we can surpass insurmountable hindrances in life with relative ease. We no longer refer to misfortunes as misfortunes. We tend to accept the bitter realities of life. It does not mean that we exercise greater control over events, it is just that we can face them better; we can get more used to them. The helplessness of man is poignantly presented here.

یُوں ہی گر روتا رہا غالبؔ تو اَے اہلِ جہاں
دیکھنا اِن بستیوں کو تُم کہ ویراں ہو گئیں

yūñ hi gar rotā rahā ġhālib to ai āhl-e jahāñ
dekhnā in bastioñ ko tum kih vīrāñ ho gaī'ñ (112:16; #680)

If this is how Ghalib keeps weeping, then O! Dwellers of the world,
You would see that these settlements would turn into ruins.

Settlements would degrade into ruins, as flooding from tears will wash away homes. The lover has begun to weep and thus the dwellers of the world are forewarned. There is a plea to do something about it lest the responsibility be theirs, not that of the poet. Of course, they can best help by arranging his meeting with the beloved to help him control his tears.

113

دیوانگی سے دوش پہ زُنّار بھی نہیں　　یعنی، ہمارے جیب میں اِک تار بھی نہیں

dīvāngī se dosh pa(h) zunnār bhī nahīñ
ya'nī, hamāre jeb meñ ik tār bhī nahīñ (113:1; #681)

The lunacy has left not even the sacred thread on the shoulder;
Meaning, not even a single thread is left in our collar slit.

dosh: shoulder; *zunnār*: sacred black string worn by Hindus over the shoulder or around the neck while visiting the temple; *jeb*: pocket, collar, collar slit; *tār:* thread, wire.

In a fit of lunacy, I ripped my clothes and left not a strand on my body that we could have used as *Zunnar*, which would have identified me as a worshipper of my beloved. (Note that Hindus worship idols; I worship my idol and hence the *Zunnar*.) The sorrow expressed here is not for the loss of all assets, but for not being identified as a lover of idol beauty.

دل کو نیازِ حسرتِ دیدار کر چکے　　دیکھا تو ہم میں طاقتِ دیدار بھی نہیں

dil ko niyāz-e ḥasrat-e dīdār kar chuke
dekhā to ham meñ ṭāqat-e dīdār bhī nahīñ (113:2; #682)

Having sacrificed the heart as an offering for her glimpse,
I found that I do not even have the strength left to look at her.

niyāz: offering; *ḥasrat:* longing; *dīdār*: glimpse.

Having offered and lost my heart, longing for a glimpse of her, I now realize that it was futile. Even if I had gotten the chance, I would not have the strength to look at her, anyway. Sacrificing the heart was therefore not such a prudent idea. This verse points out a poignant reality of life; when we strive too hard to reach a goal, we may not be able to appreciate it once it is achieved.

ملنا ترا اگر نہیں آساں تو سہل ہے　　دشوار تو یہی ہے کہ دشوار بھی نہیں

milnā terā āgar nahiñ āsāñ to sahl hai
dushvār to yahī hai kih dushvār bhī nahīñ (113:3; #683)

Meeting you, if it were not easy, it would have gone easy on me;
The difficulty is that it is not too difficult to meet with you.

Had it been impossible to meet with you, I would have given up trying and accepted the fact. However, it is not difficult to meet with you, for you meet the rival. I keep trying, in jealousy and in vain, and it makes it so much more difficult for me to accept my fate. I could have tolerated the pain of separation (not meeting with you). My burning jealousy is making it too difficult. There is a play of words between, "easy" and "difficult" here.

بے عشق عمر کٹ نہیں سکتی ہے اور یہاں　　طاقت بہ قدرِ لذتِ آزار بھی نہیں

be 'ishq 'umr kaṭ nahiñ saktī hai āur yahāñ
ṭāqat ba(h) qadr-e lażżat-e āzār bhī nahīñ (113:4; #684)

Without love, it is not possible to go through life, but here,
Even the energy needed to savor the ecstasy of pain is gone.

ba(h) qadr: required for; *lażżat-e āzār:* ecstasy of pain.

Devotion to a goal keeps life flowing. Loving you allows me to bear many sorrows, many difficulties, and perpetual disappointments. True devotion requires that we not only bear hardship, but also enjoy the ecstasy of pain to prove our sincerity to the beloved. However, this requires a great deal of energy, both physical and emotional. With this energy gone, we now wander aimlessly. The key to success in life is not just to bear difficulties but also to develop a taste for whatever the world doles out to us. Note that the poet is pointing to enjoying pain, not just bearing it, as a tool to success in life.

شوریدگی کے ہاتھ سے ہے سر وبالِ دوش   صحرا میں اے خدا کوئی دیوار بھی نہیں

shorīdgī ke hāth se hai sar-o-bāl-e dosh
ṣaḥrā meñ ai ḳhudā ko'ī dīvār bhī nahīñ (113:5; #685)

In the hands of my lunacy, the head has become a heavy burden on the shoulders;
O! God, there is not even a wall in the desert.

shor: lunacy.

My lunacy has made my shoulders become tired of my head. One solution is to smash it (the head) against the wall, but I am unable to find one. There is no wall in the desert, I know, but my lunacy questions this fact: why is not there a wall in the desert? The ultimate sign of total lunacy is displayed here.

گنجائشِ عداوتِ اغیار یک طرف   یاں دل میں ضعف سے ہوسِ یار بھی نہیں

gunjāish-e ʿdāvat-e aġhyār yak ṭaraf
yāñ dil meñ ẓoʿf se ḥavas-e yār bhī nahīñ (113:6; #686)

Setting aside any room for enmity to my rivals,
Here, in the heart, even the desire of the beloved is gone, because of our frailty.

gunjāish: concession, room; *ʿdāvat*: enmity; *zoʿf:* weakness, frailty; *ḥavas:* desire; *yār:* beloved.

How can I plan any enmity towards my rivals while my frailty is so great that I do not even have the energy left to think of my beloved? How can I fight my rivals?

ڈر نالہ ہاے زار سے میرے، خدا کو مان   آخر نواے مرغِ گرفتار بھی نہیں

ḍar nālah hāi zār se mere, k̤hudā ko mān
āk̤hir navāe murġh-e giraftār bhī nahīñ (113:7; #687)

Be afraid of the heart-rending plaints; do come to believe in God.
After all, aren't these even the calls of a caged rooster?

k̤hudā ko mān: fear God; *murġh*: rooster.

Fear God and pay attention to my wailing. It is as if these laments are less significant than those of caged birds. It is hard to believe that animals are released out of sympathy, but I am not. Trying to put the fear of God into the beloved's heart, the lover beseeches that even caged birds that are in pain are freed and here I am in your perpetual bondage with no attention from you whatsoever. God will not like this cruelty. A subtle hint that unlike the freed bird, I will not fly away is also given here.

دل میں ہے یار کی صفِ مژگاں سے روکشی   حالانکہ طاقتِ خلشِ خار بھی نہیں

dil meñ hai yār kī ṣaf-e mizhgāñ se rūkashī
ḥālāñkih ṭāqat-e k̤halish-e k̤hār bhī nahīñ (113:8; #688)

In my heart, are spread out the lines of beloved's eyelashes,
Even though the patience to bear the pain of even a thorn is gone.

rūkashī: coating, surface; *ṣaf-e mizhgāñ*: row of eyelashes; *k̤halish*: pain; *k̤hār:* thorn.

I do not even have the patience to bear the pain of the prick of thorns, yet the thought of her eyelashes remains alive in my heart. The poet is taking more than he can handle.

اِس سادگی پہ کون نہ مر جائے اَے خُدا   لڑتے ہیں اُور ہاتھ میں تلوار بھی نہیں

is sādgī pe kaun na(h) mar jāe āe ḳhudā
laṛte haiñ āur hāth meñ talvār bhī nahīñ (113:9; #689)

Who would not die, O! God, at the naïveté
Of fighting and not even having a sword in the hand.

laṛte: battling.

Who would not die, O God, at her simplicity and innocence? Even without the swords of ornament and makeup, she proves to be a killer. This proves that she is not naïve but extremely cunning for she got what she wanted—my dead body—with or without a sword. Here the beloved is accused of cunning, not admired for being naïve.

دیکھا اسد کو خلوت و جلوت میں بارہا
دِیوانہ گر نہیں ہے تو ہُشیار بھی نہیں

dekhā Asad ko ḳhalvat-o-jalvat meñ bāṛhā
dīvāna(h) gar nahīñ hai to hushyār bhī nahīñ (113:10; #690)

We have seen Asad in privacy as well as in public.
Lunatic if he is not, then he is not a clever one, either.

How the lover behaves in private with his beloved is not clever for he fails to take advantage of her. In public, he hides his lunacy and tries to appear clever.

114

نہیں ہے زخم کوئی بخیے کے درخور مرے تن میں ہُوا ہے تارِ اشکِ یاس رِشتہ چشمِ سوزن میں

nahiñ hai zaḳhm ko'ī baḳhye ke dar ḳhūr mere tan meñ
hu'ā hai tār-e āshk-e yās rishta(h) chashm-e sozan meñ (114:1; #691)

Not a single wound is left in my body that could be stitched,
As the thread in the eye of the needle has turned into a string of tears of despondency.

baḳhye ke dar ḳhūr: capable of being stitched; *rishta(h)*: thread; *chashm-e sozan*: eye of needle.

There is not a wound left that can be stitched on my entire tattered body. Despairing at this sight, the thread in the eye of the needle has turned into a thread of tears (continuous tears), an expression of great desperation. Being unable to stitch the wound, the needle is crying at its failure. The continuity of flowing tears is compared to thread; the eye of the needle is the eye shedding tears. Another way to interpret this verse is that with no wounds left to repair, the needle is crying because it cannot cause more hurt.

ہُوئی ہے مانعِ ذوقِ تماشا خانہ ویرانی کفِ سیلاب باقی ہے بہ رنگِ پنبہ روزن میں

hu'ī hai mānī-e zauq-e tamāshā ḳhāna(h) vīrānī
kaf-e sailāb bāqī hai ba(h) rang-e pañmba(h) rauzan meñ
(114:2; #692)

It has prevented the "desire" to see the ruining of my home;
The foam of the flood has plugged the holes in the wall like cotton balls.

mānī̕: impediment; *żauq:* desire, taste; *tamāshā:* spectacle; *ḳhāna(h):* house; *kaf* foam, bubbles; *sailāb:* flood; *bāqī:* remaining; *ba(h) rang:* like; *pañmba(h):* cotton wool; *rauzan:* hole in the wall, casement window.

The flooding of my tears has inundated my home and made holes in the walls. These holes have been filled with bubbles and dirt brought in by the flooding water that block my view to the inside of the house. I wanted to see the destruction of my home. The flood's foam that fills the holes is compared to wet cotton wool. Note that cotton wool is white like the foam.

ودیعت خانۂ بیدادِ کاوشہاے مژگاں ہوں
نگینِ نامِ شاہد ہے، مرا ہر قطرہ خوں تن میں

vadī̕at ḳhāna(h)' bedād-e kāvish hāi mizhgāñ hūñ
nagīn-e nām-e shāhid hai, merā har qaṭra(h) ḳhūñ tan meñ
(114:3; #693)

I am the keeper of the tyrannies of the efforts of eyelashes;
Each drop of my blood is a seal engraved with the name of the beloved.

vadī̕at: trust; *bedād:* tyranny; *kāvish*: effort; *nagina(h)*: gem

I am keeping the tyrannies of her eyelashes as close as each drop of my blood that is like a gem engraved with her name. Her eyelashes have pierced every part of my body and I am keeping this as a souvenir. The drops of blood refer to lost desires.

بیاں کس سے ہو ظلمت گستری میرے شبستاں کی
شبِ مہ ہو، جو رکھ دیں پنبہ دیواروں کے روزن میں

bayāñ kis se ho ẓulmat gustarī mere shabistāñ kī
shab-e mah ho, jo rakh deñ pañmba(h) dīvāroñ ke rauzan meñ
(114:4; #694)

To whom shall I relate the spreading of darkness in my bedroom? It will be like a moonlit night if I were to put cotton wool in the holes in the walls.

shabistāñ: bedroom; *ẕulmat gustarī:* spreading of darkness; *rauzan:* holes in wall, casement window; *pañmba(h):* cotton wool.

To whom and how should I tell the intense bleakness of my sleeping abode? A piece of cotton wool placed in the holes in the wall lights up the room like a moonlit night. In extreme darkness, anything white appears glowing. My hopelessness is so intense that even a minuscule flicker of hope cheers me.

نکوہش مانعِ بے ربطیٔ شورِ جنوں آئی   ہُوا ہے خندۂ احباب بخیہ جیب و داماں میں

nikūhish mānī-e be rabṯī' shor-e junūñ ā'ī
hu'ā hai ḳhanda(h)' āḥbāb baḳhya(h) jeb-o-dāman meñ (114:5; #695)

The reproach constrained the erratic frenzy of my madness; The laughter of friends has stitched the tear in my collar and lap.

nikūhish: reproach; *be rabṯ*: erratic; *shor-e junūñ:* tumult of frenzy; *ḳhand'a(h) aḥbāb*: laughter of friends; *baḳhya(h)*: stitch.

The reproach of my friends made me put a stop to my tumult and frenzy. By laughing at me, they helped me to sew my wounds and regain my senses. The display of teeth in laughter is compared to the stitches needed to repair the collar and shirt.

ہوئے اُس مہروش کے جلوۂ تمثال کے آگے   پَر افشاں جوہر آئینے میں مثلِ ذرّہ روزن میں

hu'e us maharvash ke jalva(h)' timṡāl ke āge
par āfshāñ johar āine meñ miṡl-e żārra(h) rauzan meñ (114:6; #696)

Confronting the display of splendor of that sun-like beloved, The mirror coating dissipated like the dust in a casement window.

maharvash: resembling sun; *jalva(h)*: splendor; *timṡāl*: show, display; *puraḟshāñ*: damaged, hurt; *johar*: mirror coating; *żarrah*: particle; *rauzan*: holes in wall, casement window.

When my sparkling beloved looked into the mirror, the coating of the mirror evaporated into fine, shiny particles in the air like a ray passing through a hole in the wall illuminates the dust particles in its path. *Ġhālib* was fascinated with dust particles that illuminated the path of a ray of light, particularly from a window, as is proven by how often he has made reference to this subject.

نہ جانوں نیک ہوں یا بد ہوں، پر صحبت مخالف ہے
جو گل ہوں تو ہوں گلخن میں جو خس ہوں تو ہوں گلشن میں

na(h) jānūñ nek hūñ yā bad hūñ, par ṣoḥbat muḳhālif hai
jo gul hūñ to hūñ gulḳhan meñ jo ḳhas hūñ to hūñ gulshan meñ
(114:7; #697)

I do not know if I am good or bad but surely, my environs are contradictory.
If I am a flower then I am in the waste-bin; if I am straw, I languish in the garden.

ṣoḥbat: company; *gulḳhan*: waste-bin, furnace-type heater in old bathrooms; *ḳhas*: straw.

The circumstances around me are not conducive to my well-being. If I am good like a flower, I should be decorating the tresses of the beloved, not being thrown into the garbage incinerator. If I am as worthless as a piece of straw, I am kept in the garden, though I should be thrown away. They punish me when they should not and they reward me when I do not deserve it. This verse points to the many inequities of life: some people reach places they do not deserve while many deserving ones keep getting pushed aside. The "I" in this verse is used in a collective manner.

ہزاروں دل دیے جوشِ جنونِ عشق نے مجھ کو   سیہ ہو کر سویدا ہو گیا ہر قطرۂ خوں تن میں

hazāroñ dil diye josh-e junūn-e ʿishq ne mujh ko
siyāh ho kar suvaidā hogayā har qatra(h) ḳhūñ tan meñ (114:8; #698)

The frenzy of love has given me a thousand hearts;
Every drop of blood in my body is charred into black spots of heart.

siyāh: black; *suvaidā*: a black dot, black spot of heart.

The frenzy of love burns the heart of lovers and leaves a black spot there. That is ordinary lunacy. In my case, every drop of blood has turned black (burned) and now there are thousands of black spots in my heart. Now I have many hearts, thanks to the frenzy of love. The compound construction between heart and dark dots also refers to the heart's core and original sins.

اسد زندانیِ تاثیرِ الفت ہائے خوباں ہوں
خمِ دستِ نوازش ہو گیا ہے طوق گردن میں

Asad zindānī' tāsīr-e ulfat hāi ḳhubāñ hūñ
ḳham-e dast-e navāzish hogayā hai tauq gardan meñ (114:9; #699)

Asad, I am a captive of the effects of beloved's affection.
The arches of arms of affection have turned into a collar of slavery.

zindānī: prisoner, captivated; *tauq*: badge of slavery, collar of slavery.

The beloved has put her arms around the lover and that has proven to be the collar of slavery. Such is the effect of her affection. Notice the use of arms around neck and a collar around neck for their similarity of shape.

115

مزے جہان کے، اپنی نظر میں خاک نہیں
سوائے خونِ جگر، سو جگر میں خاک نہیں

maze jahān ke, apnī naẕar meñ ḳhāk nahīñ
sivāe ḳhūn-e jigar, so jigar meñ ḳhāk nahīñ (115:1; #700)

The. pleasures of the world are nothing but dust before my eyes,
Except for blood in the liver, there is nothing left in the liver.

There is no greater pleasure in this world than to have enough blood in one's liver to be able to cry tears of blood. Once the liver is emptied of blood, life appears desolate. The construction of this verse is transposed requiring a 3:1 connection to read like this: except for the blood in the liver, there is no worthy pleasure.

مگر، غبار ہوئے پر ہوا اڑا لے جائے
وگرنہ تاب و تواں بال و پر میں خاک نہیں

magar, ġhubār hu'e par havā uṛā le jāe
vagarna(h) tāb-o-tavāñ bāl-o-par meñ ḳhāk nahiñ (115:2; #701)

Though turned to dust, per chance, if only the wind will carry me away,
Or else, there is not much strength and power left in my body to fly.

Lest I turn to dust and the wind takes me away, the strength of my wings bites dust. This means that I barely have the strength to fly on my own. If I die, though, then my dust will fly freely with the wind, and I will have the ultimate freedom. The hidden meaning here is that the poet wanted to reach the doorstep of his beloved but could not. The only way to reach there would be after death, when the wind blows the dust of his body to the beloved's door.

یہ کس بہشت شمائل کی آمد آمد ہے
کہ غیرِ جلوۂ گل رہگزر میں خاک نہیں

yih kis bihisht shamā'il kī āmad āmad hai
kih ġhair-e jalva(h)' gul rahguzar meñ ḳhāk nahīñ (115:3; #702)

The arrival of "who," the paradise-natured being is imminent
That except for the display of roses, there is not anything else in the path?

bihisht: paradise; *shamā'il*: nature; *ġhair*: except.

The beloved is sophisticated so in anticipation of her arrival, her path has been decorated with roses, and nothing else, to welcome her. She is like Paradise where roses are abundant. The display of roses is there to make her feel at home.

بَھلا اُسے نہ سہی کچھ مُجھی کو رحم آتا
اَثر مرے نَفَسِ بے اَثر میں خاک نہیں

bhalā use na(h) sahī kuchh mujhī ko raḥm ātā
asar mere nafas-e be āṡar meñ ḳhāk nahīñ (115:4; #703)

May be not her but at least I should have been compassionate to myself,
Knowing that there is no impact left in my ineffective breath.

Why would she be moved by my lamenting when I myself was not moved? When my own breath (lament) has become ineffective, how could it affect anyone? If not her, then at least I should have been kind to myself and left off wailing. When we are not sincere, how can we expect anyone, especially our beloved, to be moved by our sighs? On a more melancholic note, the poet is giving the benefit of doubt to the beloved.

خیالِ جلوۂ گل سے خراب ہیں میکش
شراب خانے کے دیوار و در میں خاک نہیں

ḳhayāl-e jalva(h)' gul se ḳharāb haiñ maikash
sharāb ḳhāne ke dīvār-o-dar meñ ḳhāk nahiñ (115:5; #704)

The drinkers with the thought of the display of flowers are intoxicated;
Otherwise, there is nothing special about the walls and doors of the tavern.

ḳharāb: intoxicated, tipsy.

Drinkers with the thought of flowers imagine spring, the season of drinking. It is not the thought of the tavern that makes them joyful—it is the thought of drinking wine that intoxicates them. It is the thought that intoxicates, not the doors and walls of the tavern. This illustrates that where you drink is not important.

ہوا ہوں عشق کی غارت گری سے شرمندہ
سوائے حسرتِ تعمیر گھر میں خاک نہیں

hu'ā hūñ 'ishq kī ġhārat garī se sharminda(h)
sivāe ḥasrat-e ta'mīr ghar meñ ḳhāk nahīñ (115:6: 705)

I have been shamed by the destructive nature of love,
Nothing is left except for the stifled desire to reconstruct my home.

ġhārat garī: destructive nature.

Love has destroyed me. I had wished to rebuild my home, but that remains an unfulfilled desire due to lack of resources and energy. Had I been able to build it again, I could offer it to my beloved to destroy again. Not being able to do it, I am embarrassed. Love has destroyed me and I do not have the energy to pull myself up to receive love's wrath again.

ہمارے شعر ہیں اب صرف دل لگی کے اسدؔ
کھُلا کہ فائدہ عرضِ ہنر میں خاک نہیں

hamāre sha'r haiñ ab ṣirf dil lagī ke Asad
khulā kih fā'ida(h) 'arẓ-e hunar meñ ḳhāk nahīñ (115:7; #706)

My verses are now only for petty amusement, Asad;
It became obvious that there is little gain in the pursuit of talent.

dil lagī: heart pleasing; *'arz-e hunar*: adducing talent, enhancing talent; *fāida(h):* benefit.

As it became obvious to me that few people can understand and appreciate my verses, I began writing frivolous verses for light-hearted enjoyment without any depth or meaning. There is hardly anything to be gained from the pursuit of the art of writing. This verse refers to a cynical feeling that *Ġhālib* had when he was little appreciated and even ridiculed for his choice of lofty words and difficult construction. Many of his contemporaries urged him to ease off in his diction. The present collection of *Ġhālib*'s *ġhazal*s excludes many verses that were considered to be too difficult to decipher.

116

دل ہی تو ہے، نہ سنگ و خشت، درد سے بھر نہ آئے کیوں   روئیں گے ہم ہزار بار، کوئی ہمیں ستائے کیوں

dil hī to hai, na(h) sang-o-ḳhisht, dard se bhar na(h) āe kioñ
roeñ ge ham hazār bār, ko'ī hameñ satāe kioñ (116:1; #707)

It is, after all a heart, not a stone or brick, that would not fill with sorrow.
We will cry a thousand times for why should anyone tease us?

At the insistence that the lover should bear more pain, he responds that, after all, he is a human being, not made of brick or stone, so he must feel pain. Despite the admonishment of the beloved, he must release his emotions and cry as much as he needs. Finally, the poet says, why would "anyone" tease me? This "anyone," of course, is the beloved, giving an impression that she is a stranger for only a stranger can tease this way.

دیر نہیں، حرم نہیں، در نہیں، آستاں نہیں   بیٹھے ہیں رہگزر پہ ہم، غیر ہمیں اٹھائے کیوں

dair nahiñ, ḥaram nahiñ, dar nahiñ āstāñ nahiñ
baiṭhe haiñ rahguzar pa(h) ham, ġhair hameñ uṭhāe kioñ (116:2; #708)

It is not a temple, nor *Ka'bā*, neither a gate, nor a threshold;
We are merely sitting by the roadside, so why should anyone ask us to move?

āstāñ: threshold.

I am not sitting in front of a Hindu temple where the priest would object. I am not waiting at the door of *Ka'bā* where the keepers would object. I am not waiting at the door of the beloved, nor camping at the threshold of her home, where the other lovers might find it objectionable. I am merely sitting by the roadside and the rivals have no right to tell me to get up and leave. Why would they not just leave me alone?

جب وہ جمالِ دل فروز صورتِ مہرِ نیم روز   آپ ہی ہو نظارہ سوز پردے میں منہ چھپائے کیوں

jab vuh jamāl-e dil furoz ṣurat-e mahr-e nīm roz
āp hī ho naẕẕāra(h) soz parde meñ munh chhupāe kioñ (116:3; #709)

When that heart-illuminating beauty, like the sharp afternoon sun
Being a burning spectacle herself, why should she hide her face behind the veil?

dil furoz: heart illuminating; *mehr-e nīm roz:* afternoon sun; *naẕẕāra(h) soz:* burning spectacle.

The afternoon sun and its slanted rays are hard to look at directly, just like looking at my beloved. She need not wear a veil because no one would be able to see her for her dazzling beauty would burn the sight of the spectator.

دشنۂ غمزہ جاں ستاں، ناوکِ ناز بے پناہ   تیرا ہی عکسِ رخ سہی سامنے تیرے آئے کیوں

dashna(h)' ġhamza(h) jāñ sitāñ, nāvak-e nāz be pana(h)
terā hī a'ks-e ruḳh sahī sāmne tere āe kioñ (116:4; #710)

The daggers of amorous glances are life-taking and the arrows of coquetry without limits;
Even if it is a reflection of your own face, why should it confront you?

a'ks: reflection; *dashna(h)*: dagger: *ġhamz'a(h)*: amorous glance; *nāvak*: arrow; *jāñ sitāñ*: killing.

The beloved's face is dangerous; it kills. The lover is advising the beloved not to look into the mirror, lest it might hurt her as well.

قیدِ حیات و بندِ غم اصل میں دونوں ایک ہیں   موت سے پہلے آدمی غم سے نجات پائے کیوں

qaid-e ḥayāt-o-band-e ġham aṣl meñ donoñ ek haiñ
maut se pahle ādmī ġham se najāt pāe kioñ (116:5; #711)

The bondage of life and the succession of sorrows are actually one and the same,
Before death, how can man hope to be free of the clutches of sorrow?

qaid-e ḥayāt: bondage of life; *band-e ġham*: succession of sorrow.

The duration of our life is fixed, but living means having feelings. Since all acts of living lead to sorrow and are interspersed with moments of joy, the sorrow continues until we die. Death offers the only freedom from sorrow. Life is bondage and continuous sorrow a sign of life.

حسن اور اس پہ حسنِ ظن، رہ گئی بوالہوس کی شرم   اپنے پہ اعتماد ہے غیر کو آزمائے کیوں

ḥusn āur us pa(h) ḥusn-e ẓan, ra(h) ga'ī bulhavas kī sharm
apne pa(h) i'timād haī ġhair ko āzmāe kioñ (116:6; #712)

The beauty and her self-appreciation spared the shame to the capricious ones;
Being confident of herself, she need not test others.

ḥusn-e ẓan: self-appreciation; *bulhavas*: whimsical, capricious; *i'timād*: confident.

The beloved is so sure that all of her lovers are sincere, that she is not testing the rival. She spares him the shame of being exposed as a capricious lover. The lover does not want his beloved to test the rival but at the time wishes, he would be exposed.

واں وہ غرورِ عز و ناز، یاں یہ حجابِ پاسِ وضع　　راہ میں ہم ملیں کہاں، بزم میں وہ بلائے کیوں

vāñ vuh ġhurur-e i̊zz-o-nāz, yāñ yih ḥijāb-e pās-e vaẓ'a
rāh meñ ham mileñ kahāñ, bazm meñ vuh bulāe kioñ (116:7; #713)

There she has pride and haughtiness; here I have regards for etiquette. I would rather not meet her on the road, and she would rather not invite me to her assembly.

pās-e vaẓ': regard for elegance, etiquette.

It is against her haughty nature to invite me to her assembly and it is against my tradition and values to meet her by the roadside. Therefore it seems unlikely that we will ever meet. The poet had a conservative upbringing where talking to people in public places is considered impolite. The beloved, on the other hand, just wants to say a few words in a public place so the lover would not have the chance to start wailing to her. The fact is that the lover is merely creating a scenario to be invited to her assembly. He will gladly speak to her anywhere she would prefer.

ہاں وہ نہیں خدا پرست، جاؤ وہ بے وفا سہی　　جس کو ہو دین و دل عزیز اُس کی گلی میں جائے کیوں

hāñ vuh nahiñ ḳhudā parast, jā'o vuh bevafā sahī
jis ko ho dīn-o-dil 'azīz uskī galī meñ jāe kioñ (116:8; #714)

Yes, she does not believe in God; move on if she is unfaithful. Whosoever keeps his heart and life dear, why should he go into her alley?

Friends admonish the poet that his beloved is not only a disbeliever; she is also unfaithful and treacherous. Loving her would mean losing both your religion (faith) and your life (for she will kill you). At this point, the poet interrupts by saying that no one who is strong in faith and loves life need enter her alley. I accept; I am willing to give both.

غالبِ خستہ کے بغیر کون سے کام بند ہیں
روئیے زار زار کیا، کیجیے ہائے ہائے کیوں؟

Ġhālib-e ḳhasta(h) ke baġhair kaun se kām band haiñ
ro'iye zār zār kyā, kijīye hāi hāi kioñ (116:9; #715)

Without *Ġhālib*, the tired one, what works have been stopped?
Why should one lament profusely and why should one cry in mourning?

ḳhasta(h): tired; *zār zār:* bitterly, severely.

Why should anyone weep and lament over the death of *Ġhālib*? Hardly anything has changed. Work has not stopped because he is no longer here. He was a tired, distressed man anyway, unable to do much in the world so his departure has had little impact on anything. He will not be missed.

117

غنچۂ ناشگفتہ کو دور سے مت دکھا، کہ یوں   بوسے کو پوچھتا ہوں میں منہ سے مجھے بتا، کہ یوں

ġhuncha(h)' nā shagufta(h) ko dūr se mat dikhā, kih yuñ
bose ko puchhtā huñ maiñ muñh se mujhe batā kih yūñ (117:1; #716)

Do not show me from distance like this, that unopened flower;
I am asking for a kiss, so show this to me with your lips, like that.

ġhunchah nā shagufta(h): unopened flower, a bud; *mat*: no;
shagufta(h): bloom; *bosa*: kiss.

Do not show me a flower bud to show how lips close when kissing. I want to share a kiss. Come and show me with your mouth, not through these clues. The beloved is supposed to have a small, bud-like mouth and thus the poet makes this comparison. A witty beloved is present here.

پرسشِ طرزِ دلبری کیجیے کیا کہ بن کہے   اس کے ہر اک اشارے سے نکلے ہے یہ ادا، کہ یوں

pursish-e ṭarz-e dilbarī kijīye kyā kih bin kahe
us ke har ik ishāre se nikle hai yih adā kih yūñ (117:2; #717)

What to ask of her style of stealing hearts, it goes without saying
That in all of her gestures is a blandishment coming out, "that's how?"

dilbarī: heart stealing; *pursish*: inquiry.

How the beloved steals hearts is a redundant question. All her styles and gestures are capable of stealing hearts..

رات کے وقت مے پیے، ساتھ رقیب کو لیے   آئے وہ یاں خدا کرے، پر نہ کرے خدا کہ یُوں!

rāt ke vaqt mai pīye, sāth raqīb ko līye
ā'e vuh yāñ ḳhudā kare, par na(h) kare ḳhudā kih yūñ (117:3; #718)

In the night, having imbibed wine and taking the rival along;
I pray to God that she would come to me, but O! God, not like this.

At a nighttime vigil, the beloved is drunk while in the company of the rival. The poet wants her to come and visit him but then changes his mind once he realizes that she might let the rival accompany her.

غیر سے رات کیا بنی، یہ جو کہا تو دیکھیے   سامنے آن بیٹھنا اور یہ دیکھنا کہ یُوں!

ġhair se rāt kyā banī, yih jo kahā to dekhiye
sāmne ān beṭhnā āur yih dekhnā kih yūñ (117:4; #719)

When asked, "How did it go with the rival last night?"
She boldly sat in front of me, with a puzzled look.

When I asked her how it went with the rival last night, she sat before me and looked at me as if to ask, "Is that a question to ask?" This verse handles a very difficult emotional situation. The beloved has made love to the rival and the lover knows it, but still wants her to give him a flimsy hope that nothing happened between them.

بزم میں اُس کے رُوبرُو کیوں نہ خموش بیٹھیے   اُس کی تو خامشی میں بھی ہے یہی مُدعا کہ یُوں

bazm meñ us ke rū-ba-rū kioñ na(h) ḳhamosh baiṭhīye
us kī to ḳhamshī meñ bhī hai yahī muddu'ā kih yūñ (117:5; #720)

Why shouldn't we just stay quiet before her in the assembly?
In her silence, it is implied that everyone should stay like this.

When the beloved sits quietly, perhaps she wants me to be quiet as well.

میں نے کہا کہ بزمِ ناز چاہیے غیر سے تہی   سُن کے ستم ظریف نے مجھ کو اُٹھا دیا کہ یُوں

maiñ ne kahā kih bazm-e nāz chāhiye ġhair se tahī
sun ke sitam ẓarīf ne mujh ko uṭhā diyā kih yūñ (117:6; #721)

I pleaded with her to "clear out the strangers from the assembly."
Hearing this, that cruel humorist showed me the way out just like that.

sitam ẓarīf: humor in cruelty, bad luck; *tahī*: without

In her assembly, I suggested to the beloved that she remove the strangers. She agreed with me and told me to leave. What a cruel joke this is. It is as if she is asking me, "Is that how you wanted it?"

مجھ سے کہا جو یار نے جاتے ہیں ہوش کس طرح   دیکھ کے میری بیخودی چلنے لگی ہوا کہ یُوں

mujh se kahā jo yār ne jāte haiñ hosh kis ṭarḥ
dekh ke merī beḳhudī chalne lagī hvā kih yūñ (117:7; #722)

As the beloved asked me, "How do you lose your senses?"
Seeing my delirium, the wind began blowing to say "'tis like this."

Just as the beloved asked me how I lose my senses, I lost my senses, the wind began blowing, as if it was answering, "that's how."

کب مجھے کوئے یار میں رہنے کی وضع یاد تھی   آئینہ دار بن گئی حیرتِ نقشِ پا کہ یُوں

kab mujhe kūe yār meñ rahne kī vaẓa' yād thī
ā'ina(h)dār ban gaī ḥairat-e naqsh-e pā kih yūñ (117:8; #723)

When did I remember the etiquette of living in the alley of beloved?
The surprised footprint is reflecting to show "that's how?"

ā'ina(h) dār: reflective; *ḥairat-e naqsh-e pā*: surprise of footprint.

I had forgotten the etiquette of living in her alley. Seeing this, the footprint became very surprised and told me, pointing towards itself, "That is how; like a footprint," it said. To enter her alley means entering into a love relationship. Going through it is like merging with dust, as a footprint does, giving up all you have, ego included, and spending the rest of your life in a state of total shock, looking at her beauty. A footprint, as it stays put, is supposed to be in a stunned state. A frozen footprint is likened to a state of wondering, "When I look at a footprint, I come to know who I am."

گر ترے دل میں ہو خیال، وصل میں شوق کا زوال   موج محیطِ آب میں مارے ہے دست و پا کہ یوں

gar tere dil meñ ho ḳhayāl, viṣl meñ shauq kā zavāl
mauj, muḥīt-e āb meñ māre hai dast-o-pā kih yūñ (117:9; #724)

If you think in your heart that in union, your yearning desire will decline, then see how
The ocean waves keep beating their hands and feet like this.

zavāl: decline; *muḥīt-e āb*: ocean.

If you think consummation with the beloved would result in a decline of desire, look at the ocean waves. Though they have merged with the ocean, they keep struggling, splashing water, and exhibiting a constant desire to merge with the ocean again and again. That is how lover's heart feels.

جو یہ کہے کہ ریختہ کیوں کہ ہو رشکِ فارسی
گفتۂ غالب ایک بار پڑھ کے اسے سنا کہ یوں

jo yih kahe kih reḳhta(h) kioñ kih ho rashk-e fārsī
gufta(h)' Ġhālib ek bār paṛh ke use sunā kih yūñ (117:10; #725)

To those who says, "How can *Urdū ġhazal* be envy of Persian?",
Just once recite to them the verses of *Ġhālib*, "that's how."

Some question whether *Urdū ġhazals* are better than *Persian ġhazals*.
To prove it, read *Ġhālib*'s *Urdū ġhazals*. Then you will know the answer!

118

حسد سے دِل اگر افسُردہ ہے، گرمِ تماشا ہو
کہ چشمِ تنگ شاید کثرتِ نظّارہ سے وا ہو

ḥasad se dil āgar āfsurda(h) hai, garm-e tamāshā ho
kih chashm-e tang shāyad kas̈rat-e naz̤z̤āra(h) se vā ho (118:1; #726)

If the heart is saddened with jealousy, then get busy observing,
So that perhaps your narrow vision might broaden by the abundance of the spectacle.

ḥasad: jealousy; *afsurda(h)*: saddened; *tamāshā*: spectacle; *kas̈rat:* abundance; *naz̤z̤āra(h)*: sight; *tang:* narrow; *vā*: open.

If the feeling of jealousy saddens you, then do something about it. Look around again and again. This will broaden your narrow vision and you will see that there are people more unfortunate than you. Our vision will broaden by observing things around us frequently, and closely, not just looking at them casually.

بہ قدرِ حسرتِ دل، چاہیے ذوقِ معاصی بھی
بھروں یک گوشۂ دامن، گر آبِ ہفت دریا ہو

ba(h) qadr-e ḥasrat-e dil chāhiye żauq-e ma'āṣī bhī
bharūñ yak gosha(h)' dāman, gar āb-e haft daryā ho (118:2; #727)

Proportionate to the longing of the heart is required the taste for sins also.
It will only fill a corner of the lap, if these were the waters of the seven seas.

ma'āṣī: sin; *āb-e haft daryā*: water of seven oceans.

The desire to commit sins must precede the taste for them as well. My desire and taste are both unlimited. If my sins were equivalent to the water of the seven oceans, then I would only wet a corner of my skirt with them. This means that I am capable of holding (committing) a lot more sins. This is an exaggeration of desire and taste for sin.

اگر وہ سرو قد، گرمِ خرامِ ناز آجاوے
کفِ ہر خاکِ گلشن، شکلِ قمری، نالہ فرسا ہو

agar vo sarv qad, garm-e ḳhirām nāz ājāve
kaf-e har ḳhāk-e gulshan, shakl-e qumrī, nāla(h) farsā ho (118:3; #728)

If that cypress stature beauty comes strolling in coquettishly,
The blowing dust of the garden would begin to plaint, like the ringdove.

sarv: cypress; *qad:* stature; *garm:* hot; *ḳhirām;* walk; *nāz*: coquetry; *kaf* bubbling foam; *qumrī:* ringdove (a dust colored bird).

If that tall beloved of mine walks in with her coquettish gait, the dust of the garden will blow and lament like a ring-necked dove lamenting to the moon. The lament of the ring-necked dove is taken as a sign of lunacy, meaning that everything in the garden will go crazy as she enters with her coquettish walk. The comparison of garden dust with a ring-necked dove is not coincidental: the ring-necked dove looks at the moon with great desperation, moans, and is of dusty color.

119

کعبے میں جا رہا، تو نہ دو طعنہ، کیا کہیں
بھولا ہوں حقِ صحبتِ اہلِ کنشت کو؟

Kaʿbe meñ jā rahā, to na(h) do taʿna(h), kyā kahīñ
bhūlā hūñ ḥaqq-e ṣoḥbat-e āhl-e kunisht ko (119:1; #729)

Having moved in *Kaʿbā*, taunt me not to say that
I have forgotten the companion rights of natives of temple?

ḥaqq-e ṣoḥbat: rights of companions; *kunisht*: temple, church synagogue.

Yes, I have moved to *Kaʿbā* to live, but I have not forgotten about my mates from the temple. Do not taunt that I have forgotten them. Changing one's living place does not mean you break off all devotional and emotional connection to people and places of yore. The question arises, what rights of compatriot idolaters can be recognized? Clearly, I am not supposed to give up supplicating before the beloved. The compatriots from the house of idols are the lover's colleagues. The argument in the verse circles around the connection between *Kaʿba*, where at one time used to be idols placed for supplication, supplicating before idols being prohibited in Islam, the beloved being called an idol and the lover changing his abode but not his ways.

طاعت میں تا، رہے نہ مے و انگبیں کی لاگ
دوزخ میں ڈال دو کوئی لے کر بہشت کو

ṯāʿt meñ tā, rahe na(h) mai vāñgbīñ kī lāg
dozakh meñ ḍāl do koʾī le kar bahisht ko (119:2; #730)

So in the prayers, there shall remain no temptation for wine and honey,
Would someone take the Paradise and throw it in the hell?

ṭā't: devotion, prayer; *mai vāñgbīñ*: wine and honey; *lāg*: affection, temptation.

The promise of wine, honey, and paradise keeps many people praying. It is better that we throw Paradise to hell, leaving no choice but to pray to God selflessly and not for any personal gain. This verse is a direct hit at those who preach the virtue of Paradise to lure people into praying.

ہوں منحرف نہ کیوں رہ و رسمِ ثواب سے
ٹیڑھا لگا ہے قط قلمِ سرنوشت کو

hu'ñ munḥarif na(h) kioñ rah-o-rasm-e ṡavāb se
ṭeṛhā lagā hai qaṭ qalam-e sar navisht ko (119:3; #731)

Why should I not rebel against the ways and mores of good deeds?
Slanted is the cut in the pen writing the story of my destiny?

munḥarif: rebel, revolting; *qaṭ*: cut (as in making bamboo reed writing instruments in finishing the nib of the pen); *sar navisht*: fate, destiny.

How can I not stray from the path of good deeds when the story of my fate is written with a slanted-cut pen? This makes my life and thus my behavior slanted as well.

غالب کچھ اپنی سعی سے لہنا نہیں مجھے
خرمن جلے، اگر نہ ملخ کھائے کشت کو

Ġhālib kuchh apnī sa'ī se lahnā nahiñ mujhe
ḳhirman jale, āgar na(h) malḳh khāe kisht ko (119:4; #732)

Ġhālib, there is little to gain from my endeavors;
The lightning burns the harvest if it is not already eaten by the locust.

sa'ī: efforts; *lahnā*: benefit; *khirman*: lightning; *malḳh*: locust; *kisht*: crop.

Regardless of our efforts in life, the end is naught. If the locusts do not devour the crops, then certainly lightning will strike and destroy the crop. How can I speak of my efforts resulting in any fruitful end? Lightning can strike from sky or come from the sparks generated from hard threshing of the crop.

120

وارستہ اس سے ہیں کہ محبت ہی کیوں نہ ہو   کیجے ہمارے ساتھ، عداوت ہی کیوں نہ ہو

vārasta(h) us se haiñ kih muḥabbat hī kioñ na(h) ho
kīje hamāre sāth aʿdāvat hī kioñ na(h) ho (120:1; #733)

I care least about why should there not be love;
Just keep dealing with me even if it is with enmity.

vārasta(h): free, careless.

I am free of the desire to have you love me as I love you. However, if not love, I would take enmity from you; it would be better than indifference. If you cannot love me, at least remain in touch, somehow, even if it is with hate. The lover is indifferent to the need of having her show any affection; he is not indifferent to the beloved. This is one of the most oft repeated themes of *Ġhālib*. See also, for example, *qataʿ kīje na(h) taʿlluq ham se, kuchh nahiñ hai to ʿadāvat hī sahī* [break not connection with me, if nothing else then let it be enmity] and *lāg ho to us ko ham samjheñ lagāʾo/ jab na(h) ho kuchh bhī to dhokā khaeñ kyā.* [If there were enmity, we would think of it as affection, but when there is not anything, then how would we deceive ourselves].

چھوڑا نہ مجھ میں ضعف نے رنگ اختلاط کا   ہے دل پہ بار نقشِ محبت ہی کیوں نہ ہو

choṛā na(h) mujh meñ ẓoʿf ne rang iḳhtilāṭ kā
hai dil pa(h) bār naqsh-e muḥabbat hī kioñ na(h) ho (120:2; #734)

Feebleness has not left any flare for lovemaking in me;
A heavy heart I have, even if it is from the memory of your love.

ẓo'f: weakness; *rang:* color; *iḳhtilāṭ*: love making; *bār:* burden; *naqsh:* mark, image (used here to mean memory).

Old age has taken its toll on the strength I have to make love to you. I am so weak that I cannot bear the burden of the memory of loving you. The burden of the mark of your love is difficult for me to bear.

ہے مجھ کو تجھ سے تذکرۂ غیر کا گلہ   ہر چند بر سبیلِ شکایت ہی کیوں نہ ہو

hai mujh ko tujh se tażkira(h)' ġhair kā gila(h)
harchand barsabīl-e shikāyat hī kyoñ nā ho (120:3; #735)

I do have a complaint against you that you talk about the rival,
Even though it is for the sake of complaining about him.

ġhair: stranger, rival; *gila(h)*: complaint; *shikāyat*: complaint; *tażkira(h)'*: discussion; *harchand*: even though; *barsabīl*: for the sake of.

Say nothing about my rival to me. Not even a complaint about him. I do not want to hear his name from your lips, even for the sake of discussion because it will make you think of him and that I cannot stand.

پیدا ہوئی ہے، کہتے ہیں، ہر درد کی دوا   یوں ہو تو چارۂ غمِ الفت ہی کیوں نہ ہو

paidā hu'ī hai, kahte haiñ, har dard kī davā
yuñ ho to chāra(h)' ġham-e ulfat hī kioñ na(h) ho (120:4; #736)

It is said that a cure has been created for every pain.
If that *is* the case, then why would not there be a panacea for the sorrow of love?

It is just a cliché that there is a cure for every pain; the pain of love goes untreated.

ڈالا نہ بیکسی نے کسی سے معاملہ   اپنے سے کھینچتا ہوں خجالت ہی کیوں نہ ہو

ḍālā na(h) bekasī ne kisī se mu'āmla(h)
apne se khainchtā hūñ ḳhajālat hī kioñ na(h) ho (120:5; #737)

Being destitute prevented me from dealings with anyone;
Becoming embarrassed from myself, for why is there no embarrassment?

bekasī: destitute; *mu'āmla(h)*: dealings; *khainch*: draw, take out; *ḳhajālat*: embarrassment.

Destitute and worthless, nobody wants anything from me, nor do I have the courage to ask anyone for anything. Without any dealings with people, there is no chance of ever becoming embarrassed due to lost expectations. The only embarrassment I have now is that I have no chance to be embarrassed as no one is dealing with me.

ہے آدمی بجائے خود اک محشرِ خیال   ہم انجمن سمجھتے ہیں خلوت ہی کیوں نہ ہو

hai ādmī bajāe ḳhūd ik maḥshar-e ḳhayāl
ham anjuman samjhte haiñ, ḳhalvat hī kioñ na(h) ho (120:6; #738)

Man by himself is a composite of scattered thoughts;
We think of it as an assembly while it may well be seclusion.

ādmī: man (literally an offspring of Adam); *ḳhūd*: self; *maḥshar:* confused, composite; *ḳhalvat:* seclusion; *anjuman*: assembly; *ḳhayāl:* thought.

Our perception of ourselves, is just a collection of scattered thoughts. Therefore, even when we are in seclusion, we are not free from these thoughts, biases, and prejudices. They remain with us and provide company. Composed of scattered thoughts, man is never alone—that is what is meant here. The real seclusion is getting rid of our biases, something that is not possible. Rene Descartes' idea of "I" is exquisitely described here: "I think, therefore, I am."

ہنگامۂ زبونیٔ ہمت ہے انفعال　　حاصل نہ کیجے دہر سے، عبرت ہی کیوں نہ ہو

hangāma(h)' zabūnīē' himmat hai infe'āl
ḥāṣil na(h) kīje dahr se, 'ibrat hī kioñ na(h) ho (120:7; #739)

The display of weak courage is pitiful;
Accept it not from the world, even if it is a reproof.

hangām: big show; *zabūnī:* weakness; *infe'āl*: pitiful; *dahr:* world, a terrible place to live in; *'ibrat*: reproof.

Being influenced by others is pitiful. You should not learn anything from the experience of others, even if it is a lesson of reproof. When you learn from others, you take on their points of view and their shortcomings of thoughts.

وارستگی بہانۂ بیگانگی نہیں　　اپنے سے کر، نہ غیر سے، وحشت ہی کیوں نہ ہو

vārastagī bahāna(h)' begāngī nahiñ
apne se kar, na(h) ġhair se, vaḥshat hī kioñ na(h) ho (120:8; #740)

Freedom is no excuse for becoming oblivious to others;
Seek it from yourself, not from strangers, even if it is solitude.

vārastagī: freedom; *bahānā*: excuse; *begāngī*: obliviousness; *ġhair*: stranger; *vaḥshat*: loneliness;.

Your aloofness cannot justify distancing yourself from others. If you seek solitude, seek it from your ego and not from other human beings. Here *Ġhālib* illustrates a form of freedom that is really an excuse for obliviousness. Seek solitude from yourself and not from others.

مٹتا ہے فوتِ فرصتِ ہستی کا غم کوئی؟ عمرِ عزیز صرفِ عبادت ہی کیوں نہ ہو

miṭ tā hai faut-e furṣat-e hastī kā ġham ko'ī
'umr-e 'azīz ṣarf-e 'ibādat hī kioñ na(h) ho (120:9; #741)

Nothing erases the fear of demise of leisurely moments,
Even if this life, so dear to us, is spent just praying.

furṣat: leisure; *ġham*: sorrow; *hastī*: life; *'ibādat*: devotion; *ṣarf*: spent.

No matter how we live our life, the sorrow and fear of departing from this abode remain, even if we dedicate our dear life to praying. Poet suggests that we should go on living our daily life and not waste time in praying, not holding out hope that anything better will come.

اُس فتنہ خو کے در سے اب اُٹھتے نہیں اسد
اِس میں ہمارے سر پہ قیامت ہی کیوں نہ ہو

us fitna(h) ḳhū ke dar se ab uṭhte nahiñ Asad
is meñ hamāre sar pa(h) qiyāmat hī kioñ na(h) ho (120:10; #742)

From the doorsteps of that havoc-wreaker, I would not get up, Asad,
Even if it results in bringing Doomsday calamities on my head.

The beloved is known to wreak havoc on the poet's life. He is now sitting at her threshold and refuses to leave even if it results in making her really upset with him and getting him into a great deal of trouble. The Doomsday is supposed to be a time of havoc, thus he calls the beloved "havoc-wreaker. Regardless of our efforts in life, the end is naught. If the locusts do not devour the crops, then certainly lightning will strike to destroy it. How can I speak of my efforts resulting in any fruitful end?

121

قفس میں ہوں، گر اچھا بھی نہ جانیں میرے شیون کو   مرا ہونا برا کیا ہے نواسنجانِ گلشن کو

qafas meñ huñ, gar achhā bhī na(h) jāneñ mere shevan ko
merā honā burā kyā hai navāsanjān-e gulshan ko (121:1; #743)

**They do not like my lamenting, even though I am caged now.
Why is my existence so burdensome to my singing mates in the garden?**

shevan: grief, lamentation; *navāsanjān-e gulshan*: singing birds in garden.

I have been caught and caged; yet, my fellow birds that roam free in the garden continue to malign me. They do not like my grieved utterances; I do not understand how they can hate someone who is removed from them and imprisoned. Why are they after my life? A great observation on human nature is expounded here.

نہیں گر ہمدمی آساں، نہ ہو، یہ رشک کیا کم ہے   نہ دی ہوتی خدایا آرزوئے دوست، دشمن کو

nahiñ gar hamdamī āsāñ, na(h) ho, yih rashk kyā kam hai,
na(h) dī hotī ḳhudāyā ārzū'e dost dushman ko. (121:2; #744)

**If intimacy is not possible, so be it, this jealousy alone is too much.
O! God, you should not have given to my rival, yearning for the beloved.**

hamdamī: closeness; *rashk*: jealousy; *ḳhudā*: God; *ārzū*: yearning; *dost*: beloved; *dushman*: enemy, rival;.

It does not matter if it is difficult for me to get close to my beloved. What makes it unbearable for me is my jealousy towards my rival, in whose heart you have, O' my Lord, put a desire for my beloved as well. I wish I alone longed for my beloved.

نہ نکلا آنکھ سے تیری اِک آنسو اُس جراحت پر　　کیا سینے میں جس نے خُونچکاں مژگانِ سوزن کو

na(h) niklā āñkh se terī ik āñsū us jirāḥat par
kiyā sīne meñ jis ne ḳhuñchukāñ mizhgān-e sozan ko (121:3; #745)

Not a single tear came out of your eye looking at that wound,
Which caused the eyelashes of the needle in my chest to get bloodstained.

jirāḥat: wound; *mizhgān-e sozan*: eyelashes of needle.

How callous can the beloved be? When the needle stitching my wounded chest began shedding blood-tears, the beloved remained oblivious. The needle, when it looked at my pathetic wounds, began crying blood.

خُدا شرمائے ہاتھوں کو کہ رکھتے ہیں کشاکش میں　　کبھی میرے گریباں کو کبھی جاناں کے دامن کو

ḳhudā sharmāe hāthoñ ko kih rakhte haiñ kashākash meñ
kabhī mere garebāñ ko kabhī jānāñ ke dāman ko (121:4; #746)

God should put my hands to shame when in a dilemma, they grab,
At times, my own collar and at others, my sweetheart's lap.

kashākash: dilemma, struggle.

Pulling my own collar, I am called a lunatic. Pulling her lap of skirt gets me thrown out of her assembly. I need to discipline my hands.

ابھی ہم قتل گہ کا دیکھنا آساں سمجھتے ہیں　　نہیں دیکھا شناور جُوئے خُوں میں تیرے توسن کو

abhī ham qatl gah kā dekhnā āsāñ samajhte haiñ
nahiñ dekhā shināvar jū-e ḳhūñ meñ tere tausan ko (121:5; #747)

So far we think it will be easy to bear the sight of killing-fields; Not yet having seen your agile horse swimming in the river of blood.

qatlgah: killing field; *shināvar*: swimmer; *jū-e ḳhūñ*: river of blood; *tausan*: a young unbroken horse, a high-blooded steed.

The killing fields of love are no ordinary places. The beloved's horse that swims through blood tells the whole story. The verse points to hardships that we do not foresee before embarking on a courageous act. The imagery of the verse is superbly colorful in depicting the beloved's cruelty and our inability to anticipate the hardships before us.

ہُوا چرچا جو میرے پانوْ کی زنجیر بننے کا   کیا بے تاب کاں میں جُنبشِ جوہر نے آہن کو

hu'ā charchā jo mere pāoñ kī zanjīr banne kā
kiyā betāb kāñ meñ juñmbish-e johar ne āhan ko (121:6; #748)

As the word got around that a chain is being built for my feet, The iron ore in the mine became impatient with the restlessness of its atoms.

charchā: popular talk; *kān*: mine; *juñmbish*: movement; *āhan*: iron; *johar*: atoms, components; *betāb*: impatient.

It is a great honor to be part of a chain that contains the biggest lunatic of all. This causes the iron atoms in the mine to become excited which makes the ore impatient from longing to be part of this chain.

خوشی کیا، کھیت پر میرے اگر سَو بار ابر آوے   سمجھتا ہوں کہ ڈھونڈے ہے ابھی سے برق خرمن کو

ḳhushī kyā, khet par mere āgar sau bār abr āve
samajhtā huñ kih ḍhunḍe hai abhī se barq ḳhirman ko (121:7; #749)

What joy there is to see the clouds coming over my fields a hundred times;
I know that the lurking lightning is already seeking the collected crop.

The clouds bring rain to the crop, a good omen, but it may be just a façade for the lightning to hunt for new crops. "Already," meaning that as rain pours, it is time for the lightning to target where the crop will grow. A very realistic visualization of a façade is adduced here.

وفاداری بشرطِ اُستواری اصلِ ایماں ہے   مرے بُت خانے میں تو کعبے میں گاڑو برہمن کو

vafādārī bashart̤-e ustuvārī, aṣl-e īmāñ haī
mare but ḳhane meñ to ka'be meñ gāṛo brahman ko (121:8; #750)

Faithfulness, provided it is permanent, is the real belief.
If he dies in the temple of idols, bury the Brahmin in *Ka'ba*.

bashart̤: conditional; *ustuvārī,*: permanence; *gāṛo*: to bury; *brahman*: Hindu men of high caste, Brahmin.

It matters to *Ġhālib* that Hindus do not bury their dead but instead send them to pyre and that *Ka'ba* is not a graveyard. He asserts that if a Brahmin is faithful, he deserves to be honored, for the real test of any belief is faithfulness to God, not which religion you follow. Moreover, if someone holds a real belief, God will accept him regardless of his religious affiliation. Verses like this can be very explosive if they are taken as sacrilege by the devout.

شہادت تھی مری قسمت میں جو دی تھی یہ خُو مجھ کو   جہاں تلوار کو دیکھا، جُھکا دیتا تھا گردن کو

shahādat thī merī qismat meñ, jo dī thī yih ḳhū mujh ko
jahañ talvār ko dekhā, jhukā detā thā gardan ko (121:9; #751)

It was in my fate to become a martyr, as I was given the habit that,
Wherever I would see a sword, I would lower my neck to it.

When you know what is written in your fate, you should not resist the inevitable but welcome it instead. The belief in fate gives courage and courage makes the impossible happen.

نہ لٹتا دن کو تو کب رات کو یوں بے خبر سوتا　　رہا کھٹکا نہ چوری کا دعا دیتا ہوں رہزن کو

na(h) luṭ tā din ko to kab rāt ko yūñ be ḳhabar sotā
rahā khaṭkā na(h) chorī kā du'ā detā huñ rahzan ko (121:10; #752)

Had I not been robbed during the day, how could I have slept so well in the night?
Now with the fear of theft gone, I pray to bless the robber.

du'ā: prayer; *rahzan*: highway robber.

Daytime refers to early life and thanks are extended to the daytime robber, not the nighttime thief. The use of the word "*khatkā*" has deeper meaning here. It means something that is not supposed to happen—a fear of something implausible or anticipatory. We do not anticipate a thief coming into our home; we fear he might come. *Ġhālib* has used this word very craftily elsewhere: "*thā zindagī meñ marg ka khaṭkā lagā hu'a.*" (While alive, I was in fear of death all the time.) Using daytime as a reference to early life means, I have lost everything earned. I can now be contented in my later years.

سخن کیا کہہ نہیں سکتے کہ جویا ہوں جواہر کے؟　　جگر کیا ہم نہیں رکھتے کہ کھودیں جا کے معدن کو؟

suḳhan kyā kah nahiñ sakte kih jūyā huñ javāhir ke
jigar kyā ham nahiñ rakhte kih khodeñ jāke ma'dan ko (121:11; #753)

Can I not write poetry that I must go seeking for jewels?
Do I not have a liver that I must go on to digging mines?

suḳhan: poetry; *jūyā*: seeker; *ma'dan*: mine.

Verses are compared to jewels and diction to mining jewels. In his eternal self-confidence, the poet asserts that his words are jewels, precious and bright. His heart (liver) is a mine of verses and he need not go elsewhere to enrich himself. He need not dig mines to unearth jewels. He can bring it out all from within.

مرے شاہِ سلیماں جاہ سے نسبت نہیں غالب
فریدون و جم و کیخسرو و داراب و بہمن کو

mere shāh-e sulaimāñ jāh se nisbat nahiñ Ġhālib
firidun-o-jam-o-kaiḳhusrau-o-dārāb-o-bahman ko (121:12; #754)

O! *Ġhālib*, my king like Sulaiman has no relationship with Faridun, Jam, Kaikhusro, Darab and Bahman.

The kings of Persia may be great, but they cannot be compared to my king who has the power and dignity of *Haẓrat Sulaima*. The second line names the most prominent Persian emperors. This is an extremely exaggerated ode to the King.

122

دھوتا ہوں جب مَیں پینے کو اُس سیم تن کے پاؤں   رکھتا ہے ضِد سے، کھینچ کے باہر لگن کے پاؤں

dhotā huñ jab meñ pīne ko us sīm tan ke pāuñ
rakhtā hai ẓid se, khaiñch ke bahar lagan ke pā'uñ (122:1; #755)

Whenever I wash the feet of that white-complexioned beauty, to drink,
With great arrogance, she pulls her feet out of the pail.

sīm tan: white complexioned; *ẓid*: arrogance; *lagan*: pail; *pauñ dho kar pīnā*: to be extremely respectful, to drink feet washings.

The beloved is arrogantly pulling her feet out of the pail as the lover offers to wash her feet so that he can drink the washings. He actually wants to touch her feet and lures her into allowing him to do so. To drink the water leftover from foot washing is also an expression of extreme respect.

دی سادگی سے جان، پڑوں کوہکن کے پاؤں   ہَیہات! کیوں نہ ٹوٹ گئے پیرزن کے پاؤں

dī sādgī se jān, paṛūñ kohkan ke pāuñ
haihāth! kioñ na(h) ṭūṭ ga'e pīrzan ke pa'uñ (122:2; #756)

Giving life in naïveté, I should kiss the feet of the mountain digger.
Alas! Why didn't the feet of the old lady break?

kohkan: mountain digger, *Farhād*; *haihāth*: Begone! Away!, Alas!, Woe to me!; *pīrzan*: old lady, referring to the man who disguised himself as an old lady when he came to give the false news of *Shīrīn*'s death to *Farhād*,

To show my regard for the foolish nature of *Farhād*, I must kiss his feet. The poet wishes that the old lady's feet were broken so she could not have come to see *Farhād*. The use of the seldom-used Persian word "*haihāth*" to express sorrow is made to rhyme with the word "*hāth*," meaning hand.

بھاگے تھے ہم بہت، سو اُسی کی سزا ہے یہ   ہو کر اسیر دابتے ہیں راہزن کے پانو

bhāge the ham bahut, so isī kī sazā hai yih
ho kar asīr dābte haiñ rāhzan ke pa'uñ (122:3; #757)

It is the punishment for our running away too far, that,
Now, in bondage, we comfort the feet of the highway robber.

rāhzan: highway robber; *asīr:* in bondage; *pauñ*: feet.

I was foolish to run away from her, because I soon find myself returned to her bondage, sit by her feet, and massage them. She is a robber, having robbed me of my freedom to run away from her. How daringly she did it! It was as if she were a roadside robber.

مرہم کی جستجو میں پھرا ہوں جو دور دور   تن سے سوا فگار ہیں اِس خستہ تن کے پانو

marham kī justajū meñ phirā huñ jo dūr dūr
tan se sivā figār haiñ is ḳhasta(h) tan ke pā'uñ (122:4; #758)

Having wandered far and beyond looking for a cure,
Now the feet of this tired body hurt more than the body.

marham: cure; *justajū:* search; *dūr:* distant; *tan:* body; *sivā*: except; *ḳhasta(h)*: wounded; *figār:* wounded, hurting.

I have wandered far and wide in search of a cure for my body, but now my feet are more blistered and broken than my body. Now that I cannot go any further to find a cure, I have ended up with an ailment that can no longer be cured. I have traded a lesser ailment for a major one because of my desperate desire to cure myself of minor pain. This illustrates how we are so desperate to ward-off minor ills that we end up with incurable ones. This verse also points to the useless search for a panacea.

اللہ رے ذوقِ دشت نوردی، کہ بعدِ مرگ　　ہلتے ہیں خود بخود مرے اندر کفن کے پاؤں

allah re żauq-e dasht navardī, kih ba'd-e marg
hilte haiñ ḳhud baḳhud mere andar kafan ke pā'uñ (122:5; #759)

Oh! Lord, what a desire for wandering the desert that even after death,
My feet keep moving on their own inside the shroud.

My desire to wander the wilderness did not end with my death. My feet were so used to the rough terrain of the wilderness that they kept moving even inside the shroud. Note a common observation illustrated here; when we sit idly, engrossed in some thought, we sometimes find our feet moving.

ہے جوشِ گل بہار میں یاں تک کہ ہر طرف　　اڑتے ہوئے، الجھتے ہیں مرغِ چمن کے پاؤں

hai josh-e gul bahār meñ yāñ tak kih har t̤araf
ut̤e hu'e, ulajhte haiñ murġh-e chaman ke pā'uñ (122:6; #760)

The blooming of flowers in the spring is so widespread that
The flying birds of the garden are getting their feet entangled in them.

josh-e gul: blooming of flowers; *murġh-e chaman:* birds of garden.

The garden has become so dense, and the flowering trees have grown so tall, the flying birds are getting their feet caught in them. Another explanation is that since the garden has become so attractive, the birds are reluctant to fly out and getting their feet caught.

شب کو کسی کے خواب میں آیا نہ ہو کہیں   دُکھتے ہیں آج اُس بُتِ نازک بدن کے پاؤں

shab ko kisī ke ḳh(v)āb meñ āyā na(h) ho kahiñ
dukhte haiñ āj us but-e nāzuk badan ke pāuñ (122:7; #761)

I wonder if last night she appeared in someone's dream?
For today, the feet of that delicate-body idol are aching.

How tender is a body if appearing in someone's dream makes the feet ache? This is indeed a unique *Ġhālib*ian construction.

غالب! مرے کلام میں کیونکر مزہ نہ ہو
پیتا ہوں دھو کے خُسروِ شیریں سخن کے پاؤں

Ġhālib! mere kalām meñ kioñ kar maza(h) na(h) ho
pītā huñ dho ke ḳhusrav-e shirīñ suḳhan ke pā'uñ (122:8; #762)

***Ġhālib*, why shouldn't there be savor in my verses**
For I drink the washings of the feet of Khusaro, a poet with sweet diction?

ḳhusro: Amir Khusrao, the famous *Urdū* poet, often regarded as the first *Urdū* poet; *shirīñ suḳhan*: sweet diction.

Comparing himself to other poets, *Ġhālib* elevates his own status. There is a particular flavor to his verses because he gives much attention to how Khusrao wrote poetry. The idiom,"to drink the washings of the feet," means to hold someone in high esteem. Elsewhere, *Ġhālib* says,"*haiñ āur bhī duniyā meñ suḳhanvar bahut āchhe; kahte haiñ kih Ġhālib kā hai āndāz-e bayāñ āur*." (There are others who have great diction. They say, however, that *Ġhālib* has a style altogether unique.)

123

واں اُس کو ہولِ دِل ہے، تو یاں مَیں ہُوں شرمسار
یعنی، یہ میری آہ کی تاثیر سے نہ ہو

vañ us ko haul-e dil hai, to yāñ maiñ huñ sharmsār
ya'nī, yih merī āh kī tāṡir se na(h) ho (123:1; #763)

There she has palpitations of heart, and here I am ashamed;
Might it not have been caused by the effects of my sighs.

haul-e dil: palpitation of heart; *sharmsār*: ashamed.

The poet is trying to convince himself that the ill condition of the beloved is caused by his sighs and feels ashamed of causing her suffering. Preconceived notions and high self-image are displayed here. He does not want to know the real reason for the condition of the beloved. The fact is that she is in love with someone else and the poet is trying to hide it by offering an excuse, putting the blame on himself.

اپنے کو دیکھتا نہیں، ذوقِ ستم تو دیکھ
آئینہ تا کہ دیدۂ نخچیر سے نہ ہو

apne ko dekhtā nahiñ, żauq-e sitam to dekh,
ā'ina(h) tākih dīda(h)' nāḳhchīr se na(h) ho. (123:2; #764)

Look at your tyranny for not looking at yourself
Unless the mirror happens to be the eye of the hunted-catch.

dīda(h)': eye; *naḳhchīr*: catch; *tākih*: until.

The beloved does not pay attention to her beauty until the mirror acts as the eye of the catch, a new lover. Look at your cruelty, the poet points out to her. The cruelty is two-fold. First, she catches a new lover, and then she kills him by adorning herself. The poet is hurting with jealousy. The beloved's style of using the eye of the hunted-catch as the mirror is indeed unique and so is *Ġhālib*'s expanse of thoughts.

124

واں پہنچ کر جو غش آتا پئے ہم ہے ہم کو   صد رہ آہنگِ زمیں بوسِ قدم ہے ہم کو

vāñ pahuñch kar jo ġhash ātā pa'e ham hai ham ko
ṣad rah āhang-e zamiñ bos-e qadam hai ham ko (124:1; #765)

I faint again and again, upon reaching there as if
My intention were to kiss the ground under my feet a hundred times.

ġhash: fainting; *ṣad rah*: a hundred times; *āhang*: intention; *āhang-e zamiñ bos:* act of kissing ground; *zamiñ*: ground; *qadam*: footstep.

Somehow I made it to the alley of the beloved, but I have no strength to go further as I keep fainting and getting up, hundreds of times, because of the sorrow in my heart. Kissing the alley of my beloved is, therefore, my fate, my destiny. Difficult to translate and interpret, this verse conveys a condition of lover that is truly ethereal.

دِل کو مَیں اور مجھے دِل محوِ وفا رکھتا ہے   کِس قدر ذوقِ گرفتاریٔ ہم ہے ہم کو

dil ko maiñ āur mujhe dil maḥv-e vafā rakhtā hai
kis qadar żauq-e giraftārī' ham hai ham ko (124:2; #766)

I convince my heart, and my heart convinces me to stay engrossed in devotion.
What a great desire we both have to stay captive to her.

My heart and I, both keep busy speaking about the virtues of devotion. Obviously, we both take a fancy to being captured—falling in love. The heart tells me not to give up devotion, and I keep telling my heart not to let the etiquette of loving go. Both are working to stay captive to her.

ضعف سے نقشِ پئے مور ہے طوقِ گردن   تیرے کوچے سے کہاں طاقتِ رم ہے ہم کو

ẓo'f se naqsh-e pa'e mūr hai ṭauq-e gardan
tere kūche se kahāñ ṭāqat-e ram hai ham ko (124:3; #767)

The footprint of an ant is like a collar on my neck because of frailty.
How can I gather the strength to run away from your alley?

ẓo'f frailty, weakness; *pa'e mūr*: feet of ant; *ṭauq*: collar; *ram*: to flee.

My frailty makes the weight of an ant's footprint seem like a heavy collar hanging around my neck. I have no energy to flee from your alley. Comparing footprints of an ant to a collar hanging on the neck illustrates how much energy is left in the lover.

جان کر کیجے تغافل کہ کچھ امید بھی ہو   یہ نگاہِ غلط انداز تو سم ہے ہم کو

jān kar kīje taġhāful kih kuchh ummīd bhī ho
yih nigāh-e ġhalat andāż to sum hai ham ko (124:4; #768)

Ignore me intentionally so that a hope may rise.
This glance of obliviousness is like poison to me.

taġhāful: ignoring; *sum*: presenting poison.

Ignore me like people who know one another; your indifference kills me because it does not give me any hope. Look at me as if you know me, even when you show your anger. *Ġhālib* repeats this theme often.

رشکِ ہم طرحی و دردِ اثرِ بانگِ حزیں نالۂ مرغِ سحر تیغِ دو دم ہے ہم کو

rashk-e ham ṭarḥī-o-dard-e asar-e bāñg-e ḥaziñ
nālah' murġh-e saḥar teġh-e do dam hai ham ko (124:5; #769)

Envious of the similarity of style, and of the effectiveness of the sad crowing,
The plaint of the morning bird is a double-edged sword to me.

ham ṭarḥī: same style; *bāñg:* crowing; *ḥaziñ:* sad; *teġh-e do dam:* double-edge sword.

The call of the crowing rooster sounds very much like my lament, but the rooster's crowing has more impact than mine. I am envious of the rooster for having such an impressive lament because its painful diction will be heard, but not mine. People get up to go for prayers at the call of the rooster. Maybe the rooster also wakes up the beloved. No one listens to me.

سر اڑانے کے جو وعدے کو مکرر چاہا ہنس کے بولے کہ ترے سر کی قسم ہے ہم کو!

sar uṛāne ke jo va'de ko mukarrar chāhā
hañs ke bole kih tere sar kī qasam hai ham ko (124:6; #770)

When I wanted her to repeat the promise to let my head fly off,
Laughingly, she said, "I swear upon your head."

mukarrar: repeat.

I asked my beloved to repeat the promise she made to cut off my head. Instead, she said, "I swear upon your head," which means yes and no with equal emphasis. The fact that she said it laughingly indicates her wanton style. Swearing upon the head means, "God forbid" and "If I do not do it, then you will lose your head."

دل کے خوں کرنے کی کیا وجہ، ولیکن ناچار پاسِ بے رونقیِ دیدہ اہم ہے ہم کو

dil ke ḳhuñ karne kī kyā vajh, valekin nāchār
pās-e be raunaqī' đīda(h) āham hai ham ko (124:7; #771)

What is the reason to make the heart bleed except that
It is important for me to take care of my lackluster eyes.

raunaq: luster; *nāchār*: helpless, inevitable; *āham*: important.

I had no choice but to let my heart bleed so blood would flow into my eyes. That is how I will bring back the luster to my eyes, something I consider very important. Lover's eyes are also called lamps; he just wants to brighten his dark abode.

تم وہ نازک کہ خموشی کو فغاں کہتے ہو ہم وہ عاجز کہ تغافل بھی ستم ہے ہم کو

tum vuh nāzuk ke ḳhamoshī ko fuġhāñ kahte ho
ham vuh 'ājiz kih taġhāful bhī sitam hai ham ko (124:8; #772)

You are so delicate that you consider our silence to be a lament;
Here I am so weak that even your indifference is a cruelty to me.

'ājiz: weak, incapable.

Your delicate nature hears laments even in my quietness. How delicate is our nature? When you are oblivious to me, it is really an act of cruelty shown to me. You have become so sensitive that even though I have given up lamenting, it still bothers you that I stay quiet thinking about you. The lover and the beloved are at opposite ends of sensitivity.

لکھنؤ آنے کا باعث نہیں کھلتا، یعنی ق ہوسِ سیر و تماشا، سو وہ کم ہے ہم کو

Lakhna'u āne kā bā'is nahiñ khultā, ya'nī
havas-e sair-o-tamāshā, so vuh kam hai ham ko (124:9; #773)

The reason for coming to Lucknow is not clear to me.
Perhaps it is a desire for sightseeing, but that I do not have much.

I do not know why have I come to Lucknow. Most would think I came for the sightseeing, but I do not have any such desire. This verse continues into the next verse as a quatrain. Note that Lucknow was the seat of *Urdū* poetry in Uttar Pradesh, a bastion of Nawabs. The rivalry between the Lucknow and *Delhī* school of poetry went on for years. *Ġhālib* was from *Delhī*.

مقطعِ سلسلۂ شوق نہیں ہے یہ شہر عزمِ سیرِ نجف و طوفِ حرم ہے ہم کو

maqṭa'-e silsila(h)' shauq nahiñ hai yih shahar
'azm-e sair-e Najaf-o-ṭauf-e ḥaram hai ham ko (124:10; #774)

The destination of my desire is not this city;
What I intend to do is to see Najaf and to go circling around *Ka'ba.*

maqṭa': destination; *Najaf*: burial place of *Hazrat Alī*; *ṭaufe ḥaram*: circling around *Ka'ba*.

Lucknow is not my destination (see previous verse). I wanted to visit the burial place of *Hazrat 'Alī* (Najaf) and to circle *Ka'ba* (in Mecca). Though born in a Sunni family, *Ġhālib* always preferred to be recognized as Shia. (See Glossary. Hazarat *'Alī*)

لیے جاتی ہے کہیں ایک توقّع غالب
جادۂ رہ کششِ کافِ کرم ہے ہم کو

līye jātī hai kahīñ ek tavaqqu' Ġhālib
jāda(h)' rah kashish-e kāf-e karam hai ham ko (124:11; #775)

Taking me somewhere is this expectation, *Ġhālib*;
The attraction of the letter "k" as in kindness is the pathway to our journey.

tavaqqu': expectation; *kashish-e kāf-e karam*: attraction to letter "*kāf* " in "*karam*" (kindness).

The motivation that keeps me going is my expectation of the Lord's kindness to show me the correct path through the blessings of the letter "k," as in kindness (coincidentally matching the Urdu word, *karam*).

125

تم جانو، تم کو غیر سے جو رسم و راہ ہو
مجھ کو بھی پوچھتے رہو تو کیا گناہ ہو

tum jano, tum ko ġhair se jo rasm-o-rāh ho
mujh ko bhī puchhte raho to kyā gunāh ho (125:1; #776)

It is up to you, if you want to keep acquaintance with the rival.
It would not be a sin, however, if you keep asking about me as well.

rasm-o-rāh: acquaintance.

The beloved has broken off with the lover and established an acquaintance with the rival. In a rare display of tolerance, the lover accepts the beloved having an acquaintance with the rival as long as she keeps asking, occasionally about the lover as well. The lover, however, warns the beloved that she alone is responsible if her acquaintance with the rival brings any embarrassment to her.

بچتے نہیں مواخذۂ روزِ حشر سے
قاتل اگر رقیب ہے تو تم گواہ ہو

bachte nahiñ mu'āḳhaża(h)' roz-e ḥashr se
qātil agar raqīb hai to tum gavāh ho (125:2; #777)

There is no sparing from interrogation on the Day of Judgment;
If the rival is the murderer, then you are a witness, too.

mu'āḳhaża(h): punishment (used here as interrogation); *roze ḥashr:* Day of Judgment; *qātil:* murderer; *raqīb:* rival; *gavāh:* witness.

In connivance with my beloved, the rival has killed me. O' Beloved, since you were a witness to this murder, you will not be spared interrogation on the Day of Judgment. (This is in line with the English Law where a witness can be prosecuted for not reporting a crime.) The poet makes a subtle inference implying that it may not be widely known that you commissioned to have me murdered, but beware the Day of Judgment. God will certainly fault you for being an uncooperative witness, if not a murderer. The insecurities of the lover abound.

کیا وُہ بھی بے گُنہ کُش و حق ناشناس ہیں
مانا کہ تُم بشر نہیں، خورشید و ماہ ہو

kyā vuh bhī be gunah kush-o-ḥaq nāshinās haiñ
mānā kih tum bashar nahiñ, ḳhurshid-o-mah ho (125:3; #778)

Do they also kill the innocent or usurp the rights of others?
Admitted that you are not a human but a sun and a moon.

nāshinās: not realizing, acknowledging.

The lover says that he accepts the fact that you (the beloved) are not a human being, but are instead either the moon or the sun. But tell me, my beloved, do the sun and moon also kill people and deny their rights—rights to love you?

اُبھرا ہُوا نقاب میں ہے اُن کے ایک تار
مرتا ہوں مَیں کہ یہ نہ کِسی کی نگاہ ہو

ubhrā hu'ā niqāb meñ hai un ke ek tār
martā huñ maiñ kih yih na(h) kisī kī nigāh ho (125:4; #779)

Protruding out of her veil is a thread;
I am dying to know, might this not be someone's glance.

The equivalent of "line of sight" is "*tār-e nigāh.*" Here the poet gives the sight a palpable meaning. Someone must have looked at her. That is why the thread of a glance sticks to her veil and is seen as a ridge or ripple in her veil. The poet is jealous. The description is beyond belief.

جب میکدہ چھٹا تو پھر اب کیا جگہ کی قید
مسجد ہو، مدرسہ ہو، کوئی خانقاہ ہو

jab maikada(h) chhuṭā to phir ab kyā jagah kī qaid
masjid ho, madrasah ho, ko'ī ḳhānqāh ho (125:5; #780)

When removed from the tavern, then why should there be restriction on the place,
Whether it be a mosque, a school or a monastery.

maikada(h): tavern; *masjid*: mosque; *madrasah*: school; *ḳhānqāh*: monastery.

Drinking is not allowed in the mosque, monastery, or school, but when the tavern is no longer accessible, any place will do for drinking. Of course, as long as there was a tavern, you could have restricted me from drinking elsewhere, but now I can drink anywhere. There are hints here that if you want to contain the drinkers, keep the tavern open.

سنتے ہیں جو بہشت کی تعریف سب درست
لیکن خدا کرے وہ ترا جلوہ گاہ ہو

sunte haiñ jo bahisht kī ta'rīf sab durust
lekin ḳhudā kare vuh terā jalva(h) gāh ho (125:6; #781)

Whatever praise we hear of paradise, is totally true;
But, God willing, it should also be the place for your glorious manifestation.

There is no doubt that paradise is the most beautiful place, but its goodness is judged by whether or not you are there. Though he asks for the companionship of the beloved, this verse can be construed as devotional, asking for God's will that we could see Him.

غالب بھی گر نہ ہو تو کچھ ایسا ضرر نہیں
دنیا ہو یا رب اور مرا بادشاہ ہو

Ġhālib bhī gar na(h) ho to kuchh aisā ẓarar nahiñ
dunyā ho yā rabb āur merā bādshāh ho (125:7; #782)

If *Ġhālib* is not here, then there is no loss,
But, O' Lord, the world and my King should remain here.

ẓarar: harm, loss; *yā rabb*: O' God; *bādshāh*: King, referring to *Bahadur Shāh Zafir*.

Praying for the long life of *Bahadur Shāh Zafir*, the poet says that the world and the King must remain. Whether or not he (and others) remain is not as important.

126

گئی وہ بات کہ ہو گفتگو تو کیونکر ہو   کہے سے کچھ نہ ہوا، پھر کہو تو کیونکر ہو

ga'ī vuh bāt kih ho guftagū to kioñkar ho
kahe se kuchh na(h) hu'ā, phir kaho to kioñkar ho (126:1; #783)

Gone is the situation thinking how would I speak to her, if I ever did.
If nothing came out after having said it all, then tell me how would it be?

bāt: word, conversation, here meaning situation; *guftagū*: conversation.

Gone are the days when I used to create scenarios of how I might express myself and how she would respond when we met. Now, having said it all with no response from her, I am left to wonder, "Where do I go from here?"

ہمارے ذہن میں اِس فکر کا ہے نام وصال   کہ گر نہ ہو تو کہاں جائیں ہو تو کیونکر ہو

hamāre żahan meñ is fikr kā hai nām viṣāl
kih gar na(h) ho to kahāñ jāeñ, ho to kioñ kar ho (126:2; #784)

In my thoughts, union with the beloved is called the worry
That if it is thwarted, where shall we go and if granted, how will it work?

The only thought I have is union with the beloved. I worry about two things: If it does not happen, what will happen to me? (Perhaps I will kill myself.) In addition, if it did, how will it happen? (Will I be able to survive her beauty and the joy of consummation?) Both scenarios are worrisome.

ادب ہے اور یہی کشمکش تو کیا کیجے   حیا ہے اور یہی گومگو تو کیونکر ہو

adab hai āur yahī kash-ma-kash to kyā kīje
ḥyā hai āur yahī gūmagū to kioñ kar ho (126:3; #785)

What shall I do if reverence to her keeps me in the same dilemma
While she remains shy and inexpressive, then imagine, how would things work out?

kash-ma-kash: strife, tumult, dilemma; *gūmagū*: inexpressive, shy.

My extreme regard for her keeps me from exposing my inner feelings, but my mind keeps insisting that I must because it is an unbearable feeling. She is so shy that she is unable to utter a word. How would I handle my emotions and how would it all work out if she could not say anything? The respect part here is to save the beloved from embarrassment.

تمھیں کہو کہ گزارا صنم پرستوں کا   بتوں کی ہو اگر ایسی ہی خو تو کیونکر ہو

tumhiñ kaho kih guzārā ṣanam parastoñ kā
butoñ kī ho agar aisī hī ḳhū to kioñ kar ho (126:4; #786)

You should tell me, how the survival of the idolaters
Would work out, if the idols were endowed with your habits?

guzārā: living; *ṣanam parast*: idolaters, lover; *ḳhū:* habit.

How would lovers survive if idols began to behave like you? The idolaters of stone statues do not get any sympathy, but they also feel no pain. You, though, are just as cold as an idol but are habitually bent on destroying us. The stone statues are better than you.

اُلجھتے ہو تم اگر دیکھتے ہو آئینہ   جو تم سے شہر میں ہوں ایک دو تو کیونکر ہو

ulajhte ho tum āgar dekhte ho ā'ina(h)
jo tum se shahar meñ hoñ ek do to kioñ kar ho (126:5; #787)

You get irritated if you look at yourself in the mirror,
Imagine what would happen if there were one or two like you in the city?

ulajhte: get irritated.

She is so full of herself she cannot even tolerate seeing her own image in the mirror. If there were a couple of beauties like you in town, how would you react? Some have interpreted this to mean what would happen to the town if there were a couple of beauties like you. The verse refers to the beloved's reaction, in my opinion.

جسے نصیب ہو روزِ سیاہ میرا سا   وہ شخص دن نہ کہے رات کو تو کیونکر ہو

jise naṣīb ho roz-e siyāh merā sā
vuh shaḳhṣ din na(h) kahe rāt ko to kioñ kar ho (126:6; #788)

Whosoever is meted with gloomy days like those given to me,
Why would not that person then call his nights the days?

naṣīb: fate; *roz-e siyāh*: black or gloomy day.

Any ill-fated (black fate) person given the gloomy days of my life would think that night was day because the darkness of night is brighter than the gloominess of my days. The gloom in my life is so intense that it is darker than the darkest nights. I cannot see where I am going, just like a person walking in the dark.

ہمیں پھر اُن سے اُمید اَور اُنھیں ہماری قدر　　ہماری بات ہی پُوچھیں نہ وو تو کیونکر ہو

hameñ phir un se ummīd āur unheñ hamārī qadar
hamārī bāt hī puchheñ na(h) vuh to kioñ kar ho (126:7; #789)

I am again hopeful of her and her appreciation of me,
How would it come if she does not even ask about me?

qadar: dignity; *ummīd:* hope.

I am again hopeful (having been rejected before) that she will appreciate me. How, though, can she dignify me with her attention if she continues to ignore me? How then will she know that I am important to her? The use of the word, "again," means this feeling is not new, though the poet hopes to rekindle it.

غلط نہ تھا ہمیں خط پر گُماں تسلّی کا　　نہ مانے دیدۂ دیدار جو تو کیونکر ہو

ġhalat na(h) thā hameñ ḳhaṯ par gumāñ tasallī kā
na(h) māne dīda(h)'-e dīdār jo to kioñ kar ho (126:8; #790)

It wasn't wrong of me to feel solace upon receiving her letter
But if my eyes, wanting to see you, would not agree, then how would I have it?

gumāñ: doubt, suspicion; *tasallī*: solace, satisfaction; *dīda(h)*: eye: *dīdār*: to see.

I was hoping your letter would bring satisfying news, which it did, but unfortunately, the eyes did not agree for they wanted to see you, not just your letter. I stayed dissatisfied.

بتاؤ، اُس مژہ کو دیکھ کر، کہ مجھ کو قرار   یہ نیش ہو رگِ جاں میں فِرو تو کیونکر ہو

batāo, us miẓha(h) ko dekh kar, kih mujh ko qarār
yih nesh ho rag-e jāñ meñ firo to kioñ kar ho (126:9; #791)

Tell me, looking at those eyelashes, that repose to me,
How would I get if this sting has pierced into my jugular vein?

miẓhah: eyelash; *qarār:* repose; *nesh:* sting; *rag-e jāñ:* jugular; *firo:* pierced.

Tell me after you look at her eyelashes, how can you enjoy any repose? If her eyelashes continue to sting my jugular vein, how will I be able to settle my emotions?

مجھے جنوں نہیں غالبؔ ولے بہ قولِ حضور
"فراقِ یار میں تسکین ہو تو کیونکر ہو"

mujhe junūñ nahiñ Ġhālib vale ba(h) qaul-e ḥuẓūr
"firāq-e yār meñ taskiñ ho to kioñ kar ho" (126:10; #792)

I am not a lunatic, *Ġhālib*, but as said by his Majesty:
In the separation of the beloved, how could we get consolation?

I am not a lunatic. My impatience is fully justified because lovers in separation are restless, as said by His Majesty *Bahadur Shāh Zafar*. Because a King claims it, how could it be wrong? The second line of the verse is a quote from a poem of the King, Bahadur *Shāh Zafar*.

127

کسی کو دے کے دل کوئی نواسنجِ فغاں کیوں ہو　　نہ ہو جب دل ہی سینے میں تو پھر منہ میں زباں کیوں ہو

kisī ko de ke dil ko'ī navāsanj-e fuġhāñ kioñ ho
na(h) ho jab dil hī sīne meñ to phir muñ(h) meñ zabāñ kioñ ho
(127:1; #793)

Having given heart to someone, why should then one plead and lament?
With no heart left in the chest, then why should there be a tongue in the mouth?

navāsanj-e fuġhāñ: one who laments; *muñ(h) meñ zabāñ*: tongue in mouth, being able to speak.

When you have given your heart of your own accord, it does not make sense to lament about it. When there is nothing left inside, how can you open your mouth to talk about a distraught heart that is not there?

وہ اپنی خو نہ چھوڑیں گے، ہم اپنی وضع کیوں چھوڑیں　　سبک سر بن کے کیا پوچھیں کہ ہم سے سرگراں کیوں ہو

vūh apnī ḳhū na(h) chhoṛeñ ge, ham apnī vaẓa' kioñ chhoṛeñ
subuk sar ban ke kyā pūchheñ kih ham se sar girāñ kioñ ho
(127:2; #794)

She would not change her habits, so why should I then alter my style.
How can I turning frivolus, ask her why is she annoyed with me?

ḳhū: habit; *vaẓa'*: self-respect; *subuk sar*: frivolous; *girāñ*: upset.

The beloved remains upset with the lover who has his own self-respect. It is all right if you are upset with me; so be it. I am not going to ask you why, for that will degrade me. The delicate play of words with *subuk sar* and *sar girāñ*, both of which contain the word "head," is delightful.

کیا غمخوار نے رسوا، لگے آگ اِس محبت کو نہ لاوے تاب جو غم کی وہ میرا رازداں کیوں ہو

kīyā ġhamḳh(v)ār ne rusvā, lage āg is maḥabbat ko
na(h) lāve tāb jo ġham kī vuh merā rāzdāñ kioñ ho (127:3; #795)

The sympathizer has disgraced me, so let his sympathy go to hell. How could he be my confidant if he is incapable of bearing my woes?

rusvā: disgrace; *maḥabbat*: sympathy; *rāzdāñ*: confidant.

My sympathizer has disgraced me by telling my story (told to him in confidence by me) to others. This has caused great embarrassment to my beloved and that is disgraceful to me. The reason my sympathizer did this was because he could not bear to keep the sorrow of my story so he blurted it out. I do not need his words of kindness and sympathy if he cannot bear my sorrow. I cannot ḳeep him as my confidant.

وفا کیسی، کہاں کا عشق، جب سر پھوڑنا ٹھہرا تو پھر، اے سنگدل، تیرا ہی سنگِ آستاں کیوں ہو

vafā kaisī, kahāñ kā ʿishq, jab sar phoṛnā ṭhehrā
to phir, ai sangdil, terā hī sang-e āstāñ kioñ ho (127:4; #796)

What faithfulness and what love, when it is merely smashing head? Then, O! Stonehearted beloved, why should it even be your threshold?

Love and faithfulness require reciprocity. When that is gone then it is merely like smashing the head out of love, or wasting time. That being the case, why then should I smash my head onto your threshold? Why not any other beloved? Calling the beloved stonehearted and referring to the stone of her threshold illustrates similarities. A deeper reference is made here to saner elements of life. If destruction is my fate, then why should I go to any length to get there? It will come my way sooner or later.

قفس میں مجھ سے رُودادِ چمن کہتے نہ ڈر ہمدم!
گرا ہے جس پہ کل بجلی، وہ میرا آشیاں کیوں ہو،

قفس میں مجھ سے رُودادِ چمن کہتے نہ ڈر ہمدم   گری ہے جس پہ کل بجلی، وہ میرا آشیاں کیوں ہو

qafis meñ mujh se rūdād-e chaman kahte na(h) ḍar hamdam
girī hai jis pa(h) kal bijlī, vūh merā āshyāñ kioñ ho (127:5; #797)

Fear not telling me the story of the garden, my compatriot, as I languish in the cage.
For why should that be my home whereupon the lightning fell yesterday?

rūdād: story; *hamdam*: companion.

A bird in a cage is talking to another bird outside. It is a friend of the bird in the cage. Asked to tell how things are back in the garden, the free bird is reluctant to say anything, perhaps sitting with its head lowered, because the lightning that struck in the garden yesterday had destroyed the home of the caged bird. Sensing that something is not right, the caged bird encourages the free bird not to be afraid (to hurt my feelings), asking why lightning should have struck his home. Note that the free bird has not told the story yet. This is indeed a very delicate and melancholic presentation of a fine thread of hope, knowing full well that it is all over. This is a superbly heart-rending rendition of *Ġhālib* and perhaps the most beautiful expression of human nature.

یہ کہہ سکتے ہو، ہم دل میں نہیں ہیں، پر یہ بتلاؤ   کہ جب دل میں تمھیں تم ہو تو آنکھوں سے نہاں کیوں ہو

yih kah sakte ho, ham dil meñ nahiñ haiñ par yih batlā'o
kih jab dil meñ tumhiñ tum ho to āñkhoñ se nihāñ kioñ ho (127:6; #798)

You can say that I am not in your heart, but then do tell me,
When only you are in my heart, then why are you hiding from my eyes?

nihāñ: secret.

You say you do not trust me because I have not kept you in my heart. However, how would you explain that it is you who hides from my sight because you are the one who does not love me? There is no one except you in my heart, but when I close my eyes, I am unable to see you. Is it because you are so elusive that even your imagination runs away from me? I refute and return your allegation.

غلط ہے جذبِ دل کا شکوہ، دیکھو جرم کس کا ہے　　نہ کھینچو گر تم اپنے کو کشاکش درمیاں کیوں ہو

ġhalat hai jażb-e dil kā shikva(h), dekho jurm kis kā hai
na(h) khecho gar tum apne ko kashākash darmiyāñ kioñ ho
(127:7; #799)

Wrong is the complaint against heart's passion; just see whose crime is it?
There will be no tussle between us if only you would not pull away from me.

jażb-e dil: heart's passion; *shikva(h)*: complaint; *kashākash*: tussle.

The beloved complains of the incessant cries of the lover, which, according to the lover, is all due to her attitude of appearing strained him. Such behavior only exacerbates the situation and encourages further plaints. Therefore, if the beloved wants laments to stop, she should stop pulling away from him. The lover is trying to get closer to her while she is pushing him away. Appearing strained and pulling away are the key concepts of the verse. A tug-of-war is in the offing here.

یہ فتنہ آدمی کی خانہ ویرانی کو کیا کم ہے　　ہوئے تم دوست جس کے، دشمن اُس کا آسماں کیوں ہو

yih fitna(h) ādmī kī ḳhāna(h) vīrānī ko kyā kam hai
hu'e tum dost jis ke, dushman us kā āsmāñ kioñ ho (127:8; #800)

**This mutinous beloved is more than enough to ruin a man's home;
Whomsoever you befriend, why should the heavens be an enemy to him?**

fitna(h) : troublemaker; *ḳhāna(h) vīrānī*: desolation of home;

Friendship with you, my beloved, is bound to destroy my home and, for that matter, the home of anyone who claims to love you. The heavens, known to bring calamities, are no longer needed by anyone that you have befriended, for disaster is in that person's fate. No help is needed from the heavens when you are there to destroy it all.

یہی ہے آزمانا ، تو ستانا کس کو کہتے ہیں   عدو کے ہو لیے جب تم تو میرا امتحاں کیوں ہو

yahī hai āzmānā, to satānā kis ko kahte haiñ
ʿadū ke ho liye jab tum to merā imteḥāñ kioñ ho (127:9; #801)

**If this is testing, then what else do you call teasing?
When you have gone to my enemy, then what is left there to test me?**

āzmānā: trying; *satānā*: teasing; *ʿadū*: enemy.

You are in love with my enemy and tell me that you are just testing my sincerity and patience. Is it testing or teasing? Now that you have gone to my rival, it is irrelevant whether I succeed or fail—I have already lost it all.

کہا تم نے کہ کیوں ہو غیر کے ملنے میں رُسوائی   بجا کہتے ہو، سچ کہتے ہو، پھر کہیو کہ ہاں کیوں ہو

kahā tum ne kih kioñ ho ġhair ke milne meñ rusvāʾī
bajā kahte ho, sach kahte ho, phir kahīyo kih hāñ kioñ ho (127:10; #802)

**You say, "Why would meeting the rival bring disgrace?"
Said correctly and truly, but then tell me, why did it turn out to be so?**

bajā kahte ho: you have spoken correctly (said in submission or with sarcasm).

You wondered how your meeting with the rival could bring disgrace to you and then you went ahead and met with the rival despite my admonishing that it will bring disgrace to you. See what happened now? Of course, you were correct, totally proper, and knowing (said sarcastically, of course). The rival has disgraced the beloved and the lover is now rubbing it in.

نکالا چاہتا ہے کام کیا طعنوں سے تو غالب
ترے بے مہر کہنے سے وہ تجھ پر مہرباں کیوں ہو

nikālā chāhtā hai kām kyā ta'noñ se tū Ġhālib
tere be mahr kahne se vūh tujh par mahrbāñ kioñ ho (127:11; #803)

You are trying to make things work with taunts, *Ġhālib*.
Why would your calling her unkind make her kind towards you?

Taunting to lure compassion and kindness from the beloved is quaint and has never worked before. She knows she is cruel, so if you taunt her for being cruel she will not be moved at all. The persistence of lovers in trying anything that might work keeps them steady in their path to oblivion.

128

رہیے اب ایسی جگہ چل کر جہاں کوئی نہ ہو
ہم سخن کوئی نہ ہو اور ہم زباں کوئی نہ ہو

rahīe ab aisī jagah chal kar jahāñ ko'ī na(h) ho
ham suḳhan ko'ī na(h) ho āur ham zabāñ ko'ī na(h) ho (128:1; #804)

Lets us go now and live in a place where there will be no one,
No one to talk to, nor anyone to speak in the same tongue.

Having reached a state of total frustration with his contemporaries, the poet wants to live in total seclusion where he does not have to talk to anyone understand anyone or try to make anyone understand him. The use of the word "now" indicates something suggested as a last resort.

بے در و دیوار سا اک گھر بنایا چاہیے
کوئی ہمسایہ نہ ہو اور پاسباں کوئی نہ ہو

be dar-o-dīvār sā ik ghar banāyā chāhīe
ko'ī hamsāya(h) na(h) ho āur pāsbāñ ko'ī na(h) ho (128:2; #805)

Without doors and without walls, I must build myself a home,
Where there will be no neighbors and no one to watch the doors, either.

A home without doors and walls is desired. The connection to neighbors requires thinking. Without walls, there is no delineation of the neighbors' boundary of property and there is no need to protect it from robbers.

The poet wants to live in a state where he would not have to worry about being robbed or being required to respect his neighbors' rights. He wants a free life, not a door-less, or a wall-less structure.

پڑیے گر بیمار تو کوئی نہ ہو بیماردار
اور اگر مر جائیے تو نوحہ خواں کوئی نہ ہو

paṛye gar bīmār to ko'ī na(h) ho bīmārdār
aur agar mar jā'iye to nauḥa(h) ḳh(v)āñ ko'ī na(h) ho (128:3; #806)

If I should fall ill then no one would come to attend me
And should I die, there will be no one to mourn for me either.

The last three verses form a continuum of the poet's desire to live a detached life, one without physical or mental obligations. He does not want to be pampered when ill and wants no one to cry at his death, either. This melancholic arrangement is very much *Ġhālib*.

129

از مہر تا بہ ذرہ دل و دل ہے آئنہ
طوطی کو شش جہت سے مقابل ہے آئنہ

az mahr tā ba(h) żarra(h) dil-o-dil hai ā'ina(h)
ṭūṭī ko shish jahat se muqābil hai ā'īna(h) (129:1; #807)

From the sun to the particles, it is mirrors of the heart all around;
To the parrot, it is like mirrors facing in all directions.

ṭūṭī: parrot; *shash jahat*: six directions (all around); *muqābil*: facing.

Like the shining particles of dust illuminated by the sun, I see hearts all around. Like the parrot that begins to talk after seeing its reflection in a mirror, I write poetry as I see my reflection in these mirrors of the heart. I see the reality of the Universe and of myself in my own reflection and thus I begin talking (saying verses) as a parrot would—miming, looking at its own reflection in the mirror. Another interpretation makes this verse devotional—man seeing his own image in everything. This verse is one of the most difficult visualizations of *Ġhālib*.

130

ہے سبزہ زار ہر در و دیوارِ غمکدہ
جس کی بہار یہ ہو پھر اُس کی خزاں نہ پُوچھ

hai sabza(h) zār har dar-o-divār-e ġhamkada(h)
jis kī bahār yih ho phir us kī ḳhizāñ na(h) pūchh (130:1; #808)

Grass has spread to every wall and door of the desolate home;
If this is how spring comes then ask not about the autumn.

ġhamkada(h): house full of sorrow, desolate home.

Desolate and ruined, the lover's home has wild grass growing all around making it look like spring. Because spring spells ruin, the poet wonders what will it be like when autumn arrives?

ناچار بیکسی کی بھی حسرت اُٹھائیے
دُشواریٔ رہ و ستمِ ہمرہاں نہ پُوچھ

nāchār bekasī kī bhī ḥasrat uṭhāiye
dushvārī' rah-o-sitam-e hamrahāñ na(h) pūchh (130:2; #809)

Bear the hopelessness of the helplessness too and
Do not ask about the hardships in the path nor the tyrannies of the fellow travelers.

The road was difficult, but my fellow travelers made traveling even more impossible. I wish I were alone. I could have put up with the difficulties of the road, but now the tyrannies shown by my companions make me regret it more. Now I cannot leave the companions nor can I bear their tyrannies. This verse illustrates some of the most unfortunate and inevitable choices that we often end up with in our daily lives.

131

صد جلوہ رُو بہ رُو ہے، جو مژگاں اُٹھائیے
طاقت کہاں کہ دید کا اِحساں اُٹھائیے

ṣad jalva(h) rū-ba(h)-rū hai, jo mizhgāñ uṭhā'iye
t̤āqat kahāñ kih dīd kā eḥsāñ uṭhāiye (131:1; #810)

Hundreds of manifestations are face to face, if one would lift the eye lashes;
But where is the strength to bear the obligation of vision?

Open your eyes and you will see how God appears in hundreds of ways. Since I am unable to understand this display of clues, this display goes to waste and I get buried under the Lord's obligation of extending these favors to me. This is like a man going to God and asking Him to show Himself and having God say,"Just open your eyes." How obliging that is. He has provided us many clues. This verse can also be used in the context of Moses going to the Mount Sinai to see just one display of God; he could not even bear to see the evidence.

ہے سنگ پر براتِ معاشِ جنونِ عشق
یعنی ہنوز مِنّتِ طفلاں اُٹھائیے

hai sang par barāt-e maʿāsh-e junūn-e ʿishq
yāʿnī hanūz minnat-e t̤iflāñ uṭhāiye (131:2; #811)

Dependent on the stone is the livelihood of the love-lunatic;
Meaning, we should continue to take obligations from children.

barāt-e maʿāsh: writ of livelihood.

Children throwing stones at the lunatic oblige him to their act, as they are awarding him with his livelihood--what he deserves. The stones are thus called "wages," for which one must beg children.

دیوار بارِ منّتِ مُزدُور سے ہے خم
اے خانماں خراب نہ اِحساں اُٹھائیے

đīvār bār-e minnat-e mazdūr se hai ḳham
ae ḳhānmāñ ḳharāb na(h) eḥsāñ uṭhā'iye (131:3; #812)

Bent is the wall under the obligation of the mason.
O! You, whose homes have been ruined, do not enter into obligation to anyone.

bār: weight; *minnat*: obligation; *ḳham*: bent; *ae ḳhānmāñ ḳharāb*: O! You, whose house has been ruined.

Do not enter into obligations for they can destroy you. This is the ultimate message here. When a wall bends under the obligation of the mason, just imagine what obligations can do to humans. To someone who has lost it all, it is better to think twice before rebuilding. This will mean collecting the obligations of many. Deeper meaning comes from comparing a mason to God and the wall to all that He has created and everything that bows to His honor. Beg not from God, even though you are desolate and in need of much. *Ġhālib* relates a remarkable thought with this verse.

یا میرے زخمِ رشک کو رُسوا نہ کیجیے
یا پردۂ تبسّمِ پنہاں اُٹھائیے

yā mere zaḳhm-e rashk ko rusvā na(h) kǐiye
yā parda(h)' tabassum-e pinhāñ uṭhāiye (131:4; #813)

Either do not disgrace my wounds of envy,
Or else, lift the veil of that hidden smile.

zaḳhm: wound; *rashk:* envy; *rusvā*: dishonored; *parda(h)*: veil; *tabassum:* smile; *pinhāñ*: sheepish, hidden.

Your hidden smile tells me that you are relishing the moments you have spent with my rival. The more I see you smiling, the more curious I get. I am afraid that unless you stop, the world will come to know of my envy and thus the secret of your sheepish smile. Tell me what, if anything, happened between you and the rival. The smile can be more aptly labeled as sheepish.

132

مسجد کے زیرِ سایہ خرابات چاہیے   بھوں پاس آنکھ، قبلۂ حاجات! چاہیے

masjid ke zer-e sāya(h) ḳhirābāt chāhiye
bhauñ pās āñkh, qibla(h)' ḥājāt chāhiye (132:1; #814)

Under the shadow of mosque is needed a tavern;
Like the eye near the brow, it is needed, O! Providence.

ḳhirābāt: tavern; *qibla(h) ḥājāt*: Providence, an expression of respect generally used for God. It can also be used when showing respect to elderly persons as well.

The tavern is compared to the eye for the shape of the glasses in the tavern and mosque is compared to the eyebrow for the shape of the arches in the mosque. The tavern and mosque should be close to each other, calling attention to the Providence. Why should they be close to each other? So we can commit sin and ask for forgiveness at the same time.

عاشق ہوئے ہیں آپ بھی اِک اَور شخص پر   آخر سِتم کی کچھ تو مُکافات چاہیے

'āshiq hu'e haiñ āp bhī ik aur shak̤hṣ par
āk̤hir sitam kī kuchh to mukāfāt chāhiye (132:2; #815)

You too have fallen in love with someone else.
Finally, there must be retribution for the oppression.

mukāfāt: revenge, retribution.

The beloved has fallen in love with someone and so the poet wants her to feel pain, which she used to inflict upon others because of her cruelty. Something should be returned because she has given so abundantly to so many.

دے داد اَے فلک دلِ حسرت پرست کی   ہاں کچھ نہ کچھ تلافیٔ مافات چاہیے

de dād ai falak dil-e ḥasrat parast kī
hāñ kuchh na(h) kuchh talāfi' māfāt chāhiye (132:3; #816)

Give praise, O! Heavens, to a heart despondent.
Yes! There must be some restitution of the past acts.

dil-e ḥasrat parast: despondent heart; *talāfi māfāt*: rectification of bygone things.

O, Heavens! Praise my resolve to bear the despondence of heart. At least this much praise you can give me to rectify your injustices of the past. The poet is merely asking for recognition, not necessarily a rectification.

سیکھے ہیں مہ رخوں کیلئے ہم مصوری
تقریب کچھ تو بہر ملاقات چاہیئے

سیکھے ہیں مہ رُخوں کے لیے ہم مصوّری   تقریب کچھ تو بہرِ ملاقات چاہیے

sīkhe haiñ mah ruḳhoñ ke liye ham muṣavvirī
taqrīb kuchh to bahr-e mulāqāt chāhiye (132:4; #817)

We have learned to paint for the sake of those moon-faced beauties;
An occasion, after all, is needed to meet them.

mahruḳh: moon-face or round face as it is signified in the English language, but in *Urdū* poetry it means a shining, beautiful face; *muṣavvirī,*: painting; *taqrīb*: occasion.

The beloved has turned down all offers to let the lover see her. Now the lover pulls a new trick, stating that the only reason he wants to see her is to paint her portrait, as he is a professional artist.

مے سے غرض نشاط ہے کس رُوسیاہ کو   اِک گونہ بیخودی مجھے دِن رات چاہیے

mai se ġharaẓ nishāṯ hai kis rūsiyā(h) ko
ik gūna(h) bekhudī mujhe din rāt chāhiye (132:5; #818)

Who, the disgraced ones, seek pleasure in wine?
A state of rapture round the clock is what I want.

rūsiyā(h) : blackened-face or disgraced ones; *gūna(h):* of one color, sort, kind.

Those who drink wine for pleasure are a disgrace to humanity. We drink during the day only to lose ourselves, to bear the eternal pain of sorrow given by our peers. We drink at night to absolve ourselves from the hurt of separation from the beloved. We drink only to stay ecstatic, day and night, or else we would not be interested in wine. By calling us "disgraced" and then saying we do not seek pleasure in wine signifies that we are wrongfully labeled "disgraced."

ہے رنگِ لالہ و گل و نسریں جدا جدا   ہر رنگ میں بہار کا اِثبات چاہیے

hai rang-e lāla(h)-o-gul-o-nasrīñ judā judā
har rang meñ bahār kā is̱bāt chāhiye (132:6; #819)

The colors of tulips, roses, and jonquil flowers are all different;
In every color and shade, the spring seeks affirmation.

is̱bāt: affirmation.

There are so many different kinds of flowers, all pointing to the arrival of spring. Pay little attention to flowers and think of them as the sign of the arrival of spring. It could have been manifested many different ways.

سرِپائے خُم پہ چاہیے ہنگامِ بیخودی   ق   رُو سوئے قبلہ وقتِ مُناجات چاہیے

sar pāe ḳhum pa(h) chāhiye hangām-e beḳhudī
rū sūe qibla(h) vaqt-e munājāt chāhiye (132:7; #820)

The head should be under the feet of the decanter to seek the tumult of rapture.
The face should be facing towards *Ka'bā* when it is time to sing hymns.

ḳhum: decanter; *munājāt*: hymns singing.

When it is time to be ecstatic, we must put a decanter on our head, i.e., consider this more important. When it is time to pray, we must turn to the direction of *Ka'bā* (as Muslims do to pray) and chant our hymns. Ecstasy is a condition; wine a reality. Incantation is a condition, *Ka'bā* a reality. We should not confuse our goals with our objectives.

یعنی بہ حسبِ گردشِ پیمانۂ صفات　　　عارف ہمیشہ مستِ مئے ذات چاہیے

ya'nī ba(h) ḥasb-e gardish-e paimāna(h)' ṣifāt
'ārif hamesha(h) mast-e ma'i zāt chāhiye (132:8; #821)

To keep up with the rotation of the cup of qualities,
The enlightened ones must always stay intoxicated by themselves.

ba(h) ḥasb: in proportion; *ṣifāt*: qualities; *'ārif*: knower, enlightened.

The rotation of a cup signifies the changes in the Universe or how God manifests Himself. We should examine it, but then we should not forget to examine how we understand God by losing ourselves to wine. Those who are enlightened stay in a perpetual state of intoxication. Note the tone of a whirling *Sufi* dervish dance, the rotation of cup and perpetual intoxication to express a mood.

نشو و نما ہے اصل سے غالبؔ فروع کو
خاموشی ہی سے نکلے ہے، جو بات چاہیے

nashv-o-numā hai aṣl se Ġhālib furū' ko
ḳhāmoshī hī se nikle hai, jo bāt chāhiye (132:9; #822)

In reality, *Ġhālib*, the growth is dependent on the roots;
So come out the needed words only from silence.

furū': root.

When we see branches growing, we see them as a manifestation of roots. When we hear words spoken, we should know that these have come from quietness. First there is thought, which is a quiet form, then the words follow. Quietness is real; the words are manifestation. This last verse emphasizes that there is only one source of the Universe—the Almighty. However, the Universe displays itself in many ways, the reality being only one God. We should not forget that as we become entangled in satisfying ourselves with the many manifestations of the Universe.

133

بساطِ عجز میں تھا ایک دِل، یک قطرہ خُوں وُہ بھی
سو رہتا ہے بہ اندازِ چکیدن سرنگُوں وُہ بھی

bisāṯ-e ʿijz meñ thā ek dil, yak qaṯra(h) ḳhūñ vuh bhī
so rahtā hai ba(h) andāz-e chakīdan sar nigūñ vuh bhī (133:1; #823)

There was a heart in the state of humility, which is now a drop of blood.
Even that, with its head lowered, is ready to drip.

bisāṯ-e ʿijz: state of humility; *ba(h) andāz-e chakīdan*: with intent to drop.

I have nothing left except my heart, and even that is like a drop of blood having been consumed by grief. The last drop of blood (the heart) is now ashamed and keeps its eyes lowered for not having more to offer. This verse ranks amongst the most remarkable renditions of *Ġhālib*.

رہے اُس شوخ سے آزردہ ہم چندے تکلُّف سے
تکلُّف برطرف، تھا ایک اندازِ جُنُوں وُہ بھی

rahe us shoḳh se āzurda(h) ham chande takalluf se
takalluf barṯaraf thā ek andāz-e junūñ vuh bhī (133:2; #824)

Being in pain, we remained annoyed with the beloved.
Formality aside, that too was a style of my madness.

āzurda(h): annoyed; *junūñ*: madness; *shoḳh*: bold; *takalluf*: taking upon oneself, taking pains, gratuitousness, spontaneousness, pains, attention, perseverance, inconvenience, trouble, extravagance, formality, observing etiquette; *barṯarf*: aside; *andāz*: style.

Becoming annoyed with my beloved is just another manifestation of my insanity. Frankly speaking, what would she care? Getting annoyed with her and then getting away from her was more painful than bearing her ridicule and callousness. I learned this the hard way.

خیالِ مرگ کب تسکیں دلِ آزردہ کو بخشے
مرے دامِ تمنا میں ہے اِک صیدِ زبوں وُہ بھی

ḳhayāl-e marg kab taskiñ dil-e āzurdah ko baḳhshe
mere dām-e tamannā meñ hai ik ṣaid-e zabūñ vuh bhī (133:3; #825)

When does the thought of death console an afflicted heart?
In the snare of my desire, it is merely a weak catch.

ḳhayāl: thought; *dām*: net; *āzurda(h)*: gloomy; *tamannā*: desire; *ṣaid*: hunt; *zabūñ*: weak.

Death cannot be a panacea for my broken heart. How can the thought of death ease my heart's suffering? In the net of my desires, this is just another weak catch, its coming to fruition is not likely. Extreme pessimism is expressed here.

نہ کرتا کاش نالہ، مجھ کو کیا معلوم تھا ہمدم
کہ ہوگا باعثِ افزائشِ دردِ دروں وُہ بھی

na(h) kartā kāsh nālah, mujh ko kyā ma'lūm thā hamdam
kih hogā bā'is̤-e afzāish-e dard-e darūñ vuh bhī (133:4; #826)

I would not have lamented, had I known of it, O! Companion,
That it would only enhance my heart's pain instead.

darūñ: heart; *afzāish*: growth.

I had offered my plaint in an effort to relieve my pain but I found that, instead, it increased the pain. If he had known this, the poet advises his companion, he would have restrained himself, as he, too, seems to be falling in love.

نہ اِتنا بُرّشِ تیغِ جفا پر ناز فرماؤ
مرے دریائے بے تابی میں ہے اِک موجِ خوں وہ بھی

na(h) itnā burrish-e teġh-e jafā par nāz farmā'o
mere daryāe betābī meñ hai ik mauj-e k̤hūñ vuh bhī (133:5; #827)

Be not so haughty of the sharpness of the sword of cruelty;
In my sea of impatience, it is but one of the many waves of blood.

burrish: sharpness, cut; *teġh-e jafā*: sword of cruelty; *betābī:* impatience, tumult.

O! Beloved, be not too proud of the sharpness of your cruel sword and the cuts it makes. In the sea of my impatience, there are many waves of blood and your sword is just one of these waves. These waves keep my heart impatient and tumultuous. I have taken many blows and cuts. What you offer is not new or unusual to me. I can take a lot more. Notice the use of "waves" and the "sharp edge of sword," both being similar in their appearance.

مئے عشرت کی خواہش ساقیِ گردوں سے کیا کیجے
لیے بیٹھا ہے اِک دو چار جامِ واژگوں وہ بھی

ma'i `ishrat kī k̤h(v)āhish sāqī' gardūñ se kyā kīje
liye beṭhā hai ik do chār jām-e vāẓhgūñ vuh bhī (133:6; #828)

What good it is to ask the cupbearer of heavens to give us the wine of luxury,
While he is sitting with one, two and four glasses, even those with bottoms up?

gardūñ: sky, heaven; *vāẓhugūñ*: upside down (bottoms up).

The cupbeared of heavens has no wine to give; his seven glasses (adding the count of 1, 2 and 4) are empty (bottoms up). There are seven heavens (an anecdote goes) and in each one of them, the glasses are empty, meaning none have any wine to offer. This may also refer to seven planets. The advice in this verse is to not look towards heaven for your supply of wine. Do not look to fate to offer you fortunes. The mathematical presentation is remarkable.

میرے دل میں ہے غالبؔ شوقِ وصل و شکوۂ ہجراں
خدا وہ دن کرے، جو اُس سے مَیں یہ بھی کہوں، وہ بھی

mere dil meñ hai Ġhālib shauq-e viṣl-o-shikva(h)' hijrāñ
ḳhudā vuh din kare, jo us se meñ yih bhī kahūñ, vuh bhī
(133:7; #829)

In my heart, there is a longing for union and a complaint about separation, *Ġhālib*;
May God bring that day when I could tell her about this and about that as well.

The desire for union with the beloved and complaint of separation fill my heart, but I have not been able to tell her about these. May God bring a day when I will able to tell her both and, of course, then she will resolve both of my problems. Wishful thinking! Here *Ġhālib* has used his pseudonym with double meaning, to address himself and to mean, "to over come."

134

ہے بزمِ بُتاں میں سُخن آزردہ لبوں سے
تنگ آئے ہیں ہم، ایسے خوشامد طلبوں سے

hai bazm-e butāñ meñ suḳhan āzurda(h) laboñ se
tang āe haiñ ham, aise ḳhushāmad ṯalaboñ se (134:1; #830)

With the stifled lips in the company of idols,
I have become tired of such flattery-seekers.

ṯalab: search; *bazm-e butāñ*: company of idols or the beloveds; *suḳhan āzurda(h)*: quiet, unable to speak.

In her company, the words are refusing to come from my lips. The words want me to flatter them so that they will come out. However, to flatter them I must speak, but since my lips are sealed, I cannot do that. This irritates me for it is the perfect circular argument. Unless the words come, the words will not come—a state of frustration. An example of almost wanton writing of *Ġhālib*, this verse is also interpreted as the beloved is the flattery seeker and the lover is sick and tired of it. More likely, the poet is complaining about the shortcomings of his own speech.

ہے دَورِ قدح وجہِ پریشانیِ صہبا
یک بار لگا دو خُمِ مے میرے لبوں سے

hai daur-e qadḥ vajh-e pareshānī' ṣahbā
yak bār lagā do ḳhum-e mai mere laboñ se (134:2; #831)

The rounds of drinking are the cause of the scattering of wine.
For once, bring the decanter of wine to my lips.

daur-e qadḥ: round of drink; *ṣahbā:* wine; *ḳhum-e mai*: bottle of wine.

In group-drinking sessions, the decanter of wine rotates so the drinkers are frustrated for it reduces the impact of the wine until the next round. This is called the scattering of wine. In addition, as the wine goes around it is as if the wine were troubled by being forced to go around. What the poet wants is to bring the decanter to his lips and drink it all in one gulp giving both him and the decanter much comfort. Only habitual drinkers appreciate the value of keeping their alcohol level at a certain level in order to feel good.

رندانِ درِ میکدہ گستاخ ہیں زاہد
زنہار نہ ہونا طرف ان بے ادبوں سے

rindān-e dar-e maikada(h) gustāḳh haiñ zāhid
zinhār na(h) honā ṯaraf in be ādaboñ se (134:3; #832)

The drinkers at the door of the tavern are rude, O! Preacher.
Beware, for you should not confront these disrespectful ones.

gustāḳh: rude; *zinhār*: beware!; *be adab*: disrespectful; *ṯaraf honā*: to confront.

Beware! O' Preacher, of these drunkards lying at the door of the tavern. They are very rude and have no knowledge of etiquette. They will not listen to you; so do not tangle with them. Go inside and preach to those who have crossed the door to the tavern, the purpose being to drag the preacher inside the tavern—an exquisite example of *Ġhālib*'s wit. We can invoke many scenarios about the difference between those who drink inside the tavern and those who lay at the doorstep. In addition, calling the preacher inside brings an opportunity to entice him into drinking.

بیدادِ وفا دیکھ کہ جاتی رہی آخر
ہر چند مری جان کو تھا ربط لبوں سے

bedād-e vafā dekh kih jātī rahī āḳhir
har chand merī jān ko thā rabt̤ laboñ se (134:4; #833)

Seeing the oppression of loyalty, it departed finally,
Even though my soul was connected to my lips.

rabt̤: connection.

My loyalty to her requires that I offer my soul only to her. At the time of my death, my soul came to my lips and became attached to my lips, ready to leave. It was intolerable to her that my soul would connect to anything except her. Her cruelty demanded that my soul break this connection with my lips. To comply with this oppression of loyalty, the soul broke the connection with my lips and flew away. Another explanation is that the oppression of the beloved had kept my soul to my lips at all times, meaning that it was difficult to survive. Finally, seeing that there was no possibility of change in her attitude, the soul departed. The first explanation is more appropriate, though it is very difficult to visualize.

135

تا، ہم کو شِکایَت کی بھی باقی نہ رہے جا　　سُن لیتے ہیں، گو ذکر ہمارا نہیں کرتے

tā, ham ko shikāyat kī bhī bāqī na(h) rahe jā
sun lete haiñ, go żikr hamārā nahiñ karte (135:1; #834)

So, no room will be left for me to even complain,
She listens, but does not talk about me.

She listens to what others say about the lover and then remains quiet. This is a remarkable improvement, for now she has the patience to hear his name without going up in flames. The concession is made to appease the lover.

غالب ترا احوال سُنا دیں گے ہم اُن کو　　وہ سُن کے بُلا لیں، یہ اِجارا نہیں کرتے

Ġhālib terā aḥvāl sunā deñ ge ham un ko
vuh sun ke bulā leñ, yih ijārā nahiñ karte (135:2; #835)

***Ġhālib*, we will tell her about your condition;**
We cannot assure that she will call you upon hearing us.

ijārā: assurance

Seeing the pathetic condition of the lover, his friends, who are actually the rivals, tell him that they will do him a favor and explain his condition to the beloved. However, to make sure his hopes are not raised too high, they tell him that there is no guarantee that she will ask him to join her assembly. What is worse is the realization that these rivals have access to her and he does not.

136

گھر میں تھا کیا، کہ ترا غم اُسے غارت کرتا
وُہ جو رکھتے تھے ہم اِک حسرتِ تعمیر، سو ہے

ghar meñ thā kyā, kih terā ġham use ġhārat kartā
vuh jo rakhte the ham ik ḥasrat-e ta'mīr, so hai (136:1; #836)

What was left in the home that your sorrow would have destroyed it?
The desire to build that we had is still there.

Nothing is left in my home (heart) for her to destroy. The only thing left is my desire to rebuild my home (to strengthen my heart). Perhaps that is what she wants to destroy as well. The home is the heart of the lover and the things inside the home are the unfulfilled desires. The desire to rebuild means to regroup hopes and thus to give her another chance to destroy them. The poet retains the desire though he has not a lot of it.

137

غمِ دُنیا سے گر پائی بھی فرصت سر اُٹھانے کی
فلک کا دیکھنا تقریب تیرے یاد آنے کی

ġham-e dunyā se gar pāī' bhī furṣat sar uṭhāne kī
falak kā dekhnā taqrīb tere yād āne kī (137:1; #837)

From the woes of the world if I got a chance to lift my head,
Looking at the sky would be an occasion reminding of you.

taqrīb: cause, occasion.

The burdens of worldly sorrows have buried me. If I ever get a reprieve from them and am able to raise my head I will see the sky, which reminds me of you, and the sadness will return to my heart. Omnipotent heaven has written a destiny of sorrow in everyone's fate and any reprieve from it is merely a fleeting moment. I see that sorrow is my fate. The verse may also refer to being reminded of someone's soul, like *Ārif*, his nephew, about whom *Ġhālib* has written elsewhere. Note that sky is taken as fortune-maker and looking at it reminds us of our misfortunes as well.

کھُلے گا کس طرح مضموں مرے مکتوب کا، یا رب!
قسم کھائی ہے اُس کافر نے کاغذ کے جلانے کی

khule gā kis ṭarḥ maẓmuñ mere maktūb kā, yārabb
qasam khāī hai us kāfir ne kāġhaż ke jalāne kī (137:2; #838)

How would the contents of my letters be revealed, O! Lord,
Since that disbeliever has sworn to burn the paper?

maẓmuñ: matter, substance; *maktūb*: letters; *qasam khāī:* sworn upon.

If she swore to burn all my letters without even reading them, she will never come to know the condition of my heart. "Swearing upon" also means that she has decided not to burn my letters, though she will not read them. She will not understand the condition of my heart, nor will she see whatever may flicker in the flame that burns my letters as well. The poet prefers that she would burn his letters for this might remind her of his burning heart. Note that the poet is calling the beloved a non-believer, as swearing is more of a trait of believers.

لپٹنا پرنیاں میں شعلۂ آتش کا آساں ہے
ولے مشکل ہے حکمت دل میں سوزِ غم چھپانے کی

lipaṭnā parniyāñ meñ shola(h)' ātish kā āsāñ hai
vale mushkil hai ḥikmat dil meñ soz-e ġham chhupāne kī
(137:3; #839)

It is easy for the flame to hide inside the silk fabric,
But it is a difficult effort to hide the burning of pain in the heart.

parniyāñ: silk fabric (that catches fire quickly); *ḥikmat:* efforts; *soz-e ġham*: burning of pain.

It is easy for the flame to hide itself in an inflammable cloth; however, it is difficult to figure out how to hide the burning in my heart. How difficult is it for the fabric not to burn? It is easy, but it is easier for my heart to burn. It is more difficult for me not to show the flames of my heart than it is for the fabric to contain the flames. My heart is tenderer. Note that the poet is not comparing the intensity of the flame, but what contains it.

انھیں منظور اپنے زخمیوں کا دیکھ آنا تھا
اُٹھے تھے سیرِ گل کو دیکھنا شوخی بہانے کی

unheñ manz̤ūr apne zaḳhmīoñ kā dekh ānā thā
uṭṭhe the sair-e gul ko dekhnā shoḳhī bahāne kī (137:4; #840)

Her intent was to go and visit her wounded victims;
A coquettish excuse it was to take a walk in the garden.

manz̤ūr: intent.

The coquettish excuse of the beloved is that she wants to take a refreshing walk in the garden. In reality, she wants to know how her wounded victims are doing. Blooming red flowers in the garden remind her of the wounded hearts of lovers and thus bring much joy to her.

ہماری سادگی تھی التفاتِ ناز پر مرنا
ترا آنا نہ تھا ظالم مگر تمہید جانے کی

hamārī sādgī thī iltifāt-e nāz par marnā
terā ānā na(h) thā z̤ālim magar tamhīd jāne kī (137:5; #841)

It was my naiveté to die for the kindness of your gesture;
Your arrival was, O! Tyrant, just a prelude to your leaving.

sādgī: naïveté; *iltifāt*: attention; *tamhīd*: prelude, preamble, preface.

How naïve it was of me to think that you have come to visit me out of kindness, something, for which I would give my life. However, as soon as you arrived, you began talking about leaving. Your arrival was just a prelude to leaving. You were killing me as you announced that you wanted to leave, and here I was ready to give my life for your coming to see me. Arrival as the preamble to departure is the play on words here.

لگد کوبِ حوادث کا تحمل کر نہیں سکتی
مری طاقت کہ ضامن تھی بتوں کے ناز اٹھانے کی

lakad kob-e ḥavādis̤ kā taḥammul kar nahiñ saktī
merī t̤āqat kih z̤āmin thī butoñ ke nāz uṭhāne kī (137:6; #842)

Gone is the patience to bear being kicked around by accidents;
My strength was the assurance to appease the coquetry of idols.

lakad kob: to kick around; *taḥammul:* patience.

I can no longer bear the hardships doled out by the world. There used to be a time when I could bear even the hardship of coquetry; that strength was enough to bear the hardships given by the world as well. I can no longer bear the world's hardships.

کہوں کیا خوبیٔ اوضاعِ ابنائے زماں غالب
بدی کی اس نے جس سے ہم نے کی تھی بارہا نیکی

kahūñ kyā ḳhūbī' auẓā'-e abnā'-e zamāñ Ġhālib
badī kī us ne jis se ham ne kī thī bārhā nekī (137:7; #843)

What shall I say of the goodness of traditions of the folks in this world, *Ġhālib*?
To whomsoever I was repeatedly nice, he always wronged me.

auẓā': traditions; *abnā:* folks.

The observation of the character of people leads one to lament. It is almost a tradition that whenever you are nice to someone, they will surely turn against you.

138

حاصل سے ہاتھ دھو بیٹھ، اے آرزو خرامی　　　دل جوشِ گریہ میں ہے ڈوبی ہوئی اسامی

ḥāṣil se hāth dho baiṭh, ai ārzū ḳhirāmī
dil josh-e girya(h) meñ hai ḍubī hū'ī asāmī (138:1; #844)

Wash your hands off from any gains, O wishing!
In the tumult of tears, the heart is already a sunken commodity.

ārzū ḳhirāmī: to wish*; ḍubī hū'ī asāmī:* sunken investment, from where a levy cannot be collected, like a flooded plantation.

A heart inundated with fear is like a flooded plantation that would not yield any levy. You cannot bank on your crying to accomplish anything. The use of "washing your hands off," being inundated, tears, and sunken commodity are all juxtaposed to create a very wet situation.

اُس شمع کی طرح سے جس کو کوئی بجھا دے　　　مَیں بھی جلے ہوؤں میں ہوں داغِ ناتمامی

us shama' kī ṭaraḥ se jis ko ko'ī bujhā de
maiñ bhī jale huoñ meñ hūñ dāġh-e nātamāmī (138:2; #845)

Like the candle that has been snuffed out by someone,
I am a scar of incompleteness among those who have been burnt.

dāġh-e nātamāmī: blame of incompleteness.

I was burning with love for her and now all kindness or cruelty has been withdrawn from me leaving me incomplete. An extinguished candle is incompletely burned and is blamed here for incomplete devotion. My desires, too, have been extinguished and I, too, am blamed for giving myself incompletely unto her.

139

کیا تنگ ہم ستم زدگاں کا جہان ہے
جس میں کہ ایک بیضۂ مور آسمان ہے

kyā tang ham sitam zadgāñ kā jahān hai
jis meñ kih ek baiẓah' mūr āsmān hai (139:1; #846)

How cramped is the world of us, the oppressed people,
Wherein the sky is merely an egg of an ant.

sitam: oppression; *baiẓa(h) mūr*: egg of ant.

Do you think that the world is too small for us, the oppressed people of the world? To understand it, visualize that our sky is no bigger than an ant egg. In other words, there is no limit to oppression. This world is indeed a tight place for me. The eggs of ants are indeed small; the sky is oval shaped and so are the eggs. The comparison made here also connotes the importance given to sky (heaven).

ہے کائنات کو حرکت تیرے ذوق سے
پرتو سے آفتاب کے، ذرّے میں جان ہے

hai kā'ināt ko ḥarkat tere żauq se
partau se āftāb ke, żarre meñ jān hai (139:2; #847)

The Universe is kept in motion by its yearning for You;
From the glare of the sun, comes the life throbbing in every particle.

ḥarkat: movement.

The Universe is dancing to the tune of the Lord. By itself, it is nothing. It is only something when put in motion by the Almighty. A particle remains invisible until a ray of light illuminates it and imparts it energy to move around in space. (From a scientific standpoint, the energy of the sunrays imparts energy to particles, causing them to move; this is called the "Brownian Movement." Could *Ġhālib* have known about this fundamental principle of physics governing the kinetic energy of bodies?)

حالانکہ ہے یہ سیلیٔ خارا سے لالہ رنگ
غافل کو میرے شیشے پہ مے کا گمان ہے

ḥālāñke hai yih silī' ḳhārā se lāla(h) rang
ġhāfil ko mere shīshe pa(h) mai kā gumān hai (139:3; #848)

Though it appears rose-red from being struck repeatedly with stones,
The ignorant think that there is red wine in my goblet.

silī': blow, strike; *ḳhārā*: stone.

Because my goblet has turned red, by being stricken by a stone, those who do not know it think that the goblet is filled with red wine. There are great difficulties in interpreting this verse. Striking with stone would shatter the glass, not turn it red, unless the goblet (like my heart) has such resilience that the impact of stone striking it generates heat that turns it red before breaking it. People think I am holding a goblet of wine, wherein the red color has come from receiving extreme blows of sorrow. To understand this verse, we must look at a heart badly bruised, red-hot with agony. The world not knowing this thinks of it as a display of color. The strength of the lover depends on the heart shattered as it consumes intense heat.

کی اُس نے گرم سینۂ اہلِ ہوس میں جا
آوے نہ کیوں پسند کہ ٹھنڈا مکان ہے

kī us ne garm, sina(h)' āhl-e havas meñ jā
āve na(h) kioñ pasand kih ṭhandā makān hai (139:4; #849)

A place she has warmed up in the hearts of rivals desiring her;
Why would not she like it, for their abode is cold?

ḥavas: desire.

She has created a place for her in the hearts of those who desire her. Such hearts are cold, free of the warmth of love, and she likes a cold abode. See the connection of warming the desire in the hearts and liking a cold home. The beloved is criticized here for being foolish.

کیا خوب، تم نے غیر کو بوسہ نہیں دیا؟
بس چُپ رہو ہمارے بھی مُنہ میں زبان ہے

kyā ḳhūb, tum ne ġhair ko bosa(h) nahiñ dīyā
bas chup raho hamāre bhī muñh meñ zabān hai (139:5; #850)

How nice that you did not give a kiss to the rival?
Now be quiet, for I, too, have a tongue in my mouth.

The lover is claiming to have a tongue in his mouth (which is used to speak and to engage in kissing). By acknowledging this, he says much to provide proof that the beloved did give a kiss to the rival. In addition, he is apparently asking for a kiss, to show how the rival may have kissed her, as a demonstration, of course.

بیٹھا ہے جو کہ سایۂ دیوارِ یار میں
فرماں روائے کشورِ ہندوستان ہے

baiṭhā hai jo kih sāyah' divār-e yār meñ
firmāñravāe kishvar-e hindustān hai (139:6; #851)

He, who gets to sit in the shadow of the wall of the beloved's home,
Is indeed the exalted ruler of India.

firmāñravā: ruler; *kishvar*: exalting.

He who gets to sit in the shadow of the wall of the beloved feels exalted to the level of the ruler-ship of India. It is that much of an honor.

ہستی کا اعتبار بھی غم نے مٹا دیا
کس سے کہوں کہ داغ جگر کا نشان ہے

hastī kā ʿitibār bhī ġham ne miṭā diyā
kis se kahūñ kih dāġh jigar kā nishān hai (139:7; #852)

Grief has erased the confidence in existence;
Whom shall I tell that the scar is a sign of my liver?

hastī: existence; *ʿitibār*: trust; *jigar*: liver (heart) *ġham*: sorrow.

Prolonged sorrow has transformed me into an untrustworthy soul. Who would believe it if I showed them that a branding mark is where my liver used to be? In fact, if a mark exists, that would mean that I also exist. Nevertheless, having been totally decimated by her, I myself find it less believable. If I do not exist, then neither does the mark. (Note: liver is the sign of courage.)

ہے بارے اعتمادِ وفاداری اس قدر
غالب ہم اس میں خوش ہیں کہ نامہرباں ہے

hai bāre iʿtimād-e vafādārī is qadar
Ġhālib ham is meñ ḳhūsh haiñ kih nāmahrbān hai (139:8; #853)

Such great trust there is in my faithfulness,
I am glad that she is not kind to me, *Ġhālib*.

bāṛe: because of; *is qadar*: so much.

How much she trusts my loyalty is shown by how much cruelty she doles out to me. She believes that no matter how oppressive she gets, I will not run away from her. Is not this an unlimited vote of trust?

140

درد سے میرے ہے تجھ کو بے قراری ہائے ہائے   کیا ہوئی ظالم تری غفلت شعاری ہائے ہائے

dard se mere hai tujh ko beqarārī, hāi hāi
kyā hū'ī z̤ālim terī ġhaflat shi'ārī, hāi hāi (140:1; #854)

Impatient you are at my pain. Lament! Lament!
What happened to your obliviousness, O! Tyrant? Lament! Lament!

After seeing my pain, you became impatient and began to suffer in agony. How sad! Whatever happened to those days when I would ask for your attention and get only your obliviousness? How satisfying this situation was to me. Now, with your impatience, I am suffering more.

تیرے دل میں گر نہ تھا آشوب غم کا حوصلہ   تو نے پھر کیوں کی تھی میری غمگساری ہائے ہائے

tere dil meñ gar na(h) thā āshob-e ġham kā ḥauṣla(h)
tū ne phir kioñ kī thī merī ġhamgusārī, hāi hāi (140:2; #855)

If your heart did not have the courage to bear the storm of sorrow,
Why did you then console me? Lament! Lament!

The storm of sorrow was so intense that anyone consoling me would feel my sadness. The beloved consoling me has become saddened and that is a source of lamentation for me. If you did not have the courage to bear my anguish, you should not have asked me to tell you.

کیوں مری غمخوارگی کا تجھ کو آیا تھا خیال   دشمنی اپنی تھی میری دوستداری ہائے ہائے

kioñ merī ġhamḳh(v)ārgī kā tujh ko āyā thā ḳhayāl
dushmanī apnī thī merī dostdārī, hāi hāi (140:3; #856)

Why did the thought of consoling me ever enter your mind?
Enmity it was to yourself, your friendship to me, Lament! Lament!

dostdārī: friendship.

Consoling me made you sadder. It was a gesture of friendship toward me, but certainly an act of enmity toward you.

عمر بھر کا تو نے پیمانِ وفا باندھا تو کیا　　عمر کو بھی تو نہیں ہے پائداری ہائے ہائے

ʿumr bhar kā tū ne paimāne vafā bāndhā to kyā
ʿumr ko bhī to nahiñ hai pāʾidārī, hāi hāi (140:4; #857)

So what if you gave vows of faithfulness for life?
There is no permanence to life itself. Lament! Lament!

paimān-e vafā: vow of faithfulness; *pāʾidārī:* permanence.

Your vows of faithfulness to me could not be sustained because life itself is not permanent. The vows will come to naught with the end of life.

زہر لگتی ہے مجھے آب و ہوائے زندگی　　یعنی تجھ سے تھی اسے ناسازگاری ہائے ہائے

zahr lagtī hai mujhe āb-o-havāʾe zindagī
yaʿnī tujh se thī ise nāsāzgārī, hāi hāi (140:5; #858)

I hate the climate of living,
For it proved unsuitable to you. Lament! Lament!

āb-o-havāʾ: air and water, atmosphere, climate; *zahr lagnā:* to hate, as if it were poison; *nāsāzgārī,:* unsuitable.

I deplore what sustains life, for it did not suit you and you died. Using the idiom of "being poisonous," the poet has created a double meaning here.

گل فشانی ہائے نازِ جلوہ کو کیا ہو گیا   خاک پر ہوتی ہے تیری لالہ کاری ہائے ہائے

gul fishānī hāi nāz-e jalva(h) ko kyā hogayā
ḳhāk par hotī hai terī lāla(h) kārī, hāi hāi (140:6; #859)

What happened to the coquettish blooming of flowers?
In the dust now grow these flowers. Lament! Lament!

When alive, your appearance in the assembly brought blooming flowers. This always cheered the assembly. Now, buried in dust, the flowers are growing wild (at your grave.)

شرمِ رسوائی سے جا چھپنا نقابِ خاک میں   ختم ہے الفت کی تجھ پر پردہ داری ہائے ہائے

sharm-e rusvā'ī se jā chhupnā naqāb-e ḳhāk meñ
ḳhatm hai ulfat kī tujh par pardahdārī, hāi hāi (140:7; #860)

Hiding from the shame of disgrace in the veil of dust,
Unmatched you are in keeping the secrecy of our love. Lament! Lament!

You have taken on a veil of dust (buried) to keep our love from being disgraced. The poet's style of keeping a secret cannot be matched.

خاک میں ناموسِ پیمانِ محبت مل گئی   اٹھ گئی دنیا سے راہ و رسمِ یاری ہائے ہائے

ḳhāk meñ nāmūs-e paimān-e muḥabbat mil ga'ī
uṭh ga'ī dunyā se rāh-o-rasm-e yārī, hāi hāi (140:8; #861)

Gone into dust is the honor of our vows of love;
Gone from the world is the tradition of friendship now. Lament! Lament!

The sanctity of our vows is now buried. With that goes all etiquette and traditions of friendship.

ہاتھ ہی تیغ آزما کا کام سے جاتا رہا　　دل پہ اک لگنے نہ پایا زخم کاری ہائے ہائے

hāth hī teġh āzmā kā kām se jātā rahā
dil pa(h) ik lagne na(h) pāyā zaḳhm-e kārī, hāi hāī (140:9; #862)

The sword-wielding hand became numb,
Before inflicting a deep wound to my heart. Lament! Lament!

zaḳhm-e kārī: deep wound; *teġh āzmā:* sword-trying.

No longer is the expert hand of the sword available to inflict wounds upon my heart. It was just the beginning of our affair and I had hoped to receive many wounds from you. It is over now.

کس طرح کاٹے کوئی شب ہائے تار برشکال　　ہے نظر خو کردۂ اختر شماری ہائے ہائے

kis ṯarḥ kāṭe ko'ī shab hāi tār-e barshakāl
hai naẕar ḳhū karda(h)' aḳhtar shumārī, hāi hāi (140:10; #863)

How would anyone spend the night of continuous rain?
The eyes have become used to counting stars now. Lament! Lament!

tār-e barshakāl: continuous drizzling; *ḳhū karda(h)*: habitual; *aḳhtar shumārī*: counting stars.

I used to spend our nights of separation counting stars. Now, because of the continuous rain, I cannot even see the stars. How will I spend the night now? The rain, of course, is the lover's tear. It could also refer to the rainy season.

گوش مہجورِ پیام و چشم محرومِ جمال   ایک دل، تس پر یہ نا اُمّیدواری ہائے ہائے

gosh mahjūr-e payām-o-chashm maḥrūm-e jamāl
ek dil, tis par yih nā ummīdvārī hāi hāi (140:11; #864)

Ears forsaken from hearing your voice and the eyes deprived of seeing your beauty.
Only one heart and all of this eternal despair? Lament! Lament!

mahjūr: forsaken; *maḥrūm*: deprived.

I can no longer hear or see you. How much more devastated and hopeless can my heart be?

عشق نے پکڑا نہ تھا، غالبؔ! ابھی وحشت کا رنگ
رہ گیا، تھا دل میں جو کچھ ذوقِ خواری، ہائے ہائے

'ishq ne pakṛā na(h) thā, Ġhālib! abhī vaḥshat kā rang
rah gayā, thā dil meñ jo kuchh ẓauq-e ḳh(v)ārī, hāi hāi (140:12; #865)

Love had not yet taken the color of lunacy, *Ġhālib*;
What remained, was the leftover desire in the heart to be disgraced, Lament! Lament!

pakṛā: caught; *vaḥshat*: lunacy; *ẓauq-e ḳh(v)ārī*: desire for disgrace.

I was new to love and had not yet reached a state of lunacy. Many desires for greater deprivation and disgrace remained in my heart before you departed.

141

سر گشتگی میں عالمِ ہستی سے یاس ہے
تسکیں کو دے نوید کہ مرنے کی آس ہے

sar gashtagī meñ ʿālam-e hastī se yās hai
taskiñ ko de navīd kih marne kī ās hai (141:1; #866)

In frenzy, I have lost all hope of surviving.
Give the good news to solace that there is hope for death.

sar gashtagī: frenzy, lunacy; *yās*: hopeless; *taskiñ*: quieting, soothing.

My frenzy will keep me from a long life. This will certainly be good news to my life-long desire for comfort because after death there is nothing but comfort. The poet addresses his sense of soothing by revealing that it is almost time to be joyful. Even though *Ġhālib* has talked about death being ultimate panacea, frequently, he also questions,"What happens if we do not find solace even after death?"

لیتا نہیں مرے دلِ آوارہ کی خبر
اب تک وہ جانتا ہے کہ میرے ہی پاس ہے

letā nahiñ mere dil-e āvāra(h) kī ḳhabar
ab tak vuh jāntā hai kih mere hī pās hai (141:2; #867)

Paying little attention to my vagabond heart,
She still thinks that it is with me.

āvāra(h): vagabond.

My beloved is quite oblivious to my heart. She thinks that I still have it with me. That is not true because my heart has the nature of a vagabond and cannot stay in one place. My heart is already with the beloved. Elsewhere, *Ġhālib* has declared, "where's the heart to lose, for I found my destiny."

کیجے بیاں سرورِ تبِ غم کہاں تلک
ہر مو مرے بدن پہ زبانِ سپاس ہے

kīje bayāñ surūr-e tab-e ġham kahāñ talak
har mū mere badan pa(h) zabān-e sipās hai (141:3; #868)

How far to go to describe the ecstasy of the fever of sorrow?
Every hair on my body is a tongue expressing gratitude.

tab: fever, heat; *mū:* hair; *sipās:* gratitude.

As the body temperature rises in fever, hairs rise into goose bumps. The poet refers to the fever of love giving one goose bumps. Every hair that stands upright is actually a tongue thanking the sorrow-giver. See the comparison of hair with tongue.

ہے وہ غرورِ حسن سے بیگانۂ وفا
ہر چند اس کے پاس دلِ حق شناس ہے

hai vuh ġhurūr-e ḥusn se begāna(h)' vafā
har chand us ke pās dil-e ḥaq shanās hai (141:4; #869)

The vanity of beauty is making her oblivious to faithfulness;
Otherwise, for sure, she has in her custody, a righteous heart.

ġhurūr: vanity; *begāna(h) vafā:* oblivious to faithfulness, fidelity; *pās:* custody; *ḥaq shanās:* righteous.

Her vanity keeps her oblivious to faithfulness toward me otherwise her heart is righteous. Her beauty has veiled her eyes so it is difficult to see what the right judgment is. This is a typical example of how a lover consoles his heart, by saying that there's hope after all, thus giving the benefit of doubt to the beauty.

پی جس قدر ملے شبِ مہتاب میں شراب
اس بلغمی مزاج کو گرمی ہی راس ہے

pī jis qadar mile, shab-e mahtāb meñ sharāb
is balġhamī mizāj ko garmī hī rās hai (141:5; #870)

I drank all I could get in the moonlit night,
As warmth suits my phlegmatic disposition well.

balġham: phlegm; *mizāj*: disposition, nature.

I have a phlegmatic disposition, meaning that my chest is often congested with phlegm. If I drink all that I can, it is for medical reasons, particularly if it happens to be a moonlit night. Wine is supposed to warm the chest. Note the congested chest compared to a full moon (with its spots compared to phlegm in the lung). It is most likely to happen on a full moon and a declaration that my chest remains congested requires me to drink. Congestion of the chest refers to "tightness" or a saddened heart.

ہر اک مکان کو ہے مکیں سے شرف اسدؔ
مجنوں جو مر گیا ہے تو جنگل اُداس ہے

har ik makān ko hai makīñ se sharf Asad
majnūñ jo mar gayā hai to jangal udās hai (141:6; #871)

In every home, the honor comes from its inhabitant, Asad.
As *Majnūn* has passed away, it has saddened the jungle.

makīñ: inhabitant; *sharf*: glory.

Homes without dwellers are desolate. *Majnūn*, the jungle dweller, is gone. With him went the glory and charm of the jungle, saddening it (the jungle).

142

گر خامشی سے فائدہ اِخفاے حال ہے　　خوش ہوں کہ میری بات سمجھنی محال ہے

gar ḳhāmshī se fāi'da(h) iḳhfāe ḥāl hai
ḳhush hūñ kih merī bāt samajhnī moḥāl hai (142:1; #872)

If being quiet helps hide the condition of my heart,
Then I am glad that it is difficult to understand what I say.

iḳhfā: hiding.

People hide their thoughts, their inner-selves, by being quiet. My being vocal does not reveal anything because all that I say is impossible to decipher anyway. Few can reach the height of my thoughts and thus my inner feelings remain hidden from all. Though it is beneficial to be quiet, in my case it makes little difference. Another reason it may be difficult to understand me is because when I am frenzied, my words are incoherent.

کس کو سناؤں حسرتِ اظہار کا گلہ　　دل فردِ جمع و خرجِ زباں ہاے لال ہے

kis ko sunāūñ ḥasrat-e iẓhār kā gila(h)
dil fird-e jama'-o-ḳharj-e zabāñ hāi lāl hai (142:2; #873)

To whom shall I relate my plaints of stifled desires?
My heart is merely a record of dumb tongues.

fird-e jam'a-o-ḳharj: register of account of receipts and disbursements; *zabāñ hāi lāl*: dumb tongues.

To whom shall I complain that my desire to expose the condition of my heart remains unfulfilled? My tongue is tied and in my heart are innumerable memories that have kept me from telling my story. The poet goes on to conclude that his plea of remaining mute is hardly of interest to anyone. Who would want to hear it anyway? The heart being a record of dumb tongues refers to the lack of appropriate vocabulary to explain, or of the ability to explain the condition of the heart in words that are coherent.

کس پردے میں ہے آئینہ پرداز اے خدا   رحمت کہ عذر خواہِ لبِ بے سوال ہے

kis parde meñ hai ā'īna(h) pardāz ae ḳhudā
raḥmat kih 'uzr ḳh(v)āh-e lab-e be savāl hai (142:3; #874)

O God! Behind which curtain hides the mirror?
Have mercy, as the excuse seeker is not questioning.

pardah: curtain; *ā'īna(h):* mirror.

Oh God! Tell me behind which curtain your reflection, is hidden? Be kind to me for I am willing to accept any excuse for you not wanting to be visible to me. Give, O! God, without asking! The poet wants to know the reality of God, but does not demand it. The poet is appealing to God's kindness to those who do not assume this their right.

ہے ہے! خدا نخواستہ وہ اور دشمنی   اے شوقِ منفعل! یہ تجھے کیا خیال ہے

hai hai! ḳhudā na(h) ḳh(v)āsta(h) vuh āur dushmanī
ai shauq-e munfa'il! yih tujhe kyā ḳhayāl hai (142:4; #875)

Shame! Shame! God forbid that she would show enmity!
O! You embarrassing desire! What are your thoughts?

munfa'il: embarrassed.

Shame on you for thinking that she has become your enemy; what are you thinking? You should be embarrassed for this impolite perception! The poet addresses his "desire" which remains unfulfilled and thinks that this may be because the beloved has become his enemy. What a way to console himself, by becoming a mediator between the lover's desire and the beloved.

مشکیں لباسِ کعبہ علی کے قدم سے جان نافِ زمین ہے نہ کہ نافِ غزال ہے

mushkiñ libās-e ka'ba(h) Alī ke qadam se jān
nāf-e zamīn hai na(h) kih nāf-e ġhazāl hai (142:5; #876)

The musk odor of the cover of *Ka'bā* is due to the birth of *'Alī*,
For it is the navel of the earth, not the navel of the deer.

mushkiñ: smelling like musk; *nāf-e ġhazāl*: musk in the navel of the deer.

The musk odor of the cloth of *Ka'bā* emanates because *Hazrat 'Alī* was born there; *Ka'bā*, though it is the navel of the earth, it is not the navel of the deer. An aerial view of *Ka'bā* would show it to be a dark spot in the center of earth. In reality, any point on earth is the center of earth but in the present context, it is used to display a religious meaning.

وحشت پہ میری عرصۂ آفاق تنگ تھا دریا زمین کو عرقِ انفعال ہے

vaḥshat pa(h) merī 'arṣa(h)' āfāq tang thā
daryā zamīñ ko 'arq-e infi'āl hai (142:6; #877)

For my frenzy, the expanse of the earth was so small
That rivers appear as the sweat of embarrassment on earth.

'arṣa(h)' āfāq: boundaries of earth; *'arq-e infi'āl*: sweat of embarrassment.

The frenzy of my wanderings makes the earth look small. It appears so small that out of embarrassment it perspired, thus creating the rivers and oceans—a remarkable exaggeration.

ہستی کے مت فریب میں آجائیو اسدؔ
عالم تمام حلقۂ دامِ خیال ہے

hastī ke mat fireb meñ ājāīyo Asad
ʿālam tamām ḥalqa(h)' dām-e khayāl hai (142:7; #878)

Be not deceived by the apparent reality of your existence, O! Asad!
The entire universe is nothing but a noose of the snare of thought.

hastī: existence.

Asad, do not be fooled by your existence; the entire universe is fiction. It is the creation of your own thoughts, encircled by the net of your thoughts. *Ġhālib*, a poet-philosopher, outshines all philosophers, including other philosopher-poets.

143

تم اپنے شکوے کی باتیں نہ کھود کھود کے پوچھو
حذر کرو مرے دل سے کہ اس میں آگ دبی ہے

tum apne shikve kī bāteñ na(h) khod khod ke pūchho
ḥaẓar karo mere dil se kih is meñ āg dabī hai (143:1; #879)

Do not keep probing into my plaints;
Be careful of my heart for there is fire buried in there.

ḥaẓar karo: be prudent, be careful.

There are many complaints in my heart. Asking about them repeatedly and with curiosity is not right, for these complaints are like buried fire that can bring leaping flames again. Be careful with me. The lover was able to curb his plaints, but their wounds remained in his heart. Now the beloved reminds him of his hurt by repeatedly asking about it. It is obvious that the moment of reduced agony is not acceptable to the beloved; she wants only to provoke him into more pain.

دلا یہ درد و الم بھی تو مغتنم ہے کہ آخر
نہ گریۂ سحری ہے نہ آہِ نیم شبی ہے

dilā yih dard-o-ʿalam bhī to mug̠ẖtanam hai kih āḳhir
na(h) girya(h)' saḥarī hai na(h) āh-e nīm shabī hai (143:2; #880)

O! Heart, consider this sorrow and pain a blessing in disguise, for in the end,
There will neither be morning weeping, nor the sighs in the middle of the night.

muġhtanam: regarded as a prize.

O' My Heart! Why are you growing impatient with sorrow and pain? It is a blessing that you even experience these things, for in the end there shall be no weeping in the morning and no venting of sighs in the middle of the night. When death prevails, it will all be gone. Take this pain as a sign of life. See: "*be sadā ho jāe gā yih sāz-e hastī ek din*" [Soundless it will go, this instrument of existence one day].

144

ایک جا حرفِ وفا لکھا تھا، سو بھی مِٹ گیا
ظاہرا کاغذ ترے خط کا، غلط بردار ہے

ek jā ḥarf-e vafā likkhā thā, so bhī miṭ gayā
ẓāhiran kāġhaż tere ḳhaṯ kā, ġhalaṯ bardār hai (144:1; #881)

The word, "faithful" was written in only one place; even that is erased now.
Obviously, the paper of your letter must have been the error-erasing type.

ġhalat bardār kāġhaż: error erasable paper.

At one point in your letter, you used the word faithfulness, but by the time the letter got to me, the paper had erased it, for it was indeed a wrongly placed word. The beloved did not get the opportunity to correct these obvious mistakes, so the paper did it. This verse demonstrates *Ġhālib's* remarkable melancholic humor.

جی جلے ذوقِ فنا کی ناتمامی پر نہ کیوں
ہم نہیں جلتے، نفَس ہر چند آتش بار ہے

jī jale żauq-e fanā kī nātamāmī par na(h) kioñ
ham nahiñ jalte, nafas har chand ātishbār hai (144:2; #882)

Why would not the heart burn in anguish over the imperfection of its desire for extinction?
We do not burn even though our breath is fire spewing.

Why would I not burn inside (sulk) when my desire to burn myself into extinction is not fulfilled? Though my breath is full of fire, it does not burn me—it simply burns me inside since I am unable to bring myself to extinction. It burns that I cannot burn myself enough to qualify for "*fanā*" in the Sufi tradition. My desire was intense, but not intense enough.

آگ سے پانی میں بجھتے وقت اٹھتی ہے صدا
ہر کوئی درماندگی میں نالے سے ناچار ہے

āg se pānī meñ bujhte vaqt uṭhtī hai ṣadā
har ko'ī darmāndgī meñ nāle se nāchār hai (144:3; #883)

From the fire, there arises a scream upon its extinction,
As everyone in distress helplessly adduces plaints.

darmāndgī: misery, distress; *nāchār*: helplessness.

Fire burns quietly until it is extinguished, such as when water is thrown on it. Then it creates a sound like screaming in desperation, as if it were complaining. Lovers also burn, but when faced with extinction (water thrown on their hopes), plaints come out spontaneously. The comparison between the crackling sound of a fire being extinguished and the heart's lament is remarkable. Note that in this verse, the meaning of extinction is different than when it used in *Sufi* concept.

ہے وہی بدمستیٔ ہر ذرہ کا خود عذر خواہ
جس کے جلوے سے زمیں تا آسماں سرشار ہے

hai vuhī badmastī' har żarra(h) kā ḳhud 'użr ḳh(v)āh
jis ke jalve se zamiñ tā āsmāñ sarshār hai (144:4; #884)

He, Himself is the reason for the intoxication of every particle,
From Whose display, there is ecstasy spread from the earth to the sky.

sarshār: ecstasy; *ʿużr ḳh(v)āh*: one offers excuse.

He, whose display turns everything into ecstasy, from the earth to the sky, knows it. The particles of dust need not be apologetic about their ecstasy. He is responsible for this. Everything in this Universe is in a state of ecstasy, and any sins or mistakes committed are due to this inebriation. Can we hold any creation in the Universe responsible for their acts? No. The only being responsible for this is the One whose evidence wraps everything in ecstasy, from earth to sky. If God's will is part of man's will, then God should be responsible for man's actions. That is the gist of this verse.

مجھ سے مت کہہ: "تو ہمیں کہتا تھا اپنی زندگی"
زندگی سے بھی مرا جی اِن دنوں بیزار ہے

mujh se mat keh: "tū hameñ kahtā thā āpnī zindagī"
zindagī se bhī merā jī in dinoñ bezār hai (144:5; #885)

Tell me not "You used to say to me, you are my life,"
For these days, I am even dismayed with my own life.

Do not remind me that I used to call you "my life," for these days I am sick and tired of my life. The lover is tired of his life and is ready to kill himself. Calling the beloved,"my life," may be a bad omen. This verse is clearly in the style of *Momin*, a contemporary of *Ġhālib*.

آنکھ کی تصویر سرنامے پہ کھینچی ہے کہ تا
تجھ پہ کھل جاوے کہ اِس کو حسرتِ دیدار ہے

āñkh kī taṣvīr sar nāme pa(h) khainchī hai kih tā
tujh pa(h) khul jāve kih is ko ḥasrat-e dīdār hai (144:6; #886)

I have drawn a picture of an eye in the beginning of my letter, so that
it would reveal to you that I am longing to see you.

I have drawn an illustration of an eye on the envelope addressed to you to demonstrate how badly I want to see you. The use of "it would open [reveal] to you" is written to indicate the opening of the letter as well.

145

پینَس میں گزرتے ہیں جو کوچے سے وہ میرے
کندھا بھی کہاروں کو بدلنے نہیں دیتے

pīnas meñ guzarte haiñ jo kūche se voh mere
kandhā bhī kahāroñ ko badalne nahiñ dete (145:1; #887)

When passing through my alley in the palanquin,
She does not even allow the pallbearers to shift their shoulder burden.

pīnas: carrier, palanquin.

The beloved is in such a hurry to pass through my alley that she does not even allow the pallbearers to change their shoulders while carrying her in the palanquin. If she allows this, they may slow down and give the lover a chance to catch a glimpse of her. In olden days, palanquins that were supported by four men transported women.

146

مری ہستی فضائے حیرت آبادِ تمنّا ہے
جسے کہتے ہیں نالہ وُہ اِسی عالم کا عنقا ہے

merī hastī fazā'e ḥairat ābād-e tamannā hai
jise kahte haiñ nāla(h) vuh isī `ālam kā `unqā hai (146:1; #888)

My existence is a stunned aura where desires dwell.
What we call "plaint" is actually the nonexistent bird of this world.

Because so many of my desires remain unfulfilled, I have turned into a stunned being; dumb founded yet I do not even complain. What is called "plaint" is now just the *`unqā*, the legendary mythical bird that does not exist, in my stunned world. In reality, plaint is heard, not seen, but when you exaggerate, everything goes.

خزاں کیا، فصلِ گُل کہتے ہیں کِس کو، کوئی موسم ہو
وُہی ہم ہیں، قفس ہے، اور ماتم بال و پر کا ہے

k̤hizāñ kyā, faṣl-e gul kahte haiñ kis ko, ko'ī mausam ho
vuhī ham haiñ, qafas hai, āur mātam bāl-o-par kā hai (146:2; #889)

What is autumn? What is known as spring? It may well be any season.
It is all the same for me: the same cage and the same laments about feathers and wings.

A nightingale is lamenting at the changing of the seasons that bring so much excitement and freshness to the world. However, what would a caged bird do since nothing changes for it? It is the same cage and the same plaints against the atrocities of the world.

وفائے دلبراں ہے اتفاقی، ورنہ اے ہمدم
اثر فریادِ دل ہائے حزیں کا کس نے دیکھا ہے

vafā' dilbarāñ hai ittifāqī, varna(h) ai hamdam
āsar faryād-e dil hāi ḥazīñ kā kis ne dekhā hai (146:3; #890)

The faithfulness of the beloved is merely coincidental, or else my friend,
Who has ever seen the plaint of a sad heart come to fruition?

ḥazīñ: sadness.

The beloved is kind to the lover who is not willing to accept that this is the effect of his plaints. Plaints of a sad heart are supposed to go unheard. The lover concludes that this change in the beloved's attitude is purely coincidental for he knows that the beloved will soon return to her old, cruel ways. The lover does not want to be presumptuous about the momentary change in the behavior of the beloved. There is much disbelief expressed here.

نہ لائی شوخیِ اندیشہ تابِ رنجِ نومیدی
کفِ افسوس ملنا عہدِ تجدیدِ تمنا ہے

na(h) lā'ī shoḳhī' andesha(h) tāb-e ranj-e naummīdī
kaf-e afsos malnā 'ahd-e tajdīd-e tamannā hai (146:4; #891)

The intense disappointment did not bring the despair of helplessness;
Wringing my hands in remorse is, in reality, a sign of my renewed vows.

'ahd-e tajdid-e tamannā: pledge to renew vows; *kaf-e afsos malnā:* to rub hands in sorrow.

We wring our hands in desperation and also when we plan something new. This is like strapping on boots to take on new challenges. My disappointments were so intense that I had to tell my heart, which was in unbearable pain, that wringing my hands was actually a sign of renewing my vows to cover my disappointment—to give some consolation to my heart. This helped keep helplessness out of my heart. By creating a duality between himself and his heart, the poet is trying to find a way to vent his frustration.

147

رحم کر ظالم کہ کیا بُودِ چراغِ کُشتہ ہے
نبضِ بیمارِ وفا دُودِ چراغِ کُشتہ ہے

raḥam kar ẕālim kih kyā būd-e charāġh-e kushta(h) hai
nabẓ-e bīmār-e vafā dūd-e chirāġh-e kushta(h) hai (147:1; #892)

Be merciful! O! Tyrant, for what is the existence of a burnt-out lamp.
The pulse of the patient of loyalty is like streak of smoke from a burnt-out lamp.

būd: being; *chirāgh-e kushtah*: lamp burnt out; *dūd*: smoke.

My being is like a burnt- out lamp; I am dying. The dying pulse of this faithful patient is like the smoke coming from burnt-out lamp. It becomes almost imperceptible with time. Note the comparison between dying and the burnt-out lamp. The slow cooling of both, the trickling of smoke compared to the departure of the soul and the slowing of the pulse is remarkable. In Arabic, *dūd* is another word for a crawling insect, and dying pulse is often referred to as *dūd* as well.

دل لگی کی آرزو بے چین رکھتی ہے ہمیں
ورنہ یاں بے رونقی سُودِ چراغِ کُشتہ ہے

dil lagī kī ārzū bechain rakhtī hai hameñ
varna(h) yāñ be raunaqī sūd-e chirāġh-e kushta(h) hai (147:2; #893)

The desire of merriment keeps me impatient,
Or else, here the gloom is better for the burnt-out lamp.

dil lagī: merriment; *sūd*: profit.

My desires keep me impatient. If a lamp goes out and makes the room gloomy, it is in the best interest of the lamp to save itself (not being lit). We keep lighting our lamp of desire with new desires as some come to fruition. It is this way that we keep burning ourselves in agony. If we could only control our trail of desires, we could be content. If we want to save ourselves from destruction, we should not light our desire for joyous celebrations, for the end is always sorrowful. The happier we want to be, the sadder we end up being—that is the message here.

148

چشمِ خوباں خامشی میں بھی نوا پرداز ہے
سرمہ، تو کہوے کہ، دودِ شعلۂ آواز ہے

chashm-e khūbāñ ḳhāmshī meñ bhī navā pardāz hai
surma(h) tū kahve kih, dūd-e shola(h)' āvāz hai (148:1; #894)

The eyes of the beloved are talking even when they are quiet.
The antimony appears as the smoke of the flame of her voice.

chashm-e ḳhūbāñ: eyes of beloved; *navā pardāz*: talking; *surma(h)*: antimony (see Glossary); *sho'la(h) āvāz*: fiery sound.

The eyes of my beloved, though silent, say a lot that goes to the core of my heart. The antimony applied to the eyes is likened to the smoke of the utterance of her eyes. The antimony-decorated eyes of the beloved say a lot even though the beloved is quiet. Note that the antimony is dark and applied around the eyelashes, making it look like smoke coming from the eye. Talking eyes refers to nods, hints, gestures, winks, etc. There is another very remote connection here. Antimony, while it is applied to the eye, causes gagging if it is eaten. Here antimony enhances the flame of the eyes while they stay quiet (gagged).

پیکرِ عشاق سازِ طالعِ ناساز ہے
نالہ گویا گردشِ سیارہ کی آواز ہے

paikar-e 'ushshāq sāz-e ṭāla'-e nāsāz hai
nāla(h) goyā gardish-e sayyārra(h) kī āvāz hai (148:2; #895)

The body of the lovers is a dissonant musical instrument;
The plaint of lovers is the sound of revolving planets.

paikar: appearance; *u'shshāq:* lovers; *sāz:* apparatus, instrument; *nāsāz*: dissonant, sick; *nāla(h)*: lamenting; *goyā:* as if; *gardish:* revolution; *āvāz:* sound.

The lover's body is made up of pieces of a lonely planet. When he laments, the sound of a planet ripping through space can be heard. The critical explanation comes from interpreting the meaning of *sāz* –some say the lover's body is like a dissonant instrument, its sound like a planet in revolution. What is meant here is that lamenting is in our ill fate; we were brought into the world to do just that. The creation of lovers is the act of ill fate: their plaints sound as if planets were whirling, as in fate, thus creating strange sounds. This verse is one of the most controversial writings of *Ġhālib*. All interpreters, including this writer, give their own dissonant explanations.

دستگاہِ دیدۂ خونبارِ مجنوں دیکھنا
یک بیاباں جلوۂ گل، فرشِ پا انداز ہے

dastgāh-e dīda(h)' ḳhūñ bār-e majnūñ dekhnā
yak bayābāñ jalva(h)' gul, firsh-e pā andāz hai (148:3; #896)

See the power of the blood-filled eyes of *Majnūn*,
What a grand display of flowers it has created to unroll a welcome carpet.

dastgāh: expertise, impact, power, status; *yak bayābāñ jalva(h)' gul*: extensive spread of flowers; *firsh-e pā andāz*: rolled out red carpet.

The tears of blood from the eyes of *Majnūn* colored the entire wilderness. Now it is as if a bed of roses is laid out to welcome his beloved.

149

عشق مجھ کو نہیں، وحشت ہی سہی　　میری وحشت، تری شہرت ہی سہی

ʿishq mujh ko nahiñ, vaḥshat hī sahī
merī vaḥshat, terī shohrat hī sahī (149:1; #897)

So I love you not? Let it be solitude.
My solitariness bringing you fame, so let it be.

hī sahī: let it be (used here as an improper reluctant choice).

You say that I do not love you and that I like solitude. However, as people see me forlorn they come to know of the reason of my solitariness and this makes you famous. A taunting dialogue between the lover and the beloved, it does not lead to an appropriate use of "*hī sahī*" or "let it be,". unless, of course, we assume that a reputation to drive lovers crazy is all that she will get unless she changes her ways. The use of word, *vaḥshat* is used craftily as it means many things including wildness, fierceness, etc. All of them apply here as any unusual behavior of lover points to its cause.

قطع کیجے نہ تعلق ہم سے　　کچھ نہیں ہے تو عداوت ہی سہی

qataʿ kīje na(h) taʿluq ham se
kuchh nahiñ hai to ʿadāvat hī sahī (149:2; #898)

Break-off not the connection with me;
If nothing else, enmity, let it be.

Enmity is a connection that I would rather have if you cannot be kind to me. It is when you break our connection that I get most perturbed.

میرے ہونے میں ہے کیا رُسوائی　　اے! وہ مجلس نہیں خلوت ہی سہی

mere hone meñ hai kyā rusvāī
ai! vuh majlis nahiñ ḳhalvat hī sahī (149:3; #899)

What is the embarrassment in having me there, O! Beloved?
If it is not your gathering, then your privacy, let it be.

rusvā'ī: defamation, embarrassment; *ḳhalvat*: privacy.

How could my presence be embarrassing to you? The lover complains about not being invited, which she defends by saying that the assembly is a private one. The lover retorts that he would not be an embarrassment to her. An alternate meaning is that the beloved is afraid the lover may embarrass her in the assembly. To become "unperturbed," the lover suggests that he be invited to her private quarters. Very clever of *Ġhālib*, but the use of *hī sahī* (let it be) becomes more difficult to justify—as if the meeting in private were a reluctant, rather undesirable, choice. This entire *ġhazal* is built around the difficult choice of complex meanings of simple words.

ہم بھی دشمن تو نہیں ہیں اپنے　　غیر کو تجھ سے محبت ہی سہی

ham bhī dushman to nahiñ haiñ apne
ġhair ko tujh se muḥabbat hī sahī (149:4; #900)

I, too, am not my own enemy;
The rival may love you, so let it be.

The style of this verse is typical of Momin *Ḳhān* Momin's poetry. "I am not my own enemy, given that the rival loves you, too," is a highly convoluted statement. The poet admonishes the beloved that the rival is not in love with her, but instead expresses it on the surface. The beloved disagrees vehemently, to which the poet says that he accepts it, but there is a difference between his love and that of the rival. For me, to love you is to live, and to live is to love you and I cannot be an enemy to myself. To me, loving you is a matter of survival and I cannot do things, which are not good for me (I can not be my own enemy.) In the case of the rival, it is just that he likes you, but his life does not depend on it. Here the use of "*hī sahī*" (let it be) is appropriate.

اپنی ہستی ہی سے ہو، جو کچھ ہو　　آگہی گر نہیں غفلت ہی سہی

apnī hastī hī se ho, jo kuchh ho
āgahī gar nahiñ ġhaflat hī sahī (149:5; #901)

You are because of your existence, whosoever you are;
If it is not awareness, then ignorance, let it be.

ġhaflat: to forget.

To know oneself is to know God and so when we forget ourselves we forget God. To reach God, we must first go through ourselves. We should do this whether we are enlightened or not.

عمر ہر چند کہ ہے برق خرام　　دل کے خوں کرنے کی فرصت ہی سہی

ʿumr har chand kih haī barq ḳhirām
dil kih ḳhūñ karne kī fursạt hī sahī (149:6; #902)

No doubt, that life is like the swift lightning;
Enough time to bleed my heart, let it be.

Life passes as quickly as a flash of lightning, but it should be long enough to do the most important thing: to sacrifice my heart for my beloved. Unfortunately, there is not enough time to bleed my heart [sacrifice] for her as life passes so quickly.

ہم کوئی ترکِ وفا کرتے ہیں　　نہ سہی عشق، مصیبت ہی سہی

ham ko'ī tark-e vafā karte haiñ
na(h) sahī ʿishq, muṣībat hī sahī (149:7; #903)

Do I ever give up being faithful to you?
If it is not love, then any calamity, let it be.

We are steadfast lovers and we do not give up, come what may, even if what we get in return is just one calamity after another.

کچھ تو دے اے فلکِ ناانصاف　　آہ و فریاد کی رخصت ہی سہی

kuchh to de ai falak-e nā inṣāf
āh-o-faryād kī ruḳhṣat hī sahī (149:8; #904)

Give something, O! Unjust heaven!
Even if it is the permission to send my sighs and plaints.

ruḳhṣat: permission.

The lover complains to heaven for giving nothing but injustice as all of his desires and wishes have been turned down. As the lover continues to ask heaven to be kind, he has no time left to lament his failures. So he asks to be given a chance to air his plaints. Some have interpreted this as asking for freedom from plaints though it is exactly the opposite.

ہم بھی تسلیم کی خُو ڈالیں گے　　بے نیازی تری عادت ہی سہی

ham bhī taslīm kī ḳhū ḍāleñ ge
be niyāzī terī ʿādat hī sahī (149:9; #905)

We, too, will cultivate a habit of submissive resignation;
Obliviousness may well be your style.

Your obliviousness is incessant. After trying to change it, I now realize that I have to get used to it and accept it. The lover is not threatening, but rather submitting to his failure.

یار سے چھیڑ چلی جاے اسد
گر نہیں وصل تو حسرت ہی سہی

yār se chheṛ chalī jāe Asad
gar nahiñ vaṣl to ḥasrat hī sahī (149:10; #906)

Teasing should continue with the beloved, Asad;
If it is not union, then insistence on it, let it be.

Some connection must be remain with the beloved; if not a fight with her about her refusal for union, then let it be an ongoing insistence for it.

150

ہے آرمیدگی میں نکوہش بجا مجھے
صبح وطن ہے خندۂ دنداں نما مجھے

hai ārmīdgī meñ nikuhish bajā mujhe
ṣubḥ-e vaṭan hai ḳhanda(h)' dandāñ numā mujhe (150:1; #907)

Well-deserved are these insults in my leisurely pursuit,
As the dawn in the homeland is a display of teeth, jesting at me.

nikuhish: insults; *ḳhand'a(h)'*: laughing; *dandā numāñ*: showing teeth, being sarcastic, jesting.

People laugh at me sarcastically, though justifiably, because I left home and went into exile in order to find comfort. The connection between teeth showing and dawn is obvious. Dawn in the homeland is compared to a display of teeth because both are white. This means that with every coming day, people laugh at me. The poet created a rather difficult comparison with morning at home to the brightness of teeth.

ڈھونڈے ہے اس مغنیِ آتش نفس کو جی
جس کی صدا ہو جلوۂ برقِ فنا مجھے

ḍhūñde hai us muġhannī' ātish nafas ko jī
jis kī ṣadā ho jalva(h)' barq-e finā mujhe (150:2; #908)

The soul is searching for a singer with a fiery breath,
Whose call would come as lightning to annihilate me.

muġhannī: singer; *ātish nafas*: fiery breath.

I am looking for a singer whose voice has such impact that it melts hearts. The intensity of the call would be so intense that it would burn me into nonexistence.

مستانہ طے کروں ہوں رہِ وادیِ خیال
تا، بازگشت سے نہ رہے مدّعا مجھے

mastāna(h) ṯae karūñ hūñ rah-e vādī' ḳhayāl
tā, bāzgasht se na(h) rahe muddu'ā mujhe (150:3; #909)

In sheer ecstasy, I cross the valley of my thoughts,
So I would not have anything to do with the echo.

bāzgasht: echo, returning.

Buried deep in my thoughts is the state of ecstasy that makes me forget how I arrived at a certain feeling, a certain conclusion about where I am. Because I cannot trek back, I need not worry about the origin of this thought and accept it as it is. The echo of thought is used here as a reminder of the past. Since I cannot return to the root of my thoughts, I have no reason to harp on them in an effort to decipher them. The key to this verse lies in the ecstasy, which makes me oblivious to the past.

کرتا ہے بسکہ باغ میں تُو بے حجابیاں
آنے لگی ہے نکہتِ گل سے حیا مجھے

kartā hai baske bāġh meñ tū beḥijābiyāñ
āne lagī hai nakhat-e gul se ḥayā mujhe (150:4; #910)

While you are exposing yourself so immodestly in the garden,
I have begun to feel embarrassed from the smell of flowers.

ḥayā: shame; *beḥijāb:* without veil, immodest; *nakhat:* smell.

The beloved has unveiled herself in the garden before the flowers. The smell of flowers reminds me of her being naked, unveiling in the garden and so it embarrasses me. There is also, an indication that mixed with the scent of flowers is the scent of beloved's body, which, now, everyone could smell.

کُھلتا کِسی پہ کیوں مِرے دل کا مُعاملہ
شِعروں کے اِنتخاب نے رُسوا کیا مجھے

khultā kisī pa(h) kioñ mere dil kā mu'āmla(h)
shi'roñ ke intiḳhāb ne rusvā kiyā mujhe (150:5; #911)

How could anyone have come to know, the secrets of my heart?
The selection of my poetic verses has disgraced me.

My selection of verses told the whole story of my heart. To anyone reading the verses, it was like an open book. Now the whole world knows what a pathetic lover I am. This is a matter of great disgrace to me because it brings infamy to my beloved

151

زندگی اپنی جب اس شکل سے گزری غالبؔ
ہم بھی کیا یاد کریں گے کہ خُدا رکھتے تھے!

zindagī apnī jab is shakl se guzrī Ġhālib
ham bhī kyā yād kareñ ge kih ḳhudā rakhte the (151:1; #912)

And when my life had withered away like this, *Ġhālib*,
Then how would we appreciate that we too had belonged to God?

A life as pathetic as that of *Ġhālib*'s is enough to make one doubt that God exists. If there were a God, you would not be in this pathetic condition, for He would have taken care of you, for He loves His creation. Maybe I did not have a God. The second line has an idiomatic expression wherein, "remember how well," is used to describe an expression of significance. Since the poet has had a very difficult, miserable, and deprived life, how can he even remember God?

152

اُس بزم میں مجھے نہیں بنتی حیا کیے　　بیٹھا رہا، اگرچہ اشارے ہُوا کیے

us bazm meñ mujhe nahiñ bantī ḥayā kīye
baiṭhā rahā, agarchi(h) ishāre hūv'ā kīye (152:1; #913)

In that assembly, I cannot help being bashful;
I kept sitting idly, even though taunts kept flying.

To stay in her assembly, one has to be rather shameless. The rivals were calling me names and I had to put up with this onslaught. If I were sensitive, I would have left the assembly a long time ago. To sit there was to bear these insults; it was my choice to take these insults. I would rather be shameless than leave her assembly.

دل ہی تو ہے، سیاستِ درباں سے ڈر گیا　　مَیں اور جاؤں در سے ترے بِن صدا کیے؟

dil hī to hai, siyāsat-e darbāñ se ḍar gayā
maiñ āur jāūñ dar se tere bin ṣadā kīye (152:2; #914)

It is just a heart; it became frightened by doorkeeper's politics;
Or else, how could I have passed by your door and not raised a clamor?

The heart is such a strange thing; it claimed to be brave, yet it proved so timid that it became afraid of your doorkeeper's manipulative politics, and I left. But for a weak heart that was frightened, I could not possibly pass by your home and not let a call of plaint go in the air.

رکھتا پھروں ہوں خرقہ و سجادہ رہنِ مے　　مدت ہوئی ہے دعوتِ آب و ہوا کیے

rakhtā phirūñ hūñ ḳhirqah-o-sajjādah rahn-e mai
muddat hū'ī hai da'vat-e āb-o-havā kīye (152:3; #915)

I am going around pawning my rags and mat to get some wine;
It has been a long time since I celebrated the feast of spring.

ḳhirqah: beggar's rug; *sajjādah*: mat (meaning here floor mat): *āb-o-havā*: climate (spring season).

It is springtime: time to drink and have fun. To buy more wine to start the feast, I am going to pawn my basic possessions. The mat here is the ordinary floor mat, not the prayer mat as some have interpreted, for *Ġhālib* would have no use for that.

بے صرفہ ہی گزرتی ہے، ہو گرچہ عمرِ خضر　　حضرت بھی کل کہیں گے کہ ہم کیا کیا کیے!

be ṣarfah hī guzartī hai, ho garchi(h) u'mr-e Ḳhiẓr
haẓrat bhī kal kaheñ ge kih ham kyā kīyā kīye (152:4; #916)

It is spent uselessly, even if it is the life of *Ḳhiẓr*.
You would wonder tomorrow, Mister, "What did I accomplish?"

be ṣarfah: useless.

Haẓrat Ḳhiẓr is supposed to live forever, till the Doomsday, as the legend goes. The poet wants to question Mr. *Ḳhiẓr* tomorrow (after the Day of Judgment) about what he did with his long life and professes that regardless of how much time you get in this life, it is useless. Apparently, a jesting verse, it points sarcastically to a very deep reality regarding the humbleness of human beings. All right, Mr. *Ḳhiẓr*, so you lived a long life? Tell me, how was it? Tell me, what did you accomplish? Apparently, *Ḳhiẓr* himself will wonder.

مقدور ہو تو خاک سے پوچھوں کہ اے لئیم   تو نے وہ گنج ہائے گرانمایہ کیا کیے

maqdūr ho to ḳhāk se pūchhuñ kih ai la'īm
tu ne vuh ganj hāɛ girānmāyah kyā kīye (152:5; #917)

If I was fortunate enough, I would ask the earth, O! Miser,
What did you do with those priceless treasures?

la'īm: miser.

Referring to so many good people who died and were buried, the poet wants to know what the earth did to them? You took these treasures and did not return anything, you miser earth! This means that there is a gradual shortage of good. Elsewhere *Ġhālib* writes*: sab kahāñ, kuchh lāla(h)-o-gul meñ numāyāñ ho gaī'ñ/ ḳhak meñ, kyā ṣūrateñ hoñgī kih pinhāñ ho gaī'ñ (112:1; # 665):* not all but some appeared as tulips and roses, what manifestations may be in the dirt that remained hidden. Here *Ġhālib* is talking about the many ways earth exhibits itself—it does not refer to people buried in it; this is, however, often interpreted as tulips and flowers representing those who were buried there.

کس روز تہمتیں نہ تراشا کیے عدو   کس دن ہمارے سر پہ نہ آرے چلا کیے

kis roz tohmateñ nā tarāshā kīye a'dū
kis din hamāre sar pe nā āre chalā kīye (152:6; #918)

On which day did the rival not carve blame on me?
On which day did the saw not cut through my head?

tohmateñ: blame; *tarāsha*: carved; *a'dū*: enemies; *āre*: big saw.

My enemies kept carving blame on me every day and every day was like a saw cutting through my head—meaning that my rival kept exploiting my beloved against me, making her behavior unbearable.

See the connection between carving blame and the cutting of and carving with the saw.

صُحبت میں غَیر کی نہ پڑی ہو کہیں یہ خُو　　　دینے لگا ہے بوسہ بغیر التجا کیے

ṣoḥbat meñ ġhair kī nā paṛī ho kahiñ yih ḳhū
dene lagā hai bosah baġhair iltijā kīye (152:7; #919)

Is it not in the company of a stranger, that this habit has been picked up,
Giving kisses without the beseeching of lovers?

The lover has hundreds of ways to become suspicious of the beloved. The beloved has given a kiss to the lover without asking him to beg. This has made the lover suspicious about where she picked up this trait—perhaps in the company of the rival. Apparently, the rival has cunningly made her less bashful. Dilemma, dilemma, dilemma!

ضِد کی ہے اَور بات مگر خُو بُری نہیں　　　بھولے سے اُس نے سینکڑوں وعدے وفا کیے

ẓid kī hai āur bāt magar ḳhū burī nahiñ
bhūle se us ne sainkṛoñ vaʿde vafā kīye (152:8; #920)

Stubbornness aside, her habit is not bad
As she fulfilled hundreds of promises in her forgetfulness.

Being stubborn is her trait, but the habit of being forgetful is also not bad. When she forgets that she is stubborn, she keeps many promises. Note that the poet is not endorsing, but saying, "it is not bad." Also, as she forgets, being stubborn means that being stubborn is not in her nature but something she tries to be. As a result, the poet has great hope for a more permanent change in her habits.

غالِب تمھیں کہو کہ مِلے گا جواب کیا
مانا کہ تم کہا کیے اور وہ سُنا کیے

Ġhālib tumhīñ kaho kih mile gā javāb kyā
mānā kih tum kahā kīye āur vuh sunā kīye (152:9; #921)

Tell me yourself, *Ġhālib*, what answer would you get?
Granted that you would say it all and she would listen to it as well.

A preacher is talking to the poet. Even though the chances are remote, I accept that you will have a chance to tell her your whole story, and I accept the freak chance that she will listen to you (pay attention to you). Then, after all is said and done, what do you suppose she will say in response? The answer will still be no.

153

رفتارِ عمر قطعِ رہِ اضطراب ہے   اس سال کے حساب کو برق آفتاب ہے

raftār-e ʽumr qaṭaʽ-e rah-e iẓṭirāb hai
is sāl ke ḥisāb ko barq āftāb hai (153:1; #922)

The swift passing of life through the path of impatience is like Measuring solar years in terms of lightning.

raftār: speed; *ʽumr:* age; *qaṭaʽ:* passing; *iẓṭirāb:* perturbation; *sāl:* used here to mean age; *ḥisāb:* reckoning, accounting; *āftāb:* sun.

The age measured in solar years passes in a flash of light; such is the speed of my perturbed life. How fast life is passing in the path of impatience is like making each solar day equivalent to a flash of lightning. This is a difficult verse to expound because of its mechanical construction. The word "*sāl*"(year) is used here to describe time (life) as it refers to "*aftāb*" (sun), for we measure time in solar days, months and years. Then time is described as passing like a flash of lightning. Good times pass fast, so do the moments of impatience (when we are hurried, we move fast). Measuring time using light is a concept that was developed much later by Einstein in his famous Theory of Relativity (about 100 years later).

مینائے مے ہے سروِ نشاطِ بہارِ مے   بالِ تدرو جلوۂ موجِ شراب ہے

mīnāe mai hai sarv-e nishāṯ-e bahār-e mai
bāl-e tadrau jalva(h)' mauj-e sharāb hai (153:2; #923)

The cypress tree is the wine decanter containing the ecstatic wine of spring.
The floating clouds appear like the waves of wine.

mīnā: decanter, wine bottle; *sarv:* cypress tree; *nishāṭ:* joy; *bāl-e tadrau*: piece of cloud.

The ecstasy of spring makes me see wine in a decanter when I look at the cypress tree, and the pieces of cloud remind me of the splashing waves of wine in a decanter. The intent is to describe an extremely joyful scene wherein the poet sees wine everywhere. He is already intoxicated.

زخمی ہُوا ہے پاشنہ پائے ثبات کا   نے بھاگنے کی گوں نہ اِقامت کی تاب ہے

zaḳhmī hu'ā hai pāshna(h) pāe ṡabāt kā
ne bhāgne kī guñ na(h) iqāmat kī tāb hai (153:3; #924)

The heels of perseverance have been wounded, leaving
Neither the courage to flee nor the strength to stay.

pāshna(h): heel; *ṡabāt*: stability, perseverance; *iqāmat*: to stay; *tāb*: courage.

"Digging in heels" and "taking to heels" are the two idioms expressed here craftily. The feet of stability or perseverance are our goals, but with heels damaged, we can neither run away like a coward nor dig in to fight bravely. We are destined to fall, at best—a masterpiece of expression about the limited choices offered to man.

جاداد بادہ نوشیٔ رنداں ہے شش جہت   غافل گماں کرے ہے کہ گیتی خراب ہے

jādād-e bāda(h) noshī' rindāñ hai shash jihat
ġhāfil gumāñ kare hai kih geti ḳharāb hai (153:4; #925)

In all six directions stretches the property of wine drinkers;
The ignorant ones are paranoid that this world is a bad place.

jādād: property; *bādah*: wine; *bādah noshī*: drinking wine; *rindāñ;* the wine drinkers; *shash jihat*: in six directions, all over, the Universe; *ghāfil*: ignorant; *gumān*: doubt; *geti*: world; *ḳharāb:* bad.

The entire universe (the six directions) belongs to those who drink; those who do not drink see this world as a bad, desolate place. They are ignorant for they cannot see it through the eyes of a drinker (to whom the world appears beautiful). A remarkable philosophy is presented here, stating that reality is not important. The important thing is what we see, not what is there to see.

نظارہ کیا حریف ہو اُس برقِ حُسن کا   جوشِ بہار جلوے کو جس کے نقاب ہے

naẕẕārah kyā ḥarīf ho us barq-e ḥusn kā
josh-e bahār jalve ko jis ke niqāb hai (153:5; #926)

How can my gaze face the lightning of the beauty,
Whose true splendor is hidden behind the veil of blooming spring?

naẕẕārah: view; *josh:* zeal; *jalvah:* splendor.

How can I bear to see the dazzling display of beauty, to which the spring is merely a veil? The spring, or whatever we see, serves as a veil for the ultimate spark of truth (the Creator). Whatever dazzles us is only a veil (a façade) to the reality of the ultimate beauty, the Creator.

میں، نامُراد دل کی تسلّی کو کیا کروں   مانا کہ تیرے رُخ سے نگہ کامیاب ہے

meñ, nāmurād dil kī tasallī ko kyā karūñ
mānā kih tere ruḳh se nigah kāmyāb hai (153:6; #927)

What shall we, the defeated ones, do to console our hearts,
Given that our sight is successful in reaching your face?

nāmurād: defeated; *tasallī:* consolation; *kāmyāb*: successful.

Even though you have allowed me to have a clear look at you, this is not enough. My heart will be content only when it gets much closer to you—much, much closer, not just seeing you. Calling himself unfortunate even though he is able to see her indicates the perpetual frustration of lovers.

گزرا اسدؔ مسرتِ پیغامِ یار سے
قاصد پہ مجھ کو رشکِ سوال و جواب ہے

guzrā Asad masarrat-e paiġhām-e yār se
qāṣid pa(h) mujh ko rashk-e savāl-o-javāb hai (153:7; #928)

Asad has given up on the joy of receiving letters from the beloved;
I am envious of the messenger for exchanging the words with you.

Receiving a response from the beloved brings ultimate joy, but when I think that this means that the messenger must have engaged in conversation with the beloved, I become very envious. I am ready to give up the delight of receiving a response from the beloved so I would not feel jealous of the letter carrier. The poet knows there will be no useful response anyway and that only the messenger has benefited from the exchange.

154

دیکھنا قسمت کہ آپ اپنے پہ رشک آجائے ہے   میں اُسے دیکھوں بھلا کب مجھ سے دیکھا جائے ہے

dekhnā qismat kih āp apne pe rashk ājāe hai
maiñ use dekhūñ, bhlā kab mujh se dekhā jāe ha'i (154:1; #929)

Look at my fate that I have become envious of myself.
How would I be able to see her now that I have looked at her?

Anyone looking at her is subject to my envy, myself included. I thus keep myself deprived of the pleasure of looking at her.

ہاتھ دھو دل سے یہی گرمی گر اندیشے میں ہے   آبگینہ تندیٔ صہبا سے پگھلا جائے ہے

hāth dho dil se yahī garmī gar andeshe meñ hai
ābgina(h) tūndī' ṣehbā se pighlā jāe ha'i (154:2; #930)

Wash your hands of the heart if such is the heat of your suspicion;
The decanter is melting away with the strength of wine.

hāth dho: be ready to lose; *andeshe*: suspicion; *ābgina(h)*: drinking glass, a foil set under gems, a diamond, wine, a lover's tears, (used here to mean heart); *tūndī:* strength (stoutness)

If you continue to simmer in your suspicion, be prepared to lose your heart for the heart will consume you, like the strength (stoutness) of wine can melt away the decanter. The wine is compared to thoughts, and the heart to a decanter. If you keep thinking about life, you will lose your heart. It is better to cool your thinking. The metaphor of stoutness of wine melting the decanter is remarkable.

غیر کو یارب وہ کیونکر منعِ گستاخی کرے   گر حیا بھی اُس کو آتی ہے تو شرما جائے ہے

ġhair ko yārabb vuh kioñ kar man'-e gustāķhī kare
gar ḥayā bhī us ko ātī hai to sharmā jāe ha'i (154:3; #931)

How would she, O! Lord, tell the stranger not to take liberties with her?
For when she becomes bashful, she ends up meeker.

The stranger is teasing her, making advances towards her. The lover is asking God to tell her how to protect herself. The lover is afraid she will not be able to fend off the rival because of her timid (shy) nature. Even when the stranger embarrasses her, all she does is become sheepish, as she cannot tell him to stay away—what a painful situation.

شوق کو یہ لت کہ ہر دم نالہ کھینچے جائیے   دل کی وُہ حالت کہ دم لینے سے گھبرا جائے ہے

shauq ko yih lat kih har dam nāla(h) khinche jāi'ye
dil kī vuh ḥālat kih dam lene se ghabrā jāe ha'i (154:4; #932)

The desire is addicted to keep raising plaints all the time;
The condition of the heart is such that breathing makes it upset.

lat: addiction.

Desire is addicted to plaints; but the heart, because of its weakness, is worried about the effort needed for inhaling. The heart is dying, but desire keeps on being impatient. By separating desire from heart, the poet has created a duality.

دُور چشمِ بد تری بزمِ طرب سے، واہ واہ   نغمہ ہو جاتا ہے واں گر نالہ میرا جائے ہے

dūr chashm-e bad terī bazm-e ṯarab se, vāh vāh
nāġhma(h) ho jātā hai vāñ gar nāla(h) merā jāe ha'i (154:5; #933)

May the evil eye be kept away from your assembly of felicitations, Cheers!
My lament turns into a song upon reaching there.

In the assembly of felicitations, everything is grand and colorful. May God keep the evil eye away from this gathering! The aura of happiness at her gathering is such that even as I send a lament, it turns into a melody by the time it reaches there. If we examine the metaphor used here, the poet is saying that his laments are music to his beloved's ear.

گرچہ ہے طرزِ تغافل پردہ دارِ رازِ عشق   پر ہم ایسے کھوئے جاتے ہیں کہ وہ پا جائے ہے

garchi(h) hai ṯarz-e taġhāful pardahdār-e rāz-e ʿishq
par ham aise khoe jāte haiñ kih vuh pā jāe ha'i (154:6; #934)

Though the style of obliviousness hides the secrets of my love;
She somehow figures it out from how I appear lost.

I do not want her to know the condition of my heart, so I try to hide it. I have acquired a style of obliviousness to her when in her assembly. However, as I appear lost in myself, she quickly finds out that something is wrong. Everyone finds out the condition of my heart from my appearance, regardless of how hard I try to conceal my feelings.

اس کی بزم آرائیاں سن کر دلِ رنجور، یاں   مثلِ نقشِ مدعائے غیر بیٹھا جائے ہے

us kī bazm ārā'iyāñ sun kar dil-e ranjūr, yāñ
miṣl-e naqsh-e mudda'-e ġhair baiṭhā jāe ha'i (154:7; #935)

Hearing of the celebrations in her assembly, my saddened heart here
Keeps sinking, like the impact of the intent of the rival.

bazm ārā'iyāñ: grandeur decoration of assembly; *dil-e ranjūr:* saddened heart.

The beloved is busy celebrating and enjoying with the rival. Thinking of these celebrations, my heart sinks with sadness—the rival's false declarations of love are sinking into her heart. (Note the sinking of heart and the sinking of impressions in the beloved's heart.)

ہو کے عاشق وُہ پری رُخ اور نازک بن گیا   رنگ کُھلتا جاے ہے جتنا کہ اُڑتا جاے ہے

ho kih ʿāshiq vuh parī rukh āur nāzuk ban gayā
rang khultā jāe hai jitnā kih uṛtā jāe ha'i (154:8; #936)

Turning into a lover, that fairy-faced beloved has become more delicate;
Her complexion begins to brighten more as it takes flight.

My beloved has fallen in love and that has brought a great change in her appearance. She appears more tender and delicate while her complexion brightens more as she turns pale. Even when the beloved is in love with someone else, the lover finds her more attractive. The keen observations about the changes in the complexion of a guilty heart are remarkably presented here in a rather melancholic garb.

نقش کو اُس کے مُصوّر پر بھی کیا کیا ناز ہیں   کھینچتا ہے جس قدر اُتنا ہی کِھنچتا جاے ہے

naqsh ko us ke muṣavvir par bhī kyā kyā nāz haiñ
khīñchtā hai jis qadar utnā hī khichtā jāe ha'i (154:9; #937)

In how many ways does her painting act coy to the painter?
The more he draws her, the more she pulls away from him.

An artist is drawing her portrait, but the canvas is acting coquettish (because it now contains her image), pulling away from the artist. Similarly, as the artist—who has taken on the profession to get close to her—approaches her, she pulls away from him. (Here, in physical reality, the canvas is running away from the painter.) See also: *sīkhey haiñ mahrukhoñ ke līye ham musavvarī/ taqrīb kuchh to bahr-e mulāqāt chahiye.* We have learned to paint for the sake of those with the face of moon. /After all, an occasion is needed to meet her.

سایہ میرا مجھ سے مثلِ دُود بھاگے ہے اسد
پاس مجھ آتش بجاں کے کس سے ٹھہرا جائے ہے!

sāya(h) merā mujh se miśl-e dūd bhāge hai Asad
pās mujh ātish bajāñ ke kis se ṭhehrā jāe ha'i (154:10; #938)

My shadow is running away from me like smoke, Asad.
Who can bear to stay close to this fiery soul?

When fire burns, the smoke (an integral part of fire) runs away from it as if it could not bear the heat. My own shadow is running away from me because of my fiery nature. Note that shadow brings coolness; here the coolness is running away because of my heated disposition. Elsewhere, *Ġhālib* has talked about taking comfort in his own shadow; but here, the shadow is running away from him to seek comfort.

155

گرم فریاد رکھا شکلِ نہالی نے مجھے
تب اَمان ہجر میں دی بَردِ لیالی نے مجھے

garm-e firyād rakkhā shakl-e nihālī ne mujhe
tab amāñ hjr meñ dī bard-e liyālī ne mujhe (155:1; #939)

The gladdening images kept me adducing plaints.
That's how I sought refuge from the coldness of the night of separation.

shakl-e nihālī: gladdening image, ornamental images on bedspread; *bard-e liyālī*: coldness of nights; *amāñ*: protection, refuge.

The night of separation was too cold for me to survive. It was the visualization of the beloved that kept my heart warmed and allowed the lamentation to continue—I would have otherwise died. The warm thoughts enabled me to survive the coldness of the night of separation. Some have interpreted this verse as the lover looking at the ornamental images on the comforter of his bed, thinking of her, and thus keeping his nights warm.

نسیہ و نقدِ دو عالم کی حقیقت معلوم
لے لیا مجھ سے ، مری ہمتِ عالی نے مجھے

nasīya(h)-o-naqd-e do ʿālam kī ḥaqīqat maʿlūm
le liyā mujh se, merī himmat-e ʿālī ne mujhe (155:2; #940)

I know the reality about the currency and the credits of both worlds;
It was my great courage that kept me away from me.

nasīya(h): credit (refers to the world beyond); *naqd*: cash (meaning world); *do ʿālam*: the world and beyond (referring to this world and what is coming); *himmat*: high courage.

I know the reality about the world and the hereafter; my great courage kept me away from myself, meaning that it did not let me sell myself to either. I kept myself away from the wheeling and dealing involving cash and loans. I stayed away from those who sell this world and those who sell the hereafter (religion). Since I know the reality, I did not get involved in any dealings and was not taken in. The preaching about the world beyond does not fool the poet; those who preach the virtues of this world do not fool him either. This verse condemns all those who exploit the innocent by telling them how their virtues will be weighed in the hereafter to seek their submission in this world.

کثرت آرائیِ وحدت ہے پرستاریِ وہم
کر دیا کافر اِن اَصنامِ خیالی نے مجھے

kas̊rat ārāʾī vaḥdat hai paristārī' vahm
kar dīyā kāfir in aṣnām-e ḳhayālī ne mujhe (155:3; #941)

The superabundant signs of singularity are praying to doubts;
These fictitious idols have turned me into an infidel.

kas̊rat ārāʾī: abundance of display; *aṣnām-e ḳhayālī*: fictitious idols.

The belief that God is visible in everything around us is just fanciful imagination and creates fictitious idols. Anyone who believes in it becomes an idolater. The entire universe is God, and to say that He appears visible in everything is against the concept of singularity. When we believe that we see God everywhere, we are praying to our imagination and since there are many displays, we become a polytheist. See: "*jo dūʾī ki bū bhī hoti/ to kaheñ do chār hotā*": Had there been a whiff of duality/ I would have surely come across Him somewhere.

ہَوَسِ گُل کا تصوّر میں بھی کھٹکا نہ رہا
عجب آرام دیا بے پَر و بالی نے مجھے

havas-e gul kā taṣavvur meñ bhī khaṭkā na(h) rahā
ʿajab ārām diyā be par-o-bālī ne mujhe (155:4; #942)

The desire of flowers does not knock even in our thoughts;
Being without plumage has given me a strange sense of comfort.

par-abāl: plumage.

The desire of flowers means avarice of worldly things; the intensity of this desire is proportional to how much effort one can make. A man who can ill-afford a piece of bread is not likely to put all of his efforts behind acquiring a throne. However, in all instances, we overestimate our abilities and strive endlessly, much to our chagrin. The ability to make an effort is gone and the avarice for flowers has disappeared even in the imagination, with no suspicion of it ever returning (*khatkā*, such as a thief entering a home). This feeling brought a comfort the likes of which I had not felt before.

156

کارگاہِ ہستی میں لالہ داغ ساماں ہے
برقِ خرمنِ راحت خونِ گرمِ دہقاں ہے

ḳārgāh-e hastī meñ lālah dāġh sāmāñ hai
barq-e ḳhirman rāḥat ḳhūn-e garm-e dihqāñ hai (156:1; #943)

In the world, the assets of the tulip are its brandings;
Comforting to the peasant's toil is the lightning that strikes the crop.

ḳārgāh-e hastī: workings of existence (the world); *barq-e ḳhirman*: lightning striking the crop (See Glossary); *ḳhūn-e garm-e dihqāñ:* warm blood of peasant (peasant's toil).

In this world, the assets of the tulip are its burn spots, a display of grief. A farmer's blood warming up to toil proves to be the cause of lightning striking the crop. The thought of lightning burning the crop and thus giving comfort shows that grief is a real manifestation of existence. Lightning will not strike unless there is a crop and a crop will not come until the peasant toils. Therefore, the purpose of toil is to get the lightning to strike. Moreover, that should be comforting to peasant, for that is the ultimate goal anyway. *Ġhālib* has described the meaning of this verse in his letters; unfortunately, his description confuses us more. In this explanation, *Ġhālib* is calling the tulip flower the assembly *(dāġh sāmāñ)* containing all the secrets of existence and nonexistence. Its dark spots recognize the flower. However, this flower did not just appear—it was a result of the planting, watering, and tending by the peasant, who had to work, hard at it. Moreover, when this assembly was groomed well, destruction hit it. What *Ġhālib* means here is a theme that he has repeated elsewhere also: the destruction of things is created along with them.

غُنچہ تا شُگفتن ہا برگِ عافیت معلوم!
باوُجودِ دِل جمعی خوابِ گُل پریشاں ہے

ġhuncha(h) tā shuguftan hā barg-e ʿāfiyat maʿlūm
bāvajūd-e dil jamʿī ḳh(v)āb-e gul pareshāñ hai (156:2; #944)

The bud till it blooms has the strength of security;
Despite its collected heart, the dream of the flower is scattered.

barg: the leaf of a tree, a blade of grass, an instrument, arms, intention, aim, design end, power, strength, intellect, wealth; *ʿāfiyat*: security.

A bud before it blooms appears so contented and secure, holding petals in its control. However, this comfort lasts only until the bud turns into a flower; the petals soon begin to whither away. The apparent comfort of the bud is deceptive, for it is fearfully dreaming of its future. Things that appear calm are actually in the eye of the storm.

ہم سے رنجِ بیتابی کِس طرح اُٹھایا جاے
داغِ پُشتِ دستِ عجز، شُعلہ خَس بدنداں ہے

ham se ranj-e betābī kis ṭarḥ uṭhāyā jāe
dāġh pusht-e dast-e ʿijz, shoʿlah ḳhas badandāñ hai (156:3; #945)

How can we bear the anguish of impatience
As burn scar shows the back of its hands and the flame carries straw in its teeth?

pusht-e dast: back of hands (to express extreme regards); *ḳhas badandāñ*: holding straw in teeth (an old Hindu ritual of expressing humility).

How can I bear the pain of impatience in this world? The branding mark on my heart is showing the back of its hands to express its extreme respect, saying that it cannot tolerate more pain. The flame is carrying straw in its teeth to express humbleness that it can no longer bear the heat. The heart is begging for an end to pain. Two expressions of humility are presented: showing the back of the hand and holding straw in the teeth. Note the fragility of straw containing flame inside it; how much more flimsy can things be? Even though *Ġhālib* has used two metaphors for humbleness, it is actually the helplessness and hopelessness that is meant here.

157

اُگ رہا ہے دَر و دیوار سے سبزہ غالبؔ
ہم بیاباں میں ہیں اور گھر میں بہار آئی ہے

ug rahā hai dar-o-dīvār se sabza(h) Ġhālib
ham bayābāñ meñ haiñ āur ghar meñ bahār āī hai (157:1; #946)

The greenery is growing out of the doors and walls, *Ġhālib*.
While I am in the wilderness, spring has arrived at my home.

O! *Ġhālib*, the grass is growing all over your home as you wander in the wilderness. Your desolate and neglected home looks like spring beauty compared to the place you wander—go home. Sarcastically calling his deserted home a display of the beauty of spring, the poet refuses to accept the suggestion of returning home.

158

سادگی پر اُس کی مرجانے کی حسرت دِل میں ہے
بس نہیں چلتا کہ پھر خنجر کفِ قاتِل میں ہے

sādgī par us kī marjāne kī ḥasrat dil meñ hai
bas nahiñ chaltā kih phir k̲hanjar kaf-e qātil meñ hai (158:1; #947)

In my heart, there is a longing to give my life for her innocence;
Little I can do now that the dagger is again in the hands of the slayer.

kaf: palm.

My desperate desire to sacrifice my life because she is so innocent remains unfulfilled. Every time I express this desire, she picks up the dagger, but doing so causes her to lose her innocence, and thus the desire to have my life taken away by someone innocent remains. This is a typical contrary situation. If she does not kill me, the desire remains, but if she does, the desire remains unfulfilled for she is no longer innocent.

دیکھنا تقریر کی لذّت کہ جو اُس نے کہا
مَیں نے یہ جانا کہ گویا یہ بھی میرے دِل میں ہے

dekhnā taqrīr kī lażżat kih jo us ne kahā
meñ ne yih jānā kih goyā yih bhī mere dil meñ hai (158:2; #948)

Behold the beauty of her expression, for whatever she said,
I came to realize as if this, too, were in my heart.

Look at the beauty of her expression; whatever she says appears as if it were also in my heart. The word *goyā* (as if) is the key to the verse—as if—not that it is. A speech going straight to the heart makes a believer of you—sort of a déjà vu situation.

گرچہ ہے کس کس بُرائی سے ولے با ایں ہمہ
ذِکر میرا مجھ سے بہتر ہے کہ اُس محفل میں ہے

garchi(h) hai kis kis burā'ī se vale bā īñhama(h)
żikr merā mujh se bahtar hai kih us maḥfil meñ hai (158:3; #949)

Whereas it is with much ridicule, but at least
My discussion is better than me, for it is there in her assembly.

bā īñhama(h): with this much.

Whereas I am discussed in her assembly with every sort of ridicule, I am pleased, for if I cannot be there, at least my name is there. My discussion was more fortunate than I; at least it got in there, while I could not. To a desperate lover, it is enough that she heard my name; maybe someday, she will ask who this lunatic is, and maybe she will accept me as her lover.

بس ہُجُومِ نااُمیدی، خاک میں مل جائے گی
یہ جو اِک لذت ہماری سعئِ بے حاصل میں ہے

bas hujūm-e nāumidī, khāk meñ mil jāe gī
yih jo ik lażżat hamārī saī-e be ḥāṣil meñ hai (158:4; #950)

Stop! O! Storm of despair, it will all go to ashes;
This pleasure that I draw now from my futile efforts.

Stop! O! Storm of hopelessness, if I lose all hope, then with that will go the pleasure I draw from my futile struggles. A flicker of hope is what I want to keep alive to stay on the course of struggle, which is pleasurable, though I know it is wasteful. The poet is begging himself to leave some room of hope for himself so that he may continue with his despair of losing every day.

رنجِ رہ کیوں کھینچیے، واماندگی کو عشق ہے!
اٹھ نہیں سکتا ہمارا جو قدم، منزل میں ہے!

ranj-e rah kyoñ khinchīye, vāmāndgī ko ʿishq hai
uṭh nahiñ saktā hamārā jo qadam, manzil meñ hai (158:5; #951)

Why bear the hardships of the path as the tiredness is in love.
The step in the path to destiny cannot be lifted.

vāmāndgī: tiredness.

Why should I even bother walking when tiredness has fallen in love with my feet and thus would not let them move? "*manzil meñ*" means "in the path," whereas "*manzil pa*" means destiny; the lover wishes to stay on the path but does not necessarily seek his destiny. To lift one's feet (which I cannot because of despair) is to make an effort; I wonder why should I even bother.

جلوہ زارِ آتشِ دوزخ ہمارا دل سہی!
فتنۂ شورِ قیامت کس کی آب و گل میں ہے؟

jalvah zār-e ātish-e dozaḳh hamārā dil sahī
fitna(h)' shor-e qiyāmat kis kī āb-o-gil meñ hai (158:6; #952)

My heart may be showing leaping flames of hell,
But in whose temperament lays the source of the intensity of Doomsday?

āb-o-gil: temperament.

The beloved is telling the lover that his heart is burning like the fire of hell. The lover agrees and, in turn, asks her who has the hellish temperament to give him this condition. On Doomsday, all hell will break loose. Who will be responsible for that? That day is today.

ہے دلِ شوریدۂ غالبؔ طلسمِ پیچ و تاب
رحم کر اپنی تمنّا پر کہ کس مشکل میں ہے

hai dil-e shorida(h)' Ġhālib ṯilism-e pech-o-tāb
raḥm kar apnī tamannā par kih kis mushkil meñ hai (158:7; #953)

The frenzied heart, *Ġhālib*, is in the spell of suspicion and indecision.
Be kind to my longings for they are in a strange predicament.

shoridah': frenzied, mad; *pech-o-tāb*: suspicion and indecision.

My mad heart is under the spell of indecision: it is totally confused. Be kind to me, my beloved, if not for my sake, then for the sake of taking my longing out of this predicament. What is the predicament? Will she, or will she not?

159

دِل سے تری نگاہ جگر تک اُتر گئی　　دونوں کو اِک ادا میں رضامند کر گئی

dil se terī nigāh jigar tak utar ga'ī
donoñ ko ik adā meñ rażāmand kar ga'ī (159:1; #954)

From the heart to the liver, your glance has pierced through;
It has made both agreeable with just one coquettish move.

Your glances, the arrows of your eyes, wounded both my liver and my heart, and this has made me happy. It all happened with just one of your coquettish moves. Now my heart has enough to lament about for the rest of my life. Since my liver is also gone, there is no courage left to run away from your bondage. (The heart is supposed to be home to the emotions, and the liver to reasoning, or the courage to say no.)

شق ہو گیا ہے سینہ خوشا لذتِ فراغ　　تکلیفِ پردہ داریٔ زخمِ جگر گئی

shaq ho gayā hai sīna(h), k͟hushā lażżat-e firāġh
taklīf-e parda(h) dārī' zak͟hm-e jigar ga'ī (159:2; #955)

Rent asunder is my chest and now the pleasures of carefree living abound.
Gone at last is the trouble of hiding the wounds of the heart.

shaq: rent asunder; *firāġh*: carefree.

Extreme sorrow has ripped my chest open and now the wounds of my liver are exposed. No longer is there any need for me to hide these wounds. This has given me great pleasure, as I no longer have to worry about veiling my wounds.

وہ بادۂ شبانہ کی سرمستیاں کہاں　　اُٹھیے بس اب کہ لذتِ خوابِ سحر گئی

vuh bādah' shabāna(h) kī sar mastīyāñ kahāñ
uṭhiye bas ab kih lażżat-e ḳh(v)āb saḥar ga'ī (159:3; #956)

Where have those celebrations of nighttime drinking gone?
Get up and move on, as the pleasures of the morning sleep are gone.

Drinking all night and then falling asleep in the morning hours was the ultimate ecstasy for drinkers. With the nightlong drinking gone, the pleasures of morning sleep are gone, too. It is time to leave the tavern. The poet is telling himself to "get up;" he hasn't been told by anyone to leave. "Let's move on and find our happiness elsewhere." "Get up" is often interpreted as waking up from dreams also, but that is not what is meant here. In addition, the end of morning sleep is not late life, as interpreted by some.

اُڑتی پھرے ہے خاک مری کوئے یار میں　　بارے اب اے ہوا! ہوسِ بال و پر گئی

uṛtī phire hai ḳhāk merī kūe yār meñ
bāre ab ai havā! havas-e bāl-o-par ga'ī (159:4; #957)

My ashes keep blowing over in the alley of beloved;
At least, now O! Breeze, the desire for wings and feathers is gone.

bāre: in brief, at least.

My ashes are blowing in the alley of the beloved, which was my ultimate goal. Now all of my desires have been satisfied, O! Breeze, I no longer worry about my feathers (my well-being), as I no longer have to fly anywhere. I no longer need to worry about my existence, having been reduced to ashes that have reached their destiny—her alley.

دیکھو تو دلفریبیِ اندازِ نقشِ پا موجِ خرامِ یار بھی کیا گل کتر گئی

dekho to dilfarebī' andāz-e naqsh-e pā
mauj-e ḳhirām-e yār bhī kyā gul katar ga'ī (159:5; #958)

Look at the heart-stealing style of her footprints;
How a wave of beloved's gait has trimmed the flowers away.

ḳhirām: gait; *gul katar ga'ī:* trimmed flowers away (being a trouble maker or creating a tumult).

Every step she takes has the style that steals my heart. As she is walking in the garden, it appears as if a wave is moving, trimming away the flowers. Two meanings are possible here. First, she is flirting with the flowers as she walks; and second, her walk is creating a tumult among the lovers. Perhaps both.

ہر بُو الہوس نے حُسن پرستی شعار کی اب آبروئے شیوۂ اہلِ نظر گئی

har bulhavas ne ḥusn parastī shi'ār kī
ab ābrūe shiva(h)' ahl-e naẓar ga'ī (159:6; #959)

Every sensual one has now taken to worshipping beauty;
Now the respect for the manner of those with true passion is gone.

bulhavas: sensual, inquisite, a fool; *shiva(h)*: manner, profession; *ahl-e naẓar*: those with vision or passion, lovers

With false lovers everywhere, showing how they worship beauty, the honor code of true lovers means little. There is no appreciation left for true lovers. Truth no longer prevails in this world, is the message given here. This applies not only to lovers but to all other affairs of life as well.

نظّارے نے بھی کام کیا واں نقاب کا   مستی سے ہر نگہ ترے رُخ پر بکھر گئی

nazzāre ne bhī kām kīyā vāñ niqāb kā
mastī se har nigah tere ruḳh par bikhar ga'ī (159:7; #960)

The display of the beloved worked just like a veil;
With intoxication, every glance reaching your face got scattered.

The glances of lovers reaching your face were scattered and did not reach close enough to see your beauty, such was the dazzle of your beauty. As glances fell all at the same time, it appeared as if a veil had been knitted around your face, hiding your face; thus, your display of beauty itself proved to be a veil. When we got to see you, we were so stunned that we could not see you. The sight is also called a "line of sight" or a "wire" of vision. A physical situation, wherein all these "wires" getting to her face are knitting a mesh to make a veil, is also implied here. The ray of sight (as *Ġhālib* often talks about) hitting the face of the beloved gets deflected (more appropriately refracted) making the face invisible since the ray of light must return back to the eye for the image to appear. The scattering or refraction was caused by the brilliance of her face.

فردا و دِی کا تفرقہ یک بار مِٹ گیا   کل تم گئے کہ ہم پہ قیامت گزر گئی

firdā-o-dī kā tafriqah yak bār miṭ gayā
kal tum ga'e kih ham pe qiyāmat guzar ga'ī (159:8; #961)

The distinction between yesterday and tomorrow is erased now;
As you left yesterday, it was as if the Doomsday had passed over me.

firdā-o-dī: tomorrow and yesterday; *tafriqah*: distinction.

On Doomsday, the past and future will merge (time will come to a halt). As you left me yesterday, I lost all sense of today and tomorrow—

making your passing away the passing of Doomsday. It was terrible to see you leave. (*Ġhālib* is perhaps talking about the untimely death of the singing girl with whom he was in love.)

مارا زمانے نے اسد اللہ خاں تمہیں
وہ ولولے کہاں وہ جوانی کدھر گئی

mārā zamāne ne Asad ullah ḳhāñ tumheñ
vuh valvale kahāñ vuh javānī kidhar ga'ī (159:9; #962)

The times have taken a toll on you, *Asad Ullah Ḳhān*.
Where is your fervent vigour and where has your youth gone?

zamāna(h): time (not the moments but an era), world, fortune, revolutions of heaven.

The time has taken a toll on you, *Ġhālib*, as you have lost your vigor and youth. Writing the whole name emphasizes the meaning of his name and the aura of personality, now gone. Asad means lion and *Ḳhān* means a leader.

160

تسکیں کو ہم نہ روئیں جو ذوقِ نظر ملے
حورانِ خلد میں تری صورت مگر ملے

taskiñ ko ham na(h) ro'eñ jo żauq-e naẓar mile
ḥūrān-e ḳhuld meñ terī ṣurat magar mile (160:1; #963)

We would not cry for relief, if we get to satisfy our yen for a glance
In the nymphs of paradise a semblance of yours.

ḳhuld: Paradise.

I can be content if I see things that bring pleasure to my eyes. For example, in paradise, among the *houris*, if I see someone as beautiful as you, I will be happy. But that seems remote. Leaving all the pleasures of paradise, the poet insists only on one thing—a glimpse of her. The poet is not hoping to find someone as beautiful as the beloved, but *the* beloved.

اپنی گلی میں مجھ کو نہ کر دفن بعدِ قتل
میرے پتے سے خلق کو کیوں تیرا گھر ملے

apnī galī meñ mujh ko na(h) kar dafn ba'd-e qatl
mere pate se ḳhalq ko kioñ terā ghar mile (160:2; #964)

Bury me not in your alley after murdering me.
For why should the world find your home through my address?

ḳhalq: the world.

From the location of my grave, people will be able to find out who killed me and that will bring embarrassment to you. But those who will come to visit my grave will also come to know of your abode and thus they may try to become friendly with you. This will create a situation of jealousy for me (even though I am dead). It is, therefore, better that you bury me away from your alley where you killed me. Note that the lover's ultimate desire is to be buried in the beloved's alley, but the passion of jealousy is so strong that the lover is willing to let it go.

ساقی گری کی شرم کرو آج، ورنہ ہم
ہر شب پیا ہی کرتے ہیں مے، جس قدر ملے

sāqī garī kī sharm karo āj, varna(h) ham
har shab piyā hī karte haiñ mai, jis qadar mile (160:3; #965)

Be respectful of your bartending today, because we
Keep drinking, regardless of how much more we can get, every night.

The beloved has decided to be the cupbearer and is serving wine hesitantly. The lover wants her to give more and is telling her that every night he drinks all he can get. To give someone less than what they are used to, is a sign of cheapness on the part of the host. The beloved is challenged to give more of her kindness and not be miserly. He is also making it clear that he can take whatever is doled out to him. See: *dete haiñ bāda(h) ẓarf-e qadah kh(v)ār dekh kar.* The wine is given to drinkers based on their ability to imbibe.

تجھ سے تو کچھ کلام نہیں لیکن اے ندیم
میرا سلام کہیو اگر نامہ بر ملے

tujh se to kuchh kalām nahiñ lekin ai nadīm
merā salām kahīyo agar namah bar mile (160:4; #966)

There is no argument with you, but O! Friend,
Give my greetings to the messenger, if you come across him.

Someone referred by a friend took the lover's letter to the beloved, but before he could give the letter to her, he, too, fell in love with her. He ran to the wilderness instead of delivering the letter. Now the lover has met his friend and a discussion begins. The lover is saying that he has no argument with the friend that he sent someone so weak at heart. Anyone who would have gone to her home would have reached the same destiny. The assurance of the character of the one recommended by the friend is nothing to be embarrassed about. However, if you come across your friend, do extend my greetings to him (expressed sarcastically) and ask whatever happened to all the promises you made. And, by the way, where is my letter? *Ġhālib*'s wit shows well here.

تم کو بھی ہم دکھائیں کہ مجنوں نے کیا کیا
فرصت کشاکشِ غمِ پنہاں سے گر ملے

tum ko bhī ham dikhā'eñ kih majnūñ ne kyā kīyā
furṣat kashākash-e ġham-e pinhāñ se gar mile (160:5; #967)

To you, too, we shall show what *Majnūn* did
If we ever get a reprieve from the struggles of our hidden sorrows.

If we ever get a reprieve from our hidden sorrows, we will show you how *Majnūn* used to express his lunacy of love—by running to the wilderness and tearing his clothes. We cannot do the same as our love is a secret in our heart and we do not want the whole world to know, lest it bring embarrassment to the beloved. *Majnūn* had declared his love for *Lailā* openly, we are hiding our love. There is also an air of self-confidence that we too can do what real lovers do, only if we get a break from our daily routines. Saying that we will show it to you too implies that the lover has done it before and shown his talent to others before.

لازم نہیں کہ خضر کی ہم پیروی کریں
جانا کہ اک بزرگ ہمیں ہم سفر ملے

lāzim nahiñ kih Ḳhiẓr kī ham pairavī kareñ
jānā kih ik buzurg hameñ hamsafar mile (160:6; #968)

It is not necessary that we follow the footsteps of *Ḳhiẓr*;
We just know him as the honorable elderly fellow traveler we had met.

Ḳhiẓr lives forever (as the legend goes) and shows the path to those who are lost. Why should I care for *Ḳhiẓr*, the poet questions, if I met him? I'll just assume that we met an honorable elderly person. I cannot be impressed by his manners, for we know where we are going and do not need anyone to tell us which direction to go. Of course, being an elderly man, he will act as a preacher, telling us not to follow the path to our destruction. However, does he not know that our destiny has been fixed?

اے ساکنانِ کوچۂ دلدار! دیکھنا
تم کو کہیں جو غالبِ آشفتہ سر ملے

ai sākinān-e kūcha(h)' dildār! dekhnā
tum ko kahiñ jo Ġhālib-e āshufta(h) sar mile (160:7; #969)

Look after him, O! Fellow dwellers of the alley of the beloved,
Should you ever come across *Ġhālib*, the lunatic, anywhere.

Fellow lovers, if you come across *Ġhālib*, the lunatic, look after him. Ask him how is he doing? Take care of him. A fraternal order of lovers is requested to be in action here.

161

کوئی دِن گر زِندگانی اَور ہے
اپنے جی میں ہم نے ٹھانی اَور ہے

ko'ī din gar zindagānī āur hai
apne jī meñ ham ne ṭhānī āur hai (161:1; #970)

For a few more days, if we are to live,
In my heart, I have made some other resolutions besides.

If I have more living to do, I have set my heart on doing some other things. The poet is not telling what it is. It is certainly different from what he has been doing so far. The resolve he has made appears challenging as if he is ready to show the world that he is capable of doing something bigger. A threat is apparent here. A challenge is imminent! This verse typifies a style of *Ġhālib* where he leaves the reader wondering.

آتشِ دوزخ میں یہ گرمی کہاں
سوزِ غم ہائے نِہانی اَور ہے

ātish-e dozaḳh meñ yih garmī kahāñ
soz-e ġham hā'i nehānī āur hai (161:2 #971)

Where is such heat in the fire of hell,
The burning of hidden sorrow is something else.

The searing flames of fiery hell are agonizing, but by far, much less agonizing than the heat of secret anguish. Hell does not compare to what is going on inside my heart. Hell's heat is compared to heart's anguish, not otherwise.

بارہا دیکھی ہیں اُن کی رنجشیں
پر کچھ اب کی، سرگرانی اَور ہے

bārhā dekhī haiñ un kī ranjisheñ
par kuchh ab kī, sargarānī āur hai (161:3; #972)

Times over, we have seen her vexations,
But this time around, the anger is something else.

The beloved has become angry with me frequently and I have lived through her many vexations; but this time, she is *really* upset. In reality, this time is no different from all other previous incidents. However, to a paranoid lover, every time the beloved gets upset, it appears to be something new and unusually eventful. The lover is hoping that this time she will unleash her tyranny on him like never before.

دے کے خط مُنہ دیکھتا ہے نامہ بر
کچھ تو پیغامِ زبانی اَور ہے

de ke ḳhaṯ muñh dekhtā hai nāma(h) bar
kuchh to paeġhām-e zabānī aur hai (161:4; #973)

Having handed the letter over to me, the letter carrier is looking at my face
As if there is some additional verbal message as well?

The messenger has brought back the answer from the beloved and after giving this to the lover; he looks at him as if he wants to tell him something. Apparently, the beloved had become upset and told the messenger to convey a nasty message.

قاطعِ اعمار ہیں اکثر نجوم
وہ بلائے آسمانی اور ہے

qāta`-e ā'mār haiñ akṡar nujūm
vuh balāe āsmānī āur hai (161:5; #974)

Frequently the stars cut our lives short,
But that heavenly calamity is something else.

qāta`: cutting; *ā'mār:* lives; *nujūm:* stars.

The revolution of stars determines the measure of time, as if their movement is cutting our lives short. This eventually leads to death, the ultimate calamity. However, when we look at our beloved, we see that this heavenly calamity is much harsher and crueler in cutting our lives even shorter. The sorrow of love and the berating we endure every day is crueler than what the movements of stars inflict on us.

ہو چکیں غالبؔ بلائیں سب تمام
ایک مرگِ ناگہانی اور ہے

ho chukiñ Ġhālib balāeñ sab tamām
ek marg-e nāgahānī āur hai (161:6; #975)

Having been through all calamities, *Ġhālib*,
A death, unplanned, remains the last one.

balāeñ: calamities; *marg-e nāgahānī:* unexpected death.

I have lived through all disasters and misfortunes. There remains just one, my death, but that is something that will happen suddenly and at an unexpected time. Having survived so much in life, the poet has become very pessimistic. He welcomes the event that will relieve pain; unfortunately, that is something he must wait for.

162

کوئی اُمّید بر نہیں آتی   کوئی صُورت نظر نہیں آتی

ko'ī ummīd bar nahiñ āti
ko'ī ṣurat naẕar nahiñ āti (162:1; #976)

No hope ever comes to fruition;
No way out can I see anymore.

Showing ultimate pessimism, the poet complains that since none of his hopes have ever come to fruition, how can he see his way to resolve any of his predicaments? When nothing ever works out, why hope that something will magically work?

موت کا ایک دِن مُعیّن ہے   نیند کیوں رات بھر نہیں آتی

maut kạ aik din mo'iyan hai
nīnd kioñ rāt bhar nahiñ āti (162:2; #977)

A day has been fixed for death,
So why can I not then sleep all night?

mo'iyan: fixed.

When we know that we will die on a fixed day, as written in our destiny, then why do we lose sleep over it? Apparently, sleep is also like death that will come to us at its fixed time, but unpredictably. A remarkable observation of human behavior is made here. We worry about the future and not knowing what will happen, we continue to worry about it. We do not always wait to reach a bridge before we cross it.

آگے آتی تھی حالِ دل پہ ہنسی   اب کسی بات پر نہیں آتی

āge ātī thī ḥāl-e dil pa(h) hansī
ab kisī bāt par nahiñ ātī (162:3; #978)

Once I used to laugh at the condition of my heart;
Now, nothing makes me laugh anymore.

I used to laugh at myself, and this was of great solace to me. Now, things are so bad that I have lost my sense of humor altogether. In the beginning, I used to laugh at my follies—my foolishness—but soon things became serious. As I lost my heart and soul to my beloved, a state of melancholy took over my feelings. It is too difficult to laugh now.

جانتا ہوں ثوابِ طاعت و زہد   پر طبیعت اِدھر نہیں آتی

jāntā hūñ ṡavāb-e ṯā'ṯ-o-zohad
par tabī'at idhar nahiñ ātī (162:4; #979)

I know well the rewards of praying and piety,
But somehow I do not feel inclined towards them.

ṯā'ṯ-o-zohad: praying and piety; *ṡavāb*: heavenly rewards.

Yes, I know the rewards of being pious and offering prayers, but what good is it to follow these precepts when your heart is not in it? This is one of the pivotal verses where *Ġhālib* speaks openly of his religious belief. *Ġhālib* did not believe in rituals, and he considered all religions ritualistic. Piety has its rewards, but I want my reward now, not in the afterlife.

ہے کچھ ایسی ہی بات جو چُپ ہُوں   ورنہ کیا بات کر نہیں آتی

hai kuchh aesī hī bāt jo chup hūñ
varna(h) kyā bāt kar nahiñ ātī (162:5; #980)

Yes, there is some thing that is keeping me quiet
Or else, do I not know how to talk?

Why is the lover quiet? One can conjecture many things, ranging from fear of exposing his feelings to the reproach of the beloved. He claims that he knows how to talk, but something is keeping him from doing so. We may use our imagination to guess.

کیوں نہ چیخوں کہ یاد کرتے ہیں   میری آواز گر نہیں آتی

kioñ na(h) chīḳhūñ kih yād karte haiñ
merī āvāz gar nahiñ ātī (162:6; #981)

Why would I not scream? She calls out for me
Only when she does not hear my voice.

I should continue to send my plaints because as soon as I stop, she becomes concerned and asks what has happened to the lunatic. She wants to make sure I am not dead, for that will take away her pleasure of hearing my laments.

داغِ دل گر نظر نہیں آتا   بُو بھی اے چارہ گر نہیں آتی

dāġh-e dil gar naẓar nahiñ ātā
bū bhī ai chārahgar nahiñ ātī (162:7; #982)

If the burn scar of my heart is not visible,
Does the smell of it not get to you either, O! Savior?

naẓar: view; *dil*: heart; *dāġh*: scar; *chāra(h)*: remedy; *bū*: smell.

O' Savior, If you cannot see the burn scar of my heart, does it mean you cannot smell its charred scent? Your ignorance and bias may shield your vision, but how can it block the smell of my burning heart? How can you be a savior with such incapacities?

ہم وہاں ہیں جہاں سے ہم کو بھی   کچھ ہماری خبر نہیں آتی

ham vahāñ haiñ jahāñ se ham ko bhī
kuchh hamārī ḳhabar nahiñ ātī (162:8; #983)

I have reached a place from where,
No news of mine ever gets back to me.

We are in a state of devotion, where we have lost ourselves and are thus unable to tell where we have reached or where we have gone. It is like walking absent-mindedly, not knowing how far or in which direction one has gone.

مرتے ہیں آرزو میں مرنے کی   موت آتی ہے پر نہیں آتی

marte haiñ ārzū meñ marne kī
maut ātī hai par nahiñ ātī (162:9; #984)

Offering life in constant hope for death;
Death comes, but still it does not come.

Desperate with life, my only desire is to die. I am dying for it, but like so many other lost desires, death also does not come to me when I need it. What kind of life is worse than death? Living beyond death. I die every day from lost desire; but the desire that will end it all—death—does not come.

کعبے کس منہ سے جاؤگے غالب
شرم تم کو مگر نہیں آتی

ka'abe kis muñh se jāo ge Ġhālib
sharm tum ko magar nahiñ ātī (162:10; #985)

With what face would you go to *Ka'be, Ġhālib*?
Do you not feel ashamed, after all?

Your whole life was spent in sin. Contemplating a pilgrimage to *Ka'bā* must make you feel ashamed because it shows your hypocrisy.

163

دلِ ناداں تجھے ہوا کیا ہے   آخر اس درد کی دوا کیا ہے

dil-e nādāñ tujhe hu'ā kyā hai
āḳhir is dard kī davā kyā hai (163:1; #986)

What is ailing thee, my simpleton heart?
What is the remedy for your pain, eventually?

The tone in the first line is critical of the self; the poet is rebuking himself. What is the matter with you? Why are you in this pathetic condition? Can there be any cure for the pain of love? It is supposed to be untreatable. The lover has taken to crazy acts to relieve his pain, but he should know that it is all in vain.

ہم ہیں مشتاق اور وہ بیزار   یا الٰہی یہ ماجرا کیا ہے

ham haiñ mushtāq aur vuh bezār
yā ilāhī yih mājarā kyā hai (163:2; #987)

I am ardent and she is disgusted;
O! My Lord, what is happening here?

mushtāq: ardent, intent; *mājarā:* an accident, event, occurrence, circumstances, adventure, thing past, state.

The lover is ardently telling her the condition of his heart. All the while, the beloved is showing signs of disgust; she is not interested in listening. This situation perplexes the lover and he asks why this is happening. He expects the beloved to at least listen to him and then react. This is the dilemma of a novice lover who does not know the rules. There is innocence in asking the Lord about something that he would eventually come to know on his own.

میں بھی مُنہ میں زبان رکھتا ہوں   کاش پُوچھو کہ مُدّعا کیا ہے

maiñ bhī muñh meñ zabān rakhtā hūñ
kāsh pūchho kih mudduʿā kyā hai (163:3; #988)

I too, keep a tongue in my mouth;
I wish you would ask me what my desires are.

kāsh: wish; *mudduʿā:* desire, goal.

The beloved is ignoring the lover as others continue to tell their stories to her. After waiting a while the lover says that he, too, has a tongue in his mouth and he, too, can speak. He is hoping that she will ask him to tell his desires as well. He also knows that all other stories will pale in comparison.

جب کہ تجھ بن نہیں کوئی موجود   ق   پھر یہ ہنگامہ اَے خُدا کیا ہے

jab kih tujh bin nahiñ ko'ī maujūd
phir yih hangāmah ai ḳhudā kyā hai (163:4; #989)

When nothing exists here without You!
Then what is all this tumult about, O Lord?

So many tumultuous things: the beauty of the beloved, the blooming of flowers, and the changing of seasons. All keep man wondering at the mystery of existence. When nothing exists sans You, then why are these things created to prove Your existence. (This verse describes typically *Ġhālib*'s philosophy of the Grand Order. A question that he asks often is, Why was it necessary to create the Universe, is the theme of the first verse of *Ġhālib*'s collection of *Urdū ġhazals*.)

یہ پری چہرہ لوگ کیسے ہیں   غمزہ و عشوہ و ادا کیا ہے

yih parī chahra(h) log kaese haiñ
ġhamza(h)-o-ʿishva(h)-o-adā kyā hai (163:5; #990)

What kind of people are these fairy-faced beloveds?
What is all this winking, ogling, and coquetry?

The author is pointing to the fairy-faced (rather beguiling) beloveds who are showing such coquetry. In the first line, he asks about the character of these "people," and then asks why there is all this commotion of coquetry and breaking of hearts.

شکنِ زُلفِ عنبریں کیوں ہے   نگہِ چشمِ سُرمہ سا کیا ہے

shikan-e zulf-e 'añbariñ kioñ hai
nigah-e chashm-e surmah sā kyā hai (163:6; #991)

Why are the curls of her tresses smelling of amber?
What is the purpose of those antimony-blackened eyes?

Continuing with the previous verse, the poet goes on to describe the curls in the tresses and how they smell; the antimony-blackened eyes are matched with the curls (dark) of tresses.

سبزہ و گُل کہاں سے آئے ہیں   ابر کیا چیز ہے، ہوا کیا ہے

sabza(h)-o-gul kahāñ se āe haiñ
abr kyā chīz hai, havā kyā hai (163:7; #992)

From where have the flowers and greenery come?
What are the clouds made up of? What is the substance of air?

Expressing great curiosity, the poet asks from where the greenery, clouds, and air have come. Note that in the second line, the question raised is,"What is a cloud?" and "What is air?" meaning that the whereabouts of these things are known, but what constitutes them is questioned here.

ہم کو اُن سے وفا کی ہے اُمّید   جو نہیں جانتے وفا کیا ہے

ham ko un se vafā kī hai ʿumid
jo nahiñ jānte vafā kyā hai (163:8; #993)

I am hopeful for faithfulness from her,
Who does not even know what faithfulness is.

How foolish of me to expect faithfulness from a beloved who does not know the meaning of faithfulness. That is the more common interpretation. However, given the optimistic nature of *Ġhālib*, a more appropriate interpretation would be to place emphasis on "I am hopeful" for she still does not know the meaning of faithfulness. Once she understands the meaning, she will appreciate my efforts and come to me. In this optimism resides a great deal of joy; in this optimism is displayed a great deal of *Ġhālib*.

ہاں بھلا کر ترا بھلا ہوگا   اور درویش کی صدا کیا ہے

hāñ bhlā kar terā bhlā hogā
aur darvesh kī ṣadā kyā hai (163:9; #994)

Yes! Do good deeds to get good deeds in return;
Or what else is the call of a dervish?

A *dervish*, calling for a common happening: whatever you want from people, give the same to them. More commonly: do unto others, as you would have them do unto you.

جان تم پر نثار کرتا ہوں   میں نہیں جانتا دعا کیا ہے

jān tum par niṡār kartā hūñ
maiñ nahīñ jāntā duʿā kyā hai (163:10; #995)

I offer my life to you;
I know not what is the prayer of blessing.

Wishing you well in my prayers is a small thing compared to what I am willing to do for you—give my life. How else can I show you the sincerity of my prayers?

مَیں نے مانا کہ کچھ نہیں غالبؔ
مُفت ہاتھ آے تو بُرا کیا ہے

maiñ ne mānā kih kuchh nahiñ Ġhālib
muft hāth āe to burā kyā hai (163:11; #996)

I acknowledge that it is not much of anything, *Ġhālib*;
But it is not bad if you get it free.

I understand that I am too insignificant to be noticed by you, let alone getting the honor of being your slave. Coercing the beloved, the lover is saying that having a slave free is not all that bad and through this argument, he is hoping to reach his goal. There is another mischievous meaning hidden here, wherein *Ġhālib* says that though the beloved is not very attractive, if you get to sleep with her for free, what's wrong with that?

164

کہتے تو ہو تم سب کہ بُتِ غالیہ مو آئے   یک مرتبہ گھبرا کے کہو کوئی کہ وہ آئے

kahte to ho tum sab kih but-e ġhāliya(h) mū āe
yak martaba(h) ghabrā ke kaho koʼī kih vuh āe (164:1; #997)

You are all telling me that the idol whose tresses exude perfume is coming.
Just for once, say it shockingly that she has arrived!

ġhāliya(h): compounded perfume; *mū:* hair.

The lover is dying and friends around him console him by saying that the beloved is coming—the beloved, whose tresses are perfumed. The lover finds this difficult to believe. He tells them that he will not believe that she is coming until he sees the look of shock on their faces. The poet is pointing to a very common occurrence: when we see someone important, we are shocked and do not believe we are seeing that person. The connection to perfumed tresses is given here to denote the practice of using a strong aromatic odor to bring people out of their loss of consciousness. The friends want to remind the lover of this perfume to keep him conscious.

ہوں کشمکشِ نزع میں ہاں جذبِ محبت   کچھ کہہ نہ سکوں پر وہ مرے پوچھنے کو آئے

hūñ kash-ma-kash-e nazaʻ meñ hāñ jażb-e maḥubbat
kuchh keh na(h) sakūñ par vuh mere pūchne ko āe (164:2; #998)

In the struggling moment of death, Yes! O! Expression of love!
Though not being able to say much, I wish she would come asking for me.

naza': moment of death.

The moment of death is imminent and I am unable to speak. The only thing I can hope for is that my love will attract her and that she will come to see me. The only hope left is that the intense feeling of my love will somehow miraculously turn into an effective call.

ہے صاعقہ و شعلہ و سیماب کا عالم　　آنا ہی سمجھ میں مری آتا نہیں گو آئے

hai ṣā'eqah-o-sho'lah-o-simāb kā 'ālam
ānā hī samajh meñ merī ātā nahiñ go āe (164:3; #999)

'Tis like the lightning striking and the flames of mercury leaping.
I do not understand the reason why we came, though we did.

ṣā'eqah: falling lightning; *simāb*: mercury.

The poet paints a scene of lightning and leaping flames of mercury that creates chaotic tumult all around. This describes how we spend the brief span of our lives on this planet. He then goes on to express his inability to understand why we come into the world when all we are to do here is suffer through a few unbearable moments of living. Why have we come to this planet? Some have interpreted this verse quite differently by denoting "coming" to mean the arrival of the beloved. Her short stay is the brief moment of unbearable tumult, and the second line (changing "we" to "she") asks why it was necessary for her to come. However, the latter explanation is rather weak.

ظاہر ہے کہ گھبرا کے نہ بھاگیں گے نکیرین　　ہاں منہ سے مگر بادۂ دوشینہ کی بو آئے

ẓāhir hai kih ghabrā ke na(h) bhāgeñ ge nakīriñ
hāñ muñh se magar bādah' doshinah kī bū āe (164:4; #1000)

Obviously, wouldn't the angels flee in disgust
If the smell of last night's wine came from my mouth.

nakīriñ: the two angels, *munkir and nakīr,* who would come to question our deeds in the grave upon death; *bād'ah-e doshinah*: the wine taken the night before.

The legend goes that the two angels, *munkir* and *nakīr* (hence called together *nakīriñ*), come to question the dead in their graves and make an account of good deeds and sins. The poet is suggesting that since he had been drinking the night before his death, his mouth will inevitably smell of wine. The angels will find this very repulsive and run away. He is hoping, therefore, that there will be no accounting for him; his drinking will save him. This is an exquisite example of *Ġhālib*'s wit.

جلاد سے ڈرتے ہیں نہ واعظ سے جھگڑتے　　ہم سمجھے ہوئے ہیں اُسے، جس بھیس میں جو آئے

jallad se ḍarte haiñ na(h) vā'iẓ se jhagaṛte
ham samjhe hu'e haiñ use, jis bhes meñ jo āe (164:5; #1001)

Neither afraid of the hangman, nor do I fight with the preacher. We have understood them well; whosoever comes, in whatsoever disguise.

bhes: disguise; *jallād*: hangman; *vā'iẓ*: preacher.

The hangman, representing the punishment of the corporeal world and the preacher, representing the punishment in the hereafter, are just two disguises for people who cannot deceive me into understanding the ultimate reality. I do not fight or argue with them, for it is useless. I know the ultimate reality.

ہاں اہلِ طلب! کون سنے طعنۂ نایافت　　دیکھا کہ وہ ملتا نہیں، اپنے ہی کو کھو آئے

hāñ ahl-e ṭalab! kaun sune tā'na(h)' nāyāfit
dekhā kih vuh miltā nahīñ, apne hī ko kho āe (164:6; #1002)

O! You seeker of truth! Who wants to hear the taunts of failure? When I saw I could not find Him, I moved on to lose myself.

nāyāfit: not being able to achieve.

Addressing himself as the seeker, there are two options: go to the reality that wants us to reach God, or go to the one that makes us extinct (in the *Sufi* tradition). The third option—continuing to live without achieving—is not acceptable because that would draw taunts (taunts for failing, which would be unbearable). The reason people would taunt is because the poet has declared himself as the seeker of truth. He must, do something about it, choosing from the limited options available. He just does not want to be labeled as a hypocrite.

اپنا نہیں وہ شیوہ کہ آرام سے بیٹھیں　　اُس در پہ نہیں بار تو کعبے ہی کو ہو آئے

apnā nahiñ vuh shevah kih ārām se beṭheñ
us dar pa(h) nahiñ bār to kā'be hī ko ho āe (164:7; #1003)

It is not in my style to rest, sitting comfortably;
Not getting access to His door, I just went on to visit *Kā'bā*.

It is not my style to be complacent. If knocking on the doors of the Lord proves a futile exercise, I will not give up. Instead, I will go visit *Kā'bā*, the symbolic house of the Lord. Three things need to be emphasized here. First, the goal was to visit God (to get to know Him). Secondly, *Kā'bā* is merely a symbol of God and has no other significance. Third, the desire to reach God was incessant and failure to get there did not bring any discouragement. Note that a visit to *Kā'bā* is a major event for the believers, but it is just a formality for *Ġhālib*.

کی ہمنفسوں نے اثرِ گریہ میں تقریر　　اچھے رہے آپ اُس سے مگر مجھ کو ڈبو آئے

kī hamnafasoñ ne aṡar-e giryah meñ taqrīr
achhe rahe āp us se magar mujh ko dubo āe (164:8; #1004)

My colleagues made a plea to make my weeping more effective.
They remained in her good books, but they surely drowned me.

My well-wishers made a plea to my beloved, encouraging her to recognize my crying and pathetic condition. This turned out to be futile, as she did not budge. However, having told her of my pathetic condition, my friends degraded me in front of her, causing me to lose my self-respect while they remained in her good books. This verse points to the deceptive nature of friends. Whereas they had appeared to be kind, they actually wanted to make it worse for me. The delicate connection comes from "weeping" which is supposed to inundate, and having "sunk" the lover, meaning that they destroyed him.

اُس انجمنِ ناز کی کیا بات ہے غالبؔ
ہم بھی گئے واں اور تری تقدیر کو رو آئے

us anjuman-e nāz kī kyā bāt hai Ġhālib
ham bhī ga'e vāñ aur terī taqdīr ko ro āe (164:9; #1005)

What to say about the assembly of her coquetry, *Ġhālib*?
We too went there and cried your fate out.

In this verse, *Ġhālib*'s friends are telling him about the assembly of the beloved. In the first line, they are saying what an outstanding assembly it was, apparently to make *Ġhālib* feel bad. In the second line, they are saying that they cried his fate out there, meaning they lamented his misfortune for not being there. Acting as friends, they talked about him to the beloved, though it was not a befitting occasion. They actually tried to spoil the aura of her dazzling assembly by bringing up his name.

165

پھر کچھ اِک دل کو بے قراری ہے   سینہ جُویاے زخمِ کاری ہے

phir kuchh ik dil ko be qarārī hai
sīna(h) jūyā-e zaḳhm-e kārī hai (165:1; #1006)

Then again there is restlessness in a heart,
And the chest is seeking a deeper wound.

jūyā: seeking.

Having been through the restlessness of love and having wounded my heart, I am ready again. Either I have not learned my lesson well or I am a masochist. In either case, I am ready to face another beloved. Calling his heart, "a heart," signifies a casual mention. Some have interpreted it as seeking a repeat tyranny for the beloved; however, the idea of a new beloved and the tone of masochism are pronounced.

پھر جگر کھودنے لگا ناخُن   آمدِ فصلِ لالہ کاری ہے

phir jigar khodne lagā nāḳhūn
āmad-e fiṣl-e lālah kārī hai (165:2; #1007)

Then again, nails have begun digging into liver
'Tis the arrival of the season of tulip-blooming.

The spring season, with tulips blooming, is here, and to match the display of red flowers, my nails have begun biting deep into my wounds. The ecstasy of spring freshness brings more suffering to the feelings of lovers.

قبلۂ مقصدِ نگاہِ نیاز   پھر وُہی پردۂ عماری ہے

qibla(h)' maqṣad-e nigāh-e niyāz
phir vohī pardah ʽamārī hai (165:3; #1008)

The direction of the desiring eyes is towards the destination;
Then again, there is curtain around canopy.

qibl'a(h): Anything opposite, that part to which people direct their prayers, especially the direction of Ka'aba; *ʽamārī:* a canopied elephant-litter.

The lover's eyes are fixed on the curtain of her carriage to steal a glimpse of her as she alights. Note the emphasis on "again." The beloved is ready to leave and the lovers are desperate to catch a glimpse of her before she leaves.

چشم دلّالِ جنسِ رُسوائی   دل خریدارِ ذوقِ خواری ہے

chashm dallāl-e jins-e rusvā'ī
dil k̤haridār-e żauq-e k̤h(v)ārī hai (165:4; #1009)

The eyes are brokering for the commodity of disgrace;
The heart is a buyer of the desire of denigration.

dallāl: broker; *jins-e rusvā'ī:* commodity of disgrace; *k̤h(v)ārī;* distress, meanness, baseness.

The eyes continue to shed tears and the heart continues to send plaints. Tears coming out of my eyes are the commodities the heart wants to buy. This crying that brings me disgrace by letting the world know of my pathetic condition is making my heart appear fond of denigration.

وہی صد رنگ نالہ فرسائی   وہی صد گونہ اشکباری ہے

vohī ṣad rang nālah fursāī
vohī ṣad gūna(h) ashkbārī hai (165:5; #1010)

That same crying in hundreds of ways!
That same shedding of tears hundreds of times!

The poet is being critical of his routine of crying. The hundreds of different ways to shed tears have all gone to waste.

دل ہوائے خرامِ ناز سے پھر   محشرستانِ بے قراری ہے

dil havā'-e ḳhirām-e nāz se phir
maḥsharasitān-e beqarārī hai (165:6; #1011)

Again the heart, from its craving to see her coquettish walk
Is tumultuous like the place for the assembly of Resurrection.

maḥsharasitān: the place of assembly of resurrection.

The insatiable desire of the heart to see her walk is creating a tumult. With her every move, I go into frenzy. The use of "again" indicates that it has been going on for a while. The Day of Resurrection simile expresses chaos.

جلوہ پھر عرضِ ناز کرتا ہے   روزِ بازارِ جاں سپاری ہے

jalvah phir ʿarẓ-e nāz kartā hai
roz-e bāzār-e jāñ sipārī hai (165:7; #1012)

The beauty is again displaying coquetry;
'Tis the day of the market to make offering of life.

jāñ sipārī: the offering of life.

The beloved has begun displaying her coquettishness again—the market displaying her wares is brisk. It is the season to offer our life. It is time now for the lovers to kill themselves. The "day of the market" is used to mean that it is a special day when coquetry is displayed—a special day, a special occasion or that she controls the market.

پھر اُسی بے وفا پہ مرتے ہیں   پھر وُہی زندگی ہماری ہے

phir usī bevafā pe(h) marte haiñ
phir vohī zindagī hamārī hai (165:8; #1013)

Dying again for that unfaithful beloved.
Again it's the same life for me.

I have returned to my unfaithful beloved, desperately in love with her, and adopted my old ways of lamenting and becoming frustrated. It is all the same for her as well. The verse points to the admission of foolishness, yet relates to the helplessness of a lover.

پھر کھُلا ہے درِ عدالتِ ناز ق گرم بازارِ فوجداری ہے

phir khulā hai dar-e 'adālat-e nāz
garm bāzār-e faujdārī hai (165:9; #1014)

Then again, the doors to the court of her coquetry have opened
Speeding up the filings of criminal lawsuits.

faujdārī: criminal.

The beloved is allowing people to be heard and now hundreds are filing suit against her. Note that it is the beloved who is the judge; who is the accused. People are filing lawsuits (making plaints) just so they can tell her the condition of their hearts.

ہو رہا ہے جہان میں اندھیر   زُلف کی پھر سرِشتہ داری ہے

ho rahā hai jahān meñ andher
zulf kī phir sarishtah dārī hai (165:10; #1015)

The bleak injustice is striking around the world;
Then again, the tresses are ruling.

sarishtah dārī: ruling.

Bleak justice (injustice) rules that she becomes the judge. Note bleakness of justice and dark tresses. Saying that her tresses are ruling means that her law is ruling.

پھر دیا پارۂ جگر نے سوال   ایک فریاد و آہ و زاری ہے

phir diyā pārah' jigar ne savāl
ek firyād-o-āh-o-zārī hai (165:11; #1016)

Then again, the pieces of liver have asked the question:
What great plaint and crying is going around?

The liver was torn into many pieces, and the pieces have begun asking about this injustice. This has created a noisy situation where everyone seems to be lamenting.

پھر ہوئے ہیں گواہِ عشق طلب   اشکباری کا حکم جاری ہے

phir hu'e haiñ gavāh-e 'ishq ṯalab
ashkbārī kā ḥukm jārī hai (165:12; #1017)

Once more, the witnesses to love have been summoned;
The order to shed tears has been issued.

Continuing the theme of the beloved holding a court, those who were witness to the lover's feelings have been summoned. In the end, orders have been issued for the lover to continue to cry—the witnesses stand unrecognized.

دل و مژگاں کا جو مقدمہ تھا   آج پھر اس کی روبکاری ہے

dil-o-mizhgāñ kā jo muqaddma(h) thā
āj phir us kī rūbakārī hai (165:13; #1018)

The lawsuit that was between the heart and eyelashes
Is being brought out for hearing today in the court.

The heart had a complaint against her eyelashes for piercing it; that case has now come up for hearing. This was the real lawsuit, which the previous verses discussed at length.

بے خودی بے سبب نہیں غالب
کچھ تو ہے جس کی پردہ داری ہے

be ḳhudī be sabab nahiñ Ġhālib
kuchh to hai jis kī pardahdārī hai (165:14; #1019)

The rapture is not without a reason, *Ġhālib*;
There is surely something that you have been hiding?

You do not go into a state of ecstasy without reason, *Ġhālib*. You must be hiding something. Is it that you are trying to hide your love? Another verse where *Ġhālib* leaves reader wondering.

166

جنوں تہمت کشِ تسکیں نہ ہو، گر شادمانی کی
نمک پاشِ خراشِ دل ہے لذّت زندگانی کی

junūñ tohmat kash-e taskīñ na(h) ho, gar shādmānī kī
namak pāsh-e ḳharāsh-e dil hai lażżat zindagānī kī (166:1; #1020)

Frenzy should not be accused of seeking satisfaction if celebrating;
The joys of life sprinkle salt onto wounds of the heart.

tohmat kash: the accused; *gar shādmānī kī:* became happy, celebrated; *ḳharāsh-e dil*: wounds of heart.

If I appear happy at times, it should not be construed that I am out of my frenzy. My frenzy should not be accused of getting off-track. Happiness actually makes the feeling of sadness more acute. After a brief spell of happiness I fall back into sorrow, and the feeling is more intense for I have tasted what happiness means, albeit briefly. My destiny is sorrow; intermittent happiness only intensifies it. The happy moments renew the sadness of the past as would salt sprinkled onto my wounds.

کشاکش ہائے ہستی سے کرے کیا سعیِ آزادی
ہوئی زنجیر موجِ آب کو فرصت روانی کی

kashākash hāi hastī se kare kyā saī'-e āzādī
huv'ī zanjīr mauj-e āb ko furṣat ravānī kī (166:2; #1021)

How can one seek freedom from the struggles of life?
The waves of water, when they begin to flow, turn into chains?

kashākash: struggle, tussle; *hastī*: life.

The chains of the struggle of life cannot be broken, and our efforts to free ourselves from them are futile. See how waves are formed? Like a chain, they keep turning. It is the action of water (our efforts to free ourselves) that creates chains, which in turn create more turbulence and further rolling of water. To live is to create these chains of struggle. For as long as we live, there shall be struggle.

پس از مُردن بھی دِیوانہ زیارت گاہِ طفلاں ہے
شرارِ سنگ نے تُربت پہ میری، گُل فشانی کی

pas az murdan bhī dīvāna(h) ziyārat gāh-e t̤iflāñ hai
sharār-e sang ne turbat pa(h) merī, gulfishānī kī (166:3; #1022)

Even after death, the children visit the lunatic frequently.
The spark, from their striking stones, scatters flowers on my grave.

pas az murdan: after death; *ziyārat*: pilgrimage, visit; *gulfishānī:* seattering of flowers.

The lunatic, who used to attract children to him so that they could throw stones at him, has died. Now children are throwing stones at his grave. As these stones strike his grave, they create sparkling flares (as stones hit stone), and this appears to illuminate the grave of the lover as if the children have come to throw flowers at the grave. This is indeed an extremely creative imagination.

167

نکوہش ہے سزا فریادیِ بیدادِ دلبر کی
مبادا خندۂ دنداں نما ہو صبحِ محشر کی

nikūhish hai sazā faryādī' bedād-e dilbar kī
mubādā ḳhandah dandāñ numā ho ṣubḥ-e maḥshar kī
(167:1; #1023)

Reproach is the punishment for those who complain against the cruelty of sweetheart,
Lest the morning of the Day of Judgment show its teeth in laughter.

nikūhish: reproach, censure, blame; *faryād*: complaint; *dilbar*: sweetheart; *sazā*: punishment; *maḥshar*: Day of Judgment; *mubādā*: lest; *ḳhandah dandāñ*: like big smile, showing teeth, ridiculing laughter.

He who complains about the injustices of the beloved should be punished. On the Day of Judgment, there will be justice, and those who moaned at the injustices of their beloved will be reprimanded. It is better to receive punishment here in this world than to receive ridicule later. The mention of the morning of the Day of Judgment rhymes visually with the whiteness of teeth showing when laughing.

رگِ لیلیٰ کو خاکِ دشتِ مجنوں ریشگی بخشے
اگر بووے بجائے دانہ دہقاں نوک نشتر کی

rag-e lailā ko ḳhāk-e dasht-e majnūñ reshgī baḳhshe
agar bode bajā'e dāna(h) dahqāñ nok nishtar kī (167:2; #1024)

The dust of *Majnūn*'s desert would impart tenderness to the veins of *Lailā*
If the farmer would sow the tips of the dagger instead of seed.

reshgī: fibrousness, tenderness; *dāna(h)*: seed; *bode*: to plant; *nok*: tip; *nishtar*: dagger; *dehqān*: farmer.

Legend says that when *Lailā* slashed her veins, *Majnūn's* wrists began to bleed also. However, for *Lailā* to feel any pain at the suffering of *Majnūn*, the wound and its suffering have to be more prominent. For example, if the farmer sows the tips of dagger instead of seed in the desert, and *Majnūn* runs around in this desert, the pain of *Majnūn* might be enough to bring pain to *Lailā*. The literal meaning is that the dust of the desert where *Majnūn* wanders for miles would cause *Lailā's* vein to become prominent if the farmer sowed the tips of the dagger in the desert. This is classical *Ġhālib* imagery. No two interpreters have been able to come up with the same explanation for this verse. In one interpretation, it says that if the farmer pokes (not seeds) the tip of dagger into the desert frequented by *Majnūn* then *Lailā's* veins will begin bleeding.

پرِ پروانہ شاید بادبانِ کشتیٔ مے تھا
ہوئی مجلس کی گرمی سے روانی دَورِ ساغر کی

par-e parvāna(h) shāyad bādbān-e kashtī' mai thā
hu'ī majlis kī garmī se ravānī daur-e sāġhar kī (167:3; #1025)

Perhaps the wings of the moth had turned into sails for the boat of wine;
The warming up of the assembly has initiated the rounds of wine.

The assembly started with the lighting of a candle, which brought the moth. The fluttering wings of the moth created turbulence in air, which pushed the tray carrying the wine decanter floating in the pond.

The decanter reached the aspirants who were sitting by the pond, and thus, the drinking round began. The subject of this verse is how many ways a drinker can describe the ecstasy of his anticipation. Also, the many ways *Ġhālib* can describe the improbable is displayed here.

کروں بیدادِ ذوقِ پَرفشانی عرض ، کیا قُدرت
کہ طاقت اُڑ گئی، اُڑنے سے پہلے، میرے شہپر کی

karūñ bedād-e żauq-e parfishānī ʿarẓ, kyā qudrat
kih ṯāqat uṛga'ī, uṛne se pahle, mere shahpar kī (167:4; #1026)

How shall I describe the cruelty of the taste to flutter wings?
The power of my main wing flew away before the flight.

parfishānī: fluttering of feathers; *qudrat:* talent; *shahpar:* aileron, propeller, main wing.

I had a great taste for flying and that has been a cause of great suffering to me. So great is the suffering that I do not have the ability left to express it. Why this suffering? It is because I was unable to fly, my energy and power were taken out of me, leaving me totally helpless. What a disappointment!

کہاں تک روؤں اُس کے خیمے کے پیچھے، قیامت ہے!
مری قسمت میں یا رب کیا نہ تھی دیوار پتھر کی؟

kahāñ tak roū'ñ us ke ḳheme ke pīchhe, qiyāmat hai
merī qismat meñ yārabb kyā na(h) thī dīvār pathar kī (167:5; #1027)

For how long shall I cry behind her tent? It is like Doomsday.
Wasn't there a wall of stone assigned to me in my fate, O! Lord?

Standing behind her tent and crying, the lover is thinking it would have been better if there were a stone wall to hit himself against and thus end his life, for that would be less traumatic than this unending vigil of crying. The irony is that the lover is behind the tent, eliminating any chances of seeing the beloved walk out. This explains the reason for the length of the vigil—'tis going to be forever for he is beating at the wrong door. The lover is not in front of the tent because he does not want his vigil to end.

168

بے اعتدالیوں سے سبک سب میں ہم ہوئے   جتنے زیادہ ہو گئے اُتنے ہی کم ہوئے

be i'tidālyoñ se subuk sab meñ ham hu'e
jitne ziyādah hogae utne hi kam hu'e (168:1; #1028)

Our immoderation earned us the contempt of all;
As much we overdid it, we were reduced proportionally.

be i'tidālyañ: immoderateness; *subuk*: light, disrespected.

Crossing the limit of moderation brought much embarrassment to me and I lost the respect of all. As I advanced in my immoderate behavior, so I was pushed back in my social acceptance. This is one of the trickier verses. The connection is 1:3 and 2:4 if we break each line into two parts.

پنہاں تھا دام سخت قریب آشیان کے   اُڑنے نہ پائے تھے کہ گرفتار ہم ہوئے

pinhāñ thā dām sak͟ht qarīb āshiyān ke
uṛne na(h) pāe the kih giraftār ham hu'e (168:2; #1029)

The net was hidden too close to the nest;
We had barely managed to fly that we got trapped.

The net was laid so close, yet hidden, that before I could take flight, I was trapped. The flight appears to be a maiden flight, meaning that we were surrounded by difficulties and calamities just as we began our lives, perhaps as lovers, losing our heart at the first instance. In the first line, the closeness of the net is described as "hard close," perhaps to indicated that there was no way out; the meaning of this is difficult to translate.

ہستی ہماری اپنی فنا پر دلیل ہے یاں تک مٹے کہ آپ ہم اپنی قسم ہوئے

hastī hamārī apnī fīnā par dalīl hai
yāñ tak miṭe kih āp ham apnī qasam hu'e (168:3; #1030)

Our existence is a proof of us being nonexistent;
So much were we decimated that we became our own swear.

Being reduced over time, through humiliation, we have reached a state where our existence is only a symbol of our nonexistence. *Ġhālib* has explained this difficult verse in one of his own letters. His explanation goes as follows: "First, try to understand what is this thing you call 'swear'? How tall is its stature? How do its feet and hand appear? What is its complexion? When you are not able to tell, then you will know that a 'swear' exists not because of its physical existence but from a supposition. The existence of man is also something like a 'swear' for it cannot be seen though we suppose it exists." Thus, when *Ġhālib* says we became our own swear, he means that in this state, it is an argument that we do not exist. This is one of those classic verses where *Ġhālib*'s imagination is unprecedented and so is the difficulty in visualizing the meaning of what he is saying. He confuses us more when he explains.

سختی کشانِ عشق کی پوچھے ہے کیا خبر وہ لوگ رفتہ رفتہ سراپا الم ہوئے

saḳhtīe kushān-e 'ishq kī pūchhe hai kyā ḳhabar
vuh log rafta(h) rafta(h) sarāpā alam hu'e (168:4; #1031)

What to ask of those bearing the hardships of love?
Those people, slowly and gradually, from head to toe turned into sorrow.

saḳhtī kushan: doing hard-labor; *rafta(h):* gradually; *alam:* affliction, grief.

Do not ask what happened to those who lived through bearing the hardships of love. Slowly and gradually, they dissolved into complete sorrow. Since sorrow cannot be seen, but only felt, they, too, cannot be seen but felt only through their plaints.

تیری وفا سے کیا ہو تلافی کہ دہر میں　　　تیرے سوا بھی ہم پہ بہت سے ستم ہوئے

terī vafā se kyā ho talāfī kih dahr meñ
tere sivā bhī ham pa(h) bahut se sitam hu'e (168:5; #1032)

What recompense is there for your faithfulness in this world? Besides you, there have been other cruelties wrought upon us as well.

O! My beloved, many have been unkind and cruel to me besides you. Even if you should become faithful to me, it will not be enough. Who would compensate me for the injustice rendered by others? This is a desperate attempt to seek the beloved's sympathy while giving her a clear chance to escape without blame. The use of word to describe the world means the world being not a good place to live.

لکھتے رہے جنوں کی حکایات خوں چکاں　　　ہر چند اس میں ہاتھ ہمارے قلم ہوئے

likhte rahe junūñ kī ḥikāyāt ḳhūñ chakāñ
har chand is meñ hāth hamāre qalam hu'e (168:6; #1033)

We continued to write the bleeding tales of our madness,
Though in doing so, our hands were amputated.

ḥikāyāt: story, tale; *ḳhūñ chakāñ*: blood dripping; *qalam*: pen

I decided to write the tales of the madness of love, which were so intense that blood would drip from the words. Many tried to stop me; they even amputated my hands, but I continued. The use of "*qalam*" has a double meaning, amputation and writing pen. This verse points to the incessant struggle of many in the face of adversity.

اللہ رے تیری تندیٔ خو، جس کے بیم سے   اجزائے نالہ دل میں مرے رزقِ ہم ہوئے

allah re terī tundī' ḳhū, jis ke bīm se,
ajzāe nālah dil meñ mere rizq-e ham hu'e (168:7; #1034)

Oh! God, because of your fiery disposition,
The elements of plaints in my heart consumed each other.

tund'ī-e ḳhū,: short temper, fiery disposition; *rizq-e ham*: staple for each other; *bīm:* fear, terror.

Your fiery disposition frightens me. I could not offer my plaint because of fear. The components of my plaints were eaten up by my heart (consumed), but by doing so, the heart was itself consumed (by the fire of plaints). This verse uses a rather unorthodox way to describe that because of this fear, both my plaints and their keeper, my heart, are gone.

اہلِ ہوس کی فتح ہے ترکِ نبردِ عشق   جو پاؤں اُٹھ گئے وُہی اُن کے عَلم ہوئے

ahl-e havas kī fataḥ hai tark-e nabard-e 'ishq
jo pāoñ uṭh gae vohī un ke 'alam hu'e (168:8; #1035)

The victory of the ambitious ones is to give up the battle of love;
The feet that turned away proved to be the winning flags for them.

ahl-e havas: having desire; *fataḥ*: victory; *nabard*: war, battle.

The best thing for those who desire to win the beloved is to surrender in the battle of love and consider this their victory. For them, running from the battlefield is like raising the winning flags (*'alam*). How can running away be considered a victory? It is because at least they saved their lives, as they were not going to win. Calling feet that turned away flags is an archaic idiom, which is pushed to limit here by *Ġhālib*.

نالے عدم میں چند ہمارے سپرد تھے   جو واں نہ کھنچ سکے سو وہ یاں آ کے دم ہوئے

nāle ʿadam meñ chand hamāre supurd the
jo vāñ na(h) khich sake so vuh yāñ ākih dam hu'e (168:9; #1036)

A few plaints were assigned to me before I came into being;
The ones that I couldn't take out there, turned into breath here.

ʿadam: nonexistence, since the beginning.

At the time of my creation, I was allocated a certain number of plaints. Before coming into existence, I kept airing them and when I came into existence, the remaining plaints turned into my breath. This means that lamenting and plaints were part of my creation and should remain so for as long as I live. Having my plaints turning into breath is part of my existence, as much as breathing is part of my existence. Thus, my survival is contingent on my plaints.

چھوڑی اسدؔ نہ ہم نے گدائی میں دل لگی
سائل ہوئے تو عاشقِ اہلِ کرم ہوئے

chhoṛī Asad na(h) ham ne gadā'ī meñ dil lagī
sā'il hu'e to ʿāshiq-e ahl-e karam hu'e (168:10; #1037)

Asad, we did not quit our musings even in begging;
Turning beggar, we became the lover of the generous ones.

gadā'ī: beggary; *dil lagī:* fun, amusement, musings.

Loving was my nature. As a beggar, I continued the musings of lovers. Now I love those who give alms generously. *Ġhālib* is talking about becoming a beggar of alms of beauty.

169

جو نہ نقدِ داغِ دِل کی کرے شُعلہ پاسبانی
تو فسُردگی نہاں ہے بہ کمینِ بے زبانی

jo na(h) naqd-e dāġh-e dil kī kare shoʿlah pāsbānī
to fusurdagī nehāñ hai ba(h) kamīn-e be zabānī (169:1; #1038)

If the flame will not protect the currency of scars in the heart,
Then sadness is hiding in the ambush of my tonguelessness.

pāsbānī: sentinel, protective; *naqd*: cash; *kamīn*: ambush; *naqd-e dāġh-e dil*: currency of the scars of heart; as scars are diamond shaped, resembling the currency of the time, they are called currency here.

The flame of love keeps the scars in the heart fresh and thus keeps lovers happy. These scars are called cash or currency because this is the prime asset of the heart. Also, the shape of these scars resembles coins. The sadness is quietly sitting hiding in ambush to attack and make our hearts gloomy. Had it not been for the ongoing flame of love, the sadness would have taken over. The sadness, of course, is coming from the prolonged separation from the beloved. Sadness may lead to hopelessness and that to giving up loving the beloved. The flame of love continues to give lovers a reason to live.

مجھے اُس سے کیا توقّع بہ زمانۂ جوانی
کبھی کودکی میں جس نے نہ سُنی مری کہانی

mujhe us se kyā tavaqqoʿ ba(h) zamānahʾ javānī
kabhī kaudākī meñ jis ne na(h) sunī merī kahānī (169:2; #1039)

What expectation can I have in her youth, from
The one who never listened to my stories in the childhood?

kaudākī: childhood.

Children are more attentive to hearing stories, but my beloved never liked them—even when she was very young. How can I expect her to listen to my stories now? It is not in her nature—it has nothing to do with my stories or me. The poet gives the beloved the benefit of doubt.

یُونہی دُکھ کِسی کو دینا نہیں خُوب ورنہ کہتا
کہ مِرے عَدُو کو یارب مِلے میری زِندگانی

yūñhī dukh kisī ko denā nahiñ ḳhūb varna(h) kehtā
kih mere ʿadū ko yārabb mile merī zindigānī (169:3; #1040)

Hurting anyone without reason is not nice; otherwise, I would have said,
"O! Lord, may my enemy get my life."

ʿadū: enemy; *zindigānī*: life.

Causing pain to others is not a good thing or I would have asked God to extend the life of my enemy by adding my life to his. Since my life is full of pain, it would not have been nice. So bad is the hurt in the lover's life that he does not even want his enemy to have it. This is a remarkable expression of pain using a common statement: "I would not even wish it on my worst enemy."

170

ظلمت کدے میں میرے شبِ غم کا جوش ہے   اک شمع ہے دلیلِ سحر سو خموش ہے

zulmat kade meñ mere shab-e ġham kā josh hai
ik shama' hai dalīl-e ṣaḥar so ḳhamosh hai (170:1; #1041)

In the dark abode of mine, the night of sorrow is ebullient.
There is a candle, sign of dawn, but its already put out.

zulmat kada: dark home; *dalīl*: proof, sign.

In my dark home (my heart), there is complete and intense darkness (hopelessness) as even the candle (the sign of hope) has been put out (a hopeless situation). Generally, we put out candles in the morning; however, putting out the candle in the night makes the night bleaker. Intense sorrow prevails in my life; I have no hope left of ever seeing the morning of my desires. This is one of the most powerful verses of *Ġhālib*. A dark night with a candle put out conjures up many images of a gloomy heart—a superbly melancholic composition.

نے مژدۂ وصال نہ نظّارۂ جمال   مدت ہوئی کہ آشتیٔ چشم و گوش ہے

ne muzhdah' vis̄āl na(h) naẕẕara(h)' jamāl
muddat hu'ī kih āshtī' chashm-o-gosh hai (170:2; #1042)

Neither the good news of union, nor the display of her beauty;
For a long time there has been a truce between the eyes and the ears.

āsht'ī: truce.

If my ears had heard the news of the possibility of union with the beloved, then my eyes would have become jealous. If my eyes had seen the display of your beauty, then my ears would have become jealous. However, there is a truce between the two, with no news from the beloved and no chance to see her, either.

مے نے کیا ہے حسنِ خود آرا کو بے حجاب　　اے شوق یاں اجازتِ تسلیمِ ہوش ہے

mai ne kyā hai ḥusn-e ḳhud ārā ko be ḥijāb
ai shauq yāñ ijāzat-e taslīm-e hosh hai (170:3; #1043)

The wine has made the self-adorning beauty unveil herself;
O! Desire, you are permitted now to lose your senses.

The beloved becomes drunk and loses her veil (which is very unusual for someone who is so careful about her presentation). In this condition, it is admissible for the lover to lose his senses (they will be lost anyway looking at the beloved without her veil) and drop all formalities of discretion. It is time to take advantage of her.

گوہر کو عقدِ گردنِ خوباں میں دیکھنا　　کیا اوج پر ستارۂ گوہر فروش ہے

gohar ko ʿiqd-e gardan-e ḳhūbāñ meñ dekhnā
kyā auj par sitārah' gohar firosh hai (170:4; #1044)

Look at the necklace of jewels hung around the neck of the beloved.
How high are the stars of the jewel merchant.

gohar: jewel; *ʿiqd*: garland.

The necklace of pearls in the neck of the beloved creates an envious situation. How lucky for the jeweler to see the necklace grace the neck of the beloved. Maybe the jeweler put the jewel around her neck. (Jealousy raises its head.)

دیدار بادہ، حوصلہ ساقی، نگاہ مست　　بزمِ خیال میکدۂ بے خروش ہے

dīdār bādah, ḥauṣlah sāqī, nigāh mast
bazm-e ḳhayāl maikadah' be ḳharosh hai (170:5; #1045)

The sight of wine, the patience of cupbearer, the intoxicated eyes;
In the assembly of imagination, the tavern is without tumult.

be ḳharosh: without tumult, without noise.

An imaginary assembly is a tavern where we drink the wine of her display and drink as much as our courage allows us to drink and we stay in the state of ecstasy. This is a place with no tumult—just peace. Shown here is the drunkard's utopia.

اے تازہ واردانِ بساطِ ہوائے دل   ق   زنہار اگر تمہیں ہوسِ نائے و نوش ہے

ai tāzah vārdān-e bisāṯ-e havā-e dil
zinhār agar tumhaiñ havas-e nāe-o-nosh hai (170:6; #1046)

O! Newcomers to the land of the heart's desire,
Be aware if you desire greedily for joys of song and wine!

tāzah vārdān: new arrival; *zinhār*: beware; *nāe-va-nosh*: song and wine; *havā-e dil*: heart's desire; *bisāṯ*: floor, land.

A warning is given to new lovers as they enter the world of loving. This land is not for the joys of song and wine—you should know that it is perpetual sorrow. Beware!

دیکھو مجھے، جو دیدۂ عبرت نگاہ ہو   میری سنو، جو گوشِ نصیحت نیوش ہے

dekho muǥhe, jo đīdah' 'ibrat nigāh ho
merī suno, jo gosh-e naṣiḥat nayosh hai (170:7; #1047)

Look at me, if you have eyes with vision for admonishment;
Listen to me, if you have ears that heed advice.

¨ibrat: example, warning, to pay heed; *gosh-e naṣiḥat nayosh*: ears listening to advice.

If you have discerning vision and if you can take lessons from what you see, then look at my condition. If you have been endowed with the ability to take advice, then hark unto me. Very potent advice to new lovers, the poet is pointing to the two senses that go first when you fall in love. He says that if you still have some sense left, pay heed to me.

ساقی بہ جلوہ دشمنِ ایمان و آگہی   مطرب بہ نغمہ رہزنِ تمکین و ہوش ہے

sāqī ba(h) jalvah dushman-e imān-o-āgahī
muṭrib ba(h) naġhmah rahzan-e tamkīn-o-hosh hai (170:8; #1048)

The sight of cupbearer is enemy to belief and awareness;
The singer is stealing our pride and senses with songs.

The cupbearer is showing her wares—offering wine to destroy my faith and awareness. This will turn me into her follower and I will forget about everything around me. The singer is robbing me of my pride and senses through her song. This scenario is that of the beloved's assembly wherein she is serving wine and music is playing—a divine feeling of pleasure, in which the lover has lost his awareness and sense and has become a total slave to Cupbearer. Superbly enunciated!

یا شب کو دیکھتے تھے کہ ہر گوشۂ بساط   دامانِ باغبان و کفِ گل فروش ہے

yā shab ko dekhte the kih har goshah' bisāṭ
dāmān-e bāġhbān-o-kaf-e gulfarosh hai (170:9; #1049)

Or at night, you could see that every corner of assembly
Was like the lap of a gardener and the palm of a flower-seller.

kaf: palm.

There were flowers all over the floor of the assembly—like the gardener's skirt, full of flowers, as he plucks them and carries them around; or the palm of a flower-seller, full of his wares.

لطفِ خرامِ ساقی و ذوقِ صدائے چنگ   یہ جنتِ نگاہ وہ فردوسِ گوش ہے

luṭf-e ḳhirām-e sāqī-o-żauq-e ṣadā e chang
yih jannat-e nigāh vuh firdaus-e gosh hai (170:10; #1050)

The grace of cupbearer's gait and the taste for the harp's melody;
This was paradise for the eye and that, heaven for the ear.

Cupbearer's coquettish walk was like looking at paradise, as was the heavenly melodious sound of the harp to the ears. Beautiful view, heart-stealing sounds.

یا صبح دم جو دیکھیے آ کر تو بزم میں   نے وہ سرور و سوز نہ جوش و خروش ہے

yā ṣubḥ dam jo dekhīye ākar to bazm meñ
ne vuh surūr-o-soz na(h) josh-o-ḳharosh hai (170:11; #1051)

If you come to see the assembly in the morning,
There is neither joy nor pain; neither ebulliance nor clamor.

The scene of the beloved's assembly in the night contrasts with that of the morning. With wine beginning to show its hangover, candles extinguished, the beloved gone, and the bright rays of sun burning the eyes, all joy is lost. The lover is inviting novice lovers to the reality of where it all ends.

داغِ فراقِ صحبتِ شب کی جلی ہوئی   اک شمع رہ گئی ہے سو وہ بھی خموش ہے

dāġh-e firāq ṣoḥbat-e shab kī jalī hu'ī
ik shamaʿ rāh ga'ī hai so vuh bhī ḳhamosh hai (170:12; #1052)

Burnt from the sorrow of separation of last night's revels,
There remains just one candle and even that is extinguished.

The assembly of joy is uprooted, the sorrow of which has burned my heart. How sorrowful is it? The candle is the only thing left and even that is not burning; it is already burnt out. See the arrangement of "burnt-out candle" and "burnt heart." The poet compares his heart to a candle that is no longer burning. That is indeed sorrowful.

آتے ہیں غیب سے یہ مضامیں خیال میں
غالب صریرِ خامہ نوائے سروش ہے

āte haiñ ġhaib se yih maẓāmīñ ḳhayāl meñ
Ġhālib ṣarīr-e ḳhāmah navā'e sarosh hai (170:13; #1053)

From hidden reaches do these subjects come into my thought;
***Ġhālib*, the scratching sound of the pen is the call of angels.**

ṣarīr-e ḳhāmah: sound of scratching while writing (it is particularly loud when using a reed pen); *navā'-e sarosh*: call of angels.

The topic about which the poet writes comes to his mind through mysterious channels. The scratching sound of writing is actually a call of the angels giving him mysterious thoughts. Angels bring to me my thinking. This verse is not claiming "revelation," just that angels push his thinking to spontaneous expression. A reed pen produces a scratching sound on paper.

171

آ کہ مری جان کو قرار نہیں ہے
طاقتِ بیدادِ اِنتظار نہیں ہے

ā ḳih merī jān ko qarār nahiñ hai
ṭāqat-e bedād-e intiẓār nahiñ hai (171:1; #1054)

Come! For my soul has no patience
And no strength is left to bear the tyranny of waiting.

qarār: repose, patience.

Calling the beloved, the poet expresses his impatience. Waiting for a long time has resulted in loss of strength to face the pain of waiting, and it has become unbearable; the poet asks for an end to this cruelty.

دیتے ہیں جنت حیاتِ دہر کے بدلے
نشہ بہ اندازۂ خُمار نہیں ہے

dete haiñ jannat ḥayāt-e dahar ke badle
nashah ba(h) andāzah' ḳhumār nahiñ hai (171:2; #1055)

Giving us Paradise in lieu of life on earth,
The intoxication is not proportional to the hangover.

It is said that Paradise will offer all types of comfort after death. Those who have suffered in this life will go to Paradise to receive their recompense. The poet is questioning if this is possible, as the hardships of this world are too harsh for even Paradise to recompense them. Drunkards who frequently get a hangover know that the best recipe is to drink some more. The hardship on this earth is so great that there is not enough wine in Paradise to recompense for it.

گریہ نکالے ہے تیری بزم سے مجھ کو
ہائے کہ رونے پہ اختیار نہیں ہے

girya(h) nikāle hai terī bazm se mujh ko
hāe kih rone pa(h) iḳhtiyār nahiñ hai (171:3; #1056)

Weeping causes me to be expelled from your assembly;
Alas! I have little control over my crying.

iḳhtiyār: control; *giryah*: lamentation, weeping.

Because of crying and lamenting, I was thrown out of your assembly; how sad that I do not have any control over my tears. An additional comment: If I cannot control myself, how can I expect her to exercise any control over herself?

ہم سے عبث ہے گمانِ رنجشِ خاطر
خاک میں عشاق کی غبار نہیں ہے

ham se ʿabaṡ hai gumān-e ranjish-e ḳhāṭir
ḳhāk meñ ʿushshāq kī ġhubār nahiñ hai (171:4; #1057)

Unjustifiably you think that I hold a grudge against you;
There is no dust in the grave of lovers.

ham: together; *ʿabaṡ*: useless; *gumān:* doubt; *ranjish:* misunderstanding; *ḳhāṭir*: favor; *ḳhāk*: grave; *ġhubār*: dust, mist, grudge.

It is useless for you to doubt that we can hold any grudge of grief against you; lovers do not hold any grudges—our devotion is clear. Holding a grudge in the heart here also means clouding the heart. Since even the ashes of lovers leave no dust, how then can we have any "fog" against you in our hearts? Here *Ġhālib* has played on the duality of the meaning of the word that means both "dust" and "grudge."

دل سے اُٹھا لطفِ جلوہ ہائے معانی
غیرِ گل آئینۂ بہار نہیں ہے

dil se uṭhā lutf-e jalvah hāe mʿānī
ġhair-e gul ā'inah' bahār nahiñ hai (171:5; #1058)

Take heart in drawing pleasure from the displays of reality;
Without the flower, there is no mirror reflecting spring.

lutf-e jalvah hāe mʿānī: pleasure from meaningful conversation.

If you have a heart, then enjoy the delightful interpretations of my writings. Only a flower can reflect the reality of spring, and only your heart can know the reality of the Universe from your thoughts. My verses are like flowers—they are the spring season. As you are the reader, take delight in them.

قتل کا میرے کیا ہے عہد تو بارے
وائے اگر عہد اُستوار نہیں ہے

qatl kā mere kiyā hai ʿahd to bāre
vāe agar ʿahd ustuvār nahiñ hai (171:6; #1059)

Now that you have vowed to kill me, it will be
A pity if your vows do not prove firm.

The beloved has made a vow to kill the lover. The lover is afraid that she might not go through with her promise. The feeling is something like this: Someone promises to do something good for you, but you wonder what will happen if the promise is not kept.

تُو نے قسم میکشی کی کھائی ہے غالبؔ
تیری قسم کا کچھ اِعتبار نہیں ہے

tū ne qasm maikashī kī khā'ī hai Ġhālib
terī qasam kā kuchh ʿitibār nahiñ hai (171:7; #1060)

O! *Ġhālib*, you have taken an oath to drink,
But your vows are not very trustworthy.

Here, taking oath has a dual meaning. It can mean that *Ġhālib* has sworn to either stop drinking or start drinking. When you cannot say clearly whether you are giving up or taking up drinking, how can we trust you? If you are swearing to start drinking, that means you were not drinking before—a lie. If you are swearing that you will not drink, that is an even bigger lie.

172

ہجومِ غم سے یاں تک سرنگونی مجھ کو حاصل ہے
کہ تارِ دامن و تارِ نظر میں فرق مشکل ہے

ḥujūme gham se yān tak sarnigūni mujh ko ḥāsil hai
kih tāre dāman-o-tāre nazar meñ firq mushkil hai (172:1; #1061)

In the extreme of sorrow, my head is bowed down so low
That the line of my sight is indistinguishable from the thread of my lap.

Ġhālib considers sight (not vision) to be something coming out of the eye, like a thread—the line of sight. Using a unique analogy, the poet states that his head is bowed so low (under the burden of sorrow) into his lap that the thread of the cloth and the thread of his sight have merged. This simply means that his head is touching the skirt in his lap. The position described here is almost acrobatic, requiring much bending of the spinal cord. An emotional burden, bowing of head, and a description of how low it can get is described here most unusually.

رفوئے زخم سے مطلب ہے لذت زخمِ سوزن کی
سمجھیو مت کہ پاسِ درد سے دیوانہ غافل ہے

rafū'e zakhm se maṯlab hai lażżat zakhm-e sozan kī
samajhyo mat kih pās-e dard se dīvāna(h) ġhāfil hai (172:2; #1062)

The darning of wounds is meant to savor the delight from the wounds of the needle;
Think not that your lunatic is oblivious of the reverence of pain.

Getting wounds stitched should not be construed as an attempt to ease suffering. It is meant to inflict more pain through the passing of needles through them. Do not think for a minute that this lunatic has forgotten the value of pain.

وہ گل جس گلستاں میں جلوہ فرمائی کرے غالب
چٹکنا غنچۂ گل کا صدائے خندۂ دل ہے

vuh gul jis gulsitāñ meñ jalvah firmā'ī kare Ġhālib
chaṭaknā ġhunchah' gul kā ṣadā e ḳhandah' dil hai (172:3; #1063)

In whichever garden the flower reveals its glory, *Ġhālib*;
The call of buds opening is the sound of the heart's laughter.

The beloved is a flower, and her presence is the opening of a bud that signifies a joyful heart; this is also a sign of laughter (as petals spread). The joy of the heart is the blooming of flowers in the heart. All conventions meet well.

173

پا بہ دامن ہو رہا ہوں بسکہ میں صحرا نورد
خارِ پا ہیں جوہرِ آئینۂ زانو مجھے

pā ba(h) dāman ho rahā hūñ baska(h) maiñ ṣaḥrā navard
ḳhār-e pā haiñ johar-e ā'ina(h)' zānū mujhe (173:1; #1064)

Enough wandering in the desert; my feet are now tucked into my skirt.
The thorns in my sole are the lines in the mirror of my kneecap.

bas: sufficient, enough; *ṣaḥrā:* desert; *ā'ina(h):* mirror; *navard*: roaming; *ā'ina(h) zānū:* knee cap; *pā ba(h) dāman*: feet up in the lap, giving up.

Tired of wandering around, I have given up. With my foot placed on my knee, I sit down and remove the thorns from the soles of my feet. If I think of my knee, on which the foot is resting, as a mirror because it causes me to reflect by showing me the thorns in my feet, then the thorns are like the lines in unpolished iron mirrors. While I was wandering, I could not reflect on myself; now I can, because the painful memories help me sharpen my thinking. This is one of the most misinterpreted and misunderstood verses of *Ġhālib*. Many interpreters have tried to find meaning for "reflecting kneecap," vainly. It is better if we conclude the argument by saying that in the posture of thinking, I became more reflective.

دیکھنا حالت مرے دل کی، ہم آغوشی کے وقت
ہے نگاہِ آشنا تیرا سرِ ہر مو مجھے

dekhnā ḥālat mere dil kī, ham āġoshī ke vaqt
hai nigāh-e āshnā terā sar-e har mū mujhe (173:2; #1065)

Look at the condition of my heart at the time of embracing you!
When the tip of each strand of your hair appears familiar to my eye.

When you were in my arms, I was so close to you I became familiar with the tip of each strand of hair on your body. Can you imagine what that did to my heart?

ہوں سراپا سازِ آہنگِ شکایت، کچھ نہ پوچھ
ہے یہی بہتر کہ لوگوں میں نہ چھیڑے تو مجھے

ḥūñ sarāpā sāz-e āhang-e shikāyat, kuchh na(h) pūchh
hai yahī behtar kih logoñ meñ na(h) chheṛe tū mujhe (173:3; #1066)

Ask me not, how from head to toe, I am an instrument filled with the melody of complaint.
You had better not strike me in the presence of other people.

I am like a musical instrument that is full of melodies of complaint. Do not strike me (like striking the strings) in the presence of others because all you will hear will be my plaints; it would bring more embarrassment to you. The use of "strike me not" to state "provoke me not" is the key strength of this verse because the poet has compared himself to a musical instrument. It also means that the lover is sitting, irate and aloof ready to blow up.

174

جس بزم میں تُو ناز سے گفتار میں آوے   جاں کالبدِ صُورتِ دیوار میں آوے

jis bazm meñ tū nāz se guftār meñ āve
jāñ kā lubd-e ṣurat-e dīvār meñ āve (174:1; #1067)

In whichever assembly you begin talking with your coquettish elegance,
The hearts in the wall paintings begin throbbing with life.

jāñ kā lubd: heart, skeleton; *ṣurat-e dīvār*: pictures of the wall; *gıftār*: talk.

When the beloved speaks, the pictures on the wall come alive. The use of coquettishness is a permanent style and does not mean that it happens when she is acting coquettish. Why do the pictures come to life? The sound of her voice is so appealing that even hearts on paper warm up to it; and when the hearts wake up, life is infused into the pictures.

سائے کی طرح ساتھ پھریں سرو و صنوبر   تُو اِس قدِ دلکش سے جو گُلزار میں آوے

sā'e kī ṭarḥ sāth phireñ sarv-o-ṣanobar
tū is qad-e dilkash se jo gulzār meñ āve (174:2; #1068)

Like your shadow, the cypress and pine trees will chase you,
If with this attractive stature of yours, you would come into the garden.

sarv-o-ṣanobar: cypress and pine (fir).

If the beloved walks into the garden, the cypress and pine trees will track her like a shadow. A comparison is made here to her stature (height), but it does not mean that the beloved is as tall as a cypress or pine tree. The second line says, "with this stature," meaning with your height, in proportion to your beauty. To follow someone like a shadow also means to show great admiration. It also means to stalk.

تب نازِ گراں مایگیٔ اشک بجا ہے　　جب لختِ جگر دیدۂ خونبار میں آوے

tab nāz-e girāñ māegī' ashk bajā hai
jab lak̤ht-e jigar dīdah' k̤hūñbār meñ āve (174:3; #1069)

The pride of tear is justified for its preciousness when
The pieces of liver begin to flow out from the bloodletting eyes.

girāñ māeg'ī: valuable, precious; *bajā*: acceptable, justified.

The value of tears depends on what is being shed. Ordinary tears have no value. When the pieces of liver turn into blood, and this blood begins to flow like tears, only then can we accept that the tears have value. The liver is a symbol of courage and persistence. Turning the liver into pieces and then flowing like tears signifies extreme hardship.

دے مجھ کو شکایت کی اجازت کہ ستمگر　　کچھ تجھ کو مزہ بھی مرے آزار میں آوے

de mujh ko shikāyat kī ijāzat kih sitamgar
kuchh tujh ko maza(h) bhī mere āzār meñ āve (174:4; #1070)

Give me permission to complain, O! Oppressor!
Some pleasure you, too, get in my suffering.

The beloved is cruel to the lover, who is not allowed to complain. The lover asks for permission to complain so that the beloved will know how "good" she has been at hurting his feelings. However, the lover's complaints are bound to make the beloved angrier; thus, she will dole out more cruelty, which is what is desired here. A masochistic tone is apparent in the second line.

اُس چشمِ فسُوں گر کا اگر پاے اشارہ طُوطی کی طرح آئنہ گفتار میں آوے

us chashm-e fusūñgar kā agar pāe ishāra(h)
ṯūṯī kī tarḥ ā'ina(h) guftār meñ āve (174:5; #1071)

From those bewitching eyes, if it gets any hint,
The mirror will start talking like the parrot.

fusūñgar: magician

My beloved talks with her eyes. If she sends any glances to the mirror, it will begin talking like the parrot does when it hears others talking. The use of "bewitching eyes" is necessary since the mirror is supposed to be in a "stunned state" and only a magical feat can make it talk. It is the witchcraft of the beloved's eyes that can even make a mirror talk. There is a hint in this verse towards the traditional connection between a parrot and the mirror, as discussed by *Ġhālib* in many places. A parrot looking into mirror begins talking because it thinks that there is another parrot behind the glass.

کانٹوں کی زباں سُوکھ گئی پیاس سے یارب اِک آبلہ پا وادیٔ پُرخار میں آوے

kāñṭoñ kī zabāñ sūkh ga'ī piyās se yārabb
ik āblah pā vādī' purḳhār meñ āve (174:6; #1072)

The tongue of thorns has dried out with thirst, O! Lord,
Let someone with blistered feet come to the valley of thorns.

āblah pā: blistered feet.

The dried tongue of thorns and the pointed shape of thorns is a good simile. If someone with water-filled blisters on his feet were to walk over these thorns, they would pierce the blisters and thus quench the thirst of the thorns. But why are the thorns thirsty? It is because there have not been any devoted lovers around recently. O! Lord, inculcate true devotion in the hearts of lovers, so that the thorns may quench their thirst.

مرجاؤں نہ کیوں رشک سے جب وہ تنِ نازک
آغوشِ خمِ حلقۂ زنّار میں آوے

marjāu'ñ na(h) kioñ rashk se jab vuh tan-e nāzuk
āġhosh-e ḳham-e ḥalqa(h)' zunnār meñ āve (174:7; #1073)

Why shouldn't I die of envy, when that delicate body
Would come into the arms of the loop of holy thread?

ḳham-e ḥalq'a(h) zunnār: curl of the ring of *zunnar*, the thread worn religiously around the neck.

The beloved has wrapped around her neck the holy black thread carried on the shoulders of Brahmins. The poet wishes he were that thread.

غارت گرِ ناموس نہ ہو گر ہوسِ زر
کیوں شاہدِ گل باغ سے بازار میں آوے

ġhārat gar-e nāmūs na(h) ho gar havas-e zar
kioñ shāhid-e gul bāġh se bāzār meñ āve (174:8; #1074)

If the avarice for gold were not damaging to the reputation,
Why would then the flower watchers come down to the market?

havas-e zar: avarice for material gains; *zar*: money, gold, pollens in flower.

The word "*zar*" has two meanings: First, it means money or gold, which is needed to buy flowers in the market; second, "*zar*" is the yellowish powder of pollen that appears when buds open and turn into flowers. Buds open because of lust to show their pollen; as they become flowers, they are taken to the market for sale. This causes a great loss of honor to the flowers, for selling beauty is a cheap thing to do. If flowers did not have the lust for "*zar*," they would not be disgraced—flower lovers would come to see them in the garden and not go to the market to buy them. Note that the pollen and flowers have a sexual function, also; so it is the sexual lust of flowers that disgraces them.

تب چاکِ گریباں کا مزہ ہے دلِ نالاں!　　جب اِک نفس اُلجھا ہُوا ہر تار میں آوے

tab chāk-e girebāñ kā maza(h) hai dil-e nālāñ
jab ik nafis uljhā hu'ā har tār meñ āve (174:9; #1075)

Then, O! Plaintful heart, the joy of tearing the collar would come
When each breath comes out entangled with each thread.

Tearing the collar would be fun if the thread of the cloth were entangled with the thread of breath. Then, with each pull of the thread, breath would come out as well. Breath is called a string as it comes out—like the line of vision in *Ġhālib*'s peculiar paradigms. The true joy of tearing the collar comes when death comes with it—this is what is desired here.

آتشکدہ ہے سینہ مرا رازِ نہاں سے　　اَے وائے، اگر معرضِ اِظہار میں آوے

ātishkada(h) hai sīna(h) merā rāz-e nihāñ se
ai vāe, agar ma'raẓ-e iẓhār meñ āve (174:10; #1076)

My chest is like a fireplace with hidden secrets;
How terrible it would be if it got revealed anywhere?

ma'raẓ: place of appearance.

Holding secrets within, my chest is transformed into a fireplace. I am afraid that if these secrets come out, the heat and intensity will burn the world to ashes. The remorse is not of letting the secrets out, but of damaging the environment.

گنجینۂ معنی کا طِلِسم اُس کو سمجھیے
جو لفظ کہ غالبؔ مرے اشعار میں آوے

ganjina(h)' ma'nī kā ṭilism us ko samjhīye
jo lafẓ kih Ġhālib mere ash'ār meñ āve (174:11; #1077)

Think of it as a magical treasure of meaning:
Every word that appears in my verse, *Ġhālib*.

O! *Ġhālib*, whichever words appear in my verses, think of them as the magic of a treasure of meaning. In every word, the meaning has been packed as if it were a magical act. One must break this spell of magic, but like breaking the spells, it is difficult. Yet when it does, the treasure opens (become obvious to others).

175

حسنِ مہ گرچہ بہ ہنگامِ کمال اچھا ہے　　اُس سے میرا مہِ خورشید جمال اچھا ہے

ḥusn-e mah garchih bah hangām-e kamāl achhā hai
us se merā mah-e ḳhurshīd jamāl achhā hai (175:1; #1078)

The beauty of the full moon, is lovely,
But my sun-faced beauty is lovelier still.

mah: moon; *bah hangam-e kamāl:* when it is full (perfect); *mah-e ḳhurshīd jamāl*: sun-faced beauty.

My beloved's face is more beautiful than the full moon. Both are brilliant, but the beloved has the fiery nature of the sun as well.

بوسہ دیتے نہیں اور دل پہ ہے ہر لحظہ نگاہ　　جی میں کہتے ہیں کہ مفت آئے تو مال اچھا ہے

bosa(h) dete nahiñ aur dil pa(h) hai har laḥẓa(h) nigāh
jī meñ kahte haiñ kih muft āe to māl achhā hai (175:2; #1079)

Not giving me a kiss, yet continuously keeping an eye on my heart
Saying in the heart that if it comes free, 'tis a good deal.

The beloved is keeping an eye on the lover's heart and is ready to usurp it. The lover is reminding her that she must pay the price first, a kiss. However, the beloved is trying to outsmart the lover, saying in her heart that if she can get his heart without giving a kiss, it would surely be a better deal.

اَور بازار سے لے آئے اگر ٹوٹ گیا ساغرِ جم سے مِرا جامِ سفال اچھا ہے

aur bāzār se le āe agar ṭūt gayā
sāġhar-e jam se merā jām-e sifāl achhā hai (175:3; #1080)

More we could bring from the market, if it got broken;
My bowl of clay is better than the bowl of King Jamshed.

sāġhar-e jam: bowl of King Jamshed; *jām-e sifāl*: bowl of clay, earthen bowl.

The bowl of Persian King Jamshed in which he used to drink wine was supposed to show the future of the world and thus it was priceless. When drinking wine in it, one would always be apprehensive about breaking it and that would take away the joy of carefree drinking. A clay bowl is easily replaced and therefore it is better in providing the full pleasures of drinking. This verse points to a very deep meaning in our relationship with worldly things, how cherishing them keep us from enjoying them. It is a legend that the Persian King Jamshed discovered wine.

بے طلب دیں تو مزہ اُس میں سِوا ملتا ہے وُہ گدا جس کو نہ ہو خُوئے سوال اچھا ہے

be ṯalab deñ to maza(h) us meñ sivā miltā hai
vuh gadā jis ko na(h) ho ḳhū-e savāl achhā hai (175:4; #1081)

If they give without asking, it brings greater pleasure;
The beggar not used to asking is better.

Getting something without asking is more honorable. The habit of asking for things degrades us. We should not develop a habit of asking God, but instead, let Him give to us without asking, for it is more pleasurable and honorable. It may also mean that if the beloved were to give a kiss without asking, that would be better than begging for it.

اُن کے دیکھے سے جو آجاتی ہے مُنہ پر رَونق　　وُہ سمجھتے ہیں کہ بیمار کا حال اچھا ہے

un kih dekhe se jo ājātī hai muñh par raunaq
vuh samajhte haiñ kih bīmār kā ḥāl achhā hai (175:5; #1082)

From the radiance on my face that comes from seeing her,
She assumes that the patient has improved.

The arrival of the beloved brings such joy to me that the happiness begins to show on my face, taking away the pain of suffering, which makes her think that I am feeling better. How a face changes when facing loved ones is a common observation, but in *Ġhālib*'s world, an ordinary observation easily becomes extraordinary.

دیکھیے پاتے ہیں عُشاق بُتوں سے کیا فیض　　اِک برہمن نے کہا ہے کہ یہ سال اچھا ہے

dekhīye pāte haiñ ʿushshāq butoñ se kyā faiẓ
ik birahman ne kahā hai kih yih sāl achhā hai (175:6; #1083)

Let us see what favors the lovers will get from the idol;
A Brahmin has declared, "This is going to be a good year."

The Hindu Brahmin's almanac says that this year will prove to be good for mankind. To the lover, it is not important if there will be no famine, war or other catastrophe; he only wants to know if the beloved will be kind to him or not this year. That is the only measure of goodness he can understand. The use of "idol" in the first line and the Hindu Brahmin in the second line is well exploited, as the beloved is also called an idol.

ہم سخن تیشے نے فرہاد کو شیریں سے کیا　　جس طرح کا کہ کسی میں ہو کمال اچھا ہے

ham suḳhan teshe ne farhād ko shīrīñ se kiyā
jis t̤arḥ kā kih kisī meñ ho kamāl achhā hai (175:7; #1084)

The axe made it possible for *Farhād* to talk to *Shīrīn*;
Whoever has whatever talent is good for him.

ham sukhan: talking together.

Farhād was an ordinary soul, but he had mastered the use of the axe. It was through this skill that he got to talk to *Shīrīn*, the wife of a King. Without talent, one can get nowhere—that is the lesson given here. However, in keeping with the tradition of belittling *Farhād*, *Ġhālib* says that using the axe was the only thing *Farhād* knew how to do. Not much of a talent—but it worked for him.

قطرہ دریا میں جو مل جائے تو دریا ہو جائے   کام اچھا ہے وہ، جس کا کہ مآل اچھا ہے

qaṭrah daryā meñ jo mil jāe to daryā ho jāe
kām achhā hai vuh jis kā kih māāl achhā hai (175:8; #1085)

A drop that merges into the ocean becomes the ocean;
A deed is indeed good if it ends well.

māāl: end, result.

The goodness of any act is measured by what it produces. What ends well is done well. *Ġhālib* gives the example of a drop merging into the ocean and becoming the ocean. Left alone, it will evaporate or get lost in the sand; when merged, it becomes the entire ocean. The emphasis is in the second line with the example of the "drop" used to illustrate the point, not as an argument for the first line. Elsewhere, *Ġhālib* has invoked such arguments, but not in this verse.

خضر سلطاں کو رکھے خالق اکبر سرسبز   شاہ کے باغ میں یہ تازہ نہال اچھا ہے

khiẓr sultān ko rakhe ḳhāliq-e akbar sarsabz
shāh kih bāġh meñ yih tāza(h) nehāl achhā hai (175:9; #1086)

May the Great Lord keep *Ḳhiẓr Sultān* prosperous!
In the garden of the King, this new sapling looks good.

Well-wishing at the birth of *Ḳhiẓr Sultān*, poet prays for the "greening" of the new plant. (*Ḳhiẓr Sultān*, the 26-year-old son of *Bahadur Shāh Zafar*, was shot dead by the British in 1857 at *Delhī Darwāzā*. He was *Ġhālib*'s disciple and his writings were destroyed in the mutiny of 1857.)

ہم کو معلوم ہے جنت کی حقیقت لیکن
دل کے خوش رکھنے کو غالب یہ خیال اچھا ہے

ham ko ma'lūm hai jannat kī ḥaqīqat lekin
dil ke ḳhush rakhne ko Ġhālib yih ḳhayāl achhā hai (175:10; #1087)

We do know the reality of Paradise;
However, for consoling the heart, the idea is good, *Ġhālib*.

If you think that in Paradise, you will find *houris*, channels of milk and silk dresses, and if this thought makes you happy, then it is not a bad idea after all. The reality is that it is all a farce. See: *sataish gar hai ẓahid is qadar jis bāġh-e riẓwañ kā/ vuh ek guldasta(h) hai hum beḳhudoñ ke tāq-e nisyāñ kā/* the garden about which the preacher is so praiseful is merely a forgotten bouquet in the cupola for those in ecstasy.

176

نہ ہوئی گر مرے مرنے سے تسلی، نہ سہی
اِمتحاں اَور بھی باقی ہو تو یہ بھی نہ سہی

na(h) hu'ī gar mere marne se tasallī, na(h) sahī
imteḥāñ aur bhī bāqī ho to yih bhī na(h) sahī (176:1; #1088)

Not contented with my death? It matters not.
If there is more to test then go on, it matters not.

Death being the ultimate proof of devotion, the poet is ready for testing beyond death. Do you want to desecrate my ashes? Then go ahead, I am ready for that, too, asserts the poet. Referring to the many historic occasions when the corpses were dragged through streets to disgrace the dead, the poet is making a remarkable hint towards the history of the era.

خار خارِ اَلمِ حسرتِ دِیدار تو ہے
شوق گُلچینِ گُلستانِ تسلی نہ سہی

ḳhār ḳhār-e alam-e ḥasrat-e dīdār to hai
shauq gulchīn-e gulistān-e tasallī na(h) sahī (176:2; #1089)

The prickly pain from the desire to see you is still here.
If desire could not pluck the flowers of consolation, it matters not.

ḳhār ḳhār: thorny prickly; *alam:* pain, anguish, affliction, grief; *shauq*: desire, taste, fancy, zeal, eagerness; *gulchīn*: flower gatherer, gardener, florist; *tasallī:* consolation, solace, comfort.

If my desire could not pick the flowers from the garden of consolation, so what? I still have the prickly pain in my heart from not being able to see her. However, I could not satisfy my desire, the sorrow of not being able to see her remains. If I achieve my desire, this thorn will be removed and with that will go the joy of pain. I want something, but it is better that I do not get it. I may not be able to reach the flowers of comfort, but I have these prickly thorns of longing, which are equally comforting.

مے پرستاں! خُمِ مے مُنہ سے لگائے ہی بنے
ایک دن گر نہ ہُوا بزم میں ساقی، نہ سہی

mai parastāñ! ḳhum-e mai muñh se lagā'e hī bane
ek din gar na(h) hu'ā bazm meñ sāqī, na(h) sahī (176:3; #1090)

O! Worshippers of wine, we would have to drink straight from the decanter;
If one day the cupbearer is not present in the assembly, it matters not.

Dear drinking friends, if cupbearer does not show up in the assembly one day, then do not be distraught. Now that there is no one to fill the cups, why don't we just drink straight from the bottle? This verse refers to how the orderliness of any system breaks down in the absence of its controller. With no cupbearer, the members will not be able to apportion wine equitably and there will be no one to remind them when to stop. Therefore, they might as well go straight to the bottle without pretending that they can manage it in an orderly manner.

نفسِ قیس کہ ہے چشم و چراغِ صحرا
گر نہیں شمعِ سیہ خانۂ لیلیٰ، نہ سہی

nafis-e Qais kih hai chashm-o-chirāġh-e ṣaḥrā
gar nahiñ sham'-e siyāh ḳhānah' lailā, na(h) sahī (176:4; #1091)

The existence of *Majnūn* is a matter of pride for the desert.
If the candle from *Lailā*'s black home is not here, so be it.

chashm-o-chirāġh: eye and lamp, pride; *ḳhān'ah-e lailā*: the dark home of *Lailā*;—her tent was black, her complexion was dark, and her name meant "night."

Majnūn is indeed the source to brighten the desert. Black home, candle, and splendor, all make a remarkable comparison. The first line is based on the word "*nafas*" which means both the existence and breath; "pride" is expressed as being the eye and lamp of the desert (see the connection with fiery breath as well). If the candle from *Lailā*'s home is not in the desert, so what? The breath of *Majnūn* is enough. The candle of *Lailā*'s home indicates presence of *Lailā* herself. Note that *Lailā* had dark complexion and lived in a black tent. The verse has also been interpreted as saying: So what if *Majnūn* could not brighten *Lailā*'s home—at least he is brightening the desert!

ایک ہنگامے پہ موقوف ہے گھر کی رونق
نوحۂ غم ہی سہی نغمۂ شادی نہ سہی

ek hangāme pa(h) mauqūf hai ghar kī raunaq
nauḥ' ġham hi sahī naġhma(h)' shādī na(h) sahī (176:5; #1092)

The liveliness of a home is dependent on tumult,
Let there be lamenting of sorrow, if not the songs of happiness.

The liveliness of any abode comes either from lamenting or from singing. One or the other must exist as both bring excitement; also, there must be other people to share either sorrow or joy with. Some get sorrow, and some get happiness. There is no room for complaint, for both signify the existence of life.

نہ ستائش کی تمنا نہ صلے کی پروا
گر نہیں ہیں مرے اشعار میں معنی، نہ سہی

na(h) sitā'ish kī tamannā na(h) ṣile kī parvā(h)
gar nahiñ haiñ mere ash'ār meñ ma'nī, na(h) sahī (176:6; #1093)

Neither longing for praise nor seeking any reward;
If there are no meanings in my verses, so be it.

If my verses are indecipherable to some, so be it. I have no desire for praise or any rewards from anyone.

عشرتِ صحبتِ خوباں ہی غنیمت سمجھو
نہ ہوئی غالب اگر عمرِ طبیعی، نہ سہی

'ishrat-e soḥbat-e ḳhūbāñ hī ġhanīmat samjho
na(h) hu'ī Ġhālib agar 'umr-e tabī'ī, na(h) sahī (176:7; #1094)

The joy of intimacy with beauties, consider it a blessing.
If you did not live to your expected age, *Ġhālib*, so be it.

If we did not live as expected naturally, so what? At least we lived intimately in the company of beauties. Moreover, you should consider those years a blessing.

177

عجب نشاط سے جلاد کے چلے ہیں ہم آگے
کہ اپنے سائے سے، سر پانؤں سے ہے دو قدم آگے

ʿajab nishāṯ se jallād ke chale haiñ ham āge
kih apne sāe se, sar pāuñ se hai do qadam āge (177:1; #1095)

With great delight, we walk ahead of the hangman.
In our own shadow, our head is a couple of strides ahead of our feet.

The joy of reaching the gallows makes us walk ahead of the hangman. In my shadow falling in front of me, my head is ahead of my feet, as if it were extremely eager to be hanged.

قضا نے تھا مجھے چاہا خراب بادۂ الفت
فقط خراب لکھا، بس نہ چل سکا قلم آگے

qaẓā ne thā mujhe chāha ḳharāb-e bādah' ulfat
fiqaṯ ḳharāb likhā, bas na(h) chal sakā qalam āge (177:2; #1096)

Destiny wanted me to be ruined by the wine of love.
Just as the word, "ruined," was written the pen could not write any further.

qaẓā: Destiny.

When writing my destiny, God meant to write that I would forever stay intoxicated, which literally meant, "ruined by the wine of love," however, as soon the word ruined was written, the pen stopped and

God could not complete the sentence. I live now just ṛuined. The play of words involves the interpretation of the word "ruined."

غمِ زمانہ نے جھاڑی نشاطِ عشق کی مستی
وگرنہ ہم بھی اُٹھاتے تھے لذّتِ الم آگے

ġham-e zamāna(h) ne jhāṛī nishāṭ-e ʿishq kī mastī
vagarna(h) ham bhī uṭhāte the lażżat-e alam āge (177:3; #1097)

The sorrows of the world brushed away the intoxication from the joys of love,
Or else, we, too, used to enjoy the pleasures of sorrow.

jhāṛī: shook loose, brushed away; *āge*: before, in the past.

The sorrow of the world deprived me of the sorrow of love. The sorrow of love was sheer ecstasy blown away by the routines of life. (See: *gham-e ishq gar nā hotā, gham-e rozgār hotā.* Had there not been the sorrow of love, there would still have been the tribulations of living.)

خُدا کے واسطے داد اِس جُنُونِ شَوق کی دینا
کہ اُس کے دَر پہ پہنچتے ہیں نامہ بر سے ہم آگے

ḳhudā ke vāsṭe dād is junūn-e shauq kī denā
kih us ke dar pa(h) pahunchte haiñ nāma(h) bar se hum āge (177:4; #1098)

For God's sake, give praise to this frenzy of desire
That we reach her door before the messenger arrives.

Frenzy is difficult to describe, except in this verse, where impatience, distrust, and anxiety are all combined. Impatience to know that the letter has reached there, distrust as to whether the messenger is indeed going there, and anxiety about how the beloved will receive the letter.

یہ عُمر بھر جو پریشانیاں اُٹھائی ہیں ہم نے
تمھارے آئیو اے طُرّہ ہاے خم بہ خم آگے

yih ʻumr bhar jo pareshānīyāñ uṭhā'ī haiñ ham ne
tumhāre āiyo ae ṯurra(h) hāi ḳham ba(h) ḳham āge (177:5; #1099)

This bearing the distresses of life as we have done,
May it all come to retribution before you, O! Entwined tresses.

ṯurra(h) hāi ḳham ba(h) ḳham: entwined tresses, curl upon curl;
tumhāre āiyo āge: a curse that it will come to face you.

An apparent curse, but actually a prayer that her tresses will scatter to the joy of the lover when the times comes to take account of all injustices.

دِل وجِگر میں پَر افشاں جو ایک مَوجۂ خوں ہے
ہم اپنے زُعم میں سمجھے ہُوئے تھے اِس کو دم آگے

dil-o-jigar meñ par afshāñ jo ek mauja(h)' ḳhūñ hai
ham apne z'aum meñ samjhe hū'e the is ko dam āge (177:6; #1100)

Fluttering like wounded feathers is a wave of blood in my heart and liver, which
We had vainly misconstrued to be our breath.

z'aum: presumption; *par afshāñ*: wounded feathers.

Like the damaged feathers of a fluttering bird, the wave of blood fills my heart and liver (meaning chest) that we had erroneously thought of as our breath. The key element of this verse is misconstruing the wave of blood as breath rather presumptuously. If our breath were so strong, we would have been able to survive the rigors of the beloved's demands. The strength of breath signifies strength of courage. The real thing is the wave of blood.

قسم جنازے پہ آنے کی میرے کھاتے ہیں غالبؔ
ہمیشہ کھاتے تھے جو میری جان کی قسم آگے

qasam janāze pa(h) āne kī mere khāte haiñ Ġhālib
hamesha(h) khāte the jo merī jān kī qasam āge (177:7; #1101)

Vowing not to attend my funeral, *Ġhālib*,
Are those who always used to swear upon my life before.

Swearing not to come to my funeral are the same people who swore upon my life to protect it. In the first line, they swear never to come; the second line refers to when they swore against any harm to me. Those who loved me once are now so fed up with me that they do not even want to come to my funeral. Since swearing can be both for and against something, several permutations of the swearing can be constructed here.

178

شکوے کے نام سے بے مہر خفا ہوتا ہے   یہ بھی مت کہ، کہ جو کہیے تو گلا ہوتا ہے

shikve ke nām se be mahar ḳhafā hotā hai
yih bhī mat kah, kih jo kahīye to gilā hotā hai (178:1; #1102)

Even the mention of complaint makes that unfaithful beloved upset;
Do not even say this, for saying this will be construed as a complaint also.

My beloved, who is unloving, gets upset if I ever mention her cruelty. She does not want to hear anything of the sort. Even the mention that she gets unjustifiably upset should be refrained from, for she may take it as complaining.

پُر ہوں مَیں شکوے سے یُوں، راگ سے جیسے باجا   اِک ذرا چھیڑیے، پھر دیکھیے کیا ہوتا ہے

pur hūñ meñ shikve se yūn, rāg se jaise bājā
ik żarā chheṛīye, phir dekhīye kyā hotā hai (178:2; #1103)

I am full of plaints as an instrument is full of melody.
Just try striking me once and then see what happens.

chheṛīye: striking to play an instrument, to tease; *rāg*: one of the six modes in classical music (*rāg alāpnā* means being repetitive).

I am full of complaints against my beloved just like a musical instrument is full of melodies. Tease me and I will blurt out my song. The musical instrument is actually filled with "*rāg*," the mode of classical music which represents repetitive tones. (*rāg alapnā* means to be repetitive and also in a derogatory manner it means to sound like a broken record.) With this background, we see an interesting comparison made with the musical instrument. Further, to begin playing an instrument is also called, literally, "to tease," which the poet is using to say, "Do not tease me, or be ready to hear a broken record of complaints." The tone is threatening.

گو سمجھتا نہیں پر حُسنِ تلافی دیکھو شکوۂ جور سے سرگرمِ جفا ہوتا ہے

go samajhtā nahiñ par ḥusn-e talāfī dekho
shikva(h)' jor se sargarm-e jafā hotā hai (178:3; #1104)

Look at the elegance of how she recompenses, not realizing as
Complaining of cruelty gets her busy inflicting greater cruelty.

ḥusn-e talāfī: rectifying elegantly.

My beloved is young and naïve and thus she does not understand why I complain to her. But to recompense my complaints, she inflicts more cruelty on me. Of course, more cruelty is what the lover wants. This is an elegant solution for both the lover and the beloved.

عشق کی راہ میں ہے چرخِ مکوکب کی وہ چال سست رو جیسے کوئی آبلہ پا ہوتا ہے

'ishq kī rāh meñ hai charḳh-e makaukab kī vuh chāl
sust rau jaise ko'ī ābla(h) pā hotā hai (178:4; #1105)

In the path of love, the sky filled with stars has the gait
Of a slow walker with blisters on his feet.

charḳh: sky; *makaukab*: filled with stars.

The stars in the sky are compared to blisters on the feet and the slow movement of the sky to the slow gait of someone with blistered feet. As lovers wander, their feet get blistered, slowing them down. The poet is wondering in whose love the sky is wandering. This verse would be classified as imaginative juggling.

کیوں نہ ٹھہریں ہدفِ ناوکِ بیداد، کہ ہم   آپ اُٹھا لاتے ہیں گر تیر خطا ہوتا ہے

kioñ na(h) ṭhahreñ hadaf-e nāvak-e bedād, kih ham
āp uṭhā lāte haiñ gar tīr ḳhaṭā hotā hai (178:5; #1106)

Why shouldn't we end up becoming the target of the arrow of cruelty, for we,
Ourselves collect the fallen arrows that miss striking us?

hadaf: target; *nāvak*: arrow; *ḳhaṭā*: missed.

We are, naturally, the targets of the arrow of cruelty, for we pick up the arrows that miss and return them to the archer. Why would not we end up getting hit by them, for as we return the arrows, she knows how desperate we are to be hit by her?

خُوب تھا، پہلے سے ہوتے جو ہم اپنے بدخواہ   کہ بھلا چاہتے ہیں اور بُرا ہوتا ہے

ḳhūb thā, pahle se hote jo ham apne badḳh(v)ah
kih bhalā chāhte haiñ aur burā hotā hai (178:6; #1107)

It would be better if we wished ourselves ill from the beginning.
For as we long for good, only bad things happen to us.

Whatever we desire, the opposite happens. We want good things to happen to us, but only bad things happen. Perhaps it would have been better to be our own ill wishers from the beginning. Then, many good things would have happened to us.

نالہ جاتا تھا پرے عرش سے میرا اور اب   لب تک آتا ہے جو ایسا ہی رسا ہوتا ہے

nāla(h) jātā thā pare ʿarsh se merā, aur ab
lab tak ātā hai jo aisā hī rasā hotā hai (178:7; #1108)

My plaint used to reach beyond the heavens, but now
It reaches only to my lips, if it ever goes anywhere.

My plaints used to go beyond the heavens, but now they are all buried in my chest. Those few that do come out barely reach my lips because of my weakness and lack of sincerity.

خامہ میرا کہ وہ ہے باربدِ بزمِ سخن   شاہ کی مدح میں یوں نغمہ سرا ہوتا ہے

ḳhāma(h) merā kih vuh hai Bārbūd-e bazm-e suḳhan
shāh kī madḥ meñ yūñ naġhma(h) sarā hotā hai (178:8; #1109)

My pen is like *Bārbūd* in the assembly of poetry.
As it begins to sing like him in the praise of the King

ḳhāma(h): pen; *Bārbūd*: famous singer in the court of Emperor Khusrao Parvez of Iran, he lived near Shiraz.

Like *Bārbūd* singing praises in the court of King Khusrao, my pen (my verses)—giving up writing *ġhazals*—is now praising the King. A pen turning into a singer can sing a song, but it cannot write a *ġhazal*.

اے شہنشاہِ کواکب سپہ و مہرِ علم   تیرے اکرام کا حق کس سے ادا ہوتا ہے

ai shahanshāh-e kavākib sipah-o-mahr ʿalam
tere ikrām kā ḥaq kis se adā hotā hai (178:9; #1110)

O! Emperor, with the stars as your soldiers and the sun as your flag,
Who can repay the obligation of kindness due to you?

kavākib sipah: whose army is stars, as many soldiers as stars; *mahr ʿalam*: flag like sun; *ikrām*: kindness.

O! Emperor, with as many soldiers as the stars, and a flag as high and bright as the sun, remaining the most powerful, and reigning over the world, the honor you bestow upon people is so high that it can never be paid back.

سات اقلیم کا حاصل جو فراہم کیجے   تو وہ لشکر کا ترے نعل بہا ہوتا ہے

sāt iqlīm kā ḥāṣil jo firāham kīje
to vuh lashkar kā tere na῾l bahā hotā hai (178:10; #1111)

If we provide the net worth of the seven continents,
That is equivalent to the horseshoe money for your forces.

sāt iqlīm: seven continents (meaning the entire world); *na῾lbahā*: horseshoe price (the ransom money given to conquerors to stop them from plundering their newly-won territory).

If we add up the net worth of all the continents of the world, it will be equivalent to the ransom money for your forces meaning that you have a very large force. Imagine how rich you would be to afford them, the praise of the King continues.

ہر مہینے میں جو یہ بدر سے ہوتا ہے ہلال   آستاں پر ترے مہ ناصیہ سا ہوتا ہے

har mahīne meñ jo yih badar se hotā hai hilāl
āstāñ par tere mah nāṣiya(h) sā hotā hai (178:11; #1112)

Every month as the full moon turns into a crescent,
The moon actually rubs its forehead at your threshold.

badar: full moon; *hilāl*: crescent; *āstāñ*: threshold; *mah*: moon; *nāṣiya*: rubbing forehead.

The reason why the full moon turns into a crescent every month is because it rubs its forehead at your doorstep and gets consumed. The moon does it to show its appreciation.

میں جو گستاخ ہوں آئینِ غزل خوانی میں   یہ بھی تیرا ہی کرم ذوق فزا ہوتا ہے

maiñ jo gustāḳh hu'ñ ā'īn-e ġhazal ḳhvānī meñ
yih bhī terā hi karam żauq fizā hotā hai (178:12; #1113)

My being disrespectful of the etiquette of saying, *ġhazal*
This too is a result of your kindness in creating this style.

gustāḳh: disrespectful.

I have begun writing odes while composing *ġhazals*; this is out of etiquette, but then, this new taste for the genre of ode is a result of your being kind to me. Ode to the King continues.

رکھیو غالب مجھے اِس تلخ نوائی میں مُعاف
آج کچھ درد مرے دل میں سِوا ہوتا ہے

rakhyo Ġhālib mujhe is talḳh navā'ī meñ mu'āf
āj kuchh dard mere dil meñ sivā hotā hai (178:13; #1114)

Pardon me, *Ġhālib*, for singing bitter songs;
Today in my heart there appears nothing but pain.

talḳh navā: bitter talk, singing bitter songs.

Do not be offended by my bitter songs. I should be pardoned, for today my heart is full of sadness.

179

ہر ایک بات پہ کہتے ہو تم کہ تُو کیا ہے　　تمھیں کہو کہ یہ اندازِ گفتگو کیا ہے

har ek bāt pa(h) kahte ho tum kih tū kyā hai
tumhiñ kaho kih yih andāz-e guftagū kyā hai (179:1; #1115)

At everything said, you say, "Who art thou?"
Tell me, what kind of a talk is this?

No matter what I say, I hear "Who art thou?" spoken insultingly. That is no way to talk to anyone. If I am saying something, do not interrupt me. If you disagree, let us argue; but shutting me up laughingly, belittling me, I protest.

نہ شعلے میں یہ کرشمہ نہ برق میں یہ ادا　　کوئی بتاؤ کہ وہ شوخِ تند خُو کیا ہے

na(h) sho'le meñ yih karishma(h) na(h) barq meñ yih adā
ko'ī batāo kih vuh shoḳh-e tund khū kyā hai (179:2; #1116)

Neither the flame has this miracle, nor the lightning has this coquetry;
Would someone tell me, what *is* that coquettish ill-tempered one?

karishma: miracle ; *adā*: coquetry; *shoḳh-e tund khū*: coquettishly ill-tempered.

I wanted to compare her to a flame, but it does not have her fury. Then I tried to compare her to lightning, but it does not have her ill temper or coquetry. Would someone tell me "what" she is?

یہ رشک ہے کہ وہ ہوتا ہے ہم سخن تم سے　　وگرنہ خوفِ بدآموزیِ عدو کیا ہے

yih rashk hai kih vuh hotā hai hamsuḳhan tum se
vagarna(h) ḳhauf-e badāmozī' 'adū kyā hai (179:3; #1117)

The envy is that he is conversing with you,
Or else what fear can I have that the enemy will mislead you.

badāmoz: to mislead, to teach bad things, to lead to wrong path.

I am not afraid that my enemy will mislead you against me; I am envious that you are talking to him. Trying to hide his paranoia about the enemy saying bad things about him is a subtle attempt to tell the beloved not to be fooled by the rival. Lover's insecurity is showing abundantly.

چپک رہا ہے بدن پر لہو سے پیراہن　　ہمارے جیب کو اب حاجتِ رفو کیا ہے

chipak rahā hai badan par lahū se pairāhan
ḥamāre jeb ko ab ḥājat-e rafū kyā hai (179:4; #1118)

Sticking to the body is the attire with blood.
What need is there now to darn the collar?

jeb: collar; *rafū*: darning.

Dried out blood causes the clothing to stick to the body and keeps the torn collar in place. When the whole body is bleeding and hurting, why worry about the torn collar; meaning, why worry about the pain of frenzy and despair? The whole world knows now. This verse points to a great reality of life where bigger misfortunes make our smaller misfortunes appear trivial. This is undoubtedly one of *Ġhālib*'s most profound and melancholic presentations.

جلا ہے جسم جہاں، دل بھی جل گیا ہوگا　　کریدتے ہو جو اب راکھ جستجو کیا ہے

jalā hai jism jahāñ, dil bhī jal gayā hogā
kuredte ho jo ab rākh justajū kyā hai (179:5; #1119)

Where the body was burned, the heart too must have been consumed.
Sifting the ashes, what is it that you are searching for now?

The fire of love has burned the body and with that, the heart. Why are you sifting through ashes? If you are looking for my heart, it has gone with the body. Two situations arise: The beloved wants to make sure that the heart has also burned; or perhaps she is feeling embarrassed, sifting ashes to find out if the heart can be saved. In either case, the loss is inevitable.

رگوں میں دوڑتے پھرنے کے ہم نہیں قائل　　جب آنکھ سے ہی نہ ٹپکا تو پھر لہو کیا ہے

ragoñ meñ doṛte phirne ke ham nahiñ qā'l
jab āñkh se hī na(h) ṭapkā to phir lahū kyā hai (179:6; #1120)

We believe not in just sprinting through the veins.
What blood is it that did not drip from the eyes?

Circulating blood indicates a continuous struggle but until the struggle results in suffering, causing us to cry tears of blood, the resolve of love is not complete.

وہ چیز جس کے لیے ہم کو ہو بہشت عزیز　　سوائے بادۂ گلفام مشکبو کیا ہے

vuh chīz jis ke liye ham ko ho bahisht 'azīz
sivāe bāda(h)' gulfām-e mushkbū kyā hai (179:7; #1121)

The thing, for which the Paradise is dear to us,
Is nothing except the pink, musk-scented wine.

bād'a: wine; *gulfām*: red-like ; *mushkbū*: musk-scented.

The joys of Paradise include four canals: water, honey, milk, and wine. To us, the only reason to like Paradise is that it will offer that red-colored, musk-scented wine in abundance. The wine of Paradise will not be intoxicating, but to the poet, the sight of the red wine is intoxicating enough. There is also a subtle sarcasm at what little Paradise offers. It adds that we are not running after nymphs; we only want wine.

پیوں شراب اگر خُم بھی دیکھ لُوں دو چار   یہ شیشہ و قدح و کوزہ و سبو کیا ہے

piyūñ sharāb agar ḳhum bhī dekh lūñ do chār
yih shīsha(h)-o-qadḥ-o-kūza(h)-o-sabū kyā hai (179:8; #1122)

I will drink wine if I see a few decanters of wine.
What are this glass and bowl, goblet and tumbler?

ḳhum: decanter ; *shīsha*: glass; *qadḥ*: bowl; *kūza*: earthen goblet; *sabū*: tumbler.

Wineglass and bowl do not excite me; I need to see a few decanters of wine before I will start drinking. Drinkers know that they must drink enough, without which they remain thirsty. The poet is bragging about his ability to imbibe.

رہی نہ طاقتِ گفتار اور اگر ہو بھی   تو کس اُمید پہ کہیے کہ آرزو کیا ہے

rahī na(h) tāqat-e guftār aur agar ho bhī
to kis ummid pa(h) kahīye kih ārzū kyā hai (179:9; #1123)

Gone is the strength to speak, but even if it were there,
With what hope could one say, "What is my desire?"

Waiting for a lifetime, weakness has taken away my speech. But if I could muster enough energy, what hope would I have that my words would be heard, since they have been ignored throughout my life? Here we have a hopeless situation taking away the energy to say anything at the time of death.

ہُوا ہے شہ کا مُصاحِب، پھرے ہے اِتراتا
وگرنہ شہر میں غالبؔ کی آبرُو کیا ہے

hu'ā hai shah kā maṣāḥib, phir-e hai itrātā
vagarna(h) shahr meñ Ġhālib kī ābrū kyā hai (179:10; #1124)

Becoming a courtier to the King, he is putting on airs;
Or else, what dignity does *Ġhālib* enjoy in the city?

maṣāḥib: courtier; *itrātā*: boasting; *ābrū*: dignity.

Ġhālib is going around boasting that he has been appointed a courtier to the King to gain status in town. Had it not been for this appointment, *Ġhālib* would have no status.

180

میں اُنھیں چھیڑوں، اور کچھ نہ کہیں
چل نکلتے جو مے پیے ہوتے

maiñ unheñ cheṛūñ, aur kuchh na(h) kaheñ
chal nikalte jo mai pīye hote (180:1; #1125)

Tease her and she would not say anything?
She would have gone beyond the limit, had she been drinking.

chal nikalte: gone beyond limit.

The beloved is showing tolerance because of the etiquette of the assembly. The lover is thankful and expounds that had she been drinking, she would have gone beyond limit to punish him for his audacity. That alcohol depresses inhibition is the lesson taught here.

قہر ہو یا بلا ہو، جو کچھ ہو
کاشکے تم مرے لیے ہوتے

qahr ho yā balā ho, jo kuchh ho
kāsh ke tum mere liye hote (180:2; #1126)

A calamity, an evil spirit, whoever you are;
I wish that you were made only for me.

qahr: fury, calamity, divine wrath; *balā*: evil spirit, fiend.

The beloved responds to the lover's offer by asking him, "Do you know who I am? I am fury, a calamity, an evil spirit, "to which the lover says,

"Whoever you are, I wish you were only for me." He is willing to accept all distressing situations except the distress of jealousy.

میری قسمت میں غم گر اتنا تھا
دل بھی یا رب کئی دیے ہوتے

merī qismat meñ ġham gar itnā thā
dil bhī yārabb ka'ī diye hote (180:3; #1127)

If there was such great suffering in my destiny,
Then O! Lord, You should have given me many hearts as well.

The grief in my life is too much for one heart to bear. If this is what God intended, then He should have given me several more hearts with which to bear the pain. Remarkably, *Ġhālib* is not complaining to God about his ill fate, that is God's prerogative; he is just asking for enough courage to bear it, that is man's prerogative. This is indeed one of the most humbling and melancholic verses of *Urdū* poetry.

آ ہی جاتا وہ راہ پر غالبؔ
کوئی دن اور بھی جیے ہوتے

āhī jātā vuh rāh par Ġhālib
ko'ī din aur bhī jīye hote (180:4; #1128)

She would have come to the straight path, *Ġhālib*,
If only I had lived a few more days.

My beloved would have come to agree if I had a few more days to live. Death came too soon. Naturally, this is not your fault—you should not feel bad, the poet consoles himself. This is contrary to many other verses where *Ġhālib* says that things would have remained the same if he had lived longer, or that he would have faced greater calamities if he had lived longer.

181

غیر لیں محفل میں بوسے جام کے
ہم رہیں یوں تشنہ لب پیغام کے

ġhair leñ maḥfil meñ bose jām ke
ham rahaiñ yūñ tashna(h) lab paiġhām ke (181:1; #1129)

While the strangers would kiss the goblet in your assembly,
We shall, like this, remain thirsty for invitation.

tashna(h) lab paiġhām: thirsty for invitation.

When strangers are drinking happily in your assembly, we are desperately awaiting your invitation. Drinking by strangers is contrasted with thirsty life. The tone of this verse is that of benign sarcasm.

خستگی کا تم سے کیا شکوہ، کہ یہ
ہتکھنڈے ہیں چرخِ نیلی فام کے

ḳhastagī kā tum se kyā shikva(h), kih yih
hathkanḍe haiñ charḳh-e nīlī fām ke (181:2; #1130)

Why complain to you of my ruination? For these
Are the trickeries of the blue colored sky.

ḳhastagī: exhaustion, ruination, wounded heart; *hathkanḍe*: trickery; *charḳh*: sky; *nīlī fām*: blue color.

How can I complain to you about my misfortune? It was my fate, for it was the trickery of the heavens against me. There was little that anyone could do about it—including you, my beloved.

خط لکھیں گے گرچہ مطلب کچھ نہ ہو
ہم تو عاشق ہیں تمھارے نام کے

ḳhaṯ likheñ ge garchih maṯlab kuchh na(h) ho
ham to ʿāshiq haiñ tumhāre nām ke (181:3; #1131)

Though meaningless, we shall keep writing letters, for
We are the lovers of your name.

maṯlab kuchh na(h) ho: without much substance.

We will keep writing you letters even if there is not anything new to say. The purpose of writing to you is to write your name often, for that's what we are in love with.

رات پی زمزم پہ مے اور صبح دم
دھوئے دھبّے جامۂ احرام کے

rāt pī zamzam pa(h) mai aur subḥ dam
dho'e dhabbe jāma(h)' aḥrām ke (181:4; #1132)

All night we kept drinking at the Zamzam well and at dawn,
We washed the stains from our pilgrim's garb.

zamzam: famous well a few yards away from *Kā'bā*, the place of Muslim pilgrimage; *aḥrām*: to deny yourself, two plain white sheets used to wrap oneself when performing pilgrimage, a strict code of conduct that requires denying many things until this cloth is removed.

Sitting at the well of Zamzam, we drank wine (which is forbidden), and in the morning, we washed the stain of our sins off our garb. This means that we committed sins wherever we went, but by going to *Kaʿbā* (Haj), we washed off all our sins. At least that is what we thought we were doing.

دِل کو آنکھوں نے پھنسایا کیا مگر
یہ بھی حلقے ہیں تمھارے دام کے

dil ko āñkhoñ ne phañsāyā kyā magar
yih bhī ḥalqe haiñ tumhāre dām ke (181:5; #1133)

How my eyes have trapped my heart, but
These too are the rings of your snare.

phañsāyā: trapped; *kyā*: what; *dām*: snare.

My eyes saw you and my heart fell in love with you. I was trapped because of my eyes, which actually are the rings of your snare. You have other snares also.

شاہ کے ہے غُسلِ صحت کی خبر
دیکھیے کب دِن پھریں حمام کے

shāh ke hai ġhusl-e ṣeḥat kī ḳhabar
dekhiye kab din phireñ ḥammām ke (181:6; #1134)

The news is that the King will take his bath of recuperation;
See when the fortune of the bath will turn.

ġhusl-e ṣeḥat: bathing after recovery from illness; *din phireñ*: turning of fortune; *ḥammām*: bath, Turkish bath.

(In July 1853, King *Bahadur Shāh Zafir* fell ill; the illness was prolonged. He took his bath of recovery on 23 November 1853. This verse was written in September 1853.)

There is a rumor in town that the King will soon take his bath of recovery. This is certainly a matter of great fortune for the bath; let us see when its healing powers will come to frution. This verse wishes the King well.

عشق نے غالبؔ نکما کر دیا
ورنہ ہم بھی آدمی تھے کام کے

'ishq ne Ġhālib nikammā kar diyā
varna(h) ham bhī ādmī the kām ke (181:7; #1135)

Love has rendered you, *Ġhālib*, of no use,
Or else we, too, were a person of great use.

nikammā: useless, of no use.

Loving has done wrong to you, rendering you totally useless; you were not like that before.

182

پھر اِس انداز سے بہار آئی   کہ ہُوئے مہر و مہ تماشائی

phir is andāz se bahār ā'ī
kih hu'e mahr-o-ma(h) tamāshāī' (182:1; #1136)

Again the spring season has arrived with such style
That the even the sun and moon have become its spectators.

This *ġhazal* is a detailed description of the arrival of spring season. We all look at the sun and moon to relish their beauty, but for them to be attracted to the display of the spring season is indeed a rarity; it must be the most beautiful sight in the universe.

دیکھو اے ساکنانِ خطۂ خاک   اِس کو کہتے ہیں عالم آرائی

dekho ai sākinān-e ḳhittah' ḳhāk
is ko kahte haiñ 'ālam ārāī' (182:2; #1137)

Look, you dwellers of the earth,
This is what is called decorating the world.

sākinān: inhabitants; *ḳhittah'*: piece; *ḳhāk*: dust.

Addressing the inhabitants of earth, the poet pointing to the many ways the spring season has brightened the earth.

کہ زمیں ہو گئی ہے سر تا سر   رُوکشِ سطحِ چرخِ مینائی

kih zamīñ hoga'ī hai sar tā sar
rūkash-e saṭḥ-e charḳh-e mīnāī' (182:3; #1138)

That earth has turned such that from corner to corner
It is putting to shame the face of blue coloured sky.

rūkash: putting to shame; *charḳh-e mīnā'ī*: blue colored sky; *saṭḥ*: surface, face.

Such is the depth of earth's beauty that it puts the infinitely deep blue beauty of sky to shame.

سبزے کو جب کہیں جگہ نہ ملی   بن گیا روئے آب پر کائی

sabze ko jab kahīñ jaga(h) na(h) milī
ban gayā rūe āb par kāī' (182:4; #1139)

When the grass did not find room to grow anywhere,
It turned into green algae on the surface of the water.

kā'ī: algae, fungus on water, scum.

Calling the green algae on surface of water greenery indicates that everything is displaying the color of spring season. Notice how keenly the poet is expressing the growth of life in the spring season. There is greening everywhere, even on the surface of water.

سبزہ و گل کے دیکھنے کے لیے   چشمِ نرگس کو دی ہے بینائی

sabza(h)-o-gul ke dekhne ke liye
chashm-e nargis ko dī hai bināī' (182:5; #1140)

To look at the greenery and flowers,
The eye of the narcissus has been given sight.

nargis: narcissus; *bināī'*: vision.

Narcissus is an eye-shaped flower that has been given sight to look around and appreciate the beauty of spring. Note that narcissism is self-appreciation, and thus, for one who is a narcissist to appreciate other things, it must be supremely beautiful.

ہے ہوا میں شراب کی تاثیر   بادہ نوشی ہے بادپیمائی

hai havā meñ sharāb kī tāsīr
bāda(h) noshī hai bād paimāī' (182:6; #1141)

The breeze is full of the effects of wine;
Inhaling air is just like drinking wine.

bād paimā'ī: to eat (inhale) air.

The breeze in the garden is so exhilarating that it causes us to become intoxicated without even drinking wine. It seems that inhaling air is sufficient to get drunk now.

کیوں نہ دُنیا کو ہو خوشی غالب
شاہِ دیندار نے شفا پائی

kioñ na(h) dunyā ko ho ḳhushī Ġhālib
shāh-e dīñdār ne shifā pāī' (182:7; #1142)

Why would not the world be happy, *Ġhālib*?
Our religious King has recovered from his illness.

dīñdār: religious; *shifā*: recovery from illness.

This *ġhazal* is a continuous impression of the poet looking to the arrival of the spring season. How many ways a poet can see things in ordinary happenings is remarkably well depicted here.

183

تغافل دوست ہوں ، میرا دماغ عجز عالی ہے
اگر پہلو تہی کیجے تو جا میری بھی خالی ہے

taġhāful dost hūñ, merā damāġh-e 'ijz 'ālī hai
agar pahlū tahī kije to jā merī bhī ḳhālī hai (183:1; #1143)

I like being indifferent, for my humble mind is of a high order.
If you pull away from me, then my place shall remain vacant.

dost: friend; *damāġh*: mind; *tahī*: empty; *pahlū tahī*: to avoid; *taġhāful*: obliviousness, carelessness, indifference; *'ijz*: humbleness; *'ālī*: high.

I am proud that my humbleness makes me indifferent. As you are determined to remain aloof, I will not stick around, either; and thus, this place shall remain empty. You will not find anyone else, who, like me, loves indifference.

رہا آباد عالم اہل ہمت کے نہ ہونے سے
بھرے ہیں جس قدر جام و سبو میخانہ خالی ہے

rahā ābād 'ālam ahl-e himmat ke na(h) hone se
bhare haiñ jis qadar jām-o-sabū maiḳhāna(h) ḳhālī hai
(183:2; #1144)

The world remained populated for they were not the courageous ones;
The fuller the goblet and decanter stay, the more the tavern appears deserted.

Courageous here means those who pay little attention to worldly things. It is the absence of such people that keeps the world so crowded. This is compared with an empty tavern, where the goblets and decanters shall remain filled because there is no one to drink wine. If there were enough people who would reject the world, it would turn into ruin. But that is not the case. The key to understanding this very difficult verse comes from the connection between a crowded planet and the people courageous enough to reject and thus leave the world. Since there are still so many around, these must be few courageous ones. The comparison with the tavern is made to show the taste of the wine of reality. Also, note the similarity between round earth and round goblet, both full. The reason the earth is full of people is because they do not have the courage to leave it, though they know well how bad it is.

184

کب وہ سنتا ہے کہانی میری — اور پھر وہ بھی زبانی میری

kab vuh suntā hai kahānī merī
aur phir vuh bhī zabānī merī (184:1; #1145)

When does she ever listen to my story,
Let alone in my own words?

The beloved does not want to hear anything about me from anyone. The chance that she will ever hear my story in my own words is indeed remote.

خلشِ غمزۂ خونریز نہ پوچھ — دیکھ خوننابہ فشانی میری

ḳhalish-e ġhamza(h)' ḳhūñrez na(h) pūchh
dekh ḳhunnāba(h) fishānī merī (184:2; #1146)

Ask not of the pain of her killing amorous glances;
Just look at the blood dripping from my eyes.

Ḳhūñrez: murderous

Why do you ask how badly I've been hurt by her killing glances? Do you not see the blood dripping from my eyes? A glance and an eye dripping blood create an appropriate scene, but "blood is dripping from my eyes" signifies extreme pain.

کیا بیاں کر کے مرا روئیں گے یار — مگر آشفتہ بیانی میری

kyā bayāñ kar ke merā ro'eñ ge yār
magar āshufta(h) bayānī merī (184:3; #1147)

What would my friends say while lamenting at my death,
Except for my lunatic style of expression?

To cry means to talk at the wake. Which quality of mine would they think worth remembering? The only thing that they can point out is how I used to talk incoherently in my lunacy.

ہوں زِ خود رفتۂ بَیداے خیال   بھول جانا ہے نشانی میری

hūñ zikḥud rafta(h)' baidā e ḳhayāl
bhūl jānā hai nishānī merī (184:4; #1148)

I am on my own, wandering in the desert of thought.
Getting lost is the trait that distinguishes me.

baidā: a desert.

Drifting in the wilderness of thought, I am recognized for being forgetful.

مُتقابِل ہے مُقابِل میرا   رُک گیا دیکھ روانی میری

mutaqābil hai muqābil merā
ruk gayā dekh ravānī merī (184:5; #1149)

My opponent and I are facing each other;
Hearing my flowing speech has stifled him.

mutaqābil: confronting rival; *ruk gayā*: kept quiet; *ravānī*: flow of speech.

My confronting rival, upon hearing my speech, becomes stifled due to its fluency and impact.

قدرِ سنگِ سرِ رہ رکھتا ہوں   سخت ارزاں ہے گرانی میری

qadar-e sang-e sar-e rah rakhtā hūñ
sahḳt arzāñ hai girānī merī (184:6; #1150)

My value is that of a stone lying along the path:
Extremely light is my heaviness.

arzāñ: light, cheap; *girānī*: heavy, expensive, dearness.

A heavy stone along a path does not get kicked around, but stays there for people to walk over, making it extremely cheap. It is the heaviness of the stone that makes it cheap (because it cannot be moved). I am not a lightweight poet that can be bounced around. That's why I take so many insults from people—because, like the rock, I am here to stay. It is my weight in poetry that causes people to criticize me. No one would pay attention if I were a lightweight. The play of words comes in the second line: light vs. heavy, and cheap vs. expensive.

گرد بادِ رہِ بیتابی ہوں   صرصرِ شوق ہے بانی میری

gird bād-e rah-e betābī hūñ
ṣarṣar-e shauq hai bānī merī (184:7; #1151)

A whirlwind in the path of restlessness I am;
I have been created by the dust storm of desire.

gird bād: whirlwind; *betābī*: restlessness; *ṣarṣar*: dust storm.

As tumultuous as a whirlwind of dust, I am unable to rest because I am a creation of a storm (a storm of desire). As long as this storm lingers, I shall remain restless.

دہن اس کا جو نہ معلوم ہوا   کھل گئی ہیچمدانی میری

dahan us kā jo na(h) ma'lūm hu'ā
khul ga'ī hechmadānī merī (184:8; #1152)

Her mouth that could not be discovered,
Exposed my not knowing anything.

hechmadānī: not knowing anything, ignorance.

I should have known that the mouth of the beloved is so small that it does not exist. Trying to find it—and failing—exposed my ignorance. A play on words.

کر دیا ضعف نے عاجز غالب
ننگ پیری ہے جوانی میری

kar diyā zo'f ne 'ājiz Ġhālib
nang-e pirī hai javānī merī (184:9; #1153)

My weakness has humbled me, *Ġhālib*;
Disgrace to old age is my youth.

zo'f: weakness; *'ājiz*: humble.

Though still in my youth, my feebleness is disgraceful—even to older people.

185

نقشِ نازِ بتِ طنّاز بہ آغوشِ رقیب
پائے طاؤس پئے خامۂ مانی مانگے

naqsh-e nāz-e but-e ṭannāz ba(h) āġhosh-e raqīb,
pāe ṭā'ūs pa'e ḳhāma(h)' mānī māñge. (185:1; #1154)

The painting of the playful idol in the arms of the rival
Requires peacock's feet for the brush of *Mānī*.

naqsh: picture, painting; *ṭannāz*: taunting, frank, playful; *ḳhām'a(h)*: pen, brush; *Mānī*: famous artist, citizen of Babylon who declared prophethood and was exiled. He spent much of his life in Turkey and China and lived in Iran during the time of Shahpur; *pāe ṭā'ūs*: feet of a peacock.

Regardless of how beautiful and coquettish, in the arms of the rival, it is an ugly picture of beloved, worth drawing only with the ugliest brush. The feet of peacocks are considered very ugly. This is an expression of extreme jealousy. Using "*Mānī*" in place of any other artist may have some significance, but it does not cause any difficulty of expression.

تو وہ بدخو کہ تحیّر کو تماشا جانے
غم وہ افسانہ کہ آشفتہ بیانی مانگے

tū vuh badḳhū kih taḥaiyyur ko tamāshā jāne
ġham vuh afsāna(h) kih āshufta(h) bayānī māñge (185:2; #1155)

You are so ill-mannered getting amused at my amazement
While sorrow is a story that demands lunacy to express itself.

bad ḳhū: ill-mannered; *taḥaiyyur*: astonishment, amazement, surprise, stunned; *āshufta*: lunacy.

The beloved has the bad habit of acting bemused at the stunned expression of the lover, but the lover can only express his sorrow rightly in a lunatic tone to let every one know his condition. The beloved does not like this, and it creates a dilemma for the lover—how can he keep the beloved amused while venting his grief! Another aspect is that the beloved considers his story of sorrow as lunatic babbling and gets upset with him. The reason the beloved wants the lover to stay in a state of shock is that, when in shock, he will not talk about his problems.

وُہ تپِ عشق، تمنّا ہے کہ پھر صُورتِ شمع
شُعلہ تا نبضِ جگر ریشہ دَوانی مانگے

vuh tab-e ʿishq, tamannā hai kih phir ṣurat-e shamaʿ
shoʿla(h) tā nabẓ-e jigar resha(h) davānī māñge (185:3; #1156)

I long again for that fever of love, which, like the heat of the candle flame,
Would demand spreading through the veins to reach the pulse of the liver.

nabẓ: pulse; *resha*: vein, roots, tissue; *davānī*: running.

Like the heat of the flame of the candle that seeps down the spine of the wick, the heat of my love should reach the heart (liver) to warm the soul.

186

گلشن کو تری صحبت از بسکہ خوش آئی ہے
ہر غنچے کا گل ہونا آغوش کشائی ہے

gulshan ko terī ṣoḥbat az baskih ḳhush āī hai
har ġhunche kā gul honā āġhosh kushāī' hai (186:1; #1157)

The garden has become so enamored with your presence that
The buds are turning into flowers to embrace you in their arms.

ġhunche: bud; *gul*: flowers; *āġhosh kushā'ī*: to open arms to embrace.

As the beloved arrives in the garden, the buds have begun to turn into flowers as if opening their arms to embrace her.

واں کنگرِ استغنا ہر دم ہے بلندی پر
یاں نالے کو اور اُلٹا دعوے رسائی ہے

vāñ kungur-e istiġhnā har dam hai balandī par
yāñ nāle ko aur ulṭā da'vā e rasāī' hai (186:2; #1158)

There the parapet of obliviousness is reaching new heights every minute.
Here, in response, the plaint claims to be able to reach there.

kungur: decorative facade of a cupola, parapet; *istiġhnā*: obliviousness.

A competitive situation develops here. The beloved raises her obliviousness to new heights and the lover asserts that his plaints have enough power to reach *any* height.

ازبسکہ سکھاتا ہے غم ضبط کے اندازے
جو داغ نظر آیا اک چشم نمائی ہے

azbaske sikhātā hai ġham ẓabṭ ke andāze
jo dāġh naẓar āyā ik chashm numāī' hai (186:3; #1159)

Whereas sorrow teaches the style of patience,
The scars appearing represent glances of reproof.

chashm numāī: dirty look, glance of reproof.

Sorrow is teaches love to be patient. Any new scar in the heart results from an admonishing glance.

187

جس زخم کی ہو سکتی ہو تدبیر رفو کی
لکھ دیجیو یا رب اُسے قسمت میں عدو کی

jis zaḳhm kī hosaktī ho tadbīr rafū kī
likh dījiyo yārabb use qismat meñ ʿadū kī (187:1; #1160)

The wound that could possibly be stitched,
Write it in the fate of my enemy, O! Lord.

rafū: repair, darn, stitch.

If there is a wound that can be repaired, give it to my rival. I want wounds that cannot be closed. This is one way to wish ill upon the rival.

اچھا ہے سر انگشتِ حنائی کا تصوّر
دِل میں نظر آتی تو ہے اِک بُوند لہُو کی

achhā hai sar angusht-e ḥinā'ī kā taṣavvur
dil meñ naẓar ātī to hai ik būnd lahū kī (187:2; #1161)

Great is the thought of her henna-tipped finger;
At least I can see a drop of blood in my heart.

sar angusht-e ḥinā: tip of *henna*-stained finger.

Thinking about her *henna*-stained fingertips reminds me of a drop of blood [referring to how tiny her fingers are]. Crying tears of blood, I have lost all the blood in my heart; looking at her *henna*-stained fingertips brings the warmth of blood to my heart. Note that blood keeps the heart warm.

کیوں ڈرتے ہو عُشّاق کی بے حوصلگی سے
یاں تو کوئی سنتا نہیں فریاد کسو کی

kioñ darte ho ʿushshāq kī be ḥauṣlagī se
yāñ to ko'ī suntā nahiñ firyād kisū kī (187:3; #1162)

Why are you afraid of the lover's lack of ambition?
Here nobody listens to the plaints of anyone.

be ḥauṣlagī: spiritless, dispirited, lack of ambition.

Afraid that the lovers are unable to bear the cruelty of the beloved and that they might complain to God, the poet assures the beloved that regardless of how much lovers complain, they will not be heard. The poet makes a sarcastic comparison: You did not listen to your lovers, so why would God listen to them? No one listens here, for if anyone did, they could not have missed the strong plaints of lovers.

دشنے نے کبھی مُنہ نہ لگایا ہو جگر کو
خنجر نے کبھی بات نہ پُوچھی ہو گلُو کی

dashne ne kabhī muñh na(h) lagāyā ho jigar ko
ḳhanjar ne kabhī bāt na(h) pūchī ho gulū kī (187:4; #1163)

The dagger may not have offered countenance to the liver;
The knife may not have cared to ask about the throat.

dashne: dagger; *muñh lagāyā*: to countenance; *ḳhanjar*: knife; *bāt pūchī*: to ask; *gulū*: throat.

See the next verse for explanation.

صد حیف وہ ناکام کہ اک عمر سے غالب
حسرت میں رہے ایک بت عربدہ جو کی

ṣad ḥaif vuh nākām kih ik ʿumr se Ġhālib
ḥasrat meñ rahe ek but-e ʿarbada(h) jū kī (187:5; #1164)

Alas, a hundred times for that failure, *Ġhālib*, who for a long time
Kept wishing for a quarrelsome beloved?

nākām: defeated, abortive, unrealized, unsuccesful. *ʿarbada(h) jū:* fighter.

The two verses above form a *q'ita*, a quatrain. It is sad that *Ġhālib* could not find a quarrelsome beloved who would use her daggers and knives of coquetry to kill him.

188

سیماب پُشت گرمیٔ آئینہ دے ہے، ہم
حیراں کیے ہوئے ہیں دلِ بیقرار کے

sīmāb pushtgarm'ī ā'ina(h) de hai, ham
hairāñ kiye hu'e haiñ dil-e beqarār ke (188:1; #1165)

The mercury gives character to the mirror, as we
Are thrown into amazement by our tumultuous heart.

sīmāb: mercury; *pushtgarm*: aid, support.

The mercury coating on a glass makes it a mirror, as if it were supporting the reflective nature of the mirror. My heart, which is just as tumultuous as mercury, keeps me amazed. These things support a mirror in one case and stunned state in another. But keeping me in a stunned state, my heart also stays unstable, contrary to what happens to the mercury. Mercury on a plate keeps vibrating and moving; coated on a mirror it stays put. The posture we take when we are totally amazed or stunned is that of freezing, like a frozen image in the mirror. My heart is mercury and I am the mirror.

آغوشِ گُل کشودہ برائے وداع ہے
اے عندلیب چل، کہ چلے دن بہار کے

āġhosh-e gul kushuda(h) barā'e vadā' hai
ai ʻandlīb chal, kih chale din bahār ke (188:2; #1166)

The arms of the flowers have opened to bid farewell
O! Nightingale, move on for the days of the spring season are over.

vadā: farewell.

Opening of flowers is an indication of the departure of spring. Come, nightingale, let us move on. A bud turns into a flower with open petals, which then wither away as the spring season ends.

189

ہے وصل ہجر عالمِ تمکین و ضبط میں
معشوقِ شوخ و عاشقِ دیوانہ چاہیے

hai vaṣal hjr ʿālam-e tamkīn-o-ẓabṯ meñ
maʿshūq-e shokh-o-ʿāshiq-e dīvāna(h) chāhiye (189:1; #1167)

Dignity and control in union is just like being in separation.
A sprightly beloved and a lunatic lover is what we need.

tamkīn: dignity; *ẓabṯ*: control.

Union with the beloved is just as gruesome as separation if the beloved sits gracefully and the lovers express great control over themselves. I say that the beloved should show coquetry and the lover should lose control at the sight of her. That's union!

سائے کی طرح ساتھ پھریں سرو و صنوبر   تو اِس قدِ دلکش سے جو گلزار میں آوے

us lab se mil hī jāe gā bosa(h) kabhī to, hāñ
shauq-e fuẓūl-o-jurr'at-e rindāna(h) chāhiye (189:2; #1168)

From those lips, I will sometime surely get a kiss, yes!
An exuberant desire and the courage of drunkards are needed.

shauq-e fuẓūl: exuberant desire; *jurr'at-e rindāna*: courage of drunkard.

I will definitely get a kiss from the lips of the beloved, eventually, if I keep my desire alive, which can only happen if I have excessive or exuberant desires since many of them will be killed anyway and have the courage of a drunkard. Drinking alcohol suppresses inhibition and makes one appear rather courageous.

190

چاہیے اچھوں کو ، جتنا چاہیے   یہ اگر چاہیں تو پھر کیا چاہیے

chāhiye achhoñ ko, jitnā chāhiye
yih agar chāheñ to phir kyā chāhīye (190:1; #1169)

One must love the beautiful ones, as much as one can.
And if they love you back, then what else can you want?

achhoñ: good ones, beauties.

The poet encourages all novice lovers to love the beauties and not worry about whether they love you back or not. If they do, you are lucky; but if they don't, the effort must not be stifled.

صحبتِ رنداں سے واجب ہے حذر   جائے مے ، اپنے کو کھینچا چاہیے

ṣoḥbat-e rindāñ se vājib hai ḥażar
jāe mai, apne ko khaiñchā chāhīye (190:2; #1170)

Shunning the company of drunkards is advisable;
One should retreat from wine in the tavern.

vājib: necessary, obligatory; *ḥażar*: caution, prudence; *khaiñchā*: to retreat.

It is better to avoid the company of drunkards. It is better not to drink in the tavern. Drinking is our habit and we do not need the formality of a tavern or the company of other drinkers to fulfill it; it only brings us bad name.

چاہنے کو تیرے کیا سمجھا تھا دل؟ بارے اب اِس سے بھی سمجھا چاہیے!

chāhne ko tere kyā samjhā thā dil
bāre ab is se bhī samjhā chāhīye (190:3; #1171)

What did the heart think about loving you?
Now this, too, must be admonished.

samjhā: admonish, understood.

How simple of my heart to think that loving you would be easy. For this mistake, we should admonish the heart. We should ask for an explanation.

چاک مت کر جَیب، بے ایّامِ گُل کُچھ اُدھر کا بھی اِشارا چاہیے

chāk mat kar jeb, be ayyām-e gul
kuchh udhar kā bhī ishārā chāhīye (190:4; #1172)

Tear not your collar unless 'tis a season of flowers;
As some signs must come from there too.

The coming of spring causes many to tear their collars. Flowers and lovers go hand in hand. The lover is advised not to tear his collar until there is an indication of the arrival of spring.

دوستی کا پردہ ہے بیگانگی مُنہ چھپانا ہم سے چھوڑا چاہیے

dostī kā parda(h) hai begāngī
muñh chhupānā ham se chhoṛā chāhīye (190:5; #1173)

The veil of friendship is obliviousness.
Hiding your face from us should be stopped.

When you hide your face from me, people notice it and think that there must be something between us. If you really want to show your indifference to me, then drop the veil. Here we have a playful attempt by the lover to catch a glimpse of the beloved.

دشمنی نے میری، کھویا غیر کو   کس قدر دشمن ہے، دیکھا چاہیے

dushmanī ne merī, khoyā ġhair ko
kis qadar dushman hai, dekhā chāhīye (190:6; #1174)

Enmity towards me made the rival lose out.
How great an enemy he is, we must see.

My rival used to tell the beloved derogatory things about me. Finally, the beloved got tired of it and got rid of him. My rival was such a great enemy to me that he accepted his total devastation, just to wish me ill.

اپنی، رسوائی میں کیا چلتی ہے سعی   یار ہی ہنگامہ آرا چاہیے

āpnī, rusvā'ī meñ kyā chaltī hai sa'ī
yār hī hangāma(h) ārā chāhīye (190:7; #1175)

What works out in our efforts to disgrace ourselves?
A friend of the riotous type is what is needed.

rusvā'ī: disgrace; *sa'ī*: effort; *hangāma(h) ārā*: riotous.

My efforts to lose my honor proved fruitless. This requires the presence of a riotous beloved, who can excite the lovers by her coquetry.

منحصر مرنے پہ ہو جس کی امید   نا امیدی اس کی دیکھا چاہیے

munḥaṣir marne pe ho jis kī ummīd
nā ummīdī us kī dekhā chāhīye (190:8; #1176)

The one whose only hope depends on death;
His hopelessness must be worth seeing.

How hopeless can you be when your only hope is to die? Anyone hoping for death to end all woes is indeed hopeless.

غافل ، اِن مہ طلعتوں کے واسطے   چاہنے والا بھی اَچھّا چاہیے

ġhāfil, in mah ṯalaʿtoñ kih vāsṯe
chāhne vālā bhī achhā chāhīye (190:9; #1177)

O! Ignorant, for these moon-faced beauties,
The lover must also be a good-looking one.

ṯala: face.

See the next verse for explanation.

چاہتے ہیں خُوبرُویوں کو اسؔد
آپ کی صُورت تو دیکھا چاہیے

chāhate haiñ ḵhūbrūyoñ ko Asad
āp kī ṣurat to dekhā chāhīye (190:10; #1178)

Wanting those pretty beloveds, Asad.
You must look at your own face first.

The last two verses from a *qi'ta* (quartrain). The poet is being sarcastic, reminding himself that in order to befriend the beautiful ones, you should have something to offer. Look at your own face and be ashamed.

191

ہر قدم دوریِ منزل ہے نمایاں مجھ سے   میری رفتار سے، بھاگے ہے بیاباں مجھ سے

har qadam dūrī' manzil hai numāyāñ mujh se
merī raftār se, bhāge hai bayābāñ mujh se (191:1; #1179)

Each step makes it more apparent, the distance to my destination;
With my speed, the wilderness is running away from me.

numāyāñ: apparent.

As one moves forward, the destination gets closer; but in my case, it is the opposite. As I move forward, my destination appears farther to me. The wilderness, my destiny, runs away form me just as fast as I run towards it, keeping it the same distance from me. Simply, it means that I have no way of reaching where I want to go; it is not in my destiny.

درسِ عنوانِ تماشا بہ تغافل خوشتر   ہے نگہ رشتۂ شیرازۂ مژگاں مجھ سے

dars-e 'unvān-e tamāshā ba(h) taġhāful k̤hushtar
hai nigāh rishta(h)' shīrāza(h)' mizhgāñ mujh se (191:2; #1180)

It is better to browse the headlines of display with obliviousness;
The sight is the thread that binds my eyelashes.

tamāshā: display of beloved; *k̤hushtar*: better; *nigāh*: sight; *shīrāz'a*: binding, thread; *mizhgāñ*: eyelashes.

The world is like a book, and we should just browse through its headings without going into detail. For this reason, my sight has been contained inside my eyes, as if it has become a thread that is binding (keeping closed) my eyelashes. Note how "thread" and "sight" act as the "thread that binds." The reason we should not get into the depths of matters is because if we get entangled in the details, we will not be able to see and appreciate the bigger picture, the Creator.

وحشتِ آتشِ دل سے شبِ تنہائی میں　　صورتِ دُود رہا سایہ گریزاں مجھ سے

vaḥshat-e ātish-e dil se shab-e tanhā'ī meñ
ṣurat-e dūd rahā sāya(h) gurezāñ mujh se (191:3; #1181)

From the wildness of fire in my heart, in the night of loneliness,
My shadow kept evading me like the smoke.

gurezāñ: evading.

As the flames leap, the smoke appears running away from them. The fire in the heart in the night of loneliness is so strong that its smoke has run away from it. In my craziness, as I run madly, my shadow appears to be running away from me. If you run in all directions, with the light source from one direction, you will see your shadow on and off. This condition describes the craziness of the lover who runs in all directions and finds no shadow anywhere.

غمِ عُشّاق نہ ہو سادگی آموزِ بُتاں　　کس قدر خانۂ آئینہ ہے ویراں مجھ سے!

ġham-e 'ushshāq na(h) ho sādgī āmoz-e butāñ
kis qadar ḳhāna(h) ā'ina(h) hai vīrāñ mujh se (191:4; #1182)

The grief of lovers should not make the beloved turn to simplicity;
How desolate the house of the mirror has become because of me?

sādgī āmoz: adapting simplicity.

God forbid, that the beloved would cease adorning herself because of the lovers' grief. With my death, she has done this, and the mirror is now desolate. The house of mirrors can also be the world, and thus, the simplicity of beloved has destroyed the beauty of world.

اثرِ آبلہ سے جادۂ صحراے جنوں   صورتِ رشتۂ گوہر ہے چراغاں مجھ سے

aṡar-e āblah se jādah' ṣaḥrā e junūñ
ṣurat-e rishta(h)' gohar hai charāġhāñ mujh se (191:5; #1183)

From the appearance of blisters, the path to the wilderness of frenzy
Has been illuminated like a string of pearls, because of me.

rishta(h)-e gohar: string of pearls.

My feet had blisters and I was walking in the wilderness of frenzy. The blisters on the feet are compared to pearls and track where the poet walks to a thread on which the pearls (blisters) are stringed. In contrast to pearls, the blisters have warmth in them, resulting in illumination—as if lamps were lit in the wilderness. The blisters are compared to a string of pearls as well. Imagine a wilderness; imagine a narrow track running through it; imagine this path strewn with pearls; imagine these pearls glowing; imagine the wilderness illuminated; and then imagine that this wilderness is the realm of frenzy. Now, imagine how it was all created!

بیخودی! بسترِ تمہیدِ فراغت ہو جو!   پُر ہے سائے کی طرح میرا شبستاں مجھ سے

bekḥudī! bistar-e tamhīd-e firāġhat ho jo
pur hai sā'e kī ṯaraḥ merā shabistāñ mujh se (191:6; #1184)

Ecstasy! Begin arrangements to delve into leisure,
As my bedchamber is filled with me like my shadow.

sāya(h): shadow; *be ḳhudī*: ecstasy; *bistar*: bed, to make arrangements; *shabistāñ*: bed chamber; *firāġhat*: leisure; *tamhīd*: preamble.

Addressing ecstasy, the poet calls for arrangements for a leisurely life. My sleeping quarters are filled with my shadow, meaning I have reached the place of comfort and have given up my wanderings. Now my ecstasy will unfold, as I have lost myself and reached the ultimate stage of *nirvana*.

شوقِ دیدار میں گر تو مجھے گردن مارے ہو نگہ مثلِ گلِ شمع، پریشاں مجھ سے

shauq-e ďīdār meñ gar tū muȷhe gardan māre
ho nigah, miśl-e gul-e shama̔, pareshāñ muȷh se (191:7; #1185)

If, for the desire of your glimpse, you would behead me,
My sight would spread like the flared flame from a trimmed candlewick.

gardan māre: to behead; *pareshāñ*: spread, scattered; *gul-e shama̔*: flower of candle, trimming the wick to make the flame brighter.

Beheading is compared to the clipping of a wick. After beheading for the crime of wanting to see you, my vision will become more acute, and it will spread. Beheading, here, is not taken in the literal sense. It means inflicting cruelty, to enhance my resolve that I will look for you all around, more and more.

بیکسی ہائے شبِ ہجر کی وحشت، ہے ہے! سایہ خورشیدِ قیامت میں ہے پنہاں مجھ سے

bekasī hāi shab-e hȷr kī vaḥshat, hai hai
sāyah ḳhurshid-e qiyāmat meñ hai pinhāñ muȷh se (191:8; #1186)

The wildness of the desperation of the night of separation;
Alas! Alas!
My shadow is hiding from me, shunning the sun of Doomsday.

bekasī: desperation; *shab-e hȷr*: night of separation; *qiyāmat*: Doomsday; *pinhāñ*: hiding; *vaḥshat:* wildness.

Utter loneliness of the night of separation frightened me, brought desperation and frenzy. So bad was my condition that even my shadow took refuge from me, as one might do to get away from the sun of Doomsday. My condition is truly pathetic.

گردشِ ساغرِ صد جلوۂ رنگیں تجھ سے   آئینہ داریِ یک دیدۂ حیراں مجھ سے

gardish-e sāġhar-e ṣad jalva(h)' rangīñ tujh se
ā'ina(h) dārī yak dīda(h)' ḥairāñ mujh se (191:9; #1187)

The rotation of goblets with hundreds of colorful displays is because of you;
While my stunned eyes are like display of mirror.

ā'ina(h) dārī: holding mirror.

In your assembly, there are colorful celebrations full of joy (rotation of cup meaning wine going around), all because of your presence, my beloved. I am however, stunned that you can have such delight without the presence of your true lovers. How surprised are my eyes? They are like a mirror (which is like a composite of frozen images).

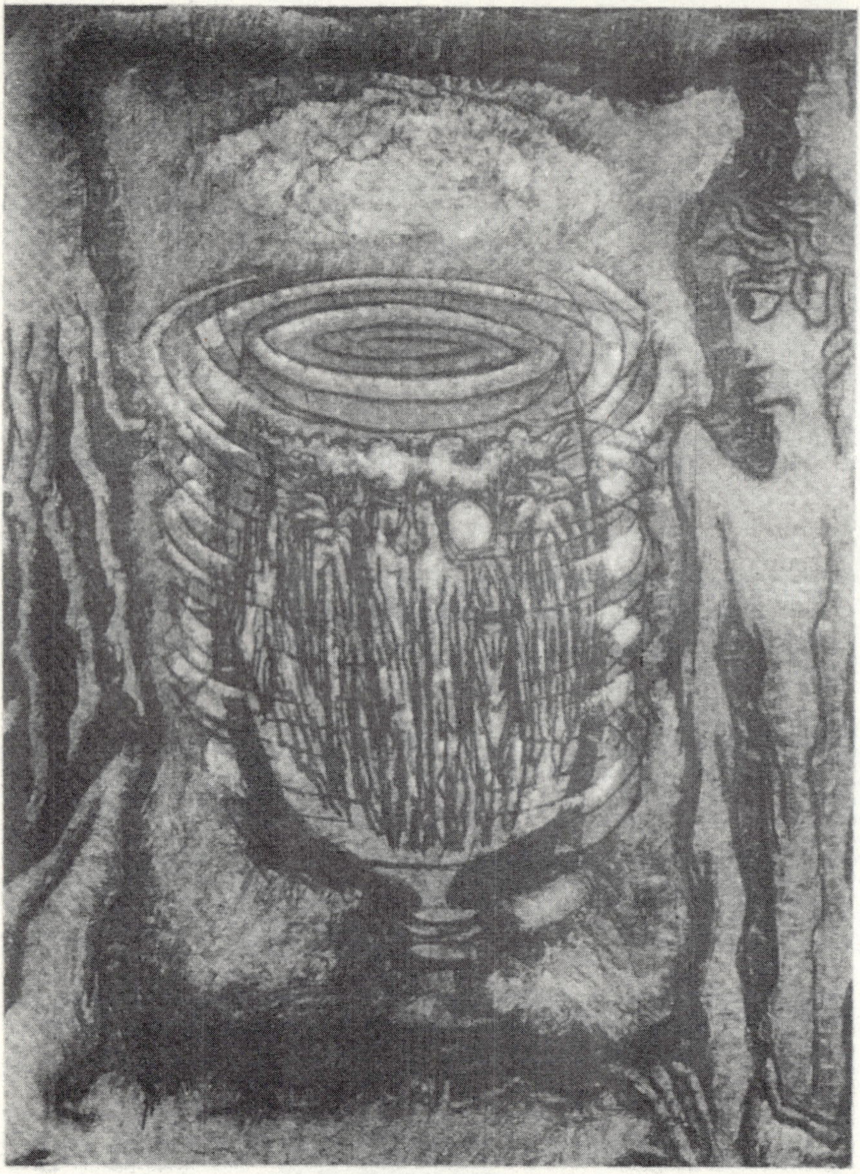

گردشِ ساغرِ صد جلوۂ رنگیں تجھ سے
آئینہ داریٔ یک دیدۂ حیراں مجھ سے

نگہِ گرم سے اِک آگ ٹپکتی ہے اسد
ہے چراغاں خس و خاشاکِ گلستاں مجھ سے

nigah-e garm se ik āg ṭapaktī hai Asad
hai charāġhāñ ḳhas-o-ḳhāshāk-e gulistāñ mujh se (191:10; #1188)

What a fire is coming out of those angry eyes, Asad,
That the garden litter is set afire because of me.

nigah garm: angry eyes; *ṭapaktī*: dripping; *ḳhas-o-ḳhāshāk*: litter; *ik*: a, used here in conjunction with "dripping" to mean " what a dripping."

I made her angry; her angry eyes began spreading the fire that burned the litter in the garden as she looked at it. Note that flowers and greenery were not burned; only the useless things like the lovers in her assembly were burned down.

192

نکتہ چیں ہے، غمِ دل اُس کو سنائے نہ بنے   کیا بنے بات، جہاں بات بنائے نہ بنے

nukta(h) chīñ hai, ġham-e dil us ko sunā'e na(h) bane
kyā bane bāt, jahāñ bāt banā e na(h) bane (192:1; #1189)

A caviller she is; it is difficult to make her listen to the heart's woes.
What success could I possibly have if I could not even state them craftily?

nukta(h) chīñ: a caviller, carper; *sunā'e na(h) bane*: no way to be heard; *bane bāt*: to succeed; *bāt banā-e*: to say craftily.

The beloved incessantly criticizes the lover; the interruptions make it difficult for him to make a coherent presentation to her. He laments how things will work out if he cannot even convey the feelings of his heart to begin with.

میں بلاتا تو ہوں اُس کو مگر اے جذبۂ دل   اُس پہ بن جائے کچھ ایسی کہ بن آئے نہ بنے

maiñ bulātā to hūñ us ko magar ai jazba(h)' dil
us pa(h) ban jā'e kuchh aisī kih bin ā'e na(h) bane (192:2; #1190)

I am calling her, but O! Cravings of my heart,
May something happen to her such that she could not resist coming to me.

ban jā'e: forced into.

I am asking her to come, but obviously there is no hope. O! Passionate craving of my heart, pray that something will happen that will force her to come. What is that thing? Obviously, if she, too falls in love, she will come running. How foolish can a heart be to hope for that? The desire of my heart should be strong enough to melt her heart. Naturally, if she decides not to come, it is the fault of my desire.

کھیل سمجھا ہے، کہیں چھوڑ نہ دے، بھول نہ جاے   کاش یُوں بھی ہو کہ بِن میرے سَتاے نہ بنے

khel samjhā hai, kahīñ chhoṛ nā de, bhūl na(h) jāe
kāsh yūñ bhī ho kih bin mere satā'e na(h) bane (192:3; #1191)

Thinking of it a mere play, I am afraid she might quit it and forget about it,
I wish it happened that she could not resist tormenting me.

The beloved thinks of love as just a game and the lover is afraid that, as children do, she might just quit the game and forget about it. He hopes that she will begin to enjoy the tormenting, become addicted to it, and continue the game. The lover knows it is just a game, and this is acceptable to him.

غیر پھرتا ہے لیے یُوں ترے خط کو کہ اگر   کوئی پُوچھے کہ یہ کیا ہے تو چھُپاے نہ بنے

ġhair phirtā hai liye yūñ tere ḳhaṯ ko kih agar
ko'ī pūche kih yih kyā hai to chhupā'e na(h) bane (192:4; #1192)

The stranger roams around, flaunting your letter so that
If someone were to ask him what it is, he would not be able to hide it.

The lover complains to the beloved that the rival is flashing her letter, and reminds her that this is bound to bring infamy to her. What a way to conceal jealousy! There is a suspicion here that the rival got a chance to talk to her, and the only thing left to do is to hide the feeling of jealousy.

اس نزاکت کا بُرا ہو، وہ بھلے ہیں تو کیا!   ہاتھ آویں تو اُنھیں ہاتھ لگائے نہ بنے

is nazākat kā burā ho, vuh bhale haiñ to kyā
hāth āveñ to unheñ hāth lagā'e na(h) bane (192:5; #1193)

Damned be that tenderness, so what if she is beautiful.
That should she come in my arms and I could not touch her.

The beloved is beautiful. That is fine, but the problem is that she is so delicate that even if I were to get hold of her, it would not be possible for me to touch her for fear of hurting her. The poet consoles himself by asking, what good is this beauty if you cannot touch it?

کہہ سکے کون کہ یہ جلوہ گری کس کی ہے؟   پردہ چھوڑا ہے وہ اُس نے کہ اُٹھائے نہ بنے

kah sake kaun kih yih jalva(h) garī kis kī hai
parda(h) chhoṛā hai vuh us ne kih uṭhā'e na(h) bane (192:6; #1194)

Who can say, whose glorious revelation this is?
He has dropped down a curtain that cannot be lifted.

Nature has put a veil of understanding between its display and our ability to see what it means. This being the case, how can we tell what the display represents, who is behind it, and what it means? This verse also refers to the *Qur'anic* verse where God declares "We have put a veil on their eyes." How can we understand Him, if He does not want us to?

موت کی راہ نہ دیکھوں؟ کہ بِن آئے نہ رہے   تم کو چاہوں؟ کہ نہ آؤ تو بُلائے نہ بنے

maut kī rāh na(h) dekhūñ? kih bin ā'e na(h) rahe
tum ko chāhūñ kih na(h) ā'o to bulā'e na(h) bane (192:7; #1195)

Not waiting for death? For it is bound to come.
Not wanting you to come? I could not resist calling you.

Why shouldn't I wait for death? It is inevitable and thus my wait will not go to waste. Because calling you is a wasted wish, I would rather not call, but then how can I control my heart that still wants to call you? The lover has many unfulfilled desires; the only one he is sure of winning is his wish for death.

بوجھ وہ سر سے گرا ہے کہ اُٹھائے نہ اُٹھے   کام وہ آن پڑا ہے کہ بنائے نہ بنے

bojh vuh sar se girā hai kih uṭhā'e na(h) uṭhe
kām vuh ān paṛā hai kih banā'e na(h) bane (192:8; #1196)

Such a burden has fallen off my head that I am unable to lift it;
Such a situation has developed that it cannot be worked out.

I was carrying the great burden of love over my head; it fell, and now I am unable to lift it and put it back. I am humbled and helpless. It is a situation that I cannot resolve.

عشق پر زور نہیں، ہے یہ وہ آتش غالب
کہ لگائے نہ لگے اور بجھائے نہ بنے

'ishq par zor nahīñ, hai yih vuh ātish Ġhālib
kih lagā'e na(h) lage aur bujhā'e na(h) bane (192:9; #1197)

There is no control over love; it is that fire, *Ġhālib*,
That can neither be started nor can it be extinguished.

One has no control over love. It just happens. Once it happens, it is not something you can escape. Facing love, man has little control over his fate. This is one of the most oft-quoted verses of *Ġhālib*.

193

چاک کی خواہش اگر وحشت بہ عُریانی کرے
صُبح کے مانند زخمِ دل گریبانی کرے

chāk kī ḳh(v)āhish agar vaḥshat ba(h) ʿuryānī kare
ṣubḥ ke mānind zaḳhm-e dil girebānī kare (193:1; #1198)

If my frenzy desires to tear the collar, exposing my nudity,
Like the daybreak, the wound of my heart is ready to turn into a collar.

girebānī: to turn into a collar.

Tearing the collar is such a delight that the wound of my heart, already shaped like a slit (tear), is ready to become a collar so that it can be torn again. In the state of nudity, when there is no cloth on the body to tear, the wound of the heart offers itself as a collar. All of this effort is to satisfy the desire to achieve the greatest delight from the tearing of the collar. The daybreak, the slit of the wound, and the slit collar are all stitched together to portray an uncontrollable frenzy in this verse.

جلوے کا تیرے وہ عالم ہے کہ گر کیجے خیال
دیدۂ دل کو زیارت گاہِ حیرانی کرے

jalve kā tere vuh ʿālam hai kih gar kīje ḳhayāl
dīda(h)ʾ dil ko ziyārat gāh-e ḥairānī kare (193:2; #1199)

The splendor of your beauty is such that just thinking of it
My eyes turn my heart into a shrine of amazement.

Your beauty is so stunning that even imagining it, let alone seeing you in person, stuns my eyes. The eyes make the heart a place of pilgrimage where people will come to see what it means to be stunned.

ہے شکستن سے بھی دل نومید، یارب کب تلک
آبگینہ کوہ پر عرضِ گرانجانی کرے

hai shikastan se bhī dil naumīd, yārabb kab talak
ābgina(h) koh par ʿarẓ-e giranjānī kare (193:3; #1200)

The heart remains hopeless of being broken. For how long, O! Lord,
Should the glass express niggardliness of the mountain?

shikastan: breaking; *ābgina(h)*: glass; *koh*: mountain; *ʿarẓ*: express; *giranjānī*: sluggishness, parsimony, stinginess, niggardliness.

The beloved is stonehearted and, thus, she is a mountain; the heart of the lover is a glass. A small piece of rock can shatter a piece of glass, but here, the entire mountain cannot break the heart. The heart has given up hope of ever being shattered. The lover has taken all kinds of hardships from the beloved, but he is ready to take a lot more and so deserves a broken heart. He is challenging her niggardliness.

میکدہ گر چشمِ مستِ ناز سے پاوے شکست
موئے شیشہ دیدۂ ساغر کی مژگانی کرے

maikada(h) gar chashm-e mast-e nāz se pāve shikast
mūe shīsha(h) dīdah' sāġhar kī miẓhgānī kare (193:4; #1201)

If the coquettish intoxicating eyes defeat the tavern,
The hairline crack in the goblet would become the eyelashes of the eyes.

maikada(h): tavern, bar; *chashm*: eye; *mast*: intoxicated; *dīda(h)*: eye; *mūe shisha(h)*: hairline crack in the glass; *sāġhar*: goblet.

The intoxication from the eyes of the beloved far exceeds the intoxication from any amount of drinking. This is a matter of embarrassment to the tavern, since the goblet has lowered its eyes in shame. The goblet shows its embarrassment by developing a crack in it that appears like the eyelashes. The similarity between eyes and goblet, the eyelashes and the crack in the glass, are plays on words.

خطِّ عارض سے لکھا ہے زُلف کو اُلفت نے عہد
یک قلم منظور ہے جو کچھ پریشانی کرے

ḳhatt̤-e ʿāriz se likhā hai zulf ko ulfat ne ʿahd
yak qalam manzūr hai jo kuchh pareshānī kare (193:5; #1202)

The down on the face is the written commitment of love to the tresses,
Saying that it is all acceptable, whatever dishevels them.

ḳhatt̤-e ʿāriz: hairline or down on the face of youth; *yak qalam*: full, also means sideburns (*qalam*).

The beloved has developed hairline (perhaps a male beloved); this is actually a writing of devotion to my beloved's tresses that no matter how disturbing this is, (as expressed by disheveled tresses; the word used here also means, "to worry.") I will accept it and continue to love you. This means that even if the charm of your tresses has lessened, my love will not. This message is sent is through the appearance of hairline growth on the face. The use of "*yak qalam*" has profound meaning. First, "*qalam*" is a pen, which writes; and secondly, it means, "sideburns." This is one of those verses where the beloved is a young male beginning to develop facial hair.

194

وہ آکے خواب میں تسکینِ اضطراب تو دے
ولے مجھے تپشِ دل مجالِ خواب تو دے

vuh āke ḳh(v)āb meñ taskīn-e iẓt̤irāb to de
vale mujhe tapish-e dil majāl-e ḳh(v)āb to de (194:1; #1203)

She would come in my dreams to console my restlessness;
If only the throbbing of heart would let me fall asleep.

ḳh(v)āb: dream, sleep; *tapish*: beating, palpitation, pulsating, throbbing; *majāl*: ability.

The beloved will never actually come, but there is hope that she will appear in my dreams to console my frenzy. Even that is not possible though, because I am too restive to fall asleep. The use of "*to*" (meaning "perhaps") in both lines is very meaningful. In the first line it makes the propositions hopeful; in the second line, it connotes that it is difficult to fall asleep. "*ḳh(v)āb*" means, "dream" in the first line and "sleep" in the next.

کرے ہے قتل، لگاوٹ میں تیرا رو دینا
تری طرح کوئی تیغِ نگہ کو آب تو دے

kare hai qatl, lagāvaṭ meñ terā ro denā
terī tarḥ ko'ī teġh-e nigah ko āb to de (194:2; #1204)

It kills me, sword of the eyes like you?

lagāvaṭ: teasing; *āb*: water, edge of sword, luster.

My complaining to you has caused you to cry; this is killing me. Not all the perfect beauties in the world would know how to give the cutting edge to their eyes. The water in the eyes (tears) has become the sharp cutting edge of the sword of the eyes. No one can have tears do this to their eyes—make them so killing when they are wet. Note that eyes have the same shape as the curved sword. The glitter of tears is giving a shine to the edge of the sword: "*āb* giving *āb*."

دِکھا کے جُنبشِ لب ہی تمام کر ہم کو
نہ دے جو بوسہ تو مُنہ سے کہیں جواب تو دے

dikhā kih juñmbish-e lab hī tamām kar ham ko
na(h) de jo bosa(h) to muñh se kahīñ javāb to de (194:3; #1205)

Finish us off by just showing a quiver of your lips;
If you are not giving a kiss, then give us any response from your mouth.

If there is no hope of a kiss from your lips, then at least let your lips tell me "no." This movement of lips would be enough to kill me.

پلا دے اوک سے ساقی! جو ہم سے نفرت ہے
پیالہ گر نہیں دیتا، نہ دے، شراب تو دے

pilā de auk se sāqī! jo ham se nafrat hai
piyāla(h) gar nahiñ detā, na(h) de sharāb to de (194:4; #1206)

O' Cupbearer, make me drink through my cupped hands if you hate me.
If you would rather not give me a cup, so be it, but at least give me some wine.

auk: cupped hands to hold drinks.

It is not important how you give me wine. Cups and goblets are not necessary, for I am ready to drink through my cupped hands. Do not hold back the wine even if you hate me and consider my touching your utensils unholy. Brahmin Hindus do not let lower caste people touch their utensils, and give water to them in their cupped hands. The poet just wants wine, if not in a cup then in his cupped hands.

اسدؔ خوشی سے مِرے ہاتھ پانْو پھُول گئے
کہا جو اُس نے: "ذرا میرے پانْو داب تو دے"

Asad ḳhushī se mere hāth pāuñ phūl ga'e
kahā jo us ne: "żarā mere pāuñ dāb to de" (194:5; #1207)

Asad, with joy, my hands and feet got goose bumps,
Just as she said, "O! Massage my feet for a little while."

hāth pāuñ phūlna: swelling of hands and feet in excitement; *pāuñ dāb*: massage feet.

When the beloved asked the lover to comfort her feet by massaging them, his hands and feet froze with joy; her request brought such happiness to him. This resulted in lover not being able to have this joy of touching her body. The idiom about feet and hands becoming puffed up is synonymous with freezing their motion.

195

تپش سے میری وقفِ کشمکش ہر تارِ بستر ہے
مرا سر رنجِ بالیں ہے مرا تن بارِ بستر ہے

tapish se merī vaqf-e kash-ma-kash har tār-e bistar hai
merā sar ranj-e bālīñ hai merā tan bār-e bistar hai (195:1; #1208)

The palpitation of heart has entangled every thread of my bed.
My head is afflicting the pillow, as my body has become a burden to the bed.

tapish: beating, palpitation, pulsating, throbbing; *vaqf*: dedicated; *kash-ma-kash*; puzzled, pulled around; *tār-e bistar*: thread of bed; *bālīñ*: pillow, head rest of the bed.

Tossing and turning in bed because of a tormented and throbbing heart brought on by separation from the beloved, every thread of the bed wonders what to do to the lover. Crying on the pillow has made it sad and he has become a burden to the bed.

سرشکِ سر بہ صحرا دادہ، نور العینِ دامن ہے
دلِ بے دست و پا افتادہ، برخوردارِ بستر ہے

sirishk-e sar ba(h) ṣaḥrā dāda(h), nūrulʿain-e dāman hai
dil be dast-o-pā uftāda(h), barḳhurdār-e bistar hai (195:2 #1209)

Tears gone to wilderness are so dear to my lap.
My shiftless, miserable heart has enjoined the bed.

sirishk:tears; *sar ba(h) ṣaḥrā dāda(h)*: gone to wilderness, vagrant, gone crazy; *nūrulʿain:* sparkle of eye, very dear*; dāman*: lap; *be dast-o-pā:* shiftless, gawky; *uftād*: misery; *barḳhurdār:* possessing; *bistar*: bed.

The home for tears is in the eye; when shed, they go vagrant. Falling into the lap of the lover, the tears make it sparkle. The sparkle of eye is now sparkling the lap of lover. The heart without head or feet (meaning shiftless) has merged with the bed (meaning it is resting) having given up the tumultuousness.

خوشا اقبالِ رنجوری، عیادت کو تم آئے ہو
فروغِ شمعِ بالیں طالعِ بیدارِ بستر ہے

ḳhushā iqbāl-e ranjūrī, ʿiyādat ko tum āe ho
faroġh-e shamaʿ-e bālīñ ṭālaʿ-e bedār-e bistar hai (195:3 #1210)

Good news! How lucky is my sickness that you came to ask about my condition.
Flaring of the candle by the headrest has woken up the fate of my bed.

iqbāl: good luck; *ranjūrī*: sickness; *ʿiyādat*: visiting a sick person; *shamaʿ-e bālīñ*: candle at the head of bed; *ṭālaʿ*: luck; *bedār*: waking.

The brightening of the candle by the headrest has woken (brightened) the fate of the bed. Sickness proved to be a good omen, bringing the beloved to ask the lover about his heart. Seeing the beloved at the bedside of the lover made the candle jealous and so it began burning brighter, enhancing the illumination of the bed (meaning abode). Briefly, the arrival of beloved is very fortunate for me. It has brightened my future.

بہ طوفاں گاہِ جوشِ اضطرابِ شامِ تنہائی
شعاعِ آفتابِ صبحِ محشر تارِ بستر ہے

ba(h) ṯufāñ gāh-e josh-e iẓṯirāb-e shām-e tanhā'ī
shuaʿ-e āftāb-e subḥ-e maḥshar tār-e bistar hai (195:4; #1211)

With the intensity of restlessness raising a storm in the night of separation,
The threads of my bed have turned into the morning sun of Doomsday.

josh: intensity; *iẓṯirāb*: tumult.

Chaos and tumult on Doomsday is compared to the tumult in the heart of the lover on the night of separation. A bed woven with the morning rays of Doomsday's sun would be very stormy. That is the condition of my heart on the night of separation.

ابھی آتی ہے بُو بالش سے اُس کی زُلفِ مشکیں کی
ہماری دید کو خوابِ زُلیخا عارِ بستر ہے

abhī ātī hai bū, bālish se, us kī zulf-e mushkīñ kī
hamārī đīd ko ḳh(v)āb-e zulaiḳhā ʿār-e bistar hai (195:5; #1212)

Still the smell of her perfumed tresses pervades the pillow.
To me, *Zuleḳhā* dreaming of her beloved is shameful to my bed.

ār: shame; *bālish*: pillow; *đīd*: view ; *ḳh(v)āb*: dream.

Zuleḳhā used to dream of Joseph (See Glossary). Our dreaming is more powerful than that of *Zuleḳhā*. It is so real I can smell the beloved's perfumed tresses emanating coming from my pillow, as if she were here in reality. This means that my power of imagination is superior to *Zuleḳhā*'s.

کہوں کیا، دِل کی کیا حالت ہے ہجرِ یار میں غالب
کہ بیتابی سے ہر یک تارِ بستر خارِ بستر ہے

kahūñ kyā, dil kī kyā ḥālat hai hijr-e yār meñ Ġhālib
kih betābī se har yak tār-e bistar ḳhār-e bistar hai (195:6; #1213)

What shall I say is the condition of my heart in separation from the beloved, *Ġhālib*?
From desperation, every thread of my bed has become a thorn of my bed.

My bed is a bed of thorns on the night of separation. That is the best way to describe the condition of my heart this night.

196

خطر ہے رشتۂ الفت رگِ گردن نہ ہو جاوے   غرورِ دوستی آفت ہے، تُو دشمن نہ ہو جاوے

khaṭar hai rishtah' ulfat rag-e gardan na(h) ho jāve
ġhurūr-e dostī āfit hai, tū dushman na(h) ho jāve (196:1; #1214)

The fear is that the amorous relationship might turn into jugular.
This pride in friendship would be calamitous, if this turns you enemy.

rishta(h): relationship; *gardan*: neck; *ġharūr*: pride; *āfit*: disaster; *rag-e gardan*: neck vein, jugluar vein.

I am afraid that my amorous relationship with you will make me very proud and haughty (giving me a stiff neck) and this pride of my relationship with you will make you, my beloved, my enemy. As I perceive my love for you, I feel proud, and that might irritate you.

سمجھ اِس فصل میں کوتاہیٔ نشو و نما غالب   اگر گُل سرو کے قامت پہ پیراہن نہ ہو جاوے

samajh is faṣl meñ kotāhī' nashv-o-numā Ġhālib
agar gul sarv ke qāmat pa(h) pairāhan na(h) ho jāve (196:2; #1215)

Consider it a shortcoming of the growth potential of this season, *Ġhālib*,
If the flowers do not grow tall enough to overshadow cypress tree,

nashv-o-numā: growth and increase.

If the spring season does not impart the flowers fast growth, it is the shortcoming of the season, not the fault of flowers.

197

فریاد کی کوئی لے نہیں ہے
نالہ پابندِ نے نہیں ہے

faryād kī ko'ī lae nahiñ hai
nālah pāband-e nae nahiñ hai (197:1; #1216)

There is no tune in complaints;
The plaints depend not on the flute.

lae: flute, tune.

Melodies and tunes are for songs and music. They have nothing to do with laments and plaints. When playing the flute, one must observe certain rules of the scale, but when sending plaints, it should go as it comes. It is a remarkable comparison to say that spontaneity is what produces these plaints, and that this must stay as it is.

کیوں بوتے ہیں باغبان تونبے
گر باغ گدائے مے نہیں ہے

kioñ bote haiñ bāġhbān tuñbe
gar bāġh gadā-e mai nahiñ hai (197:2; #1217)

Why do gardeners sow bitter pumpkins
If the garden is not a beggar of wine?

tuñbe: bitter pumpkin which was hollowed out and dried and used to store and drink wine; also used to make begging bowls. Bowls made from these pumpkins are light, easily available and handled, and do not break.

Why have so many pumpkins been planted? Is it that the gardener is begging for wine? If this is not the case, why are there so many pumpkin bowls? Note that beggars use pumpkin bowls to beg.

ہر چند ہر ایک شے میں تُو ہے
پر تجھ سی تو کوئی شے نہیں ہے

harchand har ek shai meñ tū hai
par tujh sī to ko'ī shai nahīñ hai (197:3; #1218)

Although You are manifest in everything,
But there is not a thing that is like You.

Undoubtedly, the image of God is present in everything. However, we cannot say that there is anything that resembles God.

ہاں کھائیو مت فریبِ ہستی
ہر چند کہیں کہ ہے، نہیں ہے

hāñ khā'iyo mat fareb-e hastī
harchand kahaiñ kih hai, nahīñ hai (197:4; #1219)

Yes, do not be deceived by the illusion of existence;
Howsoever we state that it is, but it is not.

Watch out! Do not be deceived by the illusion of your own existence. No matter how anyone tries to convince you that you exist, do not believe it.

شادی سے گزر کہ غم نہ ہووے
اُردی جو نہ ہو تو دَے نہیں ہے

shādī se guzar kih gham na(h) hove
urdī jo na(h) ho to dai nahīñ hai (197:5; #1220)

Let go of happiness so you will not become saddened.
If there is no spring, then there will be no autumn either.

shādī: happiness; *guzar*: let go; *urdī*: 2nd month of Persian calendar (meaning spring); *dai*: 10th month of Persian calendar (fall).

If you do not want to be sad, give up being happy. It is only when you have lived through spring, that you realize the coming of fall. In many places, *Ġhālib* has alluded to sadness being a more permanent state; a brief respite of happiness (like spring) makes it worse to live through it (fall).

کیوں ردِّ قدح کرے ہے زاہد!
مے ہے یہ مگس کی قے نہیں ہے

kioñ radd-e qadḥ kare hai zāhid
mai hai yih magas kī qai nahiñ hai (197:6; #1221)

Why do the devout ones reject the bowl of wine?
It is only wine, not the vomit of the honeybees.

radd: reject; *qadḥ*: bowl of wine; *zāhid*: abstinent, devout; *magas kī qai*: honey (vomit of honeybees).

O! Abstinent one, do not feel offended by the wine; it is not the vomit of the honeybee (vomit here means honey). By calling it the vomit of a honeybee, the poet creates an offensive element in the image of honey, similar to what the preacher relates to wine. Wine is not the vomit that you must shun. Drink it.

ہستی ہے نہ کچھ عدم ہے غالب
آخر تُو کیا ہے، اے نہیں ہے!

hastī hai nā kuchh ʿadam hai Ġhālib
āḳhir tū kyā hai, ai "nahiñ hai" (197:7; #1222)

There is nothing that exists, including nonexistence, *Ġhālib*.
But then, what are you, O! "Is not."

hastī: existence; *ʽadam*: nonexistent.

O! *Ġhālib*, we cannot say that you exist in reality nor can we say that you do not exist as a character. If we say that you are not, it would not be improper. Tell us who can and cannot exist at the same time.

198

نہ پوچھ نسخۂ مرہم جراحتِ دل کا
کہ اُس میں ریزۂ الماس جُزوِ اعظم ہے

na(ḥ) pūchh nusḳha(ḥ)ʼ marham jirāḥat-e dil kā
kih us meñ rezahʼ almās juzv-e āʼzam hai (198:1; #1223)

Ask not the composition of the ointment for the heart's wounds,
For in there is the dust of the diamond as its major ingredient.

almās: diamond; *juzv-e āʼzam*: major component.

Ask not how I make my heart's wound deeper. I use an ointment in which the major component is ground diamond, which cuts deeper into the wound.

بہت دنوں میں تغافل نے تیرے پَیدا کی
وہ اِک نگہ کہ بہ ظاہر نگاہ سے کم ہے

bahut dinoñ meñ taġhāful ne tere paidā kī
vuh ik nigah kih ba(ḥ) ẓāhir nigāh se kam hai (198:2; #1224)

After a very long time did your indifference produce
That one glance that is apparently less than a full glance.

After a long period of being oblivious, the beloved has begun to look at the lover, but only with a half glance. The trickery in the verse is her glance being less than a full glance.

199

ہم رشک کو اپنے بھی گوارا نہیں کرتے
مرتے ہیں، ولے اُن کی تمنّا نہیں کرتے

ham rashk ko apne bhī gavārā nahiñ karte
marte haiñ, vale un kī tamannā nahiñ karte (199:1; #1225)

We do not tolerate even the envy with ourselves;
We would rather die than long for her.

If I unite with her, I will become envious of myself. For this reason, I would rather die than long for her.

در پردہ اُنھیں غیر سے ہے ربطِ نہانی
ظاہر کا یہ پردہ ہے کہ پردا نہیں کرتے

dar parda(h) unhaiñ ġhair se hai rabṯ-e nihānī
ẕāhir kā yih parda(h) hai kih pardā nahiñ karte (199:2; #1226)

Behind the veil, she has a secret association with the rival;
It is a façade of a veil that you do not take a veil.

nihānī: hidden.

The beloved has developed a secret association with my rival. To mislead me, she says that the reason she meets him openly is because she has nothing to hide; she has no relationship with him. She is actually pulling a veil over my eyes.

یہ باعثِ نومیدیٔ اربابِ ہوس ہے
غالب کو بُرا کہتے ہو اچھا نہیں کرتے

yih bā'is-e naumīdī' arbāb-e havas hai
Ġhālib ko burā kahte ho achhā nahiñ karte (199:3; #1227)

This is a source of hopelessness for the desiring colleagues;
Calling *Ġhālib* bad is not a good thing to do.

If you call *Ġhālib*, bad, imagine what would the rivals think? It will be a matter of great disappointment to them. The poet is beseeching the beloved not to, lest her other lovers take flight. If *Ġhālib* is treated like this when he is the devoted one, they will surely wander. The real argument is that the poet does not want to be called bad.

200

کرے ہے بادہ ترے لب سے کسبِ رنگِ فروغ
خطِ پیالہ سراسر نگاہِ گلچیں ہے

kare hai bāda(h) tere lab se kasb-e rang-e furoġh
ḳhaṭ-e piyāla(h) sarāsar nigāh-e gulchīñ hai (200:1; #1228)

From your lips, the wine takes a splendid color indeed;
The meniscus in the cup all around, is the eye of the flower-picker.

kasab: to acquire; *furoġh*: splendid, bright; *sarāsar:* all over, throughout; *gulchīñ*: flower-picker.

As you drink the wine it takes on the fiery color of your lips. Now the measuring level in the goblet takes on the appearance of the flower-picker's eyes (as he hunts for flowers). Wine taking color means developing the properties, which are characteristic of wine: the color, the body, and the sparkle. As the wine tries to reach your lips, it is like a flower-picker trying to reach the flowers. That's how the level (the meniscus) of the wine in the goblet is appearing.

کبھی تو اس دلِ شوریدہ کی بھی داد ملے
کہ ایک عمر سے حسرت پرستِ بالیں ہے

kabhī to is dil-e shorīda(h) kī bhī dād mile
kih ek ʽumr se ḥasrat parast-e bālīñ hai (200:2; #1229)

When would an appreciation be handed to this frenzied heart?
For a lifetime, it is longing for the pillow.

dil-e shorida(h): lunatic heart; *dād*: appreciation; *bālīñ*: pillow.

I have been living with a longing for comfort of pillow (perhaps for the beloved to come and place her head on it.) When will I become acknowledged for my lifetime of tribulations?

بجا ہے، گر نہ سُنے نالہ ہاے بُلبُلِ زار
کہ گوشِ گُل نمِ شبنم سے پنبہ آگیں ہے

bajā hai, gar na(h) sune nāla(h) hāi bulbul-e zār
kih gosh-e gul nam-e shabnam se pañba(h) āgīñ hai (200:3; #1230)

It is understandable why it does not hear the plaint of the nightingale
As to the ears of flowers, the dew is the cotton wool stuffed in them.

pañba(h) āgīñ: stuffed with cotton wool.

If flowers do not hear the plaint of the poor nightingale, it is understandable because their ears have been plugged with the dew, as if there were cotton wool stuffed in their ears.

اسدؔ ہے نزع میں، چل بے وفا برائے خُدا
مقامِ ترکِ حجاب و وداعِ تمکیں ہے

Asad hai naza' meñ, chal be vafā barāe ḳhudā
muqām-e tark-e ḥijāb-o-vidā'-e tamkīñ hai (200:4; #1231)

Asad is dying; move on you unfaithful, for God's sake,
It is time to quit all bashfulness and bid goodbye to your pride.

naza': last breath; *ḥijāb*: bashfulness; *vidā'*: bidding good-bye; *tamkīñ*: pride.

This verse is an address to the beloved, asking her to give up her pride at the time of the lover's death and come to him.

201

کیوں نہ ہو چشمِ بُتاں محوِ تغافل، کیوں نہ ہو
یعنی اِس بیمار کو نظّارے سے پرہیز ہے

kioñ na(h) ho chashm-e butāñ maḥv-e taġhāful, kioñ na(h) ho
ya'nī is bīmār ko naẓẓāre se parhez hai (201:1; #1232)

Why would the eyes of the idol not be oblivious? Why should they not be?
Meaning that to this sick lover, abstinence from the display has been advised.

parhez: abstinence, avoidance (as in the diet of sick).

The beloved's eyes are oblivious to the lover. The lover assumes that this is because he has been prescribed abstinence from her beauty and so she is doing him a favor by not letting him see her eyes. The lover is assuring himself that she is kind to him that is why she is keeping away from him.

مرتے مرتے، دیکھنے کی آرزو رہ جاے گی
واے ناکامی کہ اُس کافر کا خنجر تیز ہے

marte marte, dekhne kī ārzū rah jāe gī
vāe nākāmī kih us kāfir kā ḳhanjar tez hai (201:2; #1233)

While being slain, the desire to see her shall remain unfulfilled.
Alas! The bad luck is that the dagger of the idol is sharp.

The beloved murders the lover with a sharp dagger. Had the dagger been less sharp (blunt), it would have taken longer to slit his throat, and would have given the lover a few extra moments to look at her. Apparently, this is the only instance when he is going to see her so close. Slow death would have been more painful and thus more pleasurable.

عارضِ گل دیکھ رُوئے یار یاد آیا اسد
جوششِ فصلِ بہاری اِشتیاق انگیز ہے

'āriẓ-e gul dekh rū'e yār yād āyā Asad!
joshish-e fiṣl-e bahārī ishtiyāq angez hai (201:3; #1234)

Seeing the cheeks of flowers reminded me of my beloved's face, Asad!
The eruption of the spring season is exciting the eagerness.

joshish: eruption; *ishtiyāq angez*: exciting eagerness.

In every flower I see my beloved. With flowers all around during Spring, I see my beloved's face everywhere, thus enhancing my desire to unite with her even more.

202

دیا ہے دل اگر اُس کو، بشر ہے، کیا کہیے   ہُوا رقیب تو ہو، نامہ بر ہے، کیا کہیے

diyā hai dil agar us ko, bashar hai kyā kahīye
hu'ā raqīb to ho, nāma(h) bar hai, kyā kahīye (202:1; #1235)

If he gave his heart to her, what can I say, for he, too, is a human being;
If he turns rival, what shall we say, he is a messenger.

bashar: human being.

Ġhālib's messenger falls in love with the beloved and so turns into his rival. *Ġhālib* is not surprised and concludes that the messenger, too, is a human being. Since no human being can resist her, of course the messenger could not either. This verse shows *Ġhālib*'s ongoing row with his messenger.

یہ ضد کہ آج نہ آوے اور آئے بن نہ رہے   قضا سے شکوہ ہمیں کس قدر ہے کیا کہیے

yih ẓid kih āj na(h) āve aur āe bin nā rahe
qaẓā se shikva(h) hameñ kis qadar hai kyā kahīye (202:2; #1236)

This insistence on not coming today, but not keeping from coming;
With death, I have so many complaints. What to say?

I want to die today but death refuses, saying it will come at its fixed time. What can I say if I have too many complaints against death?

رہے ہے یوں گہ و بے گہ کہ کوئے دوست کو اب   اگر نہ کہیے کہ دشمن کا گھر ہے، کیا کہیے؟

rahe hai yuñ gah-o be gah kih kūe dost ko ab
agar na(h) kahiye kih dushman kā ghar hai, kyā kahīye
(202:3; #1237)

He loiters around the beloved's alley so routinely now
That if we do not call it the "home of the enemy," then what shall we call it.

My rival is found loitering around the beloved's alley all the time, so if we call the beloved's alley, "home of the enemy," it would not be wrong.

زہے کرشمہ کہ یوں دے رکھا ہے ہم کو فریب   کہ بن کہے ہی اُنھیں سب خبر ہے، کیا کہیے

zihe karishma(h) kih yūñ de rakhā hai ham ko fireb
kih bin kahe hī unhaiñ sab ḳhabar hai, kyā kahīye (202:4; #1238)

It's through the bounty of miracle that she has kept me deceived
That without telling she knows it all, what can I say?

karishma(h): miracle.

The beloved says that, miraculously, she knows what is in my heart so there is no need for me to say anything. This way she keeps from listening to me and is able to deceive me.

سمجھ کے کرتے ہیں بازار میں وہ پرسشِ حال   کہ یہ کہے کہ سرِ رہگزر ہے کیا کہیے

samajh kih karte haiñ bāzār meñ vuh pursish-e ḥāl
kih yih kahe kih sar-e rahguzar hai kyā kahīye (202:5; #1239)

Smartly, she asks me of my condition only in the bazaar,
So that this lover will say, "It is by the roadside, what can I say here?"

Upon meeting each other by chance in the bazaar, my beloved asks how I am (to be polite)? She hopes that I will keep it short, for this is not the place or time to speak about my heart. There are two things of importance here. The beloved is cunning and also knows that proper manners require the lover to refrain from speaking in a public place.

تمھیں نہیں ہے سرِ رشتۂ وفا کا خیال　　ہمارے ہاتھ میں کچھ ہے، مگر ہے کیا؟ کہیے!

tumhaiñ nahiñ hai sar-e rishta(h)' vafā kā ḳhayāl
hamāre hāth meñ kuchh hai, magar hai kyā kahīye (202:6; #1240)

You think not much of my initiation of faithfulness;
I have something in my hand, but what is it? Tell me!

sar-e risht'a(h): end of thread, beginning of faithfulness.

The beloved has no regard for the faithfulness of the lover. The lover shows his closed fist and asks, "What is in there?" This refers to the game wherein one holds a thread in a closed fist and asks a child to guess which hand hides the thread. The key to this verse is the word, "*sar-e risht'a(h),*" which means "beginning of faithfulness" and also, "end of thread." In both cases, interesting meanings can be drawn as to why the lover wants her to guess what is in his hands. He is beginning his faithfulness, and to tell this, the lover wants to play a game to gain her attention.

انھیں سوال پہ زعمِ جنوں ہے، کیوں لڑیے؟　　ہمیں جواب سے قطعِ نظر ہے، کیا کہیے!

unheñ savāl pa(h) zo`m-e junūñ hai, kioñ laṛye
hameñ javāb se qaṯ`a-e naẕar hai, kyā kahīye (202:7; #1241)

She presumes my questioning is craziness; why go into a brawl;
Why mention it as I pay no attenion to answers anyway.

zo`m*: presumption; *junūn:* craziness; *qaṯ`a-e naẕar: connivance, indifference, irrespective.

When I ask her for anything (like a kiss), she replies, "You are mad." Listening to this, I have decided not to question, for there is no sense in quarreling with her. The lover is not giving up his desire to express; he just does not want to fight with her. He knows of who will lose the fight.

حسد سزائے کمالِ سخن ہے کیا کیجے! ستم بہائے متاعِ ہنر ہے کیا کہیے!

ḥasad sazāe kamāl-e suḳhan hai kyā kīje
sitam bahāe matāʿ-e hunar hai kyā kahīye (202:8; #1242)

Jealousy is the punishment for excellence in diction, what can we do?
Oppression is the price for goods of talent, what can we say?

bahā: price.

Those with literary skills often make other jealous, who are not as apt. This is a lament about how the world treats its creative and skilled members.

کہا ہے کس نے کہ غالبؔ برا نہیں، لیکن
سوائے اس کے کہ آشفتہ سر ہے، کیا کہیے

kahā hai kis ne kih Ġhālib burā nahiñ, lekin
sivāe is ke kih āshufta(h) sar hai, kyā kahīye (202:9; #1243)

Who has said that *Ġhālib* is not bad, however,
Except for the fact that he is a lunatic, what else is there to say?

āshufta(h) sar: lunatic.

Who says *Ġhālib* is not bad? Say that he is bad if you must, but also say that he is a lunatic, for lunatics cannot be called good or bad.

203

دیکھ کر درپردہ گرمِ دامن افشانی مجھے   کر گئی وابستۂ تن میری عریانی مجھے

dekh kar darparda(h) garm-e dāman afshānī mujhe
kar gaī' vābasta(h)' tan merī 'uryānī mujhe (203:1; #1244)

Seeing me secretly busy shaking loose my skirt,
My nudity went on to tie me down to my body.

darparda(h): unrevealed, hidden, behind the veil; *garm*: busy; *dāman afshānī*: shaking skirt lose, leaving the world; *vābasta(h):* associated; *tan*: body; *'uryānī:* nudity.

I had decided to give up all material things, i.e., to become nude by letting all layers of physical need go. However, being nude made it all the more obvious that I could not survive without my needs and so nudity again connected my body to what I was hoping to give up. Briefly, when my inner self saw that I was going to give up worldly things, it gave me more worldly reasons not to. This was necessary because my inner self knew I could not give it all up. In other words, no matter how hard we try, as long as we have a body to take care of, its needs shall remain.

بن گیا تیغِ نگاہِ یار کا سنگِ فساں   مرحبا میں! کیا مبارک ہے گرانجانی مجھے

ban gayā teġh-e nigāh-e yār kā sang-e fasāñ
marḥabā maiñ! kyā mubārak hai girānjānī mujhe (203:2; #1245)

Becoming the whetstone for the beloved's sword of glance.
Bravo to me! How lucky is my stinginess for me?

fasāñ: whetstone; *girāñjāni*: stinginess.

The beloved repeatedly sends her killer glances, which I keep inside me (as if I were stingy) turning me into a sharpening stone. This way she keeps her skills sharp and I stay connected to my beloved.

کیوں نہ ہو بے التفاتی، اُس کی خاطر جمع ہے　　جانتا ہے محوِ پرسش ہائے پنہانی مجھے

kioñ na(h) ho be iltifātī, us kī ḳhāt̤ir jamaʿ hai
jāntā hai maḥv-e pursish hāi pinhānī mujhe (203:3; #1246)

Why would not there be obliviousness; she is content
To know that I keep asking about her in my thoughts secretly.

ḳhāt̤ir jama: to one's satisfaction, heart's content; *pursish:* question, interrogation, visiting the sick; *pinhānī:* concealment.

The beloved is oblivious, but at the same time feels satisfied that her coming to me in my dreams is enough to make me happy. That being the case, why shouldn't she continue with her obliviousness? She knows that I continue to think about her and she believes that is sufficient.

میرے غم خانے کی قسمت جب رقم ہونے لگی　　لکھ دیا منجملۂ اسبابِ ویرانی مجھے

mere ġhamḳhāne kī qismat jab raqam hone lagī
likh diyā minjumla(h)ʾ asbāb-e vīrānī mujhe (203:4; #1247)

When the fate of my house of sorrow was being written down,
I was written down as the sole cause of its desolation.

minjumla(h)ʾ: totally

My name, among other things, brings desolation to my abode. Written in fate was a dark home and I was the reason for it.

میرے غم خانے کی قسمت جب رقم ہونے لگی
لکھ دیا منجملۂ اسبابِ ویرانی مجھے

بد گماں ہوتا ہے وُہ کافِر، نہ ہوتا کاش کے   اِس قدر ذوقِ نوائے مُرغِ بُستانی مجھے

bad gumāñ hotā hai vuh kāfir, na(h) hotā kāsh ke
is qadar żauq-e navā'e murġh-e bustānī mujhe (203:5; #1248)

That disbeliever has become suspicious; I wish I did not have
Such intense desire to listen to the songs of nightingale.

murġh-e bustānī: garden bird, nightingale.

My beloved is so distrustful of me that when she sees me listening to the songs of the nightingale, she becomes suspicious. I wish that I did not like listening to the nightingale so much. The beloved had begun thinking that I was talking to someone else. The theme is the same; the beloved wants my undivided attention.

وائے، واں بھی شورِ محشر نے نہ دم لینے دیا   لے گیا تھا گور میں ذوقِ تن آسانی مجھے

vāe, vāñ bhī shor-e maḥshar ne na(h) dam lene diyā
le gayā thā gor meñ żauq-e tan āsānī mujhe (203:6; #1249)

Alas! Even there, the noise of the Doomsday did not let me rest in peace;
Taking me to my grave was my desire for rest.

tan āsānī: desire for rest.

Desiring rest means getting good sleep, and for that I went to the grave tired from my many sleepless nights while still living. In the grave I was awakened by the tumult of Doomsday. (Note: On Doomsday, the dead will rise). It did not prove fruitful to seek rest in the grave. This means that rest cannot be achieved anywhere. There is another point of sarcasm raised here. Life is full of tumult, but death brings its own kind of tumult. So seek not refuge in death for your woes. It is better to face it here while living.

وعدہ آنے کا وفا کیجے یہ کیا انداز ہے　　تم نے کیوں سونپی ہے میرے گھر کی دربانی مجھے

vaʿda(h) āne kā vafā kīje yih kyā andāz hai
tum ne kioñ saunpī hai mere ghar kī darbānī mujhe (203:7; #1250)

Make good on your promise to come. What is this style?
Why have you assigned to me the guarding of my own house?

saunpī: given, assigned.

While waiting for you to come as promised, I pace back and forth, as if I were guarding my house. Why have you given me this task? What is your style?

ہاں نشاطِ آمدِ فصلِ بہاری، واہ واہ　　پھر ہوا ہے تازہ سودائے غزل خوانی مجھے

hāñ nishāṭ-e āmad-e faṣl-e bahārī, vāh vāh
phir hu'ā hai tāza(h) saudā'e ġhazal ḳh(v)ānī mujhe (203:8; #1251)

Yes, the joy of the arrival of spring is great! Cheers!
It has again refreshed in me, the frenzy of saying *ġhazals*.

With the arrival of spring, my frenzy of writing *ġhazals* has returned. It appears to be a routine every season.

دی مرے بھائی کو حق نے از سرِ نو زندگی
میرزا یوسف ہے غالب، یوسفِ ثانی مجھے

dī mere bhāī ko ḥaq ne az sar-e nau zindagī
Mirzā Yūsuf hai Ġhālib, yūsuf-e s̤ānī mujhe (203:9; #1252)

The Lord has blessed my brother with a new lease on life.
O! *Ġhālib*, *Mirzā Yūsuf* is *Yūsuf* the second to me.

Ġhālib's brother, Yousef, had brief relief from his mental disorder in 1854, but he died in 1857. He was two years younger than *Ġhālib*. Here a simile is drawn with *Haẓrat* Yousef (Joseph) who was famous for his "beauty."

204

یاد ہے شادی میں بھی ہنگامۂ "یارب!" مجھے
سبحۂ زاہد ہُوا ہے خندہ زیرِ لب مجھے

yād hai shādī meñ bhī hangāma(h)' "yārabb!" mujhe
subḥ' zāhid huvā hai ḳhanda(h) zere lab mujhe (204:1; #1253)

Even in happiness, I remember and keep saying aloud, "O! Lord!"
Hidden in my lips is the smile like the rosary of the devout.

shādī: happiness; *subḥ':* rosary; *zāhid:* devout religious person.

"Oh, My God!" is an expression used to lament as well as to express gratitude. Mumbling an ode to the Lord goes on all the time with me. My teeth appear to be rosary beads of the devout.

ہے کشادِ خاطرِ وابستہ در رہنِ سخن
تھا طلسمِ قفلِ ابجد، خانۂ مکتب مجھے

hai kushād-e ḳhāt̤ir-e vābasta(h) dar rahn-e suḳhan
thā t̤ilism-e qufl-e abjad, ḳhāna(h)' maktab mujhe (204:2; #1254)

The opening of the doors to my saddened heart is indebted to my poetry;
The sorcery of the numeric lock taught me a great deal.

suḳhan: words, poetry; *kushād*: open; *ḳhāt̤ir vābasta(h)*: pain and suffering, suffering heart; *t̤ilism:* magic, sorcery.

By opening the doors of my heart through speech—my poetry—I am able to vent my feelings of sorrow and pain. I understand now that one must verbalize something in order to open the magic lock of "*abjad*" (combination lock). It is only when I begin to say something that the lock to my heart opens. The right combination of words makes this work for me.

یارب اِس آشُفتگی کی داد کِس سے چاہیے
رشک آسائش پہ ہے زندانیوں کی اب مجھے

yārabb is āshuftagī kī dād kis se chāhīye
rashk āsāish pa(h) hai zandānīyoñ kī ab mujhe (204:3; #1255)

O! Lord, from whom shall I seek the appreciation for my lunacy?
Now I get envious thinking of the comfort of prisoners.

zandānīyoñ: prisoners.

When I was in prison, I wanted freedom. Now that my desire has come to fruition, I am envious of how restful the prisoners were. My lunacy is such that whatever condition or state I am in, I remain dissatisfied.

طبع ہے مُشتاقِ لذّت ہائے حسرت، کیا کروں
آرزو سے ہے شِکستِ آرزو مطلب مجھے

ṭabaʿ hai mushtāq-e lażżat hāi ḥasrat, kyā karūñ
ārzū se hai shikast-e ārzū maṯlab mujhe (204:4; #1256)

My nature savors the delight of grief. What shall I do?
When the desire for unfulfilled desires is what I desire.

ṭabaʿ: nature; *ḥasrat*: grief; *shikast-e ārzū*: loss of desire; *maṯlab*: desire.

What shall I do with my grief-seeking nature? My greatest desire is that my desire not come true.

دل لگا کر آپ بھی غالب مجھی سے ہو گئے
عشق سے آتے تھے مانع میرزا صاحب مجھے!

dil lagā kar āp bhī Ġhālib mujhī se hogae
'ishq se āte the mān'e mīrzā ṣāḥib mujhe (204:5; #1257)

By falling in love, *Ġhālib*, you too have become like me,
Once you used to keep me restrained from loving, *Mirzā Sāhib*.

Mirzā Sāhib: *Ġhālib*; *mān'e*: keep from, refrain.

Now that *Mirzā Sāhib* (the poet) is himself involved in a matter of the heart, he has become like me, even though he used to advise against it. Once involved, all admonishing is gone. The use of "*Mirzā Sāhib*," is meant to be sarcastic; it is also how the poet was often addressed as.

205

حضورِ شاہ میں اہلِ سخن کی آزمائش ہے　　چمن میں خوشنوایانِ چمن کی آزمائش ہے

ḥuẓūr-e shāh meñ ahl-e suḳhan kī āzmāi'sh hai
chaman meñ ḳhūshnavāyān-e chaman kī āzmāish hai (205:1; #1258)

In the honor of the King, there is a contest among the poets;
In the garden, there is a contest going on amongst the good singers.

ahl-e suḳhan: poets.

This *ġhazal* was read in the presence of King *Bahadur Shāh Zafar*. Today the poets will try out their creations. The *musha'ira* is a garden where good singers will sing.

قد و گیسو میں قیس و کوہکن کی آزمائش ہے　　جہاں ہم ہیں وہاں دار و رسن کی آزمائش ہے

qad-o-gesū meñ Qais-o-kohkan kī āzmāish hai
jahāñ ham haiñ, vahāñ dār-o-rasan kī āzmāish hai (205:2; #1259)

Through their stature and tresses is the trial of Qais and the mountain digger,
But where we are, 'tis by the gallows and the hanging noose that we are tested.

qad-o-gesū: stature and tresses; *kohkan*: mountain digger, *Farhād*; *dār-o-rasan*: altar and hanging rope, gallows and noose.

The dealings of *Qais (Majnūn)* and *Farhād* (the mountain digger) were limited to the beauty and tyranny of their beloved's heights and tresses. What we are dealing with is a matter of gallows and a noose—a much more serious and difficult matter. See the comparison between gallows and stature, noose and tresses.

کریں گے کوہکن کے حوصلے کا امتحاں آخر   ہنوز اُس خستہ کے نیروے تن کی آزمائش ہے

kareñ ge kohkan ke ḥauṣale kā imteḥāñ āḳhir
hanūz us ḳhasta(h) ke nirūe' tan kī āzmāish hai (205:3; #1260)

We will test the resolve of the mountain digger later;
Still we are testing the physical strength of the tired man.

ḳhasta: poor, tired; *nirūe'*: strength.

The task given to *Farhād* (the mountain digger) to dig the channel of milk from the mountain is just the test of his physical strength. The real test of his resolve comes later, regarding his failure. When he was given the news of the death of his beloved, he hit himself with an axe and died. He failed by not bearing this sorrow. The real test of a man is in bearing grief, not his physical resolve.

نسیمِ مصر کو کیا پیرِ کنعاں کی ہوا خواہی   اُسے یُوسف کی بُوئے پیرہن کی آزمائش ہے

nasīm-e miṣr ko kyā pīr-e kan'āñ kī havā ḳh(v)āhī
use yūsuf kī būe' pairhan kī āzmāish hai (205:4; #1261)

Why should the breeze from Egypt bring comfort to the old man from Canaan?
It was just testing the smell from the clothes of Joseph.

nasīm: breeze; *miṣr*: Egypt; *havā ḳh(v)āhī*: well wishing, sympathy; *pīr-e kan'āñ*: the old man of Canaan; *Haẓrat*: the honorable; *pairhan*: clothes.

In the *Qur'an* (Surah Yousuf), Joseph gives his shirt to his brother, asks him to place it on the face of his blind father (Jacob), and his sight returns. As the brothers leave Egypt with Joseph's shirt, on their way back to Canaan, Jacob says, "I can smell Joseph's body smell." The breeze from Egypt is not concerned about how Jacob feels; it just wants to see if the smell will reach from Egypt to Canaan. How permanent is the smell that would last through the journey to Canaan? What effect would it have when it reached there?

وہ آیا بزم میں، دیکھو، نہ کہیو پھر کہ غافل تھے　　شکیب و صبرِ اہلِ انجمن کی آزمائش ہے

vuh āyā bazm meñ, dekho, na(h) kahīyo phir ki(h) ġhāfil the
shikeb-o-ṣabr-e ahl-e anjuman kī āzmāish hai (205:5; #1262)

She has arrived in the assembly. See, do not complain later that you were unaware,
As the control and patience of those present in the assembly is being tested.

shikeb-o-ṣabr: control and patience.

An oft-repeated theme of the beloved walking into an assembly and testing the patience of her lovers has been presented here in an exquisite manner. She has arrived! First comes the announcement. Then, watch out next comes the warning. Finally, do not complain if you were not ready. If you were not ready, you should not have been there in the first place.

رہے دل ہی میں تیر اچھا، جگر کے پار ہو بہتر　　غرض شستِ بتِ ناوک فگن کی آزمائش ہے

rahe dil hī meñ tīr achhā, jigar ke pār ho bahtar
ġharaẓ shast-e but-e nāvak figan kī āzmāish hai (205:6; #1263)

'Tis good if it stays in the heart, 'tis better if it goes through the liver.
For the bow of that arrow-firing idol is being tested.

shast: bow

The heart is for love, the liver for patience. If the arrow stays in the heart, it keeps hurting and reminding me of the beloved. The liver should be destroyed for I do not need patience to tell me to hold back. Elsewhere *Ġhālib* has said, "*yih khalish kahañ se hotī, jo jigar ke pār hotā.*" (From where would have this pain come, had it gone through the liver.)

نہیں کچھ سُبحہ و زُنّار کے پھندے میں گیرائی　　وفاداری میں شیخ و برہمن کی آزمائش ہے

nahiñ kuchh subḥ-o-zunnār ke phande meñ gīrā'ī
vafādārī meñ shaikh-o-birhman kī āzmāish hai (205:7; #1264)

The loop of the rosary and the sacred thread cannot hold anyone;
The real test of Shaikh and Brahmin is in their faithfulness.

sabḥ: rosary; *gīrā'ī*: hold; *subḥ-o-zunnār:* rosary and sacred thread.

Both the rosary and *zunnār* (black sacred thread) have a thread in common. What is the ability of this thread to hold things together, keep the *Shaikh* and the *Brahmin* tied down to the tradition? The real test is how you use it. The *Shaikh* rotates the rosary and the *Brahmin* wears *zunnār* to show their resolve. What counts is their strength of belief, not their display of rituals.

پڑا رہ اے دلِ وابستہ، بیتابی سے کیا حاصل　　مگر پھر تابِ زُلفِ پُرشکن کی آزمائش ہے؟

paṛā rah aī dil-e vābasta(h), betābī se kyā ḥāṣil
magar phiṛ tāb-e zulf-e pur shikan kī āzmāish hai (205:8; #1265)

Stay put O! Captive heart. What is to be gained from impatience?
But then, it may be the testing of the strength of the curled tresses again.

zulf-e pur shikan: curled tresses.

Curls in the tresses are rings that keep the lover captured. Do you want to test their strength again? It is better to stay put without being impatient and hoping to be freed.

رگ و پے میں جب اُترے زہرِ غم تب دیکھیے کیا ہو   ابھی تو تلخیِ کام و دہن کی آزمائش ہے

rag-o-pae meñ jab utre zahr-e ġham, tab dekhīye kyā ho
abhī to talḳhī' kām-o-dahan kī āzmāish hai (205:9; #1266)

You will know what happens when the poison of sorrow creeps into the veins and nerves;
So far we are only testing its bitterness in the mouth and throat.

kām: throat; *dahan*: mouth.

Poisons are bitter even when we have only tasted them. The effect becomes more evident as the poison (sorrow of love) creeps through our veins and body. We have just begun to feel the taste of love. When the poison of sorrow seeps through our body, only then will we know that our resolve is being tested.

وہ آویں گے مرے گھر؟ وعدہ کیسا، دیکھنا غالب
نئے فتنوں میں اب چرخِ کہن کی آزمائش ہے

vuh āveñ ge mere ghar? va'da(h) kaisā, dekhnā Ġhālib
na'e fitnoñ meñ ab charḳh-e kohan kī āzmāish hai (205:10; #1267)

She would come to my home? What promise? Let us see *Ġhālib*
How with new mischief the sky is testing me.

charḳh-e kohan: the sky, the celestial sphere, the fortune; *fitnoñ:* mischiefs.

Yes, she had promised, but how is it possible that she will come? Is she giving me false hope? Is the sky testing me with new afflictions?

206

کبھی نیکی بھی اُس کے جی میں گر آجاے ہے مُجھ سے
جفائیں کرکے اپنی یاد شرما جاے ہے مُجھ سے

kabhī nekī bhī us ke jī meñ gar ājāe hai mujh se
jafā'eñ kar ke āpnī yād sharmā jāe hai mujh se (206:1; #1268)

If ever any kindness finds its way into her heart for me,
Remembering her cruelties to me, she turns coy with me.

jafāeñ: cruelties.

Remembering how cruel she has been to me makes her shy away from me. She hides her face and is rendered unable to extend her kindness to me, even if every once in a while, she really feels like it. Just another way to give benefit of doubt to the beloved.

خدایا جذبۂ دل کی مگر تاثیر اُلٹی ہے
کہ جتنا کھینچتا ہُوں اور کھنچتا جاے ہے مُجھ سے

ḳhudāyā jazbah' dil kī magar tāsīr ulṭī hai
kih jitnā khainchtā huñ aur khichtā jāe hai mujh se (206:2; #1269)

O! God! The feelings of my heart have the opposite effect.
The more I pull her towards me, the more she pulls away from me.

An appeal is being made to God to confirm why everything goes wrong. Pulling her towards me makes her move further away from me.

وہ بد خو اور میری داستانِ عشق طولانی
عبارت مختصر، قاصد بھی گھبرا جائے ہے مجھ سے

vuh bad ḳhū aur merī dāstān-e ʿishq t̤ūlānī
ʿibārat muḳhtaṣir, qāṣid bhī ghabrā jāe hai mujh se (206:3; #1270)

She is ill tempered and the story of my love is rather long;
Written briefly, even the messenger gets tired of me.

vuh: that—meaning beloved.

My beloved has a bad temper. Her impatience makes it difficult for me to believe that she will listen to my long story of woes. If my messenger gets tired of hearing these, what can I say about the beloved?

اُدھر وہ بدگمانی ہے، اِدھر یہ ناتوانی ہے
نہ پوچھا جائے ہے اُس سے، نہ بولا جائے ہے مجھ سے

udhar vuh badgumānī hai, idhar yih nātavānī hai
na(h) pūchā jāe hai us se, na(h) bolā jāe hai mujh se (206:4; #1271)

There is that mistrust and here is this weakness.
Neither is she able to ask me, nor am I able to say anything.

The beloved does not believe that I love her and she is reluctant to ask about my feelings. I have become so weak that I do not have the energy to prepare my arguments to convince her.

سنبھلنے دے مجھے اے ناامیدی، کیا قیامت ہے
کہ دامانِ خیالِ یار چھوٹا جائے ہے مجھ سے

sanbhalne de mujhe ai nāumidī, kyā qiyāmat hai
kih dāmān-e ḳhayāl-e yār chūṭā jāe hai mujh se (206:5; #1272)

**Let me settle, O! Hopelessness! What is this tumult all about?
That the hemline of the thought of the beloved is slipping away
from me.**

dāmān: skirt, hemline, lap.

Be kind to me, Oh helplessness! It is a shame that even the thought of the beloved fades away from me in despair. What will be left if that, too, is gone? The construction,"hemline of the thought of the beloved," is an exquisite *Ġhālib*ian construction, which has many deep meanings. The hemline of beloved's skirt, the hemline of the thoughts of beloved has been tightly knit in this verse together.

تکلف برطرف، نظارگی میں بھی سہی لیکن
وہ دیکھا جائے، کب یہ ظلم دیکھا جائے ہے مجھ سے

*takalluf barṯarf naẕẕārgī meñ bhī sahī lekin
vuh dekhā jāe, kab yih ẕulm dekhā jāe hai mujh se (206:6; #1273)*

**Formalities aside, though I am watching her too, but
How can I tolerate this cruelty that others would look at her as well?**

naẕẕārgī: watching; *ẕulm dekhā*: to tolerate cruelty.

Can I witness her being watched by others, even though I, too, am one of the watchers? This is too much cruelty to share gazing upon her.

ہوئے ہیں پانو ہی پہلے نبردِ عشق میں زخمی
نہ بھاگا جائے ہے مجھ سے، نہ ٹھہرا جائے ہے مجھ سے

*huv'e haiñ pāuñ hī pahle nabard-e 'ishq meñ zaḳhmī
na(h) bhāgā jāe hai mujh se, na(h) ṭhahrā jāe hai mujh se
(206:7; #1274)*

The feet have become wounded in the beginning of the battle of love.
I can neither run, nor can I stay put now.

Right at the beginning, when I entered the battlefield of love, I wounded my feet. Now I can neither run nor remain standing. It's best that I lay down my arms (my resolve) and take the blows lying down. Wounded feet refer to lost resolve to resist the beloved's cruelties.

قیامت ہے کہ ہووے مدعی کا ہم سفر غالب
وہ کافر جو خدا کو بھی نہ سونپا جائے ہے مجھ سے

qiyāmat hai kih hūve mudda'ī kā ham safir Ġhālib
vuh kāfir jo ḳhudā ko bhī na(h) saunpā jāe hai mujh se
(206:8; #1275)

'Tis Doomsday that the rival would be the travel companion, O! *Ġhālib*
Of that disbeliever, whom I could not even leave in God's custody.

mudda'ī: rival.

The beloved is going traveling with the rival so the lover faces the dilemma of how to wish her well. Customarily she would be given into the custody of God, but because of her cruelty and not believing in kindness, (the traits of God), the beloved qualifies as a disbeliever. It is a good omen to wish that people go in the custody of God. However, since the beloved is a disbeliever, she has little to do with God, and so the lover does not want to wish her that. In addition, there is a dilemma involved here. If the lover wishes her well, she will enjoy time with the rival, if the lover wishes her ill, this will negate his love for her!

207

زبسکہ مشقِ تماشا جنوں علامت ہے
کشاد و بستِ مژہ سیلیِ ندامت ہے

zabaskih mashq-e tamāshā junūñ ʿalāmat hai,
kushād-o-bast-e mizha(h) sīlī' nadāmat hai (207:1; #1276)

Whereas to keep looking around is a sign of insanity,
The fluttering eyelashes is like a slap of embarrassment.

zabaskih: because, whereas; *tamāshā*: to see; *sīl'ī*: slap; *kushād-o-bast*: opening and closing; *nadāmat*: embarrassment.

To simply look at the world, not for the sake of learning anything from it, but for the attraction of it, is a sign of insanity. If we see it correctly, we will know of its impermanence. Otherwise, just fluttering the eyelashes, watching the world in amazement, is like a slap of embarrassment. This means that anyone who watches the things around him with amazement (fluttering eyes) gets slapped with the label of being insane, a matter of great embarrassment. Notice how the movement of eyelashes are like hands striking together.

نہ جانوں کیونکہ مٹے داغ طعنِ بدعہدی
تجھے کہ آئنہ بھی ورطۂ ملامت ہے

na(h) jānūñ kioñ kih miṭe dāġh-e ta'n-e bad ʿahadī
tujhe kih ā'ina(h) bhī varṯa(h)' malāmat hai (207:2; #1277)

I do not know how the scars from taunts of breaking promises will be erased
When the mirror has also turned into a whirlpool of curse to you.

dāġh: scar; *taʿn*: blame, taunt; *bad*: wicked; *malāmat*: rebuke, curse; *bad ʿahadī*: breaking the promise, perfidy; *āʾina(h)*: mirror; *varṭa(h)*: whirlpool.

The lover addresses the beloved by warning her that she has earned a bad reputation as a promise-breaker; so much so that even her own mirror is cursing her. The curse from a mirror comes from looking at her inner self. How can you handle the world around you when your own soul curses you?

بہ پیچ وتابِ ہوس سلکِ عافیت مت توڑ
نگاہِ عجز سرِ رشتۂ سلامت ہے

ba(h) pech-o-tāb-e havas silk-e ʿāfiyat mat toṛ
nigāhe ʿijz sar-e rishta(h)ʾ salāmat hai (207:3; #1278)

From the twist and twirl of avarice, break not the connection to well being.
The vision of humility is the beginning of the thread of protection.

pech-o-tāb: twist and twirl, perplexity (used here in the context of getting involved); *silk-e ʿāfiyat*: relationship to comfort and rest.

Incessant pursuit of your desire is a sure way to lose your peace of mind and life. A humble eye, meaning not desiring more, is the beginning of the thread of protection—hold it. *Ġhālib* has often talked about vision being akin to a thread coming from the eyes.

وفا مقابل و دعوائے عشق بے بنیاد
جنونِ ساختہ و فصلِ گل، قیامت ہے

vafā muqābil-o-da'vā-e 'ishq bebunyād
junūn-e sāķhta(h)-o-fiṣl-e gul, qiyāmat hai (207:4; #1279)

The fidelity confronting the claim of love has no foundation.
It is a calamity to pretend frenzy in the spring season.

The beloved is ready to extend her fidelity, but her claim of love has no truth to it. The hypocrisy of it is as painful as Doomsday. The frenzy of love must be present naturally before we can display our feelings. To true lovers, frenzy comes naturally with the arrival of spring; to pretend that you are frenzied, and thus you are a lover, is indeed calamitous.

208

لاغر اِتنا ہُوں کہ گر تُو بزم میں جا دے مجھے
میرا ذِمّہ ، دیکھ کر گر کوئی بتلا دے مجھے

lāġhar itnā hūñ kih gar tū bazm meñ jā de mujhe
merā zimma(h), dekh kar gar koī' batlāde mujhe (208:1; #1280)

So frail have I grown that if you would allow me a place in your assembly,
I assure you that no one would notice me, if they looked for me.

merā zimma(h): my guarantee, assurance.

The beloved has told the lover that his presence is a source of embarrassment. To this the lover retorts, "I have become so weak that if I am allowed to come to your assembly, no one will notice me because of my frail stature. This saves you any embarrassment from the complaints of my rivals." Just another technique to dupe the beloved into letting him come to her assembly.

کیا تعجّب ہے کہ اُس کو دیکھ کر آجاے رحم
واں تلک کوئی کسی حیلے سے پہنچا دے مجھے

kyā ta'jub hai kih us ko dekh kar ājāe raḥem
vāñ talak koī' kisī ḥīle se pahuñchā de mujhe (208:2; #1281)

It will not be a surprise if seeing my wretched state, she would become kind to me,
If only someone would take me to her with any excuse.

ḥīle: excuse, pretext.

My condition is so pathetic that almost everyone who sees me begins to feel pity. If my friends really feel sympathetic towards me, they should take me to her under some pretext. Maybe, upon seeing my wretched state, she may begin to feel pity for me. This is an example of audacious thinking.

مُنہ نہ دِکھلاوے، نہ دِکھلا، پر بہ اندازِ عتاب
کھول کر پردہ ذرا آنکھیں ہی دِکھلا دے مجھے

munh na(h) dikhlāve, nā dikhlā, par ba andāz-e ʿitāb
khol kar parda(h) żarā ānkheñ hī dikhlāde mujhe (208:3; #1282)

Not showing the face, so be it not, but just to show your displeasure,
Part the veil a bit and show me your angry eyes at least.

ānkheñ hī dikhlāde: to get angry, to show eyes.

If you are not willing to show me your face, then at least give me an angry look. The lover is hoping that as she removes part of her veil to give him a dirty look he will be able to see more than just her angry eyes.

یاں تلک میری گرفتاری سے وُہ خوش ہے کہ مَیں
زُلف گر بن جاؤں تو شانے میں اُلجھا دے مجھے

yāñ talak merī giriftārī se vuh ḳhūsh hai kih meñ
zulf gar ban jāūñ to shāne meñ uljhā de mujhe (208:4; #1283)

So delighted is she with my capture, that
If I were the locks of her tresses, she will keep me entangled in her comb.

shāne: comb.

The beloved is thrilled to see him in captivity and would rather not let him go. She keeps him entangled just like, her hair that she catches in the comb.

209

بازیچۂ اطفال ہے دنیا مرے آگے   ہوتا ہے شب و روز تماشا مرے آگے

bāzīcha(h)' aṭfāl hai dunyā mere āge
hotā hai shab-o-roz tamāshā mere āge (209:1; #1284)

The world is merely a children's playground to me;
I watch its whirling display all day and night.

bāzīcha(h): playground.

I view the world as child's play; whatever happens around me I do not take it seriously. It is just Nature's play. *Ġhālib* has expounded upon a very serious side of God's creation in this deep verse. Maybe to God it was just a game to create the Universe, but to us it is an altogether different matter. Because I know the reality, I know why I should not take it seriously.

اک کھیل ہے اورنگِ سلیماں مرے نزدیک   اک بات ہے اعجازِ مسیحا مرے آگے

ik khel hai aurang-e sulemāñ mere nazdīk
ik bāt hai `ĵāz-e masīḥā mere āge (209:2; #1285)

The throne of Solomon is only a game to me;
The miracles of Jesus are mere talk to me.

aurang-e sulemāñ: throne of Solomon, riding which, he flew in the air; *`ĵāz-e masīḥā:* miracles of Jesus such as raising dead to life.

Soloman's flying in the air is just a play to me, a façade. The miracle of Jesus raising the dead is just hype, just talk to me. Jesus used to whisper to the dead to make them come alive.

whisper to the dead to make them come alive. See the connection between the talk and Jesus whispering.

جز نام نہیں صورتِ عالم مجھے منظور   جز وہم نہیں ہستیِ اشیا مرے آگے

juz nām nahīñ ṣurat-e ʻālam mujhe manẕūr
juz vahm nahīñ hastī'-e ashyā mere āge (209:3; #1286)

Except for its name, the existence of the Universe is not acceptable to me;
Except for an illusion, the existence of things is not a reality to me.

hastī'-e ashyā: existence of things.

The Universe has no reality except that there is a name given to it. Things do not exist except in our imagination.

ہوتا ہے نہاں گرد میں صحرا مرے ہوتے   گھستا ہے جبیں خاک پہ دریا مرے آگے

hotā hai nihāñ gard meñ ṣaḥrā mere hote
ghistā hai jabīñ ḳhāk pe daryā mere āge (209:4; #1287)

The dust raised in wandering conceals the existence of the desert;
The river rubs its forehead in the dust before me.

My wanderings in the desert are so intense that from the dust I raise, it covers the desert. Rubbing one's forehead in the dust is an extreme expression of humbleness. The river does this to acknowledge that compared to the flow of my tears, the river is nothing. Play on words using "dust," to mean several things.

مت پوچھ کہ کیا حال ہے میرا ترے پیچھے   تو دیکھ کہ کیا رنگ ہے تیرا مرے آگے

mat pūchh kih kyā ḥāl hai merā tere pīchhe
tū dekh kih kyā rang hai tera mere āge (209:5; #1288)

The thought of you turning coy and looking pale while facing me is too hurtful to think in your absence. Another meaning can be deduced if we read "complexion" as anger. When confronting your angry face, I feel comforted. Now that you are no longer unleashing your anger, I am saddened.

سچ کہتے ہو خودبین و خود آرا ہوں نہ کیوں ہوں   بیٹھا ہے بتِ آئنہ سیما مرے آگے

sach kehte ho ḳhud bīn-o-ḳhud ārā hūñ, na(h) kiyoñ huñ
baiṭhā hai but-e ā'ina(h) sīmā mere āge (209:6; #1289)

Correctly said that I am self-centered and self-adorning. Why shouldn't I be,
When I am sitting in front of an idol appearing like a mirror?

ḳhud bīn: self-centered, self-admiring, haughty, narcissist; *ḳhud ārā:* self-adorning; *ā'ina(h) sīmā:* appearing like mirror.

The beloved taunts the lover by saying that he has become conceited and self-centered. To that the lover says, "Why not, if the beloved that shines like a mirror sits in front of me?" I must keep looking into this mirror and keep pretending to dress myself with the proud ecstasy of seeing her before me. There is a play on the word "mirror" as beloved and what the lover looks into for self-adornment. The self-elevation comes from being close to the beloved.

پھر دیکھیے اندازِ گل افشانیٔ گفتار   رکھ دے کوئی پیمانۂ صہبا مرے آگے

phir dekhīye andāz-e gul afshānī'-e guftār
rakh de koī' paimāna(h)' ṣehbā mere āge (209:7; #1290)

You will then see the style of my flowery speech
If only someone would put a goblet of wine in front me.

gul afshānī: scattering of flowers.

Looking at the goblet of wine before me, my whole perspective changes. If you want to see me spread the flowers of good poetry around, just put a glass of wine in front of me.

نفرت کا گماں گزرے ہے، میں رشک سے گزرا   کیونکر کہوں لو نام نہ اُن کا مرے آگے

nafrat kā gumāñ guzre hai, meñ rashk se guzrā
kioñ kar kahūñ lo nām na(h) un kā mere āge (209:8; #1291)

Giving an impression of hatred, I had better let go of this envy.
How shall I beg them not to utter her name in front of me?

I was so intensely envious that I would not let anyone even utter her name in front of me. She and others have misconstrued this to mean that I hate her. That is terrible; I would rather give up my envy.

ایماں مجھے روکے ہے، جو کھینچے ہے مجھے کفر   کعبہ مرے پیچھے ہے، کلیسا مرے آگے

īmāñ mujhe roke hai, jo khainche hai mujhe kufr
ka'aba(h) mere pīchhe hai, kalīsā mere āge (209:9; #1292)

The belief holds me back, while disbelief pulls me towards it;
The *Kā'bā* is behind me and the temple before me.

kalīsā: church [used here, perhaps erroneously, to indicate a Hindu temple.]

As a believer, my religion keeps me from approaching the unbelievers, the idolaters. I am caught in a dilemma between the *Kā'bā* and the Hindu temple. Note that the Hindu temple contains idols. (Christians are not disbelievers or *kāfirs.*) The word, *kalīsā* [church], confuses the verse. The poet is saying that he is torn between choosing to become a believer or an unbeliever. Note that the beloved is addressed as an idol. This is tantamount to the poet becoming a disbeliever.

عاشق ہوں پہ معشوق فریبی ہے مرا کام　　مجنوں کو برا کہتی ہے لیلیٰ مرے آگے

'āshiq huñ pa(h) ma'shūq firebī hai mera kām
majnūñ ko burā kehtī hai lailā mere āge (209:10; #1293)

A lover I am, but deceiving the beloved is my trade;
Even *Lailā* calls *Majnūn* "no good" in front of me.

I entice my beloved with steadfast devotion and intense sacrifices to her. So much so that the sacrifices of the legendary lover *Majnūn* appear minuscule, to the point where *Lailā*, comparing me to *Majnūn*, begins calling him "no good."

خوش ہوتے ہیں پر وصل میں یوں مر نہیں جاتے　　آئی شب ہجراں کی تمنا مرے آگے

ḳhush hote haiñ par vaṣl meñ yūñ mar nahiñ jāte
āī shab-e hijrāñ kī tamannā mere āge (209:11; #1294)

Happy we become in the union, but not die like this.
The longings of the nights of separation came to fruition for me.

Undoubtedly, union with the beloved is such a fortunate event that it will make any lover extremely joyful, but not so much that it will kill him. Now that my desire to unite with the beloved has come true, I am faced with my longings during nights of separation that I used to have—of giving my life if I could unite with her. I did give in to my longings and died.

ہے موجزن اک قلزم خوں کاش یہی ہو　　آتا ہے ابھی دیکھیے کیا کیا مرے آگے

hai maujzan ik qulzum-e ḳhūñ kāsh yahī ho
ātā hai abhī dekhīye kyā kyā mere āge (209:12; #1295)

A sea of blood is surging to high tides; wish this would be it?
Let us see what more comes next before me?

maujzan: taking to high tides; *qulzum:* ocean, red sea; *kāsh*: wish.

A river of blood has come out of my eyes. This is painful and I hope it does not go beyond this. I am not sure, though, for I cannot know what else fate will dole out to me in the future.

گو ہاتھ کو جنبش نہیں آنکھوں میں تو دم ہے   رہنے دو ابھی ساغر و مینا مرے آگے

go hāth ko junbish nahiñ ānkhoñ meñ to dam hai
rehne do abhī sāġhar-o-minā mere āge (209:13; #1296)

Though the hands are listless, the eyes still have life.
Just leave the decanter and goblet before me.

The time of death is near. I have become so listless that I cannot move my hand to pour wine into the goblet, yet I want it left there for me to see. The poet is not asking anyone to pour wine for him for he does not have enough energy left to imbibe. Looking at the wine allows him to reminisce about the days of wine and dance, days when he used to enjoy living. This is a comforting thought for someone facing his time of death.

ہم پیشہ و ہم مشرب و ہم راز ہے میرا
غالب کو بُرا کیوں کہو، اچھا! مرے آگے

ham pesha(h)-o-ham mashrab-o-ham rāz hai merā
Ġhālib ko burā kioñ kaho, achhā! mere āge (209:14; #1297)

He is of the same profession, a drinking companion and a confidant;
All right, so why do you call *Ġhālib* names before me?

Ġhālib and I share many things: our profession, the taste for wine, and secrets. Do not call him bad, but if you must, then at least, not in front of me.

210

کہوں جو حال تو کہتے ہو مُدّعا کہیے تمہیں کہو کہ جو تُم یُوں کہو تو کیا کہیے؟

kahūñ jo ḥāl to kehte ho mudda‘ā kahīye
tumhīñ kaho kih jo tum yūñ kaho to kyā kahīye? (210:1; #1298)

If I tell you about my condition, you retort, "Just state the purpose."
You tell me now, if you talk to me like this, what can I possibly say?

The lover gives a detailed presentation of his condition to the beloved, who admonishes the lover to cut the story short and get to the point. The lover, in turn, expounds that if you cannot listen to my whole story, you cannot develop any sympathy for me, which is my ultimate goal. Also, if you cannot see my condition and the efforts I am making, then you cannot understand my story; it is thus useless to tell you anything.

نہ کہیو طعن سے پھر تُم کہ ہم سِتمگر ہیں مجھے تو خُو ہے کہ جو کچھ کہو، بجا کہیے

na(h) kahīyo ta‘n se phir tum kih ham sitamgar haiñ
mujhe to ḳhū hai kih jo kuchh kaho bajā kahīye (210:2; #1299)

Do not say again, sarcastically, "So, I am a tyrant";
It is my habit to say, "yes indeed" to whatever you say.

ta‘n: taunt, sarcasm.

The lover complains to the beloved that she is cruel. Irritated, the beloved sarcastically says, "Yes! I am a tyrant." The lover is telling her not to do this because he has a habit of saying "yes" to whatever she says and he would just second whatever she is saying, unintentionally confirming it.

وہ نیشتر سہی پر دل میں جب اُتر جاوے　　نگاہ ناز کو پھر کیوں نہ آشنا کہیے

vuh nīshtar sahī par dil meñ jab utar jāve
nigāhe nāz ko phir kyoñ na(h) āshnā kahīye (210:3; #1300)

They may well be lancets, but when they enter the heart,
Why shouldn't then we call those coquettish glances friendly?

Undoubtedly, the glances of the beloved are like lancets. When these lancets enter my heart, they become part of my existence. We begin to love them and they become part of our existence.

نہیں ذریعۂ راحت جراحتِ پیکاں　　وہ زخمِ تیغ ہے جس کو کہ دلکشا کہیے

nahiñ żarīah' rāḥat jirāḥat-e paikāñ
vuh zaḳhm-e teġh hai jis ko kih dilkushā kahīye (210:4; #1301)

The wound caused by the tip of the arrow is not a source of comfort
It is only the wound of the sword that can be called heart opening.

żarī'ah: source; *rāḥat*: comfort; *paikāñ*: tip of arrow; *zaḳhm-e teġh*: wound from sword; *dilkushā*: heart opening, glad tidings of heart.

The small wound from the tip of the arrow is not enough to bring comfort to me. It takes a deep wound of the sword to open my heart. This has two meanings. First, to make it happy and second, to expand it and make it bigger. A big heart takes more pain and thus makes it happier. Note that *Ġhālib* has often described the opening of the wound as lips parted in joy.

جو مُدّعی بنے اُس کے نہ مُدّعی بنیے   جو ناسزا کہے اُس کو نہ ناسزا کہیے

jo mudda'ī bane us ke na(h) mudda'ī banīye
jo nāsazā kahe us ko na(h) nāsazā kahīye (210:5; #1302)

Do not be a complainant to the one who is a complainant
Do not curse him back, if someone curses you.

mudda'ī: complainant; *nāsazā:* curse.

We should not live a life of reactive stance. If someone has become your enemy, do not return the animosity; if someone calls you names, do not call him names in return. This reflects the teachings of Eastern philosophies such as Buddhism.

کہیں حقیقتِ جانکاہیٔ مرض لکھیے   کہیں مُصیبتِ ناسازیٔ دوا کہیے

kahīñ ḥaqīqat-e jānkāhī' marẓ likhīye
kahīñ muṣībat-e nāsāzī' davā kahīye (210:6; #1303)

At times we write about our own soul-wasting malady;
At other times we talk about the disasters of the ineffective medicine.

jānkāhī: soul-wasting.

We often assert that our illness is terminal, yet we continue to complain about the medicine not being effective. This is not accepting the reality. This verse illustrates the lover's dilemma wherein he knows he is doomed, yet he keeps hoping that something will work out.

کبھی شکایتِ رنجِ گراں نشیں کیجے   کبھی حکایتِ صبرِ گُریز پا کہیے

kabhī shikāyat-e ranj-e girāñ nashīñ kīje
kabhī ḥikāyat-e ṣabr-e gurez pā kahīye (210:7; #1304)

At times, we complain of sorrow setting in heavily;
At other times we tell the tale of patience being ready to flee.

girāñ nashīñ: settling heavy, not easy to move; *gurez pā:* running feet

Sometimes we talk about grief setting in and at other time we talk about lack of patience.

رہے نہ جان تو قاتل کو خوں بہا دیجے   کٹے زبان تو خنجر کو مرحبا کہیے

rahe na(h) jān to qātil ko ḳhūñbahā ďije
kaṭe zabān to ḳhanjar ko marḥbā kahīye (210:8; #1305)

When life is gone, give blood money to the slayer;
When the tongue has been slashed, then give blessings to the dagger.

ḳhūñbahā: blood-money.

The arrival of death calls for repaying the slayer, or extending thanks to the slayer. Note that the one who commits murder, not the murdered one, gives the blood money. However, since we have wrought this upon us, the blood money is due to the slayer. Similarly, if our tongue is slashed, we should utter blessings for the dagger responsible for it. There is a play on words in this verse—a dead person offering blood money and a slashed tongue trying to speak.

نہیں نگار کو الفت، نہ ہو، نگار تو ہے   روانیٔ روش و مستیٔ ادا کہیے

nahiñ nigār ko ulfat, na(h) ho, nigār to hai
ravānī' ravish-o-mastī' adā kahīye (210:9; #1306)

If the beloved no longer loves me, so be it, she is still my beloved.
Her flowing gait and her intoxicating coquetry are enough for me.

ravān'ī-e ravish: flowing gait.

Not returning my love is not important to me if she remains my beloved. I enjoy seeing her swaying walk and her coquetry, which pleases me though I know well that she has no feelings for me.

نہیں بہار کو فُرصت، نہ ہو، بہار تو ہے! طراوتِ چمن و خُوبیِ ہَوا کہیے

nahiñ bahār ko furṣat, na(h) ho, bahār to hai
ṭarāvat-e chaman-o-khūbī' havā kahīye (210:10; #1307)

If the spring has no time to stay longer, so be it; at leası there is spring.
Let us talk of the freshness of the garden and the goodness of the breeze.

Spring may be short-lived, but we should not lament about it. We should enjoy the freshness (here called wetness) of the flowerbeds and the good air they impart while it lasts. Enjoy your blessings, though they may be short lived.

سفینہ جب کہ کنارے پہ آ لگا غالب
خُدا سے کیا سِتم و جَورِ ناخُدا کہیے!

safina(h) jab kih kanāre pe ālagā Ġhālib
ḳhudā se kyā sitam-o-jaur-e nāḳhudā kahīye (210:11; #1308)

When the boats have come ashore, *Ġhālib*,
Why complain to God about the cruelties and excesses of the boat commander?

safina(h): boat; *nāḳhudā*: boat commander.

Having survived the excesses of the boat commander, what good is it now to complain about him when the ship has come ashore? What is done is done, and it cannot be undone regardless of what happens to the commander of the boat now. It is better, therefore, to forget all about it and not complain about what the world has done to you in the past.

211

رونے سے اور عشق میں بیباک ہو گئے   دھوئے گئے ہم اتنے کہ بس پاک ہو گئے

rone se aur 'ishq meñ bebāk ho gae,
dho'e gae ham itne kih bas pāk hogae (211: 1; #1309)

Crying in love, we have become bolder;
Washed so thoroughly, we have become totally cleansed.

bebāk: bold; *pāk*: pious, cleansed, purified.

Our secret love was not known to anyone until we started crying. Once we began crying incessantly, the whole world came to know of it. With that went the need to hold any emotions back; we became bold by telling the world of our heart's ailment as we got rid of our fear that others would find out about our inner feelings. Here, cleansing means getting rid of hypocrisy.

صرفِ بہائے مے ہوئے آلاتِ میکشی   تھے یہ ہی دو حساب سو یوں پاک ہو گئے

ṣarf-e bahāe mai hue' ālāt-e mai kashī
the yih hī do ḥisāb so yūñ pāk hogae (211:2; #1310)

The drinking implements were bartered in lieu of the cost of wine;
These were the only two accounts left that thus got settled.

ṣarf: spent; *bahā*: price, cost; *ālāt-e mai kashī*: utensils of wine drinking.

I was concerned that I owed money for wine. In addition, I had to bear the physical burden of the wine drinking implements: the goblet, the decanter, etc., while I was homeless. To rid myself of both burdens,

I bartered the implements to pay for the money I owed for the wine. Now, all accounts are settled. There is sarcasm in this verse that does not come out easily. If these were the only problems in life, life would not be that bad. On the other hand, if these were the only accounts left to resolve, it means that all else has already been lost. Another interpretation is that there were two issues: to drink wine and to get rid of the burden of carrying drinking implements. We bartered the drinking implements to buy wine.

رسوائے دہر گو ہوئے آوارگی سے تم   بارے طبیعتوں کے تو چالاک ہو گئے

rusvāe dahar go huv'e āvārgī se tum
bāre ṯabī'atoñ ke to chālāk ho gae (211: 3; #1311)

Though the vagabond nature brought you notoriety;
But this did make your nature cunning as well.

rusvā: infamous; *dahar*: world (intended in a slighting manner); *āvārgī*: vagabond, vagrant; *ṯabī'atoñ*: nature, disposition, temperament; *chālāk:* clever, smart.

The beloved has become a vagabond, which has earned her a bad reputation. The lover, though, is looking at another angle altogether. He is saying that this has made her smarter and cleverer so now the rival will not be able to trick her. The clever use of the word temperament in this verse (used in the plural form), refers to the many faces of the beloved.

کہتا ہے کون نالۂ بلبل کو بے اثر   پردے میں گل کے لاکھ جگر چاک ہو گئے

kehtā hai kaun nālah' bulbul ko be aṡar
parde meñ gul kih lākh jigar chāk hogae (211:4; #1312)

Who says that the cry of the nightingale has no impact?
In the veil of the rose, a hundred thousand livers have been sliced open.

lākh: hundred thousand; *chāk*: sliced open.

Who are those people who claim that the cry of the nightingale is wasted? Do they not see that behind the veil of roses lie millions of livers sliced open? A red rose and its petals signify slashed organs. The liver is the source of strength and reasoning. Though it may not show, the cry of the nightingale has caused many to lose their strength and resolve and to make them fall in love.

پُوچھے ہے کیا وُجُود و عدم اہلِ شوق کا   آپ اپنی آگ کے خس و خاشاک ہوگئے

pūchhe hai kyā vujūd-o-'adam ahl-e shauq kā
āp apnī āg ke ḳhas-o-ḳhāshāk hogae (211: 5; #1313)

Why ask about the existence and nonexistence of the desiring ones?
They proved to be the leaves and straws for their own pyre.

vujūd-o-'adam: existence and non-existence; *ḳhas-o-ḳhāshāk*: leaves and straw.

Those who love burn in their own fire. Love makes them humble like leaves and straw and they burn in their humbleness. However, it is this burning that elevates them to the stage of nonexistence—the stage of *fana*; the stage of reaching out to the Lord. The use of the word "existence" in this verse is key to understanding the verse. The burning leads to the Lord. Only lovers can do this, for they have given up all ego and have turned into leaves and straw, worthless, dry, and ready to burn.

کرنے گئے تھے اُس سے تغافل کا ہم گِلہ   کی ایک ہی نگاہ کہ بس خاک ہوگئے

karne gae the us se taġhāful kā ham gila(h)
kī ek hī nigāh kih bas ḳhāk hogae (211: 6; #1314)

We went there to complain of her indifference,
But with just one glance, we were reduced to dust.

taġhāful: indifference; *ḳhāk*: dust.

We had suffered so much from her being oblivious to us that one day we decided to go and tell her about her tyranny. Having listened to our story, she turned to us and her first glance reduced us to dust. We could not bear to see her beauty. This verse can also be interpreted as a reference to Moses going to see God and then passing out when God displayed His power.

اِس رنگ سے اُٹھائی کل اُس نے اسدؔ کی نعش
دشمن بھی جس کو دیکھ کے غمناک ہو گئے

is rang se uṭhāī kal us ne Asad kī n'ash
dushman bhī jis ko dekh ki(h) ġhamnāk hogae (211:7; #1315)

Yesterday the corpse of Asad was raised with such disrespect
That even the enemies, seeing this, became melancholic.

is rang: with this color or style (here meaning disrespect); *ġhamnāk*: sad, melancholic; *n'ash*: corpse (also written as *l'ash*)

In the Muslim tradition, a dead body is carried in an open coffin-style bed on the shoulders of those who attend the funeral. The corpse of Asad, the poet, was raised with such disrespect, perhaps even being dragged in the street, that even the archenemies of Asad became sad. This concept is dwelt upon elsewhere, in addition, wherein the poet begs that his corpse be dragged through the alley of the beloved so that she will come to know what happened to her lover.

212

نشہ ہا شاداب رنگ و ساز ہا مستِ طرب   شیشۂ مے سروِ سبزِ جوئبارِ نغمہ ہے

nasha(h) hā shādāb-e rang-o-sāz hā mast-e ṯarab
shisha(h)' mai sarv-e sabz-e jū'bār-e naġhma(h) hai (212:1; #1316)

With a refreshing tone of intoxication, the musical instruments are drunk with ecstasy;
The decanter is the green cypress tree by the bank of the river of melody.

shādāb: refreshing; *mast-e ṯarab*: drunk with ecstasy; *sarv*: cypress tree; *jū'bār*: river.

The poet has created an extremely emotive spring scene. There is a stream of melodies running and the musical instruments have become drunk and ecstatic from playing pleasing tunes for her. The decanter appears as a cypress tree. Notice the shape of the cypress tree and decanter. In addition, the lover often imagines the cypress tree to be a facsimile of his beloved.

ہم نشیں مت کہہ کہ برہم کر نہ بزمِ عیشِ دوست   واں تو میرے نالے کو بھی اعتبارِ نغمہ ہے

ham nashīñ mat kah kih barham kar na(h) bazm-e 'aish-e dost
vāñ to mere nāle ko bhī i'tibār-e naġhma(h) hai (212: 2; #1317)

O! My companion, do not tell me not to disrupt the beloved's assembly of celebrations,
There even my plaints are trusted as songs.

barham: disrupt, clash; *i'tibār*: trust, assumed.

My friends tell me not to disturb the celebrations and singing at the assembly of the beloved with my wailing and complaints. I tell my friends to stop preaching to me because my plaints are like a melodious song to the ear of my beloved; hearing my plaints makes her happy. It can also mean that there is so much celebrating that my plaints would be lost in the melodies.

213

عرضِ نازِ شوخیٔ دنداں برائے خندہ ہے
دعویٔ جمعیتِ احباب جائے خندہ ہے

'arẓ-e nāz-e shoḳhī' dandāñ barā'e ḳhanda(h) hai
ďavī' jam'iyat-e iḥbāb jā'e ḳhanda(h) hai (213: 1; #1318)

The prideful, playful display of teeth is for a good laugh.
The claim of camaraderie of friends is a laughing matter.

nāz: pride; *shoḳh*: playful; *ḳhanda(h)*: laughter; *ďavī*: claim; *jam'iyat*: groupings.

Her playful display of teeth is meant to draw laughter (joy) from her lovers because they believe that her big smile is for them. She is teasing them. Collectively, they should be laughed at instead. There is also another possible meaning here. Friends getting together claiming brotherhood is a matter to be laughed at. Like teeth, they will fall out as well. In addition, there is a simile between a gathering and a display of teeth.

ہے عدم میں غنچہ محوِ عبرتِ انجامِ گل
یک جہاں زانو تأمل در قفائے خندہ ہے

hai 'adam meñ ġhuncha(h) maḥv-e 'ibrat-e anjām-e gul
yak jahāñ zānū tā'mmul dar qafā'e ḳhanda(h) hai (213: 2; #1319)

In its nonexistence, the bud is pondering on the fate of the flower
With its head on the knee, 'tis thinking of the laughter to follow.

'adam: nonexistence, losing, being deprived; *anjām*: fate, conclusion; *'ibrat*: admonition; *gul*: flower; *yak*: one; *jahāñ*: the world; *qafā*: nape of the neck, following, pursuit; *yak jahāñ zānū tā'mmul*: intense contemplation keeping head on the knees.

Before a bud becomes a flower, it is (as a bud) engrossed in thinking about its pathetic future. The laughter (the opening of the bud) leading to the withering away of the petals is worth pondering deeply. There is a bit of admonishing here that laughter always brings gloom afterwards; we should know better. Holding one's head on the knees is a posture of deep introspection. This is one of the most difficult verses to interpret. In simple words, a bud is a nonexistent flower; upon coming to existence, it finds that it is on the way to nonexistence (petals withering away) and how the world will laugh at it.

کلفتِ افسردگی کو عیشِ بیتابی حرام
ورنہ دنداں در دل افشردن بنائے خندہ ہے

kulfat-e afsurdagī ko 'aish-e betābī ḥarām
varna(h) dandāñ dar dil afshurdan bināe' ḳhanda(h) hai
(213:3; #1320)

The luxury of restlessness is forbidden in the pain of sadness,
Or else laughter comes after digging the teeth into heart.

kulfat: pain, distress; *afsūrdagī*: dejection, sadness; *betābī*: restlessness; *ḥarām*: forbidden; *dandāñ dar dil afshurdan*: to dig teeth into heart (a Persian idiom used to indicate extreme patience and tolerance).

Restlessness, pacing, and tumult all show motion and thus a means of relieving tension; when the pain of sadness is felt in the heart, restlessness appears like a luxury. It is not permitted to feel this luxury when the purpose is to bear the pain of sadness, which all lovers should do. This is my condition now. This situation is compared to laughter after bearing intense pain can pass. However, to some, like the poet, such transition is not possible; they stay in pain forever.

سوزشِ باطن کے ہیں احباب منکر ورنہ یاں
دل محیطِ گریہ و لب آشنائے خندہ ہے

sozish-e bāṯin ke haiñ aḥbāb munkir varna(h) yāñ
dil muḥīt-e giryah-o-lab āshnā-e' khanda(h) hai (213: 4; #1321)

The friends ignore the hidden fire or else here,
The heart is an endless ocean of tears, though the lips are used to laughing.

sozish: burning; *bāṯin*: hidden; *aḥbāb*: friends; *munkir*: denier; *muḥīt*: encircling (in Persian, it is used to mean an endless ocean since water has encircled the land all around); *āshnā*: intimate; *khanda(h)*: laughter.

Seeing my outward condition, laughing and joking, my friends refuse to believe that I have any inner burning of the heart. If only they knew, then they would come to know what I am holding inside—an endless ocean of tears. My laughter is a façade for the world.

حسنِ بے پروا خریدارِ متاعِ جلوہ ہے
آئنہ زانوئے فکرِ اختراعِ جلوہ ہے

214

حسن بے پروا خریدار متاع جلوہ ہے   آئنہ زانوے فکر اختراع جلوہ ہے

ḥusn-e be parvā(h) ḳharīdār-e matā'-e jalva(h) hai
ā'ina(h) zānūe fikr-e iḳhtirā'-e jalva(h) hai (214: 1; #1322)

The unconcerned beauty is the buyer of the goods of display
Mirror on the knee, she ponders new way to manifest.

be parvā(h): careless, oblivious; *matā*: commodity; *ā'ina(h) zānū*: the mirror of knee (while pondering people often put their head on the knee, thus Persian construction calls the knee a mirror); *iḳhtirā*: discovery, ingenuity.

Undoubtedly, the beauty is oblivious and careless, yet it still desires to display itself. This means that the beauty is an ongoing customer of the commodity of display. When she puts a mirror on her knees to adorn herself, she is actually thinking about how she can discover new way to display herself. Note that the knee is also called a mirror, where people put their head to think and to ponder.

تا کجا اے آگہی رنگ تماشا باختن   چشم وا گر دیدہ آغوش وداع جلوہ ہے

tā kujā ai āgahī rang-e tamāshā bāḳhtan
chashm-e vā gar dīda(h) āġhosh-e vidā' jalva(h) hai (214: 2; #1323)

How long, O! Awareness, will you keep losing, playing with colorful displays?
An open eye is the embrace that bids goodbye to splendor.

tā kujā: for how long; *rang*: color; *tamāshā*: spectacle; splendor; *bāḳhtan*: to lose at play.*chashm*: eye; *vā*: open; *dīda(h)*: the eye; *āġhosh*: embrace; *vidā'*: farewell; *jalva(h)*:

The poet addresses his own sense of observation by asking, "O' Awareness, when will you stop judging the value of what you see? You know well that as soon as you open your eyes (know the real meaning of things), the spectacle will disappear. Notice how the closing of eyelids forms an embrace like that of arms.

215

جب تک دہانِ زخم نہ پیدا کرے کوئی   مشکل کہ تجھ سے راہِ سخن وا کرے کوئی

jab tak dahān-e zaḳhm na(h) paidā kare ko'ī
mushkil kih tujh se rāh-e suḳhan vā kare ko'ī (215: 1; #1324)

Until one creates a mouth to the wound,
It is difficult for one to open path to communicate with you.

rāh-e suḳhan: means of communication.

The mouth of a wound connotes a chronic wound, a wound that is not healing. One has to develop a real desire for you O! Lord, before being able to communicate with You. The play on words here is between the lips of an open wound and lips that speak. To be able to speak, we must have lips; the lips of an open wound tell the whole story without saying a word.

عالم غبارِ وحشتِ مجنوں ہے سربسر   کب تک خیالِ طرّۂ لیلیٰ کرے کوئی

'ālam ġhubār-e vaḥshat-e majnūñ hai sarbasar
kab tak ḳhayāl-e ṯurra(h)' lailā kare ko'ī (215: 2; #1325)

The entire world is a dust storm raised by the frenzy of *Majnūn*.
For how long can one keep thinking about the ringlets of *Lailā*?

ġhubār-e vaḥshat: dust of frenzy; ; *sarbasar*: totally; *ṯurra(h)*: ringlets of hair.

Lover's frenzy turns the universe tumultuous. The storm it creates is the deception that the lover will reach his destiny. The "dust storm" is more like a smokestack that hides the realities of the universe from the lover. How long should a lover keep thinking about his beloved? The use of "ringlets of *Lailā*" means the corporeal beloved. Since the storm of dust keeps us thinking that there is reality behind, we remain enamored by the physical things around us. Once this screen clears, we will know that the reality is the Lord and not the material world. The dust storm raised by the frenzy of lovers hides the realities of the Universe from them.

افسردگی نہیں طرب انشائے التفات　　ہاں درد بن کے دل میں مگر جا کرے کوئی

afsurdagī nahiñ ṭarab inshā-e iltifāt
hāñ dard ban kih dil meñ magar jā kare ko'ī (215: 3; #1326)

Sadness cannot create happiness even with her amorous attention;
But only if someone would turn into pain and make a place in my heart.

afsurdagī: sadness; *ṭarab inshā*: someone creating happiness; *iltifāt*: being amorous.

The state of my sadness and dejection is such that nothing can relieve it, including the amorous attention of the beloved. My sadness demands more hurting. Yes, if my beloved enters my heart as pain and stays there, then perhaps I can get some relief. This verse refers to how perpetual gloom makes a person seek more sadness.

رونے سے اے ندیم ملامت نہ کر مجھے　　آخر کبھی تو عقدۂ دل وا کرے کوئی

rone se aī nadīm malāmat na(h) kar mujhe
ākhir kabhī to 'uqda(h)' dil vā kare ko'ī (215: 4; #1327)

Reproach me not, O! Friend, at my weeping,
After all, at times, one has to undo the knots in the heart.

malāmat: reproach, reprimand; *'uqda(h)*: knot.

The lover addresses his close companions after they have become increasingly critical of his incessant weeping. How long can I put up with the knot in my heart? I had to arrange to undo this knot; crying works best for me. A lump in the throat and a knot in the heart illustrate how we respond to extremely aggravating situations; the poet has depicted this exquisitely. The second line shows extreme desperation.

چاکِ جگر سے جب رہِ پُرسش نہ وا ہوئی   کیا فائدہ کہ جیب کو رُسوا کرے کوئی

chāk-e jigar se jab rah(e) pursish na(h) vā hu'ī
kyā fā'idah kih jeb ko rusvā kare ko'ī (215: 5; #1328)

When tearing off my liver did not get her attention
Then what is the use for anyone to disgrace the collar?

pursish: attention.

To show her my feelings, I ripped my heart (liver) out, but she did not notice it. What use is it now to rip my collar, for this is of much less value? The poet refers to a choice of efforts. When what is most dramatic does not get results, waste not your time with petty efforts. The philosophy described here is much deeper than the lament of the lover. It refers to the human strife and wishful thinking. When our best and most desperate efforts bring no favorable results, then it might be better not to go on struggling.

لختِ جگر سے ہے رگِ ہر خار شاخِ گل   تا چند باغبانیِ صحرا کرے کوئی

laḳht-e jigar se hai rag-e har ḳhār shāḳh-e gul
tā chand bāġhbānī' saḥrā kare ko'ī (215: 6; #1329)

The pieces of my liver turn the veins of thorns into branches of flowers.
How long shall one continue this gardening of the desert?

laḳht: piece; *tā chand*: how long.

The lover is wandering in the desert and watering the thorns of the desert with the blood from the pieces of his liver (patience). As a result, there has been a greening of the desert. The lover is questioning how long he can continue this job. He is not saying that he is giving it up, he is just asking himself how long it will go on, knowing well, though, that it is a proposition for eternity. Elsewhere in one of his Persian verses, *Ġhālib* says: "We have laced every thorn in the desert with the blood of our heart and thus we have established a rule concerning how to garden in the desert." [*āġhushta aīm har sare ḳhār-e ba(h) ḳhūne dil, qānūn-e bāġhbānī-e sahrā navishta(h) aīm*]

ناکامیٔ نگاہ ہے برقِ نظارہ سوز　　　تُو وُہ نہیں کہ تجھ کو تماشا کرے کوئی

nākāmī' nigāh hai barq-e naẕẕārah soz
tū vuh nahiñ kih tujh ko tamāshā kare koī (215: 7; #1330)

The failure of sight proves to be the lightning that burns the spectacle;
You are not the one Whose display can be observed by anyone.

It is not possible for anyone to see You. The sight that comes from the eyes searching You, returns (rebounds). Having failed, the lightning destroys my vision as it strikes me back. This means that the more we try looking around us, the less we can see. It is not possible to see you. The physical description will be akin to a mirror reflecting a ray of light. *Ġhālib* has also often described sight as being something that comes out of the eye, like a string or a wire.

ہر سنگ و خشت ہے صَدَفِ گوہرِ شکست　　　نُقصاں نہیں جُنوں سے جو سودا کرے کوئی

har sang-o-ḳhisht hai ṣadaf-e gohar-e shikast
nuqṣāñ nahiñ, junūñ se jo saudā kare ko'ī (215: 8; #1331)

Every rock and brick is a shell containing the pearl of defeat;
There is no loss if one trades in with madness.

ṣadaf: shell; *gohar-e shikast*: pearl of defeat.

Dealing in frenzy is not a losing proposition. You get rocks thrown at you, but these rocks are like gift of pearls to lunatics for they cause severe bodily harm—a reward better than jewels. This is one of those tricky verses where the meaning is very difficult to grasp. In the first verse, "defeat" means a shattering of the head, and the rocks are actually seashells. In reality, the lover, though rocks are thrown at him, is actually getting pearls—not the kind that are found in necklaces, but those that come from a broken head and limbs. Though it appears to be a losing proposition, it is not, because this is the real intent of the lover.

سربر ہوئی نہ وعدۂ صبر آزما سے عمر   فرصت کہاں کہ تیری تمنا کرے کوئی

sarbar huī' na(h) va'da(h)' ṣabr āzmā se 'umr
furṣat kahāñ kih terī tammanā kare ko'ī. (215: 9; #1332)

This lifetime was not enough for your patience-demanding promises.
Who has the time left to long for you?

The beloved's promises demand patience, but now that I am dead, the question of longing for you has become redundant. Who can live long enough to see your promises come true? Elsewhere, *Ġhālib* writes: *kaon jītā hae terī zulf ke sar hote tak.* (Who lives long enough to win your tresses?)

ہے وحشتِ طبیعتِ ایجاد یاس خیز   یہ درد وہ نہیں کہ نہ پیدا کرے کوئی

hai vaḥshat-e ṭabī'at-e ījād yās ḳhez
yih dard vuh nahiñ kih na(h) paidā kare ko'ī (215: 10; #1333)

The frenzy of creative personality brings hopelessness;
This is not a pain that one could produce consciously.

yās: hopelessness, also name of a flower.

The frenzy of being creative results in hopelessness. This is an innate personality trait; it cannot be adopted. An unrecognized scientist becomes hopelessly disappointed and so do unsuccessful lovers. Those with a creative disposition and those in frenzy do not always follow the rules; their act, however, often results in disappointment.

بیکاریٔ جنوں کو ہے سر پیٹنے کا شغل　　جب ہاتھ ٹوٹ جائیں تو پھر کیا کرے کوئی

bekārī' junūñ ko hai sar pīṭne kā shaġhl
jab hāth ṭūṭ jāeñ to phir kyā kare ko'ī (215: 11; #1334)

The idleness of frenzy is busy striking the head;
If hands are broken, then what can anyone do?

The frenzy of lunacy requires giving up everything and running to the wilderness where there is nothing to do except keep hitting one's head with one's own hands. But if in lunacy we lose our hands, then how would one keep busy in the wilderness? Breaking hands also has the connotation of being made helpless.

حسنِ فروغِ شمعِ سخن دور ہے اسدؔ
پہلے دلِ گداختہ پیدا کرے کوئی

ḥusn-e furoġh-e shama'-e suḳhan dūr hai Asad
pahle dil-e gudāḳhtah paidā kare ko'ī (215: 12; #1335)

The beauty of the brightness of the candle of poetry is far-fetched Asad,
First, one should create a heart that is molten.

ḥusn: beauty; *furoġh*: brightness, luminous; *gudāḳhtah*: molten.

A tender, sensitive heart is what you need to write poetry. To let the candle of poetry burn, you must have a molten heart to feed. See the comparison of sorrow to burnt candle, sad poetry, melting of the heart, vis-à-vis melting of a candle.

216

ابنِ مریم ہُوا کرے کوئی   میرے دُکھ کی دَوا کرے کوئی

ibn-e maryam hu'ā kare ko'ī
mere dukh kī davā kare ko'ī (216: 1; #1336)

Son of Mary, let there be someone;
Would someone cure my pain as well?

Jesus may be famous for raising the dead, but that does not help me. Curing my pain will demand a greater miracle than raising the dead. Is there anyone who can perform this miracle?

شرع و آئین پر مَدار سہی   اَیسے قاتل کا کیا کرے کوئی

shar'a-o-ā'īn par madār sahī
aise qātil kā kyā kare ko'ī (216: 2; #1337)

Given that the constitution and religious laws bind us,
But what shall one do with a murderer like that?

shar'a: Muslim religious laws; *ā'īn*: constitution.

I know I will get justice in the court of law, whether it is based on the civil law or the laws of religion. However, to convict her, we need proof of a murder weapon, something impossible to find because she has killed me with her glances. What shall we do to a killer like that?

چال جیسے کڑی کمان کا تیر   دِل میں اَیسے کے جا کرے کوئی

chāl jaise kaṛī kamān kā tīr
dil meñ aise ke jā kare ko'ī (216: 3; #1338)

The gait like an arrow shot from a fully strung bow;
In a heart like that, how would one create a place for oneself?

She walks like an arrow shot from a full-strung bow: straight, fast, and unwavering; that *is* her personality. With such inflexibility, how can one hope to make room in her heart?

بات پر واں زبان کٹتی ہے وُہ کہیں اور سُنا کرے کوئی

bāt par vāñ zabān kaṭtī hai
vuh kahaiñ aur sunā kare ko'ī (216: 4; #1339)

There is a rude interruption at everything said.
She would rather talk and everyone would just listen.

zabān kaṭtī: interrupting rudely, cutting tongue.

She rudely interrupts everything we say, and gets upset. I think it is better to just let her talk while we quietly listen to her.

بک رہا ہُوں جُنُوں میں کیا کیا کُچھ کُچھ نہ سمجھے خُدا کرے کوئی

bak rahā hūñ junūñ meñ kyā kyā kuchh
kuchh na(h) samjhe ḳhudā kare ko'ī (216: 5; #1340)

I do not know what I am babbling in my frenzy.
O! God, I only hope no one will understand it.

bak rahā: making idle talk, babbling.

In the frenzy of madness, I talk gibberish and have no idea what am I saying. Just in case I say anything about my beloved, I hope no one will understand it. She might be embarrassed lest anyone make any sense out of it.

نہ سنو، گر بُرا کہے کوئی نہ کہو، گر بُرا کرے کوئی

na(h) suno, gar burā kahe ko'ī
na(h) kaho, gar burā kare ko'ī (216: 6; #1341)

Listen not, if someone would call you bad;
Say nothing, if one does wrong to you.

If someone calls you "bad", pay no attention to it. It will drag you into an unnecessary retort that will only make your heart heavy. If someone does something wrong to you, do not respond for it may sadden him and even persuade him to retaliate against you. This verse conveys the spirit of "Hear no evil, speak no evil". The poet is simply explaining how to stay out of trouble and keep your sanity.

روک لو، گر غلط چلے کوئی بخش دو، گر خطا کرے کوئی

rok lo, gar ġhalaṯ chale ko'ī
baḳhsh do, gar ḳhaṯā kare ko'ī (216: 7; #1342)

Stop him, if one goes on a wrong path.
Forgive him, if one makes a blunder.

This is a continuation of the above verse. *Ġhālib* is encouraging others to try and keep from going down the wrong path and forgiving them if they make a blunder or else they will never return to the righteous path.

کون ہے جو نہیں ہے حاجتمند کس کی حاجت رَوا کرے کوئی

kaun hai jo nahiñ hai ḥājatmand
kis kī ḥājat ravā kare ko'ī (216: 8; #1343)

Who is there that is not a needy one?
Who can fulfill the needs of anyone?

If you take your needs to someone and they remain unfulfilled, complain not. You must realize that everyone has needs and that it is not possible for one person to fulfill all of them. What is being taught here is a lesson in being content.

کیا کیا خضر نے سکندر سے اب کسے رہنما کرے کوئی

kyā kiyā Ḳhiẓr ne Sikandar se
ab kise rahnumā kare ko'ī (216: 9; #1344)

What was it that Khizr did to Alexander?
Now whom can we accept as our guide?

ḳhiẓr: Legend has it that *Haẓrat Ḳhiẓr* was to guide Alexander to the Fountain of Eternity. Instead, he abandoned Alexander and got there on his own and was given perpetual life (see Glossary); *rahnumā*: guide.

See what *Ḳhiẓr* did to Alexander? *Ḳhiẓr* was a highly respected man. If he can do this to his disciple, imagine what the world would do to you. It certainly is difficult for us to choose our leaders.

جب توقع ہی اٹھ گئی غالب
کیوں کسی کا گلا کرے کوئی

jab tuvaqqu' hī uṭh gaī Ġhālib
kioñ kisī kā gilā kare ko'ī (216: 10; #1345)

When all hope is gone, *Ġhālib*,
Why should one complain about someone?

tuvaqqu': hope.

A complaint is made only when there is hope of it being heard. With all hope gone, what good it is to continue to plead or implore?

217

بہت سہی غمِ گیتی، شراب کم کیا ہے؟
غلامِ ساقیِ کوثر ہوں مجھ کو غم کیا ہے!

bahut sahī ġham-e getī, sharāb kam kyā hai
ġhulām-e sāqī' kauṡar hūñ mujh ko ġham kyā hai
(217: 1; #1346)

The sorrows of the world may be in abundance, but there is no shortage of wine either;
A slave of the cupbearer of Paradise, why should I worry?

getī: world; *kauṡar*: a fountain in Paradise, meaning here Paradise.

Regardless of how deep the wound is that was given to me by the world, I can bear it by losing myself in wine. I am a servant to the cupbearer who serves wine in Paradise; certainly this connection can wash away my sorrows. It is interesting to note that the wine of the fountains of Paradise is not intoxicating; it is a symbolic wine. Being a servant to the cupbearer certainly deserves some favors, like getting all the leftover drinks. Only pious ones will enter Paradise and get wine from the cupbearer of Paradise. The poet is making certain assumptions here, one of which is that when so many woes are given in this world, certainly God will take care of me, as compensation, in my next abode.

تمھاری طرز و رَوِش جانتے ہیں ہم، کیا ہے
رقیب پر ہے اگر لُطف، تو سِتم کیا ہے؟

tumhārī ṯarz-o-ravish jānte haiñ ham, kyā hai
raqīb par hai agar lutf to sitam kyā hai (217: 2; #1347)

We know well your style and your ways; so what
If there is kindness towards the rival, what is the tyranny in it?

ṯarz: style: *ravish*: ways, manners, mode, style.

I know your style of cruelty includes declining my claim that you are cruel to me. Nevertheless, look at your kindness toward my rivals. Do you not suppose this counts as cruelty towards me? Another meaning is that we know your style and sooner or later, your kindness towards the rival will turn into cruelty.

سُخن میں خامۂ غالبؔ کی آتش اَفشانی
یقیں ہے ہم کو بھی، لیکن اب اُس میں دَم کیا ہے!

sukhan meñ ḳhāma(h)' Ġhālib kī ātish afshānī
yaqīñ hai ham ko bhī, lekin ab us meñ dam kyā hai (217: 3; #1348)

In poetry, the pen of *Ġhālib* scatters fire all around;
We too believe that, but is there any energy left in him?

sukhan: poetry; *ḳhāma(h)*: pen; *ātish afshānī:* scattering flames; *dam*: breath, energy.

Yes, *Ġhālib* has written great poetry, but he no longer has the energy to write more. The use of scattering fire means fiery breath, meaning here fiery verses. Note that it takes a lot of energy to spew fiery breath.

218

باغ پا کر خفقانی یہ ڈراتا ہے مجھے
سایۂ شاخِ گل افعی نظر آتا ہے مجھے

bāġh pā kar ḳhafqānī yih ḍarātā hai mujhe
sāya(h)' shāḳh-e gul afa'ī naẓar ātā hai mujhe (218: 1; #1349)

The garden scares me finding me weak at heart;
The shadow of branch appears like a black snake to me.

ḳhafqānī: patient suffering from palpitation of heart, hysterical; *afa'ī*: black snake, cobra.

Due to my condition of having a weak heart, I am frightened by shadows in the garden. Even the shadow of the tree branches began to appear like black snakes to me. The question arises, why is the poet frightened? In this case, the garden provided everything that reminds the lover of the beloved; the black snake reminds the lover of her black tresses. How can the lover be frightened by the thought of the beloved's tresses, though? It is because he knows that she would never come to the garden, so even if it looks like her tresses, it must be a snake.

جوہرِ تیغ بہ سر چشمۂ دیگر معلوم!
ہوں میں وہ سبزہ کہ زہراب اُگاتا ہے مجھے

johar-e teġh ba(h) sar chashma(h)' dīgar ma'lūm
hūñ meñ vuh sabzah kih zahrāb ugātā hai mujhe (218: 2; #1350)

The edge of the sword is like the banks of a brook;
I am the greenery that the poisonous waters cultivate.

johar: edge, luster, substance; *teġh*: sword; *ba(h)*: with; *sar*: head; *chashma(h)*: brook; *ma'lūm*: known, obvious; *zahrāb*: dirty, stagnant or envenomed water.

If we consider the sword to be a brook, then its sharp edge is like the greenery at its bank. I am like the grass growing out of poisoned water (meaning sorrow and pain), which is the cause of my existence. Some difficulties arise in interpreting this verse. Often the sword is dipped in poisonous water to make it more potent which leaves a green coating on the sword. Like the green edge of the sword drenched in poison, I, too, am created out of the poisonous water; the way the poisoned edge can kill, I, too, kill the feelings of others by giving them my sadness, as I am a product of bitterness.

مدعا محوِ تماشائے شکستِ دل ہے
آئینہ خانے میں کوئی لیے جاتا ہے مجھے

muddaʿā maḥv-e tamāshā-e shikast-e dil hai
ā'inah ḳhāne meñ ko'ī liye jātā hai mujhe (218: 3; #1351)

The intent is engrossed in watching the breaking of heart,
As if someone were taking me to a house of mirrors.

muddaʿā: purpose, intent; *maḥv:* engrossed; *shikast-e dil*: breaking of heart; *ā'inah ḳhāne*: house of mirrors.

My heart is broken into hundreds of pieces as if it were a shattered mirror. Now the reflection of my intent is visible in each of these pieces as if it were in a house of mirrors. The purpose was, of course, to have a broken heart. My desire is to intently observe what is happening to my heart; I see mirrors all around as if I were in a house of mirrors.

Who is taking the lover to this house of mirrors? It is his own desire. Note that "I" and "desire" are the same.

نالہ سرمایۂ یک عالم و عالم کفِ خاک
آسماں بیضۂ قمری نظر آتا ہے مجھے

nāla(h) sarmāya(h)' yak 'ālam-o-'ālam kaf-e ḳhāk
āsmāñ baiẓa(h)' qumrī naẓar ātā hai mujhe (218: 4; #1352)

Plaint is the capital of this world, and the world merely a fistful of dust.
The sky appears like an egg of the ringdove to me.

sarmāya(h): capital; *baiẓa(h)*:egg; *kaf* fist; *ḳhāk*: dust; *qumrī*: ring-dove.

The plaint of suffering is what this world is made of. That is the capital of the world; that is the currency of this world; that is what circulates in this world. In being so worthless, the world is merely a fistful of dust. The insignificance of the world can be seen by how it compares to the ring-necked dove's egg. Notice that the shape of the egg is the shape of the sky and the color of the ring-necked dove's egg is sandy.

زندگی میں تو وہ محفل سے اُٹھا دیتے تھے
دیکھوں اب مر گئے پر کون اُٹھاتا ہے مجھے

zindagī meñ to vuh maḥfil se uṭhā dete the
dekhūñ ab margae' par kaun uṭhātā hai mujhe (218: 5; #1353)

While living, she would tell me to rise and leave her assembly.
Let us see who would raise me now that I am dead.

Playing on the use of the words, "rise" and "raise," the poet is asking who would raise his coffin and carry his corpse to the graveyard? When alive, the beloved would tell him to rise and leave. Now dead, let us see who would raise my coffin. Another meaning is that now I am dead, she cannot tell me to rise and leave.

219

روندی ہوئی ہے کوکبۂ شہریار کی   اترائے کیوں نہ خاک سرِ رہگزار کی

raundī hu'ī hai kaukaba(h)' shahryār kī
itrāe kioñ na(h) ḳhāk sar-e rahguzār kī (219: 1; #1354)

It is trampled by the royal pageantry of the King.
Why would not the dust of the pathway boast?

raundī: trampled; *kaukaba(h)*: royal pageantry; *shahryār*: King; *itrāe*: boast.

The dust en route to the King's pageantry feels fortunate to be trampled by the royal horses.

جب اُس کے دیکھنے کے لیے آئیں بادشاہ   لوگوں میں کیوں نمُود نہ ہو لالہ زار کی

jab us ke dekhne ke liye āeñ bādshāh
logoñ meñ kioñ numūd na(h) ho lāla(h) zār kī (219: 2; #1355)

When the King himself would come to see it,
Why would not then people take pride in the garden of tulips.

numūd: exhibition (meant here as pride); *lāla(h) zār*: garden of tulips.

When the King himself comes to see the garden of tulips, why then would not the garden of tulips be be liked by the people? People love what the King likes.

بھُوکے نہیں ہیں سیرِ گلستاں کے ہم ولے   کیونکر نہ کھائیے کہ ہوا ہے بہار کی

bhūke nahiñ haiñ sair-e gulistāñ ke ham vale
kioñkar na(h) khāīye kih havā hai bahār kī (219: 3; #1356)

We are not hungry to take a stroll in the garden.
Why would not we consume it, for it is the air of spring season?

I am not hungry for the garden, but then it is spring. Why should not we go out and inhale some fresh air? The first line means that "we are not desperate to take a stroll," but the poet has created a play on words with being hungry and eating or consuming (inhaling) air.

220

ہزاروں خواہشیں ایسی کہ ہر خواہش پہ دم نکلے　　بہت نکلے مرے ارمان لیکن پھر بھی کم نکلے

hazāroñ kh(v)āhisheñ aisī kih har ḳh(v)āhish pe dam nikle
bahut nikle mere armān lekin phir bhī kam nikle (220:1; #1357)

A thousand such desires that upon each one I would rather die,
Though many of my longings were fulfilled, many so remained.

dam nikle: to have intense desire for its quick completion, dying, impatience.

For every desire, I am willing to lay my life; I want it so badly. While many longings of mine have come to fruition, most have remained and new ones keep taking the place of old desires. The emphasis is on how new desires keep arising just as fast as the old ones are fulfilled.

ڈرے کیوں میرا قاتل، کیا رہے گا اُس کی گردن پر　　وہ خوں، جو چشمِ تر سے عُمر بھر یُوں دم بہ دم نکلے؟

ḍare kioñ merā qātil, kyā rahe gā us kī gardan par
vuh khūñ, jo chashm-e tar se ʻumr bhar yūñ dam ba dam nikle
(220:2; #1358)

Why should my slayer be afraid? Why should it remain on her neck,
The blood, which kept flowing continuously from wet eyes
throughout life?

chashm-e tar: wet eye; *dam ba dam*: all the time, continuously.

Though she is a slayer, the blood does not remain on her neck (head) because it has been flowing through my eyes all along. Everyone thinks that I bled to death through my eyes, not by the beloved slaying me. She need not be worried about the legal and moral complications of the act of slaying me.

نکلنا خلد سے آدم کا سنتے آئے ہیں لیکن   بہت بے آبرو ہو کر ترے کوچے سے ہم نکلے

nikalnā ḳhuld se ādam kā sunte āe haiñ lekin
bahut be ābrū ho kar tere kūche se ham nikle (220:3; #1359)

We have long been hearing about Adam's expulsion from Paradise but
With greater disgrace, however, we came out of your alley.

ḳhuld: paradise; *bahut*: more: *be ābrū*: disgrace; *kūche*: alley.

The poet is calling the expulsion of Adam from Paradise a disgrace (after Adam ate the forbidden fruit; see Glossary), but is calling his own expulsion from the beloved's alley a greater disgrace. A comparison is made here between Paradise and the beloved's alley. The beloved's alley was a more desired place, so the disgrace was more terrible.

بھرم کھل جائے ظالم تیرے قامت کی درازی کا
اگر اس طرۂ پر پیچ و خم کا پیچ و خم نکلے

بھرم کھل جائے ظالم، تیرے قامت کی درازی کا
اگر اس طرۂ پرپیچ و خم کا پیچ و خم نکلے

bharam khul jāe z̤ālim, tere qāmat kī darāzī kā
agar is t̤urrah' pur pech-o-ḳham kā pech-o-ḳham nikle
(220:4; #1360)

It will shatter the myth of the height of your stature, O! Cruel one,
If only the curls of your dangling forelock would unfurl.

bharam: myth; *z̤ālim*: cruel: *qāmat*: stature; *darāzī:* height; *t̤urrah:* dangling forelock.

The beloved takes much pride in her tallness, but she also wears her tresses braided. The poet is telling her that if she would only let down her dangling tresses, they would put to shame her height. This means that as they hang beyond her feet, she will look petite. Note that the lover is not saying that the beloved is short, just that her tresses are longer.

مگر لکھوائے کوئی اس کو خط تو ہم سے لکھوائے
ہوئی صبح اور گھر سے، کان پر رکھ کر قلم نکلے

magar likhvāe koī us ko ḳhat̤ to ham se likhvā'e
hu'ī ṣubḥ aur ghar se, kān par rakh kar qalam nikle (220:5; #1361)

Whosever wants it written to her should let me do the writing;
Every morning I come out of my home with a pen stuck behind my ear.

The poet suspects that most of his neighbors are corresponding with the beloved. He is anxious to know what they say in their letters because through this he will come to know what the beloved has been writing to them as well. He has taken the profession of "street clerk" to write letters on behalf of those who cannot write a letter themselves.

This was and continues to be a common tradition in uneducated societies. It was also a common tradition to keep the pen over the ear. By offering to write letters for his rivals, the lover is cleverly able to misrepresent them in the writing as well. *Ġhālib*'s wit shows well here.

ہوئی اِس دَور میں مَنسُوب مجھ سے بادہ آشامی　　پھر آیا وُہ زمانہ جو جہاں میں جامِ جم نکلے

hu'ī is daur meñ mansūb mujh se bāda(h) āshāmī
phir āyā vuh zamāna(h) jo jahāñ meñ jām-e jam nikle
(220:6; #1362)

In this era, the wine drinking has become associated with me;
The time has come for the goblet of Jamshed to appear in the world again.

daur: era, round; *mansūb:* associated; *bāda(h) āshāmī:* drinking wine; *jām-e jam*: goblet of King Jamshed.

King Jamshed was famous for the discovery of wine and so his goblet was associated with wine drinking (see Glossary). Today, my name is synonymous with wine drinking. After a long time, the tradition of Jamshed has been renewed. Just like when they used to look at the Jamshed's goblet and think of wine, now they look at me and speak of wine drinking. It is as if the goblet of Jamshed has reappeared. Self-praise and assertions are intended here.

ہوئی جن سے تَوَقُّع خستگی کی داد پانے کی　　وہ ہم سے بھی زیادہ خستۂ تیغِ سِتم نکلے

hu'ī jin se tuvaqqu' k̟hastagī kī dād pāne kī
vuh ham se bhī ziyāda(h) k̟hastah' teġh-e sitam nikle (220:7; #1363)

Those from whom I had expected appreciation of my wounds
They turned out to be more wounded than me by the sword of tyranny.

*tuvaqqu*ʿ: expectation; *ḳhastagī:* hurt, wounded; *dād*: appreciation, accolade; *teġh-e sitam*: sword of cruelty, tyranny.

How can I expect any consolation from those who are more hurt than I am? How can those who could not take care of their own wounds give me any help? Note that the lover was hoping to receive accolades for his wounds, not just sympathy. Upon realizing that others are in even worse condition, the lover is taken aback. A delicate point arises here. Others are more hurt because they are less resilient, not because more cruelty was doled out to them. They are weaker souls.

محبت میں نہیں ہے فرق جینے اور مرنے کا
اسی کو دیکھ کر جیتے ہیں جس کافر پہ دم نکلے

muḥabbat meñ nahiñ hai farq jīne aur marne kā
usī ko dekh kar jīte haiñ jis kāfir pa(h) dam nikle (220:8; #1364)

There is no difference between living and dying when it comes to love;
We live to see the same idol, for whom we would die.

We will die if we do not see her and when we do see her we are ready to give our life to her. Love erases the boundary between life and death. We continue to love on the hope of seeing her, the one for whom we are ready to lay down our lives.

کہاں میخانے کا دروازہ غالبؔ اور کہاں واعظ
پر اتنا جانتے ہیں، کل وہ جاتا تھا کہ ہم نکلے

kahāñ maiḳhāne kā darvāza(h) Ġhālib! aur kahāñ vāʿiẓ
par itnā jānte haiñ, kal vuh jātā tha kih ham nikle
(220:9; #1365)

Where is the door to the tavern, *Ġhālib*, and where is the preacher?
We only know that yesterday, he was going in as we came out.

The preacher preaches against drinking so it would be improbable to see him at the door of the tavern. Yesterday, though, as we were leaving, we caught him entering the tavern when the crowd had thinned out. The preacher, too, is addicted to wine but he hides it for the sake of his profession. Neither of us can stop drinking, but the preacher is a hypocrite.

221

کوہ کے ہوں بارِ خاطر، گر صدا ہو جائیے
بے تکلف، اے شرارِ جستہ! کیا ہو جائیے

koh kih hūñ bār-e ḳhāt̤ir, gar ṣadā ho jāīye
be takalluf ai sharār-e jasta(h)! kyā ho jāīye (221:1; #1366)

A burden I am to the mountains if I were to become the echo,
Frankly speaking, O! Flaming spark, what should I really be?

bār-e ḳhāt̤ir: tiresome, burden on mind; *sharār-e jasta(h)*: flaming spark.

How burdensome my existence is can be observed by noticing how a mountain returns the echo of sound. If I were to become sound, the material nature of which is nonexistent, the mountain will reject me and send me back as an echo. The poet is asking this question of a flaming spark that lasts only a fraction of a second. If, even as sound, I were too heavy for the mountain to keep me, what would tolerate my existence in this world? An expression of great humility is made in this extremely complex verse.

بیضہ آسا، ننگِ بال و پر ہے یہ کُنجِ قفس
از سرِ نَو زندگی ہو، گر رہا ہو جائیے

baiẓah āsā, nang-e bāl-o-par hai yih kunj-e qafis
az sar-e nau zindagī ho, gar rehā ho jāīye (221:2; #1367)

Like an egg, the corner of the cage is free of plummage;
It will be a fresh start of a new life, if only we get freed.

baiẓah āsā: like an egg; *nang*: free of, disgrace.

The corner of the cage is our abode, the egg is the sky under which we live, and freedom is from the ties that bind us to this world. The use of the word, "*nang*," which also means disgrace, further complicates the verse, but here it simply means "free from." Before the embryo comes out of the egg, it is practically nonexistent; coming out of the egg, it begins to show signs of life. I am also in the cage of this world; death will take me out of nonexistence and give me a new life. A chick inside an egg is free of hair and feathers and thus cannot fly. It is only when it comes out of the cage that it can fly. The world is like an egg that keeps us caged, free of hair and feather. To fly, we must first come out of this cage—a cage of material existence. To reach to the height of spiritual freedom, we must rid ourselves of wordly things. A very difficult comparison is made here between the dome of the sky, the hatching of an egg, and our own evolution into the realm of spirituality.

222

مستی، بہ ذوقِ غفلتِ ساقی، ہلاک ہے
موجِ شراب، یک مژۂ خوابناک ہے

masti, ba(h) żauq-e ġhaflat-e sāqī, halāk hai
mauj-e sharāb, yak mizhah' ḳh(v)ābnāk hai (222:1; #1368)

The intoxication is dying because of the obliviousness of cupbearer;
The wave of wine is like an eyelash dozing off.

The obliviousness of Cupbearer is destroying the intoxication of the wine because I am not getting enough of the wine of her beauty. It seems as if the wave of wine (meaning the decanter going around) is like an eyelash of a dozing eye—it is only partially open]. It is very slow in coming to me.

جز زخمِ تیغِ ناز، نہیں دِل میں آرزو
جیبِ خیال بھی ترے ہاتھوں سے چاک ہے

juz zaḳhm-e teġh-e nāz, nahiñ dil meñ ārzū
jeb-e ḳhayāl bhī tere hāthoñ se chāk hai (222:2; #1369)

Except for the wound from her sword of coquetry, there is no longing in my heart;
Your hands have even torn the collar of my thoughts.

The only thought in my mind is to have a wound of coquetry in my heart. You hold the collar of thoughts and you shred it. This means that you have complete control over my thoughts. All I can think about is you. When I think of you, I only want another wound from your amorous glance.

جوشِ جنوں سے کچھ نظر آتا نہیں، اسدؔ
صحرا ہماری آنکھ میں یک مشتِ خاک ہے

josh-e junūñ se kuchh naẓar ātā nahiñ, Asad
ṣaḥrā hamārī āñkh meñ yak musht-e ḳhāk hai (222:3; #1370)

I can see nothing in the intensity of frenzy, Asad!
The desert in my eyes is just a fistful of dust.

My frenzy has become so intense that I cannot see anything. It is as if the entire desert was turned into a fistful of dust and thrown into my eyes, blinding me. My desire to wander was so great that the desert seems no bigger than a fistful of sand, but it is in my eyes so I can no longer see where I am going. There is another side to this explanation. The desert is merely a fistful of dust in my view [eye], meaning that my frenzy to wander is so great that it makes the desert look like a fistful of dust.

223

لب عیسیٰ کی جُنبش کرتی ہے گہوارہ جُنبانی
قیامت کُشتۂ لعلِ بُتاں کا خوابِ سنگیں ہے

lab-e ʿisā kī junbish kartī hai gahvāra(h) junbānī
qiyāmat kushta(h)ʾ laʿl-e butāñ kā ḳh(v)āb-e sangiñ hai
(223:1; #1371)

The movement of the lips of Jesus is rocking the cradle;
Remarkable is the deep sleep of the victims of the beloved's lips.

lab-e ʿisā: lips of Jesus; *junbish*: movement; *gahvāra(h) junbānī*: rocking cradle (swing); *laʿl-e butāñ*: lips of beloved; *ḳh(v)āb-e sangīñ:* deep sleep.

Those who have been victims of the beloved's lips are in a deep sleep. Gently rocking the cradle puts children to sleep. To wake the dead, Jesus would say the words, "*qum bāzin allāh,*" but it seems that now the movement of his lips is proving to be the gentle rocking of a cradle and so these lovers are slipping into an even deeper sleep. Having kissed the beloved's lips, the intoxication is so strong that even Jesus, who can bring the dead back to life, cannot take us out of it. The discussion of Jesus' ability to raise the dead is brought up here to show how deep is the intoxication of those who have kissed the beloved.

224

آمدِ سیلابِ طوفانِ صدائے آب ہے
نقشِ پا جو کان میں رکھتا ہے انگلی جادہ سے

āmad-e sailāb-e ṭūfān-e ṣadā' e āb hai
naqsh-e pā jo kān meñ rakhtā hai unglī-e jāda(h) se (224:1; #1372)

The arrival of flooding is evident by the stormy reverberations of water,
Yet the footprints are still putting the fingers of the pathway in their ears.

A footprint is shaped like an ear; a narrow path is shaped like a finger. The flood front is noisy with stormy waters so to shield itself from the noise, the footprint has inserted the path in its ears, as if it were a finger. The flood will surely wipe out the footprint, but the main concern of the footprint is to avoid the noise, staying oblivious to its fate. This is one of those classic *Ġhālib* verses where there is a great deal of resonance: note the stormy sound, ear, footprint, path, etc. The basic meaning of the verse points to how we face an oncoming calamity; we often run for cover, but what we should do is face it. It is going to annihilate us anyway.

بزمِ مے وحشت کدہ ہے کس کی چشمِ مست کا
شیشے میں نبضِ پری پنہاں ہے موجِ بادہ سے

bazm-e mai vaḥshat kadah hai kis kī chashm-e mast kā
shīshe meñ nabz-e pari pinhāñ hai mauje bāda(h) se
(224:2; #1373)

Whose intoxicating eyes have turned the assembly of wine into a house of frenzy
That the wave of wine is hiding like the pulse of a fairy in the decanter?

shīshe: decanters; *nabz-e pari*: pulse of fairy; *pinhāñ*: hidden; *bāda(h)*: wine.

The pulsating motion of wine in the decanter is like a fairy. The shape of the decanter is like that of an eye. The intoxicating eyes of the beloved have waves of wine hidden in them like the fairy in the decanter. Everyone is trying to reach this fairy, creating tumultuousness in the assembly. The assembly of wine drinkers has gone wild because of the beloved, whose eyes bring intoxication to her lovers.

225

ہُوں مَیں بھی تماشائیِ نیرنگِ تمنّا
مطلب نہیں کچھ اِس سے کہ مطلب ہی بر آوے

huñ maiñ bhī tamāshāī' nairang-e tamannā
maṯlab nahiñ kuchh is se kih maṯlab hī bar āve (225:1; #1374)

I, too, am a spectator of the sorcery of longings,
But its object is not that my desires should come to fruition.

tamāshā'ī: spectator; *maṯlab:* meaning, desire, object; *nairang:* magic, sorcery.

I am watching to see what will come from my longings. My intent should not be misconstrued as my desire comes to fruition. The sorcery of longings can produce anything; it is unpredictable. I am merely a spectator. Fulfillment of desire is not my goal.

226

سیاہی جیسے گر جاوے دمِ تحریر کاغذ پر
مری قسمت میں یوں تصویر ہے شب ہائے ہجراں کی

siyāhī jaise gir jāve dam-e teḥrīr kāġhaż par
merī qismat meñ yūñ taṣvīr hai shab hāi hijrāñ kī (226:1; #1375)

As if ink has been spilled on the paper at the time of writing,
Such is the picture of the night of separation ingrained in my fate.

siyāhī: ink; *dam*: breath; *taḥrīr*: writing; *kāġhaż*: paper; *qismat*: fate; *taṣvīr*: picture; *shab*: night; *hijr*: separation.

In the written story of my life, the nights I spent waiting for her appear as a blot of ink—dark, large, and irregular. Such is the story of my separation from her. Note the darkness of ink and that of the nights of separation. The accidental spill happens at the point in the story where the lover writes his feelings about the night of separation. The pen fails to work and spills the ink in deep distress. The irregularity of the inkblot is compared to ill fate.

227

ہجومِ نالہ، حیرت عاجزِ عرضِ یک افغاں ہے
خموشی ریشۂ صد نیستاں سے خس بدنداں ہے

hujūm-e nālah, ḥairat ʿājiz-e ʿarẓ-e yak afġhāñ hai
k̤hamoshī reshah' ṣad nīstāñ se k̤has badandāñ hai (227:1; #1376)

Awed by the crowding of plaints, I am stifled, unable to air my desires,
As my silence holds hundreds of straws of reed in its teeth.

nīstāñ: reed, sugar cane; *k̤has badandāñ*: straw in teeth (to display humbleness).

I have so many plaints to make that I do not know where to begin. I am dumbstruck. To state this *Ġhālib* constructs a very difficult simile. Holding straw in one's teeth is a Persian idiom used to express humbleness and humility. Holding straw in teeth here means that he is too embarrassed to speak—actually, he is tongue-tied. The embarrassment is caused by not having the courage to routinely air these plaints so they will not accumulate. To make things more complicated, the poet is saying that the straw comes from a reed pipe, which is used to create sound.

تکلف بر طرف، ہے جاں‌ستاں تر لطفِ بدخویاں
نگاہِ بے حجابِ ناز تیغِ تیزِ عریاں ہے

takalluf bartaraf hai jāñsitāñ tar lutf-e badk̤hūīyāñ
nigāh-e be ḥijāb-e nāz teġh-e tez-e ʿuryāñ hai (227:2; #1377)

Frankly speaking, the kindness of the ill-tempered beloved is deadlier.
Her intimate glance of coquetry is like a sharp naked sword.

jāñsitāñ tar: more potent in taking life (killing); *badkḥūīyāñ*: of bad habits, ill-tempered [used here to address the beloved]; *lutf*: kindness.

Deadlier than her obliviousness is her kindness. Her amorous glances prove to be fatally sharp swords.

ہُوئی یہ کثرتِ غم سے تلف کیفیتِ شادی
کہ صُبحِ عید مُجھ کو بدتر از چاکِ گریباں ہے

hu'ī yih kas̱rat-e ġham se talaf kafiyat-e shādī
kih ṣubḥ-e 'id mujh ko badtar az chāk-e girebāñ hai (227:3; #1378)

The excess of grief has destroyed the state of happiness;
The morning of Eid, to me, is worse than ripping my collar.

The intensity of my sorrow was so deep that I could not enjoy the joys of Eid. In many ways it was worse than tearing my collars. Eid is the most celebrated event of joy and happiness for Muslims.

دِل و دیں نقد لا، ساقی سے گر سودا کیا چاہے
کہ اِس بازار میں ساغر متاعِ دستگرداں ہے

dil-o-dīñ naqd lā, sāqī se gar saudā kīyā chāhe
kih is bāzār meñ sāġhar matā'-e dastgardāñ hai (227:4; #1379)

Bring heart and faith as cash if you want to deal with the cupbearer,
For in this bazaar, the goblet is a common commodity.

dil: heart; *dīñ*: faith: *sāqī*: cup bearer; *saudā*: trade: *bāzār*: market; *dastgardāñ*: easily bought things, readily available.

If you only want to taste wine in this life, it is easily bought. If you want your beloved to give you the wine with any feeling, though, you must be ready to give your heart and your belief in payment. This means that it is easy to draw ordinary pleasures, but for true ecstasy, you must be ready to sacrifice much more. Common knowledge is easily acquired, but getting to the truth requires devotion.

غم آغوشِ بلا میں پرورش دیتا ہے عاشق کو
چراغِ روشن اپنا قلزمِ صرصر کا مرجاں ہے

ġham āġhosh-e balā meñ parvarish detā hai ʻāshiq ko
charāġh-e raushan apna qulzum-e ṣar ṣar kā marjāñ hai
(227:5; #1380)

Grief raises lovers in the arms of calamities;
Our lamps remain lit like the coral in the sea of a sandstorm.

qulzum-e ṣar ṣar: ocean of dust storm; *marjāñ*: red coral.

Lovers live a life full of constant calamities. This tends to harden them. A storm of dust cannot extinguish the lamp I carry just as the ocean's waves are unable to destroy the coral in the sea. We have been toughened to face any calamity and grief for we are true lovers. The poet makes a remarkable observation here. There is a great deal of stormy activity in the ocean bed where, like the sandstorms, the waves of the ocean traverse throughout. The bed of coral remains firmly attached just like the belief of lovers. See the comparison of a lamp with red coral.

228

خموشیوں میں تماشا ادا نکلتی ہے   نگاہ دل سے تری سرمہ سا نکلتی ہے

ḳhamoshīyoñ meñ tamāshā adā nikaltī hai
nigāh dil se terī surmah sā nikaltī hai (228:1; #1381)

In its silence, your coquetry brings out a display;
The glances coming out of your heart are antimony-laced.

tamāshā: spectacle; *adā*: charm; *nigāh*: glance; *dil*: heart; *surmah sā*: substances like that of antimony; *surmah*: black antimony powder used to decorate eyes.

Your quietness has an interesting grace and charm that mutes even your glances—such is your beauty and such is your hushed grace. Your glance, as it comes from your heart, is covered with antimony powder (used to decorate eyes). If antimony is eaten, it mutes the voice (the legend goes). The play on words come from muted glance and muted voice from consuming antimony.

فشارِ تنگیٔ خلوت سے بنتی ہے شبنم   صبا جو غنچے کے پردے میں جا نکلتی ہے

fishār-e tangī' ḳhalvat se bantī hai shabnam
ṣabā jo ġhunche ke parde meñ jā nikaltī hai (228:2; #1382)

The tightness of privacy squeezes to create dew
From the breeze that strolls into the layers of the bud.

fishār: squeeze, cut; *ḳhalvat*: retirement, solitude, privacy.

Seeping into the bud, the breeze finds itself in the privacy of the bud's layers that took the breeze into its arms and squeezed it. This caused the breeze to become embarrassed and it began sweating. This sweat appears as dew on the petals of the bud.

نہ پوچھ سینۂ عاشق سے آبِ تیغِ نگاہ　　کہ زخمِ روزنِ در سے ہوا نکلتی ہے

na(h) pūchh sīna(h)' 'āshiq se āb-e teġh-e nigāh
kih zaḳhm-e rauzan-e dar se havā nikaltī hai (228:3; #1383)

Ask not from the chest of the lover about the sharpness of the sword of her glance
That air leaks out from the wounds of windows in the doors.

The air leaking from the wounds indicates rotting wounds, meaning they are incurable. (An unintentional scientific reference is made to chronic wounds, where bacteria grow to produce gas.)

229

جس جا نسیم شانہ کشِ زلفِ یار ہے نافہ دماغِ آہوئے دشتِ تتار ہے

jis jā nasīm shāna(h) kash-e zulf-e yār hai
nāfi(h) damāġh-e āhūe dasht-e tattār hai (229:1; #1384)

Wherever the gentle breeze is busy arranging the beloved's tresses,
The mind of the deer of the Tattar desert turns into perfumed musk.

The breeze is combing and rearranging the beloved's tresses. Passing through the beloved's tresses, the breeze has picked up their perfume. This smell reaches the desert of Tattar, where it enters the mind of deer as they breathe. This causes their brains to begin bleeding, because they cannot bear the intensity of the smell. An interesting analogy is drawn here. After a deer has been shot in a hunt, it begins to bleed from the navel. Hunters immediately tie the navel down and remove the musk from it. Therefore, the smell of the beloved has turned the mind of the deer to its bleeding navel. The musk comes from the breeze that carries the perfume of the beloved's tresses. Presented here is a most remarkable flight of "aromatic" imagination by *Ġhālib*.

کس کا سراغِ جلوہ ہے حیرت کو اے خدا آئینہ فرشِ شش جہتِ انتظار ہے

kis kā surāġh-e jalva(h) hai ḥairat ko ai ḳhudā
āīna(h) firsh-e shash jihat-e intiẓār hai (229:2; #1385)

Whose glorious manifestation is amazement searching? O! Lord,
That in all six directions, the floor is mirrored in anticipation.

jalva(h): splendor; *ḳhudā*: God; *ā'īna(h)*: mirror; *intiẓār*: waiting (anxiously); *shash jihat*: universe, six directions.

What is it that my amazement is waiting to see, O! Lord? So stunned and amazed am I that the floor of the universe has turned into a mirror (a simile of being stunned). Such is your splendid luster that, having seen you once, everything is frozen in place waiting to see what comes next. Note that a mirror is supposed to contain frozen images; a stunned state is also called frozen.

ہے ذرہ ذرہ تنگیِ جا سے غبارِ شوق   گر دام یہ ہے وسعتِ صحرا شکار ہے

hai żarrah żarrah tangī' jā se ġhubār-e shauq
gar dām yih hai vusa'(t-e ṣaḥrā shikār hai (229:3; #1386)

Reduced to dust is the storm of my desire from the tightness of space;
If this is the snare, then the expanse of desert is a sure catch.

dām: snare.

The desire of my heart to wander in the desert is so strong that it cannot be fulfilled by the smallness (tightness) of the desert and is thus reduced to dust, meaning that it is destroyed. If that were how I kept my desire, then the expanse of the desert would be caught in the snare of being turned into nothing (dust) by my desire. Nevertheless, it still would not relieve my desire. The net here is the desire, which is being reduced to dust. The net of desire was supposed to reduce the desert to dust. This is an extremely dusty situation; meaning, my wandering would destroy the desert.

دل مدعی و دیدہ بنا مدعیٰ علیہ   نظارے کا مقدمہ پھر روبکار ہے

dil mudda'ī-o-dīda(h) banā mudda'ā 'alaīha
naẕẕāre kā muqaddamah phir rūbakār hai (229:4; #1387)

The heart is the plaintiff and the eyes are the defendants;
Again the trial of inspection is before the court session.

rūbakār: appearance face to face.

The heart has sued the eyes for providing circumstances that have damaged the heart irreparably. The court is in session to try the atrocities of the beloved's cruelties. Note the emphasis on this being a repeated event. This has been going on for a while.

چھڑکے ہے شبنم آئنۂ برگِ گل پر آب   اے عندلیب وقتِ وداعِ بہار ہے

chhiṛke hai shabnam ā'inah barg-e gul par āb
ai 'andlīb vaqt-e vidā'-e bahār hai (229:5; #1388)

The dew is sprinkling water on the mirror of the rose petals.
O! Nightingale, it is the time to say farewell to the spring season.

barg-e gul: flower petal, rose-petal.

This verse is based on an archaic Persian superstition of sprinkling a mirror (often on a person's back) with water. This is supposed to be a good omen for when someone leaves to travel. The flower petal is ready to leave and, as a superstition, the dew has wetted it. It is time for the arrival of autumn as the petal is ready to fall (depart). O! Nightingale, take a lesson from this observation that the spring season is about to end. You, too, should get ready to leave. Nightingales are supposed to be in the garden only through the spring season, their main purpose being to wail and look at the flowers. With the flowers gone, there is no use for nightingales in the garden. The "mirror of petals" means the shiny petals.

وہ آئے یا نہ آئے پہ یاں انتظار ہے

پچ آپڑی ہے وعدۂ دلدار کی مجھے   وہ آئے یا نہ آئے پہ یاں انتظار ہے

pach āpaṛī hai va'da(h)' dildār kī mujhe
vuh āe yā na(h) āe pa(h) yāñ intiẓār hai (229:6; #1389)

I must make good, for the heart-ravisher has made a promise;
Whether she comes or not, the waiting shall go on here.

pach āpaṛī: to try to make something work, to make good.

The beloved has promised to visit. I have little choice but to wait for her, even if she is not coming. I doubt she will fulfill her promise, but I cannot leave just in case she does. It will be embarrassing if I leave and do not wait for her. The lover is mumbling.

بے پردہ سوئے وادیٔ مجنوں گزر نہ کر   ہر ذرّے کے نقاب میں دل بے قرار ہے

be pardah sūe vādī' majnūñ guzar na(h) kar
har żarre ke niqāb meñ dil be qarār hai (229:7; #1390)

Do not go through the valley of *Majnūn*, without taking the veil, for
Behind the curtain of every particle lies hidden a tumultuous heart.

The glitter of the dust particles is the curtain that hides by dazzling the eye, the tumult of hearts in the valley of frenzy. The beloved *Lailā* is advised not to go there unveiled, or else these hearts will become too impatient to survive. There are two veils involved here: one that hides the hearts behind the glitter of particles, and the other is the veil of the beloved. If the beloved takes off her veil, the veil of particles will also be exposed and will be destroyed.

اے عندلیب یک کفِ خس بہرِ آشیاں   طوفانِ آمد آمدِ فصلِ بہار ہے

ai ʿandlīb yak kaf-e ḳhaṣ bahr-e āshīyāñ
t̤ūfān-e āmad āmad-e fiṣl-e bahār hai (229:8; #1391)

O! Nightingale! Collect a fistful of straw for making your nest, as
The arrival of a storm indicates the coming of the spring season.

kaf: fistful; *bahr-e āshīyāñ*: for the sake of nest; *ḳhaṣ:* straw.

With the arrival of rains, the spring season will arrive and turn all dried stems and leaves green again. That will make it difficult to find dried straw needed to make the nest—a warning to the nightingale to pick up the straw now.

دل مت گنوا خبر نہ سہی سیر ہی سہی   اے بے دماغ آئینہ تمثال دار ہے

dil mat gañvā, ḳhabar na(h) sahī, sair hī sahī
ai be damāġh āʿīna(h) timṡāl dār hai (229:9; #1392)

Do not waste heart; if it is not enlightenment then let it be amusement,
O! Haughty one! This mirror is holding a collection of many images.

ḳhabar: news; *sair*: amusement; *damāġh*: hauteur, pride; *timṡāl dār*: collection of images.

My haughty and proud beloved, do not waste my heart (throw it away) if it does not give you anything worthwhile. My heart is like a mirror with many impressions in it that might amuse you. This means that you are so haughty that you are not even looking into my heart to know what use it can be to you. It has got a lot more to offer you, like my poetry, my feelings, and my devotion. At least it should be worth some amusement to you. Give me the benefit of the doubt and look into it; the poet is beseeching the beloved. (Some interpret this as a devotional verse with the poet wasting his own heart if it does not have the highest feelings; however, this is not appropriate here.)

غفلت کفیلِ عمر و اسد ضامنِ نشاط
اے مرگِ ناگہاں تجھے کیا انتظار ہے

ġhaflat kafīl-e ʿumr-o-Asad ẓāmin-e nishāṯ
ai marg-e nāgahāñ tujhe kyā intiẓār hai (229:10; #1393)

Ignorance ensures longevity, while Asad is the guarantor of happiness.
O! Unexpected death what are you waiting for?

kafīl: sponsor, taking responsibility for; *ẓāmin*: guarantor; *nishāṯ*: happiness.

Our ignorance assures us a long life; a feeling that we will live forever and the poet guarantees to make it a happy one. The meaning is that we should live day-to-day, wining and dining without worrying about death. The poet is addressing death, which is always unexpected. What is it waiting for? This is the most opportune time, catch us off-guard. By asking death to come, the poet assures happiness, as we would die without experiencing the sadness of life. In our ignorance, we begin to believe that we will live forever. This way of thinking keeps us from enjoying life as we put these things aside for tomorrow. Death can spell great joy by ending all misery. So regardless of whether you live or die, there is happiness.

230

آئینہ کیوں نہ دُوں کہ تماشا کہیں جسے
ایسا کہاں سے لاؤں کہ تجھ سا کہیں جسے

ā'īna(h) kioñ na(h) dūñ kih tamāshā kaheñ jise
aisā kahāñ se lāuñ kih tujh sā kaheñ jise (230:1; #1394)

Why should I not give you the mirror for others to call it a spectacle?
From where can I bring another one that we could say is like you?

If I put a mirror in your hand, the image of your beauty will stun you. It will be a joyful sight for all those looking at you at that moment. The reason I want to give you a mirror is that I cannot find anyone as beautiful as you and I want you to know it. The lover wants to give the beloved a mirror to look into to see how beautiful she is, but the possibility that the rivals may also be watching raises the head of jealousy. The lover is not sure if he should give her a mirror.

حسرت نے لا رکھا تری بزمِ خیال میں
گلدستۂ نگاہ سُوَیدا کہیں جسے

ḥasrat ne lā rakhā terī bazm-e khayāl meñ
guldasta(h)' nigāh suvaidā kaheñ jise (230:2; #1395)

The longings have brought to your assembly of thought
A bouquet of glances, which is called heart's black spot.

bazm-e khayāl: assembly of thought, heart of lover because the beloved is always there; *suvaidā:* black part of eye, black spot of heart.

The bouquet of glances that failed to reach you is the black scar of my heart caused by grief that it did not reach you. This bouquet is displayed in an assembly of your thought, which is actually the lover's heart. This means that my heart is full of unfortunate glances that could not reach you.

پھونکا ہے کس نے گوشِ محبت میں اے خدا
افسونِ انتظار، تمنا کہیں جسے

phūnkā hai kis ne gosh-e maḥubbat meñ ai ḳhudā
afsūn-e intiẓār, tamannā kaheñ jise (230:3; #1396)

Who has blown into the ears of love, O! God
The spell of expectation, which is called desire?

afsūn: magic, charm, spell; *afsūn phūnkā:* enchanted, charmed.

Calling desire a spell of expectation is a remarkably unique construction by *Ġhālib,* though it needs some explanation. A desire is something that one expects to be completed. The expectation is the spell of desire, which compels us to pursue our goals. The effect of the spell continues until the desire is fulfilled. The real lover has no expectations. The poet wants to know who is blowing this spell into the ears of love, making it insincere (raising expectations in the heart of the lover). Love should be free of all expectations. Whosoever corrupts love is challenged here.

سر پر ہجومِ دردِ غریبی سے ڈالیے
وہ ایک مشتِ خاک کہ صحرا کہیں جسے

sar par hujūm-e dard-e ġharībī se ḍāliye
vuh ek musht-e ḳhāk kih saḥrā kaheñ jise (230:4; #1397)

Throw on the head the suffering of the pain of alienation;
That one fistful of dust, which is called desert.

hujūm: excess; *ġharībī:* being in an alien land.

Dejected in an alien land, the poet wants to pour all the sand of the desert on his head to end his woes, both of being in a foreign land and of not being home, in the desert, which is his real home. He is calling the desert a fistful of sand to belittle it. The poet wants to end his misery by destroying himself and his home.

ہے چشمِ تر میں حسرتِ دیدار سے نہاں
شوقِ عناں گسیختہ، دریا کہیں جسے

hai chashm-e tar meñ ḥasrat-e dīdār se nihāñ
shauq-e ʿināñ gusiḳhta(h), daryā kaheñ jise (230:5; #1398)

Hidden in the eye bedewed from tears of longing to see her
Is an uncontrolled desire called an ocean?

ʿināñ gusiḳhta(h): uncontrolled.

I long to see the beloved so I cry for that. It appears as if a storm of tears has erupted. This should be called an ocean for its intensity and volume. Stifling of desire has made his eyes wet with tears, but that is just the tip of iceberg. There is an ocean waiting to come out.

درکار ہے شگفتنِ گلہائے عیش کو
صبحِ بہار، پنبۂ مینا کہیں جسے

darkār hai shuguftan-e gulhāe ʿishq ko
ṣubḥ-e bahār, pan(m)ba(h)ʾ mīnā kaheñ jise (230:6; #1399)

It is required for the flowers of luxury to bloom,
On the spring morning that we can call the cotton wool of the decanter.

pan(m)ba(h): cotton wool; *mīnā*: wine decanter.

The white of the cotton wool is indicative of morning and is used here to indicate the stopper of the wine bottle (decanter). For the flower of luxury to bloom, we need a bottle of wine on a fine spring morning. Spring connotes the season of drinking. Calling on the morning of a spring day, the cotton wool used as a cork for the decanter is indeed unique and requires some imagination to enjoy the play on words and atmosphere here.

غالب بُرا نہ مان جو واعظ بُرا کہے
ایسا بھی کوئی ہے کہ سب اچھا کہیں جسے؟

Ġhālib burā na(h) mān jo vā'iẕ burā kahe
aisā bhī ko'ī hai kih sab achhā kaheñ jise (230:7; #1400)

Mind it not *Ġhālib*, if the preacher calls you bad.
Has there been anyone, whom everyone called good?

O! *Ġhālib*, do not be perturbed if the preacher tells you that you are no good; there is hardly anyone in the world whom everyone would call good. Since "anyone" includes the preacher himself, why pay heed to someone who himself is not considered good by all? If someone who is not considered good by all calls you bad, it does not matter.

231

شبنم بہ گلِ لالہ نہ خالی زِ اَدا ہے   داغِ دلِ بے درد، نظرگاہِ حیا ہے

shabnam ba(h) gul-e lālah na(h) ḳhālī ze adā hai
dāġh-e dil-e be dard, naẕargāh-e ḥayā hai (231:1; #1401)

The dew on the tulip flower is not there without significance;
The scars of heart that give no pain are a shameful sight.

dāġh-e dil-e be dard: scars of a heart without pain; *naẕargāh-e ḥayā:* a place of embarrassment.

The tulip has dark spots, which indicate not pain, but embarrassment. The dew on the tulip is actually the sweat of embarrassment from knowing that it has a heart but no feeling of pain.

دل خوں شدۂ کشمکشِ حسرتِ دیدار   آئینہ بہ دستِ بُتِ بدمستِ حنا ہے

dil ḳhūñ shuda(h)' kash-ma-kash-e ḥasrat-e dīdār
ā'ina(h) ba(h) dast-e but-e badmast-e ḥinā hai (231:2; #1402)

The heart bleeding with struggle of longing to see her
Is like the mirror in the *hennaed* hands of the intoxicated idol.

dīdār: sight; *badmast*: with intoxication.

My heart is bleeding out of desperation to catch just one glimpse of you. While you are holding a mirror in your *hennaed* hands, it hides your face from me. The mirror itself has turned red with the reflection of your face's intoxicating glow. Here the poet draws a comparison between the red glow in the mirror and the bleeding of his heart. He expresses a sense of frustration at the fortune of the mirror; they are both tinted red for different reasons. Notice that *henna*ed hands have a red color as well.

شعلے سے نہ ہوتی ہوسِ شعلہ نے جو کی　　جی کس قدر افسردگیٔ دل پہ جلا ہے

shu'le se na(h) hotī, havas-e shu'la(h) ne jo kī
jī kis qadar afsurdagī' dil pa(h) jalā hai (231:3; #1403)

The flame could not do what the desire to burn did.
How badly has my heart been burnt at the sadness of my heart?

shu'le: flame of love; *havas-e shu'la(h):* desire to burn.

I had longed to burn myself to death in the flame of love, but the sadness of my heart was so intense that it could not support my desire. This upsets me so that I am burning over it (sulking). It burns so much that I am finally burned to death. Love could not burn me, but the forsaken desire to burn myself made me burn to death inside. My desire did what love could not.

تمثال میں تیری ہے وہ شوخی کہ بصد ذوق　　آئینہ بہ اندازِ گل آغوش کشا ہے

timṡāl meñ terī hai vuh shoḳhī kih ba(h) ṣad żauq
ā'īnah ba(h) andāz-e gul āġhosh kushā hai (231:4; #1404)

Such is the playfulness of your image that with a hundred longings,
The mirror, like the rose, has flung open its arms to embrace you.

timṡāl: image; *āġhosh kushā:* open arms to embrace; *shoḳhī:* coquetry, playfulness.

The mirror, in its desire to contain your image in its bosom, has flung open its arms like a blooming rose. The beloved looks so beautiful that even the mirror wants to hold her image. Another explanation uses the mirror as a simile for the heart so that looking at your picture opens my heart's arms to embrace you.

قمری کفِ خاکستر و بلبل قفسِ رنگ　　اے نالہ! نشانِ جگرِ سوختہ کیا ہے

qumrī kaf-e ḳhākistar-o-bulbul qafis-e rang
ai nāla(h)! nishān-e jigar-e soḳhta(h) kyā hai (231:5; #1405)

The ringdove is like a fistful of dust, and the nightingale a cage of color.
O' plaint, what is the sign of an afflicted heart?

qumrī: a turtle dove, a ring-dove; *kaf-e ḳhākistar*: handful of dust; *qafis-e rang*: prison of color; *ai*: O! (here it is used as "*juz*," which means except); *jigar-e soḳhta(h)*: liver parched with thirst, afflicted, burnt liver or heart.

The ringdove is dusty in appearance, thus it is called a fistful of dust (also because of its size). The nightingale is called a cage of colors because of its fascination with colorful flowers. The proof that both are lovers comes from their lamentation: the dove laments while looking at the moon, while the nightingale laments the red blooming flowers, being reminded of slain hearts. We, too, should lament being recognized as lovers. Just as the styles are different for the dove and the nightingale, we too should create our own style. The ringdove turning into a fistful of dust and the nightingale into a colorful repertoire of laments is remarkable.

خو نے تری افسردہ کیا وحشتِ دل کو　　معشوقی و بے حوصلگی طرفہ بلا ہے

ḳhū ne terī afsurda(h) kiyā vaḥshat-e dil ko
ma'shūqī-o-beḥauṣlagī t̤urfa(h) balā hai (231:6; #1406)

Your style has cooled off my heart's frenzy.
Being a beloved and lacking courage is calamitous.

ḳhū: style; *afsurda(h)*: to reduce, to cool off; *ma'shūq*: beloved; *be ḥauṣlagī*: be cool, lack coquetry; *ṭurfa(h) balā*: calamitous

Your style of being aloof towards me is cooling my desire for you. You are the beloved and you are supposed to be coquettish, not simple, and plain. Your simplicity is proving to be worse than your coquetry. This style of yours is cooling my emotions and I do not like it—it is a great disaster for me. This verse presents one of the keenest psychological aspects of a lover. If the beloved is simple—free of coquetry—she cannot put fire into the hearts of lovers; the lover wants someone to flirt with, someone who will let him come close and then push him away. Lovers want coyness and a style that will be heart-rending. A frigid and cool beloved is hurtful to lovers. This explains why men are attracted to women who know how to steal and break their hearts.

مجبوری و دعوائے گرفتاریٔ اُلفت　　دستِ تہِ سنگ آمدہ پیمانِ وفا ہے

majbūrī-o da'vā-e giraftārī' ulfat
dast-e tah-e sang āmda(h) paimān-e vafā hai (231:7; #1407)

Compelled by the obligation of claim to stay arrested in love,
The compact of fidelity is like a hand caught under a heavy stone.

dast-e tah-e sang āmda(h): hand caught under heavy stone.

I am caught in the snare of love because of the claim I made to remain faithful. Like a hand caught under a heavy stone, we cannot run away for we do not have enough energy to move the stone—the burden of a promise made. We must live with it.

معلوم ہُوا حالِ شہیدانِ گزشتہ　　تیغِ ستم آئینۂ تصویر نُما ہے

ma'lūm hu'ā ḥāl-e shahīdān-e guzishtah
teġh-e sitam ā'ina(h)' taṣvīr numā hai (231:8; #1408)

We came to know about the condition of the martyrs of the past,
From your sword of cruelty reflecting images like a mirror.

On the sword of the beloved are reflected images of the past, what the previous martyrs went through. Having seen how she doles out cruelty, we know how the lovers before us died or survived.

اے پرتوِ خورشیدِ جہاں تاب! اِدھر بھی
سائے کی طرح ہم پہ عجب وقت پڑا ہے

ai partau-e ḳhurshīd-e jahāñ tāb! idhar bhī
sā'e kī t̤araḥ ham pa(h) ʿajab vaqt paṛā hai (231:9; #1409)

O! The brightness of the world-illuminating sun, turn towards us also.
Like a shadow, strange times have befallen upon us.

Note that light falling on an object creates a shadow. Asking the sun to illuminate the darkness of life and calling it a shadow cast by sunshine is a remarkable juxtaposition. Asking for God's reverence to remove grief is what is happening here.

ناکردہ گناہوں کی بھی حسرت کی ملے داد
یارب اگر اِن کردہ گناہوں کی سزا ہے

nākardah gunāhoñ kī bhī ḥasrat kī mile dād
yā rab agar in kardah gunāhoñ kī sazā hai (231:10; #1410)

Longing for sins not committed should be appreciated,
O! Lord! If there is punishment doled out for sins committed.

nākardah gunāh: sins not committed; *mile dād*: to get appreciation of; *kardah gunāh*: sins committed.

The sins that we wanted to commit, but did not, should balance the sins we did commit. The poet is bargaining with God. He explains that he suffered much by not doing what he really wanted to do. This suffering should suffice as punishment for the sins he did commit. What are the sins that he wanted to commit that he could not? One sin would be uniting with the beloved and suffering for not being able to. The tone in this verse is that of "could not" rather than "did not" commit.

بیگانگیٔ خلق سے بیدل نہ ہو غالب
کوئی نہیں تیرا، تو مری جان، خدا ہے

begāngī' ḳhalq se bedil na(h) ho Ġhālib
ko'ī nahiñ terā, to merī jān, ḳhudā hai (231:11; #1411)

Do not be disheartened at the obliviousness of the world, *Ġhālib*;
If no one is yours, so my dear, know that there *is* God.

This is an oft-repeated theme of lamentation about the atrocities of the world; no one appears to be a friend, but at least there is God who feels nothing but goodness towards mankind, his creation. The verse actually points to a more desperate situation, one that asserts that you should give up hope of befriending anyone in this world. Elsewhere, the poet has declared that: if this is how my life is spent, how well would we remember that we used to have a God too.

232

منظور تھی یہ شکل تجلی کو نور کی قسمت کھلی ترے قد و رخ سے ظہور کی

manẕūr thī yih shakl tajallī ko nūr kī,
qismat khulī tere qad-o-ruḳh se ẕuhūr kī. (232:1; #1412)

This face was acceptable to the splendor of light,
For through your stature and face, the fate of manifestation is revealed.

tajallī: brilliance, splendor; *ẕuhūr*: manifestation; *nūr*: light.

It was acceptable to "splendor" that a brilliant face would come into existence. With your face and stature, O! Mohammad, the meaning of manifestation became known to all. Had it not been for your coming into this world, the "light" would not have been noticed for its brilliance. People compare it with your face.

اک خونچکاں کفن میں کروڑوں بناؤ ہیں پڑتی ہے آنکھ تیرے شہیدوں پہ حور کی

ik ḳhūnchakāñ kafan meñ karoṛoñ banā'o haiñ
paṛtī hai āṅkh tere shahīdoñ pa(h) ḥūr kī (232:2; #1413)

In a blood-dripping shroud, there are millions of adornments;
The glance of houris is falling on your martyrs.

ḳhūnchakāñ: blood dripping; *kafan*: shroud; *ḥūr*: houri, nymphs in paradise.

The only thing your martyrs are left with is their shroud. Even from that, blood is dripping. This renders adornments to the shroud so that it attracts nymphs to your martyrs.

واعظ! نہ تم پیو نہ کسی کو پلا سکو　　کیا بات ہے تمھاری شرابِ طہور کی!

vā'iẓ! na(h) tum pīyo na(h) kisī ko pilā sako
kyā bāt hai tumhārī sharāb-e ṭāḥūr kī (232:3; #1414)

O! Preacher! You neither drink nor can you serve wine to others;
How "great" is your wine of Paradise?

ṭāḥūr: pure

What good is your wine (preaching) that you neither drink (benefit from it) it nor allow anyone else to (be influenced by it)? The poet is belittling the preacher. The wine of Paradise has no value if it cannot be enjoyed. Since the wine of Paradise does not produce intoxication, it is not worth much. Preaching neither helps the preacher nor others—what's the use of it? *Ġhālib* is taunting and in his own subtle way inviting the preacher to try something good.

لڑتا ہے مجھ سے حشر میں قاتل، کہ کیوں اُٹھا؟　　گویا ابھی سُنی نہیں آواز صُور کی

laṛtā hai mujh se ḥashr meñ qātil, kih kioñ uṭhā
goyā abhī sunī nahiñ āvāz ṣūr kī (232:4; #1415)

The slayer is fighting with me on the Day of Resurrection,
"Why did I rise?"
It seems that she has not yet heard the sound of the clarion.

ṣūr: horn, clarion; *Israfil:* The angel who will be ordered to blow the clarion on the Day of Judgment (see Glossary.)

Israfil will blow the horn to raise the dead on the Day of Resurrection. In her obliviousness to what is going on around her, she has not noticed that the clarion has been sounded for the Day of Judgement. She even wants to fight, as if this place were her assembly. She never permitted me to do this in her assembly. However, the reason why the beloved is mixed up is obvious. The scene of her assembly is always frenzied and she finds the Day of Judgment to be no different from her routine.

آمد بہار کی ہے جو بلبل ہے نغمہ سنج   اڑتی سی اک خبر ہے زبانی طیور کی

āmad bahār kī hai jo bulbul hai naġhma(h) sanj
uṛtī sī ik ḳhabar hai zabānī t̤uyūr kī (232:5; #1416)

'Tis the arrival of spring as the nightingale has begun singing.
A rumor is flying in the whisper of garden birds.

bahār: spring; *naġhma(h)*: melody; *sanj*: performing; *ḳhabar*: news; *zabān*: tongue.

Spring must be around the corner for the nightingale has begun to sing. She must have heard the news from the whispering of the birds flying around. The key to this verse lies in the dual meaning of "flying rumor," and flying birds.

گو واں نہیں، پہ واں کے نکالے ہوئے تو ہیں   کعبے سے ان بتوں کو بھی نسبت ہے دور کی

go vāñ nahīñ, pa(h) vāñ ke nikāle hu'e to haiñ
kaʿbe se in butoñ ko bhī nisbat hai dūr kī (232:6; #1417)

Though they are not there, they were once thrown out of there
A distant kinship there is, too, between these idols and *Kaʿbā*.

The idols were removed from *Kaʿbā*, but having been there once, it establishes some connection to *Kaʿbā* even though it is distant one. A play of words and synonyms is made here. The beloved is the idol, and although idolatry has been banned, the style of the beloved remains that of idols: cold and unresponsive. Note that the beloved is also called *kāfir*, or disbeliever, or an idol.

کیا فرض ہے کہ سب کو ملے ایک سا جواب   آؤ نہ ہم بھی سیر کریں کوہِ طور کی

kyā farẓ hai kih sab ko mile ek sā javāb
ā'o na(h) ham bhī sair kareñ koh-e t̤ūr kī (232:7; #1418)

It is not necessary that everyone should get the same answer.
Come on! Let us, too, go for an excursion to Mount Sinai.

koh-e t̤ūr: Mount Sinai.

Moses asked for the physical presence of God. God said, "You would not be able to see"; that does not mean that God would not show Himself. He just said that you would not be able to tolerate it. Then, that was Moses. It is not necessary that we, too, would get the same answer from God. Let us go there and find out. Because of the failure of others, we should not make stereotypical assumptions.

گرمی سہی کلام میں لیکن نہ اِس قدر   کی جس سے بات اُس نے شکایت ضرور کی

garmī sahī kalām meñ, lekin na(h) is qadar
kī jis se bāt us ne shikā'yat ẓarūr kī (232:8; #1419)

It is all right to have a sharp tongue, but not *such* a sharp tongue,
That whomsoever you talked to, would complain, nevertheless.

The poet is reprimanding the beloved that it is all right to be sharp-tongued, but not so much that everyone complains. Actually, he is trying to assuage her to be nice to him; he does not really care how she behaves with others.

غالب گر اِس سَفَر میں مجھے ساتھ لے چلیں
حج کا ثَواب نذر کروں گا حُضُور کی

Ġhālib gar is safir meñ mujhe sāth le chaleñ,
ḥaj kā s̈avāb nażr karūñ gā ḥuzūr kī. (232:9; #1420)

Ġhalib, if he will take me with him on this journey,
I will present the bounties of the pilgrimage to his Majesty.

The poet is asking *Bahadur Shāh Zafir* to take him in his entourage to *Kaʿbā* and if he does so, the poet will dedicate all spiritual rewards earned by him to the King.

233

غم کھانے میں بودا دلِ ناکام بہت ہے
یہ رنج کہ کم ہے مئے گلفام بہت ہے

ġham khāne meñ būdā dil-e nākām bahut hai
yih ranj kih kam hai ma'i gulfām bahut hai (233:1; #1421)

The defeated heart is too emaciated to bear any more grief;
I have much anguish because there is too little red wine.

būdā: weak, emaciated, loss of courage.

No courage is left to bear more grief, which is in abundance. The only reprieve from it is in drinking wine, but even that is in short supply. That is a matter of great anguish as well.

کہتے ہوئے ساقی سے حیا آتی ہے ورنہ
ہے یوں کہ مجھے دُردِ تہِ جام بہت ہے

kehte hu'e, sāqī se, ḥayā ātī hai varna(h)
hai yūñ kih mujhe durd-e tahe jām bahut hai (233:2; #1422)

I am ashamed to tell the cupbearer; otherwise,
The sedimentation in the goblet is quite enough for me.

durd-e tahe jām: precipitate in wine bottle or chalice.

The fact is that I am happy with the sediment in the goblet (which comes from red wine that has gone bad). I am ashamed to tell this to the Cupbearer, though, for she will think that I am willing to lower myself so much that I will accept any wine, even the sedimentation of wine. The poet is willing to accept anything offered by the cupbearer.

نے تیر کماں میں ہے، نہ صیاد کمیں میں
گوشے میں قفس کے مجھے آرام بہت ہے

ne tīr kamāñ meñ hai, na(h) sayyād kamiñ meñ
goshe meñ qafis ke mujhe ārām bahut hai (233:3; #1423)

Neither the arrow is in the bow nor is the hunter lurking in ambush.
In this corner of the cage, I am very comfortable.

sayyād: captor, hunter.

In freedom we stay alert, but are fearful of losing it. Once our freedom is lost, so goes the paranoia and we can be very comfortable. A bird is trying to run away from the captor; once caught, it sits comfortably in the cage. This is a remarkable expression illustrating how we spend our lives worrying, but when all is lost, so goes all the worry. It should be a source of solace for us that we free ourselves in bondage.

کیا زہد کو مانوں کہ نہ ہو گرچہ ریائی
پاداشِ عمل کی طمعِ خام بہت ہے

kyā zohd ko mānūñ kih na(h) ho garchi(h) riyāī'
pādāsh-e `amal kī t̤ama`-e ḳhām bahut hai (233:4; #1424)

How can I believe in piety though it appears free of hypocrisy,
The raw avarice for recompense to good deeds is too much.

zohd: piety, prayer, abstinence; *riyāī:* hypocrisy; *pādāsh*: requital, recompense; *ṭama*: avarice, greed, lust, covetousness.

People adopt piety, which is apparently free of hypocrisy, but how do I know people are not doing good deeds in order to claim rewards in the hereafter? That would make them hypocrites for praying. Praying should be for the sake of God, not self. A deeper connection is made to those who preach piety while camouflaging their hypocrisy and those who openly deny piety and thus renounce hypocrisy.

ہیں اہلِ خرد کس روشِ خاص پہ نازاں
پابستگیِ رسم و رہِ عام بہت ہے

haiñ ahl-e ķhirad kis ravish-e ķhāṣ pa(h) nāzāñ
pābastagī' rasm-o-rah-e 'ām bahut hai (233:5; #1425)

Which paths are the intelligent ones boasting about following?
Restricting to customs and populist trends is just too common.

ahl-e ķhirad: intelligent people; *pābastagī:* restrictions; *ravish*: path, trend.

Those who claim to be intelligent are not following any special trend; they, too, comply with common customs and traditions. *Ġhālib* repeatedly advocates going against traditions. In one place, the poet berates the legendary lover, *Farhād*, for being too traditional a lover. He needed a physical implement (an axe) to kill himself for he was too deeply ingrained in the traditions and customs. Here *Ġhālib* challenges the intelligent ones to see that whatever path they are taking is a common path and that they should not boast about it.

زمزم ہی پہ چھوڑو، مجھے کیا طوفِ حرم سے؟
آلودہ بہ مے جامۂ احرام بہت ہے

zamzam hī pa(h) chhoṛo, mujhe kyā ṯaof-e ḥaram se
ālūdah ba(h) mai jāmah' aḥrām bahut hai (233:6; #1426)

Leave me at Zamzam, for what do I have to do with going around *Ka'bā*?
My pilgrimage garb is too well drenched with wine.

Zamzam: the fresh water spring in *Ka'bā* considered sacred by Muslims; *ḥaram:* the cubical structure in the mosque at Makkah (Mecca); *aḥrām*: the unstitched cloth worn around the body during the rituals of pilgrimage, pilgrimage garb.

Leave me at Zamzam spring so that I can purify my clothes by washing the wine from them. Having donned the *ahrām*, the intent is to go around *Kā'ba*. The poet is conscious of his sins and wants to undo whatever he can. The depth of this verse comes in the statement that we should give up whatever sins we can before going to ask forgiveness (which should be restricted to the sins that we could not eliminate ourselves). Here is a declaration stating, "My clothes are drenched with wine, so I am in no shape to go around *Ka'bā*. Let me first cleanse myself at Zamzam spring."

ہے قہر گر اب بھی نہ بنے بات کہ اُن کو
اِنکار نہیں اور مجھے اِبرام بہت ہے

hai qahr gar ab bhī na(h) bane bāt kih unko
inkār nahiñ aur mujhe ibrām bahut hai (233:7; #1427)

It would be calamitous if even now, things do not work out,
When there is no refusal by her and I am too insistent.

ibrām: insistence.

The beloved has not refused the request to unite and the lover is ardently insistent. If it does not work out now, it would really be pathetic. Disbelief raises its head.

خوں ہو کے جگر آنکھ سے ٹپکا نہیں اے مرگ
رہنے دے مجھے یاں، کہ ابھی کام بہت ہے

ḳhūñ ho kih jigar ānkh se ṭapkā nahiñ ai marg
rahne de mujhe yāñ, kih abhī kām bahut hai (233:8; #1428)

O death! The liver, turning to blood, has not yet dripped out of the eyes;
Let me live a while longer for there is much left for me to do.

The "liver turning to blood" means extreme suffering. Dripping blood from the eyes is what the lovers need to do to show their devotion to hardship. The poet is saying that since I have not yet reached that stage—let me stay until I do. He is asking for a reprieve from death. Know that often death is the only resolution to grief. In this case, the lover wants his suffering to go on. This may also refer to the poet who cried for more time to express his abilities in his verse.

ہوگا کوئی ایسا بھی کہ غالب کو نہ جانے؟
شاعر تو وہ اچھا ہے پہ بدنام بہت ہے

hogā ko'ī aisā bhī kih Ġhālib ko na(h) jāne
shā'ir to vuh achhā hai pa(h) badnām bahut hai (233:9; #1429)

There is hardly anyone who would not know of *Ġhālib*
He is a good poet, but he is just too notorious.

Who does not know *Ġhālib*? It is not because of his poetry, but because of his infamy as a lover.

234

مدت ہوئی ہے یار کو مہماں کیے ہوئے   جوشِ قدح سے بزم چراغاں کیے ہوئے

muddat hu'ī hai yār ko mahmāñ kīye hu'e
josh-e qadaḥ se bazm charāġhāñ kīye hu'e (234:1; #1430)

Long it has been since I hosted the beloved,
Having illuminated the assembly with the fervency of goblet.

The last time my beloved came to my assembly, the goblet and wine became so excited they lit up to illuminate the assembly. It was indeed a memorable event for me to reminisce about now. Lighting up the assembly with goblets and wine also indicates a celebration.

کرتا ہوں جمع پھر جگرِ لخت لخت کو   عرصہ ہوا ہے دعوتِ مژگاں کیے ہوئے

kartā hūñ jama' phir jigar-e lakht lakht ko
'arṣah hu'ā hai da'vat-e mizhgāñ kīye hu'e (234:2; #1431)

Again I collect the pieces of my liver, one by one
Long it has been to offer a feast for her eyelashes.

When you last came to visit me, you ripped my liver into many pieces with your amorous glances. To provide a feast for your eyelashes, I am once again collecting those scattered pieces of my liver. Note that the liver is the bastion of courage. Having lost it once by succumbing to the beloved, I am again gathering my courage for you to shatter.

پھر وضعِ احتیاط سے رکنے لگا ہے دم   برسوں ہوئے ہیں چاک گریباں کیے ہوئے

phir vaẓ'e iḥtiyāt se rukne lagā hai dam
barsoñ hu'e haiñ chāk girebāñ kīye hu'e (234:3; #1432)

Then again, I have begun to suffocate at the traditions of sobriety;
Years have passed since I tore my collar away.

vaẓ' iḥtiyāt: style of caution, sobriety.

Rationality forces certain behavior that includes controlling the expression of frenzy. It is all too suffocating for lovers. They just want to tear their collar and go wandering as they used to. Why should the lover be concerned about sobriety? A torn collar will tell the whole world what ails him and that can be embarrassing to both the lover and the beloved.

پھر گرمِ نالہ ہائے شرر بار ہے نفس   مدت ہوئی ہے سیرِ چراغاں کیے ہوئے

phir garm-e nāla(h) hāi sharar bār hai nafis
muddat hu'ī hai sair-e charāġhāñ kīye hu'e (234:4; #1433)

Then again breath is active in spewing fiery plaints
Long has it been since I went to see display of lamps.

sharar: fire spark; *nafis*: breath; *chirāġhāñ:* display of lamps.

Lamps are the burn spots (scars) of the heart. With fiery plaints, the heart will burn in many places and create a display of lamps along the path of the fiery breath. It has been a long time since I saw myself in this condition. There is an element of melancholia in this expression.

پھر پرسشِ جراحتِ دل کو چلا ہے عشق   سامانِ صد ہزار نمکداں کیے ہوئے

phir pursish-e jirāḥat-e dil ko chalā hai 'ishq
sāmān-e ṣad hazār namakdāñ kīye hu'e (234:5; #1434)

The love is again inquiring about the condition of heart's wounds,
Having gathered a hundred thousand salt shakers.

It was love that created these wounds. Now it is coming to inquire, "Why aren't these wounds hurting more?" It will empty all salt shakers onto the wounds out of vengeance.

پھر بھر رہا ہوں خامۂ مژگاں بخونِ دل   سازِ چمن طرازیٔ داماں کیے ہوئے

phir bhar rahā hūñ ḳhāmah' mizhgāñ ba(h) ḳhūn-e dil
sāz-e chaman ṭarāzī' dāmāñ kīye hu'e (234:6; #1435)

Again, I am dipping my pen of eyelashes in the heart's blood,
Intending to draw decorative flowers on my hem.

chaman ṭarāz'ī: decorating flowers.

The real purpose of dipping the pen in blood is to decorate my skirt. The lover is hoping that the beloved will see it and come to praise the work.

باہم دگر ہوئے ہیں دل و دیدہ پھر رقیب   نظارہ و خیال کا ساماں کیے ہوئے

bāḥam digar hu'e haiñ dil-o-dīda(h) phir raqīb
naẓẓārah-o-ḳhayāl kā sāmāñ kīye hu'e (234:7; #1436)

Again, the heart and the eye have become rivals to each other,
Being fully readied for looking at and thinking about her.

The eye wants to see her, but the heart only imagines her. They are fighting each other but they are united and well-prepared for achieving their desires.

دِل پھر طوافِ کوئے ملامت کو جائے ہے   پندار کا صنم کدہ ویراں کیے ہوئے

dil phir ṭavāf-e kūe malāmat ko jāe hai
pindār kā sanamkadah vīrāñ kīye hu'e (234:8; #1437)

Then again, my heart goes back to the alley of reproach,
Having brought to desolation the idol-temple of my pride.

pindār: pride; *sanamkadah*: idol temple.

I was too proud to go to her alley to be disgraced. Shaking my pride, the heart is now drifting toward that alley of reproof, taking a path that will bring the wrath of many. I can do this, having emptied the temple where I used to keep my pride. Like an idol, I use to supplicate to my pride—no more.

پھر شوق کر رہا ہے خریدار کی طلب   عرضِ متاعِ عقل و دل و جاں کیے ہوئے

phir shauq kar rahā hai ḳharīdār kī ṯalab
'arẕ-e matā'-e 'aql-o-dil-o-jāñ kīye hu'e (234:9; #1438)

The desire is again demanding a buyer,
To offer the goods of wisdom, heart and life.

Of course, the only customer that can take them all is the beloved, to whom all offerings are made. The price must be very attractive, too. The lover wants to lose it all to the beloved.

دوڑے ہے پھر ہر ایک گل و لالہ پر خیال   صد گلستاں نگاہ کا ساماں کیے ہوئے

doṛe hai phir har ek gul-o-lāla(h) par ḳhayāl
ṣad gulsitāñ nigāh kā sāmāñ kīye hu'e (234:10; #1439)

Again, the imagination runs towards tulips and roses,
Embracing a hundred gardens for the spectacle.

gul-o-lāla(h): roses and tulips, beautiful gardens.

Hundreds of gardens are providing viewing opportunities and my thoughts are racing toward each and every flower. So many beauties in the world and I am running after each one of them.

پھر چاہتا ہوں نامۂ دلدار کھولنا   جاں نذرِ دلفریبیٔ عنواں کیے ہوئے

phir chāhatā huñ nāma(h)' dildār kholnā
jāñ nażr-e dilfarebī' ʿunvāñ kīye hu'e (234:11; #1440)

Then again, I want to open the letter from the beloved,
Sacrificing my life at the heart-deceiving display of the envelope.

dilfareb: attractive, heart deceiving; *ʿunvāñ*: envelope, title.

Everything that comes from the beloved is beautiful but destructive. Just the beauty of the envelope and the address written on it are enough to kill me. Imagine what would happen if I opened the letter. The use of "again" in the first line refers to being through this event before, and so the lover knows what the response would be, but he is consoling himself by saying that when the envelope is so beautiful, the letter will definitely be more so.

مانگے ہے پھر کسی کو لبِ بام پر ہوس   زلفِ سیاہ رخ پہ پریشاں کیے ہوئے

mānge hai phir kisī ko lab-e bām par havas
zulf-e siyāh ruḳh pa(h) pareshāñ kīye hu'e (234:12; #1441)

The desire again demands to see someone at the balcony,
With dark tresses disheveled about her face.

lab-e bām: edge of terrace, balcony; *zulf-e siyāh*: black tresses; *ruḳh*: face; *pareshāñ*: scattered, disheveled.

The lover desperately wants to see his beloved at the balcony with her tresses loose. This conveys an extremely creative imagination. The black tresses, of course, are the dark clouds. Being high on the balcony also reminds the lover of dark, spring clouds in the sky.

چاہے ہے پھر کسی کو مقابل میں آرزو   سرمے سے تیز دشنۂ مژگاں کیے ہوئے

chāhe hai phir kisī ko muqābil meñ ārzū
surme se tez dashna(h)' mizhgāñ kīye hu'e (234:13; #1442)

The longing again demands to confront someone,
Having daggers of eyelashes sharpened with black antimony.

surma(h): black antimony powder used to decorate eyes; *tez*: sharpened; *dashna(h)' mizhgāñ*: daggers of eyelashes.

The eyelashes are sharpened and laced with antimony powder. This is to pierce the heart of the lover; what he wants and demands again. Calling the beloved "someone" is significant. It shows that the heart is ready—let it be anyone.

اِک نَوبہارِ ناز کو تاکے ہے پھر نگاہ   چہرہ فروغِ مَے سے گلستاں کیے ہوئے

ik nau bahār-e nāz ko tāke hai phir nigāh
chehra(h) furūġh-e mai se gulistāñ kīye hu'e (234:14; #1443)

The eyes again yearn to see a coquettish fresh-as-spring beloved,
Her face brightly flushed under the influence of wine.

tāke: stare, watch.

The lover is searching again for a new beloved whose face will be red from drinking wine. The freshness of the garden, the red-colored flowers, and the flushed face of the beloved are all very intoxicating. The lover wants a beloved who likes to drink wine. Once intoxicated, the lover is hoping to take advantage of her.

پھر جی میں ہے کہ در پہ کسی کے پڑے رہیں   سر زیرِ بارِ منّتِ درباں کیے ہوئے

phir jī meñ hai kih dar pa(h) kisī kih paṛe raheñ
sar zer bār-e minnat-e darbāñ kīye hu'e (234:15; #1444)

Then again, the heart longs to keep lying at someone's doorstep,
With head burdened under the obligation of pleading to the doorkeeper.

bār: burden; *minnat*: pleading.

The lover is sitting at her doorstep and feels obliged to the doorkeeper to let him stay there. This results in his head being burdened to the point that he cannot lift it. Calling beloved "someone" shows distance from the beloved. This is a futile attempt to show obliviousness because the lover has already reached "her" doorstep.

جی ڈھونڈتا ہے پھر وہی فرصت، کہ رات دِن　　بیٹھے رہیں تصورِ جاناں کیے ہوئے

jī ḍhūnḍtā hai phir vohī furṣat, kih rāt din
baiṭhe raheñ taṣavvur-e jānāñ kīye hu'e (234:16; #1445)

The heart searches again for the leisure that round the clock,
We would keep sitting, contemplating the thoughts of sweetheart.

The often-used theme of this *ġhazal* is to repeat an experience. Apparently, the lover has had those moments of leisure when he could only think of his beloved and take joy from that; he wants those moments back. He wants to be able to sit alone in contemplation. This is one of the most widely quoted verses of *Ġhālib*, expressing eloquently the feeling of nirvana. A serious difficulty arises if this verse is read with the comma in the first line. The lover is asking for such leisure that round the clock he could contemplate the thoughts of sweetheart; he is not asking for days and nights of leisure, as often erroneously interpreted.

غالب ہمیں نہ چھیڑ کہ پھر جوشِ اشک سے
بیٹھے ہیں ہم تہیۂ طوفاں کیے ہوئے

Ġhālib hameñ na(h) cheṛ, kih phir josh-e ashk se
baiṭhe haiñ ham tahaiyya(h)' ṯūfāñ kīye hu'e (234:17; #1446)

Ġhālib! Tease me not, for again with the intensity of the tears,
I am sitting, having committed to stirring up a storm.

The lover's tears can produce a deluge, he warns. This time, he is ready to let it all go and warns others not to disturb him or else they will be responsible for the storm that will follow.

235

نویدِ امن ہے بیدادِ دوست جاں کے لیے　　رہی نہ طرزِ ستم کوئی آسماں کے لیے

navīd-e amn hai bedād-e dost jāñ ke liye
rahī na(h) t̤arz-e sitam ko'ī āsmāñ ke liye (235:1; #1447)

The tyranny of beloved is good news for life,
Leaving no other style of cruelty for the heavens to dole out.

navīd: good news; *bedād-e dost:* tyranny of beloved.

The beloved has tried all possible ways of extending her wrath and cruelty. If the heavens want to try us, it would have to be in one of her ways, ways which we are already experienced in handling. This is indeed good news for the victims of her cruelty. Repeatedly, Heaven is blamed for bringing bad luck, catastrophe, and ill fate. Now, after having gone through all hardships, whatever the heavens can dole out to us is easy for us to bear, for we have experienced all that can be experienced. Here *Ġhālib* belittles Heaven's cruelties compared to what the beloved doles out.

بلا سے اگر مژۂ یار تشنۂ خوں ہے　　رکھوں کچھ اپنی بھی مژگانِ خوں فشاں کے لیے

balā se! gar mizha(h)' yār tashnah ḳhūñ hai
rakhūñ kuchh apnī bhī mizhgān-e ḳhūñ fishāñ ke liye (235:2; #1448)

Who cares if the beloved's eyelashes are thirsty for blood?
I must keep some for my own bleeding eyelashes as well.

balā se: who cares, to hell with; *tashnah*: thirsty.

The beloved is thirsty for blood, but this is no time to give all of my blood to please her. I must keep some for my own eyelashes as well, so that when all other lovers fall by the wayside I will still have something to offer her. This is the call of an experienced lover. The lover is not keeping the blood for another beloved.

وہ زندہ ہم ہیں کہ ہیں روشناسِ خلق اے خضر　　نہ تم کہ چور بنے عمرِ جاوداں کے لیے

vuh zinda(h) ham haiñ kih haiñ rūshināṣ-e ḳhalq, ai Ḳhiẓr
na(h) tum, kih chor bane ʿumr-e jāvidāñ ke liye (235:3; #1449)

We are the ones living who do know people, O! *Khizr*!
Who, unlike you, do not hide like a thief for an eternal life?

Haẓrat Ḳhiẓr (see Glossary) lives a life of eternity, but no one knows him, as he stays hidden. Belittling him, the poet says that *Ḳhiẓr* is hiding, as thieves do. A subtle reference is made here to how *Ḳhiẓr* was instilled with eternal life - by stealing the opportunity meant for King Sikandar. A subtle play of words points to *Ḳhiẓr* not being visible and hiding is wittingly presented here. Real life is when all know who we are and we know who are they.

رہا بلا میں بھی، میں مبتلائے آفتِ رشک　　بلائے جاں ہے ادا تیری اک جہاں کے لیے

rahā balā meñ bhī, maiñ mubtilāe āfit-e rashk
balāe jāñ hai adā terī ik jahāñ ke liye (235:4; #1450)

Even in my misfortune, I continue suffering from the bane of envy;
Calamity to my life is your coquetry for the rest of the world.

balā: misfortune; *balāe jāñ*: calamity.

Your coquetry brings much suffering and misfortune to your lovers, including this one, but I am getting doubly killed because of jealousy as well. I would want that your wraths should be only for me and not for anyone else. As you dole out your coquetry to the world, I am hurt twice: once from your coquettish style and second, from knowing that others have been hurt as well. All tyranny should be for me.

فلک نہ دُور رکھ اُس سے مجھے کہ میں ہی نہیں   دراز دستیٔ قاتل کے اِمتحاں کے لیے

filak na(h) dūr rakh us se mujhe, kih maiñ hī nahiñ
darāz dastī' qātil ke imteḥāñ ke liye (235:5; #1451)

O! Heavens! Do not keep me away from her; for, I am not the only one
Left to be tested by the far-reaching arm of the killer?

darāz dast: arms length, far-reaching, cruel.

An interesting play on words is used here. *Ġhālib* uses the word to describe "far-reaching" to also mean "cruel." It is true that the test of murderers comes from seeing how far she can reach, but I would like to know why I have been chosen to test her powers. There are others available as well. Test them for the outreach of the slayer, but spare me; bring me closer and kill me.

مِثال یہ مری کوشش کی ہے کہ مُرغِ اسیر   کرے قَفَس میں فَراہم خَس آشیاں کے لیے

misāl yih merī koshish kī hai, kih murġh-e asīr
kare qafis meñ farāham ḳhas āshiyāñ ke liye (235:6; #1452)

A simile of my efforts is that of a captive bird,
Who would, even in the cage, collect straw to build a nest.

misāl: example, analogy, simile.

Melancholically, a caged bird collects straw hoping to get out one day to build a nest. That is how you can describe the condition of this lover. However, it must be iterated that the lover is not praying for freedom. He is just describing the condition of his heart, a state of self-deception hoping that someday he will succeed in melting the heart of the beloved. It is in my character to be impatient.

گدا سمجھ کے وہ چُپ تھا، مری جو شامت آئے　　اُٹھا، اور اُٹھ کے قدم مَیں نے پاسباں کے لیے!

gadā samajh ke vuh chup thā, merī jo shāmat āe
uṭhā, aur uṭh ke qadam maiñ ne pāsbāñ ke liye (235:7; #1453)

Thinking of me as a beggar, he was silent, but as bad luck would have it,
I got up and grabbed the feet of her gatekeeper.

Few verses can condense a love story as effectively as this verse does. The lover was sitting at the threshold of the beloved's home, hoping to get a glimpse of her. The gatekeeper, looking at the lover's tattered clothes and pathetic condition, thought he was a beggar and ignored him. However, as the lover could no longer sit still, he got up and fell at the feet of the doorkeeper, which, of course, resulted in havoc, as the gatekeeper recognized him and beat him up. Many explanations exist to answer why the lover did it. First, the lover felt so indebted to the doorkeeper for letting him sit there that he could not hold back. Secondly, the lover may have planned it so that the beloved might inquire what the noise was. Here we have an excellent example of *Ġhālib*'s wit.

بہ قدرِ شوق نہیں ظرفِ تنگنائے غزل　ق　کچھ اَور چاہیے وُسعت مرے بیاں کے لیے

ba(h) qadr-e shauq nahiñ ẓarf-e tangnāe ġhazal
kuchh aur chāhiye vus'at mere bayāñ ke liye (235:8; #1454)

In proportion to my fancy there is not enough room in the tight alleys of *ġhazal*.
I need some more spaciousness for my expression.

tangnāe: tight place, narrow alley.

The genre of the *ġhazal* is too narrow for my thoughts to be expressed adequately. I need another, more expansive medium to express the depth of my thoughts.

دیا ہے خلق کو بھی، تا اُسے نظر نہ لگے
بنا ہے عیش تجمّل حسین خاں کے لیے

diyā hai ḳhalq ko bhī, tā use naẕar na(h) lage
banā hai ʿaish tajammul ḥusain ḳhāñ ke liye (235:9; #1455)

Given to world as well, merely to safeguard him from the evil eye,
Or else, the luxuries were created only for *Tajammul Hussain Ḳhān*.

Praising his benefactor, *Nāwab Tajammul Hussain Ḳhān*, *Ġhālib* explains that luxuries are given to people to keep them from casting an evil eye on the *Nawāb*. God gave luxuries to others merely to keep them from becoming jealous of the luxurious style of the *Nawāb*.

زباں پہ بارِ خدایا! یہ کس کا نام آیا
کہ میرے نُطق نے بوسے مری زباں کے لیے

zabāñ pa(h) bār-e ḳhudāyā! yih kis kā nām āyā
kih mere nuṯq ne bose merī zabāñ kih liye (235:10; #1456)

Whose name has come on my tongue, O! Mighty Lord
That my speech has begun kissing my tongue.

nuṯq: diction, speech.

To take a kiss from the tongue, where the tongue gives kisses, can also be interpreted as "My words kissed my tongue." Speaking of the beloved—taking her name—caused my words and tongue to start kissing each other. The tongue creates speech that kisses the tongue. Here we have a classic tongue in cheek situation. Some have insisted that this verse is an ode to the Lord or to his prophet as the piety of the name has caused my tongue to kiss the words.

نصیرِ دولت و دیں اور معینِ ملت و ملک   بنا ہے چرخِ بریں جس کے آستاں کے لیے

naṣir-e daulat-o-dīñ aur mu'īn-e millat-o-mulk
banā hai charḳh-e barīñ jis ke āstāñ kih liye (235:11; #1457)

The defender of wealth and religion, the defender of the nation and country,
For whose threshold are the wheels of heavens made.

charḳh-e barīñ: wheel of heaven; *āstāñ*: threshold.

Referring again to *Nawāb Tajammul Hussain Ḳhān*, the first line of the verse is just the title of the *Nawāb*. The high skies are made for him, the poet asserts in the second line.

زمانہ عہد میں اُس کے ہے محوِ آرائش   بنیں گے اور ستارے اب آسماں کے لیے

zamāna(h) 'ahd meñ us ke hai maḥv-e ārāish
baneñ ge aur sitāre ab āsmāñ ke liye (235:12; #1458)

In his reign, the whole world is busy decorating itself;
Now more stars will have to be created for the skies.

Since the existing stars will be used to decorate the palace of *Nawāb Tajammul Hussain Ḳhān*, God will have to create more stars to keep the sky twinkling.

ورق تمام ہوا اور مدح باقی ہے   سفینہ چاہیے اِس بحرِ بے کراں کے لیے

varaq tamām hu'ā aur madḥ bāqī hai
safina(h) chāhiye is baḥr-e be karāñ ke liye (235:13; #1459)

The paper is finished, but the ode goes on
A fleet is needed for this endless ocean.

safina: fleet, register.

There is not enough paper to write an ode to *Nawāb Tajammul Hussain Ḳhān*. A big fleet is needed to traverse this ocean of expression. Note that the word used for fleet also means "register" which makes the connection to paper very clear.

ادائے خاص سے غالبؔ ہُوا ہے نکتہ سرا
صلائے عام ہے یارانِ نکتہ داں کے لیے

adāe ḳhāṣ se Ġhālib hu'ā hai nuktah sarā
ṣalāe 'ām hai yaran-e nuktah dāñ ke liye (235:14; #1460)

With a special style, *Ġhālib* has sung his subtle verses;
A common call it is now to my cohort critics.

nuktah sarā: singing subtleties; *nuktah dāñ:* those who understand or appreciate subtleties, critic.

A challenge is given to all those who understand and follow the unique style of *Ġhālib*. The challenge is to criticize and ultimately become a believer in him. No other verse qualifies better as the final verse of *Ġhālib*'s sonnets than this verse does. The poet has written his poetry in a totally unique style—a challenge is made to all to match it.

Appendix 1

Guide to Transliteration

Pronunciation	*Urdū* Script	Transliteration
alif-short	ا	*a, i, u*
alif-long	ا ,آ	*ā*
bay	ب	*b*
pay	پ	*p*
tay	ت	*t*
Tay (t: retroflex)	ٹ	*ṭ*
say	ث	*s*
jeem	ج	*j*
chay	چ	*ch*
hey	ح	*ḥ*
khey (kh: velar)	خ	*ḳh*
dal	د	*d*
dal (d: retroflex)	ڈ	*ḍ*
zal	ذ	*ż*
ray	ر	*r*
rhay (rh: retroflex)	ڑ	*ṛ*
zay	ز	*z*
zhay	ژ	*zh*
seen	س	*s*
sheen	ش	*sh*
suaad (saad)	ص	*ṣ*
zuaad (zaad)	ض	*ẓ*
tuay	ط	*ṯ*
zuay	ظ	*ẕ*

ain	ع	
ghain (gh: velar)	غ	*ġh*
fay	ف	*f*
qaaf	ق	*q*
kaaf	ک	*k*
gaaf	گ	*g*
laam	ل	*l*
meem	م	*m*
noon	ن	*n*
vao	و	*v, ū, o, au*
hey	ه, ھ	*h*
ye	ی	*ī*
bari ye	ے	*y, e, ai*
noon-e ghunnah (gh: vellar; nasal n)	ں	*ñ*
hamza	ء	*'*
izaafat		*-e*

For the sake of consistency, Persian words have been transliterated as they are pronounced in *Urdū*. Indic words have been treated as though they were written phonetically in *Urdū* script.

Appendix 2

A Brief History of Urdu Poetry

Poetry is an intensely personal, emotional genre making it difficult to explain intellectually; however, the following defining aspects of poetry are instructive. Poetry is:

- an expression of the heart, human experience, feelings, and thoughts.
- an expression of facts using appropriate words.
- a description of life rendered with imagination and emotion
- the most popular literary genre.
- a creative source for civilization, constitution, and different arts and crafts.
- a concoction of all knowledge and craft.
- an element of surprise to us.
- an art through which a poet can excite the emotions and feelings of others.
- an expression of an ordinary event in an illuminating, evocative writing style that creates a sharp reaction in the heart and mind of the reader.

Poetry is universal in that every language on the planet carries with it some poetic elements. Although languages differ significantly in the manner of expression, the nature of poetic expression remains remarkably consistent, indicating that poetry is more of a human phenomenon than syntactical expression. From expressions of love for a woman to revolt against a regime, poetry carries an element of subtlety and spontaneity—something created by the environs of the poet. To understand a great poet, therefore, we must first look into his mind and his subjective awareness of the milieu. Since *Ġhālib,* undoubtedly the greatest poet of the *Urdū* language, expressed himself mainly through his love sonnets, it is imperative that we examine the art of love sonnets, the language in which they are written, and the environs that prompted these poetic expressions to better understand how *Ġhālib* became a master of this genre.

In this chapter, we will examine the roots of the *Urdū* language, *Urdū* poetry, and particularly the genre of love sonnets, *ġhazals*, in *Urdū*. The following chapters will look at the life, the works and the poetry of *Ġhālib*.

Urdū—literally *camp* in Turkish—is a mixture of languages and dialects. Muslims brought various languages to India, and diluted India's languages freely with words from their own. When *Delhī* was the seat of the Muslim Empire in the late 12th century, the languages around *Delhī*, mainly *Brij Bhasha* and *Sauraseni*, became heavily mixed with Persian, the *lingua franca* of the Muslim rulers. Other languages that found their way into the languages of India were Turkish, Arabic, and, later, English. Whereas much of the vocabulary of the original languages (*Sauraseni*, for example) changed, the basic grammatical structure remained intact. In the 13th century, the language of India became widely known as *Hindvi, Hindi,* and *Brij Bhasha* and was written in the original *Devanagri* script [the Sanskrit script]. The name "*Urdū*" was given to this thriving regional language in the period of the *Muġhal* Emperor Shah Jehan (1627-1658). The language was introduced to the southern province of India, Hyderabad Deccan, by the armies and followers of the Tughlaq and Khilji Kings in the 14th century. Affected by the dialects of the south, the language became known as Deccani (after Hyderabad Deccan), having adopted the Persian script and replaced Persian in offices as the official language. Since the language was rendered in the *Devanagri* script for quite some time around *Delhī*, it had been erroneously assumed that the first *Urdū* poet was Amir Khusro (1253-1325) from the Deccan. The fact is many northern poets had already been writing *Urdū* poetry, namely

Kabir Das, Mira Bai, Guru Nanak, Malik Mohammad Jaisi, and Abdul Rahim *Ḳhān* Khanan, who lived much earlier than Amir Khusro.

Before *Amīr Ḳhusro* (1253-1325), the language of poetry was primarily the vernacular *Brij Bhasha. Amīr Ḳhusro* interspersed it with Persian as the first school of *ġhazal* poets emerged in the Deccan during the 15th and 16th centuries. Early *ġhazal* was somewhat free of structure and made use of rather simple and blunt expressions as we see in the works of the Qutub *Shahī* poets of the Deccan. *Valī* (1668-1744) contributed much to the structure of *ġhazals*. When the works of *Valī* reached *Delhī* in 1720, the town was in an uproar and, within a decade, *Urdū* became a language of poetry. The works of many minor poets like Hatim, *Najī*, *Mazmūn*, and *Abrū* actually formed the groundwork for *Urdū* poetry in the 18th century in Northern India, particularly *Delhī*. *Urdū ġhazals* became heavily Persianized and ushered in their golden age, beginning with *Mīr Taqī Mīr*. The simplicity of emotions expressed in earlier *ġhazals* underwent a metamorphosis, leading to the works of *Ġhālib*, perhaps the most difficult to read of *Urdū ġhazal* poets. This transition, taking place from the 15th to 18th century, was due not only to the maturity of technique but to changes in the social order as well. For India, the 18th century was an age of transition. The last of the strong *Muġhal* Emperors was Aurangzeb (1707), after whom the empire disintegrated. The capital was invaded and destroyed by *Nadir Shāh* and *Ahmad Shah Abdalī*, followed by others. Finally, the British crept in with their deceptive plans. All of this altered the aura of the empire, which in turn stifled human thought. The uncertainties of the time raised many questions and a revival of the arts and literature ensued for India in the 18th century, a sort of renaissance period. *Urdū* poetry benefited significantly from this revolution of thought. The doubts and the uncertainty of the 18th century continued into the 19th century, and the mutiny of 1857 against the British left many indelible marks on the social and cultural scene of Northern India, all reflected melancholically by many poets, *Ġhālib* among them. New constructions of language arose that hinged on old similes. The executioner and the rival were now the British. Christ became a symbol of the ruling elite and new meaning was afforded the *kalīsa* (church). The waning days of the dying empire became a candle ready to be extinguished as the weak, symbolic emperor, *Bahadur Shāh Zafar*, who himself was an elite poet, tried desperately to preserve the traditions of the *Muġhal Empire*. Mourning over lost glory became an oft-repeated theme in *Urdū* poetry.

Urdū poetry of the Indian subcontinent as we know it today did not take its final form until the 17th century, when *Urdū* was declared the official language of the court. The 18th century saw a phenomenal rise in *Urdū* poetry when *Urdū* replaced Persian as the *lingua franca* of the region. *Urdū* poetry, as it is derived from Persian, Turkish, and Arabic, acquired many poetic conventions from these languages. Just as Elizabethan English is characterized by social and regional realities, *Urdū* holds a remarkable wealth of the conventions of many cultures and languages. This element was given a great boost in the 18th century, when newspapers and other information media were available on a limited basis. *Urdū* poetry rose to become a more intimate form of communication as a reflection of the social and political tribulations of the time. The commonest form of communication, in line with Arabic tradition, was to read poetry in gatherings, called *musha'era,* in which poets would gather to read poems crafted in accordance with a metrical pattern, often prescribed beforehand. Not only did the poetry have to meet standards of word choice and the loftiness of thought, but also these strict metrical patterns. Competitions were held similar to those held in ancient Greek, Roman, and pre-Islamic Arabic cultures. However, the intensity and warmth of the *musha'eras* that developed in *Delhī* were indeed unique and helped popularize *Urdū* as the language of poetry in the *Muġhal* Empire. A culture built around taking lessons in writing *Urdū* poetry became fashionable for royalty, and the masters of poetry were awarded reverence worthy of kings. In all *musha'eras,* the most honored of the poets would preside and the candle that was passed from poet to poet in the order of their ranking ultimately reached the presiding poet. This impact on the tradition of respect and new cultural traits was able to take root because poets were held in such high esteem. Royalty sought out their company and poetry was sent as gift to their aristocratic friends. Whereas the 18th century produced remarkable literature in *Urdū*, it was often lost, since it was not until poets reached fame that their writings were collected and published. The writings of one of the greatest *Urdū* poets, Nazir, were collected 80 years after his death, and even the works of Zauq, the teacher of King *Bahadur Shāh Zafar*, were destroyed during the mutiny of 1857. Some of the poems written by the King in exile, *Bahadur Shāh Zafar*, were also lost.

Urdū poetry is based on a system of linguistic measure—it is a quantitative expression and its form is very rigid. The typical measures are nine, or more commonly eighteen, but by various permutation and combinations, they number over 800. The many forms of *Urdū* poetry include:

- *qasīda,* or ode of praise.
- *maṣnavī,* or long reflective poem and tale in verse.
- *marṣia,* or elegy.
- *qit'a,* or fragment, a four-line quatrain.
- *ruba'ī,* or a quatrain with specific rhyme and topic, made famous in the West by the works of Omar Khayyam.
- *ġhazal*, a lyrical poem of 6 to 26 lines, often longer; the word "*ġhazal*" is derived from the Arabic word *taġhazzul*, or "conversation with ladies" (or expression of love for women). The word "*ġhazal*" also means the agonized cry of the gazelle. The literal meaning of "*ġhazal*" is to talk to or about women or to express love to them through the description of the condition of heart.

Whereas many poets have specialized in writing one of the above types, most have attempted *ġhazal*, the most popular form, and those who have achieved the greatest fame have been poets of *ġhazal*. Since each verse of a *ġhazal* entails an independent segment and complete description of the topic (though a chain of verses may share the same theme), a great deal of ability is needed to express in few words the most complex emotions. Also, since the topic of *ġhazal* is not novel and because most people in their lifetime experience affection toward the opposite sex (or the same sex, as often portrayed), the style of expression in the *ġhazal* has to be unique to make an impact. As a result, it is easy to write a common verse but quite another thing to create a unique one.

Ġhazal became the most popular form of Persian and *Urdū* poetry, whereas *qasīda* was popular in Arabic poetry. *Qasīda* finds its roots in tribal sentiments. The rise of Islam saw a decline in the tribal structure of communities and more sophisticated, livelier expressions of society; the lover and the beloved became accepted themes in poetry. This tradition survives today, though in the chronological transition many aspects of mysticism have also surfaced. The *ġhazal* also maintains a rather platonic sense as well; juxtaposed to corporeal love, the spiritual love expressed in *Urdū ġhazal* coexists with the mundane. Understanding an *Urdū ġhazal* can be a daunting task for anyone, particularly those who are removed from the Indo-Persian and Arabic scene. The force of the images, dreams, and the strength of the analogies, combined with the subtleties of words as used colloquially, set the mood of the *ġhazal*, making it virtually impossible to translate into another language. English, though rich in vocabulary and conceptual symbolism, remains inadequate in expressing the nuances of a distant culture and language. [The same would hold true if one were to translate Shakespeare into *Urdū*.] All of this combined with the extreme brevity of a two-line verse, makes the form very difficult to understand and interpret. The poetry of *Ġhālib*, the topic of this book, is a classic example. A good *ġhazal* has to be experienced through allowing it to sink in—it cannot be read only once; it entails a slow imbibing process before the spirit of the thoughts expressed begin to "uncompress" and an abstract expression takes shape visually. The deconstruction of an apparent thought in a *ġhazal* is a slow process entailing peeling the layers like that of an onion.

The *ġhazal* is made up of *sh'ers* (verses) that consist of two hemistiches each, and may be called couplets with the difference being that the two lines rhyme only in the opening verse, or where they form a *qit'a* (quartrain) or a continuous *ġhazal*. (The word *sh'er* is derived from the Arabic meaning "of wisdom" and hence the "*shā'er*," "*shā'eri*," "*musha'era*," all representing intelligence, reasoning, knowledge, and consciousness.) A verse has *qāfiā* and *radīf* the rhyming and repeating words, except in the first verse, *matlā*, in which the *qāfiā* and *radīf* are the same. The last verse is called *maqtā*, wherein the poet normally uses his pseudonym (*takhallus*), often to create a meaning out of it or to construct a clever thought. The meter is also very specific for *ġhazals*.

A distinction from Western poetry arises here as the *she'rs* do not relate to one another and are often singularly complete in the thought, theme, or feeling they portray. Though *ġhazals* often carry a theme, they can contain such drastic changes in expression that it catches the Western reader off-guard. The measure of a *ġhazal* remains the same, and the rhyming scheme is aa, ba, ca, and so on.

The popularity of *Urdū ġhazal* comes from its varied themes. The high etiquette required in writing *ġhazal* and the thematic limits placed on the poet. The most common subjects found in the *ġhazal* include the love of the poet for his beloved, her (his, see later) indifference, the broken heart, the cruelty of fate, the difficulties in passing nights spent in separation, the impermanence of human glory, the instability of life, the meaning of God, and so on. Many similes are used to describe the varied images and themes that form the core of *Urdū ġhazals*. The nest is the lover's heart, wherein the lightning (cruelty of fate) strikes; the nightingale (*bulbul*) loving the rose; the moth burning itself on the candle; the snare and the hunted bird; and the dagger of beloved's eyelashes all are common motifs. Also intertwined in the poetic narrative are references to biblical prophets:

Jacob's patience and his suffering for Joseph; the beauty of Joseph; *Zulekhā*, the wife of Potiphar; Solomon the wise; Jesus the giver of life; Moses' challenge to God to show Himself. As well, scores of anecdotal stories and themes are oft repeated: Qaroon, the rich man who was hanged for not paying taxes; the discovery and taste for good wine of the Persian Kings Jamshed, Kaikobad, and Kaikhusro of Zoroastrian days; Alexander of Macedonia; *Shīrīn* and *Farhād*, the legendary lovers of Persia, and their Arabic counterparts, *Lailā* and *Majnūn*; the warrior *Sultān Mahmūd Ghaznī* and his beloved slave, Ayaz—these are some of the themes that must be well understood by the reader of *Urdū* poetry. In addition, the poet has many personalities, some of them figurative, that require resolution; there is a *pīr* who serves as a guide or mediator, trying to dissuade the lover from his insanity; the prayer cloth and the black string worn by religious men; the wine, the tavern, the goblet, the decanter—such images are ubiquitous. The more sublime topics include descriptions of monism, dialogues with God; and the assertion of *Sufi* doctrines. The Glossary describes the details of these and many more topics common to *Urdū ġhazal.* A deep knowledge of the holy book of Islam, the *Qur'an*, finds many references in *Ġhālib*'s *ġhazal,* as do the vedantic beliefs and Hindu philosophy of life.

Despite the diversity in topics of the *ġhazal*, the most significant mood remains melancholy and love-sickness; a heart full of sadness is the prevailing theme, and rules for this were actually laid down by Arab critics Ibn-e Rasheeq and Ibn-e Quddama in the 10th and 11th century; Persian poetry, which has had the greatest influence on *Urdū ġhazal,* reinforced this theme. Held in supreme regard is the beloved and no expression could belittle the beloved. (However, see below how *Ġhālib* got away with this.) The *ġhazal* carries a sense of nobility, idealism, sensuousness (not necessarily a sensual aura) wherein the lover is inseparable from the loved. It is more like the 16th and 17th century English lyrical poetry, wherein metaphors play a significant role. Take for example T. S. Eliot's "Love Song of J. Alfred Prufrock": Love adduced in *Urdū ġhazals* is always one-sided, unrequited love, idolizing and idealizing in the same breath. The *Urdū ġhazal* poet is not merely creating a *ġhazal* from its many blocks (*she'rs*), but also representing the time he or she lives in. The vision of the poet as affected by his or her surroundings is overtly reflected in the *ġhazal*, a concept akin to Shelley's concept wherein the poet is the "unacknowledged legislator of mankind." *Ġhālib*'s *ġhazals* have also been compared to the couplets of Alexander Pope.

A rather touchy situation for the Western reader of *Urdū* poetry arises in how the male gender is relied on for the beloved. Translations, including this one, are made difficult in this sense. (As a result, I have addressed the beloved as female). The roots of this convention go back to the ancient Persians and Greeks; the Persians, with their homosexual preferences, found the young Turkish boys taken in as slaves very attractive. In the 18th and the 19th centuries, it was fashionable to have these young companions as confidants and cupbearers (*saqī*) to the point where royalty began to profess their love for them rather openly. As a result, the poetry, which at that time was mainly for the consumption of the royalty, began to express the love of a male for a male. (The Western gay movement finds its beginning in the late 20th century.) Soon it became fashionable to address the beloved as male and the tradition continues.

In brief, the *Urdū ġhazal* finds its roots in the melancholic romantic era of the *Muġhal* period. It was through the rise of *Urdū ġhazal* as a medium of expression that the *Urdū* language rose to its significant height of popularity and evolution in a very short time.

Appendix 3

The Life, the Times and Works of *Ġhālib*

The Life

Mirzā Asadullah Beg Khān, *alias Ġhālib*, was born in Agra on December 27, 1797. Both his father and uncle, who were of Turkish ancestry, died while he was still young, and thus he spent a good part of his early boyhood with his mother's family, a situation he would regret and that inevitably affected his self-image. *Ġhālib* received tutoring at home from *Harmuzd*, a Zoroastrian from Iran who converted to Islam, and who was a devoted scholar of literature, language, and religions. (There is a controversy in the literature as to whether *Harmuzd* was a real person or a fictitious entity conjured by *Ġhālib* so he could claim he had had a traditional teacher.) *Ġhālib* received no formal education of any sort and followed the tradition of private tutoring in various subjects. *Ġhālib* openly acknowledges his academic shortcomings. He was, however, a Persian scholar and knew Arabic well. Repeatedly, he has referred to himself as a Persian poet, listing his *Urdū* contributions as side efforts. Ironically, the fame of *Ġhālib* stems from his *Urdū* poetry.

In 1810, he married into a rich family and moved to *Delhī*; he apparently never cared much for his wife. In his letters, *Ġhālib* is very forthcoming about his life. He speaks of only one love affair and that with a professional singer; however, he did admire many women. In *Delhī*, *Ġhālib* lived a life of relative comfort, though he had great difficulty maintaining his aristocratic lifestyle.

Ġhālib began writing poetry in *Urdū* at the early age of 10 without having served under any *ustād* (mentor), as was traditional. He chose the pseudonym of "*Asad*," meaning *lion*, from his name, Asadullah, which means, *Lion of God*, given to him by his parents. Incidentally, it is also one of the surnames of the fourth caliph of Islam, *Haẓrat Alī*, cousin of Prophet Mohammad[pbuh] ; the pen name "*Ġhālib*" is another surname of the same caliph: *'Alī ibn Abī Ṭālib al-Ġhālib*, the "triumphant conqueror." Thus his names pay homage to the hero of Shia Islam, the religious form to which the poet was inclined and contrary to his family, who were Sunnis. He changed his penname after discovering there was another ["cheap," according to *Ġhālib*] poet who had used this pseudonym before him. *Ġhālib*'s writings graduated from pedantic to fastidious ingenuity with great complexity, rivaling that of *Mīr Taqī Mīr* in *ġhazal* writing, all before he turned 21. *Ġhālib* changed his course of writing to Persian in the 1820s and gave up writing in *Urdū* until the mid 1840s. The later works of *Ġhālib* appear remarkably seamless with his experiments 30 years before. *Ġhālib*'s obsession with material things and his sense of personal insecurity are abundantly visible throughout his writings. *Ġhālib* was never really a part of the court except in its waning era. He could not stand *Żauq*, who was *Bahadur Shāh Zafar*'s tutor. The King and *Ġhālib* also were at odds until the death of *Żauq*, when *Ġhālib* was asked to write the history of the *Muġhal* Dynasty. During these years, until 1869, *Ġhālib*, disgusted with the British Empire after the Revolt, remained confined to his rented house while he received a stipend from the *Nawāb of Rāmpur*. *Ġhālib* died on February 15th, 1869, at the age of 72.

The Times

From the beginning, *Ġhālib*'s poetry was controversial. Full of complex arrangements and archaic Persian constructions, his work drew much sarcasm and ridicule from his peers and contemporaries, similar to what the "University Wits" had heaped on Shakespeare. His prime literary enemies of the time were the established poets, Shah *Nasīr* and *Żauq*, who did their best to discredit *Ġhālib*. But nothing could stifle his art from reaching perfection, as was demonstrated in the publication of his collection of *ġhazals* (*Divan*) at the age of 23. Published in 1821, this is known as the *Hamidīa* manuscript and includes about half of the written works of *Ġhālib* at the time, exactly 3,776 lines. *Ġhālib* had deleted much of his work that he thought would be too difficult for many to understand. Novices to *Ġhālib*'s *ġhazal* would find many versions of these *ġhazals* with different listings of his verses; generally, the *Hamidīa* manuscript is considered to be authentic, although later, *Arshī* compiled a more modern version of *Ġhālib*'s *ġhazals* (see Bibliography).

The years between 1825 and 1833 were spent in futility trying to restore *Ġhālib*'s family pension, which was jeopardized because of family feuds. After losing the case in 1833, *Ġhālib* continued his efforts until 1844, when he finally gave up all hope of recovering anything from the British. This period of continual pursuit of the British Empire brought him closer to many of his admirers and pupils, among them the rulers of Rampur and Lucknow, as he needed their help and also as he traveled to Calcutta, where the office of the East India Company was then located. Many episodes of travel find a significant place in his prolific letters. Even the ruler of the *Muġhal* Empire became one of his admirers as he asked *Ġhālib* later to write a chronicle of the *Muġhal* Empire in 1850.

Ġhālib's desire to reach the royal court was achieved only after the death of the court-poet, *Zauq*, in 1855, which appointment included substantial annuities. Unfortunately, these favors came to an abrupt halt following the mutiny in 1857. The *Muġhal* court also conferred upon him two titles and an array of honors and gifts, yet his financial troubles continued, as reflected in his often-frustrated poetry. The two greatest sorrows of *Ġhālib*'s life were the death of the singing woman he loved and that of *Zainul Abedin Ḳhān Ārif*, his adopted son and his wife's nephew, and for whom *Ġhālib* produced eloquent elegies.

Whereas much of *Ġhālib's* life remains obscure, his quintessential letters to friends reveal some colorful aspects of his life and, as such, make for excellent reading in some of the finest *Urdū* prose existent. Revealed in these letters is his philosophy of life, his ego, his pride in his nobility, his imagination and ability to make critical observations, his criticism of the indifference of people, and the sense of frustration and bitterness that he harbored throughout his life. These traits of personality and nuances of emotion flow abundantly through his verses as well.

In 1865, the British signed a treaty of ascendancy to the *Muġhal* empire. This event would mark the ultimate decay of the *Muġhal Empire*, which had a significant impact on *Ġhālib*'s poetry. Revolts, orthodoxy, and a general decay of law and order, not to mention the fall of the dignified Emperorship, prevailed in those times. Though the British had ascended, people still owed their allegiance to the *Muġhal* Emperor, knowing full well that he was merely a symbol with little authority. To assert their identity, people took to religious fervor and split into warring loyalties. While the oriental culture remained intact, the Ẇestern style slowly crept in and the general sense of morality felt threatened by the most orthodox. Poets like *Momin* and *Ġhālib* even preached a revolt against the British. Above all other poets, *Ġhālib* took this changing environment to heart and, given his remarkable imagination, it resulted in poetry that is highly structured, complex and that sets the ground for an entirely new way of expression through unusual similes, highly dramatic exaggerations, and using techniques that trace their roots to very old Persian literature. This was also the era when another school of poetry began thriving in Lucknow, which is often called the "fleshly school." Carla Pietevich's "Assembly of Rivals" examines this issue thoroughly and concludes that the differentiation between the Lucknow and *Delhī* schools was arbitrary and that it is not justified to call the Lucknow school any "fleshier" than the *Delhī* school. A rivalry between the two schools also had an impact on how poets belonging to each school maintained their identity through their selection of topics and the art and craft of presenting ideas.

Ġhālib's poetry reflects a movement of thought, the product of a civilization standing on the brink of change, as he remained fully yet remorsefully conscious of it. Given the complex personality that *Ġhālib* inherited, he put a stamp of individuality on all his verses and, as a result, founded no "school," nor did he leave any heir to his tradition of individuality. Of all things, the legacy issue separates *Ġhālib* from the sundry poets of his time, who began a style—a movement—that was often sustained even after their death. Never had there been a poet who thought like *Ġhālib* and there has not been any poet since to challenge *Ġhālib*'s individuality of expression. In the words of *Ahmad Alī*: "Only a mind like this could feel and express as he could, hammer out plastic images from a piece of steel still red-hot on the anvil." It is difficult to improve on this characterization. The only thing that needs iteration is that the age of *Ġhālib* was indeed a period of Renaissance for the *Urdū ġhazal* and that he did receive great intellectual and literary challenges to enhance and cultivate his thinking and abilities.

The social order of the 18th century saw a great freedom of expression giving rise to many critics, such as *Saudā* in his satires and *Nazīr* in his odes. Whereas *Saudā* would engage in mysticism and *Mīr* would imagine post-existence, *Ġhālib* was busy looking at what had happened to the minds of the people of India—an emotional state turned to intellectualism. A bridging gap, if we can call it that, between the 18th century poets and *Ġhālib*, comprised two of the greatest poets, *Nazīr* and *Momin*, who worked on expressing how the mind shaped emotions. *Nazīr* talked about the injustices of a society degrading man and *Momin* of the trials and tribulations of a society ransacked by invaders. *Ġhālib*, however, took a metaphysical turn in his approach. He used the richness of the language of his predecessors more sharply to the point of near nihilism. The mid-19th century was rife with unrest among the middle class as religion took a diverse turn with many factions of Islam vying for attention, and *Ġhālib* did not remain oblivious to it. He was often blamed for having a *shī'a* and atheistic bent.

The Works of *Ġhālib:*

Ġhālib's writings comprise works in Persian and *Urdū*, wherein he wrote both prose and poetry prolifically. Following is a listing of his written works:

Persian Writings

1. *Panj āhang*: This book comprises five parts as the name implies. The first part contains salutations and etiquette; the second part entails lexicon; the third part is a selection of verses from his *Urdū* collection; part four is *taqrīẕ* (meaning ode to the living); and the final part contains letters written by *Ġhālib.*
2. *Mehr nīm roz:* King *Bahadur Shāh Zafar* had commissioned *Ġhālib* to write the history of the *Taimūrī* family but later, the King modified the scope and *Ġhālib* ended up writing a history from the time of Adam up to King *Humāyūñ*.
3. *Dastanmbo:* This book was written in the revolution of 1857 and tells of the events from May 1850 to August 1858. Published in 1858, the book distinguishes itself by containing Persian words free of Arabic or any other language.
4. *Qata'-e burhān: Maulvī Mohammad Husain Tabrezvī* compiled a Persian dictionary by the same name. In 1857, *Ġhālib* reviewed the dictionary and found it to contain many errors. He corrected these and published it in 1861 from Lucknow.
5. *Darfash kādiyāni:* The second edition of the Persian dictionary (4) included many changes and was renamed in 1865.
6. *Kullīyāt-e nazm fārsī: Ġhālib*'s first collection of Persian poetry, which was called *Maiḳhanā-e ārzū* (Tavern of Desires), was first published in 1845. The second edition, containing verses written through 1859, was published in 1863; the third edition was published in 1893 and the fourth in 1924.
7. *Subd chaen:* A short collection of *Ġhālib*'s *maṡnavi, abr guhar bār,* and other writings left out of earlier collections were published in 1867.

8. *Du'a-e sabah:* The Persian translation of the Arabic prayer is known by the title, which is associated with *Hazrat Alī* and was written at the request of *Ġhālib*'s nephew, *Mirzā Abbās Baig*. This *maṡnavi* contains 131 verses and was published in Lucknow during *Ġhālib*'s lifetime.
9. *Mutafarraqāt-e Ġhālib:* Some unpublished works of *Ġhālib* compiled by *Masud-ūl Hasan Rizvī*; first published in 1947 in Rampur, the book contains some letters, some poems and *maṡnavis* written by *Ġhālib* in Calcutta, and includes the *maṡnavi* written in 1853 to defend the reputation of King *Bahadur Shāh Zafar*.

Urdū Writings

10. *Dīvān-e Urdū:* Whereas *Ġhālib* took greater pride in his Persian writings, his real fame is indebted to his collection of *Urdū* verses. *Ġhālib*'s initial writings were heavily *Persianized*, but at the advice of his associates, particularly *Maulanā Fazal Haq Ḳhairābādī*, he changed his style and made a selection of verses himself that he considered intelligible to his *Urdū* speaking audience. The first edition of *Ġhālib*'s *Urdū ġhazals* was published in 1841, followed by the second edition in 1847, which contains 1,159 verses; the third edition was published in 1861, the fourth in 1862, and the fifth in 1863. The great popularity of *Ġhālib*'s *Urdū ġhazals* necessitated publication of frequent editions and printings, which inevitably modified the verses, partly because of typographical errors and partly because of the preferences of the compilers (mostly fans of *Ġhālib*) who sought to reflect their own interpretations. The most important versions of *Ġhālibs*'s *Urdū ġhazals* are found in the *Hamidīā* and *Arshī* manuscripts.
11. *Aud-e hindī:* Collection of *Ġhālib*'s letters published in Meerut (India) in 1868.

12. *Urdū-e mu'alla:* Another collection of *Ġhālib*'s letters, the first part of which was published in March 1869, and the second (which included the first one) in 1899 under the guidance of *Maulanā Hālī*.
13. *Makatīb-e Ġhālib:* A collection of *Ġhālib*'s letters written to the court of Rampur; this was compiled by Arshi and published in 1937 and the fifth edition in 1947.
14. *Nadirāt Ġhālib:* A collection of letters written by *Ġhālib* to his friend, *Munshī Nabī Baḳhsh Haqīr*, and compiled by *Mīr Mehdi Majrūh* and *Mīr Afzal Alī*, was published from Karachi in 1949 by Afaq Dehlavi.
15. *Nukāt-e Ġhālib-o-ruqq'āt-e Ġhālib:* At the request of *Piyare Lāl Āshob*, *Ġhālib* compiled two issues of a journal which include the grammar rules of the Persian language written in *Urdū* and 15 letters written in Persian. The book was published in 1867 from *Delhī*.
16. *Qādir nāma(h):* For the children of *Ārif*, *Ġhālib*'s dear nephew, *Ġhālib* wrote this 8-page journal in which he explains the concept of God. The first verse of the writing is: *qādir āllah aur yazdāñ hai ḳhudā/ hai nabī mursil payambar rehnumā:* (Powerful is Allah and Omnipotent is God/ The Prophet is sent to bring the message of guidance).

Appendix 4

The Poetry of *Ġhālib*

Poets like *Ġhālib* are capable of converting everyday—even mundane—feelings and occurrences into momentous events. When asked to recite his favorite verse, *Ġhālib* said that he would give his entire Divan for this verse of *Momin*:

tum mere pās hote ho goyā
jab koī dūsrā nahīñ hotā

As if you are with me, just when,
There is no one else around me.

Reading the above verse repeatedly affects the reader with the depth that only emotions can achieve when expressed through a craftily written verse. A good verse travels swiftly and directly to the heart. It does have a quantitative appeal.

Ġhālib was mostly inclined toward philosophic diction and thus he is clearly the first philosophic poet of *Urdū*. There are three types of poets. First, there are poets who talk about love and beauty eloquently, such as *Momin, Daġh, Hasrat,* and *Jigar*. Then there are philosophic poets like *Ġhālib, Asġhar*, and *Fanī*, who express their poetry through their expression of a philosophy of life. The third kind is the poet philosophers, those who express philosophy through poetry like *Iqbāl, Rumī, and Bedil*. Since philosophic poets are curious by nature, they are always discovering new ways to express themselves. As a result, they rarely follow any traditional style or theme.

Though *Ġhālib* was born a Muslim, religion never suited him, and throughout his poetry he seems to be joking with the Lord:

ham ko ma'lūm hai jannat kī ḥaqīqat lekin
dil ke ḳhush rakhne ko Ġhālib yih ḳhayāl achhā hai (175:10; #1087)

We do know the reality of Paradise;
However, for consoling hearts, the idea is good, *Ġhālib*.

In one place, *Ġhālib* clearly admits that he knows the rewards of piety and praying but somehow, he says, his heart still is not inclined toward them. *Ġhālib*, however, was a staunch monotheist as he states that "*jo duī ki bū bhi hotī to kahīn̄ do chār hotā*" (Translation: Had there been even a faint smell of duality, we would then have come across Him somewhere. He believed that God and he were the same and thus to see God would mean duality). *Ġhālib* also had a great ego, with a wanton style often aimed at himself. Fond of leisure, *Ġhālib* suffered much to his heart's discontent. There is a subtle queasiness, a vein of mercurial displeasure that runs deeply throughout his poetry:

zindagī apnī jab is shakl se guzrī Ġhālib
ham bhī kyā yād kareñ ge kih ḳhudā rakhte the (151:1; #912)

And when my life had withered away like this, *Ġhālib*,
Then how would we appreciate that we too had belonged to God?

Ġhālib liked fame and took pride in being elevated with titles and positions in the court. This aspect of *Ġhālib*'s personality seems to contradict his humbleness as a "lover," but in reality the haughtiness of *Ġhālib* mixed with his desire for fame created a rather irritating personality as viewed by many. Because *Ġhālib* continuously struggled for money and fame, he seemed to have spent his life mostly in disappointment. Though he accomplished much for someone in his situation, we cannot think of *Ġhālib* as a person who preferred to live within his means.

Ġhālib's intelligence was evident in several aspects, one of which is his ability to rectify his errors quickly and without fail. One person who had singularly influenced the style of *Ġhālib* was *Maulanā Fazal Haq Khairabadī*. Had it not been for him, we would be reading verses that only *Ġhālib* himself could possibly decipher. *Ġhālib's* initial poetry is extremely difficult to understand, and he seems to have used this style to impress others as well as himself. Soon enough he realized that until he "gets into the heart of the people," he would not be recognized. As a result, he discarded a significant portion of his verses in the selection of his collection. There remain many vestiges of *Ġhālib*'s earlier style and these will be pointed out as we go along. Here is just one example, the likes of which we were mercifully saved from, thanks to the efforts of *Maulanā Fazal Haq Khairabadī:*

Asad ham vuh junūñ jaulāñ gadā e be sar-o-pā haiñ
kih hai sar panj'a(h)-e mizhgān-e āhū pusht ḳhār apnā (24:1; #156)

Asad, we are those wanderers in madness, roguish paupers,
To whom the eyelids of the deer serve as the handy back-scratching claw.

Ġhālib was also above bias and discrimination against other human beings. He had just as many Hindu friends as he had Muslim friends. This created a rather subtle love for mankind for which *Ġhālib* is well known.

The Evolution of Ġhālib's Poetry

Mirroring his personality, *Ġhālib*'s poetry is very rocky and filled with slopes and inclines, peaks and nadir. Great poets like *Mīr* and Momin had uniform styles, great diction, and excellent command of language. *Ġhālib*, on the other hand, diversified his writing, not only as a result of his life events but also through the influence of different poets at different times in his life. *Ġhālib's* poetry can be classified into four types:

- The difficult, almost indecipherable poems, as exemplified above. The style of Bedil is abundant in these poems. *Ġhālib* removed many of these verses from his collection.
- The verses that create a kind of linguistic magic out of words, lacking any great underlying concepts. Here *Ġhālib* seems to follow the style of *Nasiḳh*.
- The verses that work like arrows and daggers, rife with poetic meaning, creativity, thought, and choice of words; these are done in the style of *Mīr Taqī Mīr*.
- Finally, the expressive and emotive style of *Ġhālib* that is full of *mazmūn* and *ma'nī āfrinī*, or thematic in the style of Momin.

We can classify *Ġhālib*'s literary life into five distinct periods:

- From about 1809 to 1821, *Ġhālib*'s writing was highly influenced by the Persian language and its various formal techniques. The topics examined are unusual and there is a high degree of exaggeration in his expression. The poetic thoughts are rather flimsy and much depends on the art of "construction," rather than "creativity." *Ġhālib* admits it himself: "In the beginning, I used to write in the style of Bedil, Shaukat and Asir. From the age of 15 to 25, I wrote mainly on imaginary subjects. In ten years, a large collection was created but when I got the sense to realize it, then I let go of this collection, tore its pages and left only 10-15 verses just for the sake of a sampling in the collection." Surprisingly, when we examine the works of Hafiz, such as the following verse:

سینه از آتش دل درغم جانانه بسوخت   آتشی بود درین خانه که کاشانه بسوخت

From the fire of love in my heart, my chest got consumed in the grief for the beloved;
The fire in the house was such that it consumed the house.

(*Translation by the author.*)

And compare the work of *Ġhālib*:

دل مرا سوزِ نہاں سے بے مُحابا جل گیا
آتشِ خاموش کے مانند گویا جل گیا

dil merā soz-e nihāñ se be muḥābā'jal gayā
ātish-e ḳhāmosh ke mānind goyā jal gayā (5:1; #20)

The hidden heat of love burned my heart unkindly;
Like a smoldering fire, it withered away to ashes.

دل میں ذوقِ وصل و یادِ یار تک باقی نہیں
آگ اِس گھر میں لگی اَیسی کہ جو تھا جل گیا

dil meñ żauq-e viṣl-o-yād-e yār tak bāqī nahiñ
āg is ghar meñ lagī aisī kih jo thā jal gayā (5:2; #21)

Neither longings for bliss of union nor the memory of my beloved remain.
A fire raged such that whatever there was in this house burnt down.

We find a remarkable similarity if we combine the first line of the first verse and the second line of the second verse.

From 1821 to 1827: During this period, *Ġhālib* paid less attention to his *Urdū* poetry, but whatever he wrote was less influenced by Persian and we see the style of Naziri (d. 1614) creeping in. There are fewer imaginary situations: the lover-poet figure establishing itself and the realities of life are eloquently felt and described. A period of maturation for *Ġhālib*'s poetry.

- From 1827 to 1847: Even though *Ġhālib* continued his efforts in Persian poetry, his *Urdū* poetry excels during this period, when some of his best *Urdū ġhazals* were written. For example:

miltī hai ḳhūe yār se nār iltihāb meñ
kāfir hūñ, gar na(h) miltī ho rāḥat 'ażāb meñ (98:1; #576)

The roar of fire mimics the style of the beloved;
Disbeliever I would be if I did not find comfort in calamity.

- From 1847-1857: During this period, *Ġhālib* was associated with King *Bahadur Shāh Zafar*'s court and consequently paid more attention to his *Urdū* writings. We see a mature style, an extremely delicate choice of words, a sense of humor, and cleverness in showing some influence of the style of *Ẕauq*. The meanings of the verses are deep yet expressed with spontaneity. See for example:

vafā kaisī, kahāñ kā 'ishq, jab sar phoṛnā ṭhehrā
to phir, ai sangdil, terā hī sang-e āstāñ kioñ ho (127:4; #796)

What faithfulness and what love, when it is merely smashing head?
Then, O! Stonehearted beloved, why should it be your threshold.

- From 1857 to 1868: In this period, the simplicity of the earlier period continues and we find a greater sense of wit. Perfection prevails but age is catching up with him; unable to concoct unique ideas, *Ġhālib* relies heavily on the style of expression and smoothness of diction:

hazāroñ kh(v)āhisheñ aisī kih har ḳh(v)āhish pe dam nikle
bahut nikle mere armān lekin phir bhī kam nikle (220:1; #1357)

A thousand such desires that upon each one I would rather die,
Though many of my longings were fulfilled, many so remained.

Every poet has unique characteristics that set him apart from other poets and *Ġhālib* was no exception. We can divide his characterizing qualities into nine specific categories.

Uniqueness of Style

Ġhālib's style is easily recognized and in fact places him among the most revered of all poets. Interestingly, he was fully aware of this, as he has repeatedly described:

haiñ āur bhī dunyā meñ suḳhanvar bahut achhe
kahte haiñ kih Ġhālib kā hai andāz-e bayāñ āur (63:11; #405)

There are indeed other eloquent poets in this world as well,
But it is said that *Ġhālib*'s style of diction is something else.

adāe ḳhāṣ se Ġhālib hu'ā hai nuktah sarā
ṣalāe 'ām hai yaran-e nuktah dāñ ke liye (235:14; #1460)

With his special eloquent style, *Ġhālib* has sung his subtle verses;
A common call it is now to my cohort critics.

yih masā'il-e taṣavvuf yih terā bayān Ġhālib
tujhe ham valī samajhte jo na(h) bāda(h) ḳh(v)ār hotā (21:11; #133)

These maxims of mysticism and your sublime oration, *Ġhālib*;
We would have taken you for a saint had you not been a wine-drinker.

What we call the style of *Ġhālib*'s diction is actually composed of several unique characteristics; particularly, the innovation in simile and metaphor, the words and imagination adduced. Even the tired topics rewritten by *Ġhālib* became interesting reading because it was impossible to reach the heart of the matter simply by reciting the verse. One needs to imbibe and delve into each verse, making the vision broader and deeper. It is this need to pay great attention to his words that creates the unique style of *Ġhālib.* Let me share with you just one verse that is as simple as it is crafty:

shor-e pand-e nāṣiḥ ne zaḳhm par namak chiṛkā
āp se ko'ī pūchhe: tum ne kyā mazā pāyā (4:7; #19)

The preacher's boisterous reprimands threw salt on my wounds.
Would someone please ask him, "What savor you got out of it?"

Apparently a simple complaint against the preacher in a melancholic style, but there is nothing simple about *Ġhālib*'s writing. He chooses a word, "*shor,*" to mean "noise" or "loudness," but "*shor*" also means salt, thus justifying the subtlety of *Ġhālib*'s verses. The connection between salt and wound is well appreciated.

The creativity of *Ġhālib*'s approach left us with many unique thoughts and imaginations:

lāg ho to us ko ham samjheñ lagāo
jab na(h) ho kuchh bhī to dhokā khāeñ kyā (47:3; #289)

Enmity, if there were, I would think of it as affection,
But with no feelings at all, how would I deceive myself?

na(h) thā kuchh to ḳhudā thā, kuchh na(h) hotā to ḳhudā hotā
ḍuboyā mujh ko hone ne, na(h) hotā maiñ to kyā hotā (33:1; #204)

When there was nothing, there was God; had there been nothing, God would still have been.
Drowned because I existed, how would it have mattered if I did not exist?

baskih dushvār hai har kām kā āsāñ honā
ādmī ko bhī mayassar nahiñ insāñ honā (18:1; #102)

Whereas it is difficult for everything to work out easily,
A man cannot even afford to be a human.

Ġhālib's creativity gave us a new language of idioms, construction of compound words, and new uses of oft-repeated words. New similes and metaphors created by *Ġhālib* became very popular, though few could use them with the mastery that he did.

haiñ zavāl āmāda(h) ajzā āfrīnish ke tamām
mahar-e gardūñ hai charāġh-e rahguzār-e bād yāñ (106:2; #636)

Destined to decline are all elements of Nature;
Here the sun is like a lamp in the path swept by a tempest.

ġham-e hastī kā Asad kis se ho juz marg 'ilāj
shama' har rang meñ jaltī hai saḥar hote tak (79:7; #481)

O! Asad! What can relieve the grief of life except death?
The candle burns, as it must, till the break of dawn.

ḳārgāh-e hastī meñ lālah dāġh sāmāñ hai
barq-e ḳhirman rāḥat ḳhūn-e garm-e dihqāñ hai (156:1; #943)

In the world, the assets of the tulip are its brandings;
Comforting to the peasant's toil is the lightning that strikes the crop.

dam liya thā nā qiyāmat ne hanūz
phir tera vaqt-e safir yād āyā (36:2; #223)

The passing of the Doomsday had barely paused, when
I came to recall the time of your parting.

Even the simplest thought becomes highly creative:

būe gul, nāla(h)' dil, dūd-e chirāġh-e maḥfil,
jo terī bazm se niklā so pareshañ niklā. (6:3; #28)

The scent of a flower, the sighs of the heart and the smoke from the lamps of your assembly;
Whosoever wandered out of your gathering, departed perturbed.

Ġhālib originated creative uses of unusual similes:

na(h) choṛī ḥaẓrat-e yūsuf ne yāñ bhī ḳhana(h) ārā'ī
safaidī dīda(h)' ya'qūb kī phirtī hai zindāñ par (62:2; #388)

Honorable Joseph did not let go illuminating the home even here;
As Jacob's sclera of his eye kept wandering on the walls of the prison cell.

The Love for Difficulties

Another characteristic that separates *Ġhālib* from other poets is his love affair with thoughts which is at times difficult to understand. Referring to the defective coating of metallic mirrors (often appearing as straight lines) as the letter *alif* (ا) and comparing that to the opening of the collar is just one such example. Reminding us of the trickery of creating a chemical moon by one *Hakīm* Munnaqqay; comparing the ring around the collar of "*qumrī*" to the lock on the doors to the garden; running in the wilderness without head or feet and having one's back scratched by the eyelashes of a deer; saying that the night is dark because the moon is looking upwards as calamities descend from the sky; referring to the rust spots in the metallic mirrors as "fluttering parrots" and declaring that the beloved is jealous thinking the lover is training the parrots to talk; invoking the old Persian usage of "back of the hand," "scrolls of declaration," and "tying hearts to the sleeve"; the wine in the decanter stretching its arms in boredom; the foam of a flood blocking the windows of a home—these are just some of the examples through which *Ġhālib* shines in rendering thoughts that produce great difficulties for his readers. The irony is that even where *Ġhālib* himself has clarified his poetry in his many letters to friends, the explanations seem just as difficult to decipher if not more so. Why does *Ġhālib* use such a difficult media of expression? I revert back to the uniqueness of *Ġhālib* wherein he refused to adopt any specific style. His style, therefore, is the style of testing the resolve and intelligence of his readers.

Implicative Style

The art of compelling the reader to draw inferences and perceive implications beyond what is specifically stated in the verse is where *Ġhālib* excels and in fact supersedes all *Urdū* poets. This clearly falls into the purview of *ma'nī āfrīnī*. For example, when he says, "What desolation it is that seeing the desert, I thought of my home," the reader must imagine whether the desert resembles home or the home resembles the desert and which is more desolate. Perhaps the most classic of the implicative style is exhibited in this popular verse:

ā'īna(h) dekh apnā sā mun(h) le ke rah ga'e
ṣāḥib ko dil na(h) dene pa(h) kitnā ġhurūr thā (41:1; #256)

Looking into the mirror, you got embarrassed to see a face like your own.
Madam! How proud were you for not letting your heart go?

Here *Ġhālib* examines narcissism, wherein the beloved, in looking at her beauty, falls in love with herself and gives her heart to herself. She then realizes the vanity of her pride when her lovers asked for her heart. *Ġhālib*'s work is full of such implicative verses that provide the experts with fodder for discussing the exact meaning of the verse. The plot thickens as we look at those verses that relate to his thoughts and beliefs of monism. To interpret *Ġhālib,* one must look at his whole personality. For example, despite all the troubles he experienced, *Ġhālib* remained an optimist. In his famous verse, "I hope for faithfulness from her; who does not know what faithfulness, is" should be read as: "I *do* hope for faithfulness from her, for she does not yet know what faithfulness is." The point being that the beloved is so young, innocent, and inexperienced that she cannot fully appreciate the trials and tribulations lovers go through in expressing their faithfulness. Once she is mature enough to understand, she will extend the bounty of her love to her lovers. By creating this implication, *Ġhālib* has drawn upon another element—the element of self-deception, audacity, and false hope that is very common throughout his poetry.

Condensing Volumes

A *she'r* is a two-line verse that stands on its own, without requiring any connection to previous or subsequent verses. It is a complete thought fully expressed. No wonder *Ġhālib* excels in *ġhazal* writing, because it gives him the challenge to condense a world of philosophy, a whole story, a prophecy in its entirety into just two lines. He himself wrote, "Think of them as a magical treasure of meaning; whatever words come into my verses, *Ġhālib.*" Some verses would take a thousand words to describe the scenario, the meaning, and finally the intent. Take, for example, the verse in which two birds are talking, one inside the cage and the other that just flew in and is sitting on a branch. "Be not afraid of telling the story of the garden to me in the cage. Why would the nest where the lightning struck yesterday be mine?" A highly melancholic arrangement: self-deception, helplessness, and friendship are all condensed into two lines. One can expand the meaning of the verse, creating many scenarios, many characters, and many stories to go along with it, attesting to a profound condensation of meaning. Another verse states: "When, if ever, the goblet came to me in her assembly, I wonder if the cupbearer has mixed something in the wine." Here the poet is waiting to receive the goblet, as he always does to little end. Today, however, things were different and the goblet did reach the lover. Now the lover is becoming suspicious as to why the goblet reached him. Is it because the beloved has mixed poison in the wine and it is meant for him alone? or perhaps the wine is so strong that others cannot take much of it, leaving enough in the goblet to reach him. Of course, the wine represents the kindness of the beloved. Does it mean she is testing him? And so on.

Humor and Wit

When we talk of *Ġhālib*'s style, we speak of its uniqueness. But what is "uniqueness?" Among other traits, the humor of *Ġhālib* sets him apart from all other poets of his time and ever since. Although there are plenty of poets who use humor, *Ġhālib* was a poet-humorist and not a humorist-poet. Whether he is taunting, being clever, showing wit, or being subtly funny, the style is entirely his own. Take, for example, how *Ġhālib* laughs at himself by offering a prayer for the longevity of *Hazrat Ḳhizr* (the legendary person who lives forever; see Glossary) just to make sure that at least one of his prayers does not go to waste. *Ġhālib*'s wit is abundant not only in those verses in which he entangles the beloved, but also when he talks to God. "Whatever insult he doles out, I would take it; for the doorkeeper to her home turned out to be my old friend." Here, a complete scenario of being roughed-up up by the doorkeeper is handled [as the poet is getting up, shaking loose the dirt from his clothes] with the rationalization that we are just playing around because the doorkeeper is my old friend. Other examples include: "We will take revenge on these fairy-faced creatures in Paradise; if by the favor of God, they turned into *hourīs* (nymphs) over there." Unable to get anywhere with the beautiful women here, the poet plans to get even with them in paradise. The assumption implies that the poet will graduate to paradise [given the condition of his deeds, this seems remote]. Or in one place, *Ġhālib* says that he is learning to paint merely to create a situation in which he can get closer to his beloved. The taunt by *Ġhālib* stings when he maintains that if the wine is given to people based on their ability to hold it, then why was Moses given the audience by the Lord in the first place when Moses could not handle it? And then he talks to the preacher about his wine of paradise, which *Ġhālib* ridicules as wine the preacher can neither drink nor offer to others. Is that wine? Another verse in which *Ġhālib* shines in his wit, sarcasm, and humor is when he says, "Why should we worry if you [the beloved] are in town as we will go and bring more hearts and lives from the market?" Here a classic situation arises. As the beloved walks into town, the lovers are afraid they will lose their hearts and lives, so they have put them up for sale, causing the prices to plummet [as on the Wall Street]. With such drop in prices, the poet feels he can afford many hearts and is thus not afraid of facing the beloved. *Ġhālib*'s cleverness peaks when he says, "All right, do not give me a kiss, but then give me a rebuke; after all, you do have a tongue, if not mouth." "Let us see what benefit the lovers would get from the idols; a Brahmin has said that this is going to be a good year." Idols, Hindu Brahmin, and predictions of the almanac are beautifully juxtaposed.

Deception

Deception lurking behind a veil of words is what *Ġhālib* offers best. "Who would dare to imbibe the heady wine after my death? The cupbearer is repeating the call after my death." Two meanings are possible. First, that after my death, there are no buyers of the strong wine, and cupbearer is calling for buyers. The other meaning is that cupbearer is repeating her call, first to others and then saying it quietly in disappointment. This verse is perhaps the most vivid example of *Ġhālib*'s creativity in describing human nature. Even the cupbearer is talking to herself in disappointment, as we do all the time. "How could I keep my life away from that idol? Is not my belief dear to me?" The first meaning is that sacrificing my life for the beloved is my belief and thus I cannot keep my life dear to me. The second meaning is that if I do not keep life dear to me, then she will take my belief—a belief dearer to me than my life. "When I wanted her to repeat her promise to behead me; she said laughingly, 'I swear I would'." The first meaning is that yes she would, and the second meaning is exactly the opposite: swearing upon someone's head means to pray for its protection.

Heart Stealing

Ġhālib steals the heart right away. "The luxury of a drop is to merge with the ocean; pain going beyond limit creates a panacea." *Ġhālib* says what is already in our hearts. "Look at the beauty of the speech, for whatever she said, I realized that this too was in my heart." "How would the pain of existence go except with death? The candle burns till dawn no matter what." Different verses appeal to different people based on what they are trying to find in *Ġhālib.* Everyone from lovers to philosophers finds something that interests them. And they all end up losing their heart to *Ġhālib's* poetry.

Favorite Words

Highly influenced by *Bedil, Ġhālib* loves his vocabulary, to which only a few can compare. Since *Ġhālib* used these words frequently, a style evolved around these words. For example, he found the mirrors made from metal fascinating. These mirrors were constructed by polishing iron plates that would rust in the rainy season, leaving green spots; also during polishing, there would be straight lines left in them. He used the word "*jauhar,*" meaning shine, talent, or the sharp edge of the sword. *Ġhālib* created many revolving meanings around this word. He visualized his crying as producing flooding that would inundate his home and destroy it; he found the foam of flood fascinating and compared it to cotton (because it is white like the foam). He also loved how lightning strikes, and in one place he calls the matter that creates lightning "the hard labor of the peasant." For if he had not worked so hard, there would be no grain and thus no need to strike it to burn. On the other hand, when peasant thrashes crop it products electric spark as well.

Projection of Reality

Ġhālib was at the same time both imaginative and realistic. He studied human nature closely, which is clearly evident when he said that as the beloved has arrived at his home, he is looking at her and then at his home in disbelief repeatedly. Or, when he says that seeing the beloved, a freshness comes to his face, which gives her the impression that her lover's condition has improved. One of the most famous verses of *Ġhālib* says: "There is no control over love, for it is a fire that would not start if tried and would not extinguish once started." It takes a real lover to say this, and he surely was one. At one point, *Ġhālib* tells his beloved that it is not fair for him to complain to her for destroying him, because his fate must have had a hand in his destruction. *Ġhālib* goes on to request that God give him more than one heart to bear all the grief He has doled out to him. *Ġhālib* did not complain about being grief-stricken, he just wants some help in handling it.

Envy and Jealousy

Ġhālib handles this common theme of poetry very differently. He does it with a creativity seen in no other poet. When told that the beloved is getting friendly with his rival, he laughs about it, saying, "It is not possible for her to be kind to anyone." He abhors his rival having any desire for the beloved and feels envious (not quite jealous) of the letter carrier because he may have talked to her. He asserts, however, that the beloved should maintain some connection even if it means enmity [you can keep your love for the rival]. When the beloved puts a string around her neck, *Ġhālib* becomes jealous of the string. In one place, he is afraid to tell others where he is going as he is lost and looking for directions, fearing they might follow him and fall in love with her as well. When *Ġhālib* talks about the beloved getting jealous, thinking that the lover is trying to teach parrots to talk, he breaks through all bounds of creative exaggeration because the lover is actually looking into a mirror with green rust spots, which the beloved envisions are parrots being taught to speak. The point being that the beloved does not want the lover to do anything but suffer in desperation for her. *Ġhālib* talks about a candle becoming jealous of the beloved and wanting to remove the glass shade around in much the same manner as the beloved, who has bared herself. *Ġhālib* also feels embarrassed facing the flowers that may have seen the beloved undress.

Expression of Love

The fine trade of love poetry is handled by *Ġhālib* in a manner that puts all others to shame. "You say that you will not return my heart if you found it; where is the heart to lose, for I got my wish?" The beloved is saying she would not return the heart of the lover [she has it], whereas the lover is saying I no longer have a heart left to lose, and thus finds his wish granted. The beloved is being playful, the lover insolent. *Ġhālib* often talks about love in words only lovers can appreciate and since most of us have at one time or other shared his feelings, he talks to us intimately. When he asks how one can lose the heartache, particularly when the heart is gone (lost), he is speaking the language of lovers. *Ġhālib* has expressed love in many different ways that appeal to all, for we can always find something that strikes our heart. "Even though the pain is life-taking, how can we run away from it, for there is heart that loves pain; Had there not been the sorrow of love, there would have been the sorrow of living."

Philosophy

Ġhālib is a philosophic poet. Whether he is using deception, similes, or comparisons, he never leaves philosophy behind. From questioning why it was necessary for God to create man if the destiny was pain to the movement of dust particles in a beam of sunlight, *Ġhālib* finds something to philosophize about in everything. He was greatly bothered by the idea of proof of man's existence and talks repeatedly about us not existing when we think we do. He "fights" with God about the need to create humans and then not caring for them. He is obviously turned off by religious rituals and instead conforms only to the doctrine of monoism, which he delineates clearly and eloquently. The beginning verse of *Ġhālib*'s collection finds the poet complaining to God [a subtle devotional verse] about who wrote these words [created the universe] where we appear so humbled [not humble]. *Ġhālib*'s melancholic moods impart a unique flair for expression compared to others when he talks about the existence of man, the existence of incessant pain, man's indifference toward his brethren, and the fact that we all finally get reduced to ashes. "Why then such tumult while living," he questions frequently.

Glossary & Lexicon

ا (*Alīf, ā, a*)

āb, water, edge of sword, luster.

ābād, populated, full of inhabitants.

āb-e bar jā mānda(h), stagnant water.

ābdār, shiny, sparkling.

ābrū, sanctity, honor, dignity.

ābla(h) pā, feet with water blisters.

ābgina(h), drinking glass, a foil set under gems, a diamond, wine, lover's tears, often used to mean heart.

āb-o-gil, temperament.

āb-o-havā, weather, climate, literally, air and water.

āb-e haft daryā, water of seven oceans.

āpaṛī, wrought upon.

ātish, fire.

ātish afshānī, scattering flames.

ātish-e pinhāñ, hidden fire.

ātish-e ḳhāmosh, smoldering fire.

ātish zer pā, fire (cinders) under feet, impatient.

ātish-kada(h), fire-worshippers' temple.

ātish-e gul, fire of flowers, often used as a simile for beloved's cheek.

ātish nafas, fiery breath.

ātish nafsī: having fiery breath.

āṡar, effect.

ādmī, man, offspring of Adam (the biblical Adam, the first prophet of Islam), the symbol of humankind. See also *insān.*

āżar fishāñ, blowing fire.

ār, shame.

ārā, embellishing.

ārā'ish, adornment.

āre, big saw.

ārzū, desire, yearning, wish, longing.

ārzū ḳhirāmī, to wish.

āzād, free.

āzār, hurt, torment.

āzurda(h), annoyed, hurt, sad.

āzurdagī, grief, pain, uneasiness.

āzmānā, to test, to try.

āsāñ, easy.

āstāñ, threshold.

āstīñ, sleeve.

āsmāñ, sky, heavens.

āsht'ī, truce.

āshufta, lunatic, crazy.

āshufta(h) sar, insane, lunatic, scatter-brain.

āshuftagī, lunacy, perturbation, consternation, confusion, commotion, disorder.

āshufta(h) navā, singing distressed songs.

āshnā, friend, beloved, intimate.

āshnā dushman, enemy of friend.

āshob, tumultuousness, terror, riot.

āfat, disaster.

āftāb, sun.

āftāb parast, sun worshipper, a Zoroastrians.

āġhosh, circle of arms, embrace.

āġhosh kushā, open arms to embrace.

āgāhī, awareness.

āge, before, in the past, in front of, in the future.

ālāt-e mai kashī, utensils of wine drinking, goblet and decanter.

ālūda(h), mixed, polluted, impure.

āmūz, experience, learning, skilful.

ānkheñ dikhānā, to get angry, to intimidate.

āvārgī, wandering, being vagrant.

āvāra(h), vagabond, vagrant.

āvāz, sound, voice, tone, clamor, rumor.

āhan, iron.

āhang, intention, harmony, music.

āhū, deer.

ā'īn, constitution.

ā'īna(h), mirror, looking glass, one of the oldest and most consistently employed image in Persian and *Urdū* traditions of poetry, an image of perfect truth and clarity, indication of a frozen state. The mirror plays a complex part in the traditional imagery of the *Urdū ġhazal.* A mirror is that which reflects the true nature of things, a symbol of clarity and impartial judgment, therefore an image of disinterestedness on the one hand, and clarity of soul on the other.

ā'īna(h) bāz, mirror juggler, one showing various faces of mirror, Lord.

ā'īna-e intizār, fixation in waiting.

ā'īna(h) ḳhāne, the house of mirrors, the hall of mirror, house with mirror-work on the walls and the ceiling reflecting the image.

ā'īna(h) dār, reflective.

ā'īna(h) dārī, holding mirror.

ā'ina(h)-e zānū, the knee pan, the mirror of knee (while pondering people often put their head on the knee, thus Persian construction calls the knee a mirror).

ā'ina(h) sīmā, bright face.

ā'ina-e shish jihāt, six faced mirror, vision, revelation, heart of Mohammed[pbuh].

abr, cloud.

ibrām, insistence.

Ibrahīm, the biblical Abraham. In Islamic belief, the son of Azar (q.v.). He is called *ḳhalīl* (friend [of God]), a title which God Himself bestowed on him. He is famous for his hospitality.

abnā, folks.

apnā sā muñh, face like your own, embarrassed, abashed.

itrānā, boasting.

is̱bāt, affirmation.

ijābat, consenting, complying.

ijārā, assurance.

ajzā, components, elements, part of.

ajzā-e pareshāñ, elements of perturbation.

achhoñ, good ones, beauties.

iḥbāb, friends.

ihtizāz, movement as in ecstasy, swirling in ecstasy, joy, exultation.

aḥrām, to deny oneself, the unstitched cloth worn around the body during the rituals of pilgrimage, pilgrimage garb.

āḥmaq, fool.

aḳhtar, star.

aḳhtar shumārī, counting stars.

iḳhtirā, discovery.

iḳhtilāṭ, love making.

ikhtiyār, control.

ikhfā, hiding.

ikhlāṣ, sincerity.

adā, coquettishness, charm, to pay.

idrāk, perception, comprehension, wisdom.

arzāñ, light, cheap.

arzānī, abundance, inexpensive.

iram, the fabulous garden said to have been devised by Shaddad bin 'Ad in emulation of the garden of paradise, paradise.

armuġhāñ, souvenir, gift.

arbāb-e vafā, true lovers, sincere friends.

az bas ki(h), to such degree that.

az dast rafta(h), gone from hand.

armān, wish, longing.

urti phirai hai, is flying, or hovering around.

asbāb, reason, cause.

ustuvār, firm, strong, solid, faithful, true, perfection, equality, evenness.

istiġhnā, obliviousness.

Asad, Ġhālib's first name, which he also used in his early *Urdū* poetry as a pen-name (pseudonym); he adopted the name "*Ġhālib*" first for his Persian verses, then began using it for *Urdū* as well, when he found out there was another "cheap poet," according to *Ġhālib*, who used the same pseudonym.

Israfil, The angel to whom on the Day of Judgment, God will order to blow the trumpet to wake the dead, according to Qur'an and Bible.

is rang, with this color or style.

is qadar, so much.

Ismaīl, the son of Ibrahim (q.v.). To put Ibrahim's devotion to the test, God commanded him to sacrifice Ismail. Both father and son gladly prepared themselves to obey but at the last moment God substituted a ram for sacrifice.

asīr, in bondage.

ishārat, hints.

ishāre, indicators, hints.

ishtiyāq angez, enhancing eagerness.

aṣnām-e k̤hayālī, fictitious idols.

iẓt̤irāb, restlessness, tumult, perturbation.

i'tibār, trust, assumption.

i'tidāl, moderation, balance.

i'timād, confidence.

i'timād-e dil, trust in heart.

i'jaz, miracle.

'ijāz-e masīḥā, miracles of Jesus (raising dead to life).

a'ẓā, body parts.

uftād, misery.

af'aī, black snake (compared to beloved's tresses), cobra.

afzāish, growth.

afsurda(h), saddened, melancholic.

afshurda(h)-e angūr, wine expressed from grapes.

afsurdagī, sadness, coagulation, dejection, melancholy, the condition of being withered faded, benumbed, depressed, or dejected.

afsos, sorrow, vexation.

afsūn, magic, charm, spell.

afsūn phūnkā, to enchant, to cast spell.

afshāñ, dispersing, scattering.

iqāmat, stopping, resting, staying.

iqbāl, good luck.

ikrām, honor.

ek 'ālam, one world, extreme intensity, all around.

agle, past (sometimes used for future also).

alāmāñ, refuge, reprieve.

iltihāb, roaring of flames.

iltifāt, being amorous, kindness, attention.

ulajhte, getting irritated.

alif, first alphabet of *Urdū* (straight vertical line referring to imperfection in the polished steel mirror and also to mean beginning).

alif besh, beyond beginning.

ulfat, love, affection.

Alexander the Great, See *Ḳhiẓr*.

alam, pain, anguish, affliction, grief.

almās, diamond.

amāñ, protection, refuge.

imtiyāz, distinction.

ummat, people, followers of a prophet.

ummīd, hope.

amīn, trustee.

an-al-baḥar, "I am the ocean" (Arabic).

intiẕār, to wait.

intiẕār khainch, to wait.

anjām, fate, conclusion.

anjum, star.

anjuman, assembly, banquet, gathering.

andāz, style.

andāza(h), guess.

andāza(h)-e himmat, measure of courage.

andoh, pain, grief, sorrow.

ando(h) rubā, sorrow relieving.

andherā, darkness

andherī, dark.

andesha(h), thought, worry, fear of something happening, suspicion.

insān, man, mankind, human being, mortal. There are two words for "man" in *Urdū*: the word "*ādmī*" obviously derived from the word "Adam," is the simple word, meaning "man" in the ordinary sense of the word. The word is often capitalized to indicate a greater level of existence as "man," often word is used to indicate "mankind" or "humanity" as well; "*insān*" points to a certain sophistication, goodness, and that condition which distinguishes man from the animal level of existence without suggestion of greater rationality or intellectual power, only more humane, sympathetic, alive.

infe'āl, pitiful.

angusht, finger.

angusht-e ḥina'ī, finger tinted with *henna*.

angez, exciting.

āuj, zenith, summit, height.

auẓā', traditions, behavior, postures.

auk, cupped hands (to drink).

aurang-e sulemāñ, throne of *Haẓrat* Sulaiman (honorable Solomon), riding which he flew in the air.

ahl, qualified, deserving.

ahl-e bīnish, those having vision, wise people.

ahl-e tamannā, having desire (to sacrifice for their beloved).

ahl-e jafā, oppressors, beloveds.

ahl-e ḳhirad, intelligent people.

ahl-e dahr, those living in this world; the word "*dah*r" connotes world being a bad place.

ahl-e suḳhan, poets.

ahl-e karam, compassionate, benign.

ahl-e naẕar, those with vision or sight, connoisseur, discriminating, those with passion or lovers, who love with discrimination, or love only that which is truly beautiful.

ahl-e havas, those with desire; often used to mean lusting lovers.

āham, important.

īmā', belief, faith.

imān, belief, faith, less accurately religion or belief, a concept integral to Islam, the only concept of knowledge.

ب (Bay, b)

bāb, door, chapter.

bāb-e nabard, someone worthy of fighting.

bāt, word, conversation.

bāt banā-e, to say craftily.

bāt pūchī, to ask.

bāt kā bannā, something working out.

bāḳhtan, to play, to lose at play, to give, to bestow.

bād, breeze.

bād paimā'ī, gluttony, measuring the air

bādā-e-shabānā, wine of the night, nights of drunkenness, drunk nights, euphemism for sleep.

bāda(h), wine.

bāda(h) āshāmī, drinking wine, addiction to wine.

bāda(h) ḳh(v)ār, wine-drinker.

bāda(h)-e doshina(h), the wine drank the night before.

bādshāh, King, mostly referring to King *Bahadur Shāh Zafir*.

bāda(h) noshī, drinking wine.

baidā', a desert.

bār, chance, burden.

Bārbud, famous singer in the court of emperor Khusro Parvez of Iran, he lived near Shiraz.

bāre, by chance, in short, because of, in brief, at least.

bār-e ḳhāt̤ir, tiresome, burden on mind.

bāz, agent, to refrain.

bāzār, market.

bāzgasht, echo.

bāzīcha(h), playground.

bāt̤in, hidden, intrinsic, the secret thoughts.

bāġh, garden.

bāgh-e-rizwān, the garden of paradise.

bāqī, remaining.

bāg, leash.

bāl, wings, arms.

bāl-o-par, plumage.

bālish, pillow.

bālīñ, pillow, bed, couch.

bāl-e ṭadrau, piece of cloud.

bāl-e humā, wings of "*hŭmā,*" an anecdote states that anyone coming under the shadow of the legendary bird *humā* gets lucky to the extent of even becoming an emperor.

bāl kushā honā, to get wings ready to fly, to spread wings.

bāndhnā, to tie down.

bāndhe, composed, tied.

bāñg, crowing, call.

bāng-e tasallī, call of assurance.

bāham, together.

bāvar, to believe.

bāvajūd, despite.

ba(h) badī: in bad words, deragatorily

but, statue.

but-e āīna(h)-e seemā, an icon that resembles the subject as a reflection in a mirror resembles the person reflected.

but-e bedād fin, an idol expert on tyranny.

but ḳhana(h), house of idols.

but shikanī, breaking idols.

but-kadā(h), house of icons or idols, beloved's house, house where beautiful women live.

bajā, acceptable, justified.

bajuz, except.

baḥr, ocean, sea, river.

baḳht-e rasā, lucky, great fortune.

baḳht-e ḳhufta(h), sleeping fortune.

baḳhya(h), stitch.

baḳhye(h) ke dar ḳhūr, capable of being stitched.

bad, wicked, bad.

badāmoz, to mislead, to teach bad things, to lead to wrong path.

bad ḥālī, bad condition, poverty, being destitute.

badḳhūīyāñ, bad habits, ill-tempered beloved, coquetry.

badr, full moon.

bad 'ahadī, breaking the promise, perfidy.

badgumān, distrustful, suspicious.

badmast, intoxicated.

burrish, sharpness, cut.

barham, to disrupt, to clash.

barāt-e ma'āsh, writ of livelihood.

barḳhurdār, possessing, enjoying.

barḳhurdār-e bistar, resting in bed.

bard-e liyālī, coldness of nights.

barsāt, rainy season.

barsabīl, for the sake of, by way of.

barshikāl, rainy season.

barṭaraf aside.

barq-e ḳhirman, lightning striking the crop, electricity of un-threshed corn, dry husk giving off sparks when threshed too hard.

barq-e tajalli, the lightning luster of the beatific vision, the flash in burnt Sinai.

barg: the leaf of a tree, a blade of grass, an instrument, arms, intention, aim, design end, power, strength, intellect, wealth

barg-e 'āfiyat, strength of security.

barg-e gul, flower petal, rose-petal.

barang-e dīgar, of different shade, of different color.

barrū, face to face.

bazm, company (at a feast or entertainment), same as "*mahfil*", assembly, get-together and informal meeting, meeting of intimate friends.

bazm ārāiyāñ, grand decoration of assembly.

bazm-e butāñ, company of idols or the beloved.

bazm-e beḳhudī, state of rapture.

bazm-e khayāl, assembly of thought, heart of lover because the beloved is always there.

bazm-e qadaḥ, gathering at the tavern, wine drinking party.

bas, sufficient, enough.

bisāṭ, place, floor.

bisāṭ-e 'ijz, state of humility.

bistar, bed, to make arrangements.

baski(h), whereas, though.

bismil, wounded.

bashar, human being. See also, *insān, ādmī.*

basharṭ, conditional.

baṣad, hundreds.

baṭ, duck.

ba'īd, beyond.

baġhair yak, without one.

bak rahā, making idle talk, babbling.

balā, calamity, evil spirit, fiend, distress, affliction, misfortune, catastrophe.

balā se, who cares, to hell with.

balāeñ, calamities.

balā'-e jāñ, heart wrecking, calamity to life.

bulbuleñ, nightingales.

bulhavas, whimsical, capricious.

balġham, phlegm.

bulandī, height.

ban jā'e, worked out.

banāt-unna'sh gardūñ, the three stars in the tail of the constellation of the bear, which has seven stars, an old Persian expression, literally meaning daughters of the dead in the sky because of their appearance as pallbearers, wherein of the seven northern stars, four are in the arrangement of coffin and three hanging, the pallbearers are also called constellation of women.

band, the binding strings, to close.

band-e ġham, succession of sorrow.

bandagī, submission, obedience, prayer, paying respects, dependency.

banda(h) parvar, concerned about others.

bane bāt, to succeed.

bun-e har ḳhār, root of every thorny bush.

bū, smell, faint chance or hint.

būturāb, drenched in dust. Mohammad pbuh addressed *Hażrat Alī* "*būturāb*" once and thus, this became his nickname.

būd, was, being.

būdā, weak, emaciated, loss of courage.

bū-e gul, smell of flower.

bahā, price, bounty.

bahār, prime, bloom, glory, delight, spring.

bahār-e nāz, blossoming coyness.

bahānā, excuse.

bahisht, heaven.

bahisht-e shimāyal, heaven like.

bahr-e āshīyāñ, for the sake of nest.

bahut, more.

baid, willow.

baiża(h), egg.

baiża(h) āsā, like an egg.

baiża(h)-e mūr, egg of ant.

bā īñhama(h): although

be, without, void of.

bayābāñ, desert, wilderness.

bayābāñ navard, wanderer of wilderness.

be ābrū, disgrace, without honor, respect, dignity or repute.

be adab, disrespectful.

bebāk, bold, assertive.

bebākī, boldness, assertiveness.

be i'tidālyañ, immoderation.

be bahra(h), unaware, ignorant.

be parvā(h), careless, oblivious.

betāb, impatient.

betābī, impatience, tumult, restlessness.

be takalluf, spontaneously, informal, unhesitatingly.

bejā, undeserved, unnecessary.

beḥijāb, without veil, immodest.

beḥis, refractory, numb, insensitive.

be ḥauṣlagī, spiritlessness, dispirited, lack of ambition.

be ḳharosh, without tumult, without noise.

be ḳhud, in ecstasy, one who is beside himself, lost in the love of the divine.

be ḳhudī, ecstasy, unaware of self, rapture, without self-control.

beḳhudī-o-hushyārī, obliviousness and cunningness.

bedād, tyranny, cruelty, oppression.

bedād gar, cruel person.

bedād-e dost, tyranny of beloved.

bedār, waking.

be-dard, unsympathetic.

be dast-o-pā', without head or feet (lit), shiftless, resourceless, gawky, lubberly.

bedilī, pessimism, heartlessness.

be dimāghī, spiritlessness.

be zabān, tongueless, speechless, in a pitiable condition unable to complain.

be rabṯ, erratic, disorganized.

be rabṯī, haphazard, disorderly.

besabab āzār, pain without reason or cause.

be sabab ranj, getting upset without reason.

be sar-o-pā, without head or feet (lit), making no sense, indignant, rougish, rascal, ruffian.

be muḥābā', without attachment, unloving.

besh, more (always use as prefix).

besh az yak nafas, more than a breath, fleeting moment.

be ṣadā, without sound.

be ṣarfah, useless.

bekasī, loneliness, destitution, desperation, hopelessness.

begāngī, obliviousness.

begāna(h)-e vafā, oblivious to faithfulness or fidelity.

bīm, fear, terror.

bīmār-e dost, lover, lovesick.

bīm-e raqīb, fear of rival.

be mahr, unaffectionate, unkind, unloving.

bīnā, seeing, clear-sighted.

bīnish, insight, perspicacity.

binā'ī, vision.

boriyā, tattered rug, rag.

bosa(h), kiss.

bulhavas, sensual, inquisitive, a fool.

bharam, myth.

bhed, secret.

bhes, disguise.

bhūl, forgetfulness.

ba(h), by (always prefixed to another word), with.

ba(h) andāz-e chakīdan, with intent to drop.

ba(h) andāza(h), according to estimate.

ba(h) bād, given to breeze.

ba(h) ḥasb, in proportion.

ba(h) ḳhūñ ġhaltīdan, laced with blood.

ba(h) rang, like.

ba(h) hirza(h), futile, absurd.

ba(h) hirza(h), futile, absurd.

ba(h) faiẓ, by the grace of.

ba(h)rū-ekār, to come face to face.

ba(h) qadr, in honor of.

ba(h) qadr-e lab-o-dandāñ, in the honor of lips and teeth, for tasting only.

ba(h) mohr, closing, sealed.

brahman, Brahmin, A member of the highest Hindu case, the priestly caste, the counterpart of the Muslin sheikh, the pillar of religious orthodoxy.

پ *(Pay, p)*

pā, foot.

pā ba(h) dāman, feet up in the lap, giving up.

pā ba(h) ḥinā, henna tinted feet.

pābastag'ī, restrictions.

pābos, to kiss feet.

pādāsh, reward, requital, recompense.

pār'a(h), shatter.

pāra(h), pieces.

pārasā'ī, piety.

pāra(h) hāi dil, pieces of heart.

pās, consideration, custody.

pāsbāñ, protector, sentinel.

pāsbānī, protecting.

pās-e vaẓ, regards for elegance or etiquette.

pāsuḳh, answer.

pāsuḳh-e maktūb: answer to letter.

pāshnah, heel.

pañba(h) āgīñ, stuffed with cotton wool.

pañmba(h), cotton wool.

pauñ, feet.

pāuñ dāb, massage feet.

pauñ dho kar pīnā, to be extremely respectful, to drink feet washings (literally).

pāuñ meñ chakkar, whirling feet, incessant wandering.

pā-e afgār, wounded feet.

pā-e ṭā'ūs, feet of peacock.

pā-e sukhan, feet of talk (literally), eloquence.

pa'e mūr, feet of ant.

pā'idārī, permanence.

patthar, stone.

pach āparī, to try to make something work, to make good.

par, feather.

partau, shine, reflection, brightness, sunbeam, splendor, light.

partau-e khūr, radiance of sun.

partau-e mahtāb: moonlight.

parda(h), veil, curtain, a musical note or key.

parda(h)-e sāz, a musical tone or sound, a note, a melody; the key of an organ, harpsichord, or similar instrument.

parda(h) sanj, a musician, a singer.

parastish, worship, devotion.

pursish, attention, inquiry.

parfishānī, fluttering of feathers.

purfishānī shama', flickering of flame of candle.

purkār, clever, cunning.

parī paikar, fairy persona, with the face of a fairy, angelic, very beautiful.

parī zādoñ, off spring of fairies.

parivash, beautiful (fairy persona), nymph.

pareshāñ, perturbed, dispersed, spread in wanton, spread, scattered, disheveled, worried.

pareshānī' ḳhāṯir, for the sake of distress of heart.

parniyāñ, silk fabric.

parvāz, flight, glory, radiance.

parvāz-e shauq-e nāz, desire to go to any lengths to please the beloved.

parvānā(h), moth.

parhez, abstinence, avoidance (as in the diet of sick).

pas az murdan, after death.

pastī, humility, down fall, nadir.

pusht ḳhār, a device to scratch back.

pusht-e chashm, back of eye, to show obliviousness.

pusht-e dast, back of hands (to express extreme regards).

pusht garmī, support, help, assistance.

pashīmān honā, to be ashamed or embarrassed.

pakṛā, caught.

palang, leopard, panther.

panja-e pusht, back scratcher, back claw. See *pusht ḳhār*

pand, advice, moral admonition.

pindār, pride.

pinhāñ, hidden.

pūjtā, worships.

posh, garb, attire.

phirtī, wanders.

phir gayā, reneged.

pahlū, side.

pehlū-e andesha(h), strength of thought.

phañsāyā, trapped.

paich-o-tāb, suspicion and indecision, to be perplexed, in dilemma, being perturbed.

paida'ī, existence.

pairāhan, attire, clothes

pīr, old man.

pīrzan, old lady; referring to the man who disguised himself as an old lady when he came to give the false news of *Shīrīn*'s death to *Farhād*, at which moment *Farhād* hit himself with an axe and killed himself.

pīr-e kan'āñ, the old man of Canaan- *Haẓrat Yaqūb* (Jacob).

peshtar, before.

peshdastī, forestalling, getting ahead of, anticipation.

paiġhāra(h) jū, slanderer, abuser.

paikar, face, countenance, figure, model, form, portrait, likeliness, an idol-temple.

paikāñ, tip of arrow, a call.

paimān, promise, undertaking.

paimān-e vafā, vow of faithfulness.

pīnas, carrier, palanquin.

pevasta(h), fused, merged.

pevand, patch, connection.

ت *(tay, t)*

tāb, courage, tolerance.

tāsīr, effect.

tā chand, how long.

tāḳhīr, delay.

tār, thread, wire.

tārāj, devastation, destruction.

tār-e barshakāl, continuous drizzling.

tār-e bistar, thread of bed.

tār-e nafas, line of breath.

tār-e nigāh, line of sight.

tāza(h) vārdān, new arrival.

tāk, a vine.

tā kujā, for how long.

tāke, stare, watch.

tāki(h), until.

tālīf compiling.

tab, fever, heat.

tabassum, smile.

tabassum hāe pinhāñ, hidden smile (smiling sheepishly).

tapish, pulsation, throbbing, beating, palpitation, heat.

tapīdan, restlessness, palpitation, grow hot.

tajāhul peshgī, knowingly appear ignorant.

tajallī, luster, dazzle, brilliance, brightness, manifestation.

taḥrīr, writing.

toḥfa(h), gift.

taḥammul, patience.

taḥṣīl, acquisition.

taaḥayyur, surprise.

tażkira(h), discussion.

tadbīr, workings, solution, effort.

tarāsha, carved.

tarāwish, dripping, coming out, become evident.

tarastā, crying for, longing.

tark, give up, discard.

tarkash, quiver.

tiryākī: opium addiction.

tasbīḥ, rosary.

tasallī, consolation, solace, comfort.

taslīm, acceptance.

tishnagī, desire, thirst.

tishnagī-e żauq, thirst of desire meaning love.

tishnah, thirsty.

tishna(h)-e taqrīr, thirsty to talk, desperate to express.

tishna(h) kām, left thirsty.

tishna(h) lab paiġhām, thirsty for invitation.

taṣavvur, imagination, fancy.

taṣvīr: form, painting, picture, image, effigy, likeness, sketch, drawing.

taṣavvuf, mysticism, contemplation.

ta'n, taunt, sarcasm.

ta'ziyat, condolence.

ta'zīr, punishment.

taġhāful, unmindfulness, being unaware, indifferent, ignoring, obliviousness, carelessness, indifference, feignins ignorance.

taġhāful hāi tamkīn̄ āzmā, indifference to test patience.

taġhaiyyur, change.

taqāẓā, insistence, reason, coaxing, demanding, importuning.

taqṣīr, excuse.

taqrīb, occasion, purpose, cause.

taqrīr, expression, speech.

taqlīd, following.

taqvā, abstinence.

taf, flame, heat, warmth.

tafriqah, distinction.

takrār, argument.

takalluf formality, observance of etiquette, ceremoniously, extravagant propriety, splendor in arrangement, profusion of good things, extreme formality.

takalluf bartaraf frankly speaking, formalities aside, without mincing words, or matters.

takyā(h) gāh, place to rest against, abode.

talāfi māfāt, rectification of bygone things.

talḳh navā, bitter talk, singing bitter songs.

tamāshā, display, spectacle, to see.

tamāshā'ī, spectator.

tamāshā kijiye, to see.

timṡāl, show, display, image.

timṡāl dār, producing reflection, collection of images.

tamām, finished, end.

ta'ma(h), greed, avarice.

tamkīñ, control, pride, patience, dignity, self-possession, wisdom, ability to analyze.

tamannā, desire.

tamhīd, prelude, preamble, preface.

tumhāre āiyo āge, a curse that it will come before you.

tan, body.

tan āsānī, desire for rest.

tuñbe: bitter pumpkin used to store wine, to make begging bowls and to drink wine from them. They are very light and do not break easily.

tan-e ranjūr, weak body.

tinkā, straw.

tundī, strength, stoutness.

tund'ī ḳhū, short temper, fiery disposition.

tunuk ābī, shortage of water.

tunuk ẓarfi, low ability, lack of courage, weakness.

tang, narrow.

tangī, tightness, narrowness, hopelessness,

tangnāe, tight place, narrow alley.

tang'ī-e chashm, narrowness of vision (heart), anemic eye.

tan-e majrūḥ, wounded body.

taubāh, vow not to sin or commit crime or be unjust.

tausan: a young unbroken horse, a pure-bred steed.

taufīr, to increase, enhance.

taufīq, ability.

tavaqqu', expectation, hope.

thā, was.

thame, stayed, stopped.

tīr, arrow.

tīr-e nīm kash, half drawn arrow.

tez, sharpened.

tesha(h), axe.

teġh, sword.

teġh āzmā, sword-trying.

teġh-e jafā, sword of cruelty.

teġh-e do dam, double-edge sword.

teġh-e sitam, sword of cruelty, tyranny.

tevrī, scowl.

tahī, empty, void.

tohmat kash, the accused.

tohmateñ, false accusations, slander.

ٹ *(tay, ṭ)*

ṭapaktī, dripping.

ث (say, ṡ)

ṡabāt, stability, perseverance.

ṡavāb, heavenly rewards.

ج (jeem, j)

jāda(ly), path.

jām, goblet.

jām-e jam, goblet of King Jamshed.

jām-e sifāl, bowl of clay, earthen bowl.

jāñ, life.

jāñ dā da(ly), one who is willing to give his life.

jān-e dardmand, sympathetic beloved.

jāñ sitāñ, killing, alluring.

jāñ sipārī, the offering of life.

jānkāhī, soul-wasting.

jāñ kā lubd, heart, skeleton.

jāñ gudāz, weakening, consuming, soul-melting.

jāñ gusil, killing, heart breaking.

jāved, long-live.

jāvidānī, perpetual, perennial.

jā'dād, property.

jabīñ, forehead.

jirāḥat, wound.

jurr'at āzmā, daring, testing.

jurr'at-e rindāna, courage of drunkard.

juz, except, part.

juzv-e ā'zam, major component.

justajū, search, struggle.

josh, zeal, intensity, enthusiasm, brimming with life, bubbling when applied to wine-cup.

joshish, violent desire, boiling.

josh-e gul, blooming of flowers.

jafā, cruelty.

jigar, liver or heart.

jigar tashnah, intense longing.

jigar-e tashna(h) āzār, liver thirsty for more pain.

jigar tashna(h)-e nāz, dying to bloom.

jigar darī, patience and control.

jigar-e soḳhta(h), liver parched with thirst, afflicted, burnt liver.

jaltā, sulking, see *jalnā* below.

jallād, hangman.

jalnā, to burn, to be burnt, to be consumed by fire or heat, burning with envy, sulking.

jalva(h), splendor, display, show, indirect manifestation, in the sense of the Creator being manifest in what He creates, direct revelation, as in the story of Moses where God revealed Himself to Moses.

jalv'a(h)-e bīnish, sparkle of vision.

jalva(h) pardāz, pardāzī means,"to write," and thus "to leave an imprint" or "to adorn."

jalva(h) tamāshā, display of beauty.

jalva(h) rezī bād, wind blowing.

jalva(h)-e gul, display of flowers.

jam, King Jamshed, who according to legend, invented wine.

Jamshed, Emperor of Persia, who, according to legend, invented wine and wine cup. He is also known to have possessed or invented a wine cup in which he could see the reflection of future events.

jama-o ḳharch, record of expense.

jama'-o-ḳhirj daryā kā, extent of river flow.

jam'īyat, groups.

jāñsitāñ tar, potent in taking life or killing.

juñmbish, movement.

jannat, paradise.

jannat nigāh, heavenly scene.

jins, commodity.

jins-e rusvā'ī, commodity of disgrace.

junūñ, madness or craziness. The word goes back to the given name of *Majnūn* the man who was mad, the most famous of Arabia's ancient lovers. King Lear has never surprised readers of *Urdū* poetry: he is simply a man who gains knowledge through, and in, madness.

junūñ jaulāñ, wanderer in madness.

junūn-e nārasāñ, incomplete and ineffective devotion.

jū, river, yoke.

javāñ marg, one who died in youth.

javāñmīr, died in youth.

javāhir-e ṯarf-e kulā(h), end of cap embroidered with jewels.

jū'bār, river.

Joseph, Yousuf.

jaur, cruelty, oppression.

jaulān, sprinting.

jauhar, power, real matter, talent, lines in the steel mirror, substance, talent, mirror coating, atoms, components, edge, luster, substance, genius, real essence, the true substance, nucleus.

jauhar-e andesha(h), intensity of thought.

johar-e ā'īna(h), lines formed at the time of coating in the mirror, green spots on mirror, mirror coating that appears as lines in iron mirrors and are also called straw of mirror.

johar-e teġh, edge of sword.

jūyā, seeking.

jū-e ḳhūñ, river of blood.

jū-e shīr, channel of milk. (Referring to the legendary lover *Farhād*'s digging the channel of milk out of the mountain for King Khusrao, as a condition of having his wife, *Shīrīn*.

jhāṛī, shook loose, brushed away.

jahān, the world.

jahān tāb, that, which illuminates, lends warmth to the world.

jahān-e ḳharāb, terrible world.

jahān hangāma(h), too much tumult and uproar.

jī, heart, spirit, courage.

jeb, pocket, collar slit.

jeb-e ḳhayāl, pocket of thought.

Jesus, see Isa (ʿīsā).

چ (chay, ch)

chāra(h), resolution, remedy.

chāra(h) sāzī, resolution of problem.

chāk, rend, sliced open.

chālāk, clever, smart.

chirāġh, lamp, a special kind of lamp—a round, open bowl of dried clay, with oil and cotton wick in it.

chirāġhāñ, display of lamps.

charāġh-e ḳhānāh, lamp of house.

chirāgh-e kushtah, burnt out lamp.

charāġh-e murdah, burnt out lamp.

charāġhañ sar-e rahguzar bād, lamps lit in the face of wind.

charchā, gossip, rumor.

charḳh, heaven, sky, wheel.

charḳh-e barīñ, wheel of heaven.

charḳh-e kohan, the sky, the celestial sphere, fortune.

charḳh-e mīnā'ī, blue colored sky.

chashm, eye.

chashma(h), brook.

chashmak, hinting with eye movements, winking.

chashm-e tār, line of sight.

chashm-e tar, wet eye, bedewed eyes.

chashm-e ḳhūbāñ, eyes of the fair (beloved).

chashm-e sozan, eye of needle.

chashm-e mā roshan, my eyes are brightened, I am happy.

chashm numāī, dirty looks, glance of reproof.

chashm-o-chirāġh, eye and lamp (literally), light of the eye, dearly beloved.

chakāñ, dripping.

chal nikalte, gone beyond limit.

chaman, garden, an orchard.

chaman ṯarāz'ī, decorating flowers.

chande takalluf: for the sake of formality.

chang, a stringed musical instrument.

chīn, wrinkle.

chhallā, band worn on finger.

chheṛīye, striking to play an instrument, to tease.

ح (hey, ḥ)

ḥāl, condition.

ḥā'il, interfering, in between.

ḥubāb, bubble.

ḥijāb, veil, curtain, bashfulness.

ḥujjat, argument.

ḥujra(h), cell, enclave.

ḥadīṡ, new, newly made, history, tradition.

ḥażar; caution, prudence.

ḥazīñ, sadness.

ḥarām, forbidden.

ḥarf-e mukarrar; repeated letter.

ḥarkat, movement.

ḥaram, the black cube in the mosque at Makkah, *Ka'bā.*

ḥarīṣ, avaricious.

ḥarīf opponent in the same profession, fighting opponent, opponent.

ḥisāb, calculation, reckoning, accounting.

ḥasad, jealousy.

ḥusūd, jealous.

ḥasrat, longings, grief, desire, to pine for, longing, regret, an unfulfilled desire to have done something and the consequent regret, the regret of failure.

ḥasrat sanj, holding unfulfilled desires.

ḥusn, beauty.

ḥusn-e talāfī, rectifying elegantly.

ḥusn-e tamāshā dost, exhibitionist of beauty.

ḥusn-e z̤an, self-appreciation.

ḥusn-e 'amal, good deed.

ḥusn-e ṭalab, asking politely, gently.

ḥaẓar karo, be prudent, careful.

ḥaẓrat, "The Presence," a title given to honored personages and often used as a sarcasm, someone sharp and cunning,.

ḥaq, God, reality, fact, truth, rights.

ḥaq shanās, righteous.

ḥaqq-e ṣoḥbat, rights of companions.

ḥaqīqat, truth, reality.

ḥikāyāt, story, tale.

ḥikmat, efforts, wisdom.

ḥalqa(h), ring.

ḥalqa(h) berūn-e dar; latch on outside door.

ḥammām, bath, Turkish bath.

ḥamza(h), legendary tale of Hamza, (nothing to do with *Ḥaẓrat* Hamza).

ḥavādis̊, accidents, plural of *ḥādisā,* accident or events unfortunate ones, beyond one's control or misfortunes one has to bear.

ḥūr; houri, nymph.

ḥayā, shame.

ḥairat, surprise.

ḥairat kada(h), house of surprise (mirror).

ḥairat-e naqsh-e pā, surprise of footprint.

ḥīle, excuse, pretext.

خ *(khay, ḳh)*

ḳhātam, ring with owner's name engraved, seal.

ḳhār; thorn, prickle, thistle, a cock's spear, jealousy, grudge, wick.

ḳhārā, hard stone, a tone in music.

ḳhār ḳhār; thorny.

ḳhāshāk, garden waste.

ḳhāṯir; courtesy, mind, memory, favor.

ḳhāṯir jam'a, to one's satisfaction, heart's content.

ḳhāk, dust, ashes, grave.

ḳhāk andāz, dust pan.

ḳhākastar nashinī, humbleness.

ḳhāk bhī nahiñ, not even dust left.

ḳhāk nahiñ, not even the dust, nothing, is absent, worthless.

ḳhāl kunj-e dahan, mole at the side of mouth.

ḳhāma(h), pen, brush.

ḳhāna(h), home, house.

ḳhana(h) ḳharābī, messing up of things (lit. destruction of home).

ḳhāna(h) zād, domesticated, slaved.

ḳhanazād-e ẓulf, slave of tresses.

khānā virāni, destruction of the place where one lives, desolation of one's home.

ḳhāna(h) vīrāñ sāz, destroyer of home.

ḳhana(h) virāñ sazī, to destroy home.

ḳhānah' Lailā, the dark home of *Lailā*; her tent was black, her complexion was dark and her name meant night.

ḳhānqāh, monastery.

ḳhabar, whereabouts, news.

ḳhajālat, embarrassment.

ḳhit'ah, hindering.

ḳhūbāñ, the good, the beautiful.

ḳhūd, self.

ḳhudā, God.

ḳhud ārā, self-adorning.

ḳhudbīñ, watching self, selfish, haughty, narcissist.

ḳhuddārī, self-respect.

ḳhuddarī-e sāhil, pride of river banks.

ḳhudā ko mān, fear God.

ḳharāb, bad, rotten, too old, intoxication, intoxicants, being drunken also signifies a condition of being rather broken, or eroded.

ḳharābi, ruining, state of ruin, desolation, old age, valuelessness.

ḳharāsh, scratch, wound.

ḳharāsh-e dil, wounds of heart.

ḳhas badandāñ, holding straw in teeth (an old hindu ritual of expressing humility).

ḳhasta(h), tired.

ḳhastagī, exhaustion, ruination, wounded heart, hurt, weakness, physical and moral, that results from having failed, fatigue, brittleness, moral weariness, the feeling of having grown old, sense of failure, consumed by the effort of a doomed mission.

ḳhissat, miserly.

ḳhas-o-ḳhāshāk, leaves and straw, litter.

ḳhusro, Amir Khusro, the famous *Urdū* poet, often regarded erroneously as the first *Urdū* poet.

Ḳhusrao, the Persian King (*Ḳhusrao Pervez*), the husband of *Shīrīn*, the beauty with whom, *Farhād,* the legendary lover from Persia, fell in love. *Farhād* was told to dig and bring a canal of milk to Khusrao's palace if he wanted *Shīrīn*. He did it and then killed himself with the spade he dug the canal with when he was told of *Shīrīn*'s death in an attempt to fool him.

ḳhaṣ, straw, garden waste, grass.

Ḳhiẓr: In quranic and pre-quranic lore, *Ḥaẓrat Ḳhiẓr*, 'The Green Man', identified with the mysterious servant of Allah and holy teacher of prophet Moses spoken of in the Holy *Qur'an* ('The Cave'), is believed to be the discoverer of the *Ma'ul Hayat* or Water of Life. The heart of the '*Ḳhiẓr* region' of Serendib, is Kathirkamam or *Khizr-gama* as the place is also known among Sri Lankan Muslims, who remarkably claim to have seen the ancient living prophet, or *Ḳhiẓr*, himself. To this day, an old Islamic house occupies the reputed site of the Ma'ul Hayat in Kathirkamam prayer, also known as *Khizr Maqām*, or 'the (spiritual) station of al-*Ḳhiẓr*'. He is a mysterious figure that so many claim to have drawn inspiration and blessings from. Some even claim to have met him. Often associated with the biblical prophet Elijah and St. George, the patron saint of England, al-*Ḳhiẓr* is identified, in the Islamic tradition, as an unknown servant of Allah. This unknown servant was blessed by God 'out of His own knowledge' with exceptional wisdom and the gift of perpetual life. Prophet **Moses**, commanded by God to learn of the higher mysteries from this servant of Allah, found *Ḳhiẓr* at the place where two currents meet and merge into the sea. Local tradition maintains that the two currents are the visible Menik Ganga, or River of Gems, and the hidden, or underground, current of grace and wisdom that issues from this site on the left bank of the Menik Ganga—Al-Khidr's Fountain of Life. Even prophet Moses himself, however, could not bear patiently with *Ḳhiẓr*'s baffling lessons on the paradoxes of life. With his third failure, Moses was obliged to part with his strange teacher. According to one legend, al-*Ḳhiẓr* was a general in the army of Alexander the Great. Still other legends maintain that he was Alexander's cook. Either way, the association of al-*Ḳhiẓr* with **Iskandar** or **Alexander the Great** has persisted from pre-Islamic times and is amply testified over much of south, central, and western Asia. To this very day, encounters with al-*Ḳhiẓr* by pious believers continue to occur. The two—Iskandar and *Ḳhiẓr* — are said to have come together in search of the Fountain of Life; *Ḳhiẓr* alone discovered and tasted the divine elixir. What Iskandar doggedly sought, *Ḳhiẓr* found without seeking, they say. *Ḳhiẓr* has three characteristics: first he never dies because he found and drank the water of life (*āb-e hayāt*), secondly no one can see him and thirdly that he guides the travelers who are lost. *Ġhālib* often belittles him, arguing that he has not used his endless life to any good effect; he had been deprived of the joy of dying (for love) and is therefore not to be envied; that he is hiding like a thief as people cannot see him or know him.

ḳhirābāt, tavern.

ḳhirām, walk, stroll, gait.

ḳhirman, harvest.

ḳhirām-e yār, gate of beloved.

ḳhirqah, beggar's clothes, tattered garb.

ḳhat̠, hair line, first growth of moustache and beard in a youth, down on the face.

ḳhat̠ā, mistake.

ḳhat̠ ayāġh, glass of wine, shot glass, line on the glass.

ḳhat̠-e jām, measure mark on the glass, meniscus.

ḳhat̠t̠-e ʿāriz, hair line on face.

ḳhat̠-o-ḳhāl, lines and beauty mole or curvaceous figure.

ḳhifāī, unacknowledged.

ḳhafqānī, patient suffering from palpitation of heart, hysterical.

ḳhuld, heaven, paradise, one of the several words for paradise.

ḳhalal, defect.

ḳhalish, pinch, hurt, pain.

ḳhalq, the world.

ḳhalvat, seclusion, privacy.

ḳham, curves, curls.

ḳhum, decanter, goblet.

ḳhumār, hangover, intoxication.

khumār rusum-o qayūd, intoxication of customs and restriction.

ḳham-e ḥalq'a(h) zunnār, curl of the ring of zunnar, the thread worn religiously around the neck.

ḳhumkada(h), tavern.

ḳhum-e mai, bottle of wine.

ḳhamyāza(h), yawning, stretching, expanse.

ḳhamyāza(h) khainche, to stretch, yawn.

ḳhū, habit, style.

ḳhanda(h), smile, laughter.

ḳhand'a(h) aḥbāb, laughter of friends.

ḳhandah dandāñ, big smile, showing teeth, jest, ridiculing laughter.

ḳhanda(h)-e gul, blooming of flowers (laughter of flowers).

ḳhanda(h) hāi bejā, untimely laughter.

ḳhanjar, knife, dagger.

ḳh(v)āb, dream, sleep.

ḳh(v)āb-e ḳhūsh, carefree sleep, deep sleep without fear of interruption.

ḳh(v)āb-e sangiñ, deep sleep.

kh(v)ār, abandoned, poor, distressed.

ḳh(v)ārī, denigration, meanness, baseness.

ḳhūbāñ, beauty, beloved, excellent.

kharqā, ragged garment of a devotee.

ḳhor, sun.

ḳhūrshīd, sun.

ḳhush, happy.

ḳhushā, joyful.

ḳhushā ṭāli', happy fortune.

ḳhushtar, better.

ḳhūgar, habitual.

ḳhū karda(h), habitual.

ḳhūn, blood

ḳhūñbahā, blood money.

ḳhūnnāb, pure blood.

ḳhūnnāba(h), pure blood (meaning tears of blood).

ḳhunnāba(h) mashrab, one who likes drinking blood.

ḳhūñ chakāñ, dripping with blood.

ḳhūñgar, murderous.

ḳhūn-e garm, toil, warm blood.

ḳhūn-e garm-e dihqāñ, warm blood of peasant (peasant's toil).

ḳhun gashtā(h), unfulfilled, covered with blood, killed mercilessly and left unburied.

ḳhu-e yār, beloved's or friend's habits or style.

ḳhiyābān, bed of flowers, avenue.

ḳhayāl, thought.

khyāl-e jalvā(h)-e gul, thought of display of flowers (as a symbol of goodness, beauty, peace, etc).

ḳhairāt, charity.

ḳhair bād, good-bye.

د (daal, d)

dād, praise, appreciation, accolade.

dādḳh(v)āh, candidate for favor, demanding redress.

dād-o-sitad, wheeling-dealing.

dār-o-rasan, scaffold and hanging rope, gallows and noose.

dāġh, spot, scar, speck, stain, stigma, blemish, a mark burnt in.

dāġh-e dil-e be dard, scars of a heart without pain.

dāġh-e kohan, chronic scar.

dāġh-e nātamāmī, blame of incompleteness.

dām, net, snare.

dāman, lap, skirt.

dāman afshānī, shaking skirt lose.

dām-e tamannā, net of desire.

dām-e shunīdan, net of awareness.

dām gāh: place of catching prey, meaning here, the tavern.

dāna(h), seed.

dānish, knowledgeable.

dā'im, permanent.

dā'im alḥabas, life sentence.

dabistāñ, school.

dajla(h), a famous river of Iraq, the river Tigris. Euphrates and Tigris are the most often-mentioned rivers in the tradition of Urdu *ġhazal*, like the Ganges in Hindi. *Ġhālib* does not particularly mean Tigris; any river.

dar, door.

darāz dast, arms length, far-reaching.

darāzī, height.

dar-e ā'īna(h), door of the mirror, in the metaphor, the mirror is conceived as something that you enter and go out of, a place. The mirror plays a complex part in the traditional imagery of the *Urdū ġhazal*. A mirror is that which reflects the true nature of things, a symbol of clarity and impartial judgment, therefore an image of disinterestedness on the one hand, and clarity of soul on the other.

darbāñ, doorkeeper, guard.

dar tashnagī murdagāñ, those who died thirsty.

dar ḳhor, worthy, suitable, proper.

dar ḳhur-e 'arẓ, worth presenting.

dard, pain (of life).

durd-e tahe jām, precipitate in wine bottle or chalice.

dars, lesson.

durust, proper, correct, fixed, removed.

darparda(h), hiding of defects, secrets.

darmāndgī, helplessness, sorrow, desperation, misery, distress.

darmiyāñ, in-between.

daryā, river, ocean.

daryā āshnā, ocean friendly.

daryā-e betābī, an ocean of impatience.

daryā mauj, wave after wave.

darīġh, reluctance, stupid, foolish, denial, refusal.

direġhā, Alas!

darūñ, inside (often used to mean heart).

darvesh, poor, indigent, a dervish, monk.

dastār, turban.

dast ba(h) dast, hand to hand.

dast-e tah-e sang āmda(h), hand caught under heavy stone.

dast-e qaẓā, hand of destiny.

dastgāh, excellence, wisdom, status, power.

dastgardāñ, things bought on mortgage.

dastgirī, assistance, aid, help, defense, protection.

dasht, desert, wilderness, where nothing grows, barren or wasteland.

dasht navardī, wandering in the desert.

dushman, enemy, rival.

dashn'a(h), dagger.

dashn'a(h) mizhgāñ, daggers of eyelashes.

dushvār, difficult.

dushvār pasand, liking difficulties.

du'ā, prayer.

du'āeñ, good wishes, felicitations.

da'vā, claim.

da'vī, claimant.

dāvat-e miẓhgāñ, feat of eyelashes.

daf warding off, driving away, repelling.

daftar-e imkāñ, world of possibilities.

dafina(h), buried place, treasure.

dallāl, broker.

dil, heart.

dil āzurdgāñ, who are broken-hearted, lovers.

dil āshuftagān, heart broken, lover.

dilbar, sweetheart.

dilbarī, heart stealing.

dil bastagī, connection to heart, to please heart.

dil-e be mudda'ā, a heart without desire.

dil pażīr, settling in heart.

dil-e ranjūr, saddened heart.

dilsatāñ, one who steals heart.

dilsatānī, stealing heart.

dil-e shorida(h), lunatic heart.

dilfareb, attractive, heart deceiving.

dil furoz, heart illuminating.

dilkushā, heart opening, glad tidings of heart.

dil kā kyā rang karūñ: how shall I color my heart; difficult to translate, it means how shall I handle my heart, how shall I let my heart bleed in the meantime.

dillagī, merriment, fun, amusement, musings, fun, good humor, to joke, to give one's heart.

dil-o-dast-e shinā, swimming heart and hand, courage and energy to swim.

dalīl, proof.

dam, breath, energy.

damgāh, the brain, the palate, the nose, pride, haughtiness, consequential airs, drunkenness, wish, desire.

damāġh, mind, intellect, haughtiness, courage.

damāġh kahāñ, where is the mind or courage or tolerance.

damāġh nahīñ, intolerable.

damāġh na(h) honā, inability to bear.

din phireñ, turning of fortune.

dam-e āb-e baqā, a draught of "*āb-e ḥayāt*" (water of life).

dam ba dam, all the time.

dam-e taḥrīr; time of writing.

dam-e-sard, cold breath, sigh.

dam-e shamshir; edge of sword.

dam nikle, impatience, to have intense desire, losing breath, lose something irreplaceable.

dandāñ, teeth.

dandāñ dar dil afshurdan, to dig teeth into heart (a Persian idiom used to advise extreme patience and tolerance).

dandāñ numā, showing teeth, being sarcastic, jesting.

dunyā, world, verifiable objects.

davām, world.

davāñ, running, walking fast.

do-chār, sudden and unexpected meeting, two-four, running into someone.

dūd, cloud, smoke, dark smear cause by smoke.

dūr; remote, far, distant.

daur; era, period, a round of drinks.

daur-e qadḥ, round of drink.

dost, beloved, friend.

dostdārī, friendship.

dosh, shoulder.

do 'ālam, the world and beyond, referring to this world and the next.

dū'ī, duality, the condition of having someone else exactly like oneself, possibility of being duplicated, lending one's essence to another being, duality.

dharā, left behind.

dahānā, mouth.

dahr, time, eternity, vicissitudes of time, fortune, adverse fortune, calamity, God as a ruler of destiny, the world, the customs, the manners, the habit.

dehqān, farmer, literally, one who works on the land, hence, farmer or peasant.

Delhī, the capital of India, where *Ġhālib* lived.

dhoke meñ margayā, got killed by deception.

dhūl dhappā, being physical, a row, slapping.

dhamkī, challenge, threat.

dai, 10th month of Persian calendar (fall); *Urdū:* 2nd month of Persian calendar (meaning spring).

dīd, view.

dīdār, glimpse, sight.

dīda(h), eye.

dīd'a(h)-e bīnā, eye of vision, eye of a wise man, the eye that can see.

dīda(h)-o-dil firsh-e rāh, eyes and heart spread in the path, highest regards.

dīda(h)-e ḳhunnāba(h) fishāñ, blood crying eyes.

dīñ, faith, religion, belief in existence (of Man, God, objects). *Ġhālib* often finds himself doubting the existence of the world. Does the world really exist? Or, is it merely the creation, or reflection, of senses?.

dīñdār, religious.

dīvāre ju, looking for a wall.

dīvān, collection of verses, volume, a collection of poems by a single author. A *dīvān* is normally arranged in alphabetical order by the last letter of the *radif* (refrain)—but not by the next-to-last, so that the poet is able to make his own arrangement.

divāng'ī-e shauq, craziness of desire.

ڈ (ḍaal, ḍ)

ḍuboyā, drowned, destroyed, sank, disgraced.

ḍubī hū'ī asāmī, sunken investment, from where a levy cannot be collected.

ذ (żaal, ż)

żaa't, self, essence or radical constituent of self.

żarra(h), speck, particle.

żarī'ah, source.

żikr, discussion, story telling.

żillat, disgrace.

żalīl, mean, contemptible.

żauq, passion, taste, desire.

żauq-e asirī, desire to be captured or imprisoned.

żauq-e kāvish nāḳhūn, taste for the efforts of nails, sweet pain of the nail's laceration.

ر (ray, r)

rāḥat, comfort.

rāz, secret.

rāzdāñ, secret keeper, confidant.

rāg, one of the six modes in classical music.

rāg alapnā, being repetitive.

rāhzan, robber.

rāh-e suḳhan, means of communication.

rāh guzar, path.

rabb, God, Lord (in *Urdū* and Persian, it means someone who is the highest of all beings).

rabāb, a type of violin.

rubā'ī. Quatrain, a four-line poem in one or more of a group of traditionally prescribed meters, and usually rhyming AABA.

rutbā, place of honor, an office carrying authority and dignity.

rabṯ, connection.

raḥmat, Lord, kindness.

raḳhsh, horse (Rustam's horse).

raḳhshinda(h), bright, shining.

ruḳh, face.

ruḳhsār; cheek.

ruḳhṣat, to let go, depart.

radd, reject.

radīf refrain, in a *ġhazal*, the identically repeated word or words at the end of the second line of each two-line verse, after the *qāfiyah*. A *radīf* is extremely common but not compulsory.

radīf-e shi'r; the ending repetitive word of verse.

rizq, staple, food, that which is consumed, that which nourishes.

rasā, getting, reaching.

rastḳhez andāza(h), like the Doomsday or the Day of Resurrection, tumult.

rasm-o-rāh, acquaintance.

rusvā, disgraced, infamous, notorious, dishonored.

rusvā'ī, disgrace, defamation, embarrassment.

rusūm, traditions.

rusūm-o quyūd, traditions and restrictions.

rishta(h), relationship, connection, thread.

rishta(h)-e shama', candle wick.

rishta(h)' gohar: thread used to string pearls.

rashk, envy, jealousy.

rizvāñ, guard to heaven, the gatekeeper of paradise and keeper of its gardens.

ra'nāī' khayāl, loveliness of thought.

raft, going.

raftār, speed.

rafta(h), gone, at times used to mean *farīfta*(*h*) (in love or enamored).

rafū, darning, repair, stitch.

raqīb, beloved's lover, rival.

rakāb, saddle foot hold, stirrup.

rag, vein.

rag-e jāñ, artery of life, jugular vein.

rag-e gardan, vein in the neck.

rag-e-sang, vein or sinew of the stone.

ram, to flee.

ranjish, misunderstanding.

ranjūrī, sickness.

rindāñ, the drinkers.

rind, wine addict, a drunkard.

rang, color, presentation, state.

rang-e shikasta(h), faded colour, pale color.

rang lāve gī, would make something happen.

rau, swing, act of going.

ravā, going, restarted.

ravānī, flow.

ravānī' ravish, flowing gait.

rūbarū, face to face.

rūbakār, appearance, face to face.

roz-e jazā, Day of Judgment or Retribution.

roz-e siyāh, black or gloomy day, day of mourning.

roze ḥashr, Day of Judgment.

rauzan, small window, small openings in the wall to let the light in, casement window.

rūsiyā(h) : one whose face is blackened, someone disgraced, unfortunate, or infamous.

ravish, ways, manners, mode, style, path, trend.

roshan, bright, illuminated.

raundī, trampled.

raunaq, luster, splendor, sprightliness.

rūkash, surface, coating.

rū'edād, story, the story of that which has happened.

rū'e nigār, face of beloved.

rūḥ-e nabātī, soul of plants.

rūḥ-ul-quds, the angel of revelation, Gabriel.

rahbar, directing.

rahzan, robber.

rahguzar, path.

rahn, mortgage, pledge, pawn.

rahnumā, guide.

rahīn, dedicated, engrossed.

riyāī, hypocrisy.

reḳhte, mixture of many, it means the *Urdū* language, particularly *Urdū ġhazal.*

rezish, to fall.

resh, wound.

resha(h), vein, roots, tissue, fiber.

reshgī, fibrousness–meant here tenderness.

ز (zay, z)

zār zār, bitterly, severely.

zāhid, preacher, abstinent, devout, zealot, recluse, one who shuns the pleasures of this world.

zabān, tongue.

zabāñ hāi lāl, dumb tongues.

zabān kaṭtī, interrupting rudely, cutting tongue.

zabaskih, because, whereas.

zabūñ, weak.

zabūnī, weakness.

zaḥmat, difficulty, inconvenience.

zaḳhm, wound.

zaḳhm-e teġh, wound from sword.

zaḳhm-e kārī, deep wound.

zakāt, charity (required giving by Islamic tenet).

Zakarīa: a Prophet of Islam.

zamānā, the world, that which encompassed it, time but differentiated from "*waqt*" (time) by defining a certain length of it, an era, revolutions of heaven.

zūd pashemāñ, quick repenter, one who is quick to recognize mistakes.

z'um, presumption, pretending.

zahr, poison.

zahrāb, dirty, stagnant or envenomed water.

zahra(h), spleen, the sign of courage.

zahara(h)-e abr āb, melting out of clouds.

zahr lagnā, to be like poison, to hate, unbearable.

س (seen, s)

sāt iqlīm, seven continents, the entire world.

sādgī, simplicity, naïveté.

sādgī āmoz, adapting simplicity.

sādgī-o-purkārī, simplicity and deception.

sada(h), simple.

sāda(h) dil, simpleton at heart.

sāḥil, bank of river, beach.

sāz, apparatus, instrument.

sāz-e ṣadā-e āb, water reeds.

sāġhar, goblet.

sāġhar-e jam, bowl of King Jamshed. See Jamshed.

sāf durdī kash, wine with precipitate removed.

sāqī, the cupbearer, beloved, the beautiful youth who pours the wine, the symbol of beloved (human or divine), or love, or beauty or of any ideal that inspires.

sākinān, inhabitants.

sāl, age, year.

sāmān, cause.

sāmāñ ṭarāz, provider of things.

sāya(h), shadow.

sā'il, beggar.

sāe(h), shadow.

sabza(h), greenery, grass.

sabza(h)-e ḳhaṭ, the green tinge of hair growing on face, down on the face.

subuk, light, disrespected.

subuk dast, expert, dexterous.

sabuk-sar, humble, light headed, sober.

sabza(h)' nauḳhez, new growth of greenery.

sabū, tumbler.

subḥ', rosary.

subḥ-o-zunnār, rosary and sacred thread.

subḥ ṣad dāna(h), rosary with a hundred beads.

sipās, kindness, approval, grace, favor, gratitude.

sipand, black rue seed thrown in fire; if cracks down, it protects from evil.

satānā, teasing.

sitāish, praise.

sitam, torture, oppression.

siṯam ijād, discoverer of new cruelties.

sitam ẓarīf who practices tyranny in a subtle and dexterous way.

sitam kash, bearing cruelty.

sitamgar, punisher, tyrant.

sajjādah, floor mat, the rug or carpet on which Muslims worship.

sajda(h), supplication, prostration, a Muslim form of worship, often used to indicate a form of salute.

saḳht kam āzār, hardly giving any woes.

saḳhtī, difficulty, hardness.

saḥr, magic.

suḳhan, poetry, words.

suḳhan āzurda(h), quiet, unable to speak.

sar, head.

sarā, recitation.

sarāb, mirage.

sarāpā nāz, completely coquettish, coquettish head to toe.

sarāsar, all over, thoughout, all around.

surāġh, sign, lead, clue, tracking.

sar angusht-e ḥinā, tip of *henna* tinted finger.

sarbasar, totally, equally, head to head.

sar ta sar-e ḳhāk, entire earth.

sard, dull, cold.

sarshār, intoxicated, brimful.

sarishtah dārī, ruling.

sar karnā, to win.

sar gashtagī, frenzy, lunacy.

sar-garān, angry, person with a heavy head.

sargarm, excited, busy.

sargushta(h), lost.

sarmāya(h), asset, substance, capital.

surma(h), black antimony powder used to decorate eyes.

sarnavisht, fate, destiny, written on the forehead.

sarv, cypress tree.

sar-o-barg, resource.

sarv-e chirāġhāñ, graceful display of lamps, an ancient punishment whereby holes were drilled in the head to install candles in them.

sarv qāmat, of the stature of cypress tree (meaning tall).

sarv-o-ṣanūbar, cypress and pine (fir).

sazā, punishment.

Sa'di, the great thirteenth-century Persian poet and prose writer, especially famous for his *Gulistān*, a collection of short humorous and moral anecdotes.

sa'ī, help, endeavor, effort.

sufrah, provision prepared by men of hospitality for strangers, travelers and the poor.

saṭḥ, surface, face.

siṭvat, awe, reverence.

safaidī, whitewash.

safaidī-e dīda(h), sclera of eye.

safīna(h), fleet, notebook, boat.

silī', blow, strike.

salamander, see *samandar*.

silk-e 'āfiyat, relationship to comfort and rest.

salṯanat, kingdom.

samā', listening to music.

samand, horse, steed.

samandar, A mythical creature, Salamander, a lizard that lives in fire that had remained lit for at least a few centuries that dies if taken out of fire. From the days of Plinius, the salamander has been considered to be an extremely "cold" animal, which can extinguish fire. In Islamic folklore it is sometimes thought to have been born in fire and is, at least from the 13th century onwards, regarded as a bird, not as a reptile—perhaps confused with the Phoenix, which is reborn out of fire. This misconnect appears routinely in the majority of Persian poets in the Middle Ages when they regarded salamander as a bird. According to *Ibn Sīda*, salamander is "a creeping animal known among the Indians and Chinese." It is correct poetically though not scientifically.

samandar, ocean, Salamander, see above.

samjhā, admonished, understood.

sunā'e na(h) bane, no way to get heard.

sum, presenting poison.

Sinai, see *Tūr*, Musa.

sanj, performing.

sanjāb, mink.

sang, stone.

sang-e āstāñ, threshold stone.

soḳhtan, to burn.

sivā, except.

sau jā, hundreds of places.

sūd, profit, interest charged on loans or paid on loans.

saudā, trade, connection, dealing.

saudā(h), insane, crazy, melancholic.

sūr, image, appearance.

soz, burning.

sozan, needle.

sozish, burning.

soz-e ġham, burning of pain.

soz-e nihāñ, hidden burning or sorrow.

saunpī, given.

sūe, towards.

suvaidā, black spot, a mole, scar in heart, black part of eye.

sū'ī z̤ann, suspicion.

siyāh, black, dark.

siya(h) mast, extremely ecstatic, intoxicated.

siya(h) mastī, intense or deep ecstasy.

siyāhī, ink.

sair, amusement.

sīl'ī, slap.

sail, flood.

sailāb, flood.

sīmā, appearance.

sīmāb, mercury.

sīm tan, white complexioned body.

sīna(h), chest.

sīna(h) gudāz, that which can melt the heart, heart rending.

ش (*sheen, sh*)

shād, delighted.

shādāb, refreshing.

shādī, happiness.

shān, dignity.

shāna(h), shoulder.

shāne, comb.

shā'iba(h), mixture, impurity, suspicion, doubt.

shāyād, perhaps.

shāhid, observer, evident.

shab, night.

shabro, night time burglar.

shabistāñ, sleeping place, secluded bed chamber, private quarters, resting place.

shab-e firāq, night of separation.

shabnamistāñ, dew covered land.

sharar, spark, fire, shedding, throwing.

sharār-e jasta(h), flying spark.

sharḥ, explanation, to open.

shar'a, Muslim religious laws.

sharf glory.

sharm, embarrassment, modesty.

sharmsār, ashamed.

sharminda(h)', ashamed, regretting.

sharminda(h)' ma'nī, fulfilling its meaning.

sharm-e nārasāī', embarrassment for not reaching to God.

shash jihat, in six directions, all over, the Universe.

she'r, a distich or two-line verse, treated in the *ġhazal* as an independent poetic unit; both lines must be in the same meter and must make a complete poetic effect of their own, without regard to the rest of the poem. The second line must end in the rhyming elements (*qāfiyah* definitely, and in most *ġhazals radīf* as well).

sho'la(h), flame.

sho'la(h) āvāz, fiery sound.

sho'la(h) javāla(h), leaping flame.

shifā, recovery from illness.

shafaq, red lining of sky, orange dusk.

shaq, rent asunder.

shak, doubt.

shikāyat, complaint.

shikāyat hāi rangīñ, loud plaint.

shikast, defeat, breaking, inner discord, note of music which does not agree or harmonize with the rest.

shikast-e ārzū, defeat of desire, loss of desire.

shikast-e dil, breaking of heart.

shikast-e qīmat, loss of value.

shikasta(h), pale, weak, broken.

shikastan, breaking.

shakl-e nihālī, ornamental marks on carpet or bedspread, gladdening image.

shikeb, patience.

shikeb-o-ṣabr, control and patience.

shikva(h) sanj, complainer.

shagufta(h), blooming.

shumār, count.

shuguftagī, freshness.

shama', candle.

shama'-e bālīñ, candle at the head of bed.

shamaʿ-e kushta(h), extinguished candle, candle just put out.

shanīdan, to hear, listen, or attend to.

shināvar, swimmer.

shoḳh, playful, mischievous, bold.

shoḳhī, coquetry, playfulness.

shoḳh-e tund khū, coquettish ill-tempered, beloved.

shor, outcry, lunacy, salt.

shor-e junūñ, tumult of frenzy.

shor-e jaulāñ, noise of running horses.

shorish, confusion, tumult, rebellion, agitation, passion, direct, powerful expression of the lover's experience of life.

shoridah, frenzied, mad.

shorida(h) ḥāl, lunatic.

shauq, desire, taste, fancy, zeal, eagerness, interest, attachment, yearning, predilection for, ardor, zeal.

shauq-e fuẓūl, exuberant desire.

shahpar, aileron, propeller.

shahr-e ārzū, city of aspiration (many aspirations).

shahryār, King.

shahīd, martyr.

shāhid bāz: a whoremonger, a womanizer.

shahūd, observing or witnessing.

sheftagī, madness in love.

shīrāza(h), thread used to bind parts of book together, the sum.

shīrīñ bayānī, sweet talk.

shirīñ suḳhan, sweet diction.

Shirīñ-Farhād, the legendary tale of a mountain digger falling in love with the wife of a King in Persia. See *Farhād.*

shīsha, glass, decanter

shīsha(h) bāz, glass juggler.

shiva(h), manner, profession, style.

ص (ṣuaad, ṣ)

ṣāḥib, Mister, a title of honor and respect; *Ġhālib* has often used it sarcastically to address the beloved.

ṣā'eqah, lightning.

ṣabā, breeze.

ṣabad-e gul, flower basket.

ṣubḥ, dawn.

ṣad, hundred.

ṣadā, reverberating noise, echo, call of prayer, invitation to a marriage celebration or a feast.

ṣad dil, hundred hearts.

ṣad rah, a hundred times.

ṣaḥrā, desert.

ṣaḥrā gard, wanderer of wilderness, the character of *Majnūn*.

ṣarf spent.

ṣarṣar, dust storm.

ṣarfa(h), profitable.

ṣarīr-e ķhāma(h), sound of scratching pen while writing; it is particularly loud when using a reed pen.

ṣafā, cleanliness, spark.

ṣifāt, qualities.

ṣaf-e mizhgāñ, row of eyelashes.

ṣalā, call to come (for food, wine or prayer).

ṣanam parast, idolaters, lover.

ṣanamkada(h), idol temple.

ṣūr, horn, clarion.

ṣurat, form, appearance, figure, ways, shape.

ṣurat-e dīvār, simile of the wall, like wall.

ṣahbā, wine.

ṣoḥbat, company.

ṣaiyād, captor, hunter.

ṣaid, catch (prey), hunt.

ṣaid-e zavām jasta(h), catch that runs away after being caught.

ṣaiqal, shine, polish.

ض (*ẓuaad, ẓ*)

ẓāmin, guarantor.

ẓabṭ, control.

ẓid, arrogance.

ẓarar, harm, loss.

ẓo'f weakness, frailty, weakness.

ẓauq-e ḳh(v)ārī, desire for disgrace.

ط (*tuay, ṭ*)

ṭā't, devotion, prayer.

ṭā't-o-zohad, praying and piety.

ṭāq-e-nisyān, "*tāq*" means a vault or recess in the wall. "*nisyān*" is forgetfulness or oblivion. Despite its ambiguity, the metaphor suggests: a little vault where one may put something and then forget where one has put it; an obscure corner to which one may retire if one is intoxicated, in a state of ecstasy or oblivion; cupola of amnesia.

ṭāq, cupola.

ṭāqat rubā, taking strength away.

ṭālib-e tāsīr, desirous of effect.

ṭāla', fortune, luck.

ṭaba', nature, temperament, taste.

ṭabī'atoñ, dispositions.

ṭarāvat, wetness, freshness.

ṭarab, joy, cheerfulness.

ṭarab inshā, someone creating happiness.

ṭarz, style, manner.

ṭarz-e tapāk, welcoming style.

ṭaraf honā, to confront.

ṭurra(h), style, parade, tuft of braided, frizzled or curled hair, ringlets of hair, dangling forelock, end of turban hanging loose, anything twisted.

ṭa'na(h), taunt.

ṭalab, search.

ṭalabgār, one demanding something.

ṭila', pleasure, delight.

ṭilism, spell, magic, sorcery.

ṭama, avarice, greed, lust, covetousness.

ṭannāz, taunting, frank, playful.

ṭaufe ḥaram, circling around *Ka'bā*.

tubā, a tree in paradise, the branches of which extend so widely that there will be one in the house of every dweller there. Its branches are laden with all types of fruits and perfumes, and the branches bearing them will lower them of their accord to be plucked.

Tūr, Mount Sinai; also see *Mūsā*.

ṭurfa(h) balā, calamitous

ṭuṭī, parrot.

ṭūfānī, stirring up storms, stormy.

ṭauq, badge or collar of slavery.

ṭūl, stretch, drag, lengthen.

ṭūmār, decree, book, office.

ظ (*ẓuay, ẕ*)

ẓāhir, manifest, visible.

ẓālim, cruel.

ẓarf courage, ability, class, receptacle or goblet, forbearance, power of tolerating.

ẓulm, cruelty.

ẓulmat: darkness.

ẓulmat gustarī, spreading of darkness.

ẓuhūr, manifestation.

ẓuhūrī, a poet who remained unacknowledged during his time but became famous afterwards in the time of *Ġhālib*. The word "*ẓuhūrī*" also means something which is apparent to us.

ع (*ain,* ʿ)

ʿājiz, weak, imbecile, impotent, exhausted, defective, hopeless, powerless, dejected.

ʿār, shame.

ʿārif, enlightened, one who knows, sagacious, possessing knowledge of God, his ways, and of how to deal with them, the man to whom things have been revealed.

ʿāfīyat, comfort, security.

ʿālam, universe.

ʿālī, high, excellent, grand, supreme.

ʿibādat, devotion, praying.

ʿibārat, writing, expression.

ʿabaṡ, unnecessary, useless.

ibrat, to take warning from, warning, admonition.

'ajab, strange, unusual.

'ijz, humility.

'ijz-e himmat, low esteem.

'adāvat, enmity.

'adam, nothingness, losing, being deprived.

'adū, enemy.

'arbada(h), war, scolding.

'arbada(h) jū, fighter, quarrelsome.

'arẓ, expression.

'arẓ-e niyāz, expression of offering, supplication to beloved.

'arẓ-e hunar, adducing talent, enhancing talent, humble expression.

'arṣa(h) āfāq, boundaries of earth.

'arq, extract.

'arq-e infi'āl, sweat of embarrassment.

'arsh, heaven.

'uryāñ, naked, bare, unconcealed.

'uryānī, nudity.

'uzr, excuse.

'uzr ḳh(v)āh, one who offers excuse.

'azīz, dear.

'ishrat, happiness, joy, ecstasy.

'ishrat ga(h), place of luxury, palace.

'ushshāq, lovers.

'ishq pur 'arbada(h), fighting love.

'iṭr-e pairāhan, perfume of clothing.

'uqd'a, mystery, knot.

'uqd'a(h)-e mushkil, difficult argument, puzzle, secret.

'aqd-e gohar, string of pearls.

'uqūbat, punishment, chastisement, torment, torture.

'aqīda(h), belief, idea.

'aks, reflection, picture.

'Alī, the cousin of the prophet Muhammad pbuh and husband of his daughter, Fatimah. After the prophet's death, a caliph (Khalifa-literally, "deputy") was needed to guide the Muslim community in both spiritual and temporal affairs. Some felt that *Alī* should have been the first caliph. During his life, he fought two wars against his rivals and was finally murdered by a member of a rival sect. According to the *Shī'a* doctrine, *'Alī,* was the first *Imām* or the leader; the lineage continued to 12 *Imāms,* with the last one being Mehdi, who is hiding and will become visible sometime in the future to bring the message of God. The rivalry between the two sects of Muslims is often intense; for example, the website http://www.shia.org if searched does not reveal the names of Omar or Abu Bakar, the caliphs according to the Sunni doctrine.

'alī arraġhm, opposite.

'umr, age.

'umr-e Ḳhiẓr darāz, May *Ḳhiẓr* have long life (*a fait accompli*).

'umr-e vara', life of abstinence. See, *Ḳhiẓr.*

'anāṣir, elements.

'unqā, a mythical bird, which is believed to exist, although no one has seen it.

'inān̈ gusiḳhta(h), uncontrolled.

'inān̈gir, someone holding back, one who holds the reins.

'unvān̈, envelope, title.

'ahd, promise.

'ahd-e tajdid-e tamannā, pledge to renew vows.

'ohda(h), responsibility, position.

'iyādat, visiting a sick person.

'īsī, Christ.

ʿid-e naẓẓāra(h), sight of sheer happiness.

ʿayār, standard of weight.

ʿaish-e rafta(h), luxuries of times bygone.

ʿayūb, defects.

غ (*ghain, ġh*)

ġhāratgar, plunderer.

ġhārat garī, destructive nature.

ġhāfil, ignorant.

Ġhālib initially chose the pseudonym of "*Asad*," meaning "lion," from his name, Asadullah, which means, "Lion of God," given to him by his parents. Incidentally, that is also one of the surnames of the fourth caliph of Islam, *Alī*, cousin of Prophet Mohammad[pbuh] ; the pen name "*Ġhālib* is another surname of the same caliph: *ʿAlū ibn Abū Ṭālib al-Ġhālib,* the "triumphant conqueror." Thus his names pays homage to the hero of Shia Islam, the religious seet to which the poet was inclined, contrary to his family who were Sunnis. A change in his pen name came about after he discovered that there was another [cheap, according to *Ġhālib*] poet who had used this pseudonym before him.

ġhāliya(h), compounded perfume.

ġhubār, very fine dust like sand that goes easily in the wind, mist, dry, weightless, grudge.

ġhaẓab, outrage, indignation.

ġhaẓal, a genre of lyric poetry in Arabic, Persian, Turkish, *Urdū*, and other languages.

ġhurbat, living in alien land, see "*ġharīb,*" while away from home, the condition of being "*ġharīb,*" the condition of being destitute and away from home.

ġharīb, destitute, poor, a man who is in an alien land, a stranger, a foreigner, a man addressed pitifully.

ġharībī, being in an alien land, poverty.

ġhurūr, pride, vanity.

ġhusl-e ṣeḥat, bathing after recovery from illness.

ġhaflat, ignorance, torpor, loss of consciousness, temporary or permanent; trance as can be induced by drugs such as opiates.

ġhalat bardār kāġhaż, error erasing paper.

ġham, sorrow, grief, suffering, torment.

ġhaltida(h), laced.

ġhamkada(h), house full of sorrow, desolate home.

ġhamḳh(v)ār, consoler.

ġhamza(h), amorous glance, wink.

ġhammāzī, squealing, slander, detraction.

ġhamnāk, sad, poignant.

ġham-e rozgār, worry of livelihood.

ġhuncha(h), bud.

ġhanīmat, blessing, enough.

ġhaib, unknown, mysterious.

ġhair, stranger, unknown, rival.

ف *(fay, f)*

fāriġh, free of, without.

fāqa(h) mastī, intoxication in starvation (poverty).

fānūs, chandelier.

fāida(h), benefit.

fitna(h), commotion, tumult, commotion, trial, torment, affliction, calamity, a character on the Doomsday creating commotion, the word is often used as "raising *fitna(h),* to mean creating trouble.

fitrāk, straps of saddle, stirrup.

fatḥa, victory.

fatīla(h), wick.

firāġh, independence, freedom, being carefree.

farāġhat, leisure, freedom, idleness, termination.

fardā-o-dī, tomorrow and yesterday.

fardi jam'a-o-ḳharj, written record of finances.

fard fird, scattered, incoherent.

farsh-e pā andāz, rolling out carpet (door mat).

farishta(h), angel.

furṣat, time, leisure, time free of worries and work, time to be alone.

furqat, separation, disunion (of lovers).

farmāñravā, ruler.

firo, down, below.

furozāñ, lit.

furū', root.

furoġh, brightness, luminous, splendor, illumination, flaring.

furoġh-e ṭāli', bright fortune.

faroġh-e sho'la(h)-e ḳhas: brightness of straw flame.

Farhād, the legendary Iranian lover, who fell in love with Shirin, the wife King Khusrau and relying on his false promise, dug a canal through a mountain to bring a channel of milk to Khusrau's palace. Just when he had completed the task, a man dressed like a woman came to give *Farhād* concocted news that Shirin had died in vow of separation with him. *Farhād* could not take this and hit himself with the spade and killed himself.

faryād, cry, complaint.

faryādī, pleader, crier.

fareb, spell, deception, self-delusion.

fareb-e vafā ḳhurdgāñ, deceived by faithfulness.

fasāna(h), romance, tale.

fusūñgar, magical, bewitching, magician.

fusūn, incantation, fascination.

fusūn-e niyāz, chant of humility, offerings.

fishār, squeezed from all sides.

faṣl, crop.

fizā, atmosphere.

fuġhāñ, sigh.

figār, wounded, hurting.

faqīr, a religious mendicant, one who lives an austere, simple life of wandering and meditation.

falak, sky, heaven.

fanā, extinction, devoted, phenomena of death, decay, inevitability of death, mortal nature of existence.

fanā honā, to die, to be consumed, to become so much a part of something as to merge with it.

faujdārī, criminal.

faiẓ-e havā, beneficence of air.

ق *(qaaf, q)*

qātil, murderer.

qāṣid, letter carrier, messenger.

qāfiyah, rhyme, in a *ġhazal*, the rhyming syllable at the end of the second line of each two-line verse and is usually (though not always) followed by a *radīf* (refrain).

qāmat, stature.

qabā, long garment open in front worn by men, a kind of tunic or cloak

qibla(h), anything opposite, that part to which Muslims direct their prayers–especially the direction of *Ka'bā.*

qibla(h) ḥājāt, Providence, an expression of respect generally used for God but it also used for elderly respectable persons as well.

qatlgah, killing field.

qaḥt, famine.

qad, stature, height.

qadar, value, quantity.

qadr, dignity. worth, respect, value.

qudrat, talent, ability, courage, Nature.

qadam, footstep.

qadd-e ādam, height of a man.

qad-o-gesū, stature and tresses.

qadaḥ, bowl, bowl of wine, cup, goblet, wine-glass.

qiṣṣa(ḥ), tale.

qaṣīdah, ode, a poem with a "purpose," poems in praise of something or someone—usually a patron. But a *ḥaju* (complaint, insult) too may be technically described as a *qaṣīdah.*

qaẓā, destiny, death.

qarār, declaration, repose.

qismat, fate.

qasam khāī, sworn upon.

qasam milne kī, oath never to meet, or to meet.

qaṯ, cut (as in making bamboo reed writing instruments in finishing the nib of the pen).

qāta', cutting off, amputating, breaking off, stopping short.

qiṯ'ah, verse-sequence, cutting, section. Within a *ġhazal,* a series of verses meant to be read as a connected sequence. The first verse of the *qiṯ'ah* is traditionally marked with the letter *qāf;* the last verse is not marked. Sometimes a *qiṯ'ah* outgrows the *ġhazal* entirely and takes on an independent existence, as a unified poem in its own right; it is then usually given a title.

qaṯa'-e naẓar, to refuse, to ignore, overlook, not to take interest, to know what the answer would be, therefore, not even to argue.

qatra(h), drop.

qafā, behind, neck.

qafas, a bird's cage, coop.

qafas-e rang, prison of color.

qufl-e abjad, alpha lock ("abjd" comes from the letters in the order they are used in numerology associated with letters: abjd, hwz, huti, klmn).

qulzum, ocean, red sea.

qulzum āshāmī, to drink oceans, meaning the ability to drink beyond limits.

qulzum ḳhūñ, ocean of blood.

qulzum-e ṣar ṣar, ocean of dust storm.

qalam, pen.

qimār, playing at dice.

qimār ḳhānā(h), gambling den.

qumrī, a type of partridge with a ring around neck, turtle-dove, ringdove (a dust colored bird). Anecdotally, *qumrī* cries looking at the moon, which is frequently compared this with the cry of nightingale looking at flowers.

qanā't, contentment.

qavā, plural of strength, powers, forces.

qahr, fury, calamity, divine wrath.

qahr-o-ġhaẓab, anger and punishment.

qaid-e ḥayāt, bondage of life.

qiyās, guess.

qiyāmat, Resurrection, Doomsday.

qiyāmat kih fitne, havoc wreaker of Doomsday.

Qais, Majnūn (meaning lunatic; the legendary lover from Arabia). See, *Majnūn.*

ک (*kaaf, k*)

kār farmā, ruler, guardian, caretaker, Creator.

kārgāh-e hastī, workings of existence (the world).

kārgar, effective.

kārobār, routine, dealings, business.

kāsa(h), begging bowl.

kāsa(h) gardūñ, bowl of heaven.

kāsh, wish I had.

kāshāna(h), home.

kāġhaż, paper.

kākul, tresses.

kām, throat.

kāmil, perfect, complete.

kām-e nahang, throat of crocodile.

kāmyāb, successful.

kān, mine.

kāvish, effort.

kāvkāv, hard labor, incessant beating as done by a sharp pointed object on a surface, digging.

kā'ī, fungus on water, scum.

kāṡāfat, crudeness, dirtiness.

kaṡrat, abundance.

kaṡrat ārā'ī, abundance of display.

kuchh na(h) kī, did little.

kardah gunāh, sins committed.

karishma(h), miracle.

karam, kindness, God, benevolence.

kasab, to acquire.

kisvat, apparel, dress.

kisvat-e fānūs, mesh wrapped around the glass lamp or chandelier.

kashākash, dilemma, struggle, tussle, constant strife.

kushād, open.

kushād-o-bast, opening and closing.

kashāṉ-e ʿishq, home of love.

kash-ma-kash, sorrow, distress, pulling different ways, puzzled, pulled around.

kisht, seed, tillage, cultivation of a crop, cultivating a habit, a view of life, a permanent pattern of conduct.

kushta(h), victim, the one killed.

kushā'ish, unloosening, aperture, opening, clearness, cheerfulness, hilarity.

kishvar, a climate, country, quarter, region of the world as divided into seven climates each of which is supposed to be dependent on one of the planets. Thus, the first climate, i.e., Hindustan (India), is assigned to the planet Saturn; the second, i.e., China and Khota, to Jupiter; the third, i.e., Turkistan, to Mars; the fourth, i.e., Iraq and Khurasan, to the sun; the fifth, i.e., Transoxania, to Venus; the sixth, i.e., Greece, or the Turkish empire (Rum), to Mercury; and the seventh, i.e., the hyperborean region, to the moon.

kesh, faith.

Kā'bā, The holy place in Mecca toward which Muslims turn when they pray, the way forward, the most sacred of Muslim shrines, a pilgrimage to which is one of the essential duties of a Muslim. Muslim tradition says it was built by Ibrahim (q.v.) and his son, Ismail (q.v.).

kaf foam, bubbles, palm, fist, fistful.

kaf-e afsos malnā, to rub hands in sorrow.

kaf burdan, in the palm.

kafan, shroud.

kaf-e ḳhākistar, handful of dust.

kufr, impiety, infidelity, idolatry, paganism, blasphemy.

kafīl, sponsor, taking responsibility for.

kul, whole.

kulfat, pain, distress.

kulfat-e ḳhāt̤ir, thought of sadness, for the sake of sadness.

kalejā ṭhanḍā karnā, to draw satisfaction, to cool off liver.

kalīsā, church.

kam, less.

kamar, waist.

kamand, noose.

kamūs, second stage of digestion.

kamīñ, ambush, look out.

kinār, shore.

kināra(h) kar: move on, get aside.

kungur, decorative facade of cupola, parapet.

kanġar istaġhnā, snake (specially the one who has recently shed skin) of obliviousness.

kunisht, a synagogue, a fire temple.

kināyah, implication, penumbra of suggestion, one of the techniques of *ma'nī āfirīnī*..

kotāhī-e qismat, shortcoming of fortune.

kūcha(h), alley, street, the area in which one's house is situated, abode.

kauṡar, a legendary river in paradise, a stream in paradise in which the wine of purity will flow.

kaudākī, childhood.

kūza(h), earthen goblet.

kor'ī, devoid, blindness.

kosoñ, miles (one kose is equal to two miles).

kaukaba(h), royal pageantry.

kaund, struck.

koh, mountain.

koh-e ṭūr, mount Sinai.

khujātā, scratching.

kohkan, mountain digger, often used to mean *Farhād*.

khaṭkā, paranoia of unknown happening.

khulā, became informal, opened.

khul jā'o, open up, be intimate.

khare, straightforward.

khainch, draw, take out.

khaiñchā, pulled.

kyā, what.

kaifiyat, mood, state of being in trance, the response evoked by a certain kind of verse: an ineffable, mysterious, melancholy, romantic mood in the reader, condition.

گ (gaaf, g)

gāṛo, to bury.

gālī, abuse.

gadā'ī, beggary.

gudāḳhtah, molten.

girāñ, heavy, costly.

girāñbārī, heaviness.

girāñ māeg'ī, valuable, precious.

girāñ nashīñ, heavy, not easy to move.

giranjānī, sluggishness, parsimony, stinginess, niggardliness.

girānī, heavy, expensive.

gard, dust.

girdāb, whirlpool.
girdbād, whirlwind, tornado.
gard thā, was like dust, was of no value.
gardan, neck.
gardan māre, to behead.
gardish, rotation, revolution.
gardish-e mudām, encircling perpetually, wandering.
gardūñ, sky, heaven.
gar shādmānī kī, if I became happy.
garm, hot, busy.
girah, equivalent to 3 inches, cloth knot; money kept in a cloth knot.
girah-e nīm bāz, half opened knot.
garebāñ, collar.
girya(h), crying, lamentation, weeping.
gurez pā, running feet.
gurezāñ, avoiding, evading.
guzārā: to bear with, to have lived on, substance.
guzar gāh, passage.
guzargāh-e ķhayāl, a path or track of thought.
gustāķh, disrespectful, rude.
gustāķhī, impoliteness, disrespect.
guftār, talk.
guftagū, conversation.
gul, flowers.
gul afshānī, scattering of flowers.
gul bāz, one who plays with flowers or roses.
gulbang tasallī, the consoling note of the nightingale.
gul-e tar: fresh red rose.
gulķhan, furnace, garbage incinerator, dust-bin, waste bin.

gulchīn, flower gatherer, gardener, florist.

gul-e k̤hizānī-e shama', the autumn flower of candle; the rosette of wax remaining after the candle burns out completely, leaving a pool of wax that takes the shape of a flower (rosette).

gul dar qafā-e gul, flower behind flower.

guldasta(h), a bouquet, an anthology of formally identical *ġhazals*, often containing those recited at a formal gathering.

gulistāñ honā, to rejoice.

gulshan, garden.

gul katar ga'ī, trimmed flowers away, being a trouble maker or creating a tumult.

gul-e shama', flower of candle, trimming the wick to make the flame brighter.

gulfām, rose-like, rose-color, red or pink wine.

gulfishānī, spreading or scattering of flowers.

gul-e nāġhma(h), flower of song, happy song or melody.

gulū, throat.

gul-o-lāla(h), roses and tulips, beautiful gardens.

gila(h), complaint.

galīyoñ, alleys.

gumān, doubt.

gumbad, dome.

gūmagū, inexpressive speech

gunjāish, concession, room, small space, capacity.

ganjīna(h), treasure.

ganjfa(h), a type of playing card game wherein 56 round cards are dealt among 8 players.

gūna(h), of one color, sort, kind.

gavārā, tolerate.

gavāh, witness.

gor, grave.

gor-e ġharibāñ, stranger's grave.

gosha(h), edge.

gosh-e naṣiḥat nayosh, ears listening to advice.

goyā, as if.

gohar, pearl, jewel.

gohar bār, pearl giving.

goñ, form, kind.

ghabrānā, to be worried.

gahvāra(h)-e junbānī, rocking cradle, swing.

gayā, gone.

gīyāh, grass.

getī, world.

gīrāī', hold, grasp.

ل (laam, l)

lāg, enmity.

lāf boasting, bravado!, bragging, claim.

lākh, hundred thousand.

lālā, red flower (tulip), red poppy (the Indian poppy is smaller than the Western variety), metaphor for the heart (bleeding heart like in Shelley's poetry), or for the eye (crying and thus turning red). The dewdrops on a red poppy are the tears in the bloodshot eyes.

lāla(h) zār, garden of tulips.

la'sh, corpse.

la'īm, miser.

lauḥ, slate.

lab-e afsos, saddened lips.

lab-e bām, edge of terrace, balcony.

lab-e ḳhushk, dried, parched lip.

lab-e ḳhūnī navā, lips raising blood-filled sighs.

lab-e ʽisā, lips of Jesus.

lat, addiction.

laḳht, piece.

laḳht-e dil, pieces of heart.

lażżat, delicacy.

lażżat-e āzār, ecstasy of pain.

lażżat-e kh(v)āb-e saher, pleasure of the morning dreams, the luxury of sleeping late.

lazzat-e sang, pleasure of stone.

laraznā, flickering, shivers, trembles, to tremble with fear or envy, etc.

laṛte, battling or fighting.

lutf kindness.

laṯma(h), a blow, a cuff, a slap.

laʽl-e butāñ, lips of beloved.

laʽl-o-gohar, jewels, rubies and pearl.

lakad kob, to kick around.

lakīreñ, lines.

lagā'o, association, love.

lagan, a basin, a copper trough, love, affection.

lahnā, a fool, a stone.

lahū pānī honā, to suffer in pain and sorrow, blood turning into water.

lae, flute, tune.

(meem, m)

mātam, lament.

mātam ḳhana(h), dark homes, homes in mourning.

māl, money.

mānī, famous artist, citizen of Babul who declared prophethood and was exiled. Spent much of his life in Turkey and China and lived in Iran during the time of Shahpur.

mā'l, end.

mah, moon.

mah-e ḳhurshīd-e jamāl: sun-faced beauty.

mahruḳh, moon-face.

maharvash, resembling sun.

māh-e shab-e chār dahum, full moon, moon of the fourteenth night.

māh-e kan'āñ, moon of Canaan, Joseph.

mājarā: an accident, event, occurrence, circumstances, adventure.

mah-e nāḳhshab: a luminous appearance resembling the moon, produced from a well at the foot of mount Siyam, in the town of Nakhshab in Turkey, by the juggler *Muqanna'* every night during a period of four months; it is also called *māh-e siyām.*

mubādā, lest.

mubaddal, transformed, changed.

mat, no, don't.

matā', commodity, asset, worth.

matā'-e burda(h), robbed belongings.

matā'e hunar, goods of skills.

mutaqābil, confronting rival.

mit gayee, died, disappeared, erased.

mis̄āl, example, analogy, simile.

mas̄navī, a narrative or reflective poem, often long but of no fixed length, often romantic but with no prescribed subject matter. Its two- line verses normally rhyme AA, BB, CC, etc..

majāl, ability, courage.

majāzī ḳhudā, corporeal god.

majboori, constraint, necessity, being under compulsion.

majmū'a(h), collection.

Majnūn (the mad one) the name given to Qais, the great lover in Arab legend. He fell in love with *Lailā* when both were children. When their love became known steps were taken to prevent them meeting and Qais went roaming about the desert wastes. Sometimes *Lailā* passed that way riding in a litter on a she-camel and *Majnūn* would run after it. *Lailā* returned his love but her father married her to another man. She died of grief and when *Majnūn* heard the news, he rushed to her tomb and died there as a celebrated lover of ancient Arabia. *Majnūn* is synonymous with a great lover. His real name was "*Qais*." The word "*Majnūn*" literally means "insane" and was given to him as a second name.

muḥābā, showing respect, kind behavior, friendship.

mahjūr, forsaken.

maḥram, knowing, someone informal or close.

maḥrūm, deprived.

maḥrūmī, misfortune, deprivation.

maḥrūm'ī qismat, deprivation of fate, ill fate.

maḥshar, Doomsday, Day of Resurrection, Day of Judgment.

mehshar-e ḳhayāl, Doomsday of thought.

mehfil, assembly of friends, a get together with definite sense of rejoicing and light-heartedness.

maḥmil, carrier for riding camel, a camel litter for women, covering of the *Ka'bā.*

maḥmil bāndhā: readied a carrier for riding camel.

maḥv, engrossed.

muḥīṯ, encircles, surrounds, ocean, encompassing.

muḥīṯ āb, surrounded by water.

muḥiṯ bāda(h), surrounded by wine.

muḳhtaṣir, brief.
madār, dependent on.
madaḥ-e nāz, praise, ode to coquetry.
madrasah, school.
madfan, grave.
mudda'ā, desire, goal, whatever is meant, purpose, intent.
mudda'ā pāyā, understood well, reached the goal.
mudda'ī, complainant.
muddī, defendant, claimant.
mudda'ā ṭalabī, achieving goals.
mażkūr, mention.
marśīya(h), an elegy, a lament written to commemorate someone's death, mostly to the death of *Ḥaẓrat* Imam Husain at Karbala(h).
marjāñ, red stone, red coral.
marḥabā, welcome.
mard, man.
murdā, dead.
mardomak-e dīda(h), sclera, white part of eye.
murġh, rooster, bird.
murġh-e bustānī, garden bird, nightingale.
murġh-e chaman, birds of garden.
murġh-e giraftār, bait bird.
marġhūb, liked, desire, excellent, beautiful.
marg, death.
marg-e nāgahānī, unexpected death.
marham, cure, ointment.
mizāj, disposition, nature.
marhūn, indebted to.
mizhah, eyelashes.

mizhgāñ, eye lashes.
mizhgān-e sozan, eyelashes of needle.
muzhda(h), good news.
mizha(h) hāi darāz, long lashes.
masā'il, maxim, aphorism, problems.
mast, intoxicated, carefree.
mast-e ṯarab, drunk with ecstasy.
masjid, mosque.
masjūd, to whom bowing, supplicating.
masīḥā, healer, Jesus.
mushā'irah, a gathering at which poets read their verses in front of an audience.
mushāhida(h), observation.
musht, handful.
mushtāq, ardent, intent, desirous.
mushtamil, consist of.
mashrab: drinking, imbibing.
mushkbū, musk-scented.
mushkiñ, smelling like musk.
mashad, point of martyrdom.
mashhūd, what is observed.
maṣāḥib, courtier.
miṣr, Egypt.
miṣra', line, a single hemistich or line of poetry.
maṣlaḥat, reason.
muṣavvīrī, painting.
muẓmir, hidden.
muẓmaḥil, weak, old, lethargic.
maẓmuñ, matter, substance, topics, a poetic theme or proposition.

maẓmūn āfirīnī, proposition-creation, the making of the implicit or explicit assertions of metaphoric identity from which the *ġhazal* develops.

muṯrib, singer.

maṯlab, meaning, desire, object.

maṯlab kuchḥ na(h) ho, without much substance, to not have meaning or object.

maṯla' opening verse in a *ġhazal,* an introductory pattern-setting verse that has the rhyme (and refrain, if any) at the end of each of its two lines, where the sun rises.

muṯlaq, absolute.

maṯlūb, desired.

mu'āmla(h), dealings, interaction.

ma'āṣī, sins.

ma'ida(h), feast.

ma'dan, mine.

ma'żūr, pardonable, excusable.

ma'raẓ, place of appearance.

ma'zūl, dethroned, incapacitated.

ma'shūq, the beloved, God, The Supreme Being.

ma'lūm, known, obvious.

ma'mure, settlement, city, town.

mo'taqid, believer.

ma'nī, meaning.

ma'nī āfirīnī, creation of meaning, the multiplication and enrichment of poetic meaning, the art of creating a verse that will elicit two or more different interpretations or suggestions (*kināyah*).

mo'iyyan, fixed.

mo'in, defender.

muflisāñ, poor.

muġhtanam, regarded as a prize.

magas kī qai, honey (vomit of honeybees).

maġhfirat, forgiveness.

muġhannī, singer.

muqābil, facing.

maqbūl, accepted.

maqtal, a place of execution.

maqdam, arrival, reception.

maqdam-e sailāb, arrival of flood.

muqarrar, established, confirmed, ratified, agreed upon, fixed, settled, ascertained, undoubted, certain, unquestionable, appointed, assigned.

muqaddar, fate, destiny predestined, predetermined, decreed by God, prescribed, understood (not expressed), implied.

maqṯa', closing verse, point of cutting off, in a *ġhazal*, a verse that both include the poet's pen name and occupies the last (or sometimes next-to-last) position, destination.

maktab, school.

maktūb, letter.

mukāfāt, revenge, retribution.

makaukab, filled with stars.

mukarrar, repeat, again.

makīñ, inhabitant.

malāmat, rebuke, curse.

millat, community, nation, group.

millateñ, nations.

milñ, resembles, getting.

mile dād, to get appreciation of.

malḳh, locust.
malakulmaut, the angel of death.
munājāt, hymns singing.
minnat, pleading.
minnat kash, under obligation, pleader.
minnat khenchnā, not to take an obligation.
munḥarif rebel, revolting, distracted.
mansūb, associated with.
manṣab, position.
Manṣūr, Mansūr Hussain, who declared "*ānal ḥaq*" meaning, I am God and was put to ḋeath.
manẓar, view.
manẓūr, intended, accepted.
mānā', prohibiting.
mān'e, preventing, impediment, refrain, keep from.
munfa'il, to be embarrassed.
munkir, one who denies.
muñh par khulnā, for something to suit in terms of appearance.
muñh lagāyā, to countenance.
muñ(h) meñ zabāñ, tongue in mouth, being able to speak.
mū, hair.
mū-e ātish, heat-damaged hair (not burned), singed hair, fragile.
mū'e ātish ḋida(h), singed hair.
mū-e shisha(h), hairline crack in the glass.
mauj, wave, tide.
mauj-e rang, wave of color.
maujzan, taking to high tides, tumultuous, agitated.
maujah'-e raftār, fast wave.
mau'j-e gul, abundance of flowers (roses), wave of flowers.

mu'āḳhaża(h), punishment.

mūnis, friend.

Mūsa, The Moses of the Bible and one of the major prophets of Islam. The commonest references is to the incidence of his speaking with God near the mount of Sinai. It was here that Moses asked God to show Himself to him. In the *Qur'an* (vii), 143, God says: When Moses (Musa) came to the place appointed by Us, and his Lord addressed him he said: "Oh my Lord show (Thyself) to me that I may look upon thee," God said: "By no means canst thou see Me (direct); but look upon the mount. If it abide in its place then shalt thou see Me." When his Lord manifested His glory on the mount He made it as dust, and Moses fell down in a swoon. The mount was the mountain of *Tūr* (Sinai), which was reduced to dust by God's radiance. Moses is also called *kalīm*—literally 'one who speaks with another– because he spoke with God. At one stage in his life, he served eight years as a goatherder to the prophet *Shuaib,* who, in return, gave his daughter to Moses in marriage. When Moses led the children of Israel out of Egypt towards the Promised Land, the waters parted before them to enable them to reach the other side in safety and then closed over Pharaoh and his army and drowned them. In Muslim tradition, these were the waters of the Red Sea.

mauqūf contingent.

mund, closed.

mu(v)aḥḥid, monotheist, one who believes in the unity of God, orthodox, Unitarian.

mohar, stamp.

mahr āsāñ, like sun.

mahrbāñ, kind.

mahrbānī hāl: extreme kindness.

mohr pusht nigāh, seal of the back of the eye, eye-shaped seal.

mahr alam, flag like sun.

mahr gayā, a plant root, the possession of which brings good fortune and makes the beloved kinder (an anecdote), herb of grace.

mehr-e nīm roz, afternoon sun.

mai, wine.

mai parastī, drinking wine.

mai ḳhān'a(h) nairang, tavern of mystery, mysteries of universe.

maidāñ, field.

maikada(h), tavern, bar.

mai mard afgan, wine that will knock men out.

mai vāñgbīñ, wine and honey.

mayassar, afford, available.

minā, decanter, goblet, wine bottle, wine decanter, The shape of the Persian decanter is a slender and is compared to a shapely neck, a mark of great beauty.

merī nigāh meñ, in my plan or vision.

merā zimma(h), my guarantee, assurance.

ن *(noon, n)*

nā tavānī, weakness.

nāchār, helpless, destitute, inevitable.

nāḳhudā, boat commander.

nār, fire.

nārasā, unheard.

nāz, coquetry, pride.

nāz-e-zameeñ, air assumed by those who are loved, pride of earth.

nāzish, blandishment, boasting.

nāz-o-adā, style and coquettishness.

nāsāz, dissonant, ill.

nāsāzgārī, unsuitable, incompatibility.

nāsūr, chronic non-healing wound.

nāshināś, not realizing or acknowledging.

nāṣeḥ, preacher.

nāṣiya(h), forehead.

nāṣiya(h) firsā, one who rubs his forehead.

nā 'āqibat andesh, not concerned with future, imprudent.

nāf-e ġhazāl, musk in the navel of the deer.

nāqiṣ, faulty, defective.

nākardah gunāh, sins not committed.

nākām, defeated, abortive, unrealized, unsuccesful.

nāk meñ dam, to feel sick of something, to be irritated.

nāgahāñ, unexpected.

nāguzīr, inevitable.

nāla(h), lamenting, plaint, a cry of anguish, complaint, lament.

nā'lbahā, horseshoe price (the ransom money given to conquerors to stop them from plundering their newly-won territory).

nāla(h)-e dil, sighs of the heart.

nāma(h), letter.

nām-e ḳhudā, name of God, God bless you.

nāmurād, disappointed, defeated.

nām rakhnā, to blame.

nāmūs, sanctity, integrity, respect, purity, honor.

nāvak, arrow.

nāyāb, nonexistent, rare.

nāyāfat, not being able to achieve.

nāe-va-nosh, song and wine.

nabard, war, battle.

nabard pesha(h), fond of fighting and contests.

nabẓ, pulse.
nabz-e pari, pulse of fairy.
nabẓ-e ḳhas, pulse of straw.
najaf the city where *Haẓrat Alī* is buried.
nākhat-e gul, scent of flower.
nāḳhvat, haughtiness.
naḳhchīr, catch.
Naḳhshab, See *māh-e-naḳhshab.*
nidāmat, embarrassment.
nadīm-e dost, friend of friend.
nargis, narcissus.
nāżr, offering.
nikuhish, insults.
nirūe', strength.
nazar maiñ hai, is in sight, before one's eyes, always under consideration, all thinking.
naza', last breath, moment of death.
nuzūl, coming down, revelation.
nāsazā, curse, improper.
nasīm, breeze.
nasīya(h), delay, adjournment, credit, respite.
nistāñ, flute.
nisyāñ, amnesia, forgetfulness.
nisyā-o naqad do ālam, profit and loss in the two worlds.
nishāṯ, joy, happiness.
nishāṯ-e āhang, joy of music.
nishāṯ-e dil, joy of heart.
nishāṯ-e kār, desire to accomplish.
nishāñ, mark.

nishanī, charm, souvenir.

nishtar; knife, dagger.

nashv-o-numā, growth and increase.

nasheb-o-firāz, rise and fall, peaks and valleys.

naṣīb, good fortune, faith, destiny.

nuṭq, diction, speech.

nujūm, stars, astronomy.

naẕẕārah, sight, view, vista, sight, spectator.

naẕar; view, vision, sight, glance.

naẕar tez tez, attentive, sharp or angry glance.

naẕargāh, a place of sight or show, a tomb of a prophet or a holy man..

naġhma(h), melody.

nāġhma(h) hā'i ġham, the song of sorrow.

nafas, soul, breath, sighs.

nafas parvar, holding breath, lazy.

nafas-e i̓tr sāe gul, to breath in the smell of flowers.

nafī, denial.

naqqāsh, sculptor.

naqd, cash.

naqd-e dāġh-e dil: currency of the scars of heart as scars are shaped like the currency in circulation then.

naqsh, mark, word, spot, scar, picture, image.

naqshā or naqsha(h), condition, map, layout, design.

naqsh-e qadam, foot impression.

nukta(h) chīñ, a caviller, a carper.

nuktah dāñ, those who understand or appreciate subtleties, critic.

nuktah sarā, singing subtleties.

nikammā, useless, of no use, good for nothing.

niko, good, beautiful, a good thing.

nakhat, smell.

nakīriñ, the two angels, *munkir* and *nakīr,* who would come to question our deeds in the grave upon death.

nigār, beloved, painting.

nigāh, glance, sight.

nigāh-e surma(h) sā, eyes adorned with black antimony powder.

nigah-e garm, angry eyes.

nagina(h), gem.

numāyāñ, evident, apparent.

numū karnā, to grow, to show.

Namrūd, King of ancient Iraq who claimed that he was God. Ibrahim (q.v.) rejected his claim and Namrud had him thrown into a great fire whereupon the fire became a bed of flowers.

namūd, display, show.

nang, shame, embarrassment, disgrace.

nang-e pairāhan, disgrace to attire.

nañg-e sajda(h), disgrace of prostration.

nang-e vajūd, disgrace to existence.

nau, new.

naumidī-e javed, hopelessness of life.

navā pardāz, talking.

navāzish, kindness, politeness, courtesy.

navāsanj-e fuġhāñ, pleader of lament, one who utters loud cries of pain.

navā'-e sarosh, call of angels.

navahā-e rāz, calls from unknown world.

nūr, light.

nūrul'ain, sparkle of eye, very dear.

navard, roaming, wander, travel.

nok, tip.

navīd, good news.

nihāñ, hidden, secret.

niyāz, offering.

nairang, deception, trick, deceit, miracle, mystery, magic, strange, sorcery.

nairang-e betābī, intensity of tumultuousness and impatience.

nairang-e nazar, bewitching artfulness, magic, miracle, a fascinating performance, which appears in many colors and guises, beloved.

Naiyyar, Ziauddin Ahmad Nayyar, brother-in-law of *Ġhālib* and a master of Persian poetry.

nīstāñ, reed, sugar cane.

nīlī fām, of blue color.

nīm, half.

nīm jāñ, half-dead.

na(h) shunidan, not listening.

nesh, sting.

و (vao, v)

vā, open.

vābasta(h), associated.

vājib, necessary, obligatory.

vā ḥasratā, Alas!, statement of extreme sorrow.

vāh vāh, Bravo! Bravo!

vād'ī ḳhayāl, valley of thought.

vād'ī-e purḳhār, valley full of thorns

vāẕhugūñ, upside down (bottoms up).

vārasta(h), free, careless.

vārastagī, freedom.

vārdān, arrival

vāsṯe, for the sake of, for, connection.

vā karnā, to open.

vāq'iah, incidence.

vām, loan, borrowing.

vāmāndgī, tiredness, openness, exposure.

vāñ, there.

vāñgbīñ, honey.

vāe, Alas!.

vāe nākāmī, Alas! The bad luck.

vā'iẕ, preacher.

vabāl, disgrace, curse, divine vengeance, ruin.

vajūd, existence appearance.

vujūd-o-'adam, existence and non-existence.

vajh, cause, reason.

vahm, suspicion, supposition, imagination, doubt.

vuh 'ālam, what a spectacle.

vaḥshat, despair, solitude, frenzy.

vadia't, something in trust, vested, property in trust

va'da(h), promise.

vidā', farewell.

vidā'-e hosh, bidding farewell to senses.

vidā'-e tamkiñ, letting pride go.

varṯa(h), whirlpool.

varaq, page.

varna(h), or else.

varq gardānī', shuffling card, flipping pages.

vīrāñ, desolate place, ruin.

viṣl, union (with beloved).

vus'at-e ma'i ḳhāna(h), expanse of tavern.

vaẓa', style.

vaẓ' iḥtiyāt, style of caution, sobriety.

vaṭan, homeland.

vafā ḳhurdgāñ, deceived by faithfulness.

vafā, faithfulness.

vufūr, excess, abundance.

vaqf, dedicated to.

vaqt, time, moment.

vagarna(h), or else.

valī, Saint.

vale, but.

valekin, otherwise.

valvale, fervent vigor

vohī, that, the same.

ه (hay, h)

hāth dho, be ready to lose.

hāth pāuñ phūlna, hands and feet to up swelling in excitement.

hal min mazzīd, is there more?, taken from the *Qur'an* ("the day when we will ask the hell,"are you filled," the hell will respond,"is there more?").

hathkanḍe, trickery.

hujūm, excess, crowd.

hujūm-e āshk, crowding of tears.

hjr, separation.

hech midānī, not knowing anything, perfect ignorance.

hujūm, excess, crowd.

hujūm-e āshk, crowding of tears.

hijr, separation.

hech midānī, not knowing anything, perfect ignorance.

hadaf target.

hadīya(h), offering.

harbun, root.

harbun-e mū, root of every hair.

har chand, whereas, even though.

har sū, in all directions.

hazār bār, thousands of times.

hastī, existence, life, to have lived, being.

hastī'-e ashyā, existence of things.

hūshyārī, consciousness, cleverness, cunningness.

halāk, killed, victim.

hilāl, crescent.

ham, together, we, us.

hama(h), always.

humā, a mythical bird about which it is said that any man on whom its shadow falls will become a king.

hamārī janāb meñ, in my honor.

hamdam, companion, friend one who breathes in unison.

hamdamī, closeness.

himmat, courage.

Hamzā, the hero of one of the most famous, voluminous, old tales of *Urdū*.

ham ṭarḥī, same style.

hamdīgar, with each other.

ham suḳhan, someone who speaks the same language, one who understands, talking together.

hamnāmī, having the same name.

henna, a plant whose leaves are crushed and made into paste to apply to hands and feet to give them red color on occasions of rejoicing; lover's blood is often compared to *henna* or serves as *henna.*

hangām, time.

hangāma(h) ārā, riotous.

hanūz, yet, still.

havā, air, aspiration, desire, breeze, atmosphere, hope.

havā bāṅdhnā, to express falsely, to exaggerate, to promote self.

havā-e jalva(h) nāz, desire to see display of her grace.

havā ḳh(v)āhī, well wishing, sympathy.

havā-e dil, heart's desire.

havā-e saiqal, the polishing wind, the spring breeze that turns things green all around; "*saiqal*" refers to the old way of making mirrors by applying a metal polish that turns green in high humidity and thus comparisons are made the greening of graden in the spring season and the mildew growth stating that the natural air of spring can change color and function of things as much as the artificial polish does.

havā-e gul, desire for flowers.

havas, avarice, desire, intense longing.

havas-e bāl-o par, desire for feathers, desire to fly.

havas-e zar: lust for material gains.

havas-e shu'la(h), desire to burn.

haul-e dil, palpitation of heart.

haif, pity.

haihāth, Be gone! Away! Alas! Woe to me!.

hayūlā, constituent matter of being, real matter, basic element of any matter, nucleus, potential, possibility.

ی (ye, y)

yā, O!

yād, remembrance.

yār, beloved, friend, lover.

yā rabb, O' God.

yās, hopelessness, also name of a flower.

yak, one.

yak bayābāñ jalva(h)-e gul, large spread of flowers.

yak bayābāñ māndgī, extreme tiredness, desert of tiredness.

yaktā, unique.

yaktā'ī, singularity.

yak jahāñ zānū tā'mmul, intense contemplation keeping head on the knees.

yagāna(h), *yaktā*, alone, unique, only one of its kind.

yak qalam, throughout, altogether, full, also means sideburns (*qalam*).

Bibliography

1. *A Dance of Sparks*—Imagery of Fire in *Ġhālib*'s Poetry. Annemarie Schimmel. East-West Publications. London. 1979.
2. A History of Urdu Literature, Graham T. Bailey, Association Press, Calcutta. 1932.
3. *Ġhālib paimāī, Dr. Syed Moin-ur Rehmān. Al-Wiqār Publications*, Lahore, Pakistan 1998.
4. *Ġhālib*, 1797-1869: Life and Letters. Ralph Russel and *Ḳhurshīdul Islām* (Eds). Oxford University Press. 1994.
5. *Ġhālib, A* Critical Introduction. *Maṭbūāt-e Majlis-e yādgār-e Ġhālib, Urdū Academy,* Karachi, Pakistan. 1969.
6. *Ġhālib*, Seventeen Ninety-Seven to Eighteen Sixty-Nine: Life and Letters. Ralph Russell and *Khurshīdul Islām* (Eds). Harvard University Press. 1969.
7. *Ġhālib*: The Man, The Times. Pavan K. Varma. South Asia Books. India.1989.
8. *Ġhalib kī chand tehrīreñ. Dr. Sādāt Ali Siddiqī. Anjuman Taraqqī Urdū* (Hind). New *Delhī*. India 1990.
9. *Ġhalib*. Natalia Parigarina. *Maktabā-e-Danyāl.* Karachi, Pakistan. 1998.
10. *Ġhalib*—The Man and His Couplets. Umesh Joshi, Umesh Joshi, New Delhi, India. 1998.
11. *Ġhazals* of *Ġhālib*. Sasha Newborn, and Basho Swanner (Ed). Bandana Books. 1989.
12. *Ġhazals of Ġhālib*: Versions from the *Urdū*. Aijaz Ahmad (ed), Oxford India Paperbacks. New Delhi, India. 1995.
13. Assembly of Rivals, Carla Petievich. Vanguard Books (PVT) Ltd, New Delhi, India. 1992.
14. *Bayān-e Ġhālib: Shirḥ Dīvān-e Ġhālib.* Agha Mohammad Baqar. Azad Book Depot. Amritsar. India 1939.

15. *Dehlī kī ākhrī shama'. Mirzā Farhatullāh Beg Dehlavī. Anjuman Taraqqī Urdū* (Hind). New *Delhī*. India 1992.
16. *Faizān-e Ġhālib. Arsh Malīsānī. Ġhālib Academy*, New Delhi, India. 1977.
17. *Ghalib āshuftanavā. Dr. Aftāb Ahmed. Maktabā-e-Danyāl.* Karachi, Pakistan. 1997.
18. How Proust Can Change Your Life, Alain de Botton, Pantheon Books, New York, NY. 1997.
19. *Inshā-e Ġhālib. Maktabā-e Jamia*, New Delhi, India. 1994.
20. *Interpretations of Ghālib . J L. Kaul.* Atma Ram & Son. New Delhi, India. 1956.
21. *Karīm-ul luġhāt. Maulvī Karīmuddin Dehlavī.* Raja Ram Kumar Book Depot. India. 1861.
22. *Ghālib-His life and Persain Poetry*. Arifsha Sayyid *Gilānī*. Azam Book Corporation, Karachi Pakistan, 1956.
23. *Mirzā Ġhālib* , A Creative Biography. Natalia Parigarnaya. Oxford University Press, Karachi, Pakistan 1986.
24. *Mirzā Ġhālib* –The Poet of Poets. Sarswati Saran. Munshiram Manoharlal Publishers Ltd, New Delhi, India 1976.
25. *Mushkilāt-e Ġhālib: shirḥ dīvān-e Ġhālib. Allamā Nīāz Fatehpurī*. Halqa-e Niaz-o Nigaar. Karachi. Pakistan 1993.
26. *Navā-e sarosh—mukammal dīvān-e Ġhalib mai shirḥ. Ghulām Rasūl Mehr. Shaikh Ghulām Hussain & Sons,* Karachi, Pakistan. 1996.
27. *Nets of Awareness*. Frances W. Pritchett. University of California Press. Los Angeles, California. 1994.
28. Persian-English Dictionary. F. Steingass. Routledge & Kegan Paul plc, London. United Kingdom. 1892.
29. *Ramūz-e Ġhalib. Dr. Gyān Chand. Idārā-e Yādgār-e Ġhalib.* Karachi, Pakistan. 1999.
30. *Selected Verses of Mirzā Ġhālib. Sūfīā Sādullāh.* Darwen Finlayson Ltd, England. 1965.
31. *Shirḥ Dīvān-e Urdū-e Ġhālib. Maulvī Syed Ālī Haider Tabatabaī, Idārā-e Farūgh-e Urdū*, Lucknow, India 1984.

32. *Shirḥ-o-Matn*: *Ġhazaliat-e Ġhālib*. Dr. Farman Fatehpuri. Beacon Books, Multan. Pakistan 2000.

33. *Tafhīm-e Ġhālib* , *Shamsur Rahmān Farūqī*, *Ġhalib* Institute, New Delhi, India. 1989.

34. *The ash'ārs of Ġhālib* and 25 Masters. Umesh Joshi. Rupa & Co., Calcutta, India 1995.

35. The Concise Persian English Dictionary. *Abbās Aryānpur* and *Manūchehr Aryānpūr*. Amir Kabir Publication Organization. Tehran, Iran. 1976.

36. *The Golden* Tradition—An *anthology of Urdū Poetry*. *Ahmed 'Alī*, Columbia University, New York, NY 1973.

37. The Lightning Should Have Fallen on *Ġhālib*: Selected Poems of *Ġhālib*. Robert Bly and Sunil Dutta. The Ecco Press. USA. 1999.

38. Translations of Selected Verses of *Ġhālib*'s *Urdū Ġhazals*. *Yaqūb Mirzā*, *Ġhalib Institute, New Delhi, India. 1992.*

39. *Urdū Ġhazals of Ġhalib*, Yousuf Husain Khañ *Ġhalib Instiute, New Delhi, India. 1977.*

40. *Urdū Ġhazals*—An Anthology. K. C. Kanda. Sterling Paperbacks. New Delhi, India. 1995.

41. *Urdū* Letters of *Mirzā Asadu'llah Ḳhān Ġhālib*. *Daūd Rahbar* and Annemarie Schimmel (Ed). State University of New York Press. New York. 1987.

42. *Urdū*-English Dictionary, *Maulvī Abdul Haq*. *Anjuman Tarraqī Urdū*, Karachi, Pakistan. 1965

43. Whispers of the Angel (*Navā-e-Sarosh*). *Nizāmuddin*. Selection from 14 English translations of *Ġhālib*. *Ġhālib* Academy. *New Delhī*. India. 1969.

Dr Sarfaraz, K. Niazi has been teaching for over thirty years and has published several books, texts and articles on scientific, philosophical and literary topics. His father, Allama Niaz Fatehpuri, was a renowned author and critic of the Urdu language. Dr Niazi lives in Deerfield, Illinois.

Dr Farman Fatehpuri, who formerly held a chair of Urdu at Karachi University, is a scholar of Urdu and the author of scores of books (several on Ghalib). He is also the editor of a comprehensive dictionary of Urdu, and a renowned authority on the subject. He lives in Karachi, Pakistan.

Sadequain, a renowned artist and a fan of Ghalib, created around twenty works dealing with his own interpretation of Ghalib's verses, some of which are presented here. Sadequain developed a unique style of abstract presentation and brought the calligraphy of Quranic verses to such an expressive level that they now adorn many revered places.